Lecture Notes in Computer Science

T0253611

Vol. 88: Mathematical Foundations of Computer Science 1980. Proceedings, 1980. Edited by P. Dembiński. VIII, 723 pages. 1980.

Vol. 89: Computer Aided Design - Modelling, Systems Engineering, CAD-Systems. Proceedings, 1980. Edited by J. Encarnacao. XIV, 461 pages. 1980.

Vol. 90: D. M. Sandford, Using Sophisticated Models in Resolution Theorem Proving. XI, 239 pages. 1980

Vol. 91: D. Wood, Grammar and L Forms: An Introduction. IX, 314 pages. 1980.

Vol. 92: R. Milner, A Calculus of Communication Systems. VI, 171 pages. 1980.

Vol. 93: A. Nijholt, Context-Free Grammars: Covers, Normal Forms, and Parsing. VII, 253 pages. 1980.

Vol. 94: Semantics-Directed Compiler Generation. Proceedings, 1980. Edited by N. D. Jones. V, 489 pages. 1980.

Vol. 95: Ch. D. Marlin, Coroutines. XII, 246 pages. 1980.

Vol. 96: J. L. Peterson, Computer Programs for Spelling Correction: VI, 213 pages. 1980.

Vol. 97: S. Osaki and T. Nishio, Reliability Evaluation of Some Fault-Tolerant Computer Architectures. VI, 129 pages. 1980.

Vol. 98: Towards a Formal Description of Ada. Edited by D. Bjørner and O. N. Oest. XIV, 630 pages. 1980.

Vol. 99: I. Guessarian, Algebraic Semantics. XI, 158 pages. 1981.

Vol. 100: Graphtheoretic Concepts in Computer Science. Edited by H. Noltemeier. X, 403 pages. 1981.

Vol. 101: A. Thayse, Boolean Calculus of Differences. VII, 144 pages. 1981.

Vol. 102: J. H. Davenport, On the Integration of Algebraic Functions. 1–197 pages. 1981.

Vol. 103: H. Ledgard, A. Singer, J. Whiteside, Directions in Human Factors of Interactive Systems. VI, 190 pages. 1981.

Vol. 104: Theoretical Computer Science. Ed. by P. Deussen. VII, 261 pages. 1981.

Vol. 105: B. W. Lampson, M. Paul, H. J. Siegert, Distributed Systems – Architecture and Implementation. XIII, 510 pages. 1981.

Vol. 106: The Programming Language Ada. Reference Manual. X, 243 pages. 1981.

Vol. 107: International Colloquium on Formalization of Programming Concepts. Proceedings. Edited by J. Diaz and I. Ramos. VII, 478 pages. 1981.

Vol. 108: Graph Theory and Algorithms. Edited by N. Saito and T. Nishizeki. VI, 216 pages. 1981.

Vol. 109: Digital Image Processing Systems. Edited by L. Bolc and Zenon Kulpa. V, 353 pages. 1981.

Vol. 110: W. Dehning, H. Essig, S. Maass, The Adaptation of Virtual Man-Computer Interfaces to User Requirements in Dialogs. X, 142 pages. 1981.

Vol. 111: CONPAR 81. Edited by W. Händler. XI, 508 pages. 1981.

Vol. 112: CAAP '81. Proceedings. Edited by G. Astesiano and C. Böhm. VI, 364 pages. 1981.

Vol. 113: E.-E. Doberkat, Stochastic Automata: Stability, Nondeterminism, and Prediction. IX, 135 pages. 1981.

Vol. 114: B. Liskov, CLU, Reference Manual. VIII, 190 pages. 1981.

Vol. 115: Automata, Languages and Programming. Edited by S. Even and O. Kariv. VIII, 552 pages. 1981.

Vol. 116: M. A. Casanova, The Concurrency Control Problem for Database Systems. VII, 175 pages. 1981.

Vol. 117: Fundam
Edited by F. Gécs

Vol. 118: Mathen
Proceedings, 198
1981.

Vol. 119: G. Hirst, Anaphora in Natural Language Understanding: A Survey. XIII, 128 pages. 1981.

Vol. 120: L. B. Rall, Automatic Differentiation: Techniques and Applications. VIII, 165 pages. 1981.

Vol. 121: Z. Zlatev, J. Wasniewski, and K. Schaumburg, Y12M Solution of Large and Sparse Systems of Linear Algebraic Equations. IX, 128 pages. 1981.

Vol. 122: Algorithms in Modern Mathematics and Computer Science. Proceedings, 1979. Edited by A. P. Ershov and D. E. Knuth. XI, 487 pages. 1981.

Vol. 123: Trends in Information Processing Systems. Proceedings, 1981. Edited by A. J. W. Duijvestijn and P. C. Lockemann. XI, 349 pages. 1981.

Vol. 124: W. Polak, Compiler Specification and Verification. XIII, 269 pages. 1981.

Vol. 125: Logic of Programs. Proceedings, 1979. Edited by E. Engeler. V, 245 pages. 1981.

Vol. 126: Microcomputer System Design. Proceedings, 1981. Edited by M. J. Flynn, N. R. Harris, and D. P. McCarthy. VII, 397 pages. 1982.

Voll. 127: Y.Wallach, Alternating Sequential/Parallel Processing. X, 329 pages. 1982.

Vol. 128: P. Branquart, G. Louis, P. Wodon, An Analytical Description of CHILL, the CCITT High Level Language. VI, 277 pages. 1982.

Vol. 129: B. T. Hailpern, Verifying Concurrent Processes Using Temporal Logic. VIII, 208 pages. 1982.

Vol. 130: R. Goldblatt, Axiomatising the Logic of Computer Programming. XI, 304 pages. 1982.

Vol. 131: Logics of Programs. Proceedings, 1981. Edited by D. Kozen. VI, 429 pages. 1982.

Vol. 132: Data Base Design Techniques I: Requirements and Logical Structures. Proceedings, 1978. Edited by S.B. Yao, S.B. Navathe, J.L. Weldon, and T.L. Kunii. V, 227 pages. 1982.

Vol. 133: Data Base Design Techniques II: Proceedings, 1979. Edited by S.B. Yao and T.L. Kunii. V, 229–399 pages. 1982.

Vol. 134: Program Specification. Proceedings, 1981. Edited by J. Staunstrup. IV, 426 pages. 1982.

Vol. 135: R.L. Constable, S.D. Johnson, and C.D. Eichenlaub, An Introduction to the PL/CV2 Programming Logic. X, 292 pages. 1982.

Vol. 136: Ch. M. Hoffmann, Group-Theoretic Algorithms and Graph Isomorphism. VIII, 311 pages. 1982.

Vol. 137: International Symposium on Programming. Proceedings, 1982. Edited by M. Dezani-Ciancaglini and M. Montanari. VI, 406 pages. 1982.

Vol. 138: 6th Conference on Automated Deduction. Proceedings, 1982. Edited by D.W. Loveland. VII, 389 pages. 1982.

Vol. 139: J. Uhl, S. Drossopoulou, G. Persch, G. Goos, M. Dausmann, G. Winterstein, W. Kirchgässner, An Attribute Grammar for the Semantic Analysis of Ada. IX, 511 pages. 1982.

Vol. 140: Automata, Languages and programming. Edited by M. Nielsen and E.M. Schmidt. VII, 614 pages. 1982.

Vol. 141: U. Kastens, B. Hutt, E. Zimmermann, GAG: A Practical Compiler Generator. IV, 156 pages. 1982.

Lecture Notes in Computer Science

Edited by G. Goos and J. Hartmanis

181

Foundations of Software Technology and Theoretical Computer Science

Fourth Conference, Bangalore, India
December 13–15, 1984
Proceedings

FST and TCS 4

Edited by Mathai Joseph and Rudrapatna Shyamasundar

Springer-Verlag
Berlin Heidelberg New York Tokyo 1984

Editorial Board
D. Barstow W. Brauer P. Brinch Hansen D. Gries D. Luckham
C. Moler A. Pnueli G. Seegmüller J. Stoer N. Wirth

Editors
Mathai Joseph
Rudrapatna Shyamasundar
Computer Science Group, Tata Institute of Fundamental Research
Homi Bhabha Road, Bombay 400 005, India

CR Subject Classification (1982): B.7, D.1, D.2, F.1, F.2, F.3, F.4, H.1, H.2, I.1

ISBN 3-540-13883-8 Springer-Verlag Berlin Heidelberg New York Tokyo
ISBN 0-387-13883-8 Springer-Verlag New York Heidelberg Berlin Tokyo

This work is subject to copyright. All rights are reserved, whether the whole or part of the material is concerned, specifically those of translation, reprinting, re-use of illustrations, broadcasting, reproduction by photocopying machine or similar means, and storage in data banks. Under § 54 of the German Copyright Law where copies are made for other than private use, a fee is payable to "Verwertungsgesellschaft Wort", Munich.

© by Springer-Verlag Berlin Heidelberg 1984
Printed in Germany

Printing and binding: Beltz Offsetdruck, Hemsbach/Bergstr.
2145/3140-543210

Preface

For four years now, the FST&TCS Conferences have been providing an annual occasion for the presentation of topics of current research in India and abroad. After a hesitant start, interest and enthusiasm in the Conference has grown enormously: this year there were 58 submissions from authors in 10 countries. A large and extremely cooperative panel of referees has helped in keeping a high standard for the accepted papers. And one of the rewards of submitting a paper has been that most authors receive detailed comments whether or not their papers are accepted.

Selected papers from the first two conferences have, after revision, appeared as special issues of Theoretical Computer Science in 1983 and 1984. Another special issue with papers from the third conference is now being prepared.

Acknowledgements

We would like to thank the invited speakers, Professors Kowalski, Parikh, Sahni and Thiagarajan, for agreeing so readily to give talks. The referees deserve a great deal of gratitude for their careful attention, often at very short notice.

The major secretarial assistance for the conference came from Mrs. Asha Ramaswamy and, during her absence, from Mr. P.R. Chandrashekhar. The conference would have been difficult to organize without their assistance. And once again, Mr. T.M. Sahadevan and the staff of the TIFR Centre in Bangalore have provided valuable help.

Mathai Joseph
R.K.Shyamasundar

Conference Advisory Committee

A Chandra, IBM Armonk
B Chandrasekaran, Ohio State U
S Crespi-Reghizzi, Milan Polytech
D Gries, Cornell U
A K Joshi, U of Pennsylvania
U Montanari, U of Pisa
J H Morris, Carnegie-Mellon U
A Nakamura, Hiroshima U
R Narasimhan, NCSDCT
J Nievergelt, ETH, Zurich
M Nivat, LITP, Paris
R Parikh, Brooklyn College
S Rao Kosaraju, Johns Hopkins
B Reusch, U of Dortmund
S Sahni, U of Minnesota
R Sethi, AT&T Bell Labs
P S Thiagarajan, Aarhus U
W A Wulf, Tartan Labs

Programme Committee

M Joseph, TIFR
S N Maheshwari, IIT, Delhi
S L Mehndiratta, IIT, Bombay
K V Nori, Tata R.D.D.C.
S V Rangaswamy, IISc, Bangalore
R K Shyamasundar, TIFR
R Siromoney, Madras Christian College

LIST OF REVIEWERS

The Programme Committee would like to thank the following reviewers for their comments on papers submitted for the Conference.

S Aggarwal, AT&T Bell Labs
S Arun-Kumar, TIFR
R J R Back, Åbo Academy
J L Baer, U of Washington
A Bagchi, IIM, Calcutta
G Barua, IIT, Kanpur
M Bellia, U of Pisa
A Bernstein, SUNY Stony Brook
P C P Bhatt, IIT, New Delhi
S Biswas, IIT, Kanpur
F J Brandenburg, U Passau
P J Brown, U of Kent
R Chandrasekar, NCSDCT
B Chazelle, Brown U
M Clint, Queen's U of Belfast
S Crespi-Reghizzi, Milan PolyTech
M Crochemore, U de Haute Normandie
D M Dhamdhere, IIT, Bombay
A Finkel, U Paris-Sud
N Francez, Technion, Haifa
C Frougny, LITP, Paris
J von zur Gathen, U of Toronto
R Gerth, U of Utrecht
M G Gouda, U of Texas, Austin
D T Gray, Queen's U of Belfast
D Harel, Weizmann Inst.
M Hennessy, Edinburgh U
M Henson, U of Essex
P Hitchcock, U of Newcastle
A Joshi, U of Pennsylvania
R Kannan, Carnegie-Mellon U
D Kapur, GE Res. Labs
C M Kintala, AT&T Bell Labs
M S Krishnamoorthy, RPI, Troy
R Kuiper, U of Manchester
J L Lassez, U of Melbourne
P Lauer, U of Newcastle
K Lodaya, TIFR
S Mahadevan, TIFR
M Maher, U of Melbourne
B Mayoh, U of Aarhus
A McGettrick, U of Strathclyde
A Moitra, Cornell U
U Montanari, U of Pisa
P Mosses, U of Aarhus
S P Mudur, NCSDCT
A Nakamura, Hiroshima U
P Narendran, GE Res. Labs
P Pandya, TIFR
F Panzieri, U of Newcastle
M S Paterson, U of Warwick
G Plotkin, Edinburgh U
A Pneuli, Weizmann Inst.
T V Prabhakar, IIT, Kanpur
D K Pradhan, U of Massachusetts
V R Prasad, NCSDCT
R Ramanujam, TIFR
S P Rana, IIT, New Delhi
K Rangarajan, Madras Christian College
P Sadanandan, NCSDCT
R Sanghal, IIT, Kanpur
E M Schmidt, U of Aarhus
F Schreiber, Milan PolyTech
Z Segall, Carnegie-Mellon U
P Shankar, IISc, Bangalore
S K Shrivastava, U of Newcastle
K Sikdar, ISI, Calcutta
M K Sinha, NCSDCT
S Sokolsky, U of Gdansk
C Stirling, Edinburgh U
P S Thiagarajan, U of Aarhus
V G Tikekar, IISc, Bangalore
J Vautherin, U de Paris-Sud
C E Veni Madhavan, IISc, Bangalore
T M Vijayaraman, NCSDCT
N Viswanatham, IISc, Bangalore
K Voss, GMD, St. Augustin
P J L Wallis, U of Bath

TABLE OF CONTENTS

* Short presentation

Logic for Knowledge Representation

R. A. Kowalski
Imperial College of Science and Technology
Department of Computing
London SW7 2BZ

A formal computer-based language such as formal logic, can be judged for two properties:

- its expressiveness for knowledge representation,
- its problem-solving power.

The procedural interpretation of Horn clause logic, which is the basis of logic programming, contributes to the general advancement of formal logic in both of these areas. It contributes to knowledge representation because it shows how to represent algorithms and procedures in formal logic; and it contributes to problem-solving because it shows how goal-directed, efficient computation can be obtained as a special case of more general logical deduction.

Much of the recent interest in logic programming has focussed on improving the efficiency of its implementations, both the implementation of sequential PROLOG and the design and implementation of parallel logic programming languages. Interest in knowledge representation has concentrated on new applications to natural language processing and expert systems as well as on implementation oriented applications in system programming. Here I shall sketch some further applications of logic programming to knowledge representation in

- systems analysis,
- the formal analysis of legislation, and
- the representation of events and time.

I shall discuss some of the implications of such applications for software engineering.

Systems analysis

In his classic book [6] on structured systems analysis, DeMarco represents the software development life cycle by means of the following dataflow diagram:

Diagram: Software Development Life Cycle	(DeMarco)

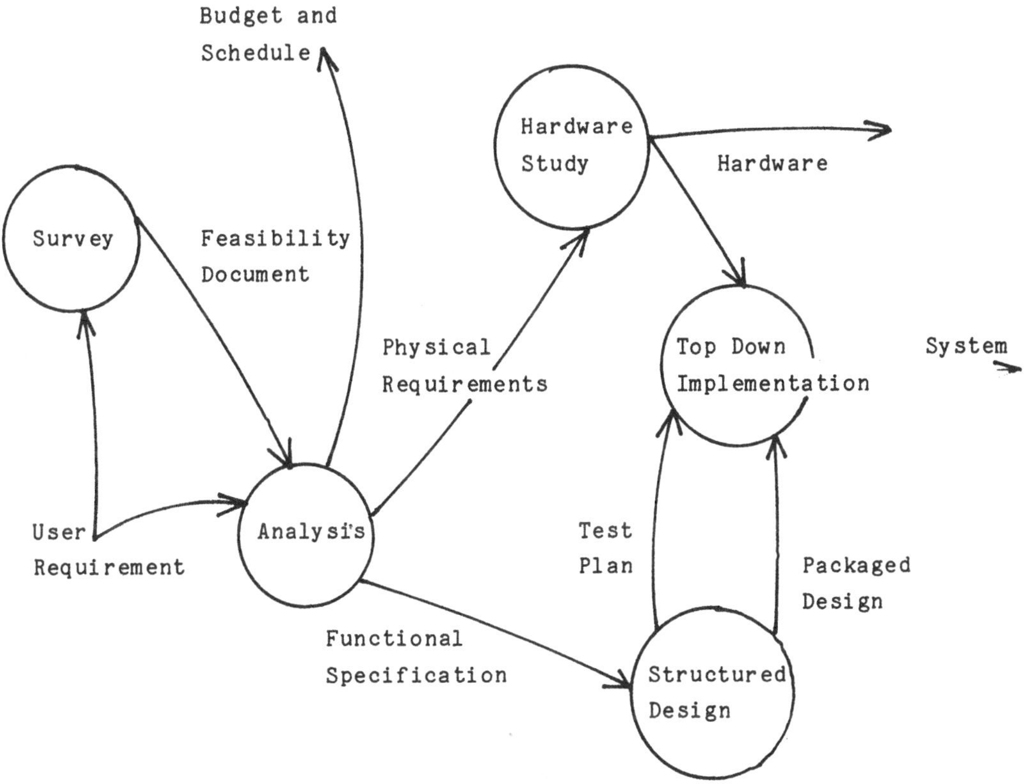

He argues compellingly for the general use of dataflow diagrams as the major tool for communicating between the user and the system analyst. Such diagrams are a graphical representation of knowledge which is easily intelligible to users without any knowledge of computers. On the other hand, it is sufficiently rigorous to communicate the results to the systems designer.

Independently of the applications to systems analysis, Kahn and MacQueen [8] showed how to execute dataflow diagrams as communicating processes; and DeLucena and van Emden [7] and Clark and Gregory [3] showed how to extend the Kahn-MacQueen results to logic programming. This can be illustrated by the following example.

Diagram: possible customer for product

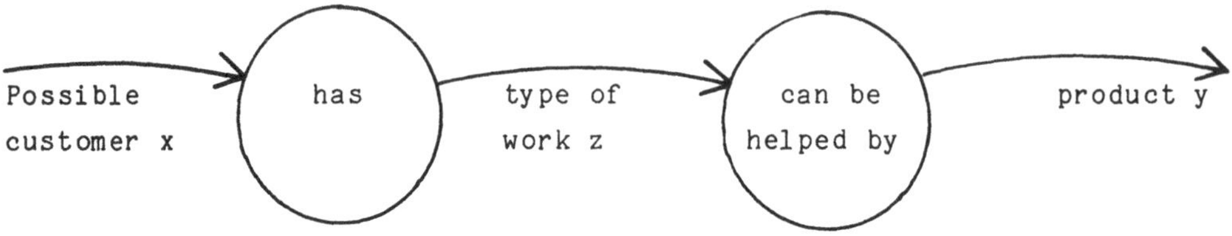

The diagram can be expressed as a Horn clause. The label of the diagram identifies the conclusion and the processes, represented by circles, identify the conditions. The communication channels, represented by arcs, identify the arguments of the predicates.

x is a possible customer for product y
if x has type of work z
and z can be helped by y

The arrows on the arcs indicate the intended direction of dataflow:

Given a possible customer,
find what kind of work he has and
find a product which can help that work.

Such directionality is more closely associated with functional programming than it is with relational, logic programming. The logic program can equally be used to find customers for a given product:

Given a product,
find what kind of work that product can help, and
find a possible customer who has that type of work.

The use of logic liberates the knowledge which is contained within the user's restricted perception of the user requirement.

James Martin in his advocacy of fourth generation languages [11] voices several criticisms of structured systems analysis, which can be resolved by representing dataflow diagrams as logic programs:

- The dataflow diagram and therefore the systems analysis can be executed, tested and debugged before the detailed specification, design and implementation of the system. In many cases the executable analysis is sufficiently efficient that it can be used as the final system in its own right.

- The logic program representation of the systems analysis is not restricted to the user's perception of the requirement. It can represent the underlying model of the problem domain and can assist the solution of unforseen problems, unanticipated requirements and unexploited opportunities.

To a limited extent, we have been able to demonstrate these characteristics of logic programming in our partial formalization [1] of the British Nationality Act and our calculus of events [10].

The formal analysis of legislation

Legislation is an especially good domain for the analysis and solution of knowledge representation problems. Although its syntax is often archaic and unnecessarily complex, it normally aims to be precise and unambiguous without being rigid and inflexible. It is a domain with a long and rich tradition of logical analysis, which is ripe for the application of modern developments in computational logic.

The very first subsection 1.1 of the British Nationality Act 1981, illustrates some of these characteristics:

> "A person born in the United Kingdom after commencement shall be a British citizen if at the time of birth his father or mother is:
>
> (a) "a British citizen; or .... "

Subsection 1.1.a, for example, might be represented at a first approximation as follows:

```
x is a British citizen if  x was born in U.K.
                        and x was born on date y
                        and y is after commencement
                        and z is parent of y
```

```
                          and z is a British citizen on date y.
```

That this is inadequate can be seen immediately, once we recognize the mismatch between the conclusion and the last condition of the rule. Implicit in the original English form of the rule is the intended conclusion that

```
x acquires British citizenship on date y.
```

Moreover, implicit in the Act as a whole is the unstated assumption:

```
x is a British citizen on date y
                    if  x acquires British citizenship on date z
                    and y is on or after z
                    and x is alive on date y
                    and x has not lost citizenship between z and y
```

But even these changes are insufficient. Elsewhere in the Act the rule for acquisition by descent, shows that the notion of British citizenship requires an additional parameter to identify the subsection of the Act by means of which x acquires British citizenship:

> "A person born outside the United Kingdom after commencement shall be a British citizen if at the time of birth his father or mother -
>   (a) is a British citizen otherwise then by descent; or ..."

To take this into account the formalization of subsection 1.1.a needs to be changed to:

```
x acquires British citizenship by subsection 1.1.a on date y
                    if x was born in U.K.
                    and x was born on date y
                    and y is after commencement
                    and z is parent of y
                    and z is a British citizen by
                    subsection u on date y.
```

This example shows that, despite its relatively formal character, legislation still contains much imprecision and avoidable ambiguity.

The analysis of legislation by means of any formal language must consequently be a trial and error process, more closely related to systems analysis than to programming or program specification. But it also shows that the formal representation of legislation is not tied to any preconceived notion of the user's requirement.

During two months in the summer of 1983, a postgraduate student, Fariba Sadri, at Imperial College under the direction of Marek Sergot represented most of the 1981 British Nationality Act as a PROLOG "program". She could fit only a relatively small, but self-contained, portion of the Act within the confines of a micro- PROLOG [4] system running on an IBM-pc. Nonetheless, the implementation was sufficiently complete to demonstrate a number of characteristics which conflict with the conventional software engineering model of software development:

- The formal analysis of the legislation, with only minor modifications to eliminate three non terminating loops by program transformation methods, ran with almost tolerable efficiency for deciding problems of citizenship within its domain.

- The formal representation is not restricted to the solution of any predetermined collection of problems. It can be used in theory not only to determine citizenship but also to test for arbitrary logical consequences of the legislation. In practice however, PROLOG with its left-to-right solution of subproblems and its sequential choice of problem solving methods is incomplete and unable to prove all the theorems which logically follow from the legislation. Nonetheless, even with such limitations, it could serve as a useful aid to drafters of legislation, not only to determine logical consequences of proposed legislation but also to sharpen, clarify and simplify the English formulation of the law.

The potential of computational logic applied to legislation has only begun to be explored. Better problem-solving strategies are needed for its more effective exploitation. But further advances are also needed in knowledge representation. How are we to represent, for example, such phrases as:

"If on an application for naturalization as a British citizen made by a person of full age and capacity, the Secretary of State is satisfied that the applicant fulfils the requirements of Schedule 1 for naturalization as such a citizen under the subsection, he may, if he thinks fit, grant to him a certificate of naturalization as such a citizen."

"... would have been so deemed if male..."

The first, as we were told by a civil servant, was designed to make that part of the Act "lawyer-proof". The second is a special case of reasoning with counter factual conditions. It may be that in both cases a faithful representation of the intended meaning can be obtained by combining object level and metalevel knowledge representation and reasoning [2].

The calculus of events and time

Fundamental to all more advanced applications of logic to knowledge representation is the representation of events and time. Two such applications which my colleague Marek Sergot and I have investigated are database updates and narratives [10]. It is, of course, also central to the formal analysis of legislation. The following narrative illustrates some of the problems which need to be solved:

(1) Mary was hired as lecturer on 10 May 1970.
(2) John left as lecturer on 1 June 1975.
(3) Mary left as professor on 1 October 1980.
(4) Mary was promoted on 1 June 1975.

The consecutive sentences of the narrative can be regarded as consecutive updates to an initially empty database. Notice, that in a narrative, unlike a conventional database, events can be reported and assimilated in an order which is independent of the order in which they actually take place. The assimilation of updates by adding and deleting information, which is characteristic of conventional databases, is inappropriate to more general narratives. Moreover, deletion, implemented as destructive assignment, does not mix well with the ordinary semantics of logic.

We treat all updates as adding potentially new knowledge to a "knowledge base". Assimilating a report that some relationship has ended is dealt with by _adding_ information about the end of the time period for which the relationship holds. Thus all time-varying relations have an associated time period which records the duration for which the relationship holds. But time periods, instead of being primitive concepts, are defined in terms of _events_ which are primitive. For example, the narrative above (in the spirit of semantic case representation of natural language) might be represented as a sequence of statements about events:

(1) E1 is an _act_ of hiring.
The _object_ of E1 is Mary.
The _destination_ of E1 is lecturer.
The _time_ of E1 is 10 May 1970.

(2) E2 is an _act_ of leaving.
The _object_ of E2 is John.
The _source_ of E2 is lecturer.
The _time_ of E2 is 1 June 1975.

(3) E3 is an _act_ of leaving.
The _object_ of E3 is Mary.
The _source_ of E3 is professor.
The _time_ of E3 is 1 October 1980.

(4) E4 is an _act_ of promotion.
The _object_ of E4 is Mary.
The _time_ of E4 is 1 June 1975.

The semantic case representation facilitates the representation of incomplete events such as E4 by means of binary relationships.

Time periods can be derived from events and named by terms which contain event names as parameters. For example, the information in (1) implies the existence of a time period, say

after(E1)

such that

"Mary has rank lecturer" holds for after(E1).

This can be derived by means of a rule formulated in a language which combines object language with metalanguage:

```
"x has rank y" holds for after(e)
                    if e is an act of hiring
                    and the object of e is x
                    and the destination of e is y
```

Similarly, and symmetrically, the information in (2) implies the existence of a time period, say

before(E2)

such that

"John has rank lecturer" holds for before(E2).

This can be derived by the rule

```
"x has rank y" holds for before (e)
                    if e is an act of leaving
                    and the object of e is x
                    and the source of e is y.
```

The start of after(E1) and the end of before(E2) can be derived by the conditionless rules

Start(after(e) e)
End(before(e) e).

It is possible to formulate the rules for promotion using negation as failure in such a way that after assimilating (4) we can derive

End(after(E1) E4)
Start(before(E3) E4).

This approach deals both with events which are identified as occurring at a particular time as well as with events which are only partially ordered. It also caters for events which happen simultaneously.

The event calculus deals with some of the problems which are handled by the situation calculus [12]. But by dealing with localized time periods rather than with global situations it avoids the worst of the inefficiencies which arise from the frame problem. Because relationships hold for time periods rather than at "time slices" the frame axiom, which causes the frame problem (and states that a relationship which holds at a time slice continues to hold at the next time slice, if it is not effected by the transition between time slices) does not arise. On the other hand, the use of the event calculus for plan-formation seems to be significantly more complicated than the use of the situation calculus.

The need for metalanguage in this formalization is very restricted and can be simulated by writing rules such as:

```
Holds(rank(x y) after(e))
        if Act(e hiring)
        and Object(e x)
        and Destination(e y)
```

which can be executed by PROLOG. Nonterminating loops can be eliminated by "program" transformation.

The calculus of events is another example, therefore, of a representation of knowledge which is closer to a system analysis than it is to a program or a program specification. As in the case of our formalization of the British Nationality Act, it is a formal analysis which, after suitable transformation, runs as a prototype program. Moreover, its application is not restricted to any previously forseen collection of user requirements.

Conclusion

The very terminology "logic programming" tends to reinforce the view that logic is another, albeit very important, tool to further the ends of the software engineer. This perhaps has distracted attention from the more revolutionary potential of logic to alter the nature of software engineering altogether. In a small and preliminary way, new applications such as those illustrated in this paper may give an indication of the longer terms possibilities.

Acknowledgements

The calculus of events is the result of joint work with Marek Sergot, who also played a leading role in our work on the British Nationality Act. We are both grateful to Fariba Sadri for her work on the BNA and for her helpful comments on the event calculus.

This work was supported by the Science and Engineering Research Council.

References

[1] British Nationality Act 1981. Chapter 61. Her Majesty's Stationary Office, London.

[2] Bowen, K. and Kowalski, R. A. (1982). Amalgamating language and metalanguage in Logic Programming. In "Logic Programming" (Eds. Clark, K. L. and Tarnlund, S.-A.) Academic Press, London, New York.

[3] Clark, K. L. and Gregory, S. (1981). A relational language for parallel programming. In "Functional Programming Languages and Computer Architecture". ACM, New York.

[4] Clark, K. L. and McCabe, F. (1984). Micro Prolog: Programming in Logic. Prentice Hall International, Englewood Cliffs, N. J.

[5] Cory, H. T., Hammond, P., Kowalski, R. A., Kriwaczek, F., Sadri, F. and Sergot, M. (1984). The British Nationality Act as a Logic Program. Dept. of Computing, Imperial College, London.

[6] DeMarco, T. (1979). Structured Analysis and System Specification. Prentice Hall, Englewood Cliffs, N. J.

[7] van Emden, M. H. and deLucena Filho, G. J. (1982). Predicate Logic as a Language for Parallel Programming. In "Logic Programming" (Eds. Clark, K. L. and Tarnlund, S.-A.) Academic Press, London, New York.

[8] Kahn, G. and McQueen, D. B. (1977). Coroutines and networks of parallel processes. Proc. IFIP 77.

[9] Kowalski, R. A. (1979). Logic for Problem Solving. North Holland. Amsterdam, New York.

[10] Kowalski, R. A. and Sergot, M. (1984). A Calculus of Events. Department of Computing, Imperial College, London.

[11] Martin, J. (1982). Application Development without programmers. Prentice Hall, Englewood Cliffs, N. J.

[12] McCarthy, J. and Hayes, P. J. (1969). Some Philosophical Problems from the Standpoint of Artificial Intelligence. Machine Intelligence 4, Edinburgh University Press, New York, (Meltzer, B. and Michie, D. Eds.), pp. 463-502.

LOGICAL SPECIFICATION AND IMPLEMENTATION

T S E Maibaum*, M R Sadler*, P A S Veloso**

* Dept. of Computing
Imperial College of Science and Technology
180 Queen's Gate, London SW7 2BZ

** Departmento de Informatica
Pontificia Universidade Catolica
Rua Marques de Sao Vicente, 225
22453 Rio de Janeiro, RJ Brazil

Abstract

It has become customary to focus attention on the semantic aspects of specification and implementation, a model theoretic or algebraic viewpoint. We feel, however, that certain concepts are best dealt with at the syntactic level, rather than via a detour through semantics, and that implementation is one of these concepts. We regard logic as the most appropriate medium for talking about specification (whether of abstract data types, programs, databases, specifications - as an interpretation between theories say, rather than something to do with the embedding of models or mapping of algebras. In this paper, we give a syntactic account of implementation and prove the basic results - composability of implementations and how to deal with structured (hierarchical) specifications modularly - for abstract data types.

Introduction

As we see it, the two key concepts in an approach to, or theory of, specification are the notions of specification (our objects if you like) and implementation (the morphisms between objects). At this stage we feel that is not as appropriate to investigate the category-theoretic properties of these notions (giving us the category(s) of specifications and implementations), as to continue to explore particular ways of looking at these notions based on various mathematical formalisms (algebra, set-theory, logic for example) and how these formalisms support more complex ideas like parameterisation and other mechanisms for structuring specifications.

Our claim is that logic, or the logical approach, with an emphasis on syntactic ideas is a particularly fruitful formalism. In this paper we show how the logical approach supports specification of abstract data types and implementations of abstract data types within other abstract data types.

Given an area of computing science an important first step for a theory of specification with respect to that area is an identification of what is (are) the basic unit(s) of specification, see [LZ]. That is, the packages that are used as the atomic building blocks for building more complex, structured specifications. Here we consider abstract data types as our units, or atoms with programming as the obvious area in mind. Similarly any formalism offers, or studies, various structures: in the case of logic, logics or theories say. Now part of what we would like for an approach to specification is a natural match, in some sense, between the formal structures and the units of specification. And this natural match should also extend to a match between on the one hand the kinds of mappings between our formal structures and on the other the ways we naturally put our specifications together to form structured specifications and implement specifications in each other.

The formal structures to study in a logical approach are the theories given by languages, L, over some fixed consequence relation $\vdash$ determining the logic. The decision to follow a logical approach appears in no way to commit one to any particular $\vdash$, other than a requirement that certain meta-theorems are provable about $\vdash$, the Craig Interpolation Lemma for example. (See 'Theorem' in the section: Using Implementations).

We choose to use an infinitary logic and this is where criticism is often focused. However we feel that such criticism misses the point. The major focus of attention should be as to whether we have this natural match between units of specification and formal structures, here between abstract data types and theories. We claim this match is obviously natural.

We cannot always expect (for any given approach) things to be so simple, for more complex objects more complex formal structures might be required. For specification of databases, for example, families of modal theories (and even families of families of modal theories) form the more appropriate formal structures, see [KMS].

Below we explain the logical approach to specification, implementation (in some detail) and how to use implementations to support the software design process.

Specifications

We begin by reviewing the approach to specification outlined in [MV]. There, structuring of specifications was defined in terms of semantic concepts but here a purely syntactic line using an extended first order logic with infinitary formulae and infinitary rules is taken. We conceive of specifications as theories within this modification of first order logic. The reader is assumed to be familiar with the concepts of first order logic, see, for example [END], [SCH], but we explain the modifications we make as the formal details are presented.

Expressiveness in our approach is determined by the use of many sorted languages. We require an equality symbol for each sort, but regard them as part of the non-logical vocabulary. Thus the equality symbols are not regarded as logical constants as in most approaches based on logic or algebra. In practice, rather than presenting such languages as lists of sorts, operations and so on, we use syntax diagrams to convey the information pictorially. For example:

L_{nat}:

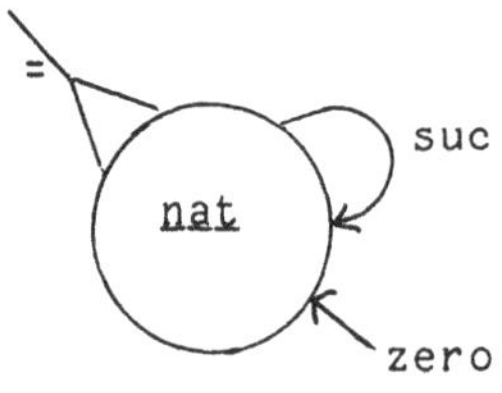

L_{nat} is an appropriate language for the natural numbers. That is, L_{nat} has one sort, nat, one constant, zero, of type (NIL,nat), a further operation, suc, of type (<nat>,nat) and a predicate symbol, =, of type <nat,nat> (where NIL is the empty string, <nat> and <nat,nat> are strings of lengths one and two respectively). For clarity, we usually suppress equality symbols from such diagrams.

The set of terms, Term(L), over a language L is defined in the usual way and we define the names, Name(L), of L to be the variable free terms in Term(L). The formulae and sentences (closed formulae) of L present our first opportunity for extending the more common first order notions. Our formulae are those of the extension to the traditional first-order language given by adding infinitary disjunctions (V). The sets of such formulae and sentences we denote by Form(L), Sent(L) respectively.

Example

for-all x ($V_{n \text{ in } N}$ x = n)

where N is an enumeration of Name(L_{nat}). Thus this formula is equivalent to:

for-all x (x=zero v x=suc(zero) v x=suc(suc(zero)) v ...).

This formula indicates that the only allowed values (up to =) over which a variable x of sort <u>nat</u> can range are the names in Name(L_{nat}). (Thus any structure satisfying this sentence will have no nonstandard values for the natural numbers.)

A **specification**, S, is a pair (L,A) where L is a many sorted language (with infinite disjunctions), A is a consistent subset of Sent(L) and where, for each sort s of L, we have:

i) L contains $=_s$ a predicate symbol of type <s,s> and A contains the usual congruence properties for $=_s$ - reflexivity, symmetry, transitivity and substitutivity. We usually drop the subscript from $=_s$ when it is clear from the context,

ii) A contains for-all x ($V_{n \text{ in Name(s)}}$ x $=_s$ n) where x is a variable of sort s, where Name(s) are the names of sort s in Name(L). (We call such sentences **namability** axioms.)

Again we usually suppress this information in presenting any specification.Note specifications need not contain boolean values and operations - these can be left as logical rather than non-logical concepts.

Examples:

NAT = (L_{nat},A_{nat}) where A_{nat} would also include:

suc(x)=suc(y) -> x=y

-(suc(x)=zero)

and where leading universal quantifiers are suppressed.

INT = (L_{int}, A_{int}) where:

L_{int}:

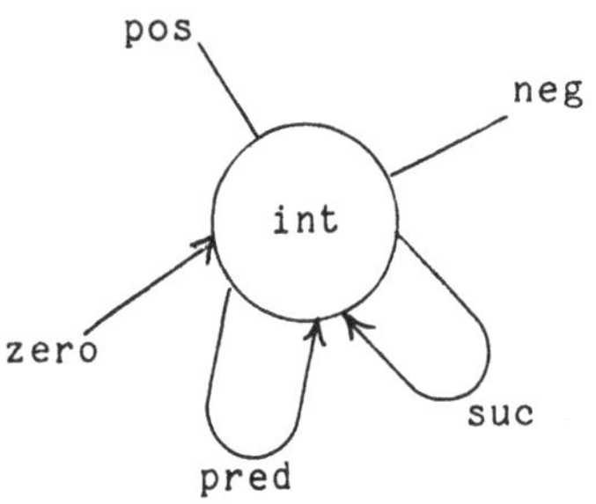

A_{int}:
suc(x)=suc(y) -> x=y
pred(x)=pred(y) -> x=y
pred (suc(x))=x
suc(pred(x))=x
pos(x) -> pos(suc(x))
neg(x) -> neg(pred(x))
pos(suc(zero)
neg(pred(zero))
-pos(zero)
-neg(zero)

A specification (L,A) defines a theory Con(A), which consists of all provable sentences, or logical consequences, of L from A where the concept of proof is based on usual first order notions together with the following omega-rule (ie, infinitary rule) or some appropriate variant:

$$\frac{\text{for-all } x\ (\ V_{n \text{ in } N}\ x=n),\ Q(n_j) \text{ for each } n_j \text{ in } J,\ J \text{ a subset of } T}{\text{for-all } x\ (\ V_{n \text{ in } N-J}\ x=n \text{ v } Q(x))}$$

That is, if we can prove some property Q for some (possibly infinite) subset J of N, then we can replace the disjuncts involving elements of J by the property Q. Thus, for example, we can derive from the above specification (L_{nat},A_{nat}) the sentence for-all x(x=zero v there-exists y (x=suc(y)). One form of the usual induction formula for the natural numbers. We use A |- Q to denote that Q is a logical consequence of A.

We can use namability axioms to help structure our specifications.

Consider, for example, the extension of NAT obtained by adding to L_{nat} the following:

L_{seq}:

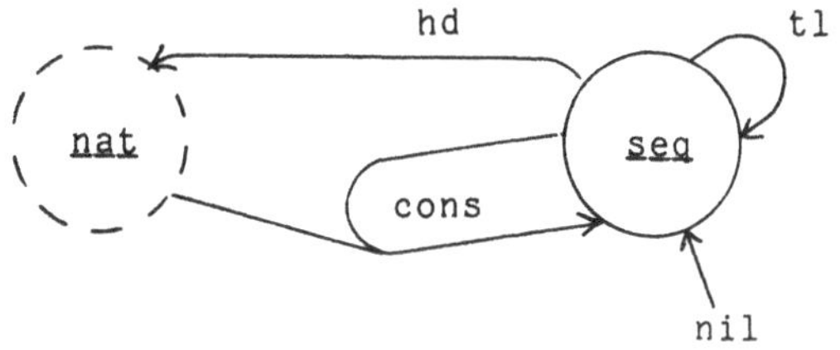

and the axioms:

A_{seq}: hd(cons(x,l))$=_{nat}$x
tl(cons(x,l))$=_{seq}$l
tl(nil)$=_{seq}$ nil
-(nil$=_{seq}$cons(x,l))
cons(x,l)$=_{seq}$cons(y,l') -> x$=_{nat}$ y & l$=_{seq}$l'
$\forall_n$ in Name(seq) l$=_{seq}$n

The (structured) specification, which we denote by (L_{seq},A_{seq})[NAT], has the property that no new natural numbers are introduced by any of the sequence operations as the namability axiom for NAT still ensures that all names for natural numbers must be of the form zero or suc(zero) or ... or equivalent to one of these. Note that this is a much weaker requirement than the sufficient completeness of [GH], [GAN], [WB], etc. Note also that the specification is partial (loose, incomplete, permissive) since no axiom tells us which natural number is the result of hd(nil). Looseness in specifications (the abandonment of a unique isomorphism class of models) has also been introduced by [BG] and [WB]. A different notion of structured specifications was also introduced in [WB] where they were called hierarchical specifications.

The above extension is in fact conservative ([END], [SCH]) - the extended theory contains no new theorems about the language being extended. That is (L_{seq},A_{seq})[NAT] has no theorems in Sent(L_{nat}) that are not provable from A_{nat}.

Semantics for specifications are provided by logical structures satisfying the axioms. Again we should point out that objects related by = symbols need not be identified in models. The namability axioms also ensure that we have only the so-called finitely generated models of [WB].

We mention the following completeness result.

Theorem:
Given a specification S and a sentence Q, then Q is valid in all models of S (ie namable models) iff Q is provable from S.

Implementation

In the corpus of work on specification of data types and programs, theories of implementation have occupied a very important place. It is via such theories that the informal software engineering notion of stepwise refinement can be incorporated into a formalisation of the programming process. Amongst the large amount of material produced on this subject, the most notable are [GTW], [HUP], [EKP], [EHR], [GAN], [EK], [SW], all of which use algebras as semantics for specifications. There is also some work on implementations using logic, as in [NOU].

Clearly, an implementation relates two specifications and the general approach used in the work referenced above is to relate the two specifications via their semantics - by applying various constructions to an algebra (model) satisfying the target specification, one can obtain an algebra satisfying the source specification. We believe that arguing in terms of models is wasteful, both formally and practically, and present a purely syntactic theory of implementation.

The concept of implementation we use is based on the logical notion of interpretation between theories. Thus, our specifications generate corresponding theories and these are related by interpretations. An interpretation shows how one can realise the concepts of one theory in terms of another - this being more or less the process described as implementation. The theories of implementation presented in other approaches do not use interpretations and hence have to resort to non-syntactic reasoning. Moreover, the composition of implementations (which needs to be defined in order to formalise the stepwise refinement process) does not have an adequate definition in any of the algebraic approaches mentioned above. This inadequacy manifests itself both in the shortcomings of the formal properties as well as in not modelling the software engineering practice which seems to work.

Formal inadequacy has been demonstrated by [PV] where it is shown that certain desirable properties are not preserved by composition as well as in [EHR], where composition is not constructive (and so inadequate for practice). Practical inadequacy can be used to illustrate what is wrong with these definitions.

Suppose that a software engineer sets out to write some program using sets. Having proved the correctness of his abstract program using the properties of set operations, he then implements sets in terms of sequences, say. Together with the abstract program, the procedures/functions defining set operations in terms of sequence operations then becomes an 'executable' implementation if the programming language has sequences as a built in data type. If not, then a further suite of procedures/functions is defined to implement sequences and the abstract program together with the set operation implementation and the sequence operation implementation constitute the final implementation. In the theories mentioned above, it is felt necessary to eliminate the equivalent of the sequence procedures (which in the program interface between the abstract program using sets and the language based constructs in terms of which sequences are implemented). This is analogous to defining recursively f in terms of g, g in terms of h, and then trying to compose the two by eliminating any occurrence of g. Often no such finite definition can be obtained by simple substitutions of definitions for symbols - hence the problems indicated in [EHR] and [PV].

When interpretations between theories are composed, no such attempt at eliminating the mediating language is made. Thus these problems are avoided.

An interpretation between theories is a translation between the underlying languages, terms, formulae, etc, which respects the properties expressed in the theory being interpreted. Thus each sort of the source language is mapped to a (tuple of) sort(s) of the target language, non-logical symbols to appropriate non-logical symbols and quantifiers to restricted quantifiers - ie, quantifiers relativised to predicates.

First an example:

We will informally discuss how to interpret INT = (L_{int},A_{int}) by means of NBOOL = (L_{NB},A_{NB}) which is an extension of NAT obtained by adding the sort bool, the symbols T, F of type (NIL,bool) and the axiom -T=F. Note that the namability axiom for bool is simply b=T v b=F.

Our intention is, of course, to represent the integer n (an abbreviation for n applications of suc to zero) by n of nat and T of bool and -n (an abbreviation for n applications of pred to zero) by n of nat and F of bool. Zero of Int can be represented in two ways (as zero and T or as zero and F). Note that, unlike other theories of data types, we do not have to create a new sort nat x bool and associated pairing and projection functions (of course we are not prevented from doing so). There is also some leeway in implementing the function symbols of L_{int}, either as a single function that returns two values (one from nat and one from bool), or as two functions each returning one value (one function having result nat and the other result bool). We choose the latter option here, but in general choose whichever option seems more appropriate for a given context.

For a term t of Term(L_{int}) we define two components $t_B{}^I$ and $t_B{}^I$ both of Term(L_{NB}) where the subscripts N and B provide us with sort information, nat and bool respectively. Thus our interpretation I consists of the following:

i) We associate with the sort int the pair of sorts nat and bool.

ii) We associate with int a relativisation predicate is_int of type <bool,nat> which we add to L_{NB} and which is defined by the following axiom:

$$\text{is\_int}(x_B, x_N)$$

This axiom says that any pair of boolean and natural number values represents some integer. (In general, we will not be so lucky. Only some values in the target of an interpretation will represent values in the source.)

iii) We associate with each function symbol (including the constants) of L_{int} a pair of function symbols which are added to L_{NB} and whose typing respects the mapping of sorts defined in (i). So we associate with zero of int the zero of nat and T of bool.

(Thus we choose one of the two possibilities mentioned above. The other, the pair zero and F will be equivalent to the pair zero and T.) To suc (pred) of L_{int} we associate sucrepN (predrepN) of type (<bool,nat>,nat), and sucrepB (predrepB) of type (<bool,nat>,bool).

iv) We associate with predicate symbols of L_{int}, predicate symbols which we add to L_{NB} and with typing which respects the mapping defined in (i). Thus to pos (neg) we associate posrep (negrep) of type <bool,nat>. To $=_{int}$ we associate =rep of type (bool,bool,nat,nat). (Note that equality is implemented like any other predicate.)

v) We associate with every variable x of sort int a corresponding pair of variables x_N and x_B of sorts nat and bool, respectively. We also add to A_{NB} axioms defining the new symbols we have added in steps (iii) and (iv). (is_int, added in step (ii), was also defined there via a new axiom added to A_{NB}). Note that =,suc,zero,T and F below are symbols in L_{NB}:

posrep(x_B,x_N) <-> (x_B=T & -x_N=zero)
negrep(x_B,x_N) <-> (x_B=F & -x_N=zero)
=rep(x_B,y_B,x_N,y_N) <-> ((x_N=y_N & x_B=y_B) v (x_N=zero & y_N=zero))

(So two pairs repesenting integers are equivalent - represent the same integer - if the pairs are identical or if the natural number element in each pair is zero.)

x_B=T -> (sucrepN(x_B,x_N)=suc(x_N) & (sucrepB(x_B,x_N)=T)
(x_B=F & -(x_N=zero)) -> (sucrepB(x_B,x_N)=F) &
there-exists y_N(sucrepN(x_B,x_N)=y_N & suc(y_N)=x_N))
(x_B=F & x_N=zero) -> (sucrepB(x_B,x_N)=T & sucrepN(x_B,x_N)=suc(zero)

(These three axioms define sucrepN and sucrepB by cases.)
We add similar axioms for predrepN and predrepB.

Having added the above symbols and axioms to NBOOL, we get a specification ENBOOL. We remark that all values in this new theory are still described by those provided by NBOOL because of the namability axioms for nat and bool. Thus models of ENBOOL can be obtained only by extending those of NBOOL without adding new objects.

(i) - (iv) above define a translation I of terms from INT to ENBOOL

Thus, for example:

$$zero_N^I = zero, \quad zero_B^I = T$$
$$(suc(t))_N^I = sucrepN(t_B^I, t_N^I)$$
$$(suc(t))_B^I = sucrepB(t_B^I, t_N^I) \quad \text{etc.}$$

We extend this translation to atomic formulae by:

$$pos(t)^I = posrep(t_B^I, t_N^I), \quad neg(t)^I = negrep(t_B^I, t_N^I)$$
$$(t=u)^I = {=}rep(t_B^I, u_B^I, t_N^I, u_N^I)$$

For sentences in general, we have to be careful because we want translated sentences to hold only for objects which really represent values in the source of the translation I. (Although we had no 'junk' elements here, in general we do.) We do this by relativising quantifiers - ie, we condition quantifiers to range only over those values which satisfy the relativisation predicates as these are meant to define such representatives. For Q and R formulae we have:

$$(-Q)^I = -Q^I, \quad (Q\&R)^I = Q^I\&R^I$$

and for Q with free variable x we have:

$$(\text{for-all}x Q)^I = \text{for-all}x_B \ \text{for-all}x_N \ (is\_int(x_B, x_N) \rightarrow Q^I)$$
$$(\text{there-exists}x Q)^I = \text{there-exists}x_B \text{there-exists}x_N \ (is\_int(x_B, x_N) \ \& \ Q^I)$$

Thus for example,

$$(\text{for-all}x \ \text{for-all}y \ (suc(x)=suc(y) \rightarrow x=y))^I$$
$$= \ \text{for-all}x_B \ \text{for-all}x_N \ \text{for-all}y_B \ \text{for-all}y_N \ (is\_int(x_B, x_N) \rightarrow$$
$$((is\_int(y_B, y_N) \rightarrow ($$
$${=}rep(sucrepB(x_B, x_N), sucrepB(y_B, y_N), sucrepN(x_B, x_N), sucrepN(y_B, y_N))$$
$$\rightarrow {=}rep(x_B, y_B, x_N, y_N) \ ) \ )).$$

To assure ourselves that our translation I is faithful in the sense of preserving the properties of integers as we have defined them, it is sufficient to show that the axioms A_{int} translate under I to theorems of ENBOOL. In particular, the namability axiom for integers

$\text{for-all}x \ (V_{z \text{ in } Z} \ x=z)$ translates to:
$$\text{for-all}x_B \text{for-all}x_N \ (is\_int(x_B, x_N)) \rightarrow V_{z \text{ in } Z} {=}rep(x_B, z_B^I, x_N, z_N^I))$$

That is, every pair of values satisfying the relativisation predicate is_int must be equivalent to the translation of an allowed name for an integer. One usually checks that the translated namability axiom is a consequence of the target theory by some sort of inductive argument based on names in the source. (We remark that the axioms defining equality also translate to relativised equality axioms.)

In general a translation as defined by (i) - (iv) above with the property that axioms of the source are translated to theorems of the target is called an interpretation between theories [END], [SCH].

Given theories (L_i,A_i) for i=1,2,3,4 and interpretations $I_i:(L_i,A_i) \to (L_{i+1},A_{i+1})$ we have the following simple properties:

a) $I_{i+1} \circ I_i$, for i=1,2,3 exists, is defined obviously in terms of mappings defined analogously to (i) - (iv) above, and is an interpretation between theories.
b) Moreover, $I_3 \circ (I_2 \circ I_1) = (I_3 \circ I_2) \circ I_1$. Thus composition of interpretations is associative.

Based on the above results, extensions of those found in [END], [SCH], we now proceed to give results that connect the two ideas of an extension and an interpretation of a specification.

When we say that we can implement specification S = (L,A) in terms of specification T = (M,B) - for example, INT in terms of NBOOL - we mean that we can extend S conservatively to $T_S[T]$ so that we can define an interpretation between theories $I:S \dashrightarrow T_S[T]$. Denoting conservative extension by >---> we have the following situation:

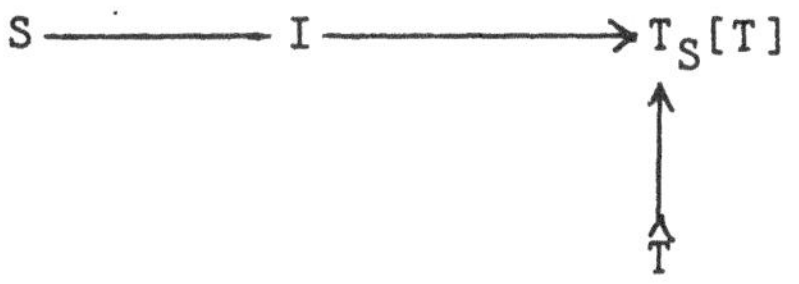

We might characterise the **implementation** of S in T by the pair $(I,T_S[T])$.

Using Implementations
In developing specifications we might now consider doing two things. Firstly, we might want to conservatively extend S and automatically

carry our extension over to the implementation of S by T. That is, we would like to be able to complete the diagram:

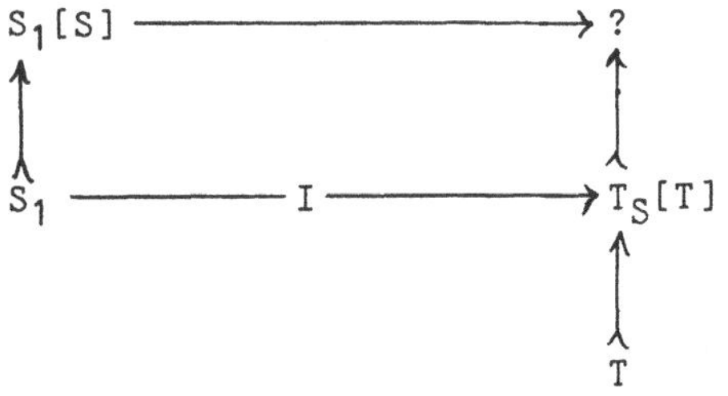

in some automatic fashion.

Secondly, we might wish to use an implementation of T in terms of U to get an implementation of S in terms of U. Graphically, this can be illustrated by the following:

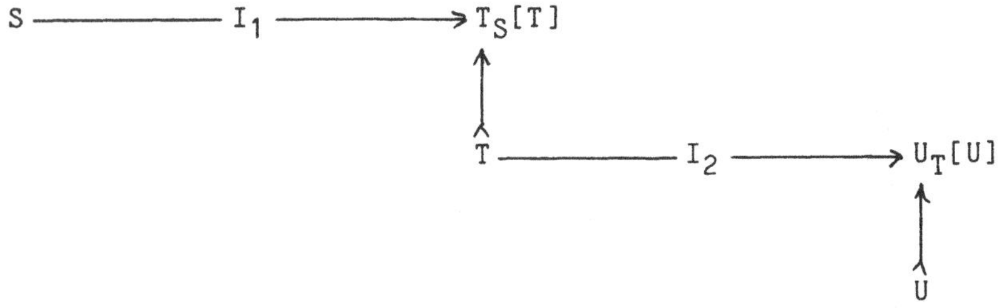

Here (I_2,$U_T[U]$) characterises the implementation of T in U. Again we see that we require the completion of the following 'rectangle'.

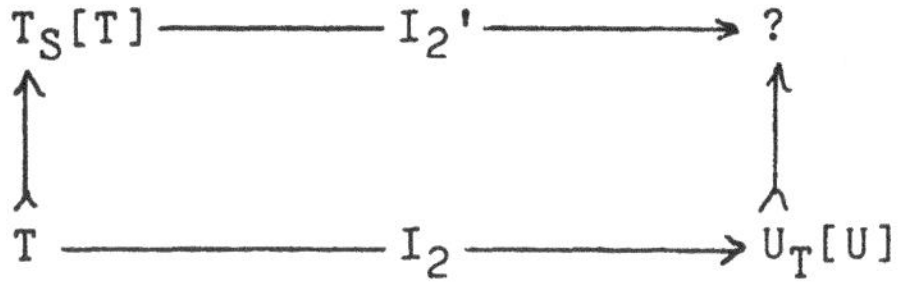

to get:

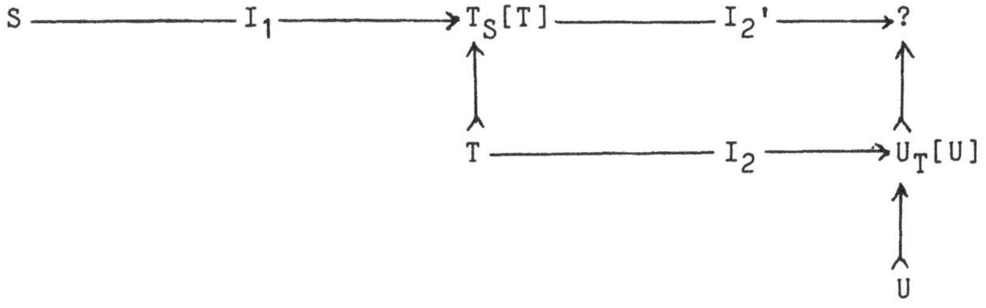

Where $I_2'oI_1$ and the target of I_2' characterise the implementation of S in U. We proceed to show that the missing specification in such rectangles can always be automatically constructed by proving a more general result.

We will say that the extension E: S-->S' is **conservative** exactly in the case that S' contains no theorems, stated only in the language of S, other than those which are provable from S.

Theorem

Suppose that S_1, S_2, S_3 are specifications, and suppose

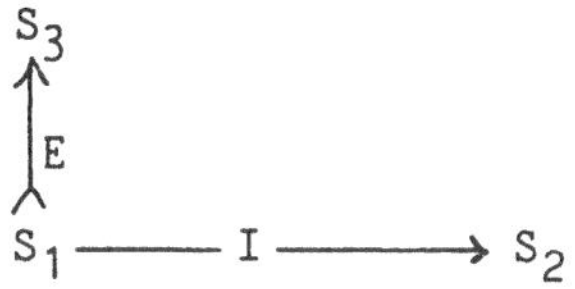

where E is a conservative extension, I an implementation, then there exists S_4 and I' such that:

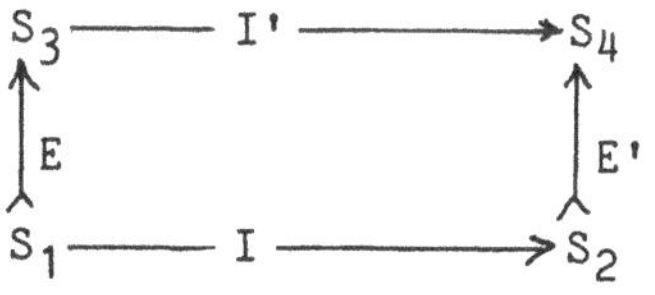

Moreover $E':S_2$-->S_4 is conservative.

Proof

Briefly, S_4 and I' are obtained by extending S_2 and I as follows: For each new sort or symbol introduced in extending S_1 to S_3, add corresponding sort or symbol to S_2. The translation I now extends to translate symbols introduced into S_3 and so we can translate terms or formulae of S_3 to those of S_4. The extension of S_2 to S_4 is completed by adding to S_2 the translations I' of the axioms introduced to get S_3 from S_1. What remains to be checked is the conservativeness of S_2-->S_4 which since S_2 is consistent gives S_4 as consistent. This is a straightforward application of the Craig Interpolation Lemma [MAK], essentially copying the proof of the Robinson Consistency Theorem from the Craig Interpolation Lemma [CK].

Further:
If $E:S_1 \dashrightarrow S_2$ is not conservative then in general S_4 and I' need not exist. For suppose S_1 has predicate p and constant a and neither p(a) nor -p(a) are in $Con(S_1)$. Suppose further that S_1 ---> S_3 and p(a) $Con(S_3)$ and $I:S_1 \rightarrow S_2$ is such that I(p)=p, I(a)=a and -p(a) is in $Con(S_2)$. Then $Con(S_4)$ would have to contain both p(a) and -p(a) which would mean that S_4 was inconsistent.

As an example, let us implement INT in NAT. We already have an implementation of INT in NBOOL (NAT extended by BOOL) and we will now implement NBOOL in NAT. We outline the necessary details below:

nat and bool of NBOOL are both mapped to nat of NAT. To nat of NBOOL we assign the relativisation predicate is_nat of type <nat> which we then define to be the identity on nat of NAT. To bool we assign the relativisation predicate is_bool of type <nat> which we then define to be:

is_bool (x) <-> x=zero v x=suc(zero).

So only zero and suc(zero) in NAT are used as boolean values. Thus this implementation produces 'junk'.

We then map zero, suc, $=_{nat}$ of NBOOL identically to zero, suc, $=_{nat}$ of NAT and we map T, F and $=_{bool}$ of NBOOL to the new symbols T', F', and $='_{bool}$ added to NAT respectively, and define them as follows:

T'=x <-> x=zero F'=x <-> x=suc(zero)
$x='_{bool}$ <-> (x=zero & y=zero) v (x=suc(zero) & y=suc(zero))

To check that this mapping is an interpretation we must check that the axioms of NBOOL translate to theorems of this extended NAT which we call ENAT. Clearly, the axioms for natural numbers in NBOOL translate to formulae logically equivalent to the same axioms in ENAT. As for the axioms concerning BOOL, $-(T=_{bool} F)$ becomes $-(T'='_{bool}F')$. (Note that there are no relativisation predicates in the resulting formulae as there are no variables in the original.) This clearly follows from the fact that in NAT, -(zero=suc(zero).) The namability axiom for bool in NBOOL is $b=_{bool}T$ v $b=_{bool}$ F). Under interpretation, this becomes: is_bool (x) -> ($x='_{bool}T'$ v $x='_{bool}F'$)). By the definitions of is_bool, $='_{bool}$, T', and F' above this is equivalent to:

(x=zero v x=suc(zero)) -> (x=zero v x=suc(zero))

which is a tautology.

Thus we have:

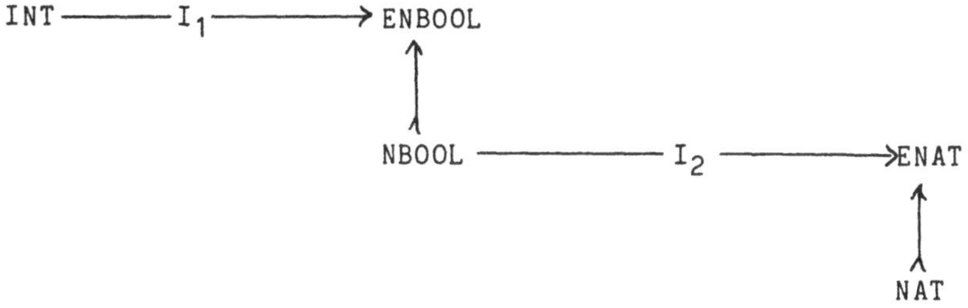

and by the above theorem we can get:

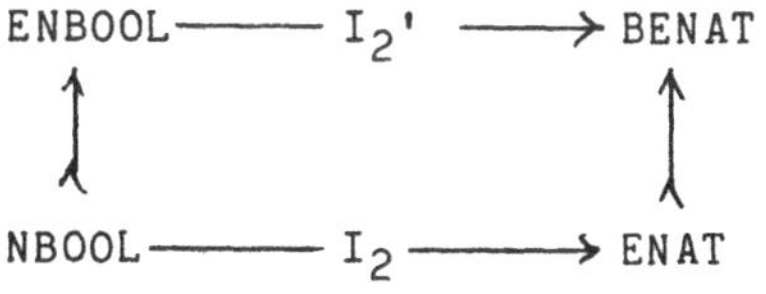

with BENAT and $I_2'oI_1$, characterising the implementation of INT in terms of NAT. The various details omitted above, are straightforward.

If we now wanted to extend INT to SINT by defining sequences of integers (as done earlier in this report for NAT) we could use the above result to carry this extension 'along' our implementation to get (unimplemented) sequences of implemented integers, SBENAT:

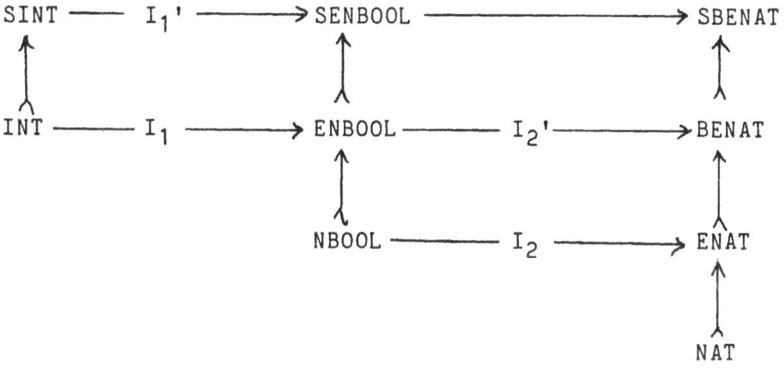

Conclusion

We feel that the theory of implementation presented above provides a simple, straightforward technical tool for reasoning about software development. The major point in its favour is the suppression of the technical flaws in earlier theories where implementations were not based on interpretations and composition was inadequately defined. The theory of specification outlined and our theory of implementation provides a wide degree of freedom in choosing implementation strategies. A structured specification can be implemented all at once into a specification which is either the same in structure or quite different from the original. Parts of the structure can be implemented independently.

Further work is in progress on a number of fronts. For example, theories are not always presented in the same formal system, as for example, the realisation of a first order specification in a conventional language like PASCAL which has a Hoare-like, modal logic. We are exploring interpretations between theories in different formal systems. We are also exploring the concept of parameterisation and defining implementations of parameterised specification. The required properties, including the commuting of implementation with parameter passing ([BG], [EK], [GAN], [PV], [SW]), turn out to be straightforwardly derivable again illustrating the suitability of our tools. Finally we are exploring the idea of 'loose implementation' as a last step to get, for example, from a specification of integers to the finite representations possible in any machine. Basically, the idea is to further restrict the relativisation predicates when we consider the translation of axioms. We partition each relativisation predicate into an interior (which respects the axioms of the source specification) and a boundary (which takes care of overflows and other boundary 'errors').

Bibliography

[BG] R M Burstall, J A Goguen. 'The Semantics of CLEAR, a Specification Language'. Proc of Advanced Course on Abstract Software Specifications, Copenhagen, LNCS86, Springer-Verlag 1980

[CK] C C Chang, H J Keisler. Model Theory. North Holland, 1977

[EHR] H-D Ehrich. 'On the Theory of Specification, Implementation and

Parameterisation of Abstract Data Types'.JACM, Vol 29, No 1, 1982

[EK] H Ehrig, H-J Kreowski. 'Parameter Passing Commutes with Implementations of Parameterised Data Types'.Proc of 9th ICALP, LNCS 140, Springer-Verlag 1982

[EKP] H Ehrig, H-J Kreowski, P Padawitz. 'Algebraic Implementation of Abstract Data Types: Concept, Syntax, Semantics and Correctness' Proc 7th ICALP, LNCS 85, Springer-Verlag, 1980

[END] H B Enderton. 'A Mathematical Introduction to Logic'. Academic Press, 1972

[GAN] H Ganzinger. 'Parameterised Specifications: Parameter Passing and Implementation'. Technical Report, Dept EECS, U Calif, Berkeley, 1980. To appear TOPLAS

[GTW] J A Goguen, J W Thatcher, E G Wagner. 'An Initital Algebra Approach to the Specification Correctness, and Implementation of Abstract Data Types'. In R T Yeh (Ed) 'Current Trends in Programming Methodology Vol IV' Prentice Hall, 1978

[GH] J V Guttag, J J Horning. 'The Algebraic Specification of Abstract Data Types'. Acta Informatica, Vol 10, No 1, 1978.

[KMS] S Khosla, T S E Maibaum, M Sadler. 'Database Specification'. Dept. Report, Imperial College, London, 1984

[LZ] B Liskov, S Zilles. 'Specification Techniques for Data Abstraction'.IEEE Trans. Software Eng. Vol SE-1, No 1, 1975

[MV] T S E Maibaum, P A S Veloso. 'A Logical Approach to Abstract Data Types'.Technical Report, Dept of Computing, Imperial College,1981 (To appear in Science of Computer Programming)

[MAK] M Makkai. 'Admissible Sets and Infinitary Logic'.Handbook of Mathematical Logic. North Holland, 1977

[NOU] F Nourani. 'Constructive Extension and Implementation of Abstract Data Types and Algorithms'. PhD thesis, Dept of Computer Science, UCLA, 1979

[PV] A Poigne, J Voss. 'Programs over abstract Data Types - On the Implementations of Abstract Data Types'. Draft Technical Report, University of Dortmund, 1983

[SCH] J R Shoenfield. 'Mathematical Logic'.Addison Wesley, 1967.

[SW] D Sanella, M Wirsing. 'Implementation of Parameterised Specifications'. Proc 9th ICALP, LNCS 140, Springer-Verlag, 1982

[WB] M Wirsing, M Broy. 'An Analysis of Semantic Models for Algebraic Specifications'. International Summer School on Theoretical Foundations of Programming Methodology, Marktoberdorf, Technical Report, Technical University, Munich, 1981

PROCESS SPECIFICATION OF LOGIC PROGRAMS

R. Ramanujam and R.K. Shyamasundar
Computer Science Group
Tata Institute of Fundamental Research
Homi Bhabha Road, Bombay 400 005.

Abstract

In this paper, we show that logic programs serve as a specification language for distributed processes. This is achieved by defining refutations with a view to use AND-parallelism and proving them sound and complete with respect to the standard semantics of logic programs given by van Emden and Kowalski.

1. Motivation

The focus of much of the research in distributed computing can be viewed in two ways:

1. a set of processes that do not share variables or a clock cooperate to achieve a global task; the problem here is one of limited information.
2. the computations of parallel processes correspond to a nondeterministic algorithm wherein several processes attempt to achieve the same task and the first successful one is said to have achieved the goal.

These two views can be called AND-parallelism and OR-parallelism respectively. In this paper, we consider only AND-parallelism.

The fundamental problem to be solved, then, is: how should a process be specified? That is, we have to define the concept of a system of processes, specify the goal to be achieved and define how the system of processes should cooperate to achieve the goal. This can be handled in general by the following two approaches:

1. write a set of equations that are "concurrently true" of the desired result and such that the equations jointly define the goal. The underlying equations could be converted to a set of processes under assumption of an appropriate parallel execution model to achieve the goal.
2. Assume the existence of processes a priori and describe how they should cooperate to achieve the task.

The first approach is called "data flow" programming, while the latter is closer in spirit to the design of concurrent programming languages.

If we should follow the second approach, what is the requirement of a specification mechanism for distributed systems? We can intuitively decide that

- it should be possible to write specifications which correspond to our a priori notion of processes
- any model for the specifications should achieve the given task
- it should provide for a clean semantics for the cooperation of processes to achieve the given task

That is, the specification mechanism should be sound and complete with respect to the task being achieved, and given a set of processes, from the semantics of cooperation it should be possible to synthesize an algorithm by which they achieve the task.

In this paper, we argue that logic programs do satisfy the above requirements. This is done by defining refutations with a view to use AND-parallelism and proving them sound and complete with respect to the standard semantics of logic programs as given in [van Emden and Kowalski 76]. We also characterize the processes defined by parallel refutations using process histories. In this sense a logic program is viewed as a specification and the computation performed is described as parallel processes.

The semantics defined here is compositional in the sense that when we have a set of Horn clauses P and a negative clause $N \equiv \leftarrow A_1,\ldots,A_n$, the refutation performed by P and N is defined in terms of the refutations performed by P and $\leftarrow A_1,\ldots,$ P and $\leftarrow A_n$. The proofs are in the style of [Apt and van Emden 82].

In a separate paper [Ramanujam and Shyamasundar 84], we show the exact derivation of a network of processes from a given logic program and relate the network execution to parallel refutations. We also establish the relationship with the networks of Dynamic CSP [Zwiers et al 83].

2. Preliminaries of Logic Program Semantics

This section is essentially a recapitulation of the standard logic programming semantics given by [van Emden and Kowalski 76]. We review all aspects of the semantics that we require.

We use $x,y,z,\ldots$ to denote <u>variables</u>, $f,g,h,\ldots,$ to denote function symbols and $P,Q,R,\ldots$ to denote <u>predicate symbols</u>. With each function symbol and predicate symbol we associate an arity. A <u>constant</u> is a function symbol of zero arity.

<u>Definition 2.1</u> A <u>term</u> is a variable or $f(t_1,\ldots, t_m)$ where f is a function symbol of arity m and $t_1,\ldots, t_m$ are terms. An <u>atom</u> is $P(t_1,\ldots, t_n)$ where P is a predicate symbol of arity n and $t_1,\ldots, t_n$ are terms.

<u>Definition 2.2</u> A <u>clause</u> is of the form

$$A_1,\ldots, A_m \leftarrow B_1,\ldots, B_n, \qquad m \geq 0,\ n \geq 0,$$

where $A_1,\ldots, A_m, B_1,\ldots, B_n$ are <u>atoms</u>. A <u>definite clause</u> has $m=1$ and a <u>negative clause</u> has $m=0$ and $n > 0$. An <u>empty clause</u> has $m=n=0$ and is denoted $\square$. A <u>program</u> is a set of definite clauses.

<u>Definition 2.3</u> <u>Substitution</u> is a set of pairs $\langle v,t\rangle$, where v is a variable, t is a term, such that if $\langle v_1,t_1\rangle \in \theta$, $\langle v_2,t_2\rangle \in \theta$ and $v_1 \equiv v_2$, then $t_1 \equiv t_2$. If V is the set of variables such that if $v \in V$ then $\langle v,t\rangle \in \theta$ for some term t, then we refer to the substitution as θ_V. If e is an expression (term, atom or clause), we write $e\theta_V$ to denote the expression obtained by uniformly replacing each variable $v \in V$ in e by the term t where $\langle v,t\rangle \in \theta_V$. $e\theta_V$ is said to be an <u>instance</u> of e.

<u>Definition 2.4</u> <u>Restriction</u> ($\setminus$) is a function $\theta_V \times V' \rightarrow \theta_{V'}$ such that

$$\theta_V \setminus V' = \theta' \quad \text{where for } v \in V \cap V',\ \langle v,t\rangle \in \theta_V \text{ implies } \langle v,t\rangle \in \theta'.$$

<u>Definition 2.5</u> A substitution θ_{V_0} is said to be <u>uniform</u> with respect to substitutions $\theta_{V_1},\ldots, \theta_{V_n}$ if

(i) $V_0 \subseteq (V_1 \cup \ldots \cup V_n)$

(ii) $\forall i, j \in \{0,\ldots,n\} : i \neq j :$

$$\theta_{V_i} \setminus (V_i \cap V_j) \equiv \theta_{V_j} \setminus (V_i \cap V_j)$$

The informal explanation of this definition can be given as follows: consider programs $P_1,\ldots, P_n$ on variables $V_1,\ldots, V_n$ respectively and a program P_0 (somehow) composed of them. Let P_0 be a program on variables V_0. Condition (i) ensures that V_0 is made up only of variables from $V_1,\ldots, V_n$. V_0 is a subset because some 'internal' variables may be 'hidden' by the composition. Condition (ii) specifies that variables 'shared' by different programs get identical values; this holds among variables $V_1,\ldots, V_n$ as well as between V_0 and any of the V_i's.

<u>Definition 2.6</u> Let P be a program. The Herbrand Base of P, denoted HB(P) is the set of all variable-free atoms having no predicate or function symbols other than those in P. An interpretation I is any subset of HB(P).

<u>Definition 2.7</u> Let I be any interpretation.

(i) a variable-free atom A is true in I iff $A \in I$

(ii) a variable-free clause $A_1,\ldots, A_n \leftarrow B_1,\ldots B_m$, $m \geq 0$, $n = 0$ or 1 is true in I iff at least one of $B_1,\ldots, B_m$ is not true in I or if $n=1$, A_1 is true in I.

(iii) a clause is true in I iff every one of its variable-free instances is true in I.

(iv) a program is true in I iff each of its clauses is true in I.

<u>Definition 2.8</u> An interpretation I such that a program P is true in I is said to be a <u>model</u> of P. The set of all models of P is denoted $\mu(P)$. We say that $\bigcap \mu(P)$ is the least model of P.

<u>Definition 2.9</u> With a program P, we associate a transformation T_p from interpretations as follows:

$A \in T_p(I)$ iff there exists a clause $B_o \leftarrow B_1,\ldots, B_m$, $m \geq 0$, in P such that $A \equiv B_o\theta$ and each $B_i\theta \in I$ for some substitution θ .

<u>Proposition 2.10</u> For a program P and interpretation I, $T_p(I) \subseteq I$ iff I is a model of P, where T_p is the transformation associated with P.

<u>Proposition 2.11</u> $\text{lfp}(T_p) = \bigcap \mu(P)$, where $\text{lfp}(T_p)$ is the least fix point of T_p.

The lattice for fix points is the powerset of the Herbrand base and the partial order of the lattice is subset inclusion. T_p is monotonic with respect to this order and the existence of least fix point follows immediately.

3. <u>SLDP-Refutations</u>

In this section, we define a variant of SLD-refutations [Apt and Van Emden 82], called SLDP-refutations, with a view towards exploiting AND-parallelism. A refutation associated with a set of clauses is a syntactic entity intended to demonstrate the unsatisfiability of these clauses.

Definition 3.1 Let P be a program and N a negative clause, where $N \equiv \leftarrow A_1, \ldots, A_n$, $n > 0$ and $A_1, \ldots, A_n$ are atoms. The SLDP-derivation of $P \cup \{N\}$ for a substitution θ is a set having n trees such that

(i) the root of the ith tree contains the negative clause $\leftarrow A_i$ and a substitution θ_i, such that θ is uniform with respect to $\theta_1, \ldots, \theta_n$.

(ii) there is a branch from a node having the clause $\leftarrow A$ to a node having the empty clause and a substitution θ' only if there exists a clause $B \leftarrow$ in P such that $A\theta' \equiv B$.

(iii) there are m branches from a node having the clause $\leftarrow A$ and a substitution θ' only if there exists a clause $B_o \leftarrow B_1, \ldots, B_m$ in P and substitutions $\theta'_1, \ldots, \theta'_m$ such that $A\theta' \equiv B_o$ and the branches lead to nodes which are roots of SLDP-derivations of $P \cup \{\leftarrow B_i\}$ for substitution θ'_i.

Definition 3.2 An SLDP-refutation is an SLDP-derivation with all finite paths and having the empty clause at each leaf node.

Intuitively, the definition of SLDP-refutations is intended to capture AND-parallelism in the following sense: at any node, if we have many branches, we only require that the substitutions on them be uniform and do not specify in what order they are found.

Definition 3.3 The success set of a program P

$$= \{ A \mid A \in HB(P) \text{ and } P \cup \{ \leftarrow A \} \text{ has an SLDP-refutation} \}$$

Theorem 3.4 The success set of a program is contained in its least model.

Proof Given an SLDP-refutation of $P \cup \{N\}$ where N is a negative clause, we have to prove that it is in the least model. By proposition 2.11, the least model is the same as the least fixpoint of T_p. Therefore we have to prove that there exists a substitution θ such that for each A in N, $A\theta \in lfp(T_p)$, the least fix point of the transformation associated with P. That is, we should show that $A\theta \in T_p^k(\phi)$ for some finite k, where ϕ denotes the empty set.

Since an SLDP-refutation consists of a set of trees each one corresponding to one atom in N, we only have to prove the theorem for one such tree.

We prove the theorem by induction on the number of non-leaf nodes in the tree.

Base case: There is only one branch from the root node, leading to a leaf node. By definition of SLDP-refutation, the leaf node contains the empty clause, which means that there exists a substitution θ such that $A\theta \in T_p(\Phi)$, because $A\theta$ matches B, and the clause is $B \leftarrow$. By definition of T_p, $T_p(\Phi)$ contains all variable-free instances of such clauses which have no premises.

Induction step: There is more than one branch from at least one node. Let this node have negative clause $\leftarrow A$ and m branches to nodes having clauses $\leftarrow B_i$ and substitution θ_i. By definition of SLDP-derivation, there exists a substitution θ uniform with respect to $\theta_1, \ldots, \theta_m$ such that $A\theta \equiv B_o$ for some clause $B_o \leftarrow B_1, \ldots, B_m$ in P. By induction hypothesis, $B_i\theta_i \in T_p^{k_i}(\Phi)$. Since T_p is monotonic, $B_i\theta_i \in T_p^k(\Phi)$ where $k = \sum_{i=1}^{m} k_i$. By definition of T_p, $A \in T_p^{k+1}(\Phi)$. This proves the theorem.

Theorem 3.5 The least model of a program is contained in its success set.

Proof Given a program P, we prove by induction on k that $A \in T_p^k(\Phi)$ implies that an SLDP-refutation exists for $P \cup \{\leftarrow A\}$.

Base step: If k=1 then $A \in T_p^k(\Phi)$ implies that A is a variable-free instance of a clause $B \leftarrow$ in P. Therefore the SLDP-refutation of $P \cup \{\leftarrow A\}$ contains a single branch from the node having $\leftarrow A$ to the node having the empty clause with substitution θ such that $A\theta \equiv B$.

Induction step: If $A \in T_p^{k+1}(\Phi)$ then by definition of T_p, there exists a variable-free instance of a clause $B_o \leftarrow B_1, \ldots, B_m$ in P such that $A \equiv B_o\theta$ and $B_1\theta, \ldots, B_m\theta \in T_p^k(\Phi)$, for some θ. Since, by induction hypothesis, there exists an SLDP-refutation of $P \cup \{\leftarrow A'\}$ whenever $A' \in T_p^j(\Phi)$, $j \leq k$, there exists a refutation of each of $P \cup \{\leftarrow B_i\theta\}$. Also, by definition of uniformity, if θ is uniform with respect to $\theta_1, \ldots, \theta_m$, there also exists a refutation of each of $P \cup \{\leftarrow B_i\theta_i\}$. The SLDP-refutation of $P \cup \{\leftarrow A\}$ consists of a node with the negative clause $\leftarrow A$ and substitution θ_i and m branches to roots of SLDP-refutations of $P \cup \{\leftarrow B_i\theta_i\}$.

Corollary 3.6 (Soundness and completeness of SLDP-refutations). The success set of a program is equal to its least model.

Now we have to consider the procedures which would perform an SLDP-refutation when it exists. This amounts to defining the processes which perform individual refutations of atoms in a negative clause, which together perform the refutation of the given negative clause with the program.

4. Processes

In this section, we consider the processes specified by logic programs. Our notion of processes involves distributed programs which interact by exchanging messages. We do not describe how the processes themselves are defined, but only define the histories generated by them. In the following, we describe a mechanism by which the processes co-operate in performing the refutation together.

Let P be a program, N a negative clause and θ a substitution. Let $P_1, \ldots, P_n$ be the predicate symbols of P. Firstly, we associate a process PR_i with each predicate symbol P_i and a process PRN with the negative clause N. Secondly, for defining process cooperation to perform the, refutation, we use histories, which are sequences of messages. Before we get on to process histories, we define the notion of service sequences on which the definition of histories is based.

Notation Let PR be any process. A message is either of the form

(i) PR! (x,y) (read 'send x to PR with signal y')

or (ii) PR? (x,y) (read 'receive x from PR with signal y').

A signal is either start or fin with the restriction that:

(a) if y = start then x = A where A is an atom

and (b) if y = fin then x = θ where θ is a substitution.

Definition 4.1 A service sequence s_i associated with process PR_i is a sequence of messages such that

(i) PR? (x,y) ε s_i if and only if there exists a service sequence say s, of process PR, such that PR_i! (x,y) ε s.
(note that PR can be anyone of $PR_1, \ldots, PR_n$, PRN).

(ii) PR? (x, start) ε s_i only if it is the first message of s_i.

(iii) PR! (θ, fin) ε s_i only if it is the last message of s_i.

(iv) s_i has only two messages PR_i? (A, start) and PR_i! (θ, fin) only if there is a clause B← in P such that $B\theta \equiv A$.

(v) PR_j! ($B_k \theta_k$, start) ε s_i only if there is a clause $B_o \leftarrow B_1, \ldots, B_m$ in P and there exist substitutions $\theta_1, \ldots, \theta_m$ uniform with respect to θ, where $A \equiv B_o \theta$ and A is in the first message of s_i, the predicate symbol of B_o is P_i and that of B_k is P_j.

The informal explanation of a service sequence can be given as follows: process PR_i receives a start signal and an atom A. If there is a clause B such that B $\theta \equiv$ A, the substitution θ is sent back as the result with a fin signal.

Otherwise, start signals are sent to subgoals and on receiving substitutions from them, the result is returned with a fin signal.

However, many service sequences can be associated with the same process. Consider a clause $B_o \leftarrow B_1, \ldots, B_m$. If any of the B_i's has the same predicate symbol as B_o, we have a service sequence associated with the subgoal and one associated with the goal, both of which refer to the same process. In this case, we combine these service sequences of the same process into the history of that process, in a manner defined below.

Definition 4.2 Let $s_{i_1}, s_{i_2}, \ldots, s_{i_{m_i}}$ be the service sequences associated with process PR_i (where $i \in \{1,\ldots,n\}$). The history H_i associated with process PR_i is a sequence of messages generated by an arbitrary interleaving of $s_{i_1}, s_{i_2}, \ldots, s_{i_{m_i}}$ in such a way that in H_i a message from s_{i_j} and one from s_{i_k} are distinguishable when $j \neq k$.

Definition 4.3 The history HN associated with process PRN is defined below: (let $N \equiv \leftarrow A_i, \ldots, A_m$, $m > o$)

(i) $PR_i!\,(A_k,$ start$) \in HN$ if and only if A_k is in N and the predicate symbol of A_k is P_i.

(ii) $PR_i?\,(\theta,$ fin$) \in HN$ if and only if there exists a service sequence s_i of PR_i such that $PRN!\,(\theta,$ fin$) \in s_i$

(iii) HN does not contain any message of the form PR? (A, start) or PR! (θ, fin)

Note that for the process PRN, its history is the same as its service sequence since there can be only one service sequence associated with process PRN.

Example Consider the program

$\{①P_1\,(b,c)\leftarrow,\ ②\ P_2\,(a,b)\leftarrow\ ,\ ③P_2(x,z)\leftarrow P_2(x,y),\ P_1(y,z)\}$ and the negative clause $N \equiv \leftarrow P_2(a,c)$. Here $<x>$ denotes the sequence x.

$HN = <PR_2!\,(P_2\,(a,c),$ start$),\ PR_2?\,(\{\ \}\ ,$ fin$)>$

$s_{2_1} = <PRN?\,(P_2\,(a,c),$ start$),\ PR_2!\,(P_2\,(a,y),$ start$),$
$PR_1!\,(P_1\,(y,c),$ start$),\ PR_1?\,(\{<y,b>\},$ fin$),\ PR_2?\,(\{<y,b>\}\ ,$
fin$),\ PRN!\,(\{\ \},$ fin$)>$

$s_{2_2} = <PR_2?\,(P_2\,(a,y),$ start$),\ PR_2!\,(\{<y,b>\},$ fin$)>$

$H_2 = <PRN?\,(P_2(a,c),$ start$),\ PR_2!\,(P_2(a,y),$ start$),\ PR_2?\,(P_2(a,y),$ start$),$
$PR_1!\,(P_1(y,c),$ start$),\ PR_1?\,(\{<y,b>\}\ ,$ fin$),PR_2!\,(\{<y,b>\}\ ,$ fin$),$
$PR_2?\,(\{<y,b>\},$ fin$),\ PRN!\,(\{\ \},$ fin$)>$

Thus, history H_2 is got by interleaving service sequences s_{2_1} and s_{2_2}.

However, we have not ensured that each process sends only such a θ as its last message which is uniform with respect to all the θ_i's it received from its subgoals. Because of this the final set of substitutions $\theta_1,\ldots,\theta_m$ in HN may well be so that no θ exists which is uniform with respect to $\theta_1,\ldots,\theta_m$.

Therefore if a process has activated subgoals at all, on receiving substitutions from them when they terminate, the process should check that there exists a θ uniform with respect to them and then sends the θ to its caller. But what if no such θ is possible? We can extend the message set by a fail signal and decree that the process sends a fail message to its caller. What should the caller do on receiving such a fail message from a subgoal? It can propagate failure to its caller and so on.

A less naive approach would be as follows:

Suppose the process finds θ_1, θ_2 such that there is no θ which is uniform with respect to them; it fixes one of them arbitrarily, say θ_1, and the other subgoal has to backtrack to find another substitution. In such a case, the subgoal which returned θ_1 can be thought of as a leader.

We modify the service sequence definition as follows, after including the messages back and fail.

Now, a message is of the form PR! (x,y) or PR? (x,y)

where (x = A and y = start or back) or

(x = θ and y = fin or fail)

With the introduction of back and fail signals, definition 4.1 is redefined as follows:

Definition 4.4 A service sequence s_i associated with a process PR_i is a sequence of messages such that

(i) PR? (x,y) $\in s_i$ iff there exists a service sequence, say s, of PR such that PR_i! (x,y) $\in$ s.

(ii) PR? (A,y) $\in s_i$ only if it is the first message in s_i

(iii) PR! (θ,y) $\in s_i$ only if it is the last message in s_i and the first message in s_i is PR? (A,x)

(iv) s_i contains only the messages PR? (A,y) and PR! (θ, fin) only if there exists a clause $B\leftarrow$ in P such that $A\theta \equiv B$.

(v) s_i contains only the messages PR? (A,y) and PR! (θ, fail) only if there exists no clause in P with goal having P_i as predicate symbol or for any such goal $B_o \leftarrow B_1, \ldots, B_m$ $(m \geq o)$ for all θ, $A\theta \not\equiv B_o$. In case y = back, only new θ's are considered. We assume that the process semantics somehow ensures memory of earlier instantiations. In this case the θ sent is an arbitrary substitution.

(vi) $PR_j! (B_k \theta_k$, start) ε s_i only if there exists a clause $B_o \leftarrow B_1, \ldots, B_m$, $m > o$ such that there exist substitutions $\theta, \theta_1, \ldots, \theta_m$, $B_o \theta \equiv A$, where A is the atom in the first message of s_i, θ is uniform with respect to $\theta_1, \ldots, \theta_m$, the predicate symbol of B_o is P_i and that of B_k is P_j.

(vii) s_i has more than two elements and PR! (θ, fin) ε s_i iff there exists a clause $B_o \leftarrow B_1, \ldots, B_m$ in $P(m > 0)$, and PR_{k_j} ? (θ_j, fin) ε s_i for all $j \in \{1, \ldots, m\}$, the predicate symbol of B_o is A (where A is the atom in the first message of s_i) and that of B_j is P_{k_j}, $B_o \theta \equiv A$ and θ is uniform with respect to $\theta_1, \ldots, \theta_m$.

(viii) $PR_j! (B_k \theta'$, back) ε s_i only if one of the following cases is true: (assume the associated clause is $B_o \leftarrow B_1, \ldots, B_m$ $(m > 0)$)

(a) $PR_{j_1}! (B_{k_1} \theta_{k_1}$, start), $PR_{j_2}! (B_{k_2} \theta_{k_2}$, start), PR_{j1}? (θ_1, y_1), PR_{j_2}? (θ_2, y_2) ε s_i such that $B_{k_1} \theta_{k_1}$ and $B_{k_2} \theta_{k_2}$ have a common variable v and there exists θ which is uniform with respect to θ_1 and θ' or θ_2 and θ' (j_1 = j or j_2 = j and y_1 = fin or y_2 = fin)

(b) the first message of s_i is PR? (A, back)

(ix) s_i has more than two elements and PR! (θ, fail) ε s_i iff for every $PR_j! (B_k \theta_k$, start) or $PR_j! (B_k \theta_k$, back) ε s_i, there exists a PR_j? (θ'_j, fail) ε s_i occuring later in s_i.

We have to redefine the history for process PRN also:

(i) $PR_j! (A_i$, start) ε HN iff the predicate symbol of A_i is P_j

(ii) PR_j? (θ_k, x) ε HN iff there exists a service sequence of PR_j, say s_j, such that PRN! (θ_k, x) ε s_j.

(iii) $PR_j! (A_k \theta'$, back) ε HN only if $PR_{j_1}! (A_{k_1}$, x), $PR_{j_2}! (A_{k_2}$, x), PR_{j_1}? (θ_1, y_1), PR_{j_2}? (θ_2, y_2) precede it in HN and there exists θ uniform with respect to θ_1 and θ' or θ_2 and θ' (j_1 = j or j_2 = j, and y_1 = fin or y_2 = fin).

If P is a program and N a negative clause, the processes $PR_1, \ldots, PR_n$ and PRN are said to perform the refutation $P \cup \{N\}$ iff there exist messages PR_j? (θ_k, fin) ε HN for all atoms A_k in N such that the predicate symbol of A_k is P_j and there exists a substitution θ which is uniform with respect to $\theta_1, \ldots, \theta_n$.

Theorem 4.5 Let P be a program, N a negative clause, θ a substitution and processes $PR_1,\ldots,PR_n$, PRN defined as above. If an SLDP refutation of $P \cup \{ N \}$ exists for θ , then there exist process histories $H_1,\ldots, H_n$ and HN such that these processes perform the refutation.

Proof Given any SLDP refutation of $P \cup \{ N\}$ for some substitution θ , we have to show that there are service sequences of processes PR_j which contain the message PRN! (θ_k, fin) and θ is uniform with respect to all the θ'_ks.

Consider each tree in the SLDP-refutation. With each non-leaf node, associate a service sequence of process PR_j where P_j is the predicate symbol of the atom on that node. We say that process PR_j is associated with this node.

Traverse the tree top-down, appending the first message PR_ℓ? (A_k, start) to each service sequence, where A_k is the atom on that node and PR_ℓ is the process associated with its parent node. In the case of root node this message is PRN? (A_k, start) . For each child node having atom A_i, add the message PR_m!(A_i, start) where PR_m is the process associated with the child node, unless the child node is a leaf node.

Now, traverse the tree bottom-up. Whenever the child node is a leaf node having substitution θ, add the final message PR_ℓ! (θ, fin), where PR_ℓ is the process associated with the parent node. If the node is not a leaf and if there are m descendants,for each ith child node having substitution θ_i and with the process associated PR_{k_i} , we add the message PR_{k_i} ? (θ_i, fin). We also add the final message PR_ℓ! (θ, fin) where θ is uniform with respect to $\theta_1,\ldots, \theta_m$ and PR_ℓ is the process associated with the parent node. In the case of root node, the final message is PRN! (θ , fin).

By definition of SLDP-refutation, such uniform substitutions are guaranteed to exist. Further we can add any number of back and fail messages consistent with the definition of service sequences, as uniform substitutions can be eventually found.

Since many nodes have service sequences associated with the same process, the process history is generated by an interleaving of these sequences, in such a way that the parent-child order of nodes is maintained. Thus, the required process histories for a given SLDP-refutation is established.

5. Discussion

An important assumption made above was that when two subgoals share a variable, they find the substitution independently. It is quite possible to have a concept of 'cooperative evaluation' of the term whereby the subgoals partially evaluate the term and together give a uniform substitution. The operational semantics has to be suitably refined to achieve this. Typically a term is thought of as a stream, on which one of the subgoal processes deposits an element and the other picks it up. [Bellia et al 82]give a semantics for parallel processes in logic using streams and lazy evaluation of terms. However, they assume one process to be the 'producer' and the other the 'consumer'. It should be noted that our transformation associated with the logic program, the SLDP-refutations and the definition of histories can be easily modified to include lazy evaluation of terms. We have to enrich the Herbrand base with $\perp$ elements for partially evaluated terms and proceed along the lines of [Bellia et al 82] . In [van Emden and Lucena Filho 82],there is a discussion on parallel logic programs which operate on streams leading to networks of processes in the style of Kahn [Kahn 74].

As we associate a process with each predicate symbol in a logic program, we should be able to directly give meanings to processes and specify the meaning of a logic program in terms of these. For this, we need to have a semantics of logic programs where the meaning of a program is explicitly defined in terms of the meanings of each of its clauses, as done in [Lassez and Maher 84] . We feel that using their approach, we can refine SLDP-refutations to give a fully compositional semantics of processes in logic programs.

The execution model of a logic program incorporating AND-parallelism has been studied by others also. The programming languages Concurrent Prolog [Shapiro 83] and Parlog[Clark and Gregory 83] are founded on this concept. While the former uses guards to specify synchronization, the latter uses clause annotation. We feel that our approach is advantageous as unification is treated as a black box and in the traditional style of semantics of distributed programs, process histories record interactions and cooperation is achieved by constraining the possible message sequences. Thus, we are able to treat logic programs as specifications of distributed systems and discuss parallel implementation at the meta-level.

We are further investigating issues of fairness and distributed failures in the setting of parallel logic programs.

Acknowledgements

We thank the referees for some insightful comments. We also thank Flory Fernandes for accurate typing.

6. References

1. Apt K.R. and M.H. van Emden : Contributions to the theory of logic programming, JACM, Vol.29, No.3, Oct. 1982.
2. Bellia M., P. Degano and G. Levi : Applicative Communicating Processes in First-Order Logic, Symposium on Programming, LNCS 137 (Springer-Verlag 1982).
3. Clark K.L. and S.A. Tarnlund (eds.): Logic Programming, Academic Press, (London, 1982).
4. Clark K.L. and S. Gregory: PARLOG : a parallel logic programming language, Imperial College Tech. Rep. (May 1983).
5. Kahn G: The semantics of a simple language for parallel programming, in J.L. Rosenfeld (ed), IFIP74, Amsterdam, 471-475 (North Holland, 1974).
6. Lassez J.L. and M.J. Maher : Closure and fairness in the semantics of programming logic, to appear in Theoretical Computer Science (1984).
7. Shapiro E : A subset of Concurrent Prolog and its interpreter, ICOT (Jan. 1983).
8. R. Ramanujam and R.K. Shyamasundar : Logic Programs for Specifying Dynamic Networks of Processes, submitted for publication, Apr. 1984.
9. van Emden M.H. and F. Lucena Filho : Predicate Logic as a Language for Parallel Programming, in [Clark and Tarnlund 82].
10. van Emden M.H. and R.A. Kowalski : The semantics of Predicate Logic as a Programming Language, JACM, Vol.23, No. 4, (Dec. 1976).
11. Zwiers J., A de Bruin and WP de Roever : A proof system for partial correctness of dynamic networks of processes, Proceedings of the 2nd Workshop on Logics of Programs, D. Kozen and E. Clarke (eds.), LNCS 164 Springer-Verlag (Heidelberg 1983).

FUNCTIONAL PROGRAMMING SYSTEMS REVISITED

Asis K. Goswami and L.M. Patnaik
School of Automation
Indian Institute of Science
Bangalore 560 012, India

ABSTRACT

Functional Programming (FP) systems are modified and extended to form Nondeterministic Functional Programming (NFP) systems in which nondeterministic programs can be specified and both deterministic and nondeterministic programs can be verified essentially within the system. It is shown that the algebra of NFP programs has simpler laws in comparison with the algebra of FP programs. "Regular" forms are introduced to put forward a disciplined way of reasoning about programs. Finally, an alternative definition of "linear" forms is proposed for reasoning about recursively defined programs. This definition, when used to test the linearity of forms, results in simpler verification conditions than those generated by the original definition of linear forms.

1. INTRODUCTION

In [1] Backus introduced a class of applicative programming systems called FP (Functional Programming) systems as an alternative to the conventional style of programming. All programs in an FP system are deterministic, and represent strict functions over some flat domain D of objects. Each FP system associates with it a finitely-generated algebra (hereinafter called FP algebra) $\langle P,\Gamma\rangle$ where P is the set of programs and Γ is a set of continuous functionals. A finite set of primitive programs is the generating set of the algebra. A remarkable aspect of the FP systems is that the rules of the FP algebra can be specified as a collection of simple laws and theorems based on functional identities. These laws and theorems can be used to reason about programs by transformations. An FP system also allows recursive definitions of programs. Algebraic methods for reasoning about recursively defined programs of several types are given in [1,2,5,6].

Any reasonably powerful FP system should have the "condition" functional to provide the programmer with a facility to define branching computations. With the boolean constants T and F (having usual meanings) as objects, this functional is defined by:

<u>Definition 1.1</u>

For all programs p, q, r, and for all objects x:

$$(p \to q;\ r):x = \begin{cases} q:x & \text{if } p:x = T, \\ r:x & \text{if } p:x = F, \\ \bot & \text{otherwise,} \end{cases}$$

where '$\bot$' is the "undefined" object (the least element of D).

The laws involving condition and other functionals are unduly complicated in the sense that any one branch of the condition reflects the essential characteristics of the laws. Also, programs requiring more than two alternative branches have to be simulated in a roundabout way by nested conditions. Complexity involved in the undue abstraction offered by the condition is also encountered in the study of "linear" forms (forms are FP program schemas), which have been introduced by Backus to reason about recursively defined programs [2]. Backus has proposed the following definition of linear forms:

<u>Definition 1.2</u>

A form H(f) (in the program variable f) is <u>linear</u> if and only if there is a form $H_t(f)$, called the <u>predicate transformer</u> of H, such that

(1) For all programs p, q, and r,

$H(p \to q;\ r) = H_t(p) \to H(q);\ H(r)$,

and

(2) For all objects x, and for all programs p,

$H(\bar{\bot}) : x \neq \bot \Rightarrow H_t(p) : x = T$

where $\bar{\bot}$ is the program such that $\bar{\bot}:x = \bot$ for all objects x.

This definition cannot always be successful as a test to determine whether a form H is linear because, if H is not linear, it cannot guarantee that H does not have a predicate transformer. Even if a form H is linear, the necessity of transforming $H(p \to q;r)$ into the form $H_t(p) \to H(q);\ H(r)$ by applying the laws of FP algebra makes the test sometimes difficult, especially if H has a complex structure. In [2] Backus has started a study of linear forms to find the relation between linearity and structure of the forms. The results of this study, as have been obtained so far, are useful, because a form can be shown linear (or, nonlinear) by examining the linearity of the components of the form. The involved object level reasoning necessitated by the aforesaid definition of linear forms tends to further complicate the study of linear forms.

In this paper we attempt to find solutions of these problems.

However, in doing so we do not remain strictly within the FP systems because, we also want to deal with nondeterministic programs. We are interested particularly in Dijkstra's "guarded commands" [3]. With these mechanisms the programmer does not have to choose between alternative computation paths (under some conditions) when there is no way to distinguish one path from another. Just as Dijkstra has used the nondeterministic "$\square$" (square) operator to combine simple conditional statements (guarded commands), we use the nondeterministic functional "∇" (union) to combine a simpler form of conditions. However, the programs written in Dijkstra's language are best reasoned about in a calculus based on first-order predicate logic [4]; whereas, we develop algebraic methods for reasoning about programs in the FP-like systems (proposed in this paper) which we call NFP (Nondeterministic FP) systems.

In Section 2 we describe NFP systems and develop the algebra of programs. In Section 3 we introduce "regular" forms and use them to indicate a disciplined way of reasoning about programs. Section 4 deals with the study of linear forms. Proofs which are relatively simple have been omitted in this paper.

2. NFP SYSTEMS

Since a program in an NFP system may be nondeterministic, we define programs as representing mappings from the set D of objects into the powerset of D. For any program p and object x, the "application" of p to x, denoted by p:x, is the set of objects into which the function represented by p maps x (Henceforth we will blur the distinction between the program p and the function represented by p).

The notion of "object" is the same as that of [1]. Given a set A of atoms, the undefined object $\perp$ (not in A) and a symbol λ (not in A), the set D is defined recursively as follows:

a) $\{\perp,\lambda\} \cup A \subseteq D$
b) If $x_1, \ldots, x_n$ are in D, then $\langle x_1, \ldots, x_n\rangle$ is in D.

The objects $\langle x_1, \ldots, x_n\rangle$ are called sequences, and the object λ is called the "empty" sequence. If for some i, $1 \leq i \leq n$, $x_i = \perp$ then $\langle x_1, \ldots, x_n\rangle = \perp$. In this paper we assume that the set A includes integers and the boolean constants T and F. As in FP systems, the object $\perp$ is used to extend all partial functions over $D-\{\perp\}$ to total functions. All programs are strict, i.e., if p is a program then $p:\perp = \{\perp\}$, $\{\perp\}$ being the least element of the powerset of D with respect to the (Egli-Milner) ordering $\sqsubseteq$: $(\forall A\subseteq D)(\forall B\subseteq D)A\sqsubseteq B \Leftrightarrow A=B \vee (\perp\in A \wedge A-\{\perp\}\subseteq B)$.

The generality and simplicity of the algebra of programs require that most of the laws involve only the interactions of the functionals. So we stipulate that all the primitive programs should be deterministic. We assume that the set of primitive programs of an NFP system includes the functions "and", "or", "not" (~) of [1] (with definitions modified as required by the functionality of NFP programs).

The set of functionals of all NFP systems includes the non-deterministic operator '∇'. In this paper we will use three other functionals. The functionals are defined below (in the definitions p, q, r, $p_1,\ldots,p_n$ stand for arbitrary programs and x stands for any object).

Functional	Definition
1. ∇ (Union)	$(p\nabla q):x = (p:x) \cup (q:x)$
2. $\circ$ (Composition)	$(p\circ q):x = \cup\{(q:y) \mid y\epsilon p:x\}$
3. Construction	$[p_1,\ldots,p_n]:x = \{<y_1,\ldots,y_n> \mid y_i\epsilon p_i:x,\ 1\leq i\leq n\}$
4. Restriction	$(p\to q):x = q:x$ if $p:x = \{T\}$,
	ϕ if $p:x = \{F\}$,
	$\bot$ otherwise.

With the help of the "empty" program Ω, which produces ϕ everywhere except at $\bot$, the relation between "restriction" and "condition" is defined by the following equalities:

$$p\to q \quad = p\to q;\ \Omega$$

$$p\to q;r = (p\to q)\nabla(p\circ\sim\to r)$$

It can be observed that the order of application of composed programs is from left to right; this deviation from the usual right-to-left ordering improves the readability of programs. The functional ∇ is associative; it can be extended to any number of arguments. In [1,2] Backus has used right- and left-insert functionals to generalize some functions defined for 2-element sequences to have sequences of arbitrary length as arguments. However, these functionals can be simulated by recursive definitions using some primitive functions of [1] and the functionals defined above. In this paper, the program "or" is assumed to take any n-element ($n\geq 2$) boolean sequence as its argument.

We now state some important laws of the algebra of programs. These laws are easily verified.

L1. a) $p\circ(\mathop{\nabla}\limits_{i=1}^{n} q_i) = \mathop{\nabla}\limits_{i=1}^{n} (p\circ q_i)$

b) $(\mathop{\nabla}\limits_{i=1}^{n} q_i)\circ p = \mathop{\nabla}\limits_{i=1}^{n} (q_i\circ p)$

L2. $[p_1,\ldots,p_{k-1}, \mathop{\nabla}\limits_{i=1}^{m} q_i, p_{k+1},\ldots,p_n]$

$= \mathop{\nabla}\limits_{i=1}^{m} [p_1,\ldots,p_{k-1},q_i, p_{k+1},\ldots,p_n]$

L3. $p\rightarrow \mathop{\nabla}\limits_{i=1}^{n} q_i = \mathop{\nabla}\limits_{i=1}^{n} (p\rightarrow q_i)$

L4. a) $(p\rightarrow f)\circ h = p\rightarrow f\circ h$.

b) $h\circ(p\rightarrow f) = h\circ p\rightarrow h\circ f$,

if h is deterministic.

L5. $[f_1,\ldots,f_{k-1}, p\rightarrow f, f_{k+1},\ldots,f_n]$

$= p\rightarrow[f_1,\ldots,f_{k-1}, f, f_{k+1},\ldots,f_n]$

L6. $p\rightarrow q\rightarrow f = ([p,q]\circ \text{ and })\rightarrow f = q\rightarrow p\rightarrow f$

3. WELL-BEHAVED PROGRAMS AND REGULAR FORMS

In this section we first identify programs of a certain type for which simple execution mechanisms exist. Programs built by construction, composition and condition have already been considered in [1]. These functionals can be used freely to construct programs. However, the functional ∇ should have programs in some restricted syntactic form as its arguments, if the execution of programs is to made made efficient. We now proceed to impose some restrictions on the use of this functional.

Definition 3.1

The program expression $\mathop{\nabla}\limits_{i=1}^{n} (p_i\rightarrow q_i)$ is called a Guarded Condition with alternatives $q_1,\ldots,q_n$ if and only if, for all objects x,

(a) if for some i, $1\leq i\leq n$, $p_i{:}x = \{\bot\}$, then for all i, $1\leq i\leq n$, $p_i{:}x=\{\bot\}$,

(b) if for all i, $1\leq i\leq n$, $p_i{:}x\neq\{\bot\}$, then $([p_1,\ldots,p_n]\circ \text{ or }){:}x=\{T\}$,

(c) for all i, $1\leq i\leq n$, if $p_i{:}x = \{T\}$, then $q_i{:}x \neq \{\bot\}\wedge q_i{:}x \neq \phi$.

Definition 3.2

A program is said to be well-behaved if and only if it is constructed from primitive programs and guarded conditions with well-behaved alternatives using only the functionals composition and construction.

The execution mechanism for guarded conditions can be described as follows: "When a guarded condition $\nabla_{i=1}^{n} (p_i \rightarrow q_i)$ is applied to an object x, if $([p_1,\ldots,p_n] \circ \text{or}):x = \{T\}$, then $q_j:x$ is evaluated, where $j \in \{i \mid p_i:x = \{T\}\}$. In all other cases the program aborts." We now introduce the concept of regular forms in order to put forward a disciplined way of reasoning about well-behaved programs.

Definition 3.3

A form is said to be a strict form if and only if it is built only by composition and construction.

Definition 3.4

The set R of regular forms is defined by:

a) Any strict form is in R.

b) If a_i, b_i $(1 \leq i \leq n)$ are strict forms then $\nabla_{i=1}^{n} (a_i \rightarrow b_i)$ is in R.

c) No other form is in R.

The following theorem can be used to reason about programs given as regular forms $\nabla_{i=1}^{n} (a_i \rightarrow b_i)$.

Theorem 3.1

If p_i $(1 \leq i \leq n)$ and q are programs then $\nabla_{i=1}^{n} p_i = q$ if and only if the following conditions hold:

a) $q \subseteq \nabla_{i=1}^{n} p_i$

b) for all i, $1 \leq i \leq n$, $p_i \subseteq q$,

where '$\subseteq$' is a relation in the set of programs defined by:
$p \subseteq q \Leftrightarrow (\forall x \in D) p:x \subseteq q:x$.

Proof: Follows immediately from the definition of ∇. □

This theorem implies that a regular program $\nabla_{i=1}^{n} (a_i \rightarrow b_i)$ can be verified by considering the terms "$a_i \rightarrow b_i$" separately. The verification procedure is further simplified by the fact that a_i and b_i are strict forms. Reasoning about programs using regular forms is illustrated by the following simple example.

Example 3.1

Consider the functions "gt" (greater than), and "ge" (greater than or equal to), over the set of 2-element sequences of integers, defined by:

$$gt : \langle x_1, x_2 \rangle = \{T\} \text{ if } x_1 > x_2 \,,$$
$$\{F\} \text{ if } x_1 \leq x_2 \,.$$
$$ge : \langle x_1, x_2 \rangle = \{T\} \text{ if } x_1 \geq x_2 \,,$$
$$\{F\} \text{ if } x_1 < x_2 \,.$$

Also consider the functions 1 and 2, over the set of 2-element sequences, defined by:

$$1 : \langle x_1, x_2 \rangle = \{x_1\}$$
$$2 : \langle x_1, x_2 \rangle = \{x_2\}$$

We want to prove that

$$(gt \rightarrow 1) \nabla (le \rightarrow 2) = (ge \rightarrow 1) \nabla (le \rightarrow 2)$$

where, $le = gt \circ \sim$.

Proof: By theorem 3.1, it is sufficient to prove that

a) $gt \rightarrow 1 \subseteq (ge \rightarrow 1) \nabla (le \rightarrow 2)$,

b) $ge \rightarrow 1 \subseteq (gt \rightarrow 1) \nabla (le \rightarrow 2)$.

Consider the following law:

If p and q are two programs such that, for all objects x, $p:x \neq \{T\} \wedge p:x \neq \{F\} \Leftrightarrow q:x \neq \{T\} \wedge q:x \neq \{F\}$

then, $[p,q] \circ \text{ or } \rightarrow r = (p \rightarrow r) \nabla (q \rightarrow r)$.

Now, the identity

$$ge = [gt, [ge,le] \circ \text{ and}] \circ \text{ or}$$

gives, by the above law,

$$ge \rightarrow 1 = (gt \rightarrow 1) \nabla ([ge,le] \circ \text{ and } \rightarrow 1).$$

Thus, $gt \rightarrow 1 \subseteq ge \rightarrow 1$.

This proves condition (a).

Similarly, the identity

$$le = [ge \circ \sim, [ge,le] \circ \text{ and }] \circ \text{ or}$$

gives $le \rightarrow 2 = (ge \circ \sim \rightarrow 2) \nabla ([ge,le] \circ \text{ and } \rightarrow 2)$.

Since $[ge,le] \circ \text{ and } \rightarrow 2 = [ge,le] \circ \text{ and } \rightarrow 1$

we have $(gt \rightarrow 1) \nabla (le \rightarrow 2) = ([gt,[ge,le] \circ \text{ and }] \circ \text{ or } \rightarrow 1) \nabla (ge \circ \sim \rightarrow 2)$
$= (ge \rightarrow 1) \nabla (ge \circ \sim \rightarrow 2)$.

Thus, $ge \rightarrow 1 \subseteq (gt \rightarrow 1) \nabla (le \rightarrow 2)$,

which is the condition (b). □

We will have to ensure that the programs which we construct can be transformed into regular forms using a small number of laws. For this purpose, we restrict ourselves to a certain subset of well-behaved programs.

Definition 3.5

A program p is called a predicate if and only if, for all objects x, the following holds:

$p:x = \{T\} \vee p:x = \{F\} \vee p:x = \{\bot\}$.

Definition 3.6

A well-behaved program is called a proper program if and only if each of its guarded conditions, $\overset{n}{\underset{i=1}{\nabla}} (p_i \to q_i)$, has all p_i's as predicates in strict forms and, further, the following conditions hold:

a) Two programs p and q are composed as $p \circ q$ if and only if, for all objects x,
$q:y \neq \{\bot\}$, for some y in p:x.

b) The program $[f_1, \ldots, f_{k-1}, \overset{n}{\underset{i=1}{\nabla}} (p_i \to q_i), f_{k+1}, \ldots, f_m]$ can be constructed if and only if, for all x, $([p_1, \ldots, p_n] \circ or):x = \{T\} \Rightarrow f_j:x \neq \{\bot\}$, for all j, $1 \leq j \leq m$, $j \neq k$.

c) The guarded condition $\overset{n}{\underset{i=1}{\nabla}} (p_i \to q_i)$ can have an alternative q_i as another guarded condition $\overset{m}{\underset{j=1}{\nabla}} (r_j \to s_j)$ if and only if, for all objects x, $r_j:x = \{\bot\} \Leftrightarrow p_i:x = \{\bot\}$ for all j, $1 \leq j \leq m$.

It can be easily verified that the set of proper programs is closed under all program transformations governed by the laws L1-L6 of the algebra of programs. A special case of this result is the following theorem (in the statement of the theorem the laws L1-L6 constitute the "Algebra of Programs"):

Theorem 3.2

The algebra of programs can transform any proper program into a regular form which is also a proper program.

Proof: Easily verified by using the conditions (a), (b) and (c) of definition 3.6 and the laws L1-L6. □

Lemma 3.1

If G is a guarded condition then, for all objects x,
$G:x \neq \phi$.

Proof: Let G be the guarded condition $\overset{n}{\underset{i=1}{\nabla}} (p_i \rightarrow q_i)$.

Now, consider any object x.

$G:x = \phi \Rightarrow (\forall i, 1 \le i \le n)(p_i \rightarrow q_i):x = \phi$

$\Rightarrow (\forall i, 1 \le i \le n) p_i:x = \{F\} (\because p_i:x = \{T\} \Rightarrow q_i:x \ne \phi)$.

We thus arrive at the contradiction that

$((\forall i, 1 \le i \le n) p_i:x \ne \{\perp\}) \Rightarrow ([p_1,\ldots,p_n] \circ or):x = \{F\}$.

So, for all objects x, $G:x \ne \phi$. □

Theorem 3.3

If G is a proper program, then, for all objects x, $G:x \ne \phi$.

Proof: Immediately follows from theorem 3.2 and lemma 3.1. □

Lemma 3.2

Let p, q be predicates and f be any program such that, for all objects x,

a) $f:x \ne \phi$

b) $p:x = \{T\} \Rightarrow f:x \ne \{\perp\}$, and $q:x = \{T\} \Rightarrow f:x \ne \{\perp\}$.

Then, $p \rightarrow f = q \rightarrow f \Leftrightarrow p = q$.

Proof: Obviously, $p = q \Rightarrow p \rightarrow f = q \rightarrow f$

To prove the reverse implication, consider any object x. If $p:x = \{F\}$, then $(p \rightarrow f):x = (q \rightarrow f):x = \phi$.

Thus, $q:x = \{F\}$, (since $f:x \ne \phi$).

If $p:x = \{T\}$, then $(p \rightarrow f):x \ne \{\perp\}$ (Since $p:x = \{T\} \Rightarrow f:x \ne \{\perp\}$).

Thus, $(q \rightarrow f):x \ne \{\perp\}$ i.e., $q:x \ne \{\perp\}$ and $q:x \ne \{F\}$.

Since q is a predicate, we have $q:x = \{T\}$.

So, we have proved that, for all objects x,

$(p:x = \{T\} \Rightarrow q:x = \{T\}) \wedge (p:x = \{F\} \Rightarrow q:x = \{F\})$.

Similarly, we can prove that, for all objects x,

$(q:x = \{T\} \Rightarrow p:x = \{T\}) \wedge (q:x = \{F\} \Rightarrow p:x = \{F\})$.

Thus, $p = q$. □

Lemma 3.3

If p is a predicate, and f and g are arbitrary programs, then

$p \to f \subseteq g \Rightarrow p \to f \subseteq p \to g$

Proof: Omitted. □

Lemma 3.4

If $\overset{m}{\underset{i=1}{\nabla}} (p_i \to f_i)$ is a deterministic proper program, then

$p_i \to \overset{m}{\underset{i=1}{\nabla}} (p_i \to f_i) = p_i \to f_i$, for all i, $1 \le i \le m$

Proof: Omitted. □

Theorem 3.4

If $\overset{m}{\underset{i=1}{\nabla}} (p_i \to f_i)$ and $\overset{n}{\underset{j=1}{\nabla}} (q_j \to g_j)$ are deterministic proper programs in regular forms, then

$$\overset{m}{\underset{i=1}{\nabla}} (p_i \to f_i) = \overset{n}{\underset{j=1}{\nabla}} (q_j \to g_j)$$

if and only if, for all i, $1 \le i \le m$, and for all j, $1 \le j \le n$,

$$[p_i, q_j] \circ \text{and} \to f_i = [p_i, q_j] \circ \text{and} \to g_j$$

and, $[p_1, \ldots, p_m] \circ \text{or} = [q_1, \ldots, q_n] \circ \text{or}$

Proof: "Only if" part: We have,

$$F = [p_1, \ldots, p_m] \circ \text{or} \to F, \text{ and } G = [q_1, \ldots, q_n] \circ \text{or} \to G,$$

where, $F = \overset{m}{\underset{i=1}{\nabla}} (p_i \to f_i)$,

$G = \overset{n}{\underset{i=1}{\nabla}} (q_i \to g_i)$.

Since F, G are proper programs, by theorem 3.3 for all objects x, $F:x \neq \phi$.

Also, $([p_1, \ldots, p_m] \circ \text{or}):x = \{T\}$

$\Rightarrow (\exists i, 1 \le i \le m)\ p_i:x = \{T\}$

$\Rightarrow (\exists i, 1 \le i \le m)\ f_i:x \neq \{\bot\}$

$\Rightarrow F:x \neq \{\bot\}$ (since all f_j are proper programs, i.e., $f_j:x \neq \phi$ for all j, $1 \le j \le m$).

Thus, by lemma 3.2, we have $F = G \Rightarrow [p_1, \ldots, p_m] \circ \text{or} = [q_1, \ldots, q_n] \circ \text{or}$.

Since F is deterministic, we have, by lemma 3.4, $p_i \to F = p_i \to f_i$ for all i, $1 \le i \le m$.

Thus, $F = G \Rightarrow p_i \to f_i = p_i \to G$ for all i, $1 \le i \le m$. (1)

By laws L3 and L6, we have $p_i \to G = \overset{n}{\underset{j=1}{\nabla}} ([p_i, q_j]\circ \text{ and } \to g_j)$ (2)
for all i, $1 \leq i \leq m$.

Formulas (1) and (2) give $p_i \to f_i = \overset{n}{\underset{j=1}{\nabla}} ([p_i, q_j]\circ \text{ and } \to g_j)$ for all i, $1 \leq i \leq m$.

Thus, $[p_i, q_j]\circ \text{ and } \to g_j \subseteq p_i \to f_i$ for all i,j, $1 \leq i \leq m$, $1 \leq j \leq n$.

By Lemma 3.3 and law L6, then

$$[p_i, q_j]\circ \text{ and } \to g_j \subseteq [p_i, q_j]\circ \text{ and } \to f_i$$

for all i,j, $1 \leq i \leq m$, $1 \leq j \leq n$.

Similarly, we can prove that

$$[p_i, q_j]\circ \text{ and } \to f_i \subseteq [p_i, q_j]\circ \text{ and } \to g_j$$

for all i, j, $1 \leq i \leq m$, $1 \leq j \leq n$.

Thus, $[p_i, q_j]\circ \text{ and } \to f_i = [p_i, q_j]\circ \text{ and } \to g_j$ for all i,j, $1 \leq i \leq m$, $1 \leq j \leq n$.

"If" part:

Consider any object x. Since F is a guarded condition, and is proper, $F:x = \{\bot\} \Rightarrow (\forall i, 1 \leq i \leq m)\ p_i:x = \{\bot\}$.

Then the second condition of the theorem implies

$$(\exists j, 1 \leq j \leq n)\ q_j:x = \{\bot\}.$$

Since G is also a guarded condition and is proper, we have

$$(\forall j, 1 \leq j \leq n)\ q_j:x = \{\bot\}.$$

Thus, $G:x = \{\bot\}$.

Now, let $F:x = \{y\}$, where $y \neq \bot$. Then,

$$([p_1, \ldots, p_m]\circ \text{ or}):x = \{T\} = ([q_1, \ldots, q_n]\circ \text{ or}):x.$$

In other words, there is some i and j, $1 \leq i \leq m$, $1 \leq j \leq n$, such that

$$p_i:x = \{T\} \wedge q_j:x = \{T\},$$

and, for that particular i and j, $f_i:x=\{y\} \wedge g_j:x=\{y\}$ (by the first condition of the theorem).

This implies, $F:x = \{y\} = G:x$.

Since we have shown that $F:x = G:x$ for all objects x,

we have, F=G. □

This theorem shows that the concept of regular forms leads to a very simple method of reasoning about deterministic proper programs.

4. LINEAR FORMS

In this section we propose an alternative definition of linear forms. We show by examples that this definition does not have the limitations of the original definition mentioned in Section 1. We will consider only deterministic proper programs. The following definition is a modified version of the definition 1.2. The modification is necessary since we are dealing only with proper programs.

Definition 4.1

A form H(f) is linear if and only if, for all predicates p and programs q and r such that $s = (p \to q) \nabla (p \circ \sim \to r)$ is a proper program and H(s) is a proper program, the algebra of programs can transform H(s) into the form $(H_t(p) \to H(q)) \nabla (H_t(p) \circ \sim \to H(r))$, and $H(\bar{\bot}):x \neq \{\bot\} \Rightarrow H_t(p) : x = \{T\}$.

Definition 4.2

A functional is said to be Ω-preserving if and only if it is $\bar{\bot}$-preserving.

The following theorem gives an alternative definition of linear forms. We assume that all forms are built only by composition, construction, union and restriction.

Theorem 4.1

A form H(f) is linear if and only if, for all predicates p and programs q and r such that $s = (p \to q) \nabla (p \circ \sim \to r)$ is a proper program, and H(s) is a proper program, the following conditions hold:

1. $H(s) = H(p \to q) \nabla H(p \circ \sim \to r)$
2. $[H_t(p) \circ \sim, b_H] \circ$ or $= H_t(p \circ \sim)$
   where $H_t(f)$ is any form such that $H(p \to q) = H_t(p) \to H(q)$,
   and b_H is a predicate associated with H, called the free predicate of H, defined by: $b_H : x = \{T\}$ if and only if $H(\bar{\bot}):x \neq \{\bot\}$.

Proof:

(a) "Only if" part: If H(f) is linear and $H_t(f)$ is its predicate transformer then

$$H((p \to q) \nabla (p \circ \sim \to r)) = (H_t(p) \to H(q)) \nabla (H_t(p) \circ \sim \to H(r)) \quad (3)$$

Since the right side of the above identity is a proper program, it is also a guarded condition. Then we have, for all objects x,

$$(H_t(p) \circ \sim):x = \{T\} \Rightarrow H(r):x \neq \{\bot\} \ . \quad (4)$$

Also, since $H((p\circ\sim\rightarrow r)\nabla((p\circ\sim)\circ\sim\rightarrow q)) = (H_t(p\circ\sim)\rightarrow H(r))\nabla(H_t(p\circ\sim)\circ\sim\rightarrow H(q))$, (5)

we have, for all objects x, $(H_t(p\circ\sim)):x = \{T\} \Rightarrow H(r):x \neq \{\bot\}$. (6)

Moreover, for all objects x, since H(r) is proper program,

$H(r):x \neq \phi$. (7)

Now, substituting Ω for q in (3) we have

$H(p\circ\sim\rightarrow r) = (H_t(p)\rightarrow H(\Omega))\nabla(H_t(p)\circ\sim\rightarrow H(r))$. (8)

We can write $H(f) = b_H\rightarrow t;\ H_1(f)$
where, $b_H:x = \{T\} \Rightarrow t:x \neq \phi$, for all objects x, and $H_1(\bar{\bot}) = \bar{\bot}$ (equivalently, $H_1(\Omega) = \Omega$).

Thus (8) becomes $H_t(p\circ\sim\rightarrow r) = (b_H\rightarrow t)\nabla(H_t(p)\circ\sim\rightarrow(b_H\rightarrow t;\ H_1(r))$
$= [H_t(p)\circ\sim, b_H]\circ\ \mathrm{or}\rightarrow H(r)$ (9)
(since, for all objects x, $b_H:x = \{T\} \Rightarrow H_t(p):x = \{T\}$) .

Similarly, substituting Ω for q in (5), we can show that, $H_t(p\circ\sim\rightarrow r) = H_t(p\circ\sim)\rightarrow H(r)$. (10)

From (9) and (10) we have $[H_t(p)\circ\sim, b_H]\circ\ \mathrm{or}\rightarrow H(r) = H_t(p\circ\sim)\rightarrow H(r)$.

By (4), (6), (7) and lemma 3.2, the above implies $[H_t(p)\circ\sim, b_H]\circ\ \mathrm{or} = H_t(p\circ\sim)$.

Condition 1 of the theorem is easily verified by using the above identity in (3). We now complete the verification of condition 2.

Let $H_t'(f)$ be another form such that $H(p\rightarrow q) = H_t'(p)\rightarrow H(q)$.

This implies, $H_t'(p)\rightarrow H(q) = H_t(p)\rightarrow H(q)$. (11)

Using condition 1 of the theorem, we see that

$(H_t'(p)\rightarrow H(q))\nabla(H_t(p\circ\sim)\rightarrow H(r))$

is a guarded conditon. So, for all objects x,

$H_t'(p):x = \{T\} \Rightarrow H(q) \neq \{\bot\}$.

Similar property for $H_t(p)$ can also be derived. By lemma 3.2, we then have from (11) $H_t'(p) = H_t(p)$.

(b) <u>"If" part</u>: Omitted. □

It is clear that the verification conditions for linearity are more relaxed than those necessitated by the original definition of linear forms. The elegance of this alternative definition is also reflected in the study of the relation between the linearity and structure of forms. We illustrate this by verifying a theorem of [2].

Theorem 4.2 (Constructed linear forms).

Given

(a) $H(f) = [E_1(f), G_1(f)]$

(b) $E_1(f) = (p\to r)\nabla(p\circ\sim\to E(f))$

(c) $G_1(f) = (q\to s)\nabla(q\circ\sim\to G(f))$

(d) E and G are linear with predicate transformers E_t and G_t

(e) $E_t = G_t$.

Then H(f) is linear with predicate transformer

$[[p,q]\circ \text{ and}, E_t(f)]\circ \text{ or}$.

Proof: First we verify condition 1 of theorem 4.1. We will write "[a,b]∘ and" simply as "a & b".

$$\text{Now, } H(f) = (p \,\&\, q\to[r,s])\nabla(p \,\&\, q\circ\sim\to[r,G(f)])\nabla(p\circ\sim \,\&\, q \to[E(f),s])$$
$$\nabla(p\circ\sim \,\&\, q\circ\sim\to[E(f),G(f)]) \qquad (12)$$

(by laws L2, L3, L5 and L6).

We have, in a similar way,

$[r,G((a\to b)\nabla(a\circ\sim\to c)] = [r,G(a\to b)]\nabla[r,G(a\circ\sim\to c)]$

(since G is linear).

$[E((a\to b)\nabla(a\circ\sim\to c)),s] = [E(a\to b),s]\nabla[E(a\circ\sim\to c),s]$

(since E is linear).

$$[E((a\to b)\nabla(a\circ\sim\to c)),G((a\to b)\nabla(a\circ\sim\to c))]$$
$$= [E(a\to b), G(a\to b)]\nabla[E(a\circ\sim\to c), G(a\circ\sim\to c)]\nabla[E_t(a)\to E(b), G_t(a\circ\sim)\to G(c)]$$
$$\nabla[E_t(a\circ\sim)\to E(c), G_t(a)\to G(b)] \,. \qquad (13)$$

Since $E_t = G_t$, we have,

$[E_t(a)\to E(b), G_t(a\circ\sim)\to G(c)]$

$= E_t(a) \,\&\, b_G\to[E(b),G(c)]$ (b_G is the free predicate of G)

$= E_t(a) \,\&\, b_G\to[E(b),G(b)]$ (since $b_G\to G(b) = b_G\to G(c)$).

Similarly, $[E_t(a\circ\sim)\to E(c),G_t(a)\to G(b)] = G_t(a) \,\&\, b_E\to[E(b),G(b)]$

(b_E is the free predicate of E)

So, the last two constructed terms of the right side of identity (13) are absorbed in the first constructed term of the right side of (13). The above results verify that

$H((a\to b)\nabla(a\circ\sim\to c)) = H(a\to b)\nabla H(a\circ\sim\to c)$.

Now, from (12) we have,

$H(a\to b) = [b',E_t(a)]\circ \text{ or}\to H(b)$ (since $E_t = G_t$)

where, $b' = p \,\&\, q$,

i.e., $H_t(a) = [b', E_t(a)] \circ or$.

Also, $b_H = [b', b_E] \circ or$.

Thus, $H_t(a \circ \sim)$

$= [b', E_t(a \circ \sim)] \circ or$

$= [b', [b_E, E_t(a) \circ \sim] \circ or] \circ or$ (since E is linear)

$= [[b', b_E] \circ or, E_t(a) \circ \sim] \circ or = [b_H, E_t(a) \circ \sim] \circ or$

$= [b_H, b_H \circ \sim \& E_t(a) \circ \sim] \circ or = [b_H, H_t(a) \circ \sim] \circ or$.

Thus H is linear with predicate transformer $[p \& q, E_t(f)] \circ or$. □

5. CONCLUSION

In this paper we have described Nondeterministic Functional Programming (NFP) systems. These are FP-like systems in which the programs are functions over sets of objects and the set of functionals includes the operator '∇' (Union). We have shown that the algebra of NFP programs is a more powerful tool than FP algebras for construction and reasoning about programs, in the sense that (a) the algebra of NFP programs consists of simpler laws, (b) the "restriction" and "union" functionals can be used to build programs with simpler symmetric structures. By introducing the concept of "regular" forms, we have shown that the algebra of programs can dispense with the laws involving nested "conditions" and yet provide the programmer with a disciplined way of reasoning about a wide class of programs. We have proposed, in the form of a theorem, an alternative definition of "linear" forms. This definition has simplified the test for linearity of forms and minimized to a great extent the object-level reasoning in the study of linear forms. Work towards formal development of NFP programs is in progress. The results of this work will be reported in a forthcoming paper.

ACKNOWLEDGEMENT

We are grateful to Julie Basu and the anonymous referees for their many useful suggestions which have helped in improving the presentation of the paper.

REFERENCES

1. Backus, J.: Can Programming be liberated from the von Neumann style? A Functional style and its Algebra of Programs. CACM 21(8) 613-641 (1978).
2. Backus, J.: The Algebra of Functional Programs: Functional level reasoning, Linear equations, and Extended Definitions. In: Lecture Notes in Computer Science, Vol.107, pp.1-43, Berlin-Heidelberg-New York: Springer-Verlag 1981.

3. Dijkstra, E.W.: A Discipline of Programming. Englewood Cliffs, N.J.: Prentice Hall, 1976.
4. Gries, D.: The Science of Programming, New York: Springer-Verlag, 1981.
5. Kieburtz, R., Shultis, J.: Transformation of FP Program Schemes. Proc. Conf. on Functional Programming Languages and Computer Architecture, 1981, Portsmouth, pp.41-48.
6. Williams, J.H.: On the Development of the Algebra of Functional Programs. ACM TOPLAS 4(4) 733-757 (1982).

Models and Transformations for Nondeterministic Extensions of Functional Programming

Thomas J. Myers and A. Toni Cohen*
University of Delaware
Newark, DE 19716

Abstract

Linguistic support of parallelism and program transformation systems both implicitly involve nondeterminism. As a result, referentially transparent languages are insufficiently expressive for these applications unless they are augmented with nondeterministic operators. This paper introduces two operators to extend FP so that it supports committed and uncommitted nondeterminism, and specifies the semantics of these operators under both strict and lenient evaluation strategies. Equational models for the four resulting systems are given individually, and two of these are merged into a combined model which supports both forms of nondeterminism under lenient evaluation. Finally, the applicability to program transformation problems is discussed.

0 Introduction

Referentially transparent languages are interesting on two counts: they implicitly support parallelism [Bryant 78] and they facilitate program transformation as a design methodology [Burstall 77]. Both of these depend on free substitutivity, i.e. on the property that any subexpression may be replaced by any other with the same value: in program transformation we try to replace terms with equivalent but cheaper ones, while in evaluation we replace terms with equivalent but simpler ones (ultimately, with their values).

Unfortunately, the attempt to make full use of either parallelism or program transformation will bring in nondeterminism, which violates referential transparency. A common use of parallelism involves a race between processors to produce acceptable, but possibly different, results. Program transformations generally begin from a specification which

* First author's work supported under National Science Foundation Grant NCS-8113250. Second author's work supported under System Development Foundation Grant G403.

fully determines the required properties of expressions, but not necessarily their values. Still less fortunate is the fact that two distinct, apparently incompatible versions of nondeterminism are involved. In the nondeterminism caused by timing uncertainties we find that once something happens it can't be changed, and failure is irrevocable. On the other hand, the choice of an approach towards solving a problem (e.g., towards finding an equivalent but more efficient version of a given program) is not irrevocable; if one path is unproductive, we are simply forced to (backtrack and) try another.

Therefore, we attempt to extend referentially transparent languages with different versions of nondeterminism, motivated by different aspects of these concerns. The substance of the paper is its development of well-behaved nondeterministic systems within which rules for program transformation can be justified.

When a programming language is extended to support nondeterminism, program output ceases to be uniquely determined by input, becoming instead a member of a set of possibilities. In this case, referential transparency is apparently destroyed: x-x might not equal 0 for indeterminate x. Thus, some program transformations within the grasp of current compilers are not feasible and, obviously, the more sophisticated transformations possible for referentially transparent languages are debarred. Historically the loss of substitutivity has been accepted phlegmatically; no attempts have been made to overcome the malignant effects.

We want to retain both the salubrious effects of referential transparency and the practical benefits of introducing nondeterminism. Our goal is an algebra of nondeterministic programs which identifies the circumstances under which transformations (rewrite rules) are valid across nondeterministic operators. We cannot achieve a fully referentially transparent system: some compromises must be made and some substitutions will be infeasible. Nor can we deal with all possible kinds of nondeterminism: the "race" situation suggested above is potentially incompatible with even the most basic transformations (e.g., the replacement of a deterministic expression with its value) unless the race is carefully regulated. However, we can perform useful transformations within mathematical systems which do not constrain implementations.

Our objective is to achieve a clean formulation which we can use for program transformations of the sort we discussed in [Cohen 82]. Our work is equational, but not completely formal; we have not yet incorporated the work of denotational semanticists on nondeterminism, although relationships between our work and theirs (such as [Park 79]'s nondeterministic merge and [Broy 81]'s denotational semantics of nondetdrminism) will be apparent to some readers. We view this paper as a necessary preliminary to complete formalization: our "semi-formal" approach is adequate to identify many difficulties in achieving a useful theory and a reasonable number of opportunities for profitable program transformation.

Two classes of nondeterministic evaluation are considered throughout the literature: **uncommitted** nondeterminism and **committed** nondeterminism. In **uncommitted** (or existential) nondeterminism, the selection mechanism is tentative so that all possible nondeterministic choices may have to be considered; evaluation is guaranteed to achieve a goal if any of the choices are guaranteed to achieve it. In **committed** (or universal) nondeterminism, the selection is irrevocable; evaluation is guaranteed to achieve a goal only if all of the choices are guaranteed to achieve it.

Both types can be considered as program design techniques: uncommitted nondeterminism was introduced in this way by [Floyd 67] and committed nondeterminism by [Dijkstra 76]. The uncommitted approach identifies a set of possibilites which contains the desired solution, while Dijkstra's methodology identifies a set of possibilites which all lead to acceptable solutions. Both approaches allow us to group programming constructs in a way which (a) corresponds to a natural grouping of ideas and (b) is not possible in conventional deterministic languages.

We introduce a system which can deal with committed and uncommitted nondeterminism within a single context. (So far as we know, this has not been done before: previous treatments of nondeterminism have assumed a single interpretation). We specify the semantics of uncommitted and committed nondeterministic operators individually, introduce extensions necessary for the languages to be useful for real computing, and then merge the two characterizations into a single mathematically respectable system. At each stage, we give a brief discussion of the model's relevance in program transformation; at the end, we attempt to characterize what we can and cannot handle.

Our base language is FP [Backus 78], with strict evaluation of determinate functions. In order to deal with parallel processing, we wish to augment FP with streams, and dealing with these requires that we introduce lazy evaluation. Streams cannot, in general, be fully evaluated, so we must permit functions which use them to converge even if it is not known whether all elements of the stream will converge. Laziness yields two other benefits: a somewhat richer set of program transformations becomes feasible (e.g., constant propagation is uniformly valid for lazy semantics), and connections between functions and functional forms become more apparent (e.g., the nondeterministic operators can be dealt with as functions.)

This paper develops notions and notations for committed and uncommitted nondeterministic operators, in strict and lazy versions of FP. We are searching for standard algebraic structures such as commutative monoids and semirings, partly to make it easier to relate our work to work by other researchers, but especially because of the availability of useful algorithms requiring only the properties of these structures: [Aho 74, Lankford 77, Stickel 81, Jerrum 82]. Our basic results are as follows:

1. Uncommitted nondeterminism ([McCarthy 67]'s *amb*) can be described by a simple model based on sets of choices to yield an abelian monoid with identity element *abort*. The strict evaluation rules of FP force us to view *amb* as a program forming operation (PFO) rather than as a function; under lazy evaluation, it could be viewed as either. Extensions of the basic system model lazy evaluation, explicitly denote divergent computation, and introduce the notation which is needed for systems supporting both committed and uncommitted nondeterminism.

2. Committed nondeterminism (e.g., [Dijkstra 76]'s guarded commands) can be described by a similar model, with a novel identity element *Skip*. This also can be handled under strict or lazy evaluation, and in either case mapped into a two-level notation.

3. The two models can be combined to form a semiring in which multiplication (uncommitted choice) distributes over addition (committed choice). Other useful relationships (e.g., each kind of nondeterminism is idempotent in isolation, and this almost holds when they are combined; the additive identity is the multiplicative zero) are readily obtained.

4. A Prolog-like *Cut* operation [Clocksin 81] can be defined to limit the amount of searching a program must do by committing to one computation path. This is important for transformations, but violates a fundamental constraint on structures of the language. We introduce a generalized inverse to *Cut*; we call it *SuperGlue*, and its effect is to undo all commitments.

5. Semiring structures can also be derived using distribution of function composition over either form of nondeterminism. These are more complex, since they depend not only on committed vs. uncommitted nondeterminism, but also on whether composition is strict or lazy. The results allow "program structuring" algorithms, such as automatic conversion of tail-recursive functions into Dijkstra-like nondeterministic iterations (much like the conversion of linear grammars into regular expressions via Arden's Lemma). These structures help in the derivation of sorting and searching algorithms.

6. Expressions in the combined systems can be modelled by forests of OR-trees. Each tree in a forest denotes one committed choice, and each leaf represents one uncommitted choice from among its trees subset of possible choices. This does not change the semantics, but does make it easier to develop an intuition for expression manipulations.

7. Transformation rules justified by the models are applied to simple problems; more complex applications are sketched.

The overall structure of the models we develop in Sections 1-3 is shown below:

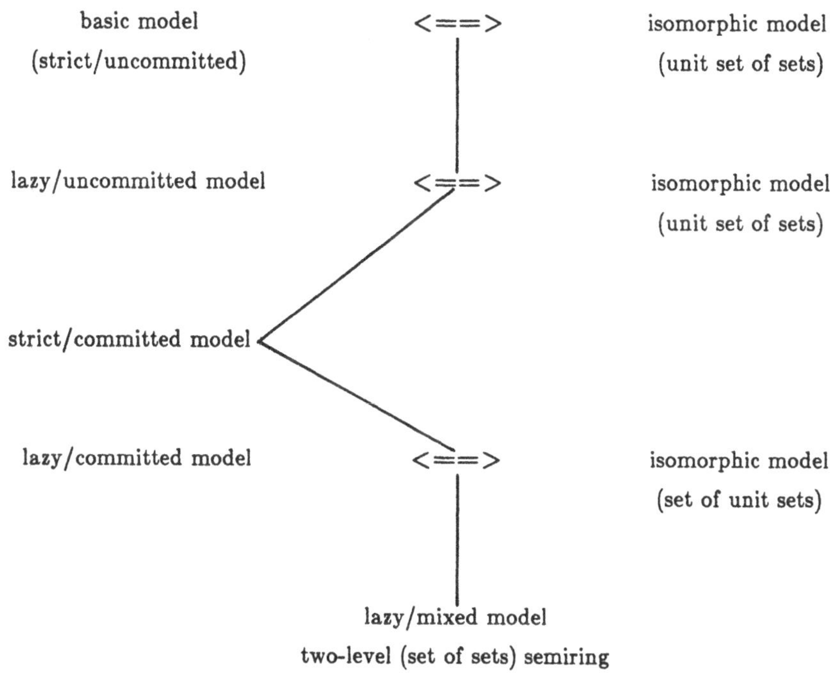

Our goal is a mixed model with lazy evaluation, (we omit the strict version, which is simpler). In this model, any expression may involve commitment to one of a set of irrevocable choices, within which uncommitted search among subordinate possibilities may take place: the set $\{\{1,2,3\},\{2,3,4\}\}$ represents an expression which commits itself to trying each of $\{1,2,3\}$ or each of $\{2,3,4\}$, but never has to explore both 1 and 4 as possible values. We lead up to this general set-of-sets construction via a construction using a set of singleton sets $\{\{a\},\{b\}\}$ for purely committed choice and another using a singleton set containing a set $\{\{a,b\}\}$ for purely uncommitted choice. Each of these is simply explained as a notational variant of a one-level model, based on a strict system. We start with the strict/uncommitted version which is closest to the original FP system.

1 Uncommitted nondeterminism

In [Cohen 82], we introduced the metalinguistic operator *Choices* which yields, for each expression E, the set of possible values (*Choices*(E)) of E. In the subsections below, we present several modifications of the original definition. These yield systems which model strict and lazy evaluation, with and without explicit failure values.

We begin with a basic model which will allow the representation of uncommitted nondeterministic choice as an extension of the strictly evaluated framework of ordinary FP. This model includes no explicit representation of failure, and, being strict, does not support streams. We then introduce a modified notation which will facilitate later extensions; this does not change the nature of the model in any way. Our third model has properties similar to those of the basic model; it contains an explicit failure element, and can thus support lazy evaluation — this model will be used later to represent committed nondeterminism. Finally, a modified notation is presented which will be compatible with this third model. The relationships between models are given by

basic model (*Choices*)	<==>	notational variant: extra set brackets (*ChoiceSets*)
+ *Fail* as a value (*LazyChoices*)	<==>	notational variant: extra set brackets (*LazyChoiceSets*)

1.1 The basic system

The basic system models strict evaluation. Each expression corresponds to a set of possible (convergent) values, i.e., to a set of normal forms to which it can be reduced. An expression fails if and only if all of its computations (reduction sequences) diverge so that this set is empty. Thus, the domains and ranges of functions are implicitly constrained and functions are always total (but it is only partially decidable if the set of values returned by an application is empty). Expressions may be atomic (constants or the uniformly divergent expression ***abort***), may be sequences $<e_1,...,e_n>$, or may result from function applications (*f:e*).

Atoms other than the unique undefined atom *abort* have unique values so that the "set of possible values" specified by *Choices* is singleton. We define

$Choices(a) \triangleq \{a\}$, except that
$Choices(abort) \triangleq \{\}$.

Our expression *abort* yields the value set {} and thus corresponds fairly closely to the traditional FP value $\bot$, but is pragmatically more general in that we view undefinedness as a special case of nondeterminism in which there are exactly zero paths yielding a value.

Sequences yield sequences as values, with one such sequence for each possible combination of values for their elements:

$$Choices(<x_1,...,x_n>) \triangleq \{<y_1,...,y_n> \mid y_i \in Choices(x_i)\}.$$

Note that this cartesian product formation implicitly requires strict evaluation; if any member of the sequence $<x_1,...,x_n>$ diverges, the cartesian product is empty.

In standard FP, a rigid distinction is drawn between objects, functions and PFO's. For our purposes, functions can be thought of as values of a higher type; so can PFO's which, subject to syntactic sugar, map sequences of functions into functions. We will apply *Choices* to expressions representing any of these; the resulting sets of values will inevitably be of the appropriate types. All primitive functions and most PFO's are deterministic and correspond to unique values, while each nondeterministic function is associated with several values. A function value, on being applied to an object, either yields a value or diverges. *Abort* always diverges; i.e.,

$$Choices(Abort{:}x) = Choices(Abort) \triangleq \{\}, \text{ for all } x.$$

Primitive functions (which are all deterministic) have unique values; they are applied to whatever value is produced by their arguments and either produce one value or diverge:

$Choices(f) \triangleq \{f\}$, for determinate f, except
$Choices(Abort) \triangleq \{\}$.

For compatibility with standard FP, we require that

$Choices(f{:}x) = \{f{:}y \mid y \in Choices(x),\ f{:}y \neq abort\}$ for determinate f;
$Choices(Abort{:}x) = \{\}$.

As noted above, in this preliminary system, there is no such value as *abort*, and the restriction $f{:}y \neq abort$ is unnecessary; we add it for clarity.

We express a general rule for the behavior of PFO's, based on our rule for sequences and our understanding of deterministic function application. From this, we derive special case rules for compositions (denoted $f{\cdot}g$), tuples $[f_1,\ldots,f_n]$, nondeterministic choices (f & g), and conditionals ($p \rightarrow f;g$). Other PFO's, such as *ApplyToAll* and *Insert*, are dealt with collectively by the general rule. We include one PFO which maps an object into a function: the constant-former denoted by @, such that $@x{:}y = x$.

Function application must satisfy a "representability law", which says that in general there could exist a higher-order (generic) function *Apply* such that

$$f{:}x = Apply{:}{<}f,x{>};$$

This constraint, combined with the basis in determinate FP, allows us to derive a rule which covers both deterministic and nondeterministic function application:

$$\begin{aligned}
Choices(f{:}x) &= Choices(Apply{:}{<}f,x{>})\\
Choices(f{:}x) &= \{Apply{:}{<}g,y{>} \mid g \in Choices(f),\ y \in Choices(x)\}\\
Choices(f{:}x) &= \{g{:}y \mid g \in Choices(f),\ y \in Choices(x)\}
\end{aligned}$$

This rule implies strict evaluation; even a constant function diverges on a divergent argument, so that $@2{:}abort = abort$.

The application of a PFO to a sequence of functions extends the general definition:

$$Choices(F{:}{<}f_1,\ldots,f_n{>}) \triangleq \{F{:}{<}g_1,\ldots,g_n{>} \mid g_i \in Choices(f_i)\}$$

where F is any of the standard (determinate) PFO's of FP.

This definition is quite restrictive in that a PFO is only applied to one of the possible meanings of a function. If a constant function @*1* is mapped over a sequence, the result must be a sequence of *1*'s. If the constant function @*2* is mapped over a sequence, the result must be a sequence of *2*'s. If the constant indeterminate function which chooses between these is mapped over a sequence, this definition requires that the result must be either a sequence of *1*'s or a sequence of *2*'s; it cannot be a mixture. This is not a failure of expressive power, since the mixture can be represented in this system by a recursive definition. However, it is not necessarily the the most useful meaning. Thus, we require

$$\begin{aligned}
&Choices(ApplyToAll\ f{:}{<}x_1,\ldots,x_n{>})\\
&\quad = \{{<}g{:}y_1,\ldots,g{:}y_n{>} \mid g \in Choices(f),\ y_i \in Choices(x_i)\}.
\end{aligned}$$

The alternative,

$$Choices(ApplyToAll\ f: <x_1,...,x_n>)$$
$$= \{<g_1:y_1,...,g_n:y_n> \mid g_i \in Choices(f),\ y_i \in Choices(x_i)\}$$

may be preferable, and can of course be introduced as a special rule for *ApplyToAll* or by a definition of metacomposition (not considered in this paper). In the terminology of [Clinger 82], we are choosing a singular semantics for functions within PFO's at present, but we expect to consider a plural semantics in future research.

By using singular semantics, we avoid some of the difficulties encountered in denotational treatments of nondeterminism (e.g., [DeBakker 80]). In particular, the iteration form (*while p f*) under singular semantics makes a single nondeterministic choice of the function to be applied. Definitions using recursive equations, however, incorporate more than one copy of the expression to be evaluated, so the problems of plural semantics are unavoidable.

A composition of functions performs successive applications: Since $(f \cdot g):x = (f:(g:x))$, we think of "·" as a dyadic PFO $Compose:<f,g>$ and find that

$$Choices(f_1 \cdot f_2) = \{g_1 \cdot g_2 \mid g_1 \in Choices(f_1),\ g_2 \in Choices(f_2)\}$$

A tuple of functions $[f_1,...,f_n]$ is similarly seen as the application of an operator $Tuple:<f_1,...,f_n>$ and therefore the application of a tuple of functions yields a sequence of values:

$$Choices([f_1,...,f_n]:x) = \{<y_1, \ldots, y_n> \mid z \in Choices(x),\ g_i \in Choices(f_i),\ y_i \in g_i:z\}$$

This is not equivalent to beta-reduction in the nondeterministic case, because it is assumed that the argument x converges (if possible) to a single value z to which all the functions are applied. It follows that $Choices[f_1,...,f_n]:x)$ is in general a subset of $Choices(<f_1:x,...,f_N:x>)$. This is the source of the failure of "where-abstraction" discussed in [Myers 82] and [Cohen 82]; to some extent, nondeterminism destroys referential transparency.

Conditional function application similarly satisfies:

$$Choices((p \rightarrow f;g):x) = \{F:X \mid P:X = true\} \cup \{G:X \mid P:X = false\}$$

where S is in $Choices(s)$ for $s = p, f, g, x$. This is doubly strict: the set is empty if x fails to converge or if x converges to y such that $p:y$ fails to converge.

Uncommitted nondeterminism is provided by a PFO which behaves in the same way as McCarthy's ambiguity function *amb*. Used as a dyadic function, *amb* is non-strict: it converges whenever at least one of its arguments does (i.e., $amb(x,\ abort) = x$ rather than *abort*).

Consequently, we must view it as a control structure (PFO) which works on functions rather than on values. We rename *amb* as *TryBoth* and represent it as the infix PFO &; these denotations were chosen to emphasize the fact that both arguments must be considered. Only one of them will be produced in the end, and authors such as [Henderson 82] therefore use an infix "or"; we reserve this for the committed nondeterministic operation which only considers one or the other of its arguments.

$$Choices(f \ \& \ g) \triangleq Choices(f) \cup Choices(g), \text{ and therefore}$$
$$Choices((f \ \& \ g){:}x) = Choices(f{:}x) \cup Choices(g{:}x).$$

This is the only nondeterministic primitive of the system and, thus, the only source of indeterminacy. Nondeterministic choice can be thought of as an indecisive conditional:

$$Choices((f \ \& \ g){:}x) = Choices(\ (@true \ \& \ @false \ \rightarrow \ f;\ g){:}x)$$

Finally, the monadic PFO's including the standard *Insert* and *ApplyToAll* and the less-standard *Constant* (and others to come) can be dealt with collectively: If "?" is a monadic PFO, then as a special case of our general rule,

$$Choices(?f) = \{?g \mid g \in Choices(f)\}$$

The system we have defined has, as promised, nice algebraic properties. & is clearly both associative and commutative with identity element *Abort*, so that

$$Choices(f \ \& \ (g \ \& \ h)) = Choices((f \ \& \ g) \ \& \ h)$$
$$Choices(f \ \& \ g) = Choices(g \ \& \ f)$$
$$Choicee(f \ \& \ Abort) = Choices(Abort \ \& \ f) = Choices(f)$$

Further, *TryBoth* is an idempotent under *Choices*:

$$Choices(f \ \& \ f) = Choices(f)$$

(More precisely, a curried operation *Curry & f* such that *Curry & f g* = *f & g* would be idempotent; the curry operation of FP, called *bu*, works on functions like + but not on PFO's such as &.)

The system (*S*, &, *Abort*), where *S* is our set of inductively defined expressions, is evidently an abelian monoid modulo equivalence under *Choices*; we will express this less formally by the assertion that (*Choices*, &, *Abort*) forms an abelian monoid.

We have specified the meanings of expressions by defining the sets of values they can assume. From an operational viewpoint, the fact that *Choices*(*E*) = *V* for some top-level expression *E* means that all untried elements of *V* will be maintained until the computation succeeds (and that the computation will fail only if there are no more elements to try).

Uncommitted nondeterminism is expensive, since alternate computation paths cannot be discarded; they must either be saved for later trial or be explored simultaneously.

1.2 Extended notation: *ChoiceSets*

In the model described in Section 1.1, failures disappear. This mirrors a reality in which failures generally arise from strictly evaluated nonterminating computations, and in which a computation fails only if all of its possible choices fail. Committed nondeterminism requires a different model: a single computation path is chosen from among the several possible, and the computation fails if that path diverges. We can define a system similar to that above, with a different nondeterministic operator (i.e., with a different evaluation strategy for nondeterminism) to model committed nondeterminism. However, we need notation which distinguishes between the two types so that we can eventually define a system which supports both of them. Thus, we introduce a second metalinguistic operator *ChoiceSets*, which interprets an expression as yielding a set of sets of values.

Operationally, the evaluator may commit itself to any of the sets of values, even if that set of values is empty; all of the values of the chosen set must be tried (if necessary) to yield a top-level value. The system we are considering contains uncommitted nondeterminism only; the evaluator must choose exactly the set *Choices*(x) to be searched. It follows that in this restricted context,

$$\mathit{ChoiceSets}(x) \triangleq \{\mathit{Choices}(x)\};$$

so that, e.g., if *Choices*(x) $= \{a,b\}$, then *ChoiceSets*(x) $= \{\{a,b\}\}$. The new operation simply adds an extra pair of enclosing brackets to the set of choices of each expression. When we introduce committed nondeterminism, the extra level of bracketing will provide a framework in which we can distinguish between the two types. The complete construction for this model will be given in Section 3.

1.3 Lazy (Uncommitted) Evaluation: *LazyChoices*

In order to represent streams, and to perform some kinds of program transformations, we broaden the system by allowing an expression to converge even when some of its subexpressions are divergent (i.e, we introduce lazy evaluation).

The most convenient way to describe the convergence of *f:x* despite the divergence of x is to introduce an explicit notation for failure: a divergent x is described as 'converging' to the unique value *Fail* rather than as having no value. (In this model, the expression *abort* uniformly converges to *Fail.*)

We will therefore define an operator *LazyChoices* which will be similar to *Choices* except that it may yield values for an expression with divergent subexpressions. This will happen, e.g., when constant functions are applied to divergent arguments (*@3:abort* = *3*) or when sequences have divergent members that are never used (*#1:<3, abort>* = *3*). In order to develop its definition, we introduce the function *FreeChoices* which behaves exactly like *Choices* except that

$FreeChoices(abort) \triangleq \{Fail\}$, and similarly

$FreeChoices(Abort) \triangleq \{@Fail\}$

We will show later that *FreeChoices* itself models a form of committed nondeterminism with lazy evaluation, and can be easily modified to model a form of committed/strict evaluation.

In order to model uncommitted/lazy evaluation, we use *FreeChoices* but then introduce a top-level function to prune out failures:

$LazyChoices(E) \triangleq FreeChoices(E) - \{Fail\}$.

The *LazyChoices* construction lacks the algebraic simplicity of the *Choices* construction, in that to have *Abort* as an identity element we must explicitly limit the behavior of functions on *Fail.* Given well-behaved functions, we have the same monoid structure as before, but we need to regulate the behaviour of the functions. Specifically, we must require that *Fail* be a unique least-defined element in some ordering for which all functions are monotonic, by, e.g., enforcing the rule that for all functions f and expressions x, *LazyChoices(f:x)* must be a superset of *LazyChoices(f:abort).* This may be a natural consequence of the usual fixpoint considerations for deterministic computations, but from our present viewpoint it is superfluous baggage. The *Choices* construction shows how such properties may be built into a strict-evaluation model at no extra charge.

Laziness does, however, have significant advantages in that we can now represent uncommitted nondeterminism at the function/object level rather than the PFO/function level, e.g. by *TryBoth* (McCarthy's *amb*):

TryBoth:<x,y> = @x & @y

or more precisely

$$TryBoth = \#1 \,\&\, \#2.$$

In a lazy system *abort* is an identity element for the abelian monoid formed around the function *TryBoth*.

1.4 Extended Notation: *LazyChoiceSets*

No additional issues are raised by defining a *LazyChoiceSets* variant such that

$$LazyChoiceSets(expr) \triangleq \{LazyChoices(expr)\}$$
$$LazyChoiceSets(expr) = \{FreeChoices(expr) - \{Fail\}\}$$

Clearly, this also forms an abelian monoid.

The *LazyChoiceSets* construction is not recursive, but can be expressed in terms of a recursive *FreeChoiceSets* construction such that

$$FreeChoiceSets(expr) \triangleq \{FreeChoices(expr)\}$$

which is recursive, i.e. it can be solved to yield a set of equations which define it without reference to *FreeChoices*, always yielding a unit set containing a set of values. For example,

$$FreeChoiceSets(a) = \{FreeChoices(a)\} = \{\{a\}\}$$
$$FreeChoiceSets(abort) = \{\{Fail\}\}$$
$$\begin{aligned} FreeChoiceSets(<x_1,\ldots,x_n>) &= \{FreeChoices(<x_1,\ldots,x_n>)\} \\ &= \{\{<y_1,\ldots,y_n> \mid y_i \in FreeChoices(x_i)\}\} \\ &= \{\{<y_1,\ldots,y_n> \mid y_i \in X_i \} \mid X_i \in FreeChoiceSets(x_i)\} \end{aligned}$$

and, more confusingly,

$$\begin{aligned} FreeChoiceSets(f \,\&\, g) &= \{FreeChoices(f \,\&\, g)\} \\ &= \{FreeChoices(f) \cup FreeChoices(g) \} \\ &= \{F \cup G \mid F,\, G \in FreeChoiceSets(f),\, FreeChoiceSets(G)\} \end{aligned}$$

The union has become a cartesian product of unions (for the present, carried out trivially over a pair of unit sets, but this is to be expanded in Section 3).

2 Committed nondeterminism

In committed (strict or lazy) nondeterminism, we intend that it will be possible to "choose to diverge" even if some choice leading to convergence is available. As with uncommitted nondeterminism, we can model the system in any of several ways, all based on set constructions. In the subsections below, we show how the *FreeChoices* construction can be interpreted as lazy committed nondeterminism (with the nondeterministic operator renamed to avoid confusion), and how an isomorphic system can be defined as a separate set of rules for *ChoiceSets*. We temporarily omit the system for strict evaluation of committed nondeterminism.

2.1 The basic system: *FreeChoices*

The *FreeChoices* function by itself yields an interpretation in which an expression may "choose" to diverge even though convergent paths exist, and may converge even if it contains divergent subexpressions. In order to refer to it without confusion, we repeat the essential axioms renaming the nondeterministic choice operator *TryOne* to represent its committed character and representing it with the infix PFO ||.

$$FreeChoices(abort) \triangleq \{Fail\}$$
$$FreeChoices(<x_1,\ldots,x_n>) \triangleq \{<y_1,\ldots,y_n> \mid y_i \in FreeChoices(x_i)\}$$
$$FreeChoices(f \parallel g) \triangleq FreeChoices(f) \cup FreeChoices(g)$$

and as an interesting consequence

$$FreeChoices((p \rightarrow f;\, g){:}x)$$
$$= \{F{:}X \mid P{:}X = true\} \cup \{G{:}X \mid P{:}X = false\} \cup \{Fail \mid P{:}X = Fail\}$$

where S is in $Choices(s)$ for $s = p,\ f,\ g,\ x$, as before.

Note that *Abort* is not an identity element for the PFO ||:

$$FreeChoices((Add1 \parallel Abort){:}2) = \{Fail, 3\}$$
$$FreeChoices(Add1{:}2) = \{3\}$$

|| is associative and commutative, but the identity for set union is still the empty set, and we therefore introduce a function *Skip* such that

$$FreeChoices(Skip) \triangleq \{\}$$

The system (*FreeChoices*, ||, *Skip*) is an abelian monoid, as promised. Interestingly, the sequence *Choices*, *LazyChoices*, *FreeChoices* seems to form an upward-compatible progression: given the same deterministic primitives in the language, any value in *Choices*(E) will appear in

LazyChoices(*E*), and any value in *LazyChoices*(*E*) using & and *Abort* will appear in *FreeChoices*(*E′*) where *E′* substitutes || for & and *Skip* for *Abort*.

Again, the lazy evaluation of the *FreeChoices* expressions allows us to lower the level of the algebra from PFO/function to function/object, introducing the function

$TryOne{:}<x,y> \triangleq @x \parallel @y$. Equivalently,
$TryOne \triangleq \#1 \parallel \#2$

2.2 Notational Variant: *FreeChoiceSets*

Again, we modify the notation to create an isomorphic system which will fit better into the extensions we intend to make later: we redefine the system *FreeChoiceSets* such that in this context (i.e., the context of the language involving || but not &)

$$FreeChoiceSets(E) \triangleq \{\{x\} \mid x \in FreeChoices(E)\}$$

and thus *FreeChoiceSets* is a set of unit sets of values. Thus, for example,

$$FreeChoiceSets(a) = \{\{a\}\}$$
$$FreeChoiceSets(abort) = \{\{Fail\}\}$$

$$\begin{aligned} FreeChoiceSets(<x_1,\ldots,x_n>) &= \{\{<y_1, \ldots, y_n>\} \mid y_i \in FreeChoices(x_i)\} \\ &= \{\{<y_1,\ldots,y_n>\} \mid y_i \in X_i,\ X_i \in FreeChoiceSets(x_i)\} \\ &= \{\{<y_1,\ldots,y_n> \mid y_i \in X_i\} \mid X_i \in FreeChoiceSets(x_i)\} \end{aligned}$$

but now

$$\begin{aligned} FreeChoiceSets(f \parallel g) &= \{\{h\} \mid h \in FreeChoices(f \parallel g)\} \\ &= \{\{h\} \quad h \in FreeChoices(f) \text{ or } h \in FreeChoices(E)\} \\ &= \{\{h\} \mid \{h\} \in FreeChoiceSets(f) \text{ or } \{h\} \text{ in } FreeChoiceSets(g)\} \\ &= FreeChoiceSets(f) \cup FreeChoiceSets(g) \end{aligned}$$

so that

$$FreeChoiceSets(@a \parallel @b) = \{\{@a\},\{@b\}\}$$

Adding the second level of bracketing does not affect the actual behaviour of this system, but will allow us (in section 3) to interpret the resulting two-level structure as indicating a committed choice of a set of values from which an uncommitted choice must be made.

3 Combined systems

The two different *FreeChoiceSets* systems can be combined to yield a system involving lazy evaluation and combining both kinds of nondeterminism. Similarly, the original *ChoiceSets* can be combined with a committed-strict system to yield one strictly evaluated system with both kinds of nondeterminism. We present the (more complex, and more useful) *FreeChoiceSets* construction in some detail, leaving the *ChoiceSets* combination as an exercise for the reader (and for the writers; like all papers on parallelism, ours includes a version of the readers-writers problem, and this is it.)

We now consider the system (*LazyChoiceSets*, &, ||, *Skip*, *Abort*), which incorporates committed and uncommitted nondeterminism: this combination is made possible by the fact that the recursive definitions of *FreeChoiceSets* are compatible.

It was the need to distinguish between the kinds of nondeterminism which led us to develop the two-layered approach of *ChoiceSets*. If the overall structure of committed (existential) and uncommitted (universal) choices is thought of as an AND/OR tree, our sets contain exactly the leaves of this tree put into disjunctive-conjunctive normal form. Within this larger system, we will obtain nontrivial sets of possible values for expressions: in general, these will be non-singleton sets of non-singleton sets. Again, an interpreter can be thought of as choosing **any** member of the outer set in a single act of committed nondeterminism; this leaves it with a set of values, **all** of which may need to be examined in order to avoid producing *Fail* as the top-level result.

We define

$$LazyChoiceSets(expr) \triangleq \{E - \{Fail\} \mid E \in FreeChoiceSets(expr)\}$$

where

$FreeChoiceSets(a) = \{\{a\}\}$, for all atoms except *abort*;
$FreeChoiceSets(abort) = \{\{Fail\}\}$.

Similarly,

$FreeChoiceSets(f) = \{\{f\}\}$, for deterministic functions;
$FreeChoiceSets(Abort) = \{\{@Fail\}\}$.

$FreeChoiceSets(Skip) = \{\}$

Sequences yield the cartesian product of all possible sequences of their values.

$$FreeChoiceSets(<x_1,...,x_n>) = \{\{<y_1,...,y_n> \mid y_i \in X_i\} \mid X_i \in FreeChoiceSets(x_i)\}.$$

f & g can search among values from F and G provided that f could search among values from F and g could search among values from G:

$$FreeChoiceSets(f \ \& \ g) = \{F \cup G \mid F \in FreeChoiceSets(f),\ G \in FreeChoiceSets(g)\}$$

$\|$ can choose to search among values from any set which could have been chosen by f or g:

$$FreeChoiceSets(f \ \| \ g) = FreeChoiceSets(f) \cup FreeChoiceSets(g)$$

The rules for function application and for the various determinate PFO's are derived as before from the sequence construction and our understanding of deterministic function application, which simply maps a set of sets of argument values (possibly including *Fail*) into the corresponding set of sets of result values (which must contain *Fail* wherever the determinate function diverges, whether the argument diverged or not). Function application tries out a set of possible values of the function applied to a set of possible values of the argument:

$$\begin{aligned} &FreeChoiceSets(f:x) \\ &\quad = \{\{g:y \mid g \in F, y \in X\} \mid F \in FreeChoiceSets(f), X \in FreeChoiceSets(x)\} \end{aligned}$$

Application of a tuple of functions yields a sequence, with the same limitation on substitutivity:

$$\begin{aligned} FreeChoiceSets([f_1,...,f_n]:x) = \{\{&<y_1, \ldots, y_n> \mid y_i = g_i:z,\ g_i \in F_i,\ z \in X\} \\ &\mid Fi \in FreeChoiceSets(fi),\ X \in FreeChoiceSets(x)\} \end{aligned}$$

Application of a conditional follows the same pattern, i.e.

$$\begin{aligned} FreeChoiceSets(p \to f;g) = \{\{&(q \to a;b) \mid q \in P, a \in F,\ b \in G\} \\ &\mid P,F,G \in FreeChoiceSets(p),...,f,...,g\} \end{aligned}$$

with the consequence that for each committed choice of P, F, G and a value-set X for the argument x we find a set of results:

$$\begin{aligned} FreeChoiceSets((p \to f;g):x) = \{&\{h:y \mid h \in F,\ y \in X,\ q \in P,\ q:y = true\} \\ &\cup \{h:y \mid h \in G,\ y \in X,\ q \in P,\ q:y = false\} \\ &\cup \{Fail \mid y \in X,\ q \in P,\ q:y = Fail\} \\ &\mid P,F,G,X \in FreeChoiceSets(p),...,f,...,g,...,x\ \} \end{aligned}$$

In the lazy context, we can add the functions *TryBoth* and *TryOne* satisfying

$$FreeChoiceSets(TryBoth) \triangleq \{\{\#1, \#2\}\}$$
$$FreeChoiceSets(TryOne) \triangleq \{\{\#1\},\{\#2\}\}$$

This gives us a function/object level system (*FreeChoiceSets, TryBoth, TryOne, skip, abort*) in exact correspondence to the PFO/function level system (*FreeChoiceSets*, &, ||, *Skip, Abort*). Statements about either system can be lifted or lowered to the other's level.

The restriction of *FreeChoiceSets* to either & or || gives us back an abelian monoid; inclusion of both gives us a semiring, because the cartesian product construction of & distributes over the union which yields ||:

$$FreeChoiceSets(f \;\&\; (g \parallel h)) = FreeChoiceSets((f \;\&\; g) \parallel (f \;\&\; h))$$
$$FreeChoiceSets(TryBoth{:}\langle a, TryOne{:}\langle b,c\rangle\rangle) = \{\{a,b\},\{a,c\}\}$$
$$FreeChoiceSets(TryOne{:}\langle TryBoth{:}\langle a,b\rangle, TryBoth{:}\langle a,c\rangle\rangle) = \{\{a,b\},\{a,c\}\}$$

and more generally

$$\begin{aligned}&FreeChoiceSets(TryBoth{:}\langle x, TryOne{:}\langle y,z\rangle\rangle)\\ &\quad = FreeChoiceSets(TryOne{:}\langle TryBoth{:}\langle x,y\rangle, TryBoth{:}\langle x,z\rangle\rangle)\end{aligned}$$

The converse is not true: *TryOne* does not distribute over *TryBoth*.

$$\begin{aligned}&FreeChoiceSets(TryOne{:}\langle a, TryBoth{:}\langle b,c\rangle\rangle)\\ &\quad = \{\{a\},\{b,c\}\}\\ &FreeChoiceSets(TryBoth{:}\langle TryOne{:}\langle a,b\rangle, TryOne{:}\langle a,c\rangle\rangle)\\ &\quad = \{\{a\},\{a,b\},\{a,c\},\{b,c\}\}\end{aligned}$$

It can easily be shown that

$$\begin{aligned}&FreeChoiceSets(TryOne{:}\langle x, TryBoth{:}\langle y,z\rangle\rangle)\\ &\quad = FreeChoiceSets(TryBoth{:}\langle TryOne{:}\langle x,y\rangle, TryOne{:}\langle x,z\rangle\rangle)\end{aligned}$$

so that one two-sided distributive law (multiplication over addition) holds, and a one-sided version of the other distributive law holds.

The system (*FreeChoiceSets*, &, ||, *Skip, Abort*) thus has (more than) all of the properties of a semiring with multiplicative element & and additive element ||; it is easy to verify additionally that the additive identity *skip* is a multiplicative zero:

$$\begin{aligned}FreeChoiceSets(TryBoth{:}\langle x, skip\rangle) &= \{A \cup B \mid A \in FreeChoiceSets(x),\ B \text{ in } \{\}\}\\ &= \{\}\\ &= FreeChoiceSets(skip).\end{aligned}$$

TryOne is idempotent, but in this context *TryBoth* is not:

$$FreeChoiceSets(TryOne{:}\langle x,x\rangle) = FreeChoiceSets(x)$$

follows directly from the idempotency of set union, but not only is *FreeChoiceSets*(*TryBoth:*$\langle x,x\rangle$) a superset of *FreeChoiceSets*(x) but every element of the former is a superset of some element of the latter. (Of course, they are equal if *FreeChoiceSets*(x) is a unit set.) The structure is therefore in some respects lattice-like, but is not a lattice.

4 Cut and SuperGlue

Nondeterministic search in Prolog can be constrained by a *Cut* operation which operationally is defined as "wait for the first non-*Fail*, then commit yourself to producing it. If it is not satisfactory (i.e., if search returns to this point because of a later *Fail*ure) then the overall search will not produce any value." In terms of *FreeChoiceSets*, we can express this by introducing

$$FreeChoiceSets(Cut{:}x) \triangleq \{\{z\}\ z \in X,\ z \neq Fail,\ X \in FreeChoiceSets(x)\}$$

Note that this violates the convention that the meaning of an application must be formed from the *FreeChoiceSets* of the function and argument in a uniform way; *FreeChoiceSets*(*Cut*) has no possible interpretation. The proof is straightforward: the cardinality of *FreeChoiceSets*(*Cut:*x) for non-divergent x is the sum of the cardinalities of *FreeChoiceSets*(x); any possible definition using the rule for applications based on a definition for *FreeChoiceSets*(*Cut*), would yield a cardinality equal to the product of the cardinalities of *FreeChoiceSets*(*Cut*) and *FreeChoiceSets*(x); there can be no n such that for all $\{m_1,\ldots,m_k\}$ it is guaranteed that $n{*}k = m_1+m_2+\ldots+m_k$.

Nonetheless *Cut* is fairly well-behaved:

$$FreeChoiceSets(Cut{:}(TryOne{:}\langle x,y\rangle)) = FreeChoiceSets(TryOne{:}\langle Cut{:}x,\ Cut{:}y\rangle)$$

$$\begin{aligned} &FreeChoiceSets(Cut{:}(TryBoth{:}\langle x,y\rangle)) \\ &\quad = \{\{z\}\ z \in X \cup Y,\ z \neq Fail,\ X,Y \in FreeChoiceSets(x),\ldots,y\} \\ &\quad = \{\{z\}\ z \in X,\ z \neq Fail,\ X \in FreeChoiceSets(x)\} \\ &\quad \cup \{\{z\}\ z \in Y,\ z \neq Fail,\ Y \in FreeChoiceSets(y)\} \\ &\qquad\qquad = FreeChoiceSets(TryOne{:}\langle Cut{:}x,\ Cut{:}y\rangle) \end{aligned}$$

Thus for example

$$FreeChoiceSets(Cut{:}(TryBoth{:}\langle a,b\rangle)) = \{\{a\},\{b\}\}$$
$$FreeChoiceSets(Cut{:}abort) = \{\}$$
$$FreeChoiceSets(Cut{:}(TryBoth{:}\langle a,abort\rangle)) = \{\{a\}\}$$

Formally,

$$Cut \cdot Abort = Skip$$

so that *Cut* essentially converts uncommitted to committed search. *Skip*, introduced as the formal identity for *TryOne*, is impossible to implement correctly in the general case; distribution must be restricted to programs which will not *abort*. Although divergence is undecidable in general, we frequently encounter situations in which the transformation is applicable since program segments which trivially terminate are commonplace, especially in a context of simple operators.

Similarly, we can define a *SuperGlue* operator which uncommits already-committed choices.

$$FreeChoiceSets(SuperGlue{:}x) \triangleq \{\{z \in X,\ X \in FreeChoiceSets(x)\}\}$$

so that

$$FreeChoiceSets(SuperGlue{:}(TryBoth{:}\langle x,y\rangle))$$
$$= FreeChoiceSets(TryBoth{:}\langle SuperGlue{:}x,\ SuperGlue{:}y\rangle)$$

$$FreeChoiceSets(SuperGlue{:}(TryOne{:}\langle x,y\rangle))$$
$$= FreeChoiceSets(TryBoth{:}\langle SuperGlue{:}x,\ SuperGlue{:}y\rangle)$$

This is of theoretical interest only, since committing to a choice in practice involves physical pruning of the evaluation tree (by removing pointers, if nothing else).

Cut and *SuperGlue* are generalized inverses, and each is idempotent.

$$Cut \cdot SuperGlue \cdot Cut = Cut$$
$$SuperGlue \cdot Cut \cdot SuperGlue = SuperGlue$$

$$SuperGlue \cdot SuperGlue = SuperGlue$$
$$Cut \cdot Cut = Cut$$

Clearly, *SuperGlue* cannot be part of a conventional run-time system, but (together with *Skip*) it can help us tame the relatively intractable but extremely important *Cut* operation.

5 Other semiring structures

The most fundamental of the standard FP PFO's is function composition, denoted by "$\cdot$". Composition is associative, since

$$((f \cdot g) \cdot h):x = f:(g:(h:x)) = (f \cdot (g \cdot h)):x, \text{ for all } f, g, h, \text{ and } x.$$

and has the identity function *id* as (left and right) identity: by definition,

$$id:x = x,$$

so that

$$(id \cdot f):x = id:(f:x) = f:x$$
$$(f \cdot id):x = f:(id:x) = f:x$$

and therefore

$$id \cdot f = f \cdot id = f$$

Thus, the set of functions under composition is a monoid (although not an abelian one). This is the source of much of the power of the standard FP algebra of programs.

An important class of laws in that algebra are distribution laws involving composition and and other operators. Some of these remain valid in the presence of nondeterminism, while others fail in that context.

Construction (tupling) generally satisfies

$$[f_1, \ldots, f_n] \cdot g = [f_1 \cdot g, \ldots, f_n \cdot g]$$

but this is not valid for nondeterministic g, since the left-hand-side applies all of the f_i to a single value, while the right-hand-side might apply distinct f_i to different values.

Left-distribution over the arms of a conditional still holds:

$$h \cdot (p \rightarrow f; g) = (p \rightarrow h \cdot f; h \cdot g)$$

Intuitively, this remains valid because only one of the copied values of h is evaluated.

The FP-valid law for right distribution,

$$(p \rightarrow f; g) \cdot h = (p \cdot h \rightarrow f \cdot h; g \cdot h)$$

fails for nondeterministic h by the general failure of beta-reduction.

Both left and right distribution succeed over both committed and uncommitted nondeterministic choice:

$$h_1 \cdot (f \ \& \ g) \cdot h_2 = (h_1 \cdot f \cdot h_2) \ \& \ (h_1 \cdot g \cdot h_2), \text{ and}$$
$$h_1 \cdot (f \ || \ g) \cdot h_2 = (h_1 \cdot f \cdot h_2) \ || \ (h_1 \cdot g \cdot h_2).$$

These rules can be viewed as special cases of the conditional rules; they escape the failure of right-distribution because the conditional functions *@true* & *@false* and *@true* || *false* ignore their arguments, except to diverge on a divergent argument under strict evaluation. Since this divergence does not affect the validity of these rules, all of the laws stated thus far are valid under either strict or lazy evaluation.

Strict and lazy semantics are distinguished, in this context, by the zero-elements to be added to the monoids. Under strict evaluation, *Abort* is a left and right zero for function composition; but under lazy evaluation, any constant function is a left zero and there can therefore be no right zero. Accordingly, under strict evaluation we get a straightforward semiring (*Choices*, ·, &, *Abort*, *Id)* and the additive identity *Abort* is the multiplicative zero. This property cannot hold (but weaker variants of it do) in the structure for ||, where the additive identity is *Skip* but the multiplicative zero is still *Abort*, or in the lazy structures for & and || where there are no multiplicative zeros. Work in progress by Paul Broome [Broome 85] uses these properties within an algorithm based on Arden's lemma: tail-recursive definitions of functions are converted into equivalent expressions in a Dijkstra-like guarded-commands language. The process (in the simplest case) is identical to the standard algorithm for conversion of right-linear grammars into regular expressions.

6 Graphical representation

This section presents a graphical technique for deriving *FreeChoiceSets*(E) for given expression E. Informally, the construction represents *FreeChoiceSets*(E) as a forest or OR-trees. There is one tree for each set in *FreeChoicesets*(E) and the leaves of each tree correspond to the elements of its set. For example, if

$$FreeChoiceSets(E)=\{\{a,b\},\{c\},\{Fail,d\}\}$$

then the associated forest is

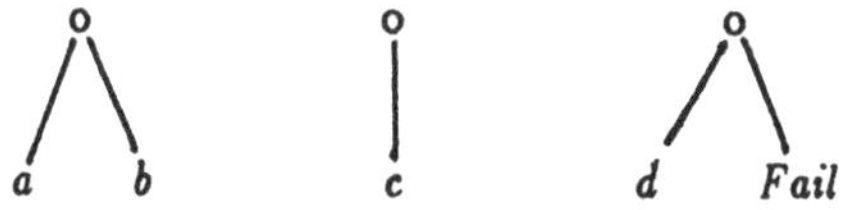

We will sketch the rules for the construction. These will be expanded and made more precise in later versions. In general, individual trees (each of which represents a committed computation path) can be developed individually, and our rules are presented as transformations on single trees.

1. For evaluation of an application *f:x*, we begin by creating a single node with the constant value *x*. Each subsequent stage involves an expression representing a function *f* and a tree to which that function is to be applied. The remaining rules therefore proceed by case analysis on *f*.

2. If *f* is deterministic, append a single branch to each leaf of the tree being expanded. Label the branch with the name of the expression being applied, and the new leaf with its value.

Given *f* = [*double, triple*], *x* = *2*, we find that

2 expands to

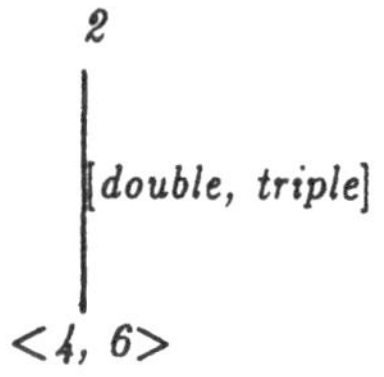

3. If the next step is application of *TryBoth*, split its arguments to form a pair of branches for each leaf of the partial tree, one for each alternative, and label appropriately.

Given *f* = *TryBoth*, *x* = <*4*,*6*> we find that

<*4*,*6*> expands to

4. If $f =$ *TryOne*, twin the tree under consideration, appending one of the alternatives to each leaf of the original and the other alternative to each leaf of the copy.

Given $f =$ *TryOne*, $x = <4,6>$

$<4,6>$ expands to *4* *6*

The forest for (*double* || *triple*) · (*double* & *triple*):@*2* is

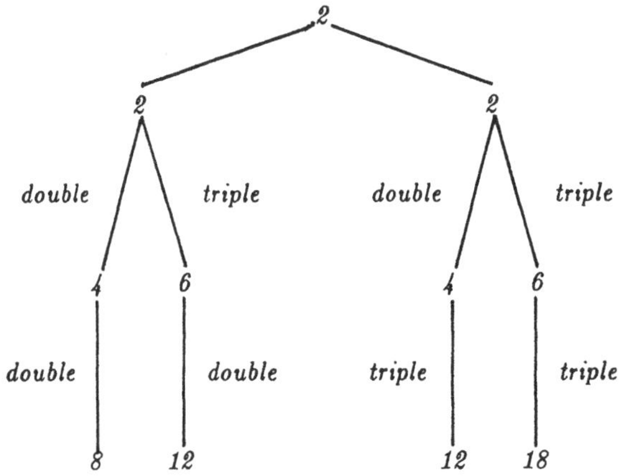

5. If the next step is the conditional $p \rightarrow f;g$, append p to each leaf (as outlined in steps 2 - 4), then apply f, g or *Abort* to each leaf (according as p applied to the argument is *true*, *false* or inappropriate).

Given $f =$ (=*4?* → *double; triple*)·(*double* & *triple*)·@*2*; x=*3*, the partial tree

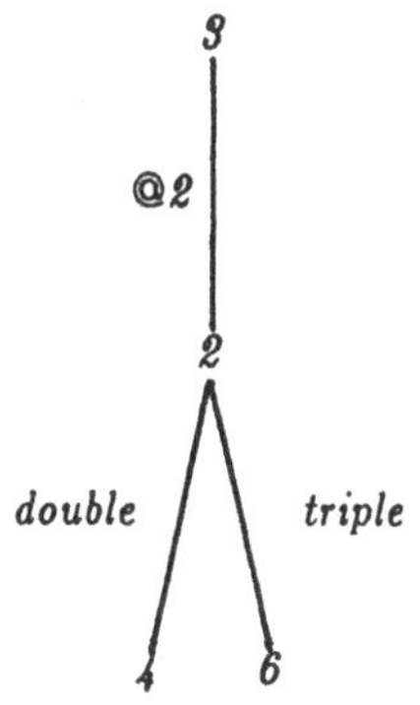

expands to

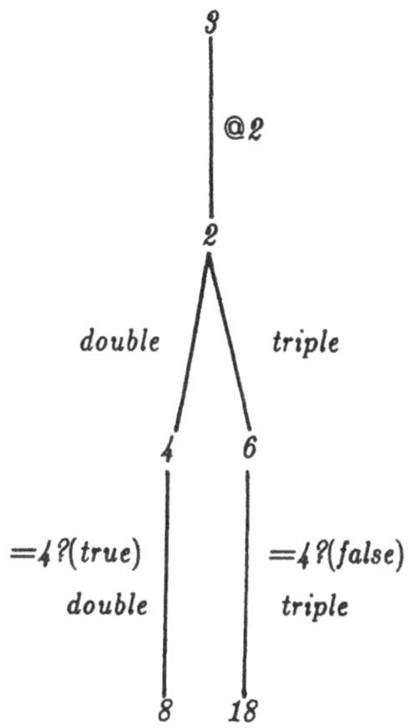

The description given above does not treat cases in which the elements of sequences or tuples do not correspond to unique values (e.g., [@*TryBoth*:<*2*,*3*>, *square*] or <*TryBoth*:<*2*,*3*>, *3*>). These involve considerable bookkeeping, but no new ideas. The tree manipulations are helpful in keeping track of the possibilities raised by an example; when the complexity of a trace becomes overwhelming, it is time to return to conventional formula-manipulation.

7 Applications

Having achieved equational characterizations of different kinds of nondeterminism under different evaluation strategies, we now turn to the problem of application: how does it help us develop programs? Our long-range goal is to manipulate programs into versions which will be semantically equivalent but which will cost less according to some architecture-dependent measure of cost. In the subsections below, we indicate the utility of our models by discussing classes of sample transformations.

7.1 Reassociations

Any associative operation with identity (e.g., *TryBoth* or *TryOne*, is subject to transformations which are beneficial almost regardless of the architecture: The insert operator "/" defined by

$$/f : <> \triangleq \textit{the identity element of } f\text{, if any}$$

$$/f : <a> \triangleq a$$

$$/f : <a_1, a_2, \ldots> \triangleq f : <a_1, /f : <a_2, \ldots>>$$

can (with associative *f*) be evaluated forwards through a sequence, saving space and bookkeeping on any architecture; alternatively, it can be evaluated on subsequences in parallel, saving time.

Moreover, the associative and commutative properties can carry over to quasifunctions (nondeterministic operations) defined in terms of the constructions used so far: a definition such as

$$\begin{aligned} ndmerge : <x,y> &\triangleq null : x \rightarrow y; \\ &\triangleq null : y \rightarrow x; \\ &\triangleq amb : <appendLeft : <hd : x, ndmerge : <tl : x, y>>, \\ &\triangleq amb : <appendLeft : <hd : y, ndmerge : <x, tl : y>>> \end{aligned}$$

allows us to establish the associativity and commutativity of *ndmerge* quite easily, as well as to establish that <> is a two-sided identity for it. *ndmerge* can therefore be used to merge collections of sequences in any order.

7.2 DisConjunctivitis

The (&,||) semiring is most easily motivated as a way to manage the degree of localization of search. On a sequential architecture, given an expression involving both || and &, it might be better to make the committed choice first since the implementation of *f&g* requires that each function wait (occupying space) while the other works. On a parallel architecture, it might be better to make the uncommitted choices first, since this utilizes (possibly idle) processors by sending them (possibly-productive) work. However, in many cases the value of a law like *f*&(*g* || *h*) = (*f*&*g*) || (*f*&*h*) will depend on the opportunities it gives for further optimizations: if we defer the uncommitted choice, we may find that it wasn't necessary. For example, *f*&(*f* || ***abort***) is not directly simplifiable, but (*f*&*f*) || (*f*&***abort***) is clearly reducible to *f*. This is not independent of the issue of managing localization: localized searches are easier to optimize.

7.3 Cut distribution

This is another (essentially quite well-known) technique for avoiding search; its use is usually based on the assumption that we want exactly one answer from a search, to which we can then commit ourselves. Prolog programmers frequently introduce *Cut* symbols into their rules, but *Cut* is not a natural part of the logical theory on which relational programming is based. We find the same problem in *Cut*'s violation of the representability criterion. Operationally, the problem is that it is difficult to handle *Skip* correctly: what we really want is to distribute *Cut* only over those terms which will not abort. Although divergence is not decidable in general, we can (in a lazy system) ascribe a *WillNotAbort* property to constant functions; this will propagate through many kinds of function applications. This is more feasible in an FP-based world than in one of recursive equations or relations, because most of the operators will allow us to propagate this property whereas arbitrary conditional recursions will not.

7.4 Distribution of composition

The distribution of composition over either sort of nondeterministic choice (but especially the uncommitted form) is important in the derivation of search algorithms because it allows us to prune search trees; in extreme cases it can prune them so far that no uncommitted nondeterminism remains. The derivation of sorting algorithms can fit this pattern: we can describe *Sort:x* as a function which uses committed nondeterminism to generate a permutation π of x, and then *Abort*s if π is not ordered. By distributing the test function across the & of the permutation generator and then simplifying with the identity *Abort*, we can derive the principal sorting algorithms directly from the definitions of permutation generators. This kind of transformation has been used for sorting in a relational context by [Clark 80] and for other examples in an equational context by [Wand 80]. Extensive transformations based on these properties (but assuming a plural semantics) are discussed in a functional context by [Cohen 82].

7.5 How does this help?

The examples given are clearly simple programs, and our transformations are "obvious". These "obvious" transformations may take the same role in a transformation system for nondeterministic programs that, e.g., the associativity of arithmetic plays in the design of an optimizing compiler: they are unlikely to be the most important tools, but they are definitely worth using.

The dominant tools will be those which can assume referential transparency and are thus more powerful. Therefore, one of the best ways to transform a nondeterministic construct must be to manipulate it so that some large part of it is deterministic. Moving nondeterminism out of and into subexpressions (e.g., by rules of the form $f.g = g'.f'$, where f and f' are determinate and g and g' are not), as discussed in [Cohen 82], thus seems extremely profitable.

This paper extends our previous work primarily by dealing with both kinds of nondeterminism simultaneously. Future efforts will be directed toward formalizing the basis we have established and extending it to incorporate plural semantics.

References

[Aho 74] A.V. Aho, J.E. Hopcroft and J.D. Ullman, *The Design and Analysis of Computer Algorithms*, Addison-Wesley, Reading, Mass. 1974.

[Backus 78] J. Backus, 'Can Programming Be Liberated from the Von Neumann Style? A Functional Style and its Algebra of Programs', CACM 1978.

[Broome 85] P. Broome, Ph.D. dissertation, in progress.

[Broy 81] M. Broy, 'A fixed point approach to applicative multiprogramming', lecture notes for the International Summer School on Theoretical Foundations of Programming Methodology, July 1981.

[Burstall 77] R.M. Burstall and J. Darlington, 'A Transformation System for Developing Recursive Programs', JACM 24:1, January 1977.

[Bryant 78] R.E. Bryant and J.B. Dennis, 'Concurrent Programming', M.I.T. Computation Structures Group Memo 148-2, June 1978.

[Clark 80] K.L. Clark and J. Darlington, 'Algorithm Classification Through Synthesis', The Computer Journal 23, 1.

[Clinger, 82] W. Clinger, 'Nondeterministic Call-by-Need is Neither Lazy nor by Name', Proceedings ACM Symposium on LISP and Functional Languages, August 1982.

[Clocksin 81] W.F. Clocksin and C.S. Mellish, *Programming in Prolog*, Springer-Verlag, 1981.

[Cohen 82] A.T. Cohen and T.J. Myers, 'Toward an Algebra of Nondeterministic Programs', Proceedings ACM Symposium on LISP and Functional Languages, August 1982.

[Dijkstra 76] E.W. Dijkstra, *A Discipline of Programming*, Prentice-Hall 1976.

[Floyd 67] R.W. Floyd, 'Nondeterministic Algorithms', JACM 14:4, 1967.

[Henderson 80] P. Henderson, *Functional Languages: Applications and Implementations*, Prentice-Hall, 1982.

[Jerrum 82] M. Jerrum and M. Snir, 'Some Exact Complexity Results for Straight-Line Computations over Semirings', JACM 29:3, July 1982.

[Lankford 77] D.S. Lankford and A.M. Ballantyne, 'Decision Procedures for Simple Equational Theories with Commutative-Associative Axioms: Complete Sets of Commutative-Associative Reductions', Technical Report, Mathematics Department, Univ. of Texas, Austin, Texas, August 1977.

[McCarthy 67] J. McCarthy, 'A Basis for a Mathematical Theory of Computation', in *Computer Programming and Formal Systems*, (ed. P Braffort and D. Hirschberg), North-Holland, 1967.

[Myers 82] T.J. Myers and A.T. Cohen, 'Through a Glass Darkly: Observations on Referential Translucency', 10th IMACS World Congress, Montreal, August 1982.

[Park 79] D. Park, 'On the semantics of fair parallelism', University of Warwick Theory of Computation Report 31, October 1979.

[Stickel 81] M.E. Stickel, 'A Unification Algorithm for Associative-Commutative Functions', JACM 28:3, July 1981.

[Wand 80] M. Wand, 'Continuation-Based Program Transformation Strategies', JACM 27:1, January 1980.

DEGREES OF NON-DETERMINISM AND CONCURRENCY:
A PETRI NET VIEW

by

M. Nielsen and P.S. Thiagarajan
Computer Science Department
Aarhus University
DK-8000 Aarhus C
Denmark

0. INTRODUCTION

The aim of this paper is to present an introduction to the theory of Petri nets. The subject matter of this theory is distributed systems and processes. In our presentation, we shall emphasise concepts at the expense of specific results and techniques. Applications of the theory, though many and varied, will not be dealt with here. Even in dealing with the concepts, we shall focus on those that we believe are relevant to the study of distributed systems in general (independent of the specific framework one might choose). In the concluding part, we will attempt a broader sketch of the scope and contents of net theory.

A main feature of this theory is that, in the study of systems, both states and changes-of-states are assigned equal importance. Moreover, both states and changes-of-states are viewed as distributed entities. A marked net (we prefer to term Petri nets as marked nets) looked upon a system model reflects these concerns. A net may be considered to be a directed bipartite graph with two kinds of nodes called S-elements and T-elements. S-elements denote the local atomic states and T-elements denote the local atomic changes-of-states (transitions). The directed arcs capture the neighbourhood relationship between S-elements and T-elements. Markings are used to represent the states of a system whose structure is modelled by a net.

A marking of a net is a distribution of objects called tokens over the S-elements. In this sense a global state is composed out of local states. In general, tokens can have a complex internal structure. This fact leads to a variety of powerful system models [13, 22, 45] that are at the forefront of applications. In this paper, given our purposes, it is sufficient to just consider marked nets in which the tokens do not have any internal structure and hence are indistinguishable from each other.

The dynamics of a marked net are captured by a firing rule. It states when and how the transitions associated with the T-elements can transform the token distribution. In general, a number of (local) transitions may proceed independent of each other at a state. In this sense, change-of-state is also a distributed entity. The chief advantage of marked nets is that they provide the means for clearly distinguishing between the three fundamental relationships that can exist between the occurrences of two transitions t_1 and t_2 of a state:

1) t_1 followed by t_2 (sequence, causal dependence)

2) t_1 or t_2 but not both (choice, conflict, non-determinism)

3) t_1 and t_2 but with no order (concurrency, non-sequentiality, causal independence)

This ability of net theory to cleanly separate - in particular - choice and concurrency has at least one important consequence. It is possible to define various mixtures of non-determinism and non-sequentiality and study the resulting sub-classes. It is this aspect of net theory which we wish to bring out in our survey.

In the next section, the basic terminology concerning marked nets is introduced. One can then identify a class of marked nets called <u>safe</u> marked nets. Our review of net theory is essentially confined to this sub-class. In Section 2, we discuss with the help of simple net diagrams the fundamental situations that can arise in the history of a distributed system. Sections 3 and 4 are the heart of the paper. We identify, by syntactic means, a hierarchy of safe marked nets. We briefly indicate the theories of well-known members of this hierarchy. Our aim is to argue that this hierarchy represents <u>one</u> way of obtaining systems that exhibit increasingly complex mixtures of choice and concurrency in their behaviour. To establish this, in Section 4, we first review the various ways of defining the behaviour of a marked net. We then adapt Milner's notion of behavioural equivalence [32] for our purposes. Finally we show that the syntactically defined hierarchy of the previous section indeed agrees with our chosen notion of behavioural equivalence. As mentioned earlier, in the concluding part we indicate the various portions of net theory that have not been dealt with in this paper.

1. TERMINOLOGY

A (directed) net is a triple $N = (S,T;F)$ where:

1) $S \cup T \neq \emptyset$; $S \cap T = \emptyset$.

2) $F \subseteq (S \times T) \cup (T \times S)$ such that $\mathrm{dom}(F) \cup \mathrm{range}(F) = S \cup T$.

S is the set of S-elements, T is the set of T-elements and F is the flow relation. Depending on the application, various interpretations can be attached to these three components of a net (see [41]). Here, we shall use S-elements to denote the local atomic states, the T-elements to denote the local transitions and the flow relation to denote the extent of changes caused by the local transitions. In what follows we will refer to S-elements as places and T-elements as transitions or as done in the next two sections, refer to S-elements as conditions and to T-elements as events.

In diagrams S-elements will be drawn as circles, T-elements as boxes and the flow relation will be represented by directed arcs. The following is an example of a representation of a net.

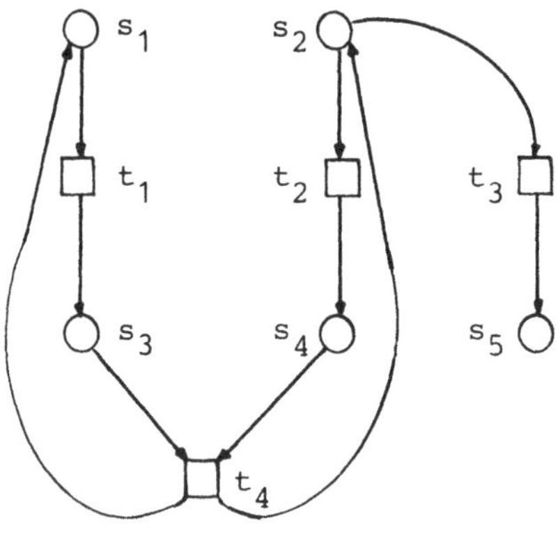

For the net N we use S_N (T_N,F_N) to denote its set of S-elements (T-elements, flow relation); $X_N = S_N \cup T_N$ is the set of elements of N. The subscript N will be dropped if N is clear from the context.

It will be very convenient to work with a 'local' representation of the flow relation. To this end let N be a net and $x \in X_N$. Then

$^{\bullet}x = \{y \in X \mid (y,x) \in F_N\}$ - the pre-set of x
$x^{\bullet} = \{y \in X \mid (x,y) \in F_N\}$ - the post-set of x.

In our example $^{\bullet}s_1 = \{t_4\}$, $t_4^{\bullet} = \{s_1,s_2\}$.

This dot notation is extended to sub-sets of X_N in the obvious way. Now it is possible to identify various sub-classes of nets by suitably (and locally) restricting the dot relation. For example the net N is said to be pure iff $\forall x \in X_N$: $^{\bullet}x \cap x^{\bullet} = \emptyset$. N is said to be simple iff $\forall x,y \in X_N$: $^{\bullet}x = {}^{\bullet}y \wedge y^{\bullet} = x^{\bullet} \Rightarrow x = y$. Our example above is both pure and simple.

In the two sections to follow we will encounter more interesting sub-classes of nets.

A marking of the net N = (S,T;F) is a function $M: S \rightarrow \mathbb{N}_0 = \{0,1,2,...\}$. In diagrams, M is represented by placing M(s) tokens (small dark dots) on each s. The transition t is enabled at the marking M iff for each $s \in {}^{\bullet}t$, $M(s) > 0$; in other words each input place of t should carry at least one token at M. The fact that t is enabled at M will be denoted by M[t>. An enabled transition may fire (occur). When t fires at M, a new marking M' is reached which is given by:

$$\forall s \in S: M'(s) = \begin{cases} M(s) - 1, \text{ if } s \in {}^{\bullet}t \setminus t^{\bullet} \\ M(s) + 1, \text{ if } s \in t^{\bullet} \setminus {}^{\bullet}t \\ M(s), \text{ otherwise.} \end{cases}$$

The transformation of M into M' by the firing of t at M is denoted as M[t>M'. Consider our example above with marking M_1, given by

$$M_1(s_1) = M_1(s_2) = 1$$
$$M_1(s_3) = M_1(s_4) = M_1(s_5) = 0$$

We then have $M_1[t_1>M_2$ where

$$M_2(s_2) = M_2(S_3) = 1$$
$$M_2(s_1) = M_2(s_4) = M_2(s_5) = 0$$

The set of markings one can reach in this way, starting from M is called the forward marking class of M. More precisely, for the net N and a marking M of N, the forward marking class of M is denoted as [M> and is the smallest set of markings of N satisfying:

1) M ∈ [M>

2) If M' ∈ [M>, t ∈ T and M" is a marking of N such that M'[t>M", then M" ∈ [M>.

Our system model is a marked net. Formally, a marked net is a quadruple $\Sigma = (S,T;F,M^0)$ where the net $N_\Sigma = (S,T;F)$ is called the underlying net of Σ and M^0 is a marking of N_Σ called the initial marking of Σ. Liveness and safety are two behavioural properties of marked nets which have traditionally received a great deal of attention in net theory. It is possible to define and study various forms of these two properties. Here we choose the 'strongest' versions.

The marked net $\Sigma = (S,T;F,M^0)$ is live iff $\forall M \in [M^0\rangle$, $\forall t \in T$: $\exists M' \in [M\rangle$ such that t is enabled at M'.

Thus in a live net no transition ever loses the possibility of becoming enabled.

The marked net $\Sigma = (S,T;F,M^0)$ is safe iff $\forall M \in [M^0\rangle$, $\forall s \in S$: $M(s) \leq 1$. Consider our example above with initial marking M_1 (exactly one token on s_1 and s_2). This marked net is then safe but not live.

In a safe net no place will ever contain more than one token. As a result, in a safe net each place can be viewed as a propositional variable. A marking is an atomic boolean valuation (1 ~ true, 0 ~ false) which then extends uniquely to a boolean valuation of the formulas built up from the propositional variables in the natural way. This view coupled with the presence of events gives rise to some obvious and pleasant links with propositional logic (see [11]) but we digress.

What is of interest here is that the basic concepts of net theory are best brought out at the level of safe marked nets. Consequently, in what follows we shall just concentrate on safe marked nets. To conclude this section, we shall adopt a few conventions. In line with tradition, we will from now on denote a safe marked net as $\Sigma = (B,E;F,M^0)$ and call B the conditions and E the events. The elements of $[M^0\rangle$ are sometimes referred to as cases. Since for each $M \in [M^0\rangle$ $M: B \to \{0,1\}$ we can and shall represent M by the set of conditions that hold at M, i.e. $\{b \in B \mid M(b) = 1\}$. Accordingly, we say that the event e is enabled at M iff $^\bullet e \subseteq M$ and so on. We conclude this section with an example of a live and safe marked net (shown in fig. 1).

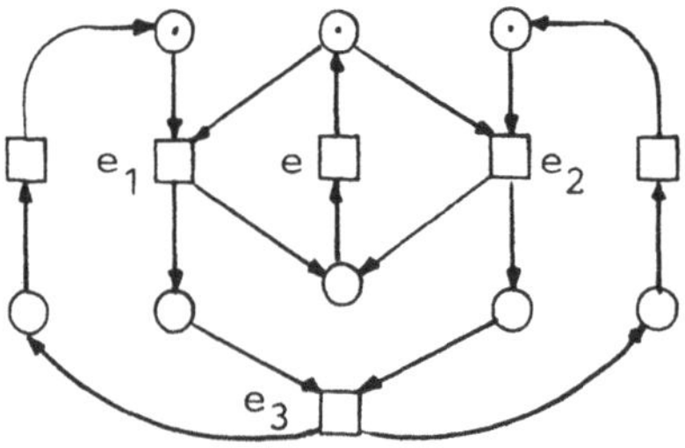

Fig. 1

2. FUNDAMENTAL SITUATION

Causality, concurrency, conflict and confusion are four basic notions of net theory. They can be brought out with the help of safe marked nets as follows.

Causality

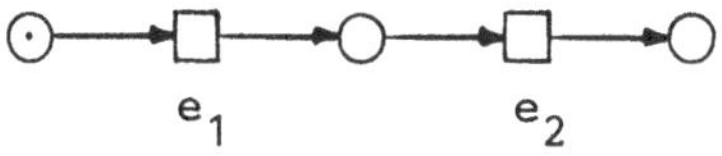

At the marking shown the occurrence e_2 must be preceded by the occurrence of e_1.

Concurrency

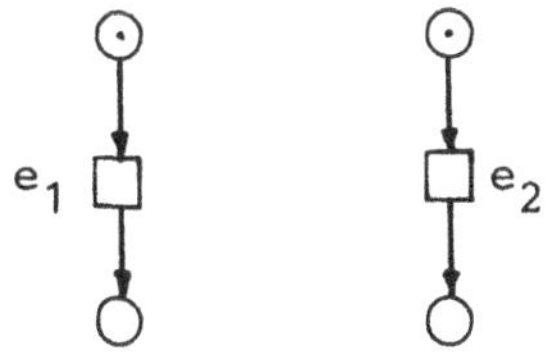

e_1 and e_2 can both occur at the marking. More importantly they can occur without 'interfering' with each other. No order is specified over their occurrences. Thus in general the occurrences of events and the resulting holdings of conditions will be partially ordered; our systems can exhibit non-sequential behaviour. One way to bring in the flavour of concurrency in the firing rule is to introduce the notion of a step.

Let $\Sigma = (B,E;F,M^0)$ be a safe net $M \in [M^0>$ and $\emptyset \neq u \subseteq E$. Then u is a step at M (denoted by M[u>) iff

1) $\forall e \in u: {}^{\bullet}e \subseteq M$ (or equivalently M[e>)

2) $\forall e_1,e_2 \in u: e_1 \neq e_2 \Rightarrow {}^{\bullet}e_1 \cap {}^{\bullet}e_2 = \emptyset$. ($e_1$ and e_2 can carry out the changes-of-states attributed to them without interfering with each other).

We say the events in u occur concurrently at M. As might be expected, M[u>M' iff M[u> and $M' = (M \setminus \bigcup_{e\in u} {}^{\bullet}e) \bigcup_{e\in u} e^{\bullet}$.

Conflict

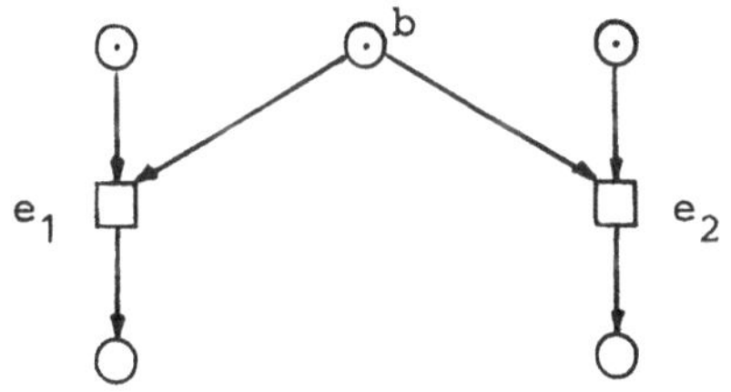

At the marking shown e_1 and e_2 can occur individually. But $\{e_1,e_2\}$ is not a step due to the shared condition b. We say e_1 and e_2 are in conflict at this marking. Non-determinism enters the picture at this stage because the choice as to whether e_1 will occur or e_2 will occur is left unspecified. One way to explain how conflict is resolved is to postulate that the environment will supply the system with the required bit of information. Conflicts and their resolutions may be thought of as the means for modelling the flow of information across the border between the system and its environment.

Confusion

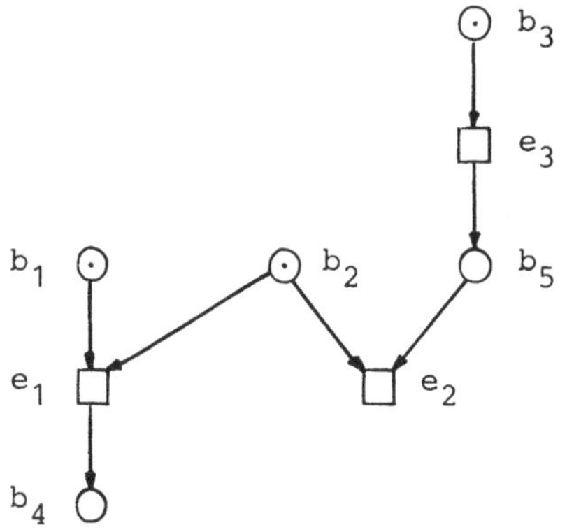

Let $M_0 = \{b_1,b_2,b_3\}$, $M_1 = \{b_4,b_5\}$ so that $M_0[\{e_1,e_3\}>M_1$. Here there could be disagreement over whether or not a conflict was resolved in going from M_0 to M_1. Two honest sequential observers O_1 and O_2 could report:

O_1 e_1 occurred first without being in conflict with any other event. And then e_3 occurred.

O_2 e_3 occurred. e_1 and e_2 got into conflict. The conflict was resolved in favour of e_1.

This is a confused situation. Confusion arises whenever conflict and concurrency 'overlap'. This phenomenon appears to be basic in nature and can be at best swept under the carpet (i.e. to a lower level of description) through temporal assumptions. In asynchronous switching circuits confusion is called the glitch problem or more appropriately the synchronisation failure problem [47].

There is a second form of confusion known as symmetric confusion. Here is an example.

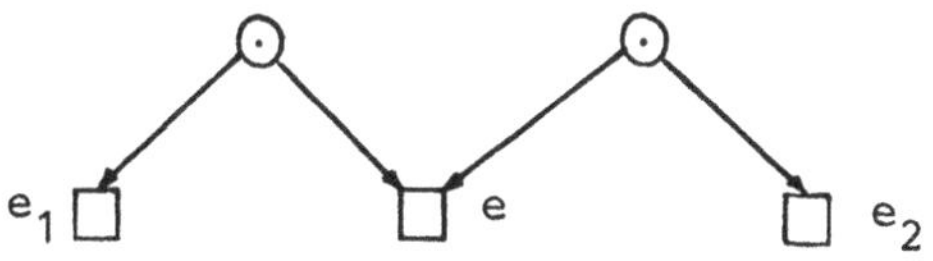

Here e_1 is in conflict with e. $\{e_1,e_2\}$ is a step. If e_2 occurs then e_1 is no longer in conflict with e. In other words e_1 gets out of conflict because of the occurrence of e_2. The whole argument of course applies to e_2 w.r.t. e_1. Hence the term symmetric confusion. Note that if the step $\{e_1,e_2\}$ occurs then there is confusion over which conflict (between e_1 and e or e_2 and e) was resolved.

3. A HIERARCHY OF SAFE NETS

We now wish to combine choice and concurrency by syntactic means and examine some of the resulting sub-classes. To this end it will be convenient to assume that our nets are finite (i.e. the set of elements is finite) and connected (in the graph theoretic sense).

S-graphs can be used to capture the structure of non-deterministic sequential systems. An S-graph is a net $N = (S,T;F)$ in which $\forall t \in T: |{}^{\bullet}t|, |t^{\bullet}| \leq 1$. A marked S-graph is a marked net whose underlying net is an S-graph. It is easy to verify that the marked S-graph $\Sigma = (S,T;F,M^0)$ is live and safe iff N_Σ is strongly-connected and $\sum_{s \in S} M^0(s) = 1$. Here is an example of an ls (live and safe) S-graph. Since liveness and safety make sense only in the presence of markings, we will from now on drop the term "marked" whenever possible.

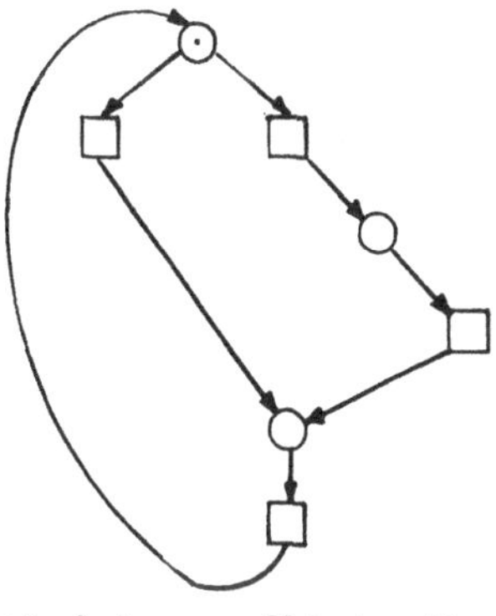

A safe S-graph can get into conflict situations; it can exhibit non-deterministic behaviour. However no two events can ever occur concurrently. In this sense safe S-graphs model non-deterministic sequential systems. Automata theory has a good deal to say about these systems. Viewed as a sub-class of distributed systems, a more appropriate theory of this class is the one constructed by Milner [32]. Note that due to the absence of concurrency, safe S-graphs are free of confusion.

It is a happy circumstance in net theory that, structurally speaking, there is a duality relation between non-deterministic sequential systems and deterministic non-sequential systems. A T-graph is a net $N = (S,T;F)$ in which $\forall s \in S$: $|{}^{\cdot}s|, |s^{\cdot}| \leq 1$. A marked T-garph is a marked net whose underlying net is a T-graph. Marked T-graphs are often called marked graphs and sometimes synchronisation graphs. Below we show an example of an ls T-graph.

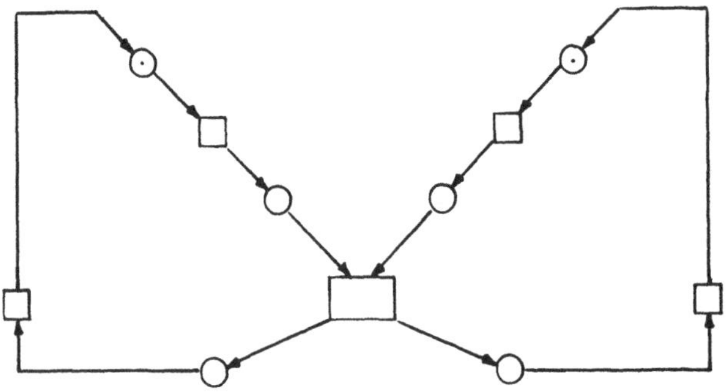

The theory of marked T-graphs is well-understood [6, 10 , 23 ,24]. Here we will just mention a characterisation of ls T-graphs. Details of the proof and other results can be found in [6 ,10].

The marked T-graph $\Sigma = (S,T;F,M^0)$ is live iff $\forall s \in S$: ${}^{\cdot}s \neq \emptyset$ and every directed circuit of N_Σ contains at least one S-element which is marked (i.e. carries at least one token) under M^0.

The live T-graph $\Sigma = (S,T;F,M^0)$ is safe iff every S-element of N_Σ is contained in a directed elementary circuit Π that carries exactly one token under M^0. In other words if S' is the set of S-elements that Π passes through then $\sum_{s \in S'} M^0(s) = 1$.

In a safe T-graph two events may occur concurrently; the behaviour can be non-sequential. But no two events can ever be in conflict. Thus safe T-graphs model deterministic non-sequential systems. Due to the absence of choice, safe T-graphs are also free of confusion. The class of systems represented by safe T-graphs is an interesting one. This class has appeared under very many disguises - with some variations on the expressive power - in the literature and will probably continue to due so. To mention just a few here Muller [33] in his work on speed independent switching circuits was the first to identify this class. This was followed by Karp and Miller [23] who explicitly used the term 'determinate'. The well known stream-processing networks of Kahn [54] are one more appealing manifestation of this class and in Milner's CCS [31] they are christened confluent systems. Finally in the land of VLSI systems, they travel under the name of systolic arrays. Clearly the reason for this commonality is that <u>deterministic</u> non-sequential systems represent the most elementary step of departure from sequential systems. Indeed we would claim that a good test for a formalism dealing with distributed systems is that it should be able to identify this sub-class in a natural way.

Systems that are both non-deterministic and non-sequential are difficult to analyse. Where confusion is present they are also difficult to synthesise. In net theory there is one particular way combining choice and concurrency that leads to a class of non-trivial and yet manageable systems. The idea - due to commoner as far as we know - is to find a common generalisation of T-graphs and S-graphs in which choice and concurrency do not 'interfere' with each other.

A <u>free choice net</u> (fc net) is a net $N = (S,T;F)$ in which

$$\forall s \in S \ \forall t \in T: (s,t) \in F \Rightarrow s^{\bullet} = \{t\} \ \vee \ \{s\} = {}^{\bullet}t.$$

Stated differently, in an fc net, if two transitions share an input place then it is the only input place for both the transitions. Thus by definition, every S-graph (T-graph) is also an fc net. And the converse is clearly not true. For easy reference we show below the sub-structures that are <u>not</u> allowed in the three sub-classes.

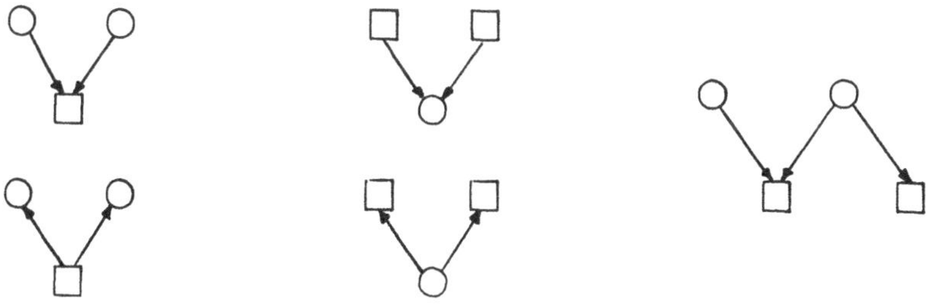

S-graph T-graph fc net

A marked fc net is a marked net whose underlying net is an fc net. An example of an lsfc net is shown below.

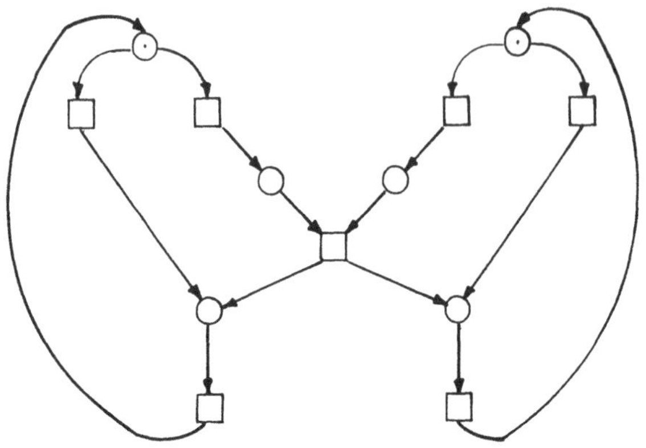

Note that a safe fc net can exhibit both non-deterministic and non-sequential behaviours. However their very structure guarantees the absence of confusion. The interested reader might wish to verify this claim.

The theory of lsfc nets is also well-developed. Indeed it is the largest sub-class of safe nets which has a relatively complete theory. Here we shall bring out a characterisation of liveness and safety. For dealing with liveness we need to identify two structural notions called deadlocks and traps. Let $N = (S,T;F)$ be a net and $S' \subseteq S$. Then S' is a deadlock iff ${}^{\bullet}(S') \subseteq (S')^{\bullet}$. Thus in a deadlock every T-element which could increase the token count on S' must, for doing so, remove at least one token from S'. The 'opposite' notion is called a trap. $S' \subseteq S$ is a trap iff $(S')^{\bullet} \subseteq {}^{\bullet}(S')$. Every T-element which would decrease the token count on S' must, for doing so, put at least one token on S'. A deadlock which is free of tokens can never acquire a token again. A trap which has acquired a token can never become free of tokens again. The liveness theorem for fc nets is:

The marked fc net $\Sigma = (S,T;F,M^0)$ is live iff every deadlock $S' \subseteq S$ contains a trap S" which is marked under M^0. In other words $S'' \subseteq S'$ and $\sum_{s \in S''} M^0(s) > 0$.

Once again we omit all proofs and the details can be found in [17]. For characterising safety, we need the notion of SM-components. Let $\Sigma = (S,T;F,M^0)$ be a marked net and $N' = (S',T';F')$ be a sub-net of N. In other words, N' is a net; $S' \subseteq S$; $T' \subseteq T$; $F' = F \cap (S' \times T' \cup T' \times S')$. Then N' is called an S-component of Σ iff

1) N' is a strongly connected S-graph.

2) The environment of each S-element in N' is complete relative to N_Σ. More precisely, $\forall s \in S'$: $^{\bullet}s \cup s^{\bullet}$ (in N') = $^{\bullet}s \cup s^{\bullet}$ (in N_Σ).

The key property of an S-component is that the total number of tokens distributed over its S-elements remains invariant through transition firings in the composite net. Finally, an SM-component of Σ is an S-component N' = (S',T';F') which satisfies $\sum_{s \in S'} M^0(s) = 1$. We can now state when a live fc net is safe.

The live fc net $\Sigma = (S,T;F,M^0)$ is safe iff it is covered by its set of SM-components. In other words $\forall s \in S$ (and hence $\forall t \in T$) there is an SM-component N' = (S'T';F') such that $s \in S'$.

lsfc nets admit an elegant and powerful decomposition theory. The classic work of Hack [17] contains the central results in this area. He identifies S-components and their dual called T-components as the major structural constituents of an lsfc net. One important consequence of this theory is that lsfc nets are, in a behavioural sense, a common generalisation of ls S-graphs and ls T-graphs. A second consequence is that in this sub-class conflict and concurrency are dual notions. In fact since we have used the term 'dual' repeatedly it might be helpful to nail it down properly.

The reverse dual (or just dual) of a net N = (S,T;F) is the net $\hat{N} = (\hat{S},\hat{T};\hat{F})$ where $\hat{S} = T$, $\hat{T} = S$ and $\hat{F} = F^{-1}$. It is easily verified that the reverse dual of an S-graph (T-graph) is a T-graph (S-graph). Interestingly enough, the reverse dual of an fc net is an fc net. Hack's decomposition theory leads to the following beautiful result.

An fc net has a live and safe marking iff its reverse dual has a live and safe marking.

Based on these results a number of additional structural and behavioural results concerning lsfc nets have been obtained in [48]. At present what is lacking is a synthesis theory. There is however a fairly satisfactory synthesis theory for a sub-class of lsfc nets called well-behaved bipolar schemes [14] which properly include ls S-graphs and ls T-graphs. These schemes also admit a computational interpretation which leads to a class of "well formed" concurrent programs [15].

At present not much is known about larger classes of safe nets (see [7, 5] for a few results). The reason we believe is the interplay between choice and concurrency resulting in varying degrees of confusion.

We shall conclude this section with a proposal to classify the remaining safe nets.

For $n \geq 1$, we shall say that a net $N = (S,T;F)$ is an <u>n-S net</u> (pronounced as "n-shared net") iff

$$\forall t \in T: |\{s \in {}^{\bullet}t \mid |s^{\bullet}| > 1\}| \leq n.$$

We say a place is <u>shared</u> if it serves as an input place to more than one transition. Note that shared places provide the means for modelling conflict. Thus in an n-S net every transition can have at most n shared input places. It is easy to verify that an fc net is a 1-S net and that the converse is not true. (Consider the marked net of fig. 1.) More generally, one readily obtains the following syntactic hierarchy of nets and hence safe nets (where the ordering relation is inclusion).

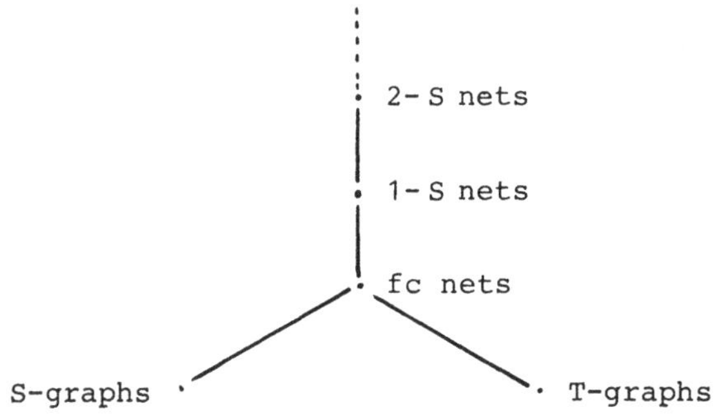

In the next section we shall argue that for safe nets, under a reasonable definition of behavioural equivalence, this is also behavioural hierarchy.

4. REPRESENTATIONS OF BEHAVIOUR

A variety of tools are available for representing the behaviour of a safe net. Before we begin discussing these tools, we would like to extend somewhat the notion of a safe net. We do so because it will enable us to provide a uniform framework for discussing behavioural notions such as processes and unfoldings. Moreover, the suppleness of the equivalence notion that we introduce is best brought out by the extended model.

The main change we propose is to consider labelled events. We assume a countable set of actions $A = \{a, a_1, \ldots, b, b_1, \ldots, c, c_1, \ldots\}$ and consider labelled safe nets of the form $\Sigma = (B, E; F, M^0, L)$ where $L: E \rightarrow A$ is the labelling function. One question that arises at once is what restrictions, if any, should be placed on L? If L is required to be injective we are back where we started. On the other hand there is something strange about two events carrying the same label occurring concurrently. If nothing else, one will have to use multi-sets (bags) rather than sets to handle steps. Hence we will compromise and demand that the labelling function L should satisfy:

$$\forall e_1, e_2 \in E: L(e_1) = L(e_2) \wedge e_1 \neq e_2 \Rightarrow \forall M \in [M^0\rangle: \{e_1, e_2\} \text{ is \underline{not} a step at } M.$$

One way to ensure this would be to require all the events that carry the same label to lie on an SM-component. Anyway, in this section we will just consider labelled safe nets whose labelling functions satisfy the above requirement. For convenience we will say just 'safe nets' and drop the term 'labelled'.

The simplest representation of behaviour is in terms of firing sequences. Let Y* be the free monoid generated by the set Y; λ the null sequence. Then $FS(\Sigma)$, the set of firing sequences of the safe net $\Sigma = (B, E; F, M^0, L)$ is smallest sub-set of E* given by:

1) $\lambda \in FS(\Sigma)$; $M^0 [\![\lambda \rangle M^0$.

2) Let $\sigma \in FS(\Sigma)$ and $M^0 [\![\sigma \rangle M$.
   If $M[e\rangle M'$ for $e \in E$ then $\sigma e \in FS(\Sigma)$; $M^0 [\![\sigma e \rangle M'$.

Thus $[\![\ \rangle$ is the three place relation $[\ \rangle$ extended to sequences of events in the natural way. The language generated by Σ is defined as:

$$\mathcal{L}(\Sigma) = \{\tilde{L}(\sigma) \mid \sigma \in FS(\Sigma)\}$$

where $\tilde{L}$ is the obvious extension of L to E*.

In general, this method of representing behaviours loses information (about concurrency and conflict). The three systems shown below will have the same set of firing sequences.

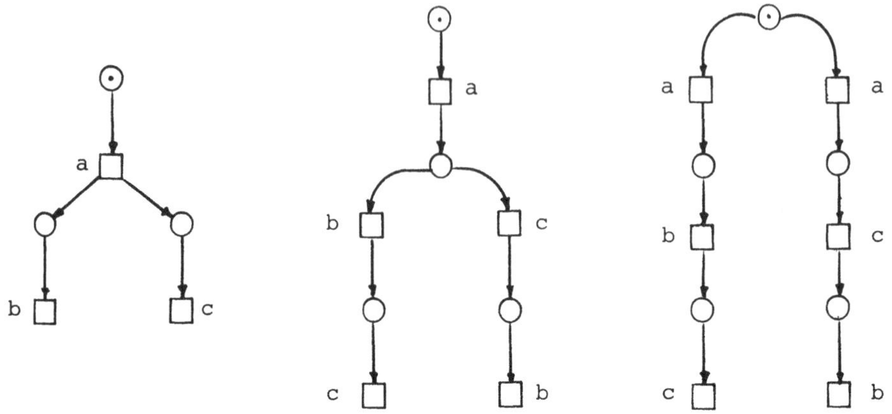

A considerable amount of work has gone into the study of languages generated by marked nets in general. The interested reader may wish to consult [18 , 37 , 49]. Though unsatisfactory as a representation of concurrency, firing sequences are an indispensable tool for proving properties of marked nets.

One generalisation of firing sequences consists of considering sequences of steps. One then obtains what is called a <u>sub-set language</u>. The idea should be clear and we will omit the details. Since a sequence of singletons in the sub-set language can be interpreted as a firing sequence, one gets, using the sub-set language, a finer behavioural representation (in case concurrency is present). The first of the above examples will be distinguished from the two others using this representation. Nevertheless the appraoch is very much rooted in formal language theory. Results concerning sub-set languages can be found in [46].

An elegant generalisation of firing sequences is the notion of a <u>trace</u> due to Mazurkiewicz [29]. Here one retains the power of string manipulating operations and yet obtains a faithful representation of concurrency. Unfortunately it would take us too far aside to explain this notion in more detail. The reader is urged to consult [30] where the full power of this concept is exploited to obtain an algebraic behavioural representation of safe nets.

In net theory corresponding to the notion of a trace, we have a <u>partially ordered</u> set of events. It will however be more convenient to first define the notion of a <u>deterministic process</u> (d-process for short). Loosely speaking, a d-process of a system $\Sigma = (B,E;F,M^0,L)$ is a record of a non-sequential run on Σ where conflicts are resolved as and when they arise. The record will thus consist of partially ordered occurrences of events and conditions. An example of a d-process of the system of fig. 1 is shown below.

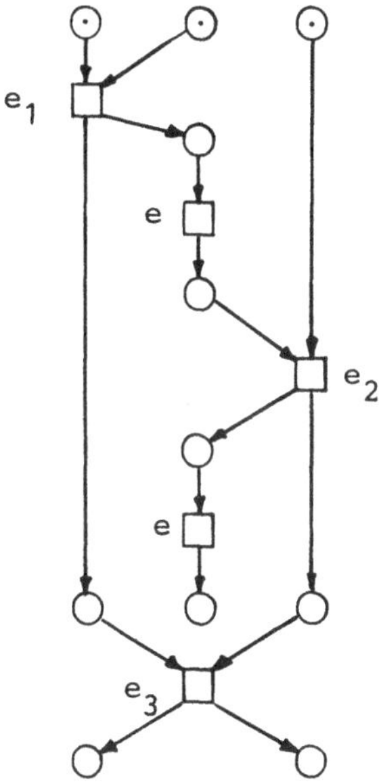

For putting down a definition we need a few notations. A <u>deterministic occurrence net</u> (d-occurrence net, for short) is a T-graph $N = (B,E;F)$ in which F^*, the transitive reflexive closure of F, is a partial ordering relation. In other words N is acyclic. F^* is usually written as $\leq_N$ and as usual the subscript is dropped whenever N is clear from the context.

Let $N = (B,E;F)$ be a d-occurrence net and $x_1, x_2 \in X_N$. Then $x_1 \text{ co } x_e$ iff $x_1 \nless x_2$ and $x_2 \nless x_1$. Let $X' \subseteq X$. Then $\downarrow X' = \{y \in X \mid \exists x \in X' \text{ s.t. } y \leq x\}$. Finally, for convenience, we shall relax the definition of a net just enough (drop the demand $S \cup T \neq \emptyset$) to permit the <u>empty</u> net $\emptyset_N = (\emptyset,\emptyset;\emptyset)$ and the corresponding labelled safe net $(\emptyset,\emptyset;\emptyset,\emptyset,\emptyset)$!.

Let $\Sigma = (B,E;F,M^0,L)$ be a safe net. Then the set of d-processes of Σ is denoted $\mathcal{DPR}(\Sigma)$ and is the smallest set of safe nets given by:

1) $\emptyset_d = (\emptyset,\emptyset;\emptyset,\emptyset,\emptyset)$ is a d-process;
   $\text{Rest}(\emptyset_d) = \{(b,\emptyset) \mid b \in M^0\}$.
   (Here and in what follows wherever necessary both F and L will be viewed as sets of ordered pairs.)

2) Let $dpr_1 = (B_1,E_1;F_1,M_1^0,L_1)$ be a d-process.
   (Part of the induction hypothesis is that a d-process is a safe net whose underlying net is a d-occurrence net.)
   Suppose $e \in E$, $B_{11} \subseteq \text{MAX}(B_1 \cup E_1)$ (w.r.t. $\leq_1 = F_1$) and $B_{12} \subseteq \text{Rest}(dpr_1)$ such that ${}^{\bullet}e = \{b \mid (b,X_b) \in B_{11} \cup B_{12}\}$.
   Then $dpr_2 = (B_2,E_2;F_2,M_2^0,L_2)$ is also a d-process of Σ where:

2a) $B_2 = B_1 \cup B_{12} \cup \{(b, \{e\} \cup B_{12} \cup \downarrow B_{11}) \mid b \in e^{\bullet}\}$.
(Once again $\downarrow$ is w.r.t. $\leq_1$)

2b) $E_2 = E_1 \cup \{(e, B_{12} \cup \downarrow B_{11})\}$.

2c) $F_2 = F_1 \cup \{((b,x_b),(e,x_e)) \mid (b,x_b) \in B_{11} \cup B_{12}, (e,x_e) \in E_2 \setminus E_1\}$
$\cup \{((e,x_e),(b,x_b)) \mid ((e,x_e) \in E_2 \setminus E_1, (b,x_b) \in B_2 \setminus (B_1 \cup B_{12})\}$

2d) $M_2^0 = M_1^0 \cup B_{12}$

2e) $\forall (e',x_{e'}) \in E_2$: $L_2((e',x_{e'})) = L(e')$.

2f) $Rest(dpr_2) = Rest(dpr_1) \setminus B_{12}$.

Thus each element of a d-process is an ordered pair. The first component is an element of N_Σ. The second component represents its 'past' in the run modelled by the d-process. In diagrams, the second component can be suppressed as done in the example shown above. We have departed violently from well established conventions in introducing the notion of a d-process. Normally what we call a d-occurrence net is called an occurrence net or a causal net. What we call a d-process is called just a process. The reason for introducing a new name is that we also wish to discuss a more general behavioural representation called the unfolding. And the unfolding of a safe net is based on a type of net which is called - yes! - an occurrence net. Moreover we wish to build up the unfolding through finite approximation which we wish to call processes. So much for terminology.

d-processes are normally defined as a mapping from a d-occurrence net to the underlying net of Σ which preserves the labels and the neighbourhood of events. For details see [12]. d-occurrence nets can be studied in their own right as a model of non-sequential processes. The fundamental ideas in this area are set out in [42] where an intuitively appealing density property called K-density is identified. Results concerning K-density and related density properties can be found in [3]. Notice that in d-occurrence nets, conflict is banished and the causality relation is particularly easy to handle, and its interaction with the concurrency relation is transparent. (Consider our definition of co.) Consequently, one can focus on the concurrency relation. Petri has made an impressive attempt to axiomatise his intuition concerning concurrency in [44]. A study of the properties identified by Petri's axioms is reported in [8]. The relationship between the properties of a system and the properties of its d-processes has been initiated in [16]. In this work, finite marked nets (i.e. the underlying nets are finite but not necessarily safe) are considered and the notion of a d-process is extended to this larger class. The major result here is that the finiteness of the state space (i.e. the set of reachable markings) of a marked net is equivalent to the K-density of its d-processes. Based on this result, a kind of liveness property of tokens at the system level and a density property called D-continuity (a generalisation, to posets, of Dedekind's definition of continuity of the reals) at the level of d-processes has been derived in [4].

Given a d-process dpr = $(B_1,E_1;F_1,M_1^0,L_1)$ of the system Σ one can strip away the conditions and obtain the labelled poset of just events $(E_1;\leq_1',L_1)$ where $\leq_1'$ is $\leq_1$ restricted to E_1. Such structures are called elementary event structures. A more general notion is called an event structure. Event structures are obtained by stripping away the conditions from an occurrence net. Occurrence nets can be used to define the processes of a safe net and a fundamental object associated with a safe net called the unfolding. This representation of behaviour is the finest and the last we shall encounter.

In going through the definitions to follow it might be helpful to consider an example of a process of the system shown in fig. 1 .

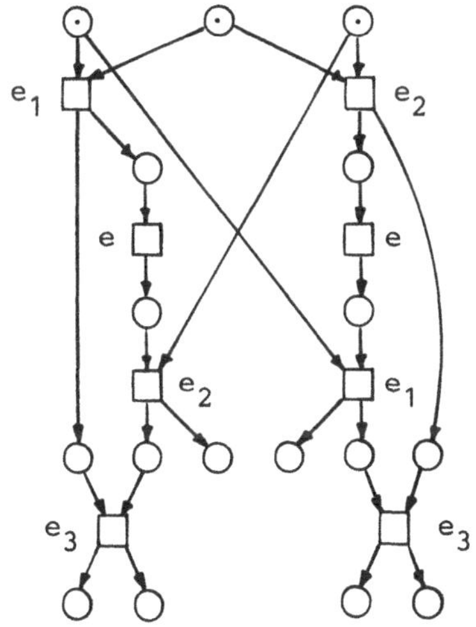

An occurrence net is a net N = (B,E;F) which satisfies:

1) $\forall b \in B$: $|{}^{\bullet}b| \leq 1$ (no backward sharing)

2) $F^* = \leq$ is a partial ordering relation (N is acyclic)

Thus every d-occurrence net is an occurrence net but the converse is clearly not true.

Let $N = (B,E;F)$ be an occurrence net. The <u>conflict relation</u> $\#_N \subseteq X \times X$ associated with N is given by:

1) $\forall b \in B\ \forall e_1,e_2 \in b^{\bullet}: e_1 \neq e_2 \Rightarrow e_1\ \#_N\ e_2$.

2) $x_1 \#_N y_1 \wedge x_1 \leq x_2 \wedge y_1 \leq y_2 \Rightarrow x_2\ \#_N\ y_2$. ($\leq\ = F^*$ as before)

Thus # is an irreflexive, symmetric relation. Note that $x_1\ \#\ x_2 \wedge x_1 < y$ would imply that $x_2\ \#\ y$.

The <u>independence relation</u> $\&_N \subseteq X \times X$ associated with N is given by:

$x\ \&\ y$ iff x co y and $\neg(x\ \#\ y)$.

Finally, $X' \subseteq X$ is a <u>&-set</u> iff $\forall x,y \in X': x\ \&\ y$. We can now generate the processes of a safe net. The set of <u>processes</u> of the safe net $\Sigma = (B,E;F,M^0,L)$ is denoted as $PR(\Sigma)$ and is the smallest set of safe nets satisfying:

1) $\emptyset_{pr} = (\emptyset,\emptyset;\emptyset,\emptyset,\emptyset)$ is a process and $Rest(\emptyset_{pr}) = \{(b,\emptyset) \mid b \in M^0\}$.

2) Let $pr_1 = (B_1,E_1;F_1,M_1^0,L_1)$ be a process of Σ. (As before, part of the inductive hypothesis is that every process is a safe net whose underlying net is an occurrence net with the associated relations $\leq$, # and &).
Suppose $e \in E$, B_{11} is a &-set of pr_1 and $B_{12} \subseteq Rest(pr_1)$ such that

$${}^{\bullet}e = \{b \mid (b,x_b) \in B_{11} \cup B_{12}\} \text{ and } (e,B_{12} \cup {\downarrow} B_{11}) \notin E_1$$

Then $pr_2 = (B_2,E_2;F_2,M_2^0,L_2)$ is also a process of Σ where:

2a) $B_2 = B_1 \cup B_{12} \cup \{(b, e \cup B_{12} \cup {\downarrow} B_{11}) \mid b \in e^{\bullet}\}$.

2b) $E_2 = E_1 \cup \{(e,B_{12} \cup {\downarrow} B_{11})\}$.

2c) $F_2 = F_1 \cup \{((b,x_b),(e,x_e)) \mid (b,x_b) \in B_{11} \cup B_{12}, (e,x_e) \in E_2 \setminus E_1\}$.
$\cup \{((e,x_e),(b,x_b)) \mid (e,x_e) \in E_2 \setminus E_1, (b,x_b) \in B_2 \setminus (B_1 \cup B_{12})\}$.

2d) $M_2^0 = M_1^0 \cup B_{12}$.

2e) $\forall (e',x_{e'}) \in E_2$: $L_2((e',x_{e'})) = L(e')$.

2f) $Rest(pr_2) = Rest(pr_1) \setminus B_{12}$.

Let $pr_1 = (B_1,E_1;F_1,M_1^0,L_1)$ be a process of Σ. Then it is quite easy to verify pr_1 is a safe net whose underlying net is an occurrence net. Moreover pr_1 (assuming that it is not the 'empty' process) has a very pleasant property. Namely $\forall e \in E_1$: $\exists M \in [M_1^0>$ such that $M[e>$ and $\forall b \in B_1$: $\exists M,M' \in [M_1^0>$ such that $b \in M$ and $b \notin M'$. In other words in a process we just record those events and condition holdings that have an occurrence (and hence the term occurrence net). The unfolding of a safe net is now obtained by 'summing up' all its processes. To nail this down, first note the set of processes of a safe net Σ, as we have defined it, is a countable set: $PR(\Sigma)$: $\{pr_0,pr_1,\ldots\}$). Assume for $i \leq 0$: $pr_i = (B_i,E_i;F_i,M_i^0,L_i)$. Then the unfolding of Σ is denoted as $\hat{\Sigma}$ and is given by:

$$\hat{\Sigma} = (\hat{B},\hat{E};\hat{F},\hat{M}^0,\hat{L}) \text{ where}$$

$$\hat{B} = \bigcup_{i=0}^{\infty} B_i,\ \hat{E} = \bigcup_{i=0}^{\infty} E_i \text{ etc.}$$

A similar route can be followed to obtain (if they exist) the infinite d-processes of a safe net. The notion of unfolding is due to the authors of [35]. Given a process $(B_1,E_1;F_1,M_1^0,L_1)$ one can strip away the conditions and obtain an event structure of the form $(E_1;\leq_1',\#_1',\&_1')$ where $\leq_1'$ $(\#_1',\&_1')$ is $\leq_1$ $(\#_1,\&_1)$ restricted to E_1. Building on the results of [35], Winskel has worked out a substantial theory of event structures and employed them to provide 'non-interleaved' semantics of CCS-like languages [51, 52].

This brings to an end our discussion of representations of behaviour. We can now define an equivalence notion.

Let $\Sigma_1 = (B_1,E_1;F_1,M_1^0,L_1)$ and $\Sigma_2 = (B_2,E_2;F_2,M_2^0,L_2)$ be two safe nets. Then $R \subseteq [M_1^0> \times [M_2^0>$ is called a bisimulation (between Σ_1 and Σ_2) iff

1) $(M_1^0,M_2^0) \in R$

2) $(M_1,M_2) \in R \Rightarrow$ a) $M_1[u>M_1'$ (in Σ_1) $\Rightarrow \exists M_2[u>M_2'$ (in Σ_2) such that $(M_1',M_2') \in R$

b) $M_2[u>M_2'$ (in Σ_2) $\Rightarrow \exists M_1[u>M_1'$ (in Σ_1) such that $(M_1',M_2') \in R$

We say that Σ_1 and Σ_2 are (bisimulation) equivalent and write $\Sigma_1 \approx \Sigma_2$ iff there is a bisimulation between them. Bisimulation is a refinement discovered by Park [36] of Milner's notion of observational equivalence. The bisimulation relation has very useful properties. Chief among them of course is that it is an equivalence relation.

It is easy but important to verify that $\hat{\Sigma} \approx \Sigma$ where Σ is a safe net and $\hat{\Sigma}$ its unfolding. The crucial feature of bisimulation is that through it one is forced to keep track of all the potential behavioural possibilities (which might lie in the distant future). A simple example might illustrate this point. The two systems shown below are not equivalent though all the other behaviours we have considered here would identify them.

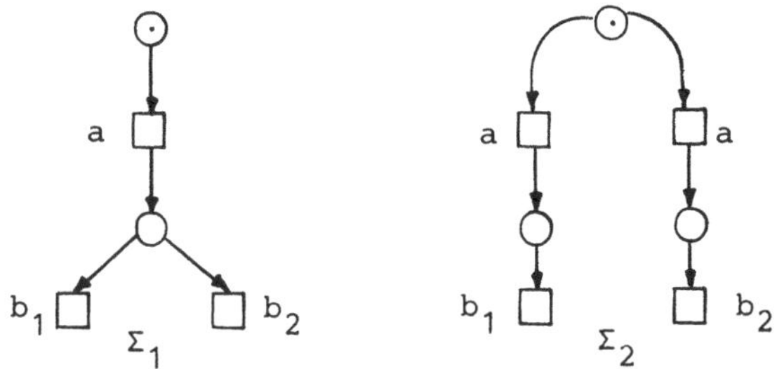

For more interesting and subtle examples the reader should consult [31]. Here we have slightly strengthened the definition in terms of steps in order to block the possibility of representing concurrency through interleaving. Given two classes of safe nets N_1 and N_2, let us define the ordering relation $\lessdot$ as follows:

$$N_1 \lessdot N_2 \text{ iff } \forall \Sigma_1 \in N_1 \colon \exists \Sigma_2 \in N_2 \text{ such that } \Sigma_1 \approx \Sigma_2.$$

$$N_1 < N_2 \text{ iff } N_1 \lessdot N_2 \text{ and } N_2 \not\lessdot N_1.$$

For convenience we will let N_T (N_S, N_{fc}) to denote the class of safe T-graphs (safe S-graphs, safe fc nets); and for n ≧ 1, N_{n-S} will stand for the class of safe n-S nets.

Consider the following systems:

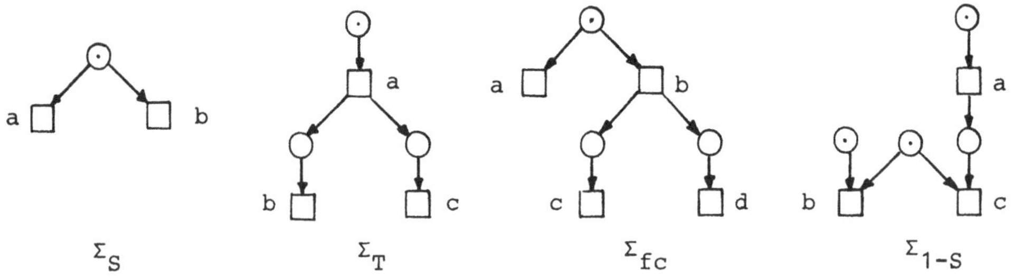

Because of Σ_S (Σ_T) in N_S (N_T) we have $N_S \not< N_T$ ($N_T \not< N_S$). From the definitions it follows that $N_S, N_T < N_{fc} < N_{1-S}$. Because of Σ_{fc} we have N_S, $N_T < N_{fc}$. And because of Σ_{1-S}, one can obtain $N_{fc} < N_{1-S}$. Once again from the definitions it follows that $\forall n \geq 1$, $N_{n-S} < N_{n+1-S}$. To show that this ordering is also strict, we consider the sequence of safe nets $\Sigma_2, \Sigma_3, \Sigma_4, \ldots$ where for $i \geq 1$, Σ_i looks as follows.

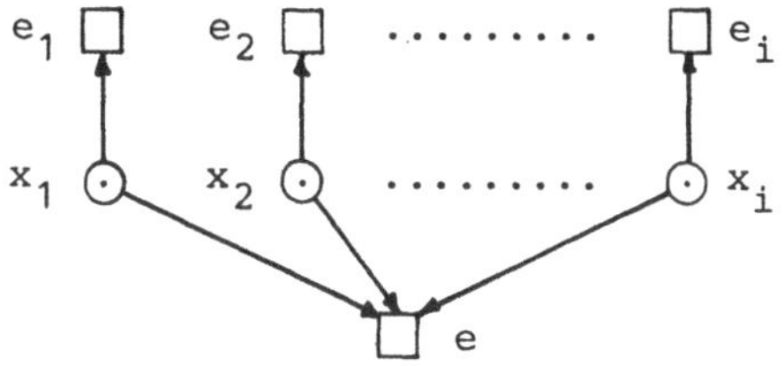

Then it is straightforward to verify that $\forall \Sigma \in N_{i-s}$: $\Sigma \not\approx \Sigma_{i+1}$. Consequently under $<$, we can get the following hierarchy.

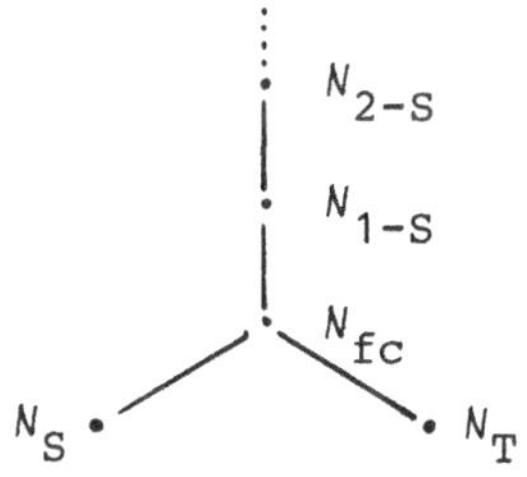

It would be nice to give some quantitative arguments to support our intuition that this hierarchy represents increasingly complex mixtures of choice and concurrency. Unfortunately, we do not have any results at present along this direction. We do wish to point out though the event structures of the form $(E; \leq, \#, \&)$ 'contained' in the various subclasses will display more and more intricate webs of $\leq$, # and & as one moves up through the hierarchy. And this fact might be helpful in obtaining the kind of result we would like to see.

We are content however that we have exhibited at least one such classification scheme. As stated in the introduction, our main aim has been to bring out some aspects of net theory while using the interplay between choice and concurrency as the topic of discussion. We hope to have succeeded in achieving this aim. We shall conclude this section with an, we think, interesting example. Actually, it is an element of a sequence of examples $\Sigma_2', \Sigma_3', \Sigma_4', \ldots$ and here we show Σ_2'. It should be easy enough to guess how the rest of the sequence looks. This sequence of examples essentially show that our hierarchy remains intact, if one adds liveness as an additional property.

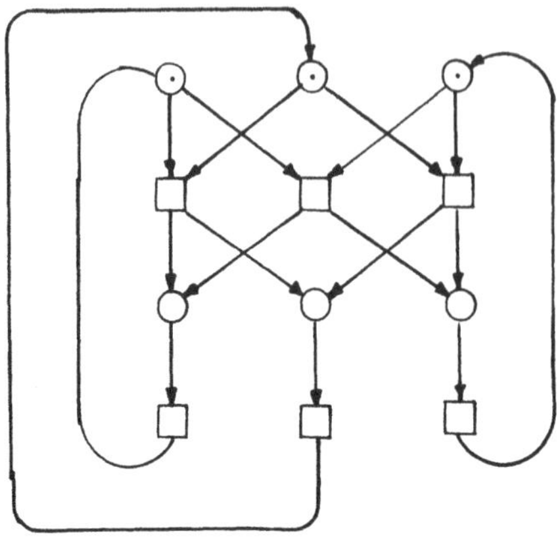

Σ_2'

5. CONCLUSION

The interplay between causality, conflict and concurrency leads to a bewildering variety of distributed systems. We feel that the chief attraction of net theory lies in its ability to represent - conceptually, mathematically and graphically - these three phenomena and their interactions. The selection of topics treated in this paper has been guided by this theme.

A more ambitious aim is to construct a comprehensive theory of distributed systems and processes based on nets. Petri - with several of his group at GMD, St. Augustin - has been pursuing this aim. Apart from initiating this systems theory [38] he has, over the years, identified a number of fundamental constructs of this theory: Information flow [39]; net morphisms [40]; completions of safe nets to obtain invariants concerning condition-holdings and event occurrences [40]; as already mentioned non-sequential processes [42] and concurrency axioms [44]. The aims and scope of this theory of systems are set out in [43] and the major details are reported in [12]. A second significant attempt to construct such a theory has been made by A.W. Holt, whose influence is less transparent (than Petri's) but nevertheless crucial. The seminal work reported in [19] is still one of the best introductions to net theory and continues to impress with its breadth and depth. Holt was also one of the first to identify confusion as a deep source of difficulties in the study of distributed systems. Finally, Holt has made a valiant - but not entirely successful - attempt to construct a theory of systems in which the continuous ('duration') and the discrete ('instant') hang together gracefully [20].

A good deal of effort has gone into the study of decision problems associated with marked nets. The classic work and results in this area are once again due to Hack [18]. The most famous problem in this area is the reachability problem (given a marked net Σ and a marking M of N_Σ, is M reachable in Σ?) and was solved recently [26, 28]. The interested reader may also wish to consult [50] for some additional decidability results.

Marked nets in which the tokens have internal structure are often called high-level Petri nets. Predicate/Transition nets [13] and coloured Petri nets [22] are the most popular versions and a related model has been proposed in [45]. A different but elegant generalisation of marked nets are called FIFO nets where the places are viewed as queues. For an introduction and a nice application see [9]. High-level nets are crucial in applications because marked nets, when used as a modelling tool, yield descriptions that are too detailed and unwieldly.

The best developed analysis tool available for both marked nets and high-level nets is S-invariants (and the related T-invariants). The notion of an S-invariant for marked nets was identified in [27] and later lifted to Predicate/Transition nets [13] and coloured nets [22]. Yet another analysis tool is the so-called reachability tree and a promising extension of this tool for high-level nets has been achieved in [21].

The ability to transform one net description into another in a consistent fashion is a crucial one. Net theory proposes to employ net morphisms for this purpose. So far though, net morphisms have been mostly used for definitional purposes (in particular, for defining d-processes) and is an important unexplored area of research. Winskel has proposed a different notion of a morphism which preserves the token game and hence several crucial behavioural properties [53]. This notion of a net morphism leads to a number of interesting results. In particular one obtains an elegant (category-theoretic) characterisation of the unfolding of a safe net and several useful operations on safe nets.

As mentioned in the introduction, we will not make an attempt to survey applications. A sample of the literature in this area can be found in [1, 2, 34].

REFERENCES

[1] Applications and Theory of Petri Nets. Eds. C. Girault and W. Reisig. Informatik-Fachberichte 52, Springer Verlag, Berlin, Heidelberg, New York (1982).

[2] Applications and Theory of Petri Nets. Eds. A. Pagnoni and G. Rozenberg, Informatik-Fachberichte 66, Springer Verlag, Berlin, Heidelberg, New York (1983).

[3] E. Best: The Relative Strength of K-density. In [34].

[4] E. Best, A. Merceron: Frozen Tokens and D-continuity. Proceedings of the 5th European Workshop on Applications and Theory of Petri Nets, Aarhus, Denmark (1984).

[5] E. Best, M.W. Shields: Some Equivalence Results on Free Choice Nets and Simple Nets and on the periodicity of Live Free Choice Nets, Proceedings of the 8th Colloquium on Trees in Algebra and Programming (CAAP), L'Aquila (1983).

[6] F. Commoner, A.W. Holt, S. Evens, A. Pnueli: Marked Directed Graphs. Journal of Computer and System Sciences 5 (1971), 511-523.

[7] F. Commoner: Deadlocks in Petri Nets. Applied Data Research Inc., CA-7206-2311, Wakefield, Mass., USA (1972).

[8] C. Fernandez, P.S. Thiagarajan: D-Continuous Causal Nets: A Model of Non-sequential Processes. Theoretical Computer Science 28 (1984), 171-196.

[9] M.P. Flé, G. Roucairol: Fair Serializability of Iterated Transactions using FIFO Nets. Proceedings of the 4th European Workshop on Applications and Theory of Petri Nets, Toulouse, France (1983).

[10] H.J. Genrich, K. Lautenbach: Synchronisationsgraphen. Acta Informatica 2 (1973), 143-161.

[11] H.J. Genrich, G. Thieler-Mevisson: The Calculus of Facts. Lecture Notes in Computer Science 45, Springer Verlag, Berlin, Heidelberg, New York (1976), 588-595.

[12] H.J. Genrich, K. Lautenbach, P.S. Thiagarajan: Elements of General Net Theory. In [34].

[13] H.J. Genrich, K. Lautenbach: System Modelling with High-level Petri Nets. Theoretical Computer Science 13, (1981), 109-136.

[14] H.J. Genrich, P.S. Thiagarajan: A Theory of Bipolar Synchronisation Schemes. Theoretical Computer Science 30 (1984), 1-78 (to appear).

[15] H.J. Genrich, P.S. Thiagarajan: Well-Formed Flow Charts for Concurrent Programming. In: Formal Description of Programming Concepts - II, Ed. D. Bjørner, North-Holland Publishing Company, Amsterdam, New York, Oxford (1983), 357-381.

[16] U. Goltz, W. Reisig: The Non-Sequential Behaviour of Petri Nets. Information and Control, 57 (1983), 125-147.

[17] M.H. Hack: Analysis of Production Schemata by Petri Nets. M.S. Thesis, TR-94, Project MAC, Cambridge, Mass., USA (1972).

[18] M.H. Hack: Decidability Questions for Petri Nets. Ph.D. Thesis, TR-161, Project MAC, Cambridge, Mass., USA (1976).

[19] A.W. Holt et al.: Information System Theory Project: Final Report. Applied Data Research Inc., RADC-TR-68-305, Princeton, N.J. (1968).

[20] A.W. Holt: A Mathematical Model of Continuous Discrete Behaviour. Unpublished Manuscript (1980).

[21] P. Huber, A.M. Jensen, L.O. Jepsen, K. Jensen: Towards Reachability Tree for High-level Petri Nets. Proceedings of the 5th European Workshop on Applications and Theory of Petri Nets, Aarhus, Denmark (1984).

[22] K. Jensen: Coloured Petri Nets and the Invariant Method. Theoretical Computer Science 14 (1981), 317-336.

[23] J.R. Jump, P.S. Thiagarajan: On the Equivalence of Asynchronous Control Structures, SIAM Journal on Computing 2, (1973), 67-87.

[24] J.R. Jump, P.S. Thiagarajan: On the Interconnection of Asynchronous Control Structures. Journal of ACM 22, (1975), 596-612.

[25] R.M. Karp, R.E. Miller: Properties of a Model for Parallel Computations: Determinacy, Termination, Queueing. SIAM Journal of Applied Mathematics 14, 6 (1966), 1390-1411.

[26] S.R. Kosaraju: Decidability of Reachability in Vector Addition Systems. Proceedings of the 14th Annual Symposium on Theory of Computing (1982).

[27] K. Lautenbach: Exakte Bedingungen der Lebendigkeit für Eine Klasse von Petri Netzen. (In German.) Berichte der GMD 82, St. Augustin, W. Germany (1973).

[28] E.W. Mayr: An Algorithm for the General Petri Net Reachability Problem. SIAM Journal on Computing 13, 3 (1984), 441-460.

[29] A. Mazurkiewicz: Concurrent Program Schemes and their Interpretations. DAIMI PB-78, Computer Science Department, Aarhus University, Aarhus, Denmark (1979).

[30] A. Mazurkiewicz: Semantics of Concurrent Systems. A Modular Fixed-Point Trace Approach. In: Advances in Applications and Theory of Petri Nets. (To appear.)

[31] R. Milner: A Calculus of Communicating Systems. Lecture Notes in Computer Science 92, Springer Verlag, Berlin, Heidelberg, New York (1980).

[32] R. Milner: A Complete Inference System for a Class of Regular Behaviours. Journal Computer and System Sciences 28 (1984), 39-466.

[33] D.E. Muller, W.S. Bartky: A Theory of Asynchronous Circuits. The Annals of the Computation Laboratory of Harvard University, 29, Harvard University Press, Cambridge, Mass., USA (1959), 204-243.

[34] Net Theory and Applications. Ed. W. Brauer, Springer Lecture Notes in Computer Science, 84, Springer Verlag, Berlin, Heidelberg, New York (1980).

[35] M. Nielsen, G. Plotkin, G. Winskel: Petri Nets, Event Structures and Domains, Part I, Theoretical Computer Science 13 (1981), 85-108.

[36] D.M. Park: Concurrency and Automata on Finite Sequences. Report, Computer Science Department, University of Warwick, Great Britain, (1981).

[37] J.L. Peterson: Petri Nets and the Modelling of Systems. Prentice-Hall, Englewood Cliffs, N.J., USA (1981).

[38] C.A. Petri: Kommunikation mit Automaten. (In German.) Schriften des IIM Nr. 2, Institute für Instrumentelle Mathematik, Bonn, W. Germany (1962).

[39] C.A. Petri: Fundamentals of a Theory of Asynchronous Information Flow, Proceedings of IFIP Congress 62 (1962).

[40] C.A. Petri: Concepts of Net Theory. Proceedings of the Mathematical Foundations of Computer Science Symposium and Summer School, High Tatras, Czechoslovakia (1973).

[41] C.A. Petri: Interpretations of Net Theory. ISF Report 75.07, GMD, St. Augustin, W. Germany (1975).

[42] C.A. Petri: Non-Sequential Processes. ISF Report 77.05, GMD, St. Augustin, W. Germany (1977).

[43] C.A. Petri: Introduction to General Net Theory. In [34].

[44] C.A. Petri: Concurrency. In [34].

[45] W. Reisig: Petri Nets with Individual Tokens. In [2].

[46] G. Rozenberg, R. Verraedt: Subset Languages of Petri Nets. In [2].

[47] C.L. Seitz: System Timing. In: Introduction to VLSI Systems, Eds. Mead, Conway, Addison-Wesley Publishing Company (1980).

[48] P.S. Thiagarajan, K. Voss: A Fresh Look at Free Choice Nets. Arbeitspapiere der GMD, 58, GMD, St. Augustin, W. Germany (1983). (Also to appear in Information and Control.)

[49] R. Valk: Infinite Behaviour of Petri Nets. Theoretical Computer Science 25 (1983), 311-341.

[50] R. Valk, M. Jantzen: The Residue of Vector Sets with Applications to Decidability Problems in Petri Nets. Proceedings of the 4th European Workshop on Applications and Theory of Petri Nets.

[51] G. Winskel: Events in Computation. Ph.D. Thesis, Department of Computer Science, University of Edinburgh, Edinburgh, Scotland (1980).

[52] G. Winskel: Event Structure Semantics for CCS and Related Languages. Lecture Notes in Computer Science 140, Springer Verlag, Berlin, Heidelberg, New York (1982), 561-576.

[53] G. Winskel: A New Definition of Morphism on Petri Nets. Lecture Notes in Computer Science 166, Springer Verlag, Berlin, Heidelberg, New York (1984), 140-150.

54] G. Kahn: The Semantics of a Simple Language for Parallel Processing. Proceedings of IFIP Congress 74 (1974).

Proof Rules for Communication Abstractions*

Gad Taubenfeld, Nissim Francez

Computer Science Department
Technion, Haifa
Israel

Abstract

A modular proof system is presented for proving partial correctness and freedom from deadlock of concurrent programs using scripts. Its applications to augmentation of CSP and subset of ADA are discussed. The proof rules are a generalization of both the procedure rule and the concurrency rules. Correctness proofs for examples are presented.

* See page number 443

A DISTRIBUTED ALGORITHM FOR DETECTING COMMUNICATION DEADLOCKS

N. NATARAJAN

National Centre for Software Development
and Computing Techniques
Tata Institute of Fundamental Research
Homi Bhabha Road, Colaba
Bombay 400 005, India

ABSTRACT

A distributed system is an interconnected network of computing elements or nodes, each of which has its own storage. A distributed program is a collection of processes. Processes execute asynchronously, possibly in different nodes of a distributed system, and they communicate with each other in order to realize a common goal. In such an environment, a group of processes may sometimes get involved in a communication deadlock. This is a situation in which each member process of the group is waiting for some member process to communicate with it, but no member is attempting communication with it. In this paper, we present an algorithm for detecting such communication deadlocks. The algorithm is distributed, i.e., processes detect deadlocks during the course of their communication transactions, without the aid of a central controller. The detection scheme does not assume any a priori structure among processes, and detection is made "on the fly" without freezing normal activities. The proposed scheme is appropriate to be implemented within runtime support or kernel of distributed programming languages.

I. INTRODUCTION

A distributed system is an interconnected network of computing elements, or nodes, each of which has its own storage which is not shared with any other node. A program that executes in the environment of a distributed system is called a distributed program. A distributed program is composed of several processes which cooperate to reach a common goal. The various processes of a distributed program may execute in different nodes of a distributed system. Since there is no shared storage between the nodes, processes executing in different nodes can cooperate only by communicating messages. If inter-process communication mode is synchronous [5] , i.e., if a process can send or receive a message only if another process is ready to perform a matching operation of receiving or sending the message, then sometimes, a group of processes may get involved in a communication deadlock. This is a situation in which each member process of the group is waiting for any one process of a subgroup to communicate with it, but no member is attempting communication with it. A communication deadlock may arise even when the communication mode is asynchronous with respect to the sender, i.e., when the sender does not wait for the message to be received. In such a case, a group of processes is involved in a communication deadlock if every member is attempting only a receive operation and there is no message in transit.

In this paper, we present a distributed scheme for detecting such communication deadlocks. The scheme is appropriate to be implemented within a kernel of a distributed programming language. Such a kernel must detect a communication deadlock when it occurs since the deadlock is a kind of communication failure. When it detects a deadlock, the kernel can report this to some member or all members of the group involved in the deadlock. Upon receiving this notification, a process can initiate appropriate action. If the deadlock is unexpected, its occurrence can be handled by processes as a fault in the design of the program. However, distributed programs can be designed such that the occurrence of a communication deadlock is not a design fault but a normal event. For example, the design of a distributed program can use the occurrence of a communication deadlock to signify the termination of a distributed computation. It has been reported that in some applications, such as distributed simulation, using the occurrence of communication deadlocks in this manner makes the implementation efficient [1] . Distributed programs for implementing relaxation algorithms can also use communication deadlocks in a similar way [8].

There have been several proposals in the literature [3], [4], [7], [9] for solving the so-called "distributed termination" problem, which is only a special case of a communication deadlock, in which all the processes of a distributed program are involved in the deadlock. In contrast, the algorithm we propose detects communication deadlocks which involve any subset of processes. Some of the solutions proposed for the detection of distributed termination assume the existence of a particular structure over all processes of a distributed program, either a spanning tree [4], or a Hamiltonian cycle [9]. Such solutions are inappropriate for communication deadlock detection, because a deadlock may involve any subset of processes, and these schemes require, for each subset, a spanning tree or a Hamiltonian cycle consisting of processes which are members of the set. This requirement makes the implementation of these schemes cumbersome, if not impossible. In contrast, our scheme does not require the existence of any particular structure among the processes. Chandy, Misra and Hass have also proposed an algorithm for detecting communication deadlocks [2]. Like our proposed scheme, their algorithm also does not require the existence of any particular structure among the processes. The major difference between their algorithm and the proposed scheme is that the additional storage required within each process for deadlock detection is much less in our scheme than theirs. Further, we assume periodic retransmission of signals for deadlock detection. We defer further comparison with this related work to a later section.

The paper is organized as follows. In section II, we outline the communication model and characterize a communication deadlock using this model. In section III, we describe the deadlock detection algorithm. In section IV, we illustrate the working of the algorithm through an example. In section V, we present an informal argument for the correctness of the algorithm and compare the algorithm with that proposed in [2]. In section VI, we summarise the merits of the proposed algorithm.

II. THE COMMUNICATION MODEL

A distributed program is a network of computing agents, and each agent executes asynchronously with respect to other agents. Computing agents operate in disjoint address spaces and they interact with each other only by communicating messages. Associated with each agent is a collection of input ports and output ports. An agent uses its output ports to send messages and input ports to receive messages. Note that an agent communicates only through its ports and it does not explicitly name the agents with which it communicates. The agents with which an agent communicates are determined by the configuration of the agent, i.e. the interconnection of the ports of the agent with ports of other agents. The configuration of an agent is specified separately from the code body or the implementation of the agent. Separation of the configuration aspects of an agent from the computation performed by it facilitates easy reconfiguration of agents. This has been discussed in detail in [8].

In the description of the configuration of an agent, an input port of the agent can be connected only to an output port of another distinct agent, and vice versa.

Definition: A communicant of a port, P, of an agent is another agent that has a port, Q, connected to P. Q is called the correspondent of P.

The configuration descriptions of agents must satisfy the following conditions:

a) Each port of an agent must have one (and only one) correspondent.

b) The configuration descriptions must be consistent with each other. Suppose, for example, the configuration of an agent A specifies that its port P has, as its correspondent, a port Q of another agent B. Then, the configuration of B must specify that its port Q has, as its correspondent, the port P of A.

Inter-agent communication is synchronous; i.e., an agent can send (receive) a message through an output (input) port, P, only if the communicant of the port is ready to receive (send) the message through the correspondent of P. To communicate with any one of its several communicants, an agent initiates a communication transaction using one or more of its ports. The ports used in a transaction of an agent are called the candidates of the agent, and the communicants of the ports are called the candidate communicants of the agent. A transaction completes when the agent synchronizes and communicates with one of the candidate communicants. A transaction fails if the agent and its candidate communicants are members of a group of agents that is communication deadlocked.

To characterize precisely a communication deadlock, we use the following definitions:

> Definition: Two communication transactions initiated by two agents do not match with each other, if no candidate of either agent is the correspondent of a candidate of the other.

> Definition: A group of agents, each of which has initiated a communication transaction, is a closed group if
>
> a) each agent in the group is a candidate communicant to some agent in the group, and
>
> b) all candidate communicants of an agent are members of the group.

A closed group of agents is deadlocked if the transaction initiated by each member agent does not match with those initiated by its candidate communicants.

A communication deadlock can be characterized in graph theoretic terms as follows. Consider a directed graph in which each node denotes an agent. There is a directed edge from one node to another, if the former agent is waiting to communicate with the latter. An agent is communication deadlocked, if the corresponding node, N, in the graph, is in a knot; i.e., all nodes that are reachable from N can also reach N. The problem of deadlock detection is thus to detect if an agent is in a knot.

III. THE DEADLOCK DETECTION ALGORITHM

Since our environment is distributed, we do not wish to designate a central controller for detecting communication deadlocks, because such a controller makes the entire system vulnerable to its failure. Instead, it should be possible for the agents themselves to detect deadlocks during the course of their communication transactions. If it is detected that a group of agents is deadlocked, the situation can be resolved by aborting the transaction of some member agent and reporting a communication failure.

For the purpose of designing a distributed deadlock detection scheme, we now characterize a communication deadlock using the states of a communicant. From the point of view of an agent, a communicant, C, of its port P, can be in one of three states:

a) C is Active if either C has not initiated a communication transaction, or C has initiated a transaction and is attempting communication with P.

b) C is Inactive if C has initiated a communication transaction but is not attempting communication with P.

c) C is Quiet if C has initiated a communication transaction but is not attempting communication with P, and further, each candidate communicant of C is in Quiet state.

An agent is involved in a communication deadlock, if it observes that each of its candidate communicants is in Quiet state. Informal reasoning to justify the above characterization is as follows:

> An agent can complete its current communication transaction only if at least one of its candidate communicants attempts a matching transaction. However, if each candidate communicant is in Quiet state, it is not attempting a transaction matching with that of the agent. Further, each candidate communicant is unable to complete its current transaction since all its candidate communicants are in Quiet state. Hence, no communication is possible and a deadlock has occurred.

In a distributed system, there is no shared memory and hence an agent cannot observe the states of its communicants directly. An agent can determine the state of a communicant only by exchanging certain control messages with the communicant. These control messages are quite distinct from the messages exchanged between agents as part of their computation. (The latter are called basic communication). It is quite simple to arrange for an agent to observe that a communicant is in Active or Inactive state: when an agent sends a control message to the communicant of a port P, the communicant can send back a response Active or Inactive depending on whether or not it has initiated a transaction for which the correspondent of P is a candidate. Depending on the response received, the agent can determine the state of the communicant.

However, a more elaborate protocol is needed to enable an agent to determine that a communicant is in Quiet state. When an agent sends a control message to a communicant, it can respond that it is in Quiet state only after it has determined that its candidate communicants are in Quiet state. This implies that a query generated by an agent to determine the state of its communicant has to be propagated successively through a chain of agents. Similarly, responses have to be propagated in the reverse direction before an agent can determine that the communicant is in Quiet state.

However, it is not necessary that every query generated by an agent need be propagated as above. Determining which queries to propagate and when to propagate them are the essential aspects of the deadlock detection scheme described below.

In the proposed scheme, in order to detect communication deadlocks, an agent uses two kinds of control messages, called signals and responses. Signals and responses are port-directed. After an agent sends a signal on a port, it waits till a response is received as reply from the communicant of the port. During this waiting period, the agent can receive signals and send responses, but it cannot send any signal on its own. In addition to responses sent as replies to signals, there are also responses not prompted by signals. We shall assume that the communication network is reliable and no message sent is lost.

An agent uses the following signals and responses:

a) Query and Detect signals to determine the states of its candidate communicants,

b) Active, Inactive, and Quiet responses as replies to Query and Detect signals received,

c) Idle response (not prompted) to indicate that it is in Quiet state.

In addition to these signals, an agent sends many other kinds of signals and responses in order to synchronize with a communicant during a transaction. However, we shall not be concerned here with these synchronizing signals. A detailed description of the synchronization scheme can be found in [8].

The deadlock detection scheme has the following salient steps:

1. When an agent initiates a communication transaction, the transaction is assigned a unique identification, called the CommId of the transaction. In addition to uniqueness, generation of CommIds for communication transactions satisfies the following property:

   When an agent initiates a communication transaction, T, the CommId assigned to T is greater than those of transactions that have sent signals or responses to the agent prior to the initiation of T.

   A simple scheme for generating CommIds is to use a logical clock (or counter) within each node, and maintain them in loose synchronization [6].

2. Each agent uses the following variables:

   a) CurrentId, which identifies the current communication transaction initiated by the agent,

   b) DeadlockId, which identifies the deadlock computation with which the agent is currently involved,

   c) Detecting, a boolean variable which, if true, indicates that the agent has either initiated or propagated a deadlock computation, and

   d) Initiator, which identifies the port of the communicant which got the agent involved in the current deadlock computation.

   Signals and responses sent by an agent include a parameter, Did, to indicate to the communicant the value of DeadlockId of the agent.

3. When an agent initiates a transaction, it does the following:

```
Detecting:=false;
DeadlockId:=CommId;
```

Thereafter, it sends Query (DeadlockId) signals periodically to its candidate communicants until either it synchronizes with one of them, or Detecting is true. When Detecting becomes true, the agent sends Detect(DeadlockId) signals instead of Query.

4. When an agent receives a Query(Did) signal on a port, P, it does:

```
if not communicating or P is a candidate
then reply Active(undef)  undef is an undefined value
else reply Inactive(DeadlockId);
```

5. When an agent receives an Active(Did) or Inactive(Did) response for a Query signal, it does:

```
if Active received
then Set state of the communicant to Active
else begin
       Set state of the communicant to Inactive;
       DeadlockId:=max(DeadlockId,Did);
       if all candidate communicants are in Inactive state
             and (CurrentId=DeadlockId)
       then begin   Initiate a deadlock computation
             Detecting:=true;
             Initiator:=self
            end
     end;
```

Note that when Detecting is true, the agent sends Detect signals periodically.

6. When an agent receives a Detect(Did) signal on a port P, it does the following:

```
if P is a candidate
then reply Active(undef)
else if not Detecting
     then begin
            if all candidate communicants are in Inactive
                state and (Did=DeadlockId)
            then begin  Propagate the deadlock computation
                Detecting:=true;
                Initiator:=the correspondent of P
                 end;
            reply Inactive(DeadlockId)
          end
     else if (Did=DeadlockId) and
                   the correspondent of P is not Initiator
          then   already propagated the computation
             reply Quiet(Did)
          else reply Inactiye(Did);
```

7. When an agent receives a response from a communicant X, after it has initiated or propagated a deadlock computation, it acts as follows:

```
if Quiet or Idle response received
then begin
        Set state of X to quiet;
        if all candidate communicants are in Quiet state
        then if Initiator=self
             then deadlock detected
             else Send Idle(DeadlockId) to Initiator
     end
else if Active response received
     then begin  Abort the deadlock computation
              Detecting:=false;
              Reset the state of all candidate communicants
              to Inactive;
              Set state of X to Active
          end
     else  Inactive response
       if Did > DeadlockId
       then begin  Abort the deadlock computation
               Detecting:=false;
               DeadlockId:=Did;
               Reset the state of all candidate communicants
               to Inactive
             end;
```

After an agent aborts its deadlock computation, it sends Query signals periodically instead of Detect signals.

IV. AN EXAMPLE OF COMMUNICATION DEADLOCK DETECTION

Let us illustrate the working of the above algorithm for detecting deadlocks in communication through an example.

There are three agents A, B, and C, each of which has three ports named A1, A2, A3, B1, B2, B3, and C1, C2, C3 respectively. A1 and B1 are connected, A2 and C1 are connected, B2 and A3 are connected, and C2 and B3 are connected.

Consider the following scenario: A has initiated a transaction (with CommId T1) using A1 and A2, B has initiated a transaction (with CommId T2) using B2, and C is currently active. Notice that the transactions of A and B do not match. Let us assume that T2 T1. Now, the agents exchange signals as follows:

1. A sends a Query(T1) to C.C1, and receives an Active(undef) response.

The situation observed by A is

```
A:: DeadlockId: T1
    State of B and C: active
```

2. After a while, A sends Query(T1) to B.B1, and receives a response Inactive(T2). The situation observed by A is

```
A:: DeadlockId: T2
    State of B: Inactive
    State of C: Active
```

3. Sometime later, B sends Query(T2) to A.A3, and receives Inactive(T2), B observes

```
B:: DeadlockId: T2
    State of A: Inactive
    Detecting: true
    Initiator: self
```

B initiates a deadlock computation by sending a Detect signal to A.A3, since its candidate communicants are Inactive and CurrentId= DeadlockId. However, when A receives that Detect signal, it does not propagate it, since one of its candidate communicants, C, is active. A replies Inactive(T2).

Thereafter, A sends Query signals, and B sends Detect signals to their candidate communicants periodically, but the responses they receive do not alter their observations.

4. After a while, C initiates a transaction (with CommId T3) using C2. Now, since C's transaction does not match with that of B, a communication deadlock has occurred. We shall demonstrate its detection through one possible sequence of exchanged signals and responses (there are many other possible sequences). Note that the CommId generation rule ensures that T3 T2.

5. C sends Query(T3) to B.B3, and receives Inactive(T2) response. C observes

```
C:: DeadlockId: T3
    State of B: Inactive
    Detecting: true
    Initiator: self
```

C initiates a deadlock computation.

6. C sends Detect(T3) to B.B3. B does not propagate it, since its DeadlockId is different from T3.

7. A sends Query(T2) to C.C1, and receives Inactive(T3). It updates its DeadlockId.

```
A:: DeadlockId: T3
    State of B and C: Inactive
```

Note that A does not initiate a deadlock computation even though its candidate communicants are Inactive, since DeadlockId is different from CurrentId.

8. B retransmits Detect(T2) to A.A3, and receives Inactive(T3). Since T3 T2, B aborts its deadlock computation.

```
B:: DeadlockId: T3
    State of A: Inactive
    Detecting: false
```

Now, DeadlockId of A, B, and C are identical, viz., T3.

9. C retransmits Detect(T3) to B.B3. Now, B propagates it.

```
B:: DeadlockId: T3
    State of A: Inactive
    Detecting: true
    Initiator: C.C2
```

10. B sends Detect(T3) to A.A3. A propagates it.

```
A:: DeadlockId: T3
    State of B and C: Inactive
    Detecting: true
    Initiator: B.B2
```

11. A sends Detect(T3) to C.C1, and receives Quiet(T3).

```
A:: DeadlockId: T3
    State of B: Inactive
    State of C: Quiet
    Detecting:  true
    Initiator:  B.B2
```

12. C retransmits Detect(T3) to B.B3. B replies Inactive(T3), since its candidates are not Quiet.

13. A sends Detect(T3) to B.B1, and receives Quiet(T3). A observes

```
A:: DeadlockId: T3
    State of B and C: Quiet
    Detecting: true
    Initiator: B.B2
```

Since all its candidate communicants are Quiet, A sends Idle(T3) to its initiator B.B2.

14. B receives Idle from A, and sets state of A to Quiet. Now, B sends Idle(T3) to C.C2, since its candidate is Quiet.

15. C receives Idle from B, and sets state of B to Quiet. Now, C detects a deadlock since all its candidate communicants are in Quiet state, and Initiator=self. As mentioned earlier, there are several other possible exchange sequences of signals and responses that will eventually result in the deadlock being detected. In all cases, only C will detect the deadlock since the CommId of its transaction is the largest.

V. REMARKS ON THE DEADLOCK DETECTION SCHEME

A correctness argument

This deadlock detection scheme is correct if it detects every communication deadlock that occurs and does not detect any false deadlock.

To show that the scheme detects every communication deadlock, we make the following observations:

1. When a group of agents is communication deadlocked, the value of DeadlockId in each member agent converges towards the maximum of the CommIds of the member agents.

   This can be proved as follows. Each agent sends Query signals to correspondents of its candidates periodically and the Inactive responses received contain the DeadlockId of the candidate communicants. When an agent receives an Inactive response, it updates its DeadlockId to max(DeadlockId,Did). Since the agents are deadlocked, they retransmit Query signals for ever and this leads to the convergence of DeadlockId.

2. When a group of agents is deadlocked, each member agent eventually observes that its candidate communicants are in Inactive state.

3. After the convergence of DeadlockId in all member agents, only one agent, called the Detector, observes that all its candidate communicants are in Inactive state, and DeadlockId=CurrentId. The deadlock computation initiated by the Detector will be propagated by all member agents. (This follows from 1 and 2). After propagation, the member agents send Quiet responses when they receive Detect signals. Each member sends Idle to its Initiator when it finds that all its candidate communicants are Quiet, and finally, Detector detects a deadlock.

To show that the scheme does not detect a false deadlock, we make the following observations:

1. After an agent sends an Idle response in a deadlock computation, it can perform a basic communication only when (or after) either the Detector or an agent which has propagated the computation performs a basic communication.

   This follows from the fact that an agent sends Idle only after it receives Quiet or Idle responses from all candidate communicants for its current deadlock computation. An agent sends Quiet only when it receives Detect in a computation that it has already propagated or initiated. Otherwise, it propagates the computation, and sends Idle to its Initiator only when it receives Idle or Quiet from all candidate communicants.

2. When an agent receives an Idle response from a communicant, C, each candidate communicant of C is either the Detector or a propagator.

   This follows directly from 1.

3. When Detector receives Idle from all candidate communicants, all of them are propagators, and they are waiting for Detector or a propagator to perform a basic communication.

   This follows from 1 and 2. It follows from 3 that when Detector receives Idle from all candidate communicants, it is involved in a deadlock.

Comparison with related work

Chandy, Misra and Hass have proposed an algorithm (hereafter referred to as the CMH scheme) for detecting communication deadlocks [2]. In their algorithm too, an "idle" process initiates a deadlock computation by sending "queries" to its "dependents", i.e., processes to which it is attempting communication. If a process receives a query when it is idle, it propagates the deadlock computation to its dependents. If a process receives a query for a computation that it has initiated or propagated, it sends a reply. When a process receives replies from all dependents for a query, it sends a reply to the process that sent the query to it, unless it has initiated the query, in which case it detects a communication deadlock.

Thus, the CMH scheme is based on the same principle that is used in our algorithm. However, there is a major difference. In the CMH scheme, an idle process, if it receives a query, always propagates the query to its dependents without checking if the initiator of the deadlock computation and the process are already waiting for each other (directly or indirectly). Because of this, in the CMH scheme, each process has to store information regarding all queries received by it. Specifically, their algorithm requires four arrays within each process, and the size of each array is equal to the total number of all processes in the system. In our scheme, we avoid these arrays, and their effect is achieved by periodic transmission of Query and Detect signals. Further, ar any time, an agent is involved in only one deadlock computation. An agent propagates a Detect signal corresponding to a deadlock computation only if the initiator of the computation and the agent are already waiting for each other. This check is accomplished by comparing DeadlockId with Did. DeadlockId of our scheme may be viewed as the identification of the knot in which the agent may potentially get involved. In the CMH scheme, the number of processes in the system must be known a priori, as this is required to fix the size of the arrays within each process. Hence, the CMH scheme is oriented towards a network of processes that is configured statically. In contrast, our scheme does not require any storage whose size is determined by the size of the network. Hence, our scheme is suitable also for an environment where agents are created dynamically.

In terms of the number of signals exchanged for detecting a communication deadlock, our scheme and the CMH scheme are quite comparable. Suppose, a group of N agents, each of which has K candidates, is deadlocked. In the CMH scheme, the computation initiated by the detector of the deadlock generates KN queries and KN replies. In our scheme, after the convergence of DeadlockId in all member agents, the computation initiated by the detector (i.e., the agent whose CurrentId=DeadlockId) generates KN Detect signals, KN responses to these Detect signals, and N-1 Idle responses. In both schemes, many more signals are generated (by other agents) and the above bound refers only to the computation initiated by the detector.

VI. SUMMARY

The proposed scheme for detecting communication deadlocks has the following merits:

1. The scheme is distributed: the agents themselves detect deadlocks during the course of their communication transactions, and there is no central controller for detecting deadlocks.

2. The scheme does not presume any a priori structure among communicating agents.

3. The deadlock detection is "on the fly" and does not require freezing of normal activities.

4. Though we have introduced specific signals, such as Query, Detect etc., this overhead can be avoided by integrating the deadlock detection scheme with the scheme for detecting communication link or agent failures. For example, a simple scheme for an agent to detect the failure of a communicant is for the agent to send a "monitoring" signal to the communicant and solicit a response from it. The agent detects a failure if no response is received within a time interval. If such a scheme is used for detecting communicant failures, then the proposed deadlock detection scheme can be made efficient by integrating the latter with the former. For instance, a Query or a Detect signal need not be sent as a separate signal, but can be combined with a monitoring signal. Then, the deadlock detection scheme has the merit that it does not require any additional overhead in terms of signals. It only requires that some additional information be sent in a monitoring signal, and a deadlock is detected using this information.

REFERENCES

1 K.M. Chandy, and J. Misra, Asynchronous Distributed Simulation via a Sequence of parallel Computations, Communications of ACM, Vol.24, No.4, April 1981, pp 198-206.

2 K.M. Chandy, J. Misra, and L.M. Hass, Distributed Deadlock Detection, ACM Transactions on Computer Systems, Vol.1, No.2, May 1983, pp 144-156.

3 E.W. Dijkstra, and C.S. Scholten, Termination Detection for Diffusing Computations, Information Processing Letters, Vol.11, No.1, August 1980, pp 1-4.

4 N. Francez, Distributed Termination, ACM Transactions on Programming Languages and Systems, Vol.2, No.1, January 1980, pp 42-55.

5 C.A.R. Hoare, Communicating Sequential Processes, Communications of ACM, Vol.21, No.8, August 1978, pp 666-677.

6 L. Lamport, Time Clocks, and the Ordering of Events in a Distributed System, Communications of ACM, Vol.21, No.7, July 1978, pp 558-565.

7 J. Misra, and K.M. Chandy, Termination Detection of Diffusing Computations in Communicating Sequential Processes, ACM Transactions on Programming Languages and Systems, Vol.4, No.1, January 1982, pp 37-43.

8 N. Natarajan, Communication and Synchronization in Distributed Programs, Ph.D. thesis, University of Bombay, November 1983.

9 S.P. Rana, A Distributed Solution to the Distributed Termination Problem, Information Processing Letters, Vol.17, No.1, July 1983, pp 43-46.

On the Existence and Construction of Robust Communication Protocols for Unreliable Channels

Saumya K. Debray Ariel J. Frank Scott A. Smolka
Department of Computer Science
SUNY at Stony Brook
Stony Brook, New York 11794
U.S.A.

Abstract: A simple necessary and sufficient condition for the existence of robust communication protocols for arbitrary alphabets and a large class of transmission errors is presented. This class of errors, called *transformation errors*, consists of those errors where symbols (messages) may be lost or corrupted to other symbols. The proof is used as the basis of a procedure for automatically constructing robust protocols for transformation errors. The protocols generated are small in size, despite not being custom-designed. The results presented generalize and expand upon those of Aho et al. [AUY79]. Two protocols are constructed to illustrate our technique, and are contrasted with those of Aho et al.

1. Introduction

A *communication protocol* is a system of communicating processes designed to ensure reliable transmission of messages over an unreliable medium. A protocol is *robust* if messages at the input will – in the absence of infinite sequences of errors – eventually be delivered correctly at the output, in the right order. The transition-model approach has been widely used for specification and verification of communication protocols. In this approach, a communication protocol is modeled as a set of finite-state machines (processes). Excellent surveys of the transition-model approach can be found in [BoS80, Dan80, Sun79].

In an unreliable communication medium, messages can be corrupted, lost, duplicated, or reordered. Duplication or reordering of messages is not considered here. We also do not consider error-detecting or correcting codes; these are usually employed in data communication systems to increase the probability of correct transmission of data. We assume that transmitted messages may be lost or corrupted beyond certain recognition at the receiving side. The notion of an unreliable medium is captured by the introduction of transmission errors that corrupt a transmitted symbol to some other symbol.

Transmission errors have not received much attention in the modeling of communication protocols. Bochmann [Boc80] presents a finite state model of a simple transmission medium that includes an *erroneous message in transit* state. This state is reachable by an *error* transition and results in an *error message* transition. Zafiropulo et al. [ZWR80] model an unreliable transmission medium as an additional process between two communicating processes. In their representation, a transition labeled by message x' represents a corruption by the medium of a valid message x. Pachl [Pac82] considers only messages that are lost by the medium. No attempt has been made, however, to define and analyze these different types of transmission errors.

This research was supported, in part, by the National Science Foundation under the grant # 2193A.

Our motivation for this paper was the handling of transmission errors by [AUY79]. They describe a communication system consisting of a transmitter–receiver pair communicating over an error-prone transmission medium. Robust communication protocols are defined for a specific alphabet and class of transmission errors. [AUY79] prove robustness of several synchronous communication protocols for this environment. The contribution of this paper is in the generalization and expansion of their results. Though we assume a similar communication system, the unreliable transmission medium is explicitly modeled. Furthermore, robust protocols for arbitrary alphabets and an entire class of transmission errors are considered. Recently, it was brought to our attention [Aho84] that a similar result appeared in [AWY82]. We also present a procedure to automatically construct protocols that are robust under such errors.

The organization of the rest of this paper is as follows. Section 2 presents our assumed model of communication; the unreliable transmission medium is especially motivated. The assumed class of transmission errors and their mappings are discussed in Section 3. Section 4 presents our procedure for constructing robust protocols; a necessary and sufficient condition for the existence of robust protocols under a class of transmission errors is given. Section 5 contrasts two robust protocols generated by our construction procedure with the corresponding ones of Aho et al. We conclude in Section 6.

2. Preliminaries

This section presents the background for the rest of the paper. First we introduce the communication model in terms of a producer–consumer pair using a protocol to communicate over channels. Our model for the channel is emphasized. This is followed by an elaboration of the notion of protocol robustness. Subsection 2.4 explains the notation used to describe protocols later in the paper.

2.1. The Communication Model

A schematic of the communication model we assume is shown in Figure 1. The nodes of the graph represent processes and the directed arcs connecting them show the direction of communication. The protocol consists of a transmitter process T and a receiver process R. The transmitter gets its input from an infinite source of symbols (the *producer*) P and the receiver writes out its output to an infinite sink of symbols (the *consumer*) C. Process communication may be synchronous or asynchronous; while we use synchronous protocols in our examples, this is done principally for simplicity, and is not fundamental to our model.

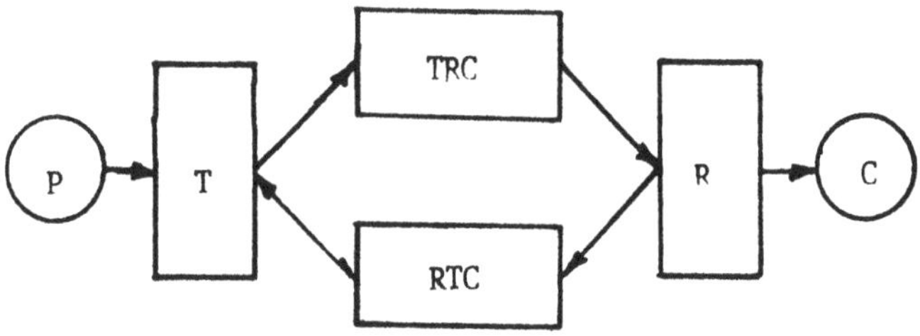

Figure 1: The Communication Model

As shown in the figure, communication between the transmitter and receiver takes place over channels (*TRC* and *RTC*) which are single slot buffers; this is sufficient for our synchronous model of communication. The channels may be unreliable, which means that messages may be corrupted in transit, in which case the message will have to be retransmitted. Correspondingly, an acknowledgement of correct reception may become corrupted or lost, resulting in unnecessary retransmissions of an old message that must be distinguished from the transmission of a new message, and discarded. It is the task of the communication protocol to guarantee correct data transfer from the producer to the consumer.

In our model, as in [ZWR80], channels are treated as processes that are connected to the transmitter and receiver by ideal communication links. Errors occurring in transmission are assumed to originate entirely in the channel process. Each message is treated as a single symbol that is sent by the transmitting side to the channel, and delivered (possibly corrupted to some other symbol) by the channel to the receiving side. The set of symbols received is thus a superset of the set sent. Thus, we define the *channel alphabet* of a protocol as the set of symbols received over a channel by a receiving side. It need not be the same as the *user alphabet*, i.e. the symbols used by the producer and consumer. It may contain, in addition to *data symbols* that convey information that the user wants transmitted, various symbols for control and status information that are internal to the protocol.

Some researchers have considered the case where all corrupted messages are *detectably* corrupted. In practice, however, detection of corruption may not always be possible. We assume a somewhat more general framework where a message symbol may be transformed into some other legal symbol. In particular, it may be changed into an *error*, or *null*, message λ [AUY79, Fra79]. We refer to this class of transmission errors as transformation errors.

In this framework, lost messages can also be modeled as being transformed into the null message λ. The rationale for this is that in practice, asynchronous processes use timeouts to detect lost messages [Har77, Sch82], while with synchronous systems, non-receipt of a message when expected is interpreted to mean that the message was lost. Both cases can be modeled by assuming that the receiver gets a null message [Lam84]. Null messages may also be used as synchronizing signals.

2.2. Protocol Robustness

A protocol is *robust* if it is both *safe* and *live* [AUY79]. Intuitively, *safety* means "bad things will not happen", e.g. erroneous outputs will not occur, while *liveness* means "good things will happen", e.g. given an input message, the protocol will eventually deliver it to its output. More formally, these criteria are defined as follows:

Safety: The sequence of messages output by the protocol is at all times a prefix of the sequence of messages input to the protocol.

Liveness: The protocol eventually delivers a message it has received if no transmission errors occur for some fixed, finite (non-zero) length of time.

Techniques for proving protocols robust include (i) the finite-state technique [AUY79], where reachability analysis is used to show that the combined machine obtained by composing all the individual machines has the required properties; (ii) the abstract program technique [Hai81], where the protocol is specified as a parallel program and verified using temporal logic; and (iii) the algebraic technique [SFD84], where algebraic transformations are used to show the protocol to be observationally equivalent to an ideal channel. In this paper, we use the finite-state technique because of its simplicity, especially when applied to synchronous protocols.

2.3. Notation

We employ finite-state machines to model communication protocols. Labels on the arcs of the transition diagram indicate the conditions governing transitions. Our notation is similar to that of [AUY79].

Notation for the Transmitter: Transitions are labeled as

$$(\alpha,\ \beta)/\gamma$$

where α indicates the symbol in the input buffer being looked at, β is the symbol received on channel RTC from the receiver and γ is the output symbol being sent to the receiver on channel TRC. If the action of the transmitter does not depend on the symbol read from the buffer, α is replaced by 'any', and similarly for β. An optional superscript of '*' indicates that the input buffer is advanced, i.e. the next symbol is read.

Notation for the Receiver: Transitions are labeled as

$$\alpha/(\beta,\ \gamma)$$

where α is the symbol received on channel TRC from the transmitter, β is the symbol being sent to the transmitter on channel RTC and γ is the symbol being written to output. The notation 'any' is used as before. If nothing is being written out, γ is replaced by '-'.

Notation for the Channels: The channels are also treated as finite-state machines. Transitions are labeled as

$$\alpha/\beta$$

where α is the symbol received from the transmitting side, and β the symbol sent to the receiving side.

2.4. The Combined Machine

The combined machine used for reachability analysis is obtained by composing the individual automata representing the transmitter, receiver and the two channels. The machine is represented by a combined transition diagram over the user alphabet; symbols used purely for internal communication between the component automata do not appear in the diagram. An example appears in Figure 3(b).

A state of the combined machine is a 4-tuple $<a, b, c, d>$, derived from the states of the component machines, and is represented pictorially as

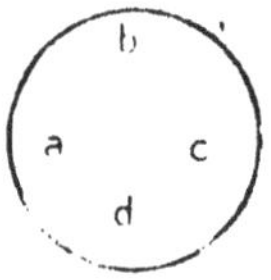

Here a is the state of the transmitter, b the state of channel TRC, c the state of the receiver and d the state of channel RTC.

The state of a channel automaton reflects the symbol last seen by it. There are n ϵ-transitions out of the initial state of the channel (see also Section 3.4), where n is the size of the channel alphabet, to model the fact that the initial contents of the channel are unknown. [AUY79] assume that the channel initially contains the null symbol λ, but such an assumption cannot be made for arbitrary alphabets.

Transitions of the combined machine are defined as follows: there is one initial step where the combined machine moves nondeterministically to one of n^2 possible initial configurations (one for each possible initial configuration of the two channels). Subsequent transitions are defined as follows: if there is a transition for the transmitter T from state t to state t' labeled $(A,B)/C$; for the channel TRC from state u to state u' labeled C/D; for the receiver R from v to v' labeled $D/(E,F)$; and for the channel RTC from state w to w' labeled E/B, then there is a global transition from state $<t, u, v, w>$ to state $<t', u', v', w'>$. Each channel introduces a unit delay between input and output. Thus, in the transition defined above, the transmitter sees the output B of the receiver (possibly corrupted) from the previous transition (which is output by RTC in this transition), while the receiver sees the output D of the transmitter from the previous transition (which is output by TRC in this transition). In the next combined transition the output C of the transmitter in this transition will be seen by the receiver, and the output E of the receiver will be seen by the transmitter.

Transitions of the combined machine are labeled as follows: transitions on which a transmission error occurs on the channel are labeled ERR for expository purposes. A transition on which a symbol α is read in from the input buffer of the transmitter is labeled 'α in', while a transition on which a symbol β is written out to the output buffer of the receiver is labeled 'β out'. Transitions which are unlabeled represent state transitions with internal communications between the automata being combined, that are not visible to the outside world (analogous to τ-transitions in the CCS model [Mil80]).

3. Modeling Transformation Errors in Channels

3.1. Error Maps

Let Σ be the channel alphabet. A ***transformation error*** is defined to occur if some $\rho \in \Sigma$ is converted to some $\sigma \in \Sigma$, $\rho \neq \sigma$. This suggests that such errors be defined as mappings over Σ. Different kinds of errors lead to different mappings. In general, there may not be a unique image of $\rho \in \Sigma$ under an error, i.e. ρ may be mapped into any member of some subset of Σ. Hence, we will model an error X as a map η_X:

$$\eta_X : \Sigma \rightarrow 2^{\Sigma},$$

so that given $\rho \in \Sigma$, $\eta_X(\rho) \subseteq \Sigma$ is the set of symbols that ρ can be changed into by the error X. If a symbol ρ is unaffected by an error X, then $\eta_X(\rho)$ is undefined.

As an example, consider the alphabet $\{0, 1, \lambda\}$, where 0 and 1 are ***data symbols***, and λ the ***null message***. [AUY79] considers three basic types of transformation errors for this alphabet: insertion, deletion and mutation. An ***insertion error*** is said to occur if the channel converts a null message λ to 0 or 1. A ***deletion*** error occurs if a message is deleted, i.e. if a 1 or a 0 is transformed into λ. A ***mutation*** error occurs if a 1 is changed into a 0, or vice versa. The corresponding error maps, η_I, η_D and η_M respectively, are

$$\eta_I = \lambda \rightarrow \{0, 1\} \qquad \eta_D = \begin{cases} 1 \rightarrow \{\lambda\} \\ 0 \rightarrow \{\lambda\} \end{cases} \qquad \eta_M = \begin{cases} 1 \rightarrow \{0\} \\ 0 \rightarrow \{1\} \end{cases}.$$

3.2. Transformation Maps

The error map tells us what happens *if* an error occurs. We cannot, of course, predict whether any given message will be corrupted. To examine the input–to–output transmission characteristics of the channel in greater detail, we use the notion of error maps to define transformation maps. A *transformation map* τ is a map

$$\tau : \Sigma \rightarrow 2^{\Sigma}$$

such that, for any input $\rho \in \Sigma$ to the channel, $\tau(\rho)$ represents the set of possible output values for ρ. In particular, for an ideal (i.e. error–free) channel, the transformation map is

$$\tau_{ideal} : \rho \rightarrow \{\rho\} \text{ for all } \rho \in \Sigma.$$

For non–ideal channels, the transformation map is obtained by composing τ_{ideal} with the appropriate error map η_X, where X is the error under consideration, as defined below:

$$\text{for all } \rho \in \Sigma, \quad \tau_X(\rho) = \begin{cases} \tau_{ideal}(\rho) \cup \eta_X(\rho), & \textit{if } \eta_X(\rho) \textit{ is defined} \\ \tau_{ideal}(\rho) & \textit{otherwise.} \end{cases}$$

Definition: A transformation map τ for a channel alphabet Σ is said to be *complete* if $\tau(\rho) = \Sigma$ for every ρ in Σ.

Note that while η is in general a partial function (in particular, for an ideal channel, η is the null function), τ is always total. Thus, for deletion errors from the previous example, we have

$$\tau_D = \begin{cases} 1 \rightarrow \{1, \lambda\} \\ 0 \rightarrow \{0, \lambda\}. \\ \lambda \rightarrow \{\lambda\} \end{cases}$$

3.3. Transformation Maps for Combinations of Errors

So far we have considered only basic types of errors. Now we extend our ideas to various combinations of these errors. We assume that for a combination of errors X and Y, an input message will possibly suffer corruption by either X *or* Y, but not both. This assumption is necessary to avoid introducing compositions of the errors under consideration into the model. Consider, for example, the combination of insertion and deletion errors. We rule out the possibility that a 0 is deleted to λ, which is transformed by an insertion error into a 1, since this is equivalent to a mutation error.

With this assumption, given a combination of errors $\{X_1, ..., X_n\}$, the output for a given input ρ will be either in $\tau_{X_1}(\rho)$, or in $\tau_{X_2}(\rho)$, ..., or in $\tau_{X_n}(\rho)$. Thus, the combined transformation map τ will be defined as

$$\text{for all } \rho \in \Sigma, \ \tau(\rho) = \bigcup_{i=1}^{n} \tau_{X_i}(\rho).$$

As an example, for the class of errors $\{$*deletion, insertion*$\}$, the transformation map is

$$\tau_{DI} = \begin{cases} 1 \rightarrow \{1, \lambda\} \\ 0 \rightarrow \{0, \lambda\} \\ \lambda \rightarrow \{\lambda, 0, 1, \} \end{cases} .$$

3.4. Deriving Finite-State Representations for the Channel

We have seen how the transformation map for any combination of errors can be derived from the error maps of the individual errors. This subsection illustrates one application of transformation maps, the automatic construction of a finite-state machine for a channel with some combination of errors. Such constructions are useful in automatic proofs of protocol robustness [SFD84]. The machine constructed acts as a one-slot buffer between the transmitter and receiver.

Let $C = \{Q, \Sigma, \delta, s, F\}$ be a nondeterministic finite-state machine representing the channel. C takes its input from the sending process and delivers its output to the receiving process. Σ is the input (channel) alphabet. Q, the set of states, is

$$Q = \{s\} \cup \{s_\rho \mid \rho \in \Sigma\},$$

while the set of final states F is empty. The state transition mapping δ is defined as follows:

(i) For every ρ in Σ, there is a transition from s to s_ρ labeled ϵ.

(ii) For every ρ_1, ρ_2 (not necessarily distinct) in Σ, and every σ in $\tau(\rho_1)$, there is a transition from s_{ρ_1} to s_{ρ_2} labeled ρ_2/σ.

The ϵ-transitions (i) model the fact that initially, the contents of the channel are undefined. Transitions (ii) handle steady-state conditions.

In the steady state, the machine is in state ρ_1 if the last symbol read was ρ_1. This follows from the fact that if it is in any state s_{ρ_1} and reads in a symbol ρ_2, it can only go to s_{ρ_2}. At every state, there is a transition that can be taken for each symbol in Σ, so that at every state, the channel can accept any input. The only transitions possible out of a state s_{ρ_1} are those that output a symbol σ that is in $\tau(\rho_1)$, and there is one such transition for each σ in $\tau(\rho_1)$. This shows that the set of possible outputs is the set of symbols that the last symbol read could have been transformed to by the channel. Together, these show that the machine C defined above represents the channel with transformation map τ. A specific example of a constructed channel is given in Figure 3(a).

4. The Existence Problem for Robust Protocols

A basic question that arises when designing a protocol is: "Given an alphabet to be transmitted over a channel under some class of errors, does there exist a robust protocol that will perform the task?" Clearly, if there *is* no robust protocol, then trying to design one is a waste of time. Moreover, even if there is no robust protocol for a particular alphabet under a given class of errors, a minor change to the alphabet may result in conditions where a robust protocol does exist. Identifying such conditions can be useful, since it can, under certain circumstances, help in the selection of an alphabet for which a robust protocol can be guaranteed.

Consider the following example: we wish to transmit the user alphabet {0, 1} over a channel where symbols may undergo deletion or mutation errors. If null messages are not used by the protocol, i.e. the channel alphabet is just {0, 1}, then – as we will show in this section – there is no robust protocol for this alphabet under this class of errors. However, if λ is also used, the channel alphabet is $\{0, 1, \lambda\}$, and robust protocols exist [AUY79].

This section investigates the conditions under which robust protocols exist for arbitrary alphabets and transformation errors. Our result is based on the existence of a robust protocol for a simple alphabet under a basic type of error. The next subsection describes this protocol and proves its robustness. In Subsection 4.2 we present the generalization of this result A procedure for constructing a robust protocol, whenever one exists, is given in Subsection 4.3.

4.1. A Robust Protocol for a Simple Alphabet

Consider the channel alphabet $\{\rho_0, \rho_1\}$, and the transformation map τ_S defined as

$$\tau_S = \begin{cases} \rho_0 \rightarrow \{\rho_0\} \\ \rho_1 \rightarrow \{\rho_0, \rho_1\} \end{cases}.$$

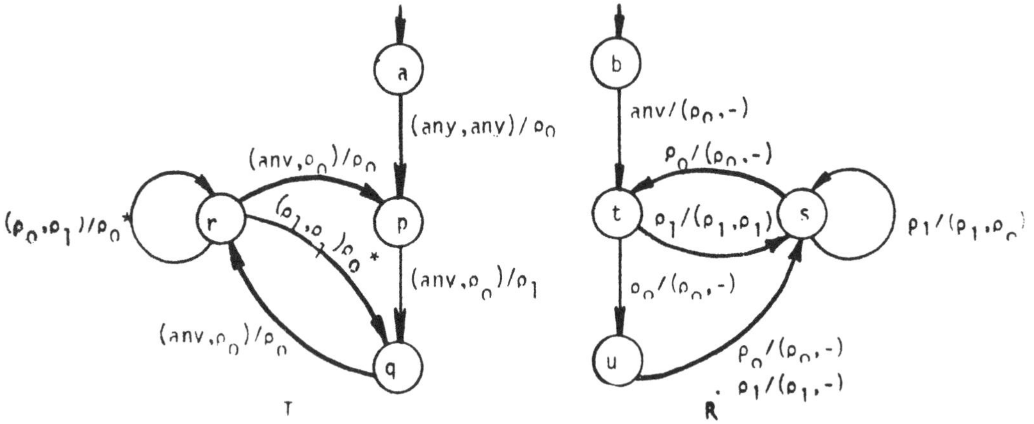

Figure 2: A Robust Protocol for the Alphabet $\{\rho_0, \rho_1\}$ and Transformation Map τ_S.

Theorem 1: There exists a robust protocol for the alphabet $\{\rho_0, \rho_1\}$ and the transformation map τ_S.

Proof: Consider the protocol of Figure 2. The channel automata *TRC* and *RTC* illustrated in Figure 3(a) are obtained from τ_S as described in Subsection 3.3. Figure 3(b) illustrates the combined transition diagram of the transmitter, receiver, and channels *TRC* and *RTC*, starting at the start state of each machine (Subsection 2.3 describes the notation for combined transition diagrams).

We use reachability analysis to prove this protocol robust for the transformation map τ_S. It can be seen that there is no combined state that has no arcs coming out of it; the existence of such a state would imply the possibility of deadlock. Every reachable combined state is fully defined, i.e. an input transition from a state of a component machine has a corresponding output transition in the state of another machine, and similarly for output actions. Every transition cycle without any errors contains input and output actions, and the longest of these is clearly bounded; this means that if no errors occur for a fixed, finite length of time, some output will be produced. These arguments prove the protocol to be *live*. Every cycle containing a *read* from the input also contains a corresponding *write* to the output. This proves the *safety* property. Since both properties hold, the protocol of Figure 2 is robust. □

The robust protocol of Figure 2 is a generalization of the protocol for deletion/mutation errors given by Aho et al [AUY79]. It uses a parity scheme based on the number of ρ_0 symbols appearing between messages. The transmitter state *a* and receiver state *b* are added to initialize the contents of both channels to ρ_0; the remaining states comprise the steady–state cycle of the protocol. The transmitter T has a minimal three state cycle that includes transmission of

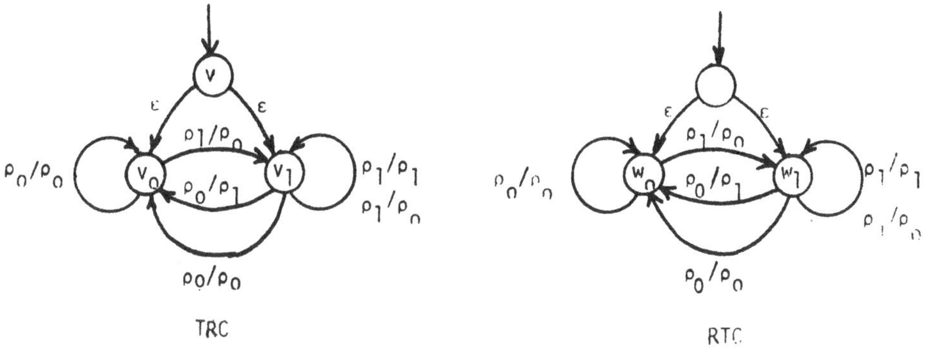

Figure 3(a): Channel Automata for Transformation Map τ_g

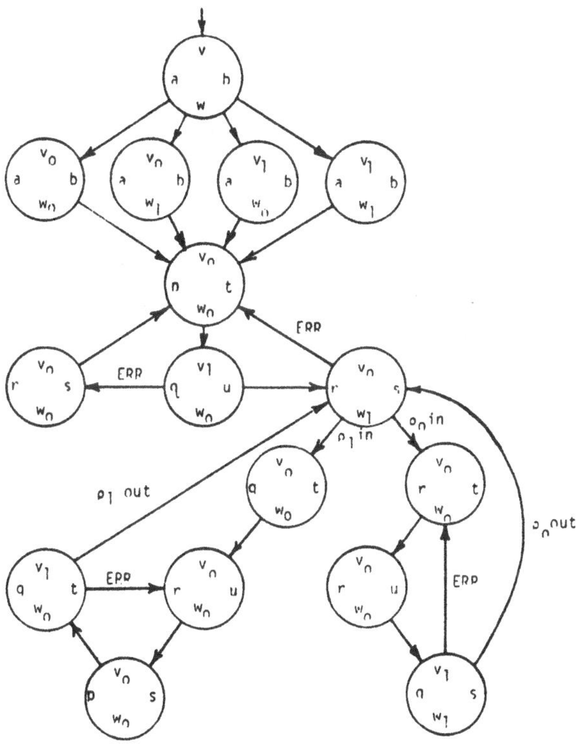

Figure 3(b): Combined Transition Diagram for the Protocol

a ρ_1 symbol (from state p) followed by two ρ_0 symbols. It sends a ρ_0 or ρ_1 message by skipping an additional one time unit (loop at state r) or two time units (r to q to r cycle), respectively. The receiver R knows the actual channel symbol corresponding to a received ρ_1 by its current state. It receives some multiple of two, three or four ρ_0 symbols preceding an unneeded retransmission (state u), a ρ_0 message (state s) or a ρ_1 message (state t), respectively.

4.2. Robustness for Arbitrary Alphabets and Error Conditions

Consider an arbitrary channel alphabet Σ and a class of errors E. We prove the following lemma:

Lemma 1: An alphabet of size N $\geq$ 2 can be transmitted reliably iff at least two symbols in the alphabet can be transmitted reliably.

Proof: The *only if* part is trivial. To prove the *if* part, note that if two symbols ρ_0, $\rho_1 \in \Sigma$ can be transmitted reliably, then any symbol $\sigma_k \in \Sigma$ can be sent reliably: the symbols of Σ are indexed so that each symbol has a unique index, and σ_k – the symbol with index k, $0 \leq k \leq$ N–1 – is sent encoded as a string of ρ_0s and ρ_1s with a ρ_0 corresponding to each 0 in the binary representation of k, and a ρ_1 corresponding to each 1, and decoded appropriately at the receiving side. □

We now state our main result:

Theorem 2: Given a channel alphabet Σ and a class of errors E, a robust protocol exists iff the transformation map τ_E is not complete.

Proof: The proof for the *only if* part is a straightforward generalization of Theorem 5 in [AUY79]. Consider two distinct symbols ρ_1 and ρ_2 in Σ. Let S be a sequence of symbols transmitted between the transmitter and receiver to communicate a single ρ_1 from the input buffer to the output buffer. Assume the length of S is n. There is some sequence of ρ_2s in the input buffer that will cause a sequence of symbols S' of length at least n to be transmitted on the channel. If τ_E is complete, then any symbol in the channel alphabet can be changed to any other symbol. This implies that for some sequence of errors, the first n symbols of S' can be changed to those of S, which will cause the receiver to erroneously output a ρ_1 even though the input contained only ρ_2s. Thus, there is no robust protocol if the transformation map is complete.

To prove the *if* part, assume that for some symbol $\rho_0 \in \Sigma$,

$$\tau_E(\rho_0) = \Sigma_0 \subset \Sigma$$

where $\subset$ denotes proper containment. This means that there must be some symbol $\rho_1 \notin \Sigma_0$.

If $\tau_E(\rho_1)$ and Σ_0 are disjoint, then the reliable transmission of ρ_0 and ρ_1 is straightforward: ρ_0 and ρ_1 are sent directly. At the receiving side, if the symbol received is in Σ_0 then the symbol transmitted must have been ρ_0, otherwise the symbol received must be in $\tau(\rho_1)$ and the symbol transmitted must have been ρ_1. It follows from Lemma 1 that all symbols in Σ can be transmitted reliably, i.e. a robust protocol exists.

If $\tau_E(\rho_1)$ and Σ_0 are *not* disjoint, then the problem is more complex. Let Σ_1 be the set Σ – Σ_0. Assume that the transmitting side sends only ρ_0s and ρ_1s. If the receiving side receives a symbol in Σ_1, then it can immediately conclude that the symbol transmitted must have been ρ_1; if the symbol received is in Σ_0, then the symbol transmitted could have been either ρ_0 or ρ_1. Since the only symbols transmitted are ρ_0 and ρ_1, we can consider all symbols in Σ_0 to be equivalent to ρ_0, and all symbols in Σ_1 to be equivalent to ρ_1. Under this equivalence, ρ_0 is received as ρ_0, but ρ_1 can either be received as ρ_1, or become corrupted and be received as ρ_0.

The transformation map under this equivalence is then

$$\tau_S = \begin{cases} \rho_0 \to \{\rho_0\} \\ \rho_1 \to \{\rho_0, \rho_1\} \end{cases}$$

By Theorem 1, a robust protocol exists for the alphabet $\{\rho_0, \rho_1\}$ and the transformation map τ_S. From Lemma 1, a robust protocol exists for alphabet Σ and transformation map τ_E. □

A similar result is outlined in [AWY82], though a detailed proof is not given. In addition, our proof takes into account the structure of the transformation map to construct more efficient protocols.

4.3. A Construction Procedure for Robust Protocols

We now present a procedure for automatically constructing a robust protocol for any channel alphabet Σ of size N, given a transformation map τ that is not complete. The protocol consists of a transmitter and a receiver, each consisting of two functionally distinct processes, E and T, and D and R respectively (see Figure 4). An infinite buffer[1] connects E to T, and similarly for D and R. Communication between E and T, and between R and D is assumed to be totally reliable. E is an encoder that reads input symbols from the producer, encodes them and gives the encoded strings to T. T is the transmitter that communicates with the receiver R over the channel. R receives the encoded strings from T and gives them to the decoder D that decodes them and produces output for the consumer. Our construction procedure is as follows:

1. Index the symbols of Σ so that each symbol has an index k, $0 \le k \le N$-1. We will denote the symbol with index k by σ_k.
2. Select two symbols $\rho_0, \rho_1 \in \Sigma$ such that $\tau(\rho_0) = \Sigma_0 \subset \Sigma$ and $\rho_1 \notin \Sigma_0$.
3. Construct the Encoder (E) and Decoder (D) processes:

   (a) E is a finite–state process that encodes symbols from the input buffer into strings of length $\log_2 N$ over $\{\rho_0, \rho_1\}$. The symbol σ_k is encoded as a string of ρ_0s and ρ_1s with a ρ_0 corresponding to each 0 in the binary representation of k, and a ρ_1 corresponding to each 1.

   (b) D is the inverse process of E: on encountering a string of length $\log_2 N$ in its input buffer, it decodes the string to output σ_k, where k is the number whose binary expansion is represented by the input string.
4. Construct the Transmitter (T) and Receiver (R) processes:

   (a) If $\tau(\rho_1)$ and Σ_0 are disjoint, then T and R are as follows: T transmits the encoded strings given to it by E. On receiving a symbol, R checks to see whether it is in Σ_0; if it is, then it writes a ρ_0 into the buffer connecting it with D, else it writes a ρ_1.

   (b) If $\tau(\rho_1)$ and Σ_0 are not disjoint, then T and R are the transmitter and receiver, respectively, of the protocol of Figure 2.

Given an indexed alphabet Σ, ρ_0 and ρ_1, designing E and D is straightforward. Note that if the user alphabet contains only two symbols, the encoding is trivial and E and D are

1. Infinite buffers are actually unnecessary, and are assumed here for conceptual simplicity. In practice, an implementation could have finite buffers of size $\log_2 N$ instead, and would use some signaling mechanism between processes to indicate full or empty buffers.

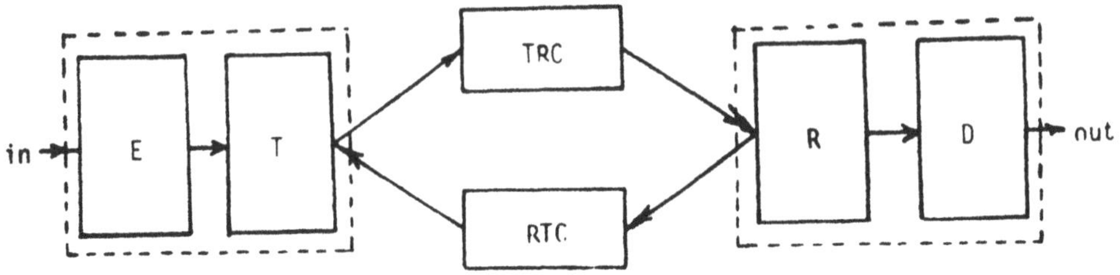

Figure 4: Schematic of Robust Protocol for Transformation Errors

unnecessary, and Step 3 in the construction can be omitted.

While robust, the protocol schema described is suboptimal in the sense that it may require more transmissions per alphabet symbol than really necessary. For example, it requires $\log_2 N$ transmissions per symbol when no errors are present, where N is the size of the user alphabet, even though one transmission per symbol would suffice. Let the ***active alphabet*** of a protocol be the set of symbols sent by a transmitting side over the channel; it is a subset of the channel alphabet (the difference being accounted for by errors). Performance can be improved by taking into account all safe symbols, a notion we define below.

Definition: A symbol ρ in the active alphabet Γ of a protocol is ***safe*** if, for all $\sigma \in \Gamma$,

$$\rho \neq \sigma \Rightarrow \rho \notin \tau(\sigma).$$

In other words, a symbol ρ is safe if no other symbol in the active alphabet can get corrupted to ρ. So, if a ρ is received, the receiver can safely assume that a ρ was sent[1]. Note that Step 4(a) of the construction procedure is based on the use of safe symbols to simplify the T and R processes.

If there are $m > 2$ safe symbols in the active alphabet, then we can encode each symbol in the user alphabet as an m-ary string using these m safe symbols, rather than as a binary string. The protocol schema above can be modified in an obvious way to take this encoding into account. The protocol now requires only $\log_m N$ transmissions per symbol. In particular, if there are no errors, then $m = N$, and only one transmission is required per symbol.

5. Examples of Robust Communication Protocols

This section illustrates our general construction procedure for robust synchronous protocols. Aho, Ullman and Yannakakis (AUY) describe synchronous protocols for various combinations of insertion, deletion and mutation errors [AUY79]. Here, we consider the same class. They assume a user alphabet of only two symbols, {0, 1}, which implies that we do not need to construct the encoder (E) and decoder (D) processes. We will consider only the transmitter (T) and receiver (R) processes.

AUY obtain lower bounds on the complexity of robust synchronous protocols. Protocol complexity is measured in terms of the number of states of the component finite-state machines. A protocol specification is of minimal complexity if its finite-state machines have the smallest number of states possible in any such protocol. The robust protocol (Figure 2)

1. **Actually, it follows from the definition that is safe to assume that a ρ was sent as long as the received symbol is in $\tau(\rho) - \bigcup_i \{\tau(\sigma_i) \mid \sigma_i \in \Gamma \wedge \sigma_i \neq \rho\}$, where Γ is the active alphabet.**

used in the construction procedure is a generalization of the AUY protocol for deletion/mutation errors, which has a complexity of 3. The protocols constructed also have a complexity of 3, if we disregard the initialization states (a, b), which are never entered in the steady-state cycle of the protocols. Protocols for the two other possible error combinations they consider are contrasted in the next two subsections.

5.1. Protocol for Deletion Errors

AUY describe an extremely simple robust protocol for deletion errors (Figure 5). The transformation map for deletion errors is given in Subsection 3.2. We choose to map ρ_0 to λ, and ρ_1 to 1 in Step 1 of our procedure. The transmitter and receiver constructed by our procedure in step 4 are given in Figure 6. AUY prove that their protocol is robust and that it has a complexity of 2, which is minimal. The constructed protocol has a complexity of 3, which is reasonable considering that it is derived automatically.

5.2. Protocol for Deletion/Insertion Errors

AUY do not explicitly give a robust protocol for deletion/insertion errors. Their existence proof for a robust protocol, however, outlines an alternating "parity symbol" strategy. They suggest such a complex strategy because of the following reasoning. Because insertion errors are allowed, there is no sense in transmitting a λ since it can be transformed to any symbol in the channel alphabet, therefore providing no differentiating information. Moreover, because deletion errors are also allowed, there is no symbol that is guaranteed to arrive as transmitted, i.e. there is no safe symbol. Consequently, there is a greater need for persistence in symbol transmission and acknowledgement at all phases; this can be achieved by the use of an alternating parity symbol. The transformation map for deletion/insertion errors is given in Subsection 3.3.

The specific strategy of their protocol is as follows. The transmitter alternates the data symbol being communicated with a parity symbol that changes with each new data symbol. The transmitter repeatedly sends the current input symbol until it is acknowledged. Only then does it change the parity symbol being transmitted. A changed parity symbol allows the receiver to distinguish between retransmissions and new symbols. The receiver acknowledges data symbols by continuously sending the current parity symbol to the transmitter. If unex-

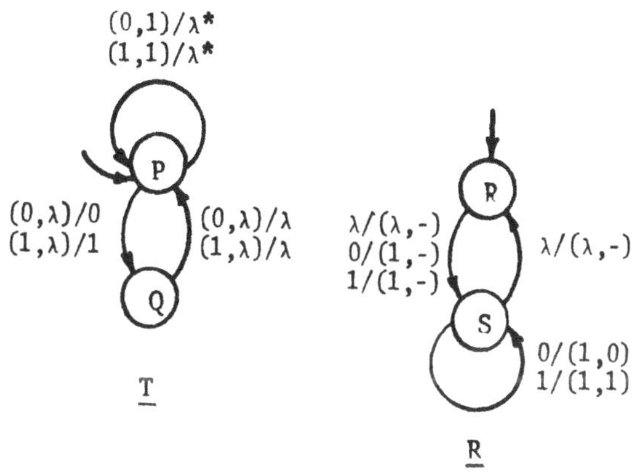

Figure 5: The AUY Robust Protocol for Deletion Errors

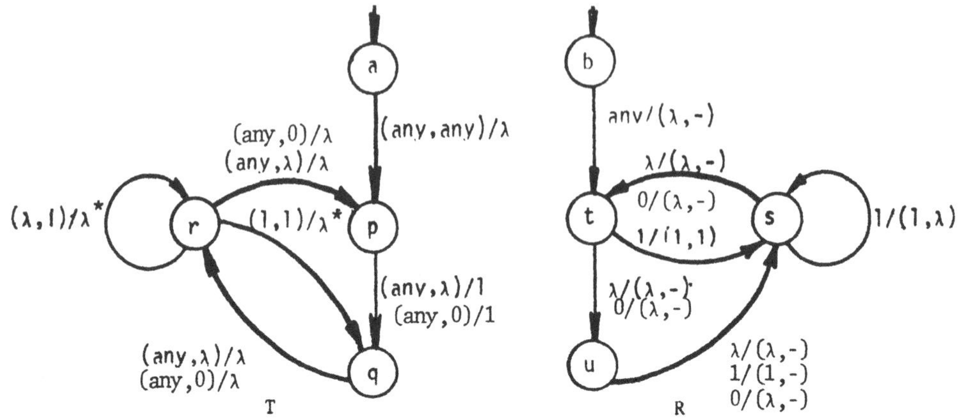

Figure 6: The Constructed Robust Protocol for Deletion Errors

pected symbols are received, the nonparity symbol is sent by the receiver to cause retransmission.

The best protocol we developed that implements their strategy is given in Figure 7. The two data symbols are used as opposing parity symbols. The initial parity symbol is 0 and it alternates with 1. The transmitter and receiver send or expect new data symbols every three time units, respectively. The transmitter persistently awaits parity symbol acknowledgements at states T and W, and only then advances the input buffer. Otherwise, it retransmits the current data symbol (at states R and U). The receiver persistently awaits specific data symbols at four states. New data symbols are expected at states I and L, and parity symbol acknowledgements at states K and N. Otherwise, it transmits the current nonparity symbol. The transmitter has 6 states, whereas the receiver is larger and has 12 states. Both transmitter and receiver are relatively large since they skip one time unit after every critical message to await the other side response in the following time unit. The receiver is twice as large since it must await specific responses at four places in contrast to only two places for the transmitter. This

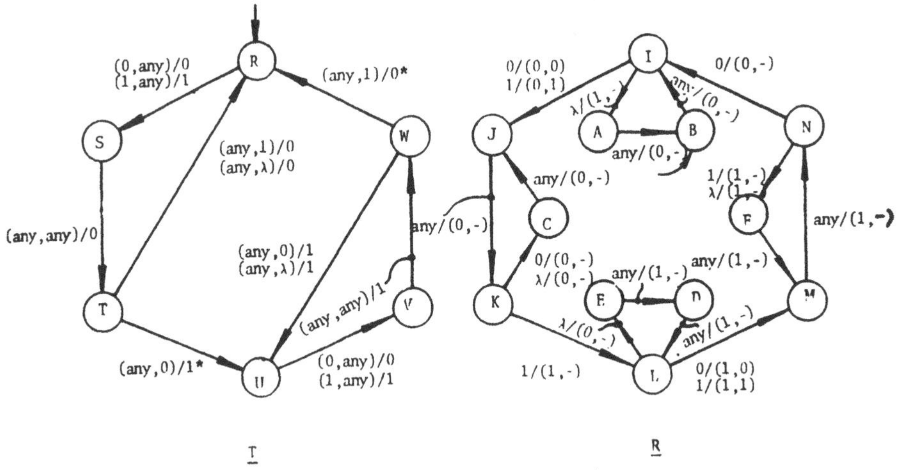

Figure 7: Suggested Protocol for Deletion/Insertion Errors

protocol has been proven robust [Fra84]. Its relatively large combined transition diagram has 81 states.

In contrast, the protocol for deletion/insertion errors that is constructed by our procedure is much simpler, since it has a complexity of 3. We choose to map ρ_0 to 0, so ρ_1 must be mapped to 1 in step 1 of the procedure. The robust protocol constructed by our procedure in Step 4 is given in Figure 8.

6. Conclusion

This paper develops a formal model for transmission errors on unreliable communication channels. A necessary and sufficient condition for the existence of robust protocols under a class of transformation errors has been presented. We used this result to describe a construction procedure that can construct robust synchronous protocols if the transformation map is not complete. Two examples of robust synchronous protocols were constructed to illustrate our technique.

The protocols constructed by our procedure are nearly as good as the corresponding, specifically designed AUY protocols, and in one case shown, even better. As noted previously, our results are a generalization of the results shown by [AUY79]. In this sense, this paper is an extension of their research on modeling communication protocols by automata.

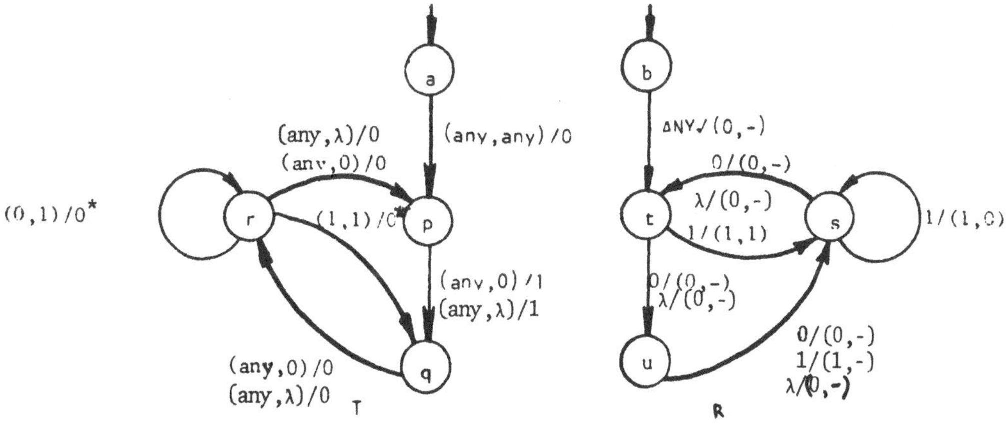

Figure 8: The Constructed Robust Protocol for Deletion/Insertion Errors

7. References

[AUY79] A. V. Aho, J. D. Ullman and M. Yannakakis, "Modeling Communications Protocols by Automata", *20th Annual Symp. on Foundations of Computer Science*, San Juan, Puerto Rico, Oct. 1979.

[AWY82] A. V. Aho, A. D. Wyner, M. Yannakakis and J. D. Ullman, "Bounds on the Size and Transmission Rate of Communications Protocols", *Comp. & Maths. with Appls.*, **8**, 3 (1982), 205-214, Pergamon Press Ltd..

[Aho84] A. Aho, in *Personal Communication*, June 1984.

[Boc80] G. V. Bochmann, "A General Transition Model for Protocols and Communication Services", *IEEE Trans. on Computers*, **COM-28**, 4 (Apr. 1980), 643-650.

[BoS80] G. V. Bochmann and C. A. Sunshine, "Formal Methods in Communication Protocol Design", *IEEE Trans. on Computers*, **COM-28**, 4 (Apr. 1980), 624-631.

[Dan80] A. A. S. Danthine, "Protocol Representation with Finite-State Models", *IEEE Trans. on Communications*, **COM-28**, 4 (April 1980), 632-643. Reprinted in "Communication Protocol Modeling", ed. C. A. Sunshine, Artech House, Dedham, Mass., 1981.

[Fra84] A. J. Frank, *Modeling Communication Protocols by Synchronous/ Asynchronous Automata*, Dept. of Computer Science, SUNY at Stony Brook, Feb. 1984. Unpublished Manuscript.

[Fra79] A. G. Fraser, "Datakit - A Modular Network for Synchronous and Asynchronous Traffic", *Proc. IEEE Int. Conf. on Communications*, Boston, June 1979.

[Hai81] B. T. Hailpern, "A Simple Protocol Whose Proof Isn't", *IBM Research Report RC8800(#38567)*, IBM Thomas J. Watson Research Center, Apr. 1981.

[Har77] J. Harangozo, "An Approach to Describing a Link-Level Protocol with a Formal Language", in *Proc. 5th. Data Communication Symp.*, Snowbird, Utah, Sept. 77. Reprinted in "Communication Protocol Modeling", ed. C. A. Sunshine, Artech House, Dedham, Mass., 1981.

[Lam84] L. Lamport, "Using Time instead of Timeout for Fault-Tolerant Distributed Systems", *ACM Trans. Prog. Lang. and Systems*, **6**, 2 (Apr. 1984), 254-280.

[Mil80] R. Milner, "A Calculus of Communicating Systems", in *Lecture Notes in Computer Science, 92*, Springer Verlag, New York, 1980.

[Pac82] J. K. Pachl, "Reachability Problems for Communicating Finite State Machines", CS-82-12, Dept. of Computer Science, Univ. of Waterloo, Waterloo, Ontario, Canada, May 1982.

[Sch82] F. B. Schneider, "Synchronization in Distributed Programs", *ACM Trans. Prog. Lang. and Systems*, April 1982, 1-24.

[SFD84] S. A. Smolka, A. J. Frank and S. K. Debray, "Proving Protocol Robustness the CCS Way", Technical Report #84/071, Dept. of Computer Science, SUNY at Stony Brook, April 1984. Proc. 4th. International Workshop on Protocol Specification, Testing and Verification, Mt. Pocono, PA, June 1984.

[Sun79] C. A. Sunshine, "Formal Techniques for Protocol Specification and Verification", *Computer*, **12**, 9 (Sep. 1979), 20-27.

[ZWR80] P. Zafiropulo, C. H. West, H. Rudin, D. D. Cowan and D. Brand, "Towards Analyzing and Synthesizing Protocols", *IEEE Trans. Commun.*, **COM-28**, 4 (April 1980), 651-661.

HEURISTIC SEARCH APPROACH TO OPTIMAL ROUTING IN A DISTRIBUTED ARCHITECTURE

Bhargab B Bhattacharya, Suranjan Ghose, Bhabani P Sinha
Indian Statistical Institute, Calcutta, India
and
Pradip K Srimani
Indian Institute of Management Calcutta, India
Current Address : Department of Computer Science
Southern Illinois University, Carbondale, ILL 62901, USA

Abstract

Recently it has been shown that the general class of De Bruijn graphs can be used to develop a fault-tolerant communication architecture for distributed processing. The present paper describes a heuristic search approach to compute the optimal path between any pair of nodes in such a distributed network.

I. Introduction

The interconnection topology plays an important role in the study of multiprocessor network design and the idea of modeling the network by an undirected graph constitutes a major part of the interconnection topology research. In this model, the nodes of the graph represent the different processors, while the edges between nodes represent the full duplex communication links between the processors. In such a network, a communication between two arbitrary processors is established via some intermediate nodes if the two processors are not connected by a direct link, and in doing so the number of intermediate nodes is kept as small as possible. Given a set of processors, the objective of designing a network graph is twofold : to keep the valency or degree of each node minimum, and to make the diameter of the graph as small as possible. Various authors [1] - [5] have investigated different families of network graphs. Some [4] - [5] of them are concerned with trivalent graphs, while others [1] - [2] consider tetravalent graphs. Recently it has been shown [1] that the general class of De Bruijn graphs [3] can be used to develop a communication architecture for distributed processors. This architecture is based on the topology which interconnects 2^n nodes by using at most 2^{n+1} links, where the maximum internode distance is n, and where each node has at most 4 I/O ports.

Given the network graph, the most important task is the computation of the shortest path between any two nodes in the network, which is required in order to minimize the inter-processor communication delay. Although a simple algorithm is given in [1] for computing a path between a pair of nodes, the length of which is less than or equal to the diameter of the given graph, in most of the cases the generated path is far from being optimal. This becomes especially crucial when we observe that there exists a significant number of nodes in the graph for which the distance is much less than the diameter. Our main objective in this paper is to apply the general theory of heuristic search [6], [7], to develop an efficient algorithm for optimal routing between any pair of nodes in the network graph. We first make a detailed investigation of the different properties that characterize the network topology, and then suitably adapt the heuristic search algorithms [7], for deriving the optimal path between any given pair of nodes. A suitable method for computing the heuristic estimate to be assigned to each node in the search graph is proposed, which later on is shown to be admissible [6], thereby infering that the proposed heuristic search algorithm will compute the optimal path in time complexity $\mathcal{O}(N^2)$, where N $(=2^n)$ denotes the total number of vertices in the graph. It has also been shown that the said family of graphs also possesses some other interesting properties like 4-colorability, and the existence of vertex-disjoint paths of total length $\leq 2n$. The latter property has been found to be useful to ensure correct communication of messages in between a pair of processors, even in presence of some faulty processor nodes. Throughout the paper we have assumed that the number (N) of nodes in the network graph be a power of 2 i.e., $N = 2^n$ as in [1].

II. Properties of De Bruijn Graphs

Let n be a fixed integer greater that 1 and let 2^n denotes the set $\left\{ s = s_0\, s_1 \ldots s_{n-1} \,\middle|\, s_i \in \{0, 1\} \right\}$. Let us define two functions f and g (mapping $2^n \rightarrow 2^n$) as follows :

$$f(s_0 \ldots s_{n-1}) = s_1 \ldots s_{n-1}\, \bar{s}_0$$

$$g(s_0 \ldots s_{n-1}) = s_1 \ldots s_{n-1}\, s_0$$

Similarly we can define the inverse functions f^{-1} and g^{-1} as in the following :

$$f^{-1}(s_o \dots s_{n-1}) = \bar{s}_{n-1}\, s_o \dots s_{n-2}$$

$$g^{-1}(s_o \dots s_{n-1}) = s_{n-1}\, s_o \dots s_{n-2}\,.$$

Clearly these functions f, g, f^{-1} and g^{-1} are all permutations of 2^n. The function f is commonly known as shuffle exchange [4].

Definition 1 : The De Bruijn graph of order n [3] is a graph G = (V,E) with the vertex set $V = 2^n$ and $(u,v) \in E$ iff $u = f(v)$ or $f^{-1}(v)$ or $g(v)$ or $g^{-1}(v)$, where u and v are any two vertices in V.

It is known that such a graph is hamiltonian, and this network topology can be very effectively used to represent a fault-tolerant communication architecture [1]. The different processors in the network are represented by the nodes of the graph while the arcs or the edges of the graph represent the direct communication links. Evidently each processor in such a network is connected to at most 4 adjacent processors and messages can be directly communicated between any pair of adjacent processors, remembering that the arcs represent two-way communication links. If a processor or vertex u wants to communicate with another vertex v, which is not adjacent to u, it is allowed to do so via other processors or vertices. A path P from s to d in the graph G is defined to be a sequence of adjacent vertices starting with the source vertex s and ending in the destination vertex d, and the length of such a path is defined to be the number of edges connecting the vertices in the sequence describing the path. Obviously from communication point of view, it is desirable to know the minimal path between any pair of nodes since greater the path length, larger is the delay in communication, and the more congested the network becomes. It has been shown in [1] that in a De Bruijn graph of order n, the diameter is n or in other words, for any given pair of vertices a path can always be found whose length is equal to or less than n. A simple algorithm has also been proposed [1] to compute such a path of length $\leq n$ for a given pair of vertices. But it can be readily observed that in such a graph G, there are in general a large number of vertex-pairs whose minimal distance is much less than n, and the algorithm of [1] fails to find the minimal path of most of the vertex-pairs in the graph, although it ensures that the length of the obtained path is within the diameter of the graph. In this paper, we formulate the problem of finding the minimal path in the heuristic search framework with 3 admissible heuristic estimates and then utilize the algorithm C [7] in order to develop an algorithm that will compute the optimal path, given any source vertex and any destination vertex in G.

Definition 2 : The run measure $r(v)$ of a given binary vector v is defined to be the total number of blocks of 0's and 1's in the vector. For example, $r(00101101) = 6$.

The following results presented below characterize a De Bruijn graph of order n.

Lemma 1 : Let r_1 and r_2 denote the run measures of two nodes v_1 and v_2 in the De Bruijn graph G. If $v_2 = f(v_1)$, then

i) $r_2 = r_1$ or r_1-1, if r_1 is even

ii) $r_2 = r_1$ or r_1+1, if r_1 is odd.

Proof : Since f consists of taking out one bit from the left end of v_1 and putting its complement at the right end of v_1 in forming v_2, it is obvious that r_2 can differ from r_1 at best by one. Again we observe that whenever a binary vector v starts and ends with same symbol, 0 or 1, $r(v)$ has to be odd, and if v starts and ends with different symbols, $r(v)$ has to be even. It then readily follows that if r_1 is even and $v_2 = f(v_1)$, r_2 can either be r_1 or r_1-1, and if r_1 is odd, r_2 can again either be r_1 or r_1+1. Q.E.D.

Remark : Lemma 1 holds also when the function f is replaced by its inverse f^{-1}.

Lemma 2 : Let r_1 and r_2 denote the run measures of two nodes v_1 and v_2 and let $v_2 = g(v_1)$. Then

$$\left| r_1 - r_2 \right| \leq 1$$

Proof : Similar to the proof of Lemma 1. Q.E.D.

Remark : Lemma 2 also holds when g is replaced by its inverse g^{-1}.

Theorem 1 : In a De Bruijn graph G, the run measures of any pair of adjacent vertices differ at most by one.

Proof : Obvious from lemma 1 and lemma 2. Q.E.D.

Theorem 2 : In a De Bruijn graph G, let v_1 and v_2 be any arbitrary pair of adjacent vertices. Then

$\left| w(v_1) - w(v_2) \right| \leq 1$, where $w(v)$ denotes the number of 1's in the binary vector v.

<u>Proof</u> : It readily follows from the fact that in one application of either of the four functions f, g, f^{-1} and g^{-1} (characterizing the arcs in the graph) the number of 1's in the vector can only either remain constant, or decrease by 1 or increase by 1. Q.E.D.

The next theorem presented below mirrors many important attributes of the function f.

<u>Theorem 3</u> : (i) If only f-transitions are considered, all the nodes in the graph are distributed into vertex-disjoint circuits.
(ii) Any vertex and its complement (with respect to the binary representation) are in the same circuit of f-transitions.
(iii) For all n, there exists at least one such circuit of length 2n.
(iv) For odd n, there exists exactly one circuit of f-transitions of length 2. For even n, no such circuit of length 2 exists.
(v) If n is prime, all but one of such circuits induced by f-transitions are of length 2n.
(vi) If n has two integer factors a and b, where a is odd, then there will exist circuits of length 2b induced by f-transitions .
(vii) If n is a power of 2, then all circuits of f transitions are of length 2n.

The proof of theorem 3 is lengthy and is therefore omitted. It however, follows from the properties of the function f and from the idea of complemented cycling registers (CCR) as indicated in [9].

<u>Corollary 1</u> : Any circuit induced by f-transitions will contain vertices the binary representations of which contain at most two values of run measures r and r + 1, where r is odd, $1 \leq r \leq n$.

<u>Theorem 4</u> : Any De Bruijn graph G of order n, $n \geq 4$, is 4-colorable.

<u>Proof</u> : Note that each node in G is of degree 4 (considering self-loops). Consider now an arbitrary node $v = s_o\ s_1\ \ldots\ s_{n-1}$. Obviously its four successors are :

$$v_1 = s_1\ \ldots\ s_{n-1}\ s_o$$

$$v_2 = s_1\ \ldots\ s_{n-1}\ \bar{s}_o$$

$$v_3 = s_{n-1}\ s_o\ s_1\ \ldots\ s_{n-2}$$

$$v_4 = \bar{s}_{n-1}\ s_o\ s_1\ \ldots\ s_{n-2}$$

Obviously v_1 and v_2 cannot be adjacent unless $s_o = s_1 = \ldots = s_{n-1}$, and similar conditions are required for adjacency of v_3 and v_4. Now note that vertices (00 ... 0) and (11 ... 1) in G have got self-loops induced by g and g^{-1}, and therefore, a complete graph of order 5 can be found nowhere in G. The rest of the proof follows from theorem 12.3 in [8]. Q.E.D.

It may be noted in this context that the De Bruijn graph exhibits certain interesting properties which enable it to be used as a fault-tolerant architecture [1]. It has been shown in [1] that in a De-Bruijn graph of order n, there exist two vertex-disjoint paths P and P' between any pair of nodes, such that the total length of P and P' is less than or equal to 4n. By virtue of the existence of two vertex-disjoint paths in G, it becomes possible to use these De Bruijn graphs as single fault-tolerant communication architecture, since if one of the paths connecting a given pair of vertices is rendered faulty, the desired communication can be resumed via the alternate path. We now claim that De Bruijn graphs are actually better. We can prove that there exist two vertex-disjoint paths of total length $\leq 2n$ between any pair of vertices in G. Before proving this, we require the following lemma.

Lemma 3 : For any vertex u in G, the following graph (as shown in Fig. 1) involving vertex u will be a subgraph of G.

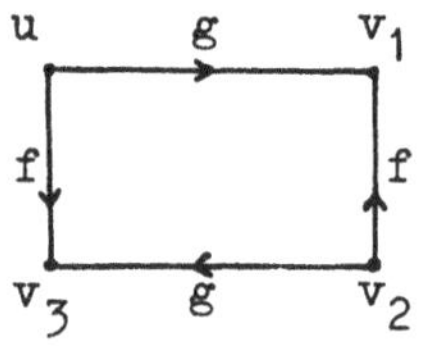

Fig. 1 : A subgraph of G (the direction shows the application of transition functions)

Proof : Immediate from the definitions of f and g. Q.E.D.

Remark : Note that in Fig. 1, vertices u and v_1 can be nondistinct i.e., $u \equiv v_1$ if and only if $u \equiv v_1 = (00 \ldots 0)$ or $(11 \ldots 1)$, and such may be the case for the pair v_2 and v_3. But $u \equiv v_1$ and $v_2 \equiv v_3$ cannot be simultaneously true for $n > 1$, since the all-0 and all-1 vertices cannot be adjacent in G whenever $n > 1$. Moreover, vertices u and v_3 can never be nondistinct, and so does the pair (v_1, v_2).

Theorem 5 : For any given source node s and destination node d, there exist at least two vertex-disjoint paths P and P' in G of order n, such that $|P| + |P'| \leq 2n$, where $|P|$ denotes the length of path P.

Proof : Consider any arbitrary source vertex $s = s_0\, s_1 \ldots s_{n-1}$ and an arbitrary destination vertex $d = d_0\, d_1 \ldots d_{n-1}$ in G. Let us now construct a binary vector $q = q_0\, q_1 \ldots q_{n-1}$, where $q_i = s_i \oplus d_i$ for all i, $0 \leq i \leq n-1$.

Construct now a control sequence (CS) of length n consisting of functions f and g as follows :

$$CS\ (s,d) = (c_o, c_1, \ldots, c_{n-1})$$
$$\text{where, } c_i = \begin{cases} g & \text{if } q_i = 0 \\ f & \text{if } q_i = 1 \end{cases}.$$

Clearly, when the functions in CS (s,d) are applied in succession to the source vector s, we arrive at the destination node d in at most n steps, i.e., a path P_1 from s to d is guaranteed to exist in G, such that $|P_1| \leq n$. What is more interesting in this context, is that the same control sequence when applied in the same order to goal node d, we arrive at the source node s along a second path P_2 such that $|P_2| \leq n$. Note that path P_1 and P_2 must be distinct for $n > 1$, since for any vertex $u \in G$, $f(u) \neq f^{-1}(u)$, and $g(u) = g^{-1}(u)$ only for all-0 and all-1 vertices. Also observe that, only functions f and g are required in defining these two paths P_1 and P_2, and we do not need the inverse functions f^{-1} and g^{-1}. To prove that there exists a pair of vertex-disjoint paths P, P' in between s, d, three cases are now to be considered.

Case 1 : P_1 and P_2 do not intersect each other than at s and d .
In this case, identify P_1 as P and P_2 as P' and therefore $|P| + |P'| \leq 2n$.

Case 2 : P_2 intersects with P_1 at some node say u, goes along P_1 towards d upto a node say v, and then traverse a vertex disjoint path upto s as shown in Fig. 2.

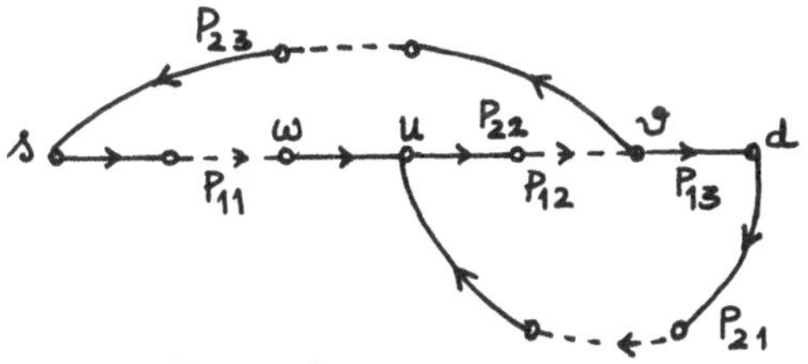

Fig. 2

Here P_1 consists of three parts P_{11} (s to u), P_{12} (u to v) and P_{13} (v to d) i.e., $P = P_{11} \| P_{12} \| P_{13}$, and P_2 consists of three parts P_{21} (d to u), P_{22} (u to v) (= P_{12}), and P_{23} (v to s), i.e., $P_2 = P_{21} \| P_{22} \| P_{23}$. Note that the path P_2 starting from d and on reaching node u, cannot proceed immediately along P_1 towards s, (say to node w), since both paths P_1 and P_2 are dictated by the control sequence CS, which is devoid of any f^{-1} and g^{-1}.

It is now obvious that $|P_{11}| + |P_{12}| + |P_{13}| \leq n$ and $|P_{21}| + |P_{22}| + |P_{23}| \leq n$. Consider now two paths P and P' from s to d such that $P = P_{11} || P_{21}$ and $P' = P_{23} || P_{13}$. Obviously, P and P' are two vertex-disjoint paths, such that $|P| + |P'| \leq 2n$. The argument can easily be generalized when the path P_2 intersects with P_1 in a similar fashion more than once.

Case 3 : Let $P_1 = (s \text{ to } v_2) || (v_2 \text{ to } u) || (u \text{ to } v_3) || (v_3 \text{ to } d)$ and $P_2 = (d \text{ to } v_4) || (v_4 \text{ to } u) || (u \text{ to } v_1) || (v_1 \text{ to } s)$, and P_2 intersects with P_1 at node u, and then P_2 proceeds to a node $v_1 \notin P_1$, as shown in Fig. 3.

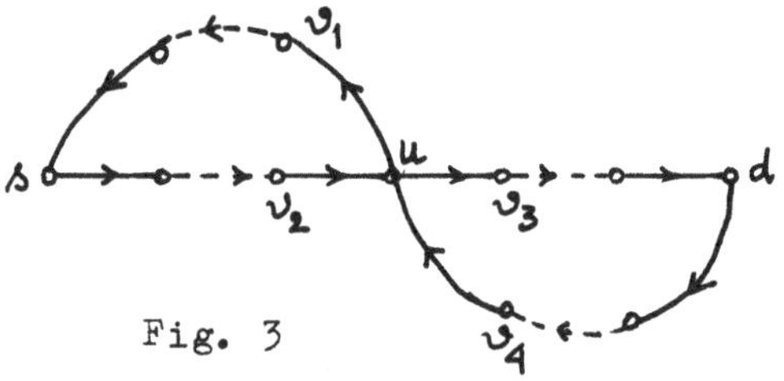

Fig. 3

Consider node u and its four adjacent vertices v_1, v_2, v_3 and v_4. The configurations of possible transition functions around node u are shown in Fig. 4.

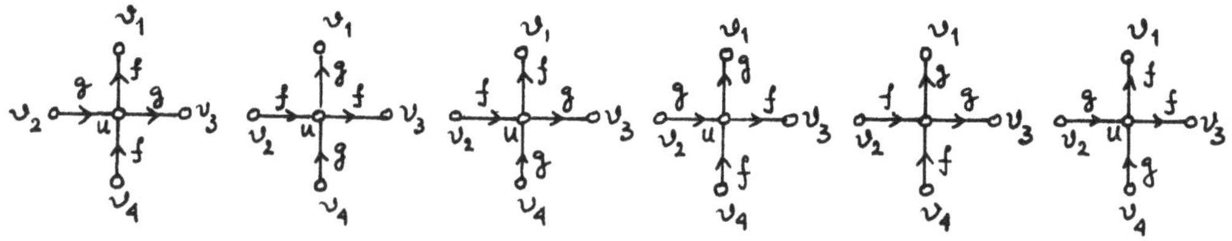

Fig.4 a b c d e f

Note that in Figs. 4e and 4f, nodes v_1 and v_3 must be nondistinct and so does the pair v_2 and v_4. Clearly, these two situations come under case-2 as described earlier. Therefore, the only configurations which are to be considered are those shown in Figs. 4a - 4d. We will be considering only the case shown in 4a, which is redrawn in Fig. 5. The proof for the rest is similar.

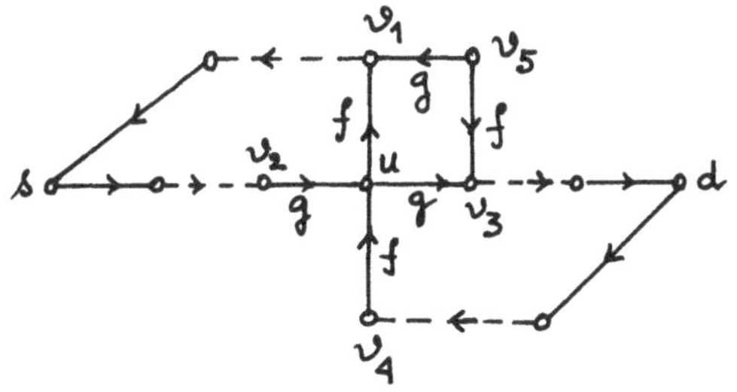

Fig. 5

If we now concentrate on node u in Fig. 5, it is quite obvious that by lemma 3, there must exist a vertex v_5 in G which is adjacent to both v_1 and v_3. Consider now two vertex-disjoint paths P and P' such that,

$$P = (s \text{ to } v_2) || (v_2 \text{ to } u) || (u \text{ to } v_4) || (v_4 \text{ to } d)$$

$$P' = (s \text{ to } v_1) || (v_1 \text{ to } v_5) || (v_5 \text{ to } v_3) || (v_3 \text{ to } d).$$

Since $|P_1| + |P_2| \leq 2n$, it immediately follows that $|P| + |P'| \leq 2n$. Also note that vertices v_1 and v_5 may be nondistinct (as pointed out in Remark, Lemma 3), but this can not jeopardize the construction of the above two paths P and P'. On the other hand, if u and v_3 are non-distinct, then $f(v_5) = f(v_4) = u$, implying that v_4 and v_5 are coincident and in that case we can make $P = P_1$ and $P' = (s \text{ to } v_1) ||$ $(v_1 \text{ to } v_4) || (v_4 \text{ to } d)$. Moreover, if v_5 is incident somewhere on P_1 or on P_2, similar vertex-disjoint paths of total length $\leq 2n$ can be constructed. The argument can also be generalized if P_2 intersects P_1 more than once. Q.E.D.

III. Optimal Routing Using Heuristic Search

Having established the above properties, we can now suitably adapt the heuristic search formulation of the problem of computing the optimal path from a given source vertex to a given destination vertex in the following way. In the graph G, consider the given source vertex s to be start node or the root node [6], and the given destination vertex d to be the goal node. All arcs in the graph are assumed to be of unit cost because the delay in communication from one processor to any of its adjacent processors is constant. We now use the algorithm C [7] to compute the optimal path from s to d. In this algorithm we use the following evaluation function $\hat{f}(v)$ for any node v in G to direct the search :

$$\hat{f}(v) = \hat{g}(v) + \hat{h}(v)$$

where $\hat{g}(v)$ is the cost of the best path currently known from the start node s to the node v, and $\hat{h}(v)$ represents the heuristic estimate assigned to this node v. The choice of this heuristic estimate for different nodes in the search graph will critically determine the search results. We propose three independent procedures to assign the heuristic estimates to the nodes, once the start node s and the destination node d are given.

Heuristic I : For a given start node s and destination node d, the heuristic estimate assigned to each node v in the graph is given by :

$$\hat{h}(v) = \left| r(v) - r(d) \right| .$$

Heuristic II : For a given start node s and destination node d, the heuristic estimate assigned to each node v in the graph is given by :

$$h(v) = \left| w(v) - w(d) \right| .$$

Heuristic III : Given a start node s and a destination node d, any other node v in G of order n, assigned a heuristic estimate h as :

$$\hat{h}(v) = [n - M(v,d)]$$

where the function M(v,d) returns the length of the maximal common subsequence existing in between the binary representations of nodes v and d.

While either of these methods is used to assign the heuristic estimates of the nodes in the graph, the search algorithm can now be framed in the light of algorithm C [7]. Here OPEN and CLOSED are two simple lists which are initially empty, and F is a real variable. By convention, the start as well as the destination node is assigned zero heuristic estimate.

Algorithm : Generation of optimal path (minimum length) from s to d.

Step 1 : OPEN $\leftarrow$ s and F $\leftarrow 0$, $\hat{g}(s) \leftarrow 0$, $\hat{f}(s) \leftarrow 0$.

Step 2 : Select a set (F_1) of nodes from OPEN, such that $F_1 = \left\{ v \mid v \in \text{OPEN, and } \hat{f}(v) \leq F \right\}$. Select node m from F_1 such that $\hat{g}(m)$ is the smallest. If F_1 is empty, consider those nodes in OPEN with minimum $\hat{f}$ value, and select from them the node m with minimum $\hat{g}$, and set $F \leftarrow \hat{f}(m)$. Ties are to be resolved arbitrarily but always in favour of a goal node. Remove m from OPEN and put it in CLOSED.

Step 3 : If m is the destination node d, then exit with $\hat{f}(m)$ as the output.

Step 4 : Expand node m to generate all its immediate successors (if none, go to step 2). For each immediate successor m' of m, set $g' \leftarrow \hat{g}(m) + 1$.

Step 5 : If m' is not already in either OPEN or CLOSED, set $\hat{g}(m') \leftarrow g'$ and $\hat{f}(m') \leftarrow g' + \hat{h}(m')$. Put m' in OPEN.

Step 6 : If m' is already in OPEN or CLOSED, and $\hat{g}(m') > g'$, then set $\hat{g}(m') \leftarrow g'$ and $\hat{f}(m') \leftarrow g' + \hat{h}(m')$. If m' is in CLOSED, remove it and put it in OPEN.

Step 7 : Go to step 2.

Definition 3 : A heuristic estimate $\hat{h}$ is admissible [7], if for all nodes $v \in G$, $\hat{h}(v) \leq h(v)$, where h(v) denotes the actual minimal cost from v to d.

Theorem 6a : Heuristic I is admissible.

Proof : We are to show that for any node v in the graph G, $\hat{h}(v) \leq h(v)$, where h(v) denotes the minimal distance of v from the destination node d. Using theorem 1, the result readily follows. Q.E.D.

Theorem 6b : Heuristic II is admissible.

Proof : Immediate from theorem 2. Q.E.D.

Theorem 6c : Heuristic III is admissible.

Proof : It immediately follows from the fact that M(d,d) = n and if v_1 and v_2 are two adjacent vertices in G, then $|M(v_1,d) - M(v_2,d)| \leq 1$. Q.E.D.

Theorem 7 : The proposed search algorithm will always compute the optimal path in between any pair of start node and destination node in G when either heuristic I or II or III is used.

Proof : Follows from theorem 3.1 [7], since under either of the heuristic estimates, the search is admissible. Q.E.D.

Theorem 8 : The proposed algorithm makes $\mathcal{O}(N^2)$ node expansions at worst, where $N(= 2^n)$ is the total number of nodes in the graph.

Proof : Same as theorem 3.3 [7]. Q.E.D.

It may be noted in this context that heuristic III requires more computational effort for assignment of the estimates to different nodes, as compared to those required in heuristic I or II. On the other hand, under heuristic III, the algorithm in general, outputs the optimal path more quickly, because this estimate, while being admissible as well, reflects a better measure of the actual minimal cost, compared to what are obtainable by the other two.

IV. Conclusion

The proposed algorithm can always compute true optimal path between any pair of nodes in the distrubuted network, and the actual message can then be communicated via this path using the same transmission mechanism, as suggested in [1]. This will result in minimum transmission delay for each message to be transmitted and consequently in minimum network congestion. Another interesting feature of this heuristic search algorithm is that it can perform equally well when any node in the graph is known to be faulty. Since by theorem 5, there exist at least two vertex-disjoint paths between any pair of nodes in G, this can be accomplished by checking the presence of any known faulty node in the list OPEN at every stage of node expansion in the algorithm and deleting it from the OPEN list unconditionally without putting it into CLOSED. However, under such a condition, the path generated by the algorithm may not be the minimal path from the given start node to the destination node if the faulty vertex lies on the minimal path.

References

[1] D.K. Pradhan and S.M. Reddy, 'A fault-tolerant communication architecture for distributed systems', IEEETC, Vol. C-31, pp. 863 - 870, Sept. 1982.

[2] D.K. Pradhan, 'Interconnection topologies for fault-tolerant parallel and distributed architectures', Proc. 1981 Int. Conf. on Parallel Processing, Aug. 1981, pp. 238 - 242.

[3] N.G. De Bruijn, 'A combinatorial problem', Proc. Akademe Van Wetenschappen, Vol. 49, part 2, 1946, pp. 758 - 764.

[4] W.E. Leland and M.H. Solomon, 'Dense trivalent graphs for processor interconnection', IEEETC, Vol. C-31, pp. 219 - 222, March 1982.

[5] B.W. Arden and H. Lee, 'A multi-tree structured network', Proc. COMPCON, Fall 1 - 78, pp. 201 - 210.

[6] N.J. Nilsson, Principles of Artificial Intelligence, Tioga, 1980.

[7] A. Bagchi and A. Mahanti, 'Search algorithmsunder different kinds of heuristics - a comparative study', JACM, Vol. 30, pp. 1 -21, January 1983.

[8] F. Harary, Graph Theory, Addison Wesley Publishing Co., 1969.

[9] S.W. Golomb, Shift Register Sequences, Holden-Day Inc., 1967.

REPLACEMENT IN MONOTONE BOOLEAN NETWORKS: AN ALGEBRAIC PERSPECTIVE.

Meurig Beynon

Dept. of Computer Science, University of Warwick,
COVENTRY CV4 7AL, UK.

ABSTRACT

Replacement rules have played an important role in the study of monotone boolean function complexity. In this paper, notions of replaceability and computational equivalence are formulated in an abstract algebraic setting, and examined in detail for finite distributive lattices - the appropriate algebraic context for monotone boolean functions. It is shown that when computing an element f of a finite distributive lattice D, the elements of D partition into classes of computationally equivalent elements, and define a quotient of D in which all intervals of the form $[t \wedge f, t \vee f]$ are boolean. This quotient is an abstract simplicial complex with respect to ordering by replaceability. Possible applications of computational equivalence in developing upper and lower bounds on monotone boolean function complexity are indicated, and new directions of research, both abstract mathematical and computational, are suggested.

Introduction.

In studying the complexity of monotone boolean networks, the notion of replaceability has proved to be a useful concept. Research in this area has been concerned with the formulation of general replacement rules (e.g.[P] and [MG]), the use of replacement techniques in proving bounds on network size (e.g.[P], [MG], [D1] and [W]), and more recently, the investigation of closed forms for particular kinds of replacement ([D2]). In this paper, which is abstracted from [B1], replaceability is studied as a relation on an algebra, rather than applied as a technique in connection with a specific class of functions or circuits. Motivation for this approach is given in §7 below.

If f, g and h are monotone boolean functions, a replacement rule has the form " when computing f, replacement of g by h is universally valid ". From the algebraic perspective of this paper, f, g and h are viewed as elements of a free distributive lattice L (see §1 below); such a rule may then be reformulated " an expression for f in terms of g and a set of generators of L, still represents f if g is replaced by h ". In this way, replaceability modulo f defines a relation on the algebra L. It can be shown that this relation is well-defined not only when a general distributive lattice is substituted for L, but when L is a general algebra. Indeed, under very general hypotheses, replaceability modulo an element f defines a pre-order (a reflexive and transitive relation $\sqsubset_f$) on an algebra L, and the equivalence relation $\Box_f$ derived by imposing anti-symmetry is an algebraic congruence called " computational equivalence modulo f ". The quotient algebra $L/\Box_f$ is then ordered by $\sqsubset_f$.

This paper formulates replaceability and computational equivalence in a general algebraic setting and outlines the results on replaceability and computational equivalence in finite distributive lattices proved in [B1]. These include generalisations and extensions of known theorems concerning replacement rules for monotone boolean networks. There are good reasons for dealing with general finite distributive lattices rather than simply the lattices of monotone boolean functions traditionally studied in theoretical computer science. This degree of generality is necessary (for instance) when reasoning about circuits to compute a representative g of a particular computational equivalence class modulo f. Besides, by its very nature, the abstract algebraic perspective on computational equivalence cannot be appreciated within the context of the specific subset of free finite distributive lattices.

For proofs of the results summarised below, the interested reader is referred to [B1]. It is worth remarking that most of the proofs use lattice-theoretic arguments based upon finiteness and distributivity, and do not require the assumption of freeness.

§1. Replaceability and computational equivalence.

Suppose that A is an Ω-algebra, and that $F \subseteq A$. A preorder relation $\sqsubseteq_F$ associated with F is defined by $h \sqsubseteq_F g$ (also written $g \sqsupseteq_F h$) if for all f in F:

" given an Ω-word w, and elements $a_1, a_2, \ldots, a_n$ in A:

if $w(g, a_1, a_2, \ldots, a_n) = f$ then $w(h, a_1, a_2, \ldots, a_n) = f$ ".

That is, for each f in F, an Ω-formula over A which represents f in terms of g still represents f when g is replaced by h.

With every preorder (reflexive, transitive relation) there is an equivalence relation defined by imposing antisymmetry. The elements g and h are *computationally equivalent* modulo F (written $g \, \Box_F \, h$) iff

$$g \sqsupseteq_F h \text{ and } h \sqsupseteq_F g;$$

the relation $\sqsupseteq_F$ then defines a partial order on the computational equivalence classes of $\Box_F$.

Note that equivalent definitions of $\sqsubseteq_F$ and $\Box_F$ are obtained if the elements $a_1, a_2, \ldots, a_n$ are constrained to lie in a particular generating set for A. For this reason, it may be assumed that $a_1, a_2, \ldots, a_n$ is a generating set for A. Intuitively, $\sqsubseteq_F$ and $\Box_F$ define replaceability and computational equivalence modulo F "relative to an input set which generates A". If $F = \{f\}$, it will be convenient to write $\sqsubseteq_f$ for $\sqsubseteq_F$, and $\Box_f$ for $\Box_F$.

Lemma 1.1.

If $f \in F \subseteq A$, then $\sqsupseteq_f$ respects the operations in Ω on A:

if $\omega \in \Omega$ has arity k, and $g_i \sqsubseteq_f h_i$ for $1 \leq i \leq k$, then

$$\omega(g_1, g_2, \ldots, g_k) \sqsubseteq_f \omega(h_1, h_2, \ldots, h_k),$$

and $\sqsubseteq_F = \bigcap \{ \sqsubseteq_f \mid f \in F \}$.

Moreover: $\Box_f$ is an Ω-congruence on A, and $\Box_F = \bigcap \{ \Box_f \mid f \in F \}$. ∎

If α is an equivalence relation on a set S, and the equivalence class of s contains a single element, s will be called *solitary under* α, or simply *solitary* where the equivalence relation is clear from the context.

Lemma 1.2.

$\sqsubseteq_F$ is the unique maximal preorder relation on A respecting the operations in Ω such that all elements in F are minimal (i.e: if $f \in F$ and $g \sqsubseteq_F f$, then $g = f$.)

$\Box_F$ is the unique maximal Ω-congruence on A such that each f in F is solitary.

Lemma 1.2 shows that computational equivalence is a trivial relation in the context of many choices of Ω. For instance, if A is a group or ring, a congruence class will be a coset of a subgroup containing 2 or more elements in a non-trivial case. In particular, if A is a Boolean algebra (where $\Omega = \{\wedge, \vee, '\}$), then $\sqsupset_f$ is trivial. Even if A is regarded as a boolean *lattice* (where $\Omega = \{\wedge, \vee\}$), $\sqsupset_f$ is still trivial, since any congruence which respects $\wedge$ and $\vee$ also respects complements.

Where computational equivalence is trivial, the preorder by replaceability may still be of interest. For instance, in a boolean lattice B, it is easy to verify by Lemma 1.2 (c.f. [B1] Cor.4.4) that:

$$\text{given } f,g,h \in B\text{: } g \sqsubset_f h \text{ iff } g+f \leq h+f,$$

where '+' denotes boolean addition. Thus $\sqsubset_f$ is an order relation in this case, and $(B, \sqsubset_f)$ is a boolean lattice isomorphic to $(B,\leq)$. Viewing B as a Boolean algebra, on the other hand, both $\sqsupset_f$ and $\sqsubset_f$ are trivial: if $\prec$ is an order on B respecting $\{\wedge, \vee, '\}$, and $g \prec h$, then

$$1 = g \vee g' \prec g \vee h' \prec h \vee h' = 1,$$

whence $h' \vee g = 1$; similarly $h' \wedge g = 0$, and $h=g$.

To illustrate the generality of the concepts introduced above, it may be observed that if g,h and f are elements of a commutative semi-group S, then

$$g \sqsubset_f h \text{ iff } gx=f \text{ in S whenever } hx=f \text{ in S.}$$

In particular, if f=4, and $S=(\mathbb{Z}_{12},\cdot)$, then the residues 2, 4, 8, and 10 are solitary, and the remaining equivalence classes for $\sqsupset_f$ are [1 7], [5 11] and [0 3 6 9]. The ordering $\sqsubset_f$ on $S/\sqsupset_f$ in this case is defined by

$$4 \sqsubset_f 10 \sqsubset_f 1 \text{ and } 8 \sqsubset_f 2 \sqsubset_f 5.$$

(For more details, see [BB].)

Replaceability and computational equivalence on finite distributive lattices are discussed below.

§2. Preliminaries on finite distributive lattices.

A distributive lattice is defined by taking $\Omega = \{\wedge, \vee\}$, where $\wedge$ and $\vee$ are associative, commutative, and idempotent binary operators, and $\wedge$ distributes over $\vee$ (and vice versa). In this context, Ω-words are frequently described as "monotone boolean functions". The family of monotone boolean functions in literals $x_1, x_2, \ldots, x_n$, ordered by "implication", form the free distributive lattice on n generators, which will be denoted by FDL(n). For background on the simple properties of finite distributive lattices cited below, see [G] or [B].

Distributive lattices form a class of algebras in which non-trivial computational equivalences can arise. As a simple example (see Fig.1), let

$D=FDL(3)$, the distributive lattice freely generated by $\{x_1, x_2, x_3\}$, and let $f = x_1 \vee (x_2 \wedge x_3)$. If $t = x_1 \wedge (x_2 \vee x_3)$, then the $\{\wedge,\vee\}$-congruence defined by $g \equiv h$ iff $g \vee t = h \vee t$ is non-trivial, and is easily identified as $\Box_f$ using Lemma 0.2. It is important to observe that computational equivalence is not necessarily preserved when a quotient is taken; this in particular justifies consideration of general rather than simply free distributive lattices. As an illustration, let D and f be as in the example above. Then

$$x_2 \wedge x_3 \, \Box_f \, T_2^3 = (x_1 \wedge x_2) \vee (x_3 \wedge (x_1 \vee x_2)),$$

but there are quotients of D in which f is identified with T_2^3 but not with $x_2 \wedge x_3$.

An element z in a lattice L is *meet-irreducible* if z is not the largest element of L, and z cannot be expressed as $a \wedge b$ where a and b are in $L \setminus \{z\}$. Dually, z is *join-irreducible* if z is not the smallest element of L, and cannot be expressed as $a \vee b$ where a and b are in $L \setminus \{z\}$.

Let D be a finite distributive lattice. In D, every element has a unique representation as a join of incomparable join-irreducibles and dually. If p is a join-irreducible of D, the complement of $p\uparrow \equiv \{z \mid z \geq p\}$ has the form

$$\tilde{p}\downarrow \equiv \{z \mid z \leq \tilde{p}\},$$

where $\tilde{p}$ is a meet-irreducible, and dually. There is a 1-1 correspondence $p \leftrightarrow \tilde{p}$ between meet-irreducibles and join-irreducibles in D; via this correspondence, the subsets of meet-irreducibles and join-irreducibles are canonically isomorphic as posets under the ordering of D. The lattice D is determined up to isomorphism by poset of meet-irreducibles Q. When the ordering on Q is trivial, D is complemented and will be referred to as a boolean lattice. Note that this term is used to refer to D as a $\{\wedge,\vee\}$-algebra, rather than a Boolean algebra.

Viewed as monotone boolean functions, the meet-irreducibles (resp. join-irreducibles) in FDL(n) are sums (resp. products) of literals, and the canonical representation of an element as a meet of meet-irreducibles (resp. join of join-irreducibles) is the CNF (resp. DNF). If p is a product of literals, then $\tilde{p}$ is the sum of those literals which do not appear in p. The subset of meet-irreducibles for FDL(n) is the set of proper subsets of an n-element set, ordered by inclusion.

Meet- and join-irreducibles have a prominent role below, and some special notation is helpful. If X is a subset of the meet-irreducibles of D, and $g \in D$, then X[g] will be used to denote

$$\{q \mid q \in X \text{ and } q \geq g\},$$

and $\tilde{X}$ the set of join-irreducibles of the form $\tilde{q}$ where $q \in X$. Dually, if Y is a subset of the join-irreducibles of D, then Y[g] will be used to denote

$$\{p \mid p \in Y \text{ and } p \leq g\},$$

and $\tilde{Y}$ the set of meet-irreducibles of the form $\tilde{p}$ where $p \in Y$.

If $S \subseteq D$ the join of all elements in S will be denoted by $\bigvee S$, and dually.

For convenience, the term "congruence" will be used as a synonym for Ω-congruence, where $\Omega = \{\wedge, \vee\}$. If α is a lattice homomorphism, the ***kernel*** of α (denoted by Ker α), is the congruence defined by

$$(a,b) \in \text{Ker } \alpha \text{ iff } \alpha(a)=\alpha(b).$$

§3. Replaceability and computational equivalence in distributive lattices.

Let D be a finite distributive lattice, and let $f \in D$. (Only replacement and computational equivalence with respect to computing a single element is considered below, but the generalisation to a subset F is easy in view of Lemma 1.1.) Define

$P_f \equiv$ set of maximal elements amongst join-irreducibles $\leq f$,

$Q_f \equiv$ set of minimal elements amongst meet-irreducibles $\geq f$.

f is then the irredundant join of the join-irreducibles in P_f, and dually.

Theorem 3.1:

$g \sqsubset_f h$ iff $P_f[g] \supseteq P_f[h]$ and $Q_f[g] \supseteq Q_f[h]$.

Thus $g \,\square_f\, h$ iff $P_f[g]=P_f[h]$ and $Q_f[g]=Q_f[h]$.

∎

Note that when D=FDL(n), the sets P_f and Q_f defined in Theorem 1.2 are the "prime implicants" and the "dual prime implicants" (or "prime clauses") of f respectively. Theorem 3.1 thus shows that if f and g are monotone boolean functions the computational role which g can play in computing f is totally determined by its relationship to the set of prime implicants and prime clauses of f.

As a particular consequence, it may be seen that if $f \in FDL[k] \subseteq FDL[n]$, then g and h in FDL[k] are computationally equivalent modulo f relative to FDL[k] iff they are computationally equivalent modulo f relative to FDL[n]. In general, if $f \in D \in K$, where D and K are finite distributive lattices, computational equivalence of elements of D modulo f relative to D and relative to K differ, since embedding D into K may alter the set of meet-irreducibles. For example, if K is the boolean closure of D, then $\square_f$ is trivial relative to K.

For monotone boolean functions, a complete description of all functional replacements which are valid when computing a fixed function f are described by Dunne in [D2] Theorem 3. The following consequence of Theorem 3.1 is the generalisation of Dunne's theorem to an arbitrary finite distributive lattice:

Cor.3.2.

$g \sqsubset_f h$ iff $g \in [\bigvee P_f[h], \bigwedge Q_f[h]]$ iff $h \in [\bigvee \tilde{Q}_f[g], \bigwedge \tilde{P}_f[g]]$

$g \Box_f h$ iff $h \in [\bigvee P_f[g] \vee \bigvee \tilde{Q}_f[g] , \bigwedge \tilde{P}_f[g] \wedge \bigwedge Q_f[g]]$.

∎

The special case when g is 0 or 1 provides generalisations of a replacement rule due to Mehlhorn (c.f. [M] and [D2]):

Cor.3.3.

For f in D, define

$$z(f) = \bigwedge \tilde{P}_f , \; u(f) = \bigvee \tilde{Q}_f , \; \mu(f) = f \vee u(f) \text{ and } \lambda(f) = f \wedge z(f).$$

If h is in D, then

$0 \sqsubset_f h$ iff $h \in [\, 0 , z(f)\,]$, and $1 \sqsubset_f h$ iff $h \in [\, u(f) , 1\,]$.

$0 \Box_f h$ iff $h \in [\, 0 , \lambda(f)\,]$, and $1 \Box_f h$ iff $h \in [\, \mu(f) , 1\,]$.

∎

Suppose that F is a subset of the finite distributive lattice D. A problem similar to that of "computing all the elements of F" is that of "computing an element of F, irrespective of which". Computational equivalence in the context of such a problem is meaningful provided that F can be a congruence class for D i.e. provided that F is an interval $[f_0, f_1]$. The appropriate quotient of D is then obtained by identifying f_0 and f_1 in D and taking computational equivalence relative to the class of f_0 and f_1, and coincides with the quotient obtained by identifying f_0 and f_1 in $D/\Box_f$. An analogue of Theorem 3.1 in which P_f and Q_f are respectively replaced by P_{f_0} and Q_{f_1} then applies.

§4. The structure of $(D/\Box_f, \leq)$.

The class of finite distributive lattices of the form $D/\Box_f$ is a special subclass, and is associated with pairs (D,f) for which the congruence $\Box_f$ is trivial on D. The results summarised in this section concern the structure of the $(D/\Box_f, \leq)$ and its relationship to D and f.

A simple corollary to Theorem 3.1 shows that the poset of meet-irreducibles of $D/\Box_f$ is isomorphic with the ordered subset $X_f \equiv P_f \,\dot{\cup}\, \tilde{Q}_f$ of D. The only possible order relations within X_f have the form $q \geq \tilde{p}$ where $p \in P_f$, $q \in Q_f$; in particular, the longest chain in X_f is of length 2. It can be deduced that all intervals of the form $[t \wedge f, t \vee f]$ in $D/\Box_f$ are boolean lattices. In fact, finite distributive lattices of the form $D/\Box_f$ are characterised by

Lemma 4.1:

$\square_f$ is trivial on D iff f↑ and f↓ are boolean.

∎

From a computational viewpoint, the map $D \to D/\square_f$ is of interest. The congruence $\square_f$ contains the pairs $(0,\lambda(f))$ and $(\mu(f),1)$, and can be shown to be generated by these pairs:

Theorem 4.2:

$D/\square_f$ and $D/\langle\lambda(f)=0,\mu(f)=1\rangle$ are isomorphic.

∎

That is (using the elementary theory of congruences on distributive lattices): $\square_f$ is the kernel of the map $e_f{:}D \to D$ defined by

$$e_f(z) = (z \vee \lambda(f)) \wedge \mu(f).$$

Since e_f is a retract it follows that $D/\square_f$ and $[\lambda(f),\mu(f)]$ are isomorphic. By Lemma 4.1, the intervals $[\lambda(f),f]$ and $[f,\mu(f)]$ are then boolean; indeed, $\lambda(f)$ is the unique minimal element in D such that $[\lambda(f),f]$ is boolean, and dually.

The above results combine to give some insight into the structure of lattices of the form $D/\square_f$, and show in particular that the appropriate algebraic model for studying the computation of a particular monotone boolean function is a distributive lattice with a particularly simple structure. In many cases, $D/\square_f$ is a boolean lattice; the problem of computing f is then equivalent to a pure set-theoretic problem of the form:

" given a target set S, and input sets $X_1, X_2, \ldots, X_n$, find a formula/circuit to represent S in terms of $X_1, X_2, \ldots, X_n$ using ∩'s and ∪'s."

As an incidental consequence of the above results, it can be shown that not all lattices of the form $D/\square_f$ arise by computational equivalence relations on a free distributive lattice; a further justification for developing the theory for general finite distributive lattices.

§5. The structure of the poset $(D/\square_f, \sqsubset_f)$.

If f and g are elements of a finite distributive lattice D, it is clear that

$$f \wedge g \sqsubset_f g \quad \text{and} \quad f \vee g \sqsubset_f g.$$

Suppose now that $\square_f$ is trivial on D. Cor.3.2 then takes the form:

$$h \sqsubset_f g \ \text{ iff } \ h \in [g \wedge f, g \vee f] \ \text{ iff } \ [h \wedge f, h \vee f] \subseteq [g \wedge f, g \vee f].$$

Thus - when $\square_f$ is trivial - the map which associates with h the interval $B(h) \equiv [h \wedge f, h \vee f]$ (a boolean lattice) identifies $(D/\square_f, \sqsubset_f)$ as the poset of intervals of the form B(h) for h in D, ordered by inclusion.

If D is a boolean lattice, and $f,g,h \in D$, then

$$g \sqsubset_f h \text{ iff } B(h) \supseteq B(g) \text{ iff } g+f \leq h+f$$

whence $(D, \sqsubset_f)$ and $(D, \leq)$ are isomorphic. In general, $(D/\Box_f, \sqsubset_f)$ is a decreasing subset of a boolean lattice, or "abstract simplicial complex." The maximal simplices in this complex are associated with elements g in $D/\Box_f$ such that $[g \wedge f, g \vee f]$ is maximal amongst intervals of this type.

Since $\sqsubset_f$ respects $\wedge$ and $\vee$, it is easy to verify that if b lies between a and c in $(D/\Box_f, \leq)$, and $a \sqsubset_f c$, then b also lies between a and c in $(D/\Box_f, \sqsubset_f)$. In particular, there are simplices in the complex $(D/\Box_f, \sqsubset_f)$ corresponding directly to the boolean intervals $f\uparrow$ and $f\downarrow$ in $(D/\Box_f, \leq)$. It also follows that $\{y \mid y \sqsubset_f z(f)\}$ is a maximal simplex (and dually); if $g \geq z(f)$ then $g \sqsupset_f 0$, whence $0 \leq g \leq z(f)$, and $g \sqsubset_f z(f)$.

The complex $(D/\Box_f, \sqsubset_f)$ has an alternative characterisation in terms of the poset of meet-irreducibles X_f of $D/\Box_f$: the simplicial complex $(D/\Box_f, \sqsubset_f)$ is isomorphic with the family of trivially ordered subsets of $P_f \,\dot\cup\, \widetilde{Q}_f$ ordered by inclusion.

The existence and nature of the ordering $\sqsubset_f$ consistent with the lattice operations on $(D/\Box_f, \leq)$ (c.f. Lemma 1.1) is perhaps the most unexpected and intriguing aspect of the study of computational equivalence and replaceabilty on distributive lattices. The characterisation of $(D/\Box_f, \sqsubset_f)$ as an abstract simplicial complex is geometric rather than algebraic, and is particularly suggestive in view of the well-established connections (see [B2], [B3] and [B4]) between simplicial complexes (resp. polyhedra) and distributive lattices (resp. vector lattices). It is reasonable to conjecture that the monotone complexity of a monotone boolean function f is related to the geometry of the complex $(FDL(n)/\Box_f, \sqsubset_f)$ and the functional classes associated with its simplices, but no simple relationship of this type is immediately apparent.

§6. The functions μ, λ, u and z.

The above results show that the computation of f in D can be interpreted within the interval $[\lambda(f), \mu(f)]$. By Theorem 4.2, this interval determines $\Box_f$ but not f, and it is of interest to examine the properties of the maps λ and μ more closely with a view to understanding which intervals $[\lambda(f), \mu(f)]$ can arise.

It can be shown that μ (resp. λ) is a $\vee$-morphism on D, whence $\mu(D)$ is a closure lattice in D. For n=4, the lattice $\mu(FDL(n))$ is depicted in Fig.1; it may be noted that the sublattice generated by $\mu(x_1)$, $\mu(x_2)$, $\mu(x_3)$ is FDL(3). The latter observation generalises to n>4, but the structure of $\mu(FDL(n)$ appears otherwise difficult to analyse.

There are a number of relations between the maps λ, μ, u and z. From Cor.3.3, the maps u and z are readily seen to be inverse bijections on D, so that (for instance) $f \vee z(f) = \mu z(f)$.

From §5, it may be seen that $(D/\square_f, \leq)$ is boolean iff $(D/\square_f, \sqsubset_f)$ is boolean iff u(f) and z(f) both represent the same class under $\square_f$ (viz. the largest element of $D/\square_f$). Since u(f) and z(f) are respectively greatest and least representatives in D for their respective computational equivalence classes, it follows that

$$D/\square_f \text{ is boolean iff } u(f) \leq z(f).$$

The subcase u(f)=z(f) is curious. In this case:

$$Q_{z(f)} = \tilde{P}_f \text{ and } Q_f = \tilde{P}_{u(f)} = \tilde{P}_{z(f)},$$

so that by Cor.3.2: $g \sqsubset_f h$ iff $h \sqsubset_{z(f)} g$. Thus $\square_f = \square_{z(f)}$, but the orderings on the equivalence complexes associated with f and z(f) are dual. As an example, let $f=(x_1 \wedge x_2) \vee (x_2 \wedge x_3) \vee (x_3 \wedge x_4)$ in FDL(4).

To complement the abstract emphasis of the above results, it is appropriate to indicate how the relationship between f, $\square_f$ and $\mu(f)$ can be connected with the computation of f. The following result is a corollary of [B1] Theorem 6.1:

Theorem 6.1:

If $FDL(n)/\square_f$ is boolean, and $V(e_1, e_2, \ldots, e_n)$ is an arbitrary boolean expression such that $V(x_1, x_2, \ldots, x_n) = f$ in $FDL(n)/\square_f$, then

$$f = (V(x_1, x_2, \ldots, x_n) \vee \lambda(f)) \wedge \mu(f).$$

■

Interpreting the theorem: if a general boolean computation computes f from the inputs $x_1, x_2, \ldots, x_n$ under hypothetical special constraints on the inputs (viz. $\lambda(f)=0$ and $\mu(f)=1$), then it computes a function $\bar{f}$ such that $f = (\bar{f} \vee \lambda(f)) \wedge \mu(f)$. Since $\lambda(f)$ and $\mu(f)$ are frequently simpler to compute than f (e.g. they may be threshold functions), the above theorem suggests one way in which the design of a general boolean circuit to compute f may sometimes be simplified without incurring a large increase in complexity.

As a corollary to Theorem 6.1:

Cor.6.2.

If $FDL(n)/\square_f$ is boolean, there exist monotone boolean functions $h_1, h_2, \ldots, h_n$ with the following property: if w is a monotone boolean expression such that $w(x_1, x_2, \ldots, x_n, h_1, h_2, \ldots, h_n) = f$ then

$$f = (w(x_1, x_2, \ldots, x_n, x_1', x_2', \ldots, x_n') \vee \lambda(f)) \wedge \mu(f).$$

§7. Further directions for research.

Much of the research described here was motivated by a search for invariants (if they exist) which determine the complexity of a monotone boolean function. As explained above, it seems likely that such invariants are associated with the algebra $(D/\square_f, \leq, \sqsubset_f)$, and might be of both an algebraic and/or geometric nature.

Specific applications of replacement techniques abound in monotone boolean function complexity, and it is to be hoped that the abstract approach adopted here lends clarity, and may allow refinement and extension of such methods.

A deeper understanding of computational equivalence is probably needed for further applications. For instance, the characterisation of monotone boolean functions f such that $FDL(n)/\square_f$ is boolean (c.f. Theorem 6.1) is obscure, and there is much scope for further algebraic and algorithmic investigation of such problems.

Finally, it would be useful to find other classes of algebras for which computational equivalence is of interest. Some initial work in this direction is described in [BB].

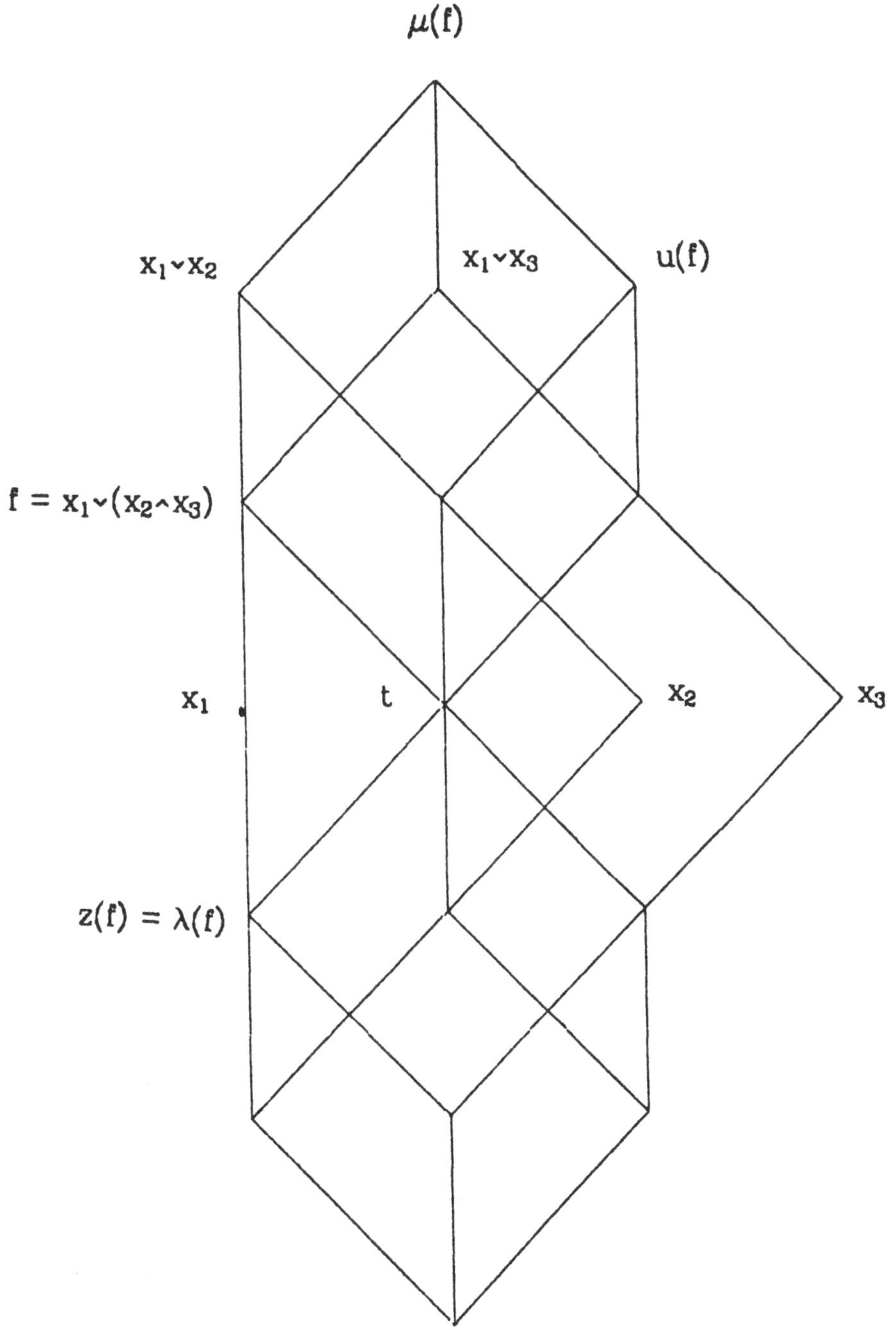

Fig 1a: $f = x_1 \vee (x_2 \wedge x_3)$ in FDL(3).

FDL(3)/ $\square_f$ is isomorphic with the interval $[\lambda(f), \mu(f)]$

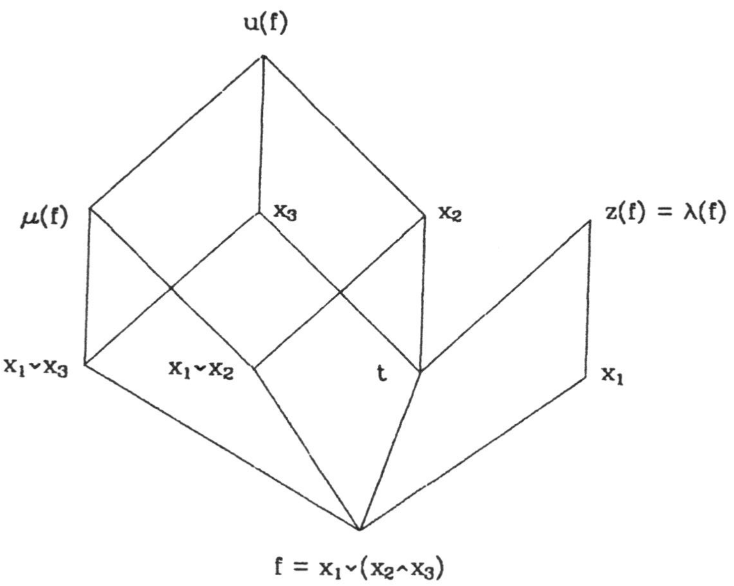

Fig 1b: The complex (FDL(3)/ $\sqsupset_f$, $\sqsubset_f$) with nodes labelled by representatives of the equivalence classes.

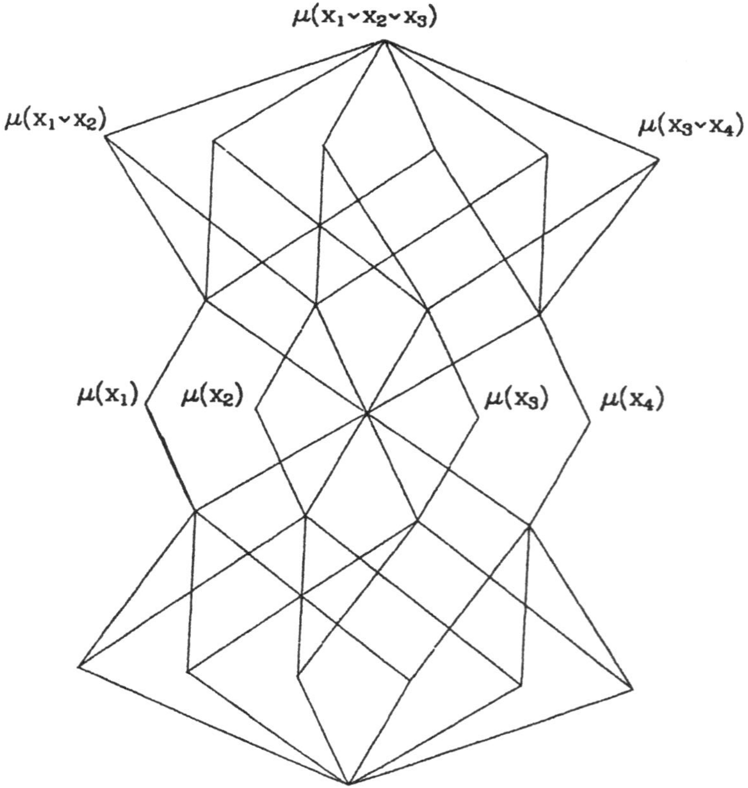

Fig.2: The closure lattice μ(FDL(4)).

References.

[B1] Beynon, W.M.
Replaceability and computational equivalence in finite distributive lattices.
Theory of Computation Report 61, Univ. of Warwick, 1984.

[B2] Beynon, W.M.
Geometric aspects of partially-ordered systems,
Ph.D. thesis, King's College, Univ. of London, 1973.

[B3] Beynon, W.M.
Duality theorems for finitely-generated vector lattices,
Proc.Lond.Math.Soc. (3) 31, 114-128, 1975.

[B4] Beynon, W.M.
Vector lattices freely generated by distributive lattices,
Math.Proc.Camb.Phil.Soc. (81), 193-220, 1977.

[BB] Beynon, W.M. & Buckle, J.F.
Computational equivalence and replaceability in commutative semigroups.
<in preparation>

[B] Birkhoff, G.A.
Lattice Theory, 3rd ed.
AMS Colloquium Publications, Vol.XXV, 1967.

[D1] Dunne, P.E.
A 2.5n lower bound on the monotone network complexity of T_3^n,
Theory of Computation Report 62, Univ. of Warwick, 1984.

[D2] Dunne, P.E.
Some results on replacement rules in monotone boolean networks,
Theory of Computation Report 64, Univ. of Warwick, 1984.

[G] Grätzer, G.
Lattice Theory: first concepts and distributive lattices,
W.H.Freeman and Co., San Francisco, 1971.

[M] Mehlhorn, K. & Galil, Z.
Monotone switching networks and boolean matrix product,
Computing (16), 99-111, 1976.

[P] Paterson, M.S.
Complexity of monotone networks for boolean matrix product,
Theoretical Computer Science (1), 13-20, 1975.

[W] Wegener, I
On the complexity of slice-functions,
Internal Report, Univ. Of Frankfurt, July 1983.

A New Characterization of BPP

Stathis Zachos
Dept. of Comp. and Inf. Sci.
Brooklyn College of the City University of New York
Brooklyn, New York 11210

Hans Heller
Techn. Universität München
München, W-Germany

Abstract

The complexity class BPP contains languages that can be solved in polynomial time with bounded error probability. It is shown that a language L is in BPP iff ($x \in L \leftrightarrow \exists_m y\ \forall z\ P(x,y,z)$) and ($x \notin L \leftrightarrow \forall y\ \exists_m z \neg P(x,y,z)$) for a polynomial time predicate P and for $|y|, |z| \leq poly(|x|)$. The formula $\exists_m y P(y)$ with the random quantifier $\exists_m$ means that the probability $Pr(\{y \mid P(y)\}) < 1/2 + \varepsilon$ for a fixed ε. Note that the weaker conditions $\exists y\ \forall z P(x,y,z)$ and $\forall y \exists z \neg P(x,y,z)$ are complementary and thus decide whether $x \in L$. Some of the consequences of the characterization of BPP are that various probabilistic polynomial time hierarchies collapse as well as that probabilistic oracles do not add anything to the computing power of classes as low as Σ_2^P. For example, $\Sigma_2^{P,\ BPP} = \Sigma_2^P$, where $\Sigma_2^{P,\ BPP}$ is the class Σ_2^P relativized to BPP.

Keywords: Probalistic algorithms, polynomial time complexity classes, oracles, polynomial hierarchies.

1. Introduction

Many arguments in the theory of cryptography make use of probabilisttic algorithms. A goal in cryptography is to construct encryption schemes, which cannot be broken by probabilistic algorithms. The assumption is that problems solvable by probabilistic algorithms are easy or tractable; supposedly well below NP-complete problems. But in reality little is known about the power of probabilistic algorithms, such as those in the class BPP. Our goal is to understand BPP and to classify it as well as possible among other polynomial time complexity classes.

Diagram 1 shows some of the known inclusion relations among polynomial time complexity classes. For detailed descriptions of the classes we refer the reader to [HU, GJ, G, Z1].

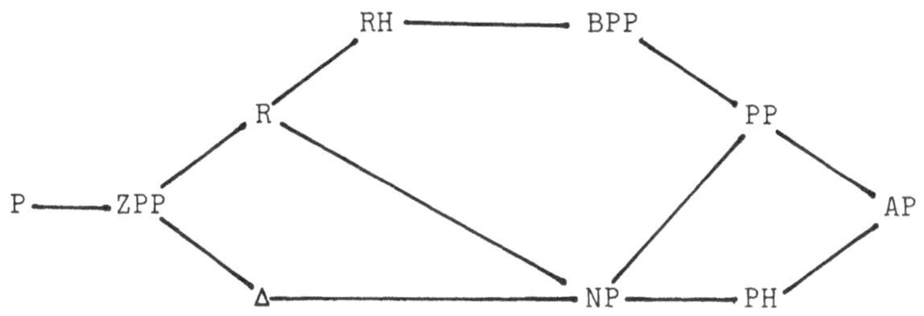

Diagram 1

We use some abbreviations:

1. In formulas describing $x \in L$ or $x \notin L$, quantifiers are restricted to to range over quantities with length at most a polynomial of the length of x. Thus for example

$$x \in L \leftrightarrow \exists y \, \forall z P(x,y,z)$$

for a polynomial time predicate P is an alternate characterization of $L \in NP^{NP}$ (NP with oracle from NP); see [St, W].

2. $\exists_m y P(x,y)$ means that there is an $\varepsilon > 0$ so that for all inputs x: $Pr(\{y \mid P(x,y)\}) > 1/2 + \varepsilon$.

Using these notations let us review the definitions of some of the above complexity classes:

<u>L in Polynomial Time P</u>: $x \in L \leftrightarrow P(x)$
for some polynomial time predicate P.

<u>L in Nondeterministic Polynomial Time NP</u>: $x \in L \leftrightarrow \exists y P(x,y)$
for some polynomial time predicate P.

<u>L in Random Polynomial Time R</u>: $(x \in L \leftrightarrow \exists_m y P(x,y))$ and
$(x \notin L \leftrightarrow \forall y \neg P(x,y))$
for some polynomial time predicate P.

$\underline{\Delta} = NP \cap \text{co-}NP$.

Zero Error Probability Polynomial time ZPP = $R \cap$ co-R

L in Bounded Error Probability Polynomial Time BPP:
$(x \in L \leftrightarrow \exists_m y P(x,y))$ and $(x \notin L \leftrightarrow \exists_m y \neg P(x,y))$
for some polynomial time predicate P.

Note that the above definition of R is decisive in the sense that $\exists y P(x,y)$ is enough to decide that $x \in L$, whereas for BPP this is not the case, because $\exists y P(x,y)$ and $\exists y \neg P(x,y)$ are not complementary.

L in Probabilistic Polynomial Time PP: $x \in L \leftrightarrow \Pr(\{y \mid P(x,y)\}) > 1/2$
for some polynomial time predicate P.

For definitions of the Polynomial Hierarchy PH, Alternating Polynomial Time AP, which is equal to PSPACE, and the Random Polynomial Hierarchy RH see [HU, CKS, Z2].

It is helpful to have an algorithmic model for the above complexity classes in order to intuitvely grasp properties of them. Nondeterministic polynomial time Turing machines are the most widely understood computing model. For precise definitions see e.g. [HU, GJ]. For example, in the case of P, all possible computation paths give the correct answer; in the case of ZPP, many paths give the correct answer, whereas the remaining paths give no answer at all (Las Vegas); in the case of Δ, there is at least one path that answers correctly, whereas the remaining paths give no answer at all; in the case of BPP many paths give the correct answer, whereas the few remaining ones may give a wrong answer (Monte Carlo). Computation trees for NP, R, PP also have the known structure.

A nondeterministic Turing machine can be augmented by a query tape and an oracle that can answer queries about some decision problem A without extra time costs. Thus for example, NP^{SAT} represents the class of problems that can be solved by a nondeterministic polynomial time Turing machine that can query an oracle for SAT. We can generalize this by allowing the oracle to be any one of some complexity class: $C_1^{C_2} = \{C_1^A \mid A \in C_2\}$. Intuitively, $C_1^{C_2}$ is the class of languages accepted by the machines that characterize the class C_1, where the machines are outfitted with oracles from C_2. $C_1^{C_2+C_3}$ is the class of languages accepted by machines for C_1 with oracles from C_2 and C_3.

It turns out that some oracle classes collapse: $P^P = P$, $ZPP^{ZPP} = ZPP$, $BPP^{BPP} = BPP$, $NP^{\Delta} = NP$, etc. For others it is known that one query to the oracle is enough to yield the whole power of the class: $NP^{NP} = NP^{NP[1]}$, $\Delta^{NP} = \Delta^{NP[1]}$, $R^R = R^{R[1]}$, $ZPP^R = ZPP^{R[1]}$, $NP^{BPP} = NP^{BPP[1]}$. $NP^{NP} = NP^{NP[1]}$ is essential for the alternate characterization of languages L in NP^{NP} as $x \in L \leftrightarrow \exists y\ \forall z P(x,y,z)$. The universal quantifier represents the single query to the oracle.

For all known inclusion relations, the relativized relations are also valid: e.g. $\Delta^R \subset NP^R$ and $NP^R \subset NP^{NP}$.
Oracle querying is associative: e.g.

$$(NP^{NP})^{NP} = NP^{(NP+NP^{NP})} = NP^{(NP^{NP})} = NP^{NP^{NP}}.$$

To persuade yourself of the above use your favorite model for NP^{NP} computations using oracles. Note that NP^{NP} is Σ_2^P.

Another property, that we will be frequently using, is the robustness property of the random quantifier $\exists_m$ (consequently of R, ZPP, BPP). The robustness property states that the following requirements for a polynomial time predicate P are equivalent:

1. for a polynomial q and for all x: $Pr(\{y \mid P(x,y)\}) > 1/2 + 1/q(|x|)$
2. for a fixed ε and for all x: $Pr(\{y \mid P(x,y)\}) > 1/2 + \varepsilon$
3. for a polynomial q and for all x: $Pr(\{y \mid P(x,y)\}) > 1 - 1/2^{q(|x|)}$.

For example, for a polynomial predicate P′ satisfying requirement 1 one can find a polynomial predicate P″ satisfying, say, requirement 2 such that for all x: $x \in P' \leftrightarrow x \in P''$.

Notice that $\exists_m$ guarantees an overwhelming majority of witnesses for some polynomial predicate P. Here it is worth mentioning that the random quantifier retains the robustness property even when used in a longer (but constant in length) sequence of alternating quantifiers in front of the polynomial time predicate. Consider for example the following language L, where P is a polynomial time predicate:

$(x \in L \leftrightarrow \exists_m x_1\ \forall x_2\ \exists_m x_3\ \forall x_4 P(x, x_1, x_2, x_3, x_4))$ and
$(x \notin L \leftrightarrow \forall x_1\ \exists_m x_2\ \forall x_3\ \exists_m x_4 \neg P(x, x_1, x_2, x_3, x_4))$.

2. A New characterization of BPP

It seems very improbable that NP is contained in BPP. Evidence for this are the following facts:

1. BPP problems can be solved in practice with arbitrary small error probability, whereas this is not known to be the case for all NP problems.
2. Using random oracles, BPP collapses to P with probability one, whereas $NP \neq P$ with probability one [BG].

3. If we assume NP BPP, we can deduce R = NP, PH BPP, and PH collapses at the second level, neither of which corresponds to our intuition (see also [K, Z2]).

Thus trying to prove $BPP \subset NP$ or $BPP \subset \sum_k^P$ for some $k > 1$, seems to be a more reasonable project. As a matter of fact, Sipser showed $BPP \subset \sum_4^P$ [Si] and Gacs [see also Si] and Lautemann [L] improved this to $BPP \subset \sum_2^P$. A simplified proof of this fact follows directly from our proof. In addition, our proof demonstrates that a poly-size argument [A] is basically enough to show $BPP \subset NP^{NP}$. We use the concept of a comb with polynomially many teeth and we then prove two lemmas about combs.

Definition: C_n a comb of size n is a collection of binary numbers (teeth of the comb), such that for all $z \in C_n$ $|z|<n$ and $card(C_n)<n$.

Remark: C_n can be encoded into one number of polynomial length and decoded from it in polynomial time (polynomial in n).

Lemma 1: If $\forall x_{|x|<n} \exists_m y_{|y|<n} P(x,y)$ then

$$\exists C_n \forall x_{|x|<n} [\text{for some tooth } y \in C_n: P(x,y)]$$

Proof:

Consider the Matrix $M[x,y] = P(x,y)$, $0 \leq x,y \leq 2^n-1$. Since all rows contain many "true", $\forall x Pr(\{y| M[x,y]=true\}) > 1/2 + \varepsilon$ and therefore $Pr(\{(x,y)| M[x,y]=true\}) > 1/2 + \varepsilon$ (M contains many "true"). It follows by a pigeon hole argument that $\exists y_1$: $Pr(\{x| M[x,y_1]=true\}) > 1/2 + \varepsilon$ (some column contains many "true"). Remove from matrix M all rows where $M[x,y_1]$=true. Remove also column y_1 and call the new matrix M'. M' has at most half as many rows as M. M' similarily contains many "true" and thus there is a column y_2 in M' that contains many "true". Proceed analogously to obtain $\{y_1,\ldots,y_n\} \doteq C_n$ and thus covering all rows of M.

q.e.d.

Roughly speaking, Lemma 1 says that we can interchange the quantifiers $\forall x$ and $\exists y$ provided that for all x there are many y. The following stronger version is also true:

Lemma 2: If $\forall x_{|x|<n} \exists_m y_{|y|<n} P(x,y)$ then

$$\exists_m C_k \forall x_{|x|<n} [\text{for some tooth } y \in C_k: \neg P(x,y)], \text{ where } k=n+2$$

Proof:

$Pr(\{C_k| \exists x_{|x|<n} [\text{for all teeth } y \in C_k: \neg P(x,y)]\}) =$

$Pr(\bigcup_{|x|<n} \{C_k| \text{ for all teeth } y \in C_k: \neg P(x,y)\}) \leq$

$\sum_{|x|<n} Pr(\{C_k | \text{for all teeth } y\in C_k\text{: } \neg P(x,y)\}) <$

$\sum_{|x|<n} (1/2)^k = 2^n(1/2)^k < 1/4 < 1/2 - \varepsilon.$

Therefore for most of the C_k $\forall x_{|x|\ n}$[for some tooth y C_k: P(x,y)] holds.
q.e.d.

Remark: If P(x,y,z) is a polynomial time predicate, then
$P'(x,C_{p(|x|)},y) = \bigvee_{z\in C_{p(|x|)}} P(x,y,z)$ is also.

Define the complexity class K by

$L\in K$: $(x\in L \leftrightarrow \exists_m y \forall z P(x,y,z))$ and $(x\notin L \leftrightarrow \forall y \exists_m z\ P(x,y,z))$
for some polynomial time predicate P.

The following theorem gives us a complete characterization of BPP.

Theorem 1: BPP = K

Proof:

Let L∈BPP, i.e. $(x\in L \rightarrow \exists_m y P(x,y))$ and $(x\notin L \rightarrow \exists_m y \neg P(x,y))$.
Assume without loss of generality that $x\in L \rightarrow Pr(\{y|P(x,y)\}) > 1-1/2^{|x|}$
and $x\notin L \rightarrow Pr(\{y|\ P(x,y)\}) < 1/2^{|x|}$
Let p(|x|) be a polynomial bound for the BPP computation on x. We will consider combs $C_{p(|x|)}$, which are shifted along the leaves of the BPP computation tree; i.e. every tooth $y_i\in C_{p(|x|)}$ is replaced by $u_i=(s+y) \bmod 2^{p(|x|)}$ for a shift s, where $s \le 2^{p(|x|)}$.

Claim 1: if x∈L then $\exists_m C_{p(|x|)} \forall$ shifts s [for a tooth y of the comb
$C_{p(|x|)}$: $P(x,(s+y) \bmod 2^{p(|x|)})$]

Proof:

Let x∈L. Since L∈BPP we know that $\exists_m y P(x,y)$. Therefore
$\forall s \exists_m y P(x,(s+y) \bmod 2^{p(|x|)})$.
Now we can apply Lemma 2 to obtain:
$\exists_m C_{p(|x|)}\ \forall s$ [for a tooth y of $C_{p(|x|)}$: $P(x,(s+y) \bmod 2^{p(|x|)})$].
This proves claim 1.

Claim 2: if x∉L then $\forall C_{p(|x|)}\ \exists_m s$ [for all teeth y of $C_{p(|x|)}$:
$\neg P(x,(s+y) \bmod 2^{p(|x|)})$]

Proof:

Let x∉L. Since L∈BPP, we have $\exists_m y \neg P(x,y)$.

Therefore for all y $Pr(\{s \mid P(x,(s+y) \bmod 2^{p(|x|)})\}) < 1/2^{|x|}$.
Thus for all $C_{p(|x|)}$ $Pr(\{s \mid$ for some tooth y in $C_{p(|x|)}$ $P(x,(s+y) \bmod 2^{p(|x|)})\}) <$

$\sum_{y \in C_{p(|x|)}} 1/2^{|x|} = p(|x|)/2^{|x|} < 1/2 - \varepsilon$.

We get $\forall C_{p(|x|)}\ \exists_m s$ [for all teeth y of $C_{p(|x|)}$: $\neg P(x,(s+y) \bmod 2^{p(|x|)})$]
This proves claim 2.

Thus

$x \in L \rightarrow \exists_m C\ \forall s R(x,C,s)$ and

$x \notin L \rightarrow \forall C\ \exists_m s \neg R(x,C,s)$

for a polynomial time predicate R, where

$R(x,C,s) \leftrightarrow$ for some z in C: $P(x,(s+z) \bmod 2^{p(|x|)})$;

i.e L in K.

On the other hand, let L be in K. Then

$x \in L \rightarrow \exists_m (y,z)$: $P(x,(y,z))$ and $x \notin L \rightarrow \exists_m (y,z)$: $\neg P(x,(y,z))$.

That means the majority of the pairs (y,z) gives the right answer.
Therefore L in BPP.

q.e.d.

Remark: Observe that using Lemma 1 instead of Lemma 2 in the previous proof yields already a Σ_2^P characterization for BPP. Therefore we have a simplified proof for this fact.

Corollary:

1. K is closed under complementation
2. $BPP \subset NP^{NP}$ and thus also $BPP \subset \Delta^{NP}$ (see [Si, L])
3. $BPP \subset R^{NP}$ and thus also $BPP \subset ZPP^{NP}$

3. Discussion and Various Consequences

Note that the characterization of BPP is decisive, that is, even if we replace $\exists_m$ quantifiers by $\exists$, the simplified clauses for $x \in L$ and $x \notin L$ are complementary and thus allow us to decide whether $x \in L$.

Another interesting fact is that possible probabilistic hierarchies built by $\exists_m \forall$ resp. $\forall \exists_m$ quantifier repetition collapse.

For example:

L$\in$BPP iff there is a polynomial time predicate P such that

$(x \in L \leftrightarrow \exists_m x_1 \forall x_2 \exists_m x_3 \forall x_4 P(x,x_1,x_2,x_3,x_4))$ and

$(x \notin L \leftrightarrow \forall x_1 \exists_m x_2 \forall x_3 \exists_m x_4 \neg P(x,x_1,x_2,x_3,x_4))$.

In other words, a fixed number of alternating quantifiers $\forall$ and $\exists_m$ does not yield more than BPP.

The insight we obtained into BPP looking at these proofs, as well as the characterization BPP = K led us to the following result:

Theorem 2: $\Sigma_2^{P,\ BPP} = \Sigma_2^P$

Sketch of a proof:

Let L be in $\Sigma_2^{P,\ BPP}$. Note that $\Sigma_2^{P,\ BPP} = NP^{NP^{BPP}}$ and that only one query per path is enough for the BPP (as well as the NP) oracle. Therefore

$$NP^{NP^{BPP}} = NP^{NP[1]^{BPP[1]}} .$$

We get

$$x \in L \leftrightarrow \exists x_1 \forall x_2 \exists_m x_3 \forall x_4 P(x,x_1,x_2,x_3,x_4)$$

With Lemma 1 we obtain

$$x \in L \leftrightarrow \exists (x_1,C) \forall x_2 \bigvee_{x_3 \in C} \forall x_4 P(x,x_1,x_2,x_3,x_4)$$

Therefore L is in Σ_2^P.

q.e.d.

This last theorem shows that using a BPP oracle does not add any computing power to classes as low as $\Sigma_2^P \cap \Pi_2^P$.

Acknowledgment: We want to thank J. Mitchell for helpful comments.

4. References

[A] Adleman, L. (1978), Two Theorems on Random Polynomial Time, FOCS 19, 75-83

[BG] Bennet, C.H., and Gill, J. (1981), Relative to a Random Oracle A $P^A \neq NP^A \neq$ co-NP^A with Probability 1, SIAM J. Comput. 10, 96-112

[CKS] Chandra, A.K., Kozen, D.C., and Stockmeyer, L.J. (1981), Alternation, JACM 28, 114-133

[GJ] Garey, M.R., and Johnson, D.S., (1979), Computers and Intractability: a Guide to the Theory of NP-Completeness, Freeman, San Francisco

[G] Gill, J., (1977), Computational Complexity of Probabilistic Turing Machines, SIAM J. Comput. 6, 675-695

[HU] Hopcroft, J.E., and Ullman, J.D., (1979), Introduction to Automata Theory, Languages, and Computation, Addison-Wesley, Reading, Mass.

[K] Ko, Ker-I,(1982), Some Observations on Probabilistic Algorithms and NP-Hard Problems, Inf. Proc. Let. 14, 39-43

[L] Lautemann, C., (1983), BPP and the Polynomial Hierarchy, Techn. Uni. Berlin, Informatik, Report 83-06

[Si] Sipser, M., (1983), A Complexity Theoretic Approach to Randomness, STOC 15, 330-335

[St] Stockmeyer, L.J., (1976), Complete Sets and the Polynomial Hierarchy, Theoret. Comp. Science 3, 23- 33

[Z1] Zachos, S., (1982), Robustness of Probabilistic Complexity Classes under Definitional Perturbations, Information and Control 54, 143-154

[Z2] Zachos, S., (1983), Collapsing Probabilistic Polynomial Hierarchies, Conf. on Comp. Compl. Th., S. Barbara, 75-81

TREATING TERMINALS AS FUNCTION VALUES OF TIME

Kamala Krithivasan

Anindya Das

Department of Computer Science and Engineering
Indian Institute of Technology
Madras - 600 036 India

ABSTRACT

Motivated by the idea of describing parquet deformations using grammars, we define in this paper a terminal weighted grammar where the terminal generated at any step of a derivation is defined as a function of time. It is seen that terminal weighted regular grammars generate exactly the class of recursively enumerable sets. Terminal weighted matrix grammars are used to describe parquet deformations. The hierarchy of families generated by putting various restrictions on the functions is studied.

1. INTRODUCTION

It has been of interest to generate various classes of pictures using grammars [1,5,7,9,10,11,12,13]. In [9], we have given a matrix model to describe digital pictures viewed as matrices (m x n rectangular arrays of terminals). In [10] we have defined an array model which generates interesting classes of pictures such as Kirsch's right triangles, letters of the alphabet of any size but with the same proportion and kolam patterns [11] (traditional picture patterns used to decorate the floor in South Indian homes) of several types. In both cases the languages generated are rectangular arrays. In [5], we have defined a developmental system called Table matrix L system.TMLS and part TMLS, particularly with coding, generate picture classes such as hollow squares, spirals etc. In [12], Siromoney and Siromoney have given radial grammars to generate circular patterns, which is an extension of the cycle languages proposed by Rosenfeld [6].

Hofstadter discusses the connection between music and visual art [2], and gives several examples of parquet deformations which are patterns of tiles that shift gradually in one dimension. We realized that these parquet deformations and similar pictures cannot be generated by our earlier models. Any of our earlier models would use only a finite number of terminals, whereas many of the parquet deformations would need an infinite number of terminals if we were to continue the pattern indefinitely. But as noted in [2], the transformation (in one direction) is gradual and somewhat resembles the gradually changing rhythms of music. He asks what is the difference between music and visual art answering it by noting that music intrinsically involves time while works of visual art do not.

In [9], we note that when a picture is described as a rectangular array of terminals, it is advantageous to assign attribute values to each member of the array, the typical attributes being intensity or grey level, color and opaqueness or transparency. Our earlier definitions very naturally allow for the description of color, texture etc. We have illustrated with the help of an example [9], taking a single attribute viz color, but extension to more attributes is straight forward ; we have only to take ordered tuples as terminals instead of single terminals.

Motivated by the idea of giving a grammar for describing parquet deformations and also for describing an infinite number of symbols starting with only a finite number, we define in this paper terminal weighted grammars, where the terminal generated at any step is defined as the value of a function of time. Each terminal a in the language generated by a grammar is replaced by $f_a(i)$ if that terminal has been generated at the ith step of derivation and f_a is a function from $\mathbb{P} \rightarrow D$ where $\mathbb{P}$ is the set of positive integers and D is a suitably defined codomain. We find that by properly defining f, we can not only generate the parquet deformations, but also several other interesting picture classes which could not be described by our earlier models.

In section 2, we define terminal weighted regular grammars and illustrate with examples. We state a few theoretically interesting results. The family of languages generated by terminal weighted grammars is exactly the family of recursively enumerable sets. We also consider terminal weighted context-free grammars at the end of this section.

In section 3, we consider terminal weighted matrix grammars where each terminal a is replaced by $f_a(i,j)$, if it has been generated in the ith step of vertical derivation starting with an intermediate generated at the jth step of horizontal derivation. We find that the parquet deformations [2] can be described using terminal weighted regular matrix grammars. We give an example to generate a pattern changing slowly in two directions.

In section 4, we consider TWRG, TWRLG and TWCFG where the codomains are all sets of strings. We put four types of restrictions on F and study the hierarchy of families generated.

2. TERMINAL WEIGHTED STRING GRAMMARS

In this section we define a terminal weighted regular grammar (TWRG) and state some theoretically interesting results. We also define a terminal weighted context-free grammar (TWCFG). We assume the reader to be familiar with the basic notions of formal language theory [4].

Definition 2.1. A regular grammar is a 4-tuple G=(N,T,P,S) where N is the set of non-terminals, T the set of terminals, S the start symbol and, P the set of production rules of the form $A \rightarrow aB$, $A \rightarrow a$ where A,B are non-terminals and a is a terminal.

Definition 2.2. A terminal weighted regular grammar (TWRG) is a two tuple (G,F) where G is a regular grammar (N,T,P,S) and if $T=\{a_1,\ldots,a_k\}$, F is a set of k functions $\{f_{a_1},\ldots,f_{a_k}\}$, $\mathbb{P}\rightarrow D_1$, $\mathbb{P}\rightarrow D_2,\ldots,$ $\mathbb{P}\rightarrow D_k$ where $D_1,\ldots,D_k$ are similar codomains (By similar we mean that if D_1 denotes a set of strings, $D_2,\ldots,D_k$ also denote a set of strings. If D_1 denotes a set of colors, $D_2,\ldots,D_k$ also denote a set of colors). We assume that f is a total function and can be computed.

A derivation in a TWRG is defined as follows. If $S \overset{1}{\Rightarrow} a_{i_1}A_1 \overset{2}{\Rightarrow} a_{i_1}a_{i_2}A_2 \overset{3}{\Rightarrow} \ldots \overset{n}{\Rightarrow} a_{i_1}\ldots a_{i_n}$ is a n-step derivation in G, then we have a 2n-step derivation in TWRG

$$S \underset{G}{\overset{1}{\Rightarrow}} a_{i_1}A_1 \underset{F}{\overset{1'}{\Rightarrow}} \alpha_{i_1}A_1 \ldots \underset{G}{\overset{n}{\Rightarrow}} \alpha_{i_1}\ldots\alpha_{i_{n-1}}a_n \underset{F}{\overset{n'}{\Rightarrow}} \alpha_{i_1}\ldots\alpha_{i_n}$$

where $\underset{G}{\overset{i}{\Rightarrow}}$ denotes a step of derivation according to G and $\underset{F}{\overset{i'}{\Rightarrow}}$ is a step where the terminal a generated at the previous step i is replaced by $f_a(i)$.

Definition 2.3. The language generated by a TWRG (G,F) is defined as $\{w \mid S \underset{G,F}{\overset{*}{\Rightarrow}} w\}$ or equivalently $\{w \mid S \underset{G}{\overset{*}{\Rightarrow}} w'$ and w is obtained from w' by applying weights to terminals$\}$.

Example 2.1 Let (G,F) be a TWRG where G=(N,T,P,S), $N=\{S\}$, $T=\{a\}$, $P=\{S\rightarrow aS, S\rightarrow a\}$ $F=\{f_a\}$, $f_a(i)=a^i$. Then a typical derivation in TWRG is given by $S \underset{G}{\Rightarrow} aS \underset{F}{\Rightarrow} aS \underset{G}{\Rightarrow} aaS \underset{F}{\Rightarrow} aaaS \underset{G}{\Rightarrow} aaaa \underset{F}{\Rightarrow} aaaaaa$. aaaaaa can also be thought of as the image of 'aaa'. The 'a' generated at the ith step is replaced by a^i.

$$L(G)=\left\{ a^{\frac{n(n+1)}{2}} \,\middle|\, n\geq 1 \right\}$$

Example 2.2 Let (G,F) be a TWRG where G=(N,T,P,S) $N=\{S\}$ $T=\{a,b\}$ $P=\{S\rightarrow aS, S\rightarrow b\}$ $F=\{f_a,f_b\}$, $f_a(i)=\epsilon$, $f_b(i)=a^{i^2}$

Then $L(G)=\{a^{n^2} \mid n\geq 1\}$

Example 2.3. Let (G, F) a be TWRG where G is given by $\{S\rightarrow aS,\ S\rightarrow a\}$ $F=\{f_a\}$, $f_a(i)$=a drawn to fit exactly in a square of side $2^{i-1}\times 2^{i-1}$ units. (One unit may be taken suitably. A typical element of L(G) is given in Fig.1).

Fig.1 : A Typical Element of Example 2.3

It is not difficult to see that several interesting types of languages can be generated by defining F suitably.

Theorem 2.1 Every recursively enumerable set can be generated by a TWRG.

Proof : Let L be a recursively enumerable set and let $w_1, w_2, \ldots$ be an enumeration of its strings. Let G be given by $\{S\rightarrow aS,\ S\rightarrow b\}$, $F=\{f_a, f_b\}$ $f_a(i)=\epsilon$ for all i, $f_b(i)=w_i$
Then it is easy to see this TWRG (G, F) generates L.

Theorem 2.2. The language generated by a TWRG is a recursively enumerable set.

Proof is by constructing a multitape Turing machine accepting the language generated by a TWRG.

We can similarly define terminal weighted CFG. As far as linear grammars are concerned, the extension is direct. If nonlinear grammars are considered, there will be a difference between leftmost derivation and non-leftmost derivations. Hence, it is necessary to stick to one type of derivation eg. leftmost derivation. It will be of interest to study the different classes of languages generated by TWCFG by putting restrictions on F. This is studied in section 4.

3. TERMINAL WEIGHTED MATRIX GRAMMARS AND PARQUET DEFORMATIONS

In this section, we define a terminal weighted matrix grammar and see how these can be used to describe parquet deformations. In [9], we defined a matrix grammar to generate rectangular arrays.

Definition 3.1. A context-free matrix grammar. (CFMG) (a regular matrix grammar (RMG)) is a two tuple $G=(G_1, G_2)$, where $G_1=(V_1, I_1, P_1, S)$ is a CFG(RG) with: V_1= a finite set of horizontal nonterminals, I_1= a finite set of intermediates= $\{S_1,\ldots,S_k\}$, P_1=a finite set of CFG (RG) production rules called horizontal production rules, and S is the start symbol. $S\in V_1$ and $V_1\cap I_1=\emptyset$. $G_2=\bigcup_{i=1}^{k} G_{2i}$ where $G_{2i}=(V_{2i},I_2,P_{2i},S_i)$, i=1,...,k are regular grammars with: I_2= a finite set of terminals, V_{2i}=a finite set of vertical nonterminals, S_i the start symbol and P_{2i} a finite set of regular production rules, $V_{2i}\cap V_{2j}=\emptyset$ if $i\neq j$. Derivations are defined as follows: First a string $S_{i_1}\ldots S_{i_n}\in I_1^*$ is generated horizontally using the horizontal production rules P_1 in G_1, i.e. $S\overset{*}{\Rightarrow}S_{i_1}\ldots S_{i_n}\in I_1^*$. Vertical derivations proceed as follows: We write

$$\boxed{S_{i_1}\ldots\ S_{i_n}}$$
$$\Downarrow$$
$$\boxed{\begin{matrix} a_{11}\ldots & a_{1n} \\ A_1 & A_n \end{matrix}}$$

if $S_{i_j}\rightarrow a_{1j}A_j$ are rules in G_2, j=1,...,n, and

$$\boxed{\begin{matrix} a_{11} & \ldots & a_{1n} \\ \vdots & & \\ a_{(r-1)1} & \ldots & a_{(r-1)n} \\ A_1 & \ldots & A_n \end{matrix}}$$
$$\Downarrow$$
$$\boxed{\begin{matrix} a_{11} & \ldots & a_{1n} \\ \vdots & & \\ a_{(r-1)1} & \ldots & a_{(r-1)n} \\ a_{r1} & \ldots & a_{rn} \\ B_1 & \ldots & B_n \end{matrix}}$$

if $A_j\rightarrow a_{rj}B_j$ are rules in G_2 for j=1,...,n. $\overset{*}{\Downarrow}$ is the transitive closure of $\Downarrow$. The derivation terminates if $A_j\rightarrow a_{mj}$ are all terminal rules in G_2.

Definition 3.2. The set of all matrices generated by G is defined to be $M(G)=\{m\times n \text{ arrays } [a_{ij}],\ i=1,\ldots,m,\ j=1,\ldots,n,\ m,n\geq 1 \mid S\underset{G_1}{\overset{*}{\Rightarrow}}S_1\ldots S_n \overset{*}{\Downarrow}_{G_2}[a_{ij}]\}$

Definition 3.3. A terminal weighted CFMG (TWCFMG) is a 2-tuple (G, F) where G is a CFMG and F= $\{f_{a_1},f_{a_2},\ldots,f_{a_k}\}$ where $\{a_1,a_2,\ldots,a_k\}$ are terminals. f_{a_i} is a function from $\mathbb{P}\times\mathbb{P}\rightarrow D_i$ where $\{D_1,\ldots,D_k\}$ are similar codomains. The derivation of any array is defined as follows : First an m x n array in L(G) is derived. Suppose the (i,j)th element is a. Then a is generated in the ith step of vertical derivation. The jth column is derived from an intermediate symbol (S_{1j} say) which might have been derived in the pth step of the horizontal derivation. Then a is replaced by $f_a(i,p)$. The functions $f_{a_1},\ldots$ should be so defined that they ensure that the resultant array is rectangular.

Remarks: 1: The functions $f_a, f_b, \ldots$ should be defined such that when applied to elements of a rectangular array generated by the CFMG, they yield another rectangular array. One way of ensuring that the resultant array is rectangular is to define f_a such that f_a consists of a single symbol.

2. It will be of interest to study what happens when F applied to some arrays yields rectangular arrays and when applied to others does not yield rectangular arrays.

3. When we consider RMG, the (i,j)th element of an array is generated in the ith step of vertical derivation starting from an intermediate generated at the jth step of horizontal derivation.

For the rest of this section we assume that the functions f_a are defined in such a way that $f_a(i,j)$ consists of a single symbol for all i,j and a.

The following CFMG generates the token T and the application of terminal weights to the token yields arrays whose typical element is shown in Fig.2.

Example 3.1. $G=(G_1, G_2)$

$G_1 = (\{S\}, \{S_1, S_2\}, \{S \to S_1 S S_1, S \to S_2\}, S)$, $G_2 = G_{21} \cup G_{22}$

$G_{21} = (\{S_1, A\}, \{., X\}, \{S_1 \to XA, A \to .A, A \to .\}, S_1)$

$G_{22} = (\{S_2\}, \{X\}, \{S_2 \to XS_2, S_2 \to X\}, S_2)$, $F = \{f_., f_X\}$

$f_X(i,j)$ = a circle of diameter d divided into 2^j equal sectors if i=1 (the first division being created by a vertical diameter)

= a circle of diameter d divided into 2^{j-i+1} equal sectors if $i \geq 2$ and $j-i+1 \geq 1$

= a circle of diameter d if $i \geq 2$ and $j-i+1 < 1$

$f_.(i,j)$ = ƀ (blank)

Fig.2 shows a typical element where the (i,j)th symbol X of the array of the CFML is replaced by a primitive with basic structure that of a circle of diameter 'd', the primitives being placed such that two horizontal neighbours and two vertical neighbours are placed with their centres at a distance 'd' from each other.

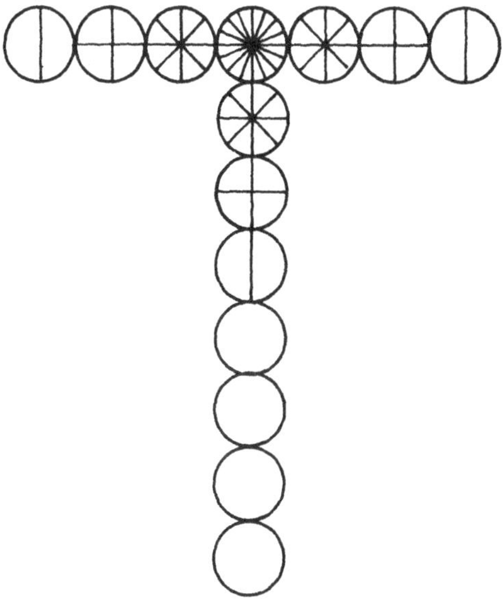

Fig 2 : A Typical Element of Example 3.1

The parquet deformation given in Fig.3 [2] can be defined by the following TWRMG.

Fig 3 : The Parquet Deformation "Fylfot FlipFlop"

Example 3.2. (G, F) is a TWRMG where G generates m x n rectangular arrays of a's with $m, n \geq 1$.

$G_1 = \{S \rightarrow S_1S, \quad S \rightarrow S_1\}$, $G_2 = \{S_1 \rightarrow aS_1, \quad S_1 \rightarrow a\}$

$F = \{f_a\}$ is defined as follows: $f_a(i,j)$ is a primitive independent of i and dependent on j only. The primitive is described with reference to a square of unit length and with the centre as the origin (Fig.4). Successive horizontal and vertical primitives are placed with a distance of unit length between their centres.

The points p_i, $1 \leq i \leq 9$ are fixed with respect to the origin. The points h_i, $1 \leq i \leq 6$ vary along the x axis and v_i, $1 \leq i \leq 6$ along the y axis as functions of time. Once the relative positions of the points p_k, h_i, v_j are known, $1 \leq k \leq 9$, $1 \leq i,j \leq 6$, the figure is defined by the line segments:

$p_1v_1, v_1p_2, p_2v_2, v_2p_3, p_3h_3, h_3p_6, p_6h_6, h_6p_9, p_9v_6, v_6p_8, p_8v_5, v_5p_7, p_7h_4, h_4p_4,$
$p_4h_1, h_1p_1, h_2p_2, h_2p_5, p_5h_5, h_5p_8, p_4v_3, v_3p_5, p_5v_4, v_4p_6.$

The coordinates of p_k, $1 \leq k \leq 9$, fixed for all t, are given by
$p_1 = (-0.5, 0.5)$, $p_2 = (0, 0.5)$, $p_3 = (0.5, 0.5)$, $p_4 = (-0.5, 0)$,
$p_5 = (0,0)$, $p_6 = (0.5, 0)$, $p_7 = (-0.5,-0.5)$, $p_8 = (0,-0.5)$, $p_9 = (0.5,-0.5)$

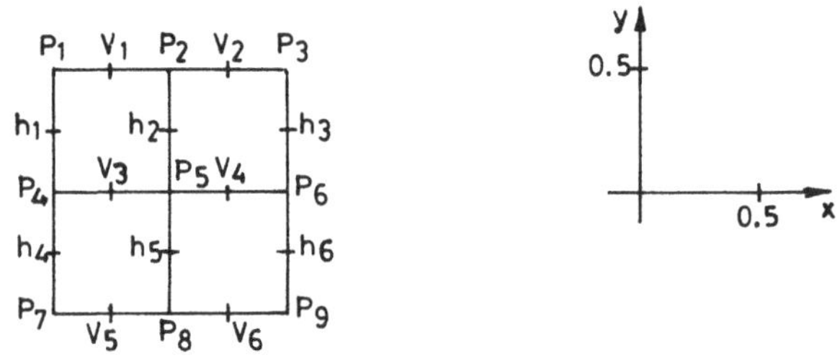

FIG 4 : The Primitive used in "Fylfot FlipFlop"

f_a is described in terms of the functions f_{v_i} and f_{h_i}. The functions $f_{v_i}: \mathbb{P} \longrightarrow I \times I$ and $f_{h_i}: \mathbb{P} \longrightarrow I \times I$, $1 \leq i \leq 6$ give the coordinates of v_i and h_i as functions of time $t \geq 1$.

$$f_{h_i}(t) = \left(C_{h_i} + \frac{1}{16}\left(\left\lfloor \frac{t+C'_{h_i}}{3} \right\rfloor \bmod 16\right), K_{h_i}\right) \text{ if } \left\lfloor \frac{t+C'_{h_i}}{3} \right\rfloor \bmod 16 \leq 8$$

$$= \left(C_{h_i} + \frac{1}{16}\left(16 - \left\lfloor \frac{t+C'_{h_i}}{3} \right\rfloor \bmod 16\right), K_{h_i}\right) \text{ if } \left\lfloor \frac{t+C'_{h_i}}{3} \right\rfloor \bmod 16 > 8$$

$$f_{v_i}(t) = \left(K_{v_i}, C_{v_i} + \frac{1}{16}\left(\left\lfloor \frac{t+C'_{v_i}}{3} \right\rfloor \bmod 16\right) \text{ if } \left\lfloor \frac{t+C'_{v_i}}{3} \right\rfloor \bmod 16 \leq 8\right.$$

$$= \left(K_{v_i}, C_{v_i} + \frac{1}{16}\left(16 - \left\lfloor \frac{t+C'_{v_i}}{3} \right\rfloor \bmod 16\right)\right) \text{ if } \left\lfloor \frac{t+C'_{v_i}}{3} \right\rfloor \bmod 16 > 8$$

$C_{h_i}, C'_{h_i}, K_{h_i}, K_{v_i}, C_{v_i}, C'_{v_i}$, $1 \leq i \leq 6$ are constants whose values can be determined (eg. $C_{\ 4} = -0.25$).

C_{v_i} and C_{h_i} represent the lowest values taken by v_i and h_i. C'_{v_i} and C'_{h_i} denote the offset from the lowest possible values so that we obtain the initial positions at time $t = 1$.

Since $f_{v_i}(t)=f_{v_i}(t+48)$ and $f_{h_i}(t)=f_{h_i}(t+48)$, the cycle repeats itself after 48 steps.

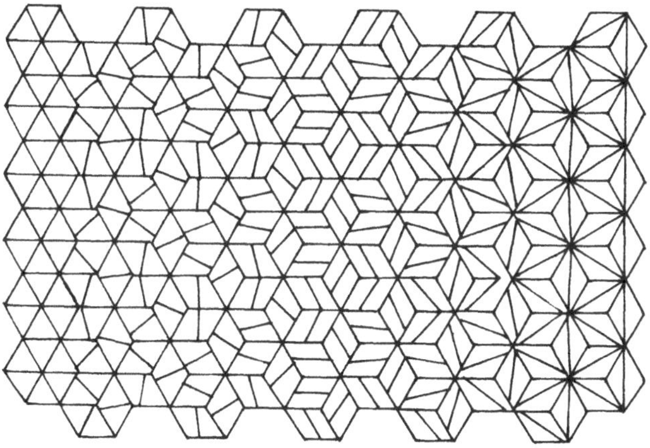

FIG 5 : The Parquet Deformation "Consternation"

The parquet deformation in Fig.5[2] can be described by the following TWRMG.

Example 3.3:(G,F) is a TWRMG where G generates arrays of the form

a . a . a . a . a	$G = (G_1, G_2)$, G_1 is given by
. a . a . a . a .	$\{ S \to S_1 S',\ S' \to S_2 S,\ S \to S_1 \}$
a . a . a . a . a	G_2 is given by $G_{21} \cup G_{22}$
. a . a . a . a .	G_{21} : $\{ S_1 \to aA,\ A \to S_1,\ A \to . \}$
a . a . a . a . a	G_{22} : $\{ S_2 \to .B,\ B \to aS_2,\ B \to a \}$
. a . a . a . a .	

$F = \{ f_a, f_. \}$

$f_.(i,j)$ = ƀ (blank)

$f_a(i,j)$ is a primitive defined with reference to a hexagonal frame (Fig.6).O is the centre of the hexagon and p_1, p_2, p_3 the centres of the three parallelograms. The line segments AB,BC,CD,DE,EF,OF,FA,OB,OD are fixed with respect to the centre O. Three line segments $x_1p_1y_1$, $x_2p_2y_2$, $x_3p_3y_3$ passing through the points p_1, p_2, p_3 and with end points on ABOF, BCDO and FODE respectively rotate clockwise around axes perpendicular to the plane of the hexagon.

Each a is replaced by a regular hexagon of side d, .'s are replaced by blanks. Two hexagons corresponding to two successive horizontal a's are placed such that their centres are 3d apart. Two hexagons corresponding to two successive vertical a's are placed such that their centres are at a distance $\sqrt{3}$ d from each other.

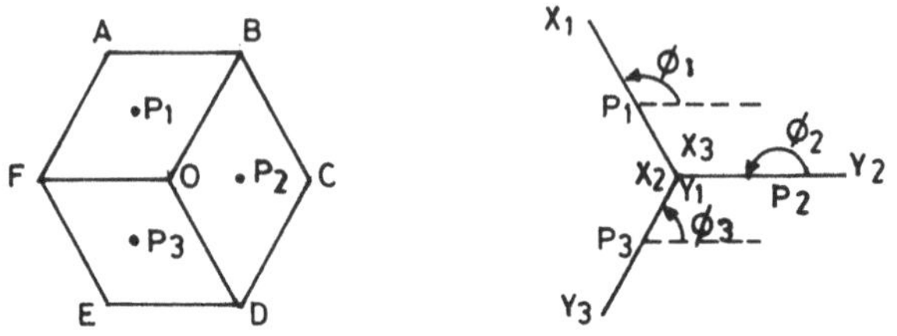

FIG 6 : The Primitive used in "Consternation"

The function $f_{p1}(i,j)$, $f_{p2}(i,j)$, $f_{p3}(i,j)$ denote the angles ϕ_1, ϕ_2, ϕ_3, described by x_1p_1, x_2p_2, x_3p_3 with respect to rays parallel to AB emanating from p_1, p_2, p_3 respectively.

$$\phi_1 = f_{p1}(i,j) = \frac{2\pi}{3} - \frac{\pi(t-1)}{20}, \quad \phi_2 = f_{p2}(i,j) = \pi - \frac{\pi(t-1)}{20},$$

$$\phi_3 = f_{p3}(i,j) = \frac{\pi}{3} - \frac{\pi(t-1)}{20}.$$

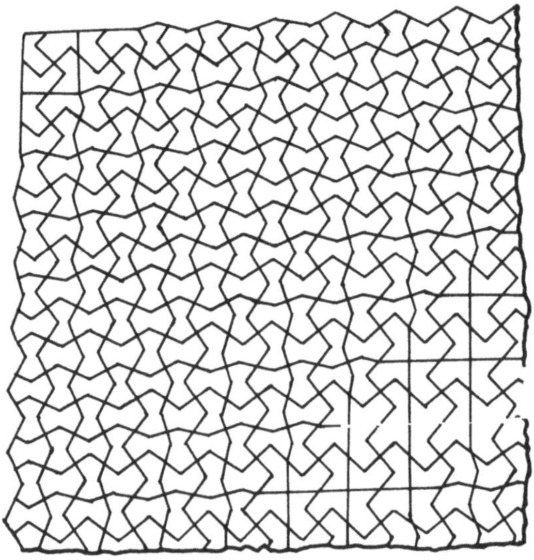

FIG 7 : The two Dimensional "Fylfot FlipFlop"

In parquet deformations, the pattern slowly changes in one direction. A pattern slowly changing in two directions can be described by the following TWRMG. This pattern is shown in Fig.7.

Example 3.4: In the TWRMG(G,F), G is the same as in example 3.2. $F=\{f_a\}$ is defined as follows: $f_a(t_1,t_2)$ is a primitive described with reference to a basic frame with points $p_i, h_j, v_k, 1\leq i\leq 9, 1\leq j\leq 6, 1\leq k\leq 6$, and with the same line segments as in example 3.2. Here $f_{v_i}(t_1,t_2)=f'_{v_i}(t_1+t_2-1)$ and $f_{h_i}(t_1,t_2)=f'_{h_i}(t_1+t_2-1)$ where f'_{v_i} and f'_{h_i} are the same as f_{v_i} and f_{h_i} in example 3.2 with minor modifications in the C'_{v_i} to ensure $f_a(t_1,t_2)=f_a(t_2,t_1)$.

In this section, we have considered only some parquet deformations. Many other parquet deformations[2] can also be described by TWRMGs, though the function F may be highly complex. **We have given the TWRMG for the parquet deformation 'Becombing Blossoms'[2]. The function F in this case is highly complex.**

4. HIERARCHY INDUCED BY RESTRICTIONS ON F

In this section, we consider TWRG, TWRLG and TWCFG where the codomains are all sets of strings (RLG has rules of the form $A\rightarrow\alpha B$, $A\rightarrow\beta$, where α,β are strings of terminals). We put four types of restrictions on F and study the hierarchy of families generated.

Definition 4.1. Let (G,F) be a TWXG(X=R, RL or CF). (G,F) is called a

i) TWXG(1) if $f_a(i)=a^{P_i}$ for all a where P_i is a positive integer

ii) TWXG(2) if $|f_a(i)| = 1$ for all a

iii) TWXG(3) if $C_a\leq |f_a(i)| \leq C'_a$, $0<C_a\leq C'_a$ for all a where C_a and C'_a are specific positive integers

iv) TWXG(4) if all f_a's are periodic functions.

We observe that $\{a^nb^n/n\geq 1\}$ and $\{a^nb^nc^n/n\geq 1\}$ can be generated by TWRG(1) but $\{ww^R/w\in(a,b)^+\}$ and $\{ww/w\in(a,b)^+\}$ cannot be generated by TWRG(1). If all the f_a's are constant functions we get a homomorphism. (Special case of TWXG(3)).

We find that the known square free words and cube free words [8,14] can be generated by TWRG(2).

Example 4.1. The following TWRG(2) generates any prefix of a cube free ω-word. $G=(\{S\}, \{a\}, \{S\rightarrow aS, S\rightarrow a\}, S)$, $F=\{f_a\}$

$f_a(i)=a$ if $n_{i-1} \bmod 2=0$

$\quad\;\; =b$ if $n_{i-1} \bmod 2=1$

where n_i is the number of 1's in the binary representation of i.

TWRG(2) can also generate the prefixes of cube free ω-word given by Wegner[14]. The pictorial representation of the problem which he calls "Rev.Back's Abbey floor" can be generated by the following TWRMG.

Example 4.2. (G, F) is given as follows:

$G=(G_1,G_2)$, $G_1=(\{S\}, \{S_1\}, \{S\rightarrow S_1S, S\rightarrow S_1\}, S)$,

$G_2=G_{21}=(\{S_1\}, \{a\}, \{S_1\rightarrow aS_1, S_1\rightarrow a\}, S_1)$, $F=\{f_a\}$

$$f_a(i,j)=f(j) \text{ if } i=1$$
$$=f(i) \text{ if } j=1$$
$$=f(j) \text{ if } f_a(1,j)=a$$
$$=\overline{f(j)} \text{ if } f_a(1,j)=b$$

where $\bar{a}=b$ and $\bar{b}=a$ and f is defined as $f(1)=a$, $f(2)=b$, for $i\geq 3$

$$f(i)=f(i-2x3^k) \text{ if } 2x3^k<i\leq 4x3^k$$
$$=f(2x(4x3^k)-i+1) \text{ if } 4x3^k<i\leq 2x3^{k+1} \text{ for some k.}$$

Next we consider some hierarchy results. TWXL(i) denotes the family of languages generated by TWXG(i).

Theorem 4.1. i) TWXL(i) $\subset$ TWXL i=1,2,3,4

ii) TWXL(2) $\subset$ TWXL(3)

iii) TWXL(4) $\subset$ TWXL(3) x=R, RL, CF

iv) TWXL(1) and TWXL(3) are incomparable but not disjoint.

v) TWRL(3) = TWRLL(3).

THeorem 4.2. i) TWXL(1) $\cap$ TWXL(2) = XL

ii) $\bigcap_{i=1}^{4}$ TWXL(i) = XL

iii) TWRL(4) = TWRLL(4) = family of regular sets.

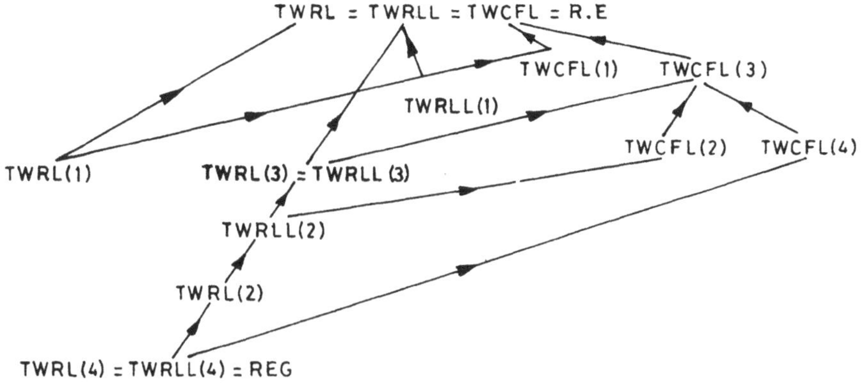

FIG 3 : The Hierarchy

Fig.8 summarises the results. A solid line indicates proper inclusion. Two families not connected are incomparable but not disjoint.

5. CONCLUSION

In this paper we have considered terminal weighted grammars and shown that terminal weighted matrix grammars can describe some parquet deformations given in [2]. [3] contains some pictures of Esher's work on metamorphosis. It may be possible to describe these also using terminal weighted grammars. We can also consider terminal weighted array grammars and terminal weighted graph grammars. These may help to describe elegantly certain classes of pictures and graphs.

REFERENCES

[1] K.S.Fu, Syntactic Pattern Recognition and Applications, Prentice-Hall, 1982.

[2] D.R.Hofstadter, Metamagical Themas : Parquet deformations : patterns of tiles that shift gradually in one dimension, **Scientific American, No.1, Vol.249, July 1983.**

[3] D.R.Hofstadter, Godel, Esher and Bach : an eternal golden braid, Vintage Books, 1980.

[4] J.E.Hopcroft and J.D.Ullman, Automata, Languages and Computation, Addison-Wesley, 1979.

[5] N.Nirmal and K.Krithivasan, Table Matrix L Systems, International Journal of Computer Mathematics, 10, 1982, 247-255.

[6] A.Rosenfeld, A note on Cycle Grammars, Computer Science Centre, University of Maryland, TR-300, April 1974.

[7] A.Rosenfeld, Picture Languages, Academic Press, 1979.

[8] A.Salomaa, Jewels of Formal Language Theory, Computer Science Press, 1981.

[9] G.Siromoney, R.Siromoney and K.Krithivasan, Abstract families of matrices and picture languages, Computer Graphics Image Processing, 1, 1972, 284-307.

[10] G.Siromoney, R.Siromoney and K.Krithivasan, Picture Languages with array rewriting rules, Inform. Contr. 22, 1973, 447-470.

[11] G.Siromoney, R.Siromoney and K.Krithivasan, Array grammars and Kolam, Computer Graphics and Image Processing, 3,1974,63-82

[12] G.Siromoney, and R.Siromoney, Radial grammars and radial L-Systems Computer Graphics Image Processing, 4, 1975, 361-374.

[13] A.L.Shaw, A formal picture description scheme as a basis for picture processing systems, Inform. Control, 14, 1969, 9-52.

[14] L.Wegner , Is $ww w^R$ cube-free, bulletin of the EATCS, 18, 1982,120.

Logics of Knowledge, Games and Dynamic Logic

Rohit Parikh

Department of Computer Science
Brooklyn College of CUNY
Bedford Ave and Avenue H
Brooklyn, NY, 11210

and

Mathematics Program
CUNY Graduate Center
33 West 42nd Street
New York, NY, 10036

Abstract: We study monotonic and non-monotonic Logics of Knowledge, giving decision procedures and completeness results. In particular we develop a model theory for a non-monotonic Logic of Knowledge and show that it corresponds exactly to normal applications of a non-monotonic rule of inference due to Mccarthy.

Introduction: While the Logic of Knowledge has traditionally been a subject for Philosophers (Cf. [W], [D], [H], [N]), recently there has been much interest in this area on the part of Computer Scientists [XW], [FHV], [M[illegible]]. This is because the analysis of Knowledge presents a real possibility of applications in Artificial Intelligence, Distributed Processing, Semantic Database Theory and Cryptography. It is natural that there will then be an interest in a more technical study of Logics of Knowledge involving not only axiomatic theories but also decision procedures and complexity results.

Traditionally, the Logic of Knowledge has been studied as a kind of Modal Logic. However, it turns out that the more powerful logical and model theoretic methods developed for Dynamic Logic and Game Logic provide us with better tools for studying both monotonic and non-monotonic Logics of Knowledge.

Non-monotonic logics of knowledge seem to have been first suggested by McCarthy. Moore [M] has pointed out that they are related to but different in character from the non-monotonic logics that arise from default reasoning [MD]. The point is that problems

---

This research was supported by NSF grant MCS 8304959 and a grant from the CUNY Faculty Research Assistance Program.

of knowledge are often given with the understanding that anything that is not explicitly stated as part of the information or implicit in it, is unknown.

Thus suppose I tell you of two numbers x and y that y is a non-trivial factor of x. If I tell you that x is 9, then from your knowledge of x you can deduce that y must be 3 and hence you also know y. If I tell you, however, that x is 6, then you do not know y and *you know that you do not know y*. Now your ignorance of y in the second case cannot be a *part of the statement* of the problem, for that tack will lead to a contradiction in case x is 9. Rather, it must be an inference of the form: if x is 6 then it cannot be proved that you know y and hence it must be concluded that you *do not* know y. Deducing things this way from what cannot be proved leads naturally to non-monotonicity.

In this paper our primary concern will be to give a coherent model theoretic and proof theoretic account of non-monotonic *many person* Logic of Knowledge. Monotonic 1 person Logic of Knowledge has been studied for a long time [H], but applications in Computer Science require an extension to many persons (processors) and the non-monotonic case has not yet been successfully tackled.However, we shall also study *monotonic* Logics of Knowledge as an easy preliminary exercise, proving completeness and decidability results.

We now proceed to discuss the language for Logics of Knowledge, which is the same for all Logics under consideration. We shall assume that we are considering n individuals who are interested not only in reality but also in each other's knowledge of it. Roughly, the language will be the Propositional calculus augmented by modal operators K_i for each of individuals i, $1 \leqslant i \leqslant n$.

Definition 1: (i) Each of the propositional variables $P_1, \ldots, P_k$ is a formula.

(ii) If A, B are formulae, so are $A \wedge B$, $A \vee B$ and $\neg A$.

(iii) If A is a formula then so is $K_i(A)$ for each individual i.

Example: The formula $K_1(P)$ says that individual 1 knows P. The formula $K_1(P) \vee K_1(\neg P)$ says that individual 1 knows P or he knows that P is false. In other words, the formula says that 1 knows *whether* P, and is not logically valid. By contrast, the formula $K_1(P \vee \neg P)$ says that 1 knows that P is either true or false and is valid. The formula $K_1(K_2(P) \vee K_2(\neg P))$ says that 1 knows that 2 knows whether P and $K_1(P \wedge \neg K_2(P))$ says that 1 knows that P and that 2 does not know that P is true. A formula $K_i(B)$ or its dual $L_i(B) = \neg K_i(\neg B)$ will be called a *knowledge formula*.

It is conventional, when setting up a logic, to offer a semantics and raise the question of a sound and complete axiom system. If possible, a completeness result should be proved. However, the notion of knowledge is insufficiently clear to have a semantics ready at hand. We shall therefore start by introducing some axioms that are usually considered and discuss them.

Axiomatisation: The following axioms and rules of inference have been considered by various researchers. We will discuss the intuitive reasons why these axioms tend to be accepted and then *only* give a Kripke model theory for them

1. All tautologies
2. $K_i(A) \wedge K_i(A \Rightarrow B) \Rightarrow K_i(B)$
3. $K_i(A) \Rightarrow A$
4. $K_i(A) \Rightarrow K_i(K_i(A))$
5. $\neg K_i(A) \Rightarrow K_i(\neg K_i(A))$

Rules of Inference

$$\frac{A \qquad A \Rightarrow B}{B} \qquad \text{(Modus Ponens)}$$

$$\frac{A}{K_i(A)} \qquad \text{(Necessitation)}$$

The axioms and rules can be intuitively justified by the following sort of informal argument. Tautologies and modus ponens do not directly involve knowledge but only truth. Of course it *is* presumed, that given A and i, $K_i(A)$ is either true or not, i.e. that individual i either knows A or not. Thus we are implicitly making the decision that classical logic applies also to statements involving knowledge.

Consider now the other axioms and rules. Axiom 3 says that something cannot be known unless it is true. Axioms 4 and 5 are justified on the grounds that whether i knows A or not is, as it were, an internal matter for i and i should know whether he knows A. Axiom 2 says that i can deduce consequences from what he knows, and finally, the rule of necessitation says that any *logically valid* argument that we can make, i can also. We shall discuss later whether these assumptions are reasonable in all contexts.

We make one technical observation before proceeding. The system as described above has the property that as soon as an axiom A is added, then $K_i(A)$ becomes a theorem. Hence it is impossible to have $P \wedge \neg K_i(P)$ be consistent. Thus the system can be used as a pure logic but is unsuitable as an applied system where one may want to say for example that, say, P is true but that i does not know this. An equivalent system can be obtained by *deleting* the generalisation rule, but *adding* the condition that if A is a (logical) axiom, then so is $K_i(A)$ for all i. This modification leaves unchanged the set of logical theorems, but now one can add an axiom A without implying $K_i(A)$ thereby. This modified system will be referred to as LK5 from now on. We shall refer to the system *without* axiom 5 as LK4. This usage parallels the notations S5 and S4 used in Modal Logic and will be justified by the close resemblance between the Modal Logics and the corresponding Logics of Knowledge. LK without a number attached to it will always mean LK5.

A Kripke Semantics: A mathematical semantics can be given for both LK4 and LK5 by considering Kripke structures. We assume given a universe W of worlds or states. Elements of W will be referred to by letters s,t etc. Then a *Kripke structure* over W assigns truth values to all atomic formulae at each state. I.e. we are given a subset $\pi(P)$ for each atomic formula P and the state s satisfies P ($s \models P$) iff $s \in \pi(P)$. Moreover, there is given for each knower i a binary relation R_i. Then the truth definition is extended to arbitrary formulae by letting:

$s \models A \vee B$ iff $s \models A$ or $s \models B$

$s \models A \wedge B$ iff $s \models A$ and $s \models B$

$s \models \neg A$ iff $s \not\models A$

$s \models K_i(A)$ iff for all t such that $(s,t) \in R_i$, $t \models A$

(If L_i is the dual of K_i, i.e. $L_i(B)$ stands for $\neg K_i(\neg B)$, then we also have $M,s\models L_i(B)$ iff there is a t such that $(s,t)\in R_i$ and $M,t\models B$.)

Sometimes we will say that there is an i arrow from s to t or that t is i-aceesible from s to indicate the fact that $(s,t)\in R_i$.

Lemma 1: A model M satisfies all axioms of LK5 if the R_i are all equivalence relations. Similarly with LK4 and partial orderings instead of equivalence relations. The set of formulae true at any state is closed under modus ponens. The set of formulae true at *all* states of M is also closed under necessitation

The proof is quite straightforward and follows the patterns of the usual (1 person) Logic of Knowledge quite closely. We give two cases. For example the formula $K_i(A)=>K_i(K_i(A))$ holds at every state s. For suppose $K_i(A)$ holds in some model M at s. Then for all t such that $(s,t)\in R_i$, A holds at t. Now the succedent $K_i(K_i(A))$ says that for all t′ such that $(s,t')\in R_i o R_i$, t′ satisfies A. But R_i is transitive and $R_i o R_i \subseteq R_i$. Hence the t′ are included among the t and the succedent is true at s.

To see closure under necessitation, suppose A is true at all states of M. Then for any s,t, if $(s,t)\in R_i$, then t satisfies A. Hence for all s, $K_i(A)$ holds. QED

It follows that all provable formulae of LK5 are true at all states of models where the R_i are equivalence relations and similarly for LK4 with partial orderings. This gives us soundness results for the LKi with appropriate models.

The intuitive justification for Kripke models is roughly that each i has a set of worlds that are possible for him. He knows A if A is true in all worlds that are possible for him. The condition that each R_i be an equivalence relation is to ensure that everything known be true and that i knows his own internal knowledge.

To obtain a completeness result it is sufficient to show that every consistent formula has a model of the appropriate kind. We shall in fact construct a *finite* model along the lines of the completeness proof in [KP]. We give the details only for LK5.

Given a consistent formula A, let F be the set of all subformulae of F and let W be the set of *all* consistent conjunctions of elements of F and their negations. Note that F has no more elements than c(A) (the number of occurrences of logical symbols and atomic predicates in A). Hence the size of W is no more than $2^{c(A)}$. Let s,t etc denote elements of W. Now define, for each P, $\pi(P)$ = {s| P is a conjunct of s}. For each individual i, let R_i = {(s,t)| for all B such that K_i(B) is in s, B is in t}. This completes our definition of the model M.

Lemma 2: Each R_i is an equivalence relation.
Proof: For each s in W, and K_i(B) in s, since K_i(B)=>B is an axiom, then ¬B cannot consistently be in s. Hence B must be. Since this is true of all K_i(B) in s, (s,s)$\in R_i$ and R_i is reflexive. Transitivity and symmetry are proved similarly using axioms 4 and 5. QED

Lemma 3: For all s in W and all B in F, s⊨B iff B is a conjunct of s.
Proof: The proof is quite straightforward and proceeds by induction on the complexity of B. the case where B is atomic holds by definition and the truth functional cases are quite easy. For eaxmple, if B∧C is in F, so are B, C and we get: s⊨B∧C iff s⊨B and s⊨C iff B is in s and C is in s. Now s contains either B∧C or ¬(B∧C). But s is consistent. Hence s contains B∧C iff it contains both B and C. Thus we get s⊨B∧C iff s contains B∧C as required.

So consider now the case of a formula K_i(B). If s contains K_i(B), then by the definition of R_i, for all t such that (s,t)$\in R_i$, t contains B. Hence for all such t, t⊨B by induction hypothesis. Thus s⊨K_i(B).

Suppose now that s does not contain K_i(B). Then it contains ¬K_i(B). We claim that the set X={C|K_i(C) is in s} is consistent with ¬B. For otherwise, X would imply B and using necessitation and axioms 2 and 4, we would get that X would imply K_i(B). But X is a subset of s and hence s would not be consistent with ¬K_i(B). Thus X∪{¬B} is consistent and extends to some element t of W. Then (s,t) is in R_i, t satisfies ¬B (by induction hypothesis) and hence s does not satisfy K_i(B). QED

The lemmas above imply the completeness theorem.

Theorem 1: The provable formulae of LK5 are precisely those that hold in Kripke structures with equivalence relations. Similarly for LK4 and partial orders.

The results above imply that LK5 is a subsystem of PDL^- and that LK4 is a subsystem of PDL.

Lemma 4: The following map θ is a faithful map from the logic LK5 of knowledge into PDL^- i.e. that for a formula A of LK, A is a theorem of LK iff $\theta(A)$ is a theorem of PDL^-. Here for each individual i, a_i is an atomic program.

1. $\theta(P)=P$ if P is an atom.
2. $\theta(\neg A) = \neg\theta(A)$
3. $\theta(A \vee B) = \theta(A) \vee \theta(B)$
4. $\theta(K_i(A)) = [(a_i \cup a_i^-)^*]\theta(A)$

The lemma is proved by the model theoretic construction above and noticing that equivalence relations are precisely the relations corresponding to the program expressions $(a \cup a^-)^*$. For clearly, if α is $(a \cup a^-)^*$, then R_α is an equivalence relation. Conversely, if R is an equivalence relation, then taking R_a to be R, we get $R_\alpha = R_a = R$.

Now we know [P1], [Pr] that PDL^- is decidable in DEXPTIME. Thus we get:

Theorem 2: LK5 is decidable in DEXPTIME.

A similar result can be proved for LK4 by replacing clause 4 above by the condition

4'. $\theta(K_i(A)) = [a_i*]\theta(A)$

Common Knowledge and Compactness: Sometimes it is convenient to introduce non-logical facts which are known to everyone. Here the important fact is not only that everyone knows these facts but also that everyone knows that everyone knows them etc. Thus if P is such a fact then P, $K_i(P)$, $K_j(K_i(P))$ $K_i(K_j(K_i(P)))$ would all have to be true. In other words, P would be true, i knows P, j knows that i knows P and i knows that j knows that i knows P. We could go on forever. If we symbolise the fact that some formula A is common knowledge as C(A), then we get the axioms $C(A) \Rightarrow K_i(A)$ and $C(A) \Rightarrow C(C(A))$ from which all these consequences can be proved.

However, there is an important difference between the logics LK4 and LK5 and the corresponding logics (call them CK4 and CK5) with common knowledge.

It is easy to see that the logics LK4 and LK5 are compact. If a set X of formulae implies some formula A, then there is a finite subset X′ of X which also implies A.

Theorem 3: LK4 and LK5 are compact.

Proof: Suppose we are given a Kripke structure M. Then M can also be thought of as a first order structure with domain W, unary predicates P_i corresponding to the atomic predicates, and binary relations R_j. Now we define a map θ which maps a formula of LK into a first order formula with one free variable.

$\theta(P)(s) = P(s)$

$\theta(A \vee B)(s) = \theta(A)(s) \vee \theta(B)(s)$

Similarly with ¬ nd ∧.

$\theta(K_i(A))(s) = (\forall t)(R_i(s,t) \Rightarrow \theta(A)(t))$

Then θ(A)(s) merely says that s⊨A in the first order structure corresponding to M.

Suppose X implies A in, say, LK5, Let E be the first order formula that says that all the R_i are equivalence relations. Then for all models M which satisfy E and all states s such that $\theta(X)=\{\theta(A)(s) \mid A \in X\}$ is true at s, s will satisfy θ(A). I.e. θ(X) together with E implies θ(A) in first order logic. But first order logic is compact. Hence some finite subset Y of θ(X) together with E implies θ(A)(s). But Y must be of the form θ(X′) for some finite subset X′ of X. Hence X′ implies A in LK5. QED

However if C is added, then compactness is lost. For let Z be the smallest set of formulae such that P is in Z and for all i and all A in Y, $K_i(A)$ is also in Z. Then Z is (semantically) equivalent to C(P) and indeed C is *explained* by saying that C(P) means Z. However, if n>1 then no finite subset of Z implies C(P).

For suppose there were such a finite subset Z′. Let m be an upper bound to the complexity of the formulae in Z′ and consider the model M with $W = \{s_0,\ldots,s_{m+1}\}$. $\pi(P) = \{s_0,\ldots,s_m\}$ and $R_i = \{(s_j,s_{j+1}) \mid j \equiv i \mod 2\}$. Then it is readily verfied that all formulae of Z′ are true at s_0 but that $D = K_2(K_1(\ldots(P)..)$ is not, where the K_1 and K_2 alternate in D and the number of K's in B is m+1. Thus Z′ did not imply D and hence cannot imply C(P).

However we do have the following result holding. Suppose that C(A) implies some formula B such that B is C free. Then there is a finite approximation to C(A) which also implies B. This follows from the fact that C(A) is effectively equivalent to an infinite set Z of C-free formulae. If C(A) implies B, then so does Z and hence by compactness, so does some finite subset of Z.

The logics of knowledge with the C operator are still translatable to PDL^-. For we can translate C as $[(a_1 \cup \ldots \cup a_n \cup a_1^- \cup \ldots \cup a_n^-)^*]$ and all the required properties hold. It would be interesting, in view of [MSM] whether there are extensions of the logic of common knowledge by axiom schemes which are undecidable or even Π_1 complete.

A Game Theoretic Semantics: We define a game theoretic semantics which gives the truth value of a formula A at an arbitrary state s of a model M.

The *positions* in the game are pairs (s,A) where s is a state and A is a formula. For convenience we will assume that all negations have been driven inwards so that A is made up from literals with $\wedge$, $\vee$, K_i and L_i where $L_i(B)$ (read, i allows B) stands for $\neg K_i(\neg B)$. (A literal is an atomic formula or its negation) There are two players I (the proponent) and II (the opponent or adversary player). A *move* consists of three parts, the current position, the choosing player and the possible new positions. If A is a literal then the game has *ended* and player I wins iff $s \models A$. The table below shows the three parts of the move for the case where A is not a literal. The current position is (s,A).

Caution: It is important to distinguish between the two players I and II and the knowers i, $i \leq n$.

Form of A	choosing player	Possible next positions
$B \wedge C$	II	(s,B), (s,C)
$B \vee C$	I	(s,B), (s,C)
$K_i(B)$	II	(t,B) with $(s,t) \in R_i$
$L_i(B)$	I	(t,B) with (s,t) in R_i.

Theorem 4: $s \models A$ iff player I has a winning strategy for the game above, starting with (s,A).

Proof: This is clear if A is a literal. Suppose A is $B \wedge C$. Then $s \models A$ iff $s \models B$ and $s \models C$ iff (induction hypothesis) there is a winning strategy for I from (s,B) and from (s,C) iff there is a winning strategy from (s,A) because I can win from both the possible next positions.

Suppose now that A is $L_i(B)$. Then $s \models A$ iff there is a t such that $(s,t) \in R_i$ and $t \models B$ iff I has a possible winning next position, But since I is the choosing player, a possible winning next position is equivalent to a winning current position. **QED**

Let the *distance* between two states (s,t) be the length d of the shortest sequence $(s_0,...,s_d)$ such that $s=s_0$, $t=s_d$ and for all $i<d$, $(s_i,s_{i+1}) \in$ some R_j. Let the *K-depth* of a formula A be the largest number of K's and L's encountered on any branch when A is written as a tree.

Theorem 5: If $M,s \models A$ and the K-depth of A is d, let M' be the part of M consisting of all states at a distance no greater than d from s. Then $M',s \models A$.

Proof: It is clear that states at a distance greater than d from s cannot be involved in the game which begins with position (s,A).

We now prove a normal form theorem for formulae. There are 8 identities of the Logic LK which allow us to eliminate a K_i or an L_i *immediately* in the scope of a K_i or an L_i. We state some of them below.

$$K_i(A \wedge K_i(B)) \iff K_i(A) \wedge K_i(B)$$
$$K_i(A \wedge L_i(B)) \iff K_i(A) \wedge L_i(B)$$
$$K_i(A \vee K_i(B)) \iff K_i(A) \vee K_i(B)$$
$$K_i(A \vee L_i(B)) \iff K_i(A) \vee L_i(B)$$

The other four are just the duals.

Let us say that a formula A is in normal form if it is made up from literals using $\wedge$, $\vee$, the K_i and the L_i and every subformula $K_i(D)$ $(L_i(D))$ of A is a truth functional combination of literals, formulae $K_j(C)$ and formulae $L_j(C)$ with $j \neq i$.

Theorem 6: Every formula is equivalent in LK5 to a normal formula.
Proof: Follows straightforwardly from the identities above.

The Nonmonotonic case: McCarthy has suggested the following non-monotonic rule of inference. See also, Reiter [R].

$$\frac{T \nvdash K_i(A)}{T \vdash \neg K_i(A)} \qquad \text{(the rule M)}$$

The intuition is that if T *includes all knowledge* that individual i has, then for any formula A such that $K_i(A)$ is not provable in T, i can conclude that (s)he does not know A. Let us refer to LK5 with this rule as NM and a theory that is closed under this rule as an NM theory. (N for non-monotonic.).

Theorem 7: (i) Every complete LK5 theory is an NM theory and vice versa.

(ii) An NM theory is complete for all knowledge formulae, i.e. formulae where every occurrence of an atom is in the scope of some K_i.

(iii) An NM theory is complete iff it is complete for all atoms P_i.

Proof: (i) Since every NM theory is an LK5 theory, it follows that a complete NM theory is also a complete LK5 theory. Conversely, let T be a complete LK5 theory. Then if $K_i(B)$ is not a theorem of T, then $\neg K_i(B)$ is.

(ii) This is obvious.

(iii) Follows immediately from (ii).

Stark [St] discusses the M rule and raises the question of a decision procedure. But first, the rule itself needs discussion. It is easy to see that the nonmonotonic M rule can lead to inconsistencies. We give some examples to provide an intuition.

Suppose that T has a single non-logical axiom $K_i(P) \vee K_i(Q)$. Then neither $K_i(P)$ nor $K_i(Q)$ will be a theorem. Now the rule yields $\neg K_i(P)$ and $\neg K_i(Q)$ and hence $\neg(K_i(P) \vee K_i(Q))$ can also be proved. But this contradicts the original assumption of $K_i(P) \vee K_i(Q)$. Thus the LK5 consistent formula $K_i(P) \vee K_i(Q)$ is NM inconsistent.

One could, of course, apply the rule *serially*. In that case, we do get consistency, for after applying it to $\vdash K_i(P)$ and getting $\neg K_i(P)$ one finds that $K_i(Q)$ is now a theorem so that $\neg K_i(Q)$ cannot be derived. Unfortunately, there is no reason other than personal taste for preferring P to Q and the other order yields a different theory.

The problem in this case was that $K_i(P) \vee K_i(Q)$ could not have been the *whole* of what was known to i. If $K_i(P) \vee K_i(Q)$ holds then i must know either P or Q and hence either $K_i(P)$ or $K_i(Q)$ must be included in the theory at the very start before we apply the non-monotonic rule. This of course is reasonable since the rule was not intended to be applied to partial information. However, there are other, subtler problems with the rule.

Suppose that T has no non-logical axioms. Then neither $K_i(P)$ nor $K_i(\neg K_i(P))$ is a theorem of T. Now, on the one hand, the rule yields $\neg K_i(P)$ and hence $K_i(\neg K_i(P))$. On the other hand the rule applied to the fact that $K_i(\neg K_i(P))$ is not provable, yields $\neg K_i(\neg K_i(P))$. These two contradict each other. Here it is clear that we have to give a preference to deducing $\neg K_i(P)$. For if there is no information from which i can know P, then it is definitely the case that he *does not know* P and hence *knows* that he does not know P.

The non-monotonic rule can also allow i to infer what *other* people know. For if $K_i(A)$ cannot be proved, then i does not know A, and hence i knows that j cannot know that i knows A. (j cannot know what is false). Thus we would infer $K_i(\neg K_j(K_i(A)))$ and *resist* the temptation to infer $\neg K_i(\neg K_j(K_i(A)))$ from the fact that $K_i(\neg K_j(K_i(A)))$ was not provable in T.

Again, the intuition is clear in this particular case, but it is not obvious what is the general paradigm for applying the rule.

Nonetheless, the M rule is intuitively a natural one. *For how else* can i find out that i does not know A except by realising that the evidence that i has is insufficient to imply A?

Can we make a systematic determination of how the rule should be applied and can we give a model theoretic reason for these choices? It turns out that we can and we now turn to a rigorous and formal investigation of non-monotonic reasoning in general and the McCarthy rule in particular.

Non-monotonic reasoning and model theory: When we use a monotonic system of deduction, the symbol $\vdash$ occurring in the rules of inference plays two distinct roles, which, by a happy coincidence, are in harmony. E.g. in the rule

$$\frac{\Gamma\vdash A \quad \Gamma\vdash A \Rightarrow B}{\Gamma\vdash B}$$

we can either say that having derived A and A=>B from Γ, we are now *allowed* to derive B. We can then define the (deductive) consequences of Γ to be the set of all formulae derivable from Γ. Call this the dynamic interpretation of the rule.

Alternately, we can think of $\vdash$ as a *relation* between Γ and certain formulae and the rule above is a condition that this relation satisfies. Call this the static interpretation of the rule.

It turns out that there is a smallest set that contains the logical axioms and the set Γ and which satisfies the conditions corresponding to the rules of inference. It is *also* the set of formulae *derivable* from Γ (and the logical axioms) using the rules. Thus the static and dynamic interpretations are in harmony and we don't usually notice that we have two interpretations of the same rule.

Of course, this harmony breaks down with non-monotonicity. When we have a rule of the form

$$\frac{\Gamma\nvdash K_i(A)}{\Gamma\vdash \neg K_i(A)}$$

the premise cannot mean that we *have not* yet derived $K_i(A)$ from Γ, but it means rather that we *cannot* derive $K_i(A)$. But knowing what we can and cannot derive from Γ requires knowing what we meant by the rule in the first place. Thus the dynamic interpretation becomes unclear and we only have the static one left. Unfortunately, there is in general no unique or even smallest set that satisfies the rules thought of as conditions on $\vdash$. The Tarski-Knaster theorem, that guarantees the existence of a smallest solution, applies only to monotonic conditions.

There is a corresponding quandary with the model theoretic aspect of the situation. Generally, the larger a set of axioms, the fewer the models. For example, the axioms for commutative groups include the ones for groups. Hence, the class of commutative groups is smaller than the class of all groups.

Generally, given a set Γ of axioms, let Mod(Γ) be all the models of Γ and given a set X of models, let Th(X) be the formulae true in all elements of X. Formally,

$\mathrm{Mod}(\Gamma) = \{M \mid \text{for all } A \in \Gamma,\ M \models A\}$

$\mathrm{Th}(X) = \{A \mid \text{for all } M \in X,\ M \models A\}$

The semantic consequences of Γ can then be defined as Th(Mod(Γ)). Now the larger the Γ, the smaller is Mod(Γ) and the larger the X, the smaller is Th(X). Both the maps Mod and Th are *anti-monotonic*, and hence Th(Mod(Γ)) is going to be *monotonic* in Γ. If we now try to set up a deductive system corresponding to this semantics, we would want that to be monotonic also. In other words if deductive consequence and semantic consequence coincide and one is monotonic, so is the other.

In terms of knowledge, it means that when more information is received, the set of axioms goes up, the set of models goes down and the set of theorems goes up. How can we break this paradigm in a sensible way?

It turns out that the problem can be understood game-theoretically. Consider what happens in the monotonic case. Given X, we define a game as follows. Player I chooses a formula A and then player II chooses a model. If the model is in X and does not satisfy A, then player II wins.

Then player I has a winning strategy which consists of choosing a formula in Th(X) and then there is no way for player II to win. Since player II is the *only* one who works with the models, if X is *decreased* then player II is worse off and player I is better off. However, in the Kripke models that we shall deal with, both players have to make moves which involve the picking of a model (=state), player II with K_i and player I with L_i, and hence a decrease in the set of models may help *either* player. Thus Kripke models are an ideal way to understand non-monotonicity.

Returning to the M rule, suppose that we have a situation where a set Γ of formulae does not imply $K_i(A)$ *in LK5*. Then there is a model M and a state s of M such that s satsifies Γ and does not satisfy $K_i(A)$, i.e. satisfies $L_i(\neg A)$. Then there is a state t and an i arrow from s to t such that t satisfies $\neg A$ in M.

Now the M rule would make $L_i(\neg A)$ a *consequence* of Γ. In other words, if there is any model in which there is such an i arrow as above, then there must be such in *all* allowed models.

Let us refer to a state t as above as an i-possibility relative to Γ. Then the M rule makes such a possibility into a necessity.

Suppose now that Γ already decides all atomic formulae. In that case we know that the NM theory of M is complete and has in some sense a unique intended model which describes for each i, how the world looks to i. This is a model in which all possibilities that Γ allows are realised *simultaneously*.

Now we see that the formula $B = K_i(P) \vee K_i(Q)$ is inconsistent bacause it allows (in M_1) an i-arrow to a state t where P is false (since $L_i(\neg P)$ is LK5-consistent with it), and also (in M_2) an i-arrow to a state t′ where Q is false. But the two arrows cannot peacefully co-exist in any LK5 model of B. (Here $s \models P \wedge Q$ in all three models.)

```
M1    s<------->t⊨¬P
          i

M2    s<------->t'⊨¬Q
          i

M    s<-┬-------->t⊨¬P
        |  i
        └-------->t'⊨¬Q
           i
```

We would certainly want that for a formula B to be NM consistent, any two LK5 models of B, glued together, should yield another LK5 model of B. But in this case, s in M does not satisfy B reflecting the fact the B is NM inconsistent.

Now we start a systematic development by defining normal models.

Definition 2: A normal model of height 0 is a truth assignment. A normal model of height d+1 consists of a truth assignment plus, for each i, at most one i-arrow to a distinct copy of each normal model of height d.

A normal model looks like a tree. It is clear that the number of normal models of height 0, #(0), is 2^m where m is the number of atomic predicates. $\#(d+1) = 2^m . 2^{n.\#(d)}$. Given a formula of knowledge depth d, if it has a model, then by standard techniques, [P2], a normal model of height d can be obtained. Unfortunately, #(d) is non-elementary in d.

Given two normal models M, M′ of height d, we shall say that $M \subseteq M'$ if they satisfy the same truth assignment at the top (the root) and M′ has all the i-arrows to models of height d−1 that M has. (We assume that the top is labelled s for both models. The theory Th(M) of a normal model M will be the set of formulae true at s)

Definition 3: Given two sets of formulae T and T′, $T \leq T'$ if for every formula A which is in just one of T and T′, A has a subformula $L_i(D)$ which is in T−T′. T<T′ if T, T′ are distinct.

Intuitively, this says that T and T′ agree on *facts* but that in T the individuals have less information than they do in T′.

Lemma 5: If $M \subseteq M'$, then $Th(M') \leq Th(M)$.

Proof: If T, T′ differ on A, take the smallest subformula of A on which Th(M) and Th(M′) differ. Since Th(M) and Th(M′) have to agree on atomic formulae, and every formula is a truth functional combination of atomic formulae and knowledge formulae, this smallest subformula must be a *knowledge* formula, say $L_i(D)$. We claim that $L_i(D)$ is in Th(M′)−Th(M).

Now M and M′ must *agree* at s on all subformulae of D. If $D \in Th(M)$ then clearly $D \in Th(M')$ and hence $L_i(D) \in Th(M')$ also. If not, there is a t and an i-arrow in M from s to t such that $M,t \models D$. We claim that $M',t \models D$ also so that M and M′ do not differ after all.

For let player I play the same strategy in M′ that he would have played in M. If he loses, that can only be through a part of M′ not in M and which can only be accessed by player II through s. Since s and t are only connected by an i-arrow, the position at that stage must be $(t, K_i(E))$ where $K_i(E)$ is a *subformula* of D. But this would have been a winning position for I in M and hence, $M,t \models K_i(E)$ so $M,s \models K_i(E)$ and since $K_i(E)$ is a subformula of D,

M′,s⊨K_i(E) so M′,t⊨K_i(E). Thus player I does not lose in M′ after all. This shows that it must have been the case that L_i(D) is true in M′ and not in M. QED

Definition 4: Suppose given two normal models M and M′, of the same height d and suppose s satisfies the same truth assignment in M and M′. The model M+M′ will be the model obtained when the two models are glued together at s and all excess i-arrows from s to two different copies of the same subtree of height d−1 are thrown away. The relations R_i are kept equivalence relations by adding any new pairs that arise.

Note that Th(M+M′) is less than either of Th(M) and Th(M′).

For the rest of this section we shall often assume that the formula B that we are considering implies (in LK5) some truth assignment on the atomic formulae, i.e. that for each P, it implies either P or ¬P. Such a formula will be called truth functionally complete or simply, t.f. complete. Note that any non-monotonic theory that contains a t.f. complete B is complete. We shall also assume for convenience that the models considered are of some fixed height d where d exceeds the knowledge depth of the finitely many (usually one or two) formulae being looked at. It is easy to show that the results do not depend on d as long as it is large enough.

Definition 5: Let B be any t.f. complete formula. We will say that B is *persistent* if for all normal models M M′ of B, M+M′ is also a model of B.

It is clear that if B is persistent, then the model obtained by gluing together *all* normal models of B is also a model of B and its theory is the least among all complete theories containing B.

Definition 6: A set X of formulae is downward closed (d.c. or Hintikka set) if whenever A∈X and C is a subformula of A, then C∈X.

Remark: The set Sub(B) of all subformulae of some B is always d.c.

Lemma 6: Let X be d.c. and let M and M′ agree on X, then so does M+M′. Moreover if L_i(D) is a formula such that all subformulae of D are in X, then L_i(D) holds in M+M′ iff it holds in one of M and M′.

Proof: Just like lemma 5, by considering winning strategies.

Lemma 7: Let X be d.c. and let B be an LK-consistent conjunction, for all $A \in X$ of A or $\neg A$. Then B is persistent.

Proof: Immediate by the lemma above.

Definition 7: A t.f. complete B has the *max property* if it has a largest normal model M_m of depth d where d is at least the knowledge depth of B. B non-monotonically *implies* some formula A if A holds at the glue state of the largest normal model of B of depth at least equal to the knowledge depth of B=>A.

A persistent formula always has the max property, But $P \wedge Q \wedge R \wedge (L_i(P) \wedge L_i(Q)) \Rightarrow L_i(R))$ has the max property but is not persistent. However it non-monotonically implies $P \wedge Q \wedge R \wedge L_i(P) \wedge L_i(Q) \wedge L_i(R)$ which is persistent.

Theorem: It is decidable whether B has the max property and whether it non-monotonically implies A.

This follows immediately from the fact that M_m if it exists is finite. However, the decision procedure is non-elementary. We shall show that there is an elementary decision procedure also.

Now we connect up our model theoretic definition of non-monotonic consequence with the M rule.

Definition 8: A *normal* non-monotonic proof of A from B in the non-monontonic system is a sequence of *monotonic* (LK) theories T_k, $0 \leq k \leq m$ such that

(i) T_0 is the LK-theory generated by B and

(ii) for each $k<m$, T_{k+1} is the LK-theory obtained by adding to T_k a formula $L_i(D)$ where $K_i(\neg D)$ is not in T_k and if D has a sub-formula $K_i(F)$ then either $K_i(F)$ or $L_i(\neg F)$ is already in T_k.

(iii) $A \in T_m$.

Theorem 8: Let B be t.f. complete.

(i) If B has the max property, then B non-monotonically implies A iff there is a normal proof of A from B and in which the formulae $L_i(D)$ added non-monotonically are all subformulae of A.

(ii) B has the max property iff among the theories containing B there is a lowest one iff there is a lowest among the finite theories which are truth assignments on the subformulae of B.

(iii) If B does not have the max property then there is a subformula C of B such that there are normal proofs of both C and ¬C and again with the same restriction on formulae $L_i(D)$ added.

Proof: (i) It is sufficient to prove this for knowledge formulae A for other formulae are merely truth functional combinations of these and atomic formulae.

Now it is clear by induction on the knowledge height of A that either A or its negation has a normal proof from B and in which the M rule is applied only to subformulae of A. For if A is (say) an L formula and ¬A is not provable after its proper subformulae have been decided, then A can be added by the (normalised) M-rule. Hence it is enough to show of every L-formula A that is added in the course of the proof that it holds in M_m.

So suppose it is added at stage k+1. Then it is LK-consistent with the formulae of stage k and hence with B. There is a model M of T_k in which A holds. We can assume by induction hypothesis that T_k holds in M_m and hence, by lemma 5, A holds in M_m+M which is essentially the same as M_m.

(ii) The proof consists of three implications.

(a) If B has a largest model then there is a smallest theory containing B (lemma 5).

(b) The intersection of this theory with the subformulae of B will be the finite theory required.

(c) Now let T be this finite theory. Then T is persistent and has a largest model M. However if M′ is any other model of B, then Th(M+M′) which is less than Th(M) must coincide with T on Sub(B). Hence M+M′ is the same as M and M is the largest model of B.

(iii) If there were a smallest among the finite theories on sub(B). then since this theory is persistent, by (iic) above, B would have the max property. So, among the finite theories on Sub(B), there are two minimal ones which are not smallest. Call them T and T′. If all formulae of both T and T′ are non-monotonically provable from B then there must be a C on which T and T′ differ. Then both C and ¬C are provable as required.

Otherwise suppose not all formulae of T can be proved. So consider the procedure like that in (i) above, which tries to prove all formulae of T from the bottom up. If at some stage there is a theory Tk⊆T and a formula Li(D) of T not in

T_k and all subformulae of D have already been decided, then $L_i(D)$ must be consistent with T_k and can be added. Similarly if there is a $K_i(D)$ which is implied by T_k or a formula which is a truth functional combination of other formulae which have already been decided.

Thus the only way we can have a deadlock is if the simplest formulae of $T-T_k$ are *all* of the form $K_i(D)$. In that case, all the formulae $L_i(\neg D)$ are consistent individually with T_k and can all be proved. If they are not consistent together with T_k, then after proving some of them non-monotonically, the negation of another one can be proved and we are done. Otherwise add *all* of them to T_k and extend to a theory T′ on Sub(B). Then T′<T contradicting the minimality of T. QED

Theorem 9: Non-monotonic consistency, the max property and non-monotonic implication are all in DEXPTIME.

Proof: The last follows immediately from the fact that LK is in DEXPTIME and that given B and A, it can be decided by the procedure above which of the K and L subformulae of A are non-monotonically implied by B.

For the first two, we just showed that the max property, non-monotonic consistency and the existence of a smallest subtheory including B on Sub(B). But the last of the three can clearly be checked in DEXPTIME. QED

Directions for Further Work: While it is true that the axioms of LK that we took as basic are widely studied, they are not universally accepted. It seems reasonable that if people (or computers) are to be knowledgeable about their own internal knowledge, then this knowledge should be confined to facts known directly and not extended to the *consequences* of directly known facts. Thus a person who knows the axioms of ZF set theory need not know all the theorems. More practically, since tautologies are an NP-complete set, it is unreasonable to expect a theory of knowledge in the context of cryptography which assumes that every one knows all tautologies. It seems that the theory we have been studying is a mathematical idealisation and a theory is needed that takes seriously the limitations on powers of reasoning and computation. Other possible directions for further research are theories that bring in probability, time and action as aspects of knowledge.

Acknowledgements: We have benefitted from incisive comments by Melvin Fitting, Joe Halpern, David Mumford and Richard Stark. We acknowledge our indebtedness to these people.

References

[D] F. Dretske, *Knowledge and the Flow of Information* MIT press 1981.

[FHV] R. Fagin, J. Halpern and M. Vardi, "A Model Theoretic Analysis of Knowledge", IEEE-FOCS 1984.

[H] J. Hintikka, *Knowledge and Belief*, Cornell U. Press 1962.

[HM] J. Halpern and Y. Moses, "Knowledge and Common Knowledge in a Distributed Environment", to appear in *ACM-PODC* 1984.

[KP] D. Kozen and R. Parikh, "An Elementary Proof of the Completeness of PDL", *Theor. Comp. Sci* 14 (1981) 113-118.

[L] D. Lehmann, "Knowledge, Common Knowledge and Related Puzzles", tp appear in *ACM-PODC* 1984.

[M2] R.C. Moore, "Semantical Considerations on Non-monotonic Logic", *Proc. 8th IJCAI* (1983) 272-279.

[MD] J. McDermott and J. Doyle, "NonMonotonic Logic" *Artificial Intelligence* 13, (1980) 41-72.

[MH] J. McCarthy, and P. Hayes "Some Philosophical Problems from the standpoint of Artificial Intelligence", in *Machine Intelligence*, ed. D. Michie, American Elsevier 1969, 463-502.

[MSM] A. Meyer, R. Streett and G. Mirkowska, "The Decucibility Problem in Propositional Dynamic Logic", *Proc 8th ICALP* Springer LNCS 115 (1981) pp 238-248.

[P1] R. Parikh, "A Completeness Result for Propostional Dynamic Logic", *MFCS '78* Springer Lecture Notes in Computer Science vol 64, 403-415

[P2] R. Parikh, "Second Order Process Logic", *IEEE-FOCS 1978*

[P3] R. Parikh, "Propositional Game Logic", *IEEE-FOCS 1983* 195-200.

[Pr] V. Pratt, "Models of Program Logics", 20th IEEE-FOCS (1979) 115-122.

[R] R. Reiter, "On Closed World Data Bases" in *Logic and Data Bases* (Ed. Gallaire and Minker) Plenum Press (1978) pp 55-76.

[St] R. Stark, "Logics of Knowledge", Zeit. Math. Logic 27 (1981) 371-374.

[XW] M. Xiwen and G. Welde, "A Modal Logic of Knowledge", *IJCAI '83* 398-401.

Persistent first class procedures are enough

Malcolm P. Atkinson and Ronald Morrison

University of Glasgow, Glasgow, Scotland G128QQ.
and
University of St Andrews, St Andrews, Scotland KY169SX.

Abstract

We describe how the provision of a persistent programming environment together with a language that supports first class procedures may be used to provide the semantic features of other object modelling languages. In particular the effects of information hiding, data protection and separate compilation are provided and a comparison of the method with more traditional techniques is examined.

Introduction

We explain what is meant by extending rights of procedures and functions in a procedural language to be consistent with those of other data types such as integer or array. This is shown to be useful and elsewhere we have demonstrated it is implementable [5].

In particular the effects of information hiding, data protection and separate compilation can be achieved without introducing new concepts such as modules and abstract types. The relative merits of the two approaches are reviewed. Separate program preparation depends on making the procedure a first class data object and providing orthogonal persistence. The power of this consistent treatment of procedures is obtained without adding to the complexity of the language. Indeed the language is simplified, there being fewer concepts for the programmer to understand.

What is persistence?

The persistence of a data object is the length of time that the object exists. In traditional programming languages data cannot last longer than the activation of the program without the explicit use of some storage agency such as a file system or a database management system. In persistent programming, data can outlive the program and the method of accessing the data is uniform whether it be long or short term data. We have discussed this concept fully elsewhere [1]. The language concepts presented in this paper depend on persistence being provided as an orthogonal property of data; all data objects, whatever their type, have the same rights to long and short term persistence.

What are first class procedures?

Most programming languages provide facilities for abstractions over expressions and statements. Indeed these abstractions, functions and procedures let us say, are often the only mechanisms for abstraction in the programming language. The power of the mechanism is derived from the fact that the user of the procedure does not require to know the details of how the procedure executes, only its effect. We use the word 'procedure' to represent both procedure and function when it is not necessary to differentiate between them.

The procedures of Algol 60[19] and Pascal[26] can only be declared, passed as parameters or executed. However, as has been pointed out by Morris [16] and Zilles [29], to exploit the device to its full potential it is necessary to promote procedures to be full first class data objects. That is, procedures should be allowed the same civil rights as any other data object in the language such as being assignable, the result of expressions or other procedures, elements of structures or vectors etc. Lisp [14] was the first language with first class procedures and other languages include Iswim [11], Pal [6], Gedanken [22], Sasl [24], ML [15] and with some restrictions Euler [25] and Algol 68 [30]. Of course the applicative programming technique revolves around the ability to have first class procedures in the language and central ideas such as partial application are impossible otherwise.

What is Closure?

The most important concept in the understanding of first class procedures is that of closure [23,9]. The closure of a procedure is all the information required to execute the procedure correctly. It is in two parts. The first part is the code to execute the procedure and the second part is its environment which contains the local and free variables of the procedure and is usually implemented by a static chain [21]. In order to execute the procedure correctly we must have both parts of the closure. We will restrict ourselves here to block structured languages with static scope rules.

In block structured languages such as Algol 60, Pascal and S-algol [17] we very rarely need both parts of the closure to be recorded explicitly for the procedure. This is because the scope rules determine that a procedure can only be called from a position in the program where all the free variables of the procedure are accessible. The local variables do not exist before and after the call so the static chain is computable at the time of the call.

This is illustrated in Figure 1 where we have a program written in S-algol. In procedure 'one' we have the free variables 'a' and 'b'. However since the procedure may only be called after its declaration in the same block or inner blocks it is always possible for the compiler to calculate the static chain of the procedure from the static chain of the block that calls it.

```
let a := 3
 .
 .
begin
```

```
     let b:= 16
     .
     .
     procedure one
     ! start of scope of procedure one
     begin
          .
          .
          write a + b
     end
     .
     .
     one
     begin
          .
          .
          one
     end
     ! end of scope of procedure one
end
```

A program where the full closure is not required

Figure 1

Algol 60, Pascal and S-algol all allow procedures to be passed as parameters to other procedures and clearly from Figure 2 it can be seen that the static chain may not always be computable from the block surrounding the call.

```
procedure A( procedure( int -> int )B )
begin
     let p := 3
     .
     .
     write B( p )
end

begin
     let b := 14 ; let c := 3
     procedure C( int a -> int ) ; b * b - 4 * a * c
     A( C )
end
```

A program requiring the full procedure closure

Figure 2

When procedure 'A' is executed in this example function 'B', which is the formal parameter, is really function 'C' in the following block. In order to execute 'C' correctly we must know about the free variables 'b' and 'c'. To do this we need both parts of the closure for 'C' to be transmitted to 'A' when 'A' is called.

The p-code implementation of Pascal [20] falls into the trap of only recording the procedure address instead of the full closure for the procedure and thus disallows the passing of procedures as parameters. A solution to the problem is given by Morrison [18].

First class procedures in relation to abstract data types.

The supporters of abstract data types [13] argue that it is essential for powerful languages to have an abstraction mechanism over data objects. In the same manner that a procedure separates the implementation of a task from its use, the abstract data type separates the representation of a data object from its use. Thus we have at once an abstraction mechanism and a protection mechanism. The abstract data type defines the operations available on the data object while only allowing the definition of the type to manipulate or access the representation. Languages which support abstract data types include Simula [4], Clu [12], Alphard [28], Euclid [10], ML[15] and Ada [8].

None of the above languages, with the exception of ML, support first class procedures. However, as has been pointed out by Horning [7], the advantages and aims of procedural and data abstraction are similar. Indeed if procedures are data objects the mechanism for both abstractions can be the same --- that of the procedure. This, of course, is not a new idea and was present in the work of Strachey [23] and Zilles [29].

The complex number example

To explain the mechanism the following program segment written in PS-algol [3] is given in Figure 3. The task it sets out to solve is to define an abstract object for a complex number and to allow only the operations of addition, printing and creation on the complex number.

```
let add := proc( pntr a,b -> pntr ) ; nullproc
let print := proc( pntr a ) ; nullproc
let complex := proc( real a,b -> pntr ) ; nullproc

begin
     structure complex.number( real rpart,ipart )

     add := proc( pntr a,b -> pntr )
            complex.number( a( rpart ) + b( rpart ),a( ipart ) + b( ipart ) )

     print := proc( pntr a )
              write a( rpart ),
              if a( ipart ) < 0 then "-" else "+",rabs( a( ipart ) ),"i"

     complex := proc( real a,b -> pntr )
                complex.number( a,b )
end

let a = complex( -1.0,-2.8 ) ; let b = complex( 2.3,3.2 )
print( add( a,b ) )
```

The definition of an abstract type for complex numbers in PS-algol

Figure 3

In PS-algol a structure class is a tuple of named fields with any number of fields of any type. The **structure** statement adds to the current environment a binding in the closest enclosing scope for the class name ('complex.number' in this example), and a binding for each field name ('ipart' and 'rpart' in this case). When an instance of a structure class is created (by complex.number(a,b) above), it yields an object of that class which may be assigned to an object of type **pntr**. The class of a pointer is not determined at compile time but at run time and since the structure class is similar to a type definition in other languages this gives a degree of polymorphism to PS-algol.

The structure declaration in the example

structure complex.number(**real** rpart,ipart)

defines a structure with two real fields 'rpart' and 'ipart'. To create an object of this class we may use the expression

complex.number(3.2,5.4)

The fields of the structure may then be accessed by using a pointer expression followed by the structure field name in brackets. e.g.

a(rpart)

The example, in Figure 3, shows three procedure variables being declared and in the following block being assigned values. The representation of the complex number is encapsulated in the block and is not available to other parts of the program. Since the field names of the representation of the complex number are local to the block only the procedures defined in the block may use these names. Outside the block the names are invisible. Thus we have completely separated the representation of the data object from its use and achieved one of the aims of abstract data types. Indeed the block could be rewritten to represent the complex number in polar co-ordinates without changing the external meaning. Furthermore we have demonstrated that the traditional block structure and scope rules of Algol 60 with the addition of first class procedures are sufficient to support abstract data types. Figure 4 shows how the block can be made into a function itself perhaps to be located elsewhere in the program or separately compiled.

```
structure complex.arithmetic( proc( pntr,pntr -> pntr )cadd ;
                              proc( pntr )cprint ;
                              proc( real,real -> pntr )ccomplex )

let complex.arith = proc( -> pntr )
begin
     structure complex.number( real rpart,ipart )

     complex.arithmetic(
     proc( pntr a,b -> pntr )
     complex.number( a( rpart ) + b( rpart ),a( ipart ) + b( ipart ) ),

     proc( pntr a )
     { write a( rpart ),
             if a( ipart ) < 0 then "-" else "+",rabs( a( ipart ) ),"i" },

     proc( real a,b -> pntr )
     complex.number( a,b ) )
end !of complex.arith

!main program --- redo the names
let t = complex.arith()
let add = t( cadd ) ; let print = t( cprint ) ; let complex = t( ccomplex )

let a = complex( 1.2,0.3 ) ; let b = complex( 9.4,-3.2 )
print( add( a,b ) )
```

The complex number package

Figure 4

The structure class 'complex.arithmetic' contains three procedures as elements. The notation

proc(**pntr**,**pntr** -> **pntr**)

denotes the type of a function from two pointer parameters to an object of type pointer. Whereas **proc**(**pntr**) denotes the type of a procedure with one pointer parameter.

In the main part of the program an application of the function 'complex.arith' yields a structure of class 'complex.arithmetic' which is assigned to the name 't'. In this procedure the same three procedures as before are defined and their closures exported via a structure. This is slightly more complex than the last version in that there is an extra dereference to obtain the same names but that is a syntactic problem which can easily be overcome if necessary.

Data protection

Morris [16] specified three ways in which a data object may be used in a manner not intended. They are

"1. Alteration : An object that involves references may be changed without use of the primitive functions provided for the purpose.
2. Discovery : The properties of an object might be explored without using the primitive functions.
3. Impersonation : An object, not intended to represent anything in particular, may be presented to a primitive function expecting an object representing something quite specific."

The first two problems are overcome by the methods already demonstrated in PS-algol. Since the names of the fields in the structure class are only known to the primitive procedures, by the scope rules, then the objects can never be accessed except by the primitive procedures. However impersonation is a problem in PS-algol because structure class pointers are checked at run time. It is not that the impersonation will not be discovered but that it will cause a hard failure at run time. The solution to the problem is to check the class of the object before allowing any operation on it. Thus we can define the program's action if an impersonation does take place. In our example the procedure 'complex.arithmetic' may be rewritten as in Figure 5.

```
let complex.arith = proc( -> pntr )
begin
     structure complex.number( real rpart,ipart )
     let error = proc( pntr a -> bool )
                 if a isnt complex.number then
                 begin
                      write error.message
                      true
                 end else false
     complex.arithmetic(
     proc( pntr a,b -> pntr )
     if error( a ) or error( b ) then nil else
```

```
      complex.number( a( rpart ) + b( rpart ),a( ipart ) + b( ipart ) ),
   proc( pntr a )
   if error( a ) then write "This is not a complex number"
   else { write a( rpart ),
                if a( ipart ) < 0 then "-" else "+",rabs( a( ipart ) ),"i" },
   proc( real a,b -> pntr )
   complex.number( a,b ) )
end !of complex.arith
```

The complex number package with impersonation checks

Figure 5

Comparison of first class procedures and abstract data types

Figure 6 below shows how the abstract type for complex numbers may be declared in ML. We ignore the fact that ML does not have **real** as a base type for this example.

```
abstype comp = comp of real # real
with
    val add( comp( r1,i1 ) ) ( comp( r2,i2 ) ) = comp ( ( r1 + r2 ),( i1 + i2 ) )
    and print( comp( r,i ) ) = ( output( terminal,stringofreal( r ) ) ;
        output( terminal, if i < 0.0 then "-" else "+" ) ;
        output( terminal,stringofreal( realabs( i ) ) ) ;
        output( terminal,"i" ) )
    and complex r i = comp ( r,i )
end
```

An example abstract datatype declaration written in ML

Figure 6

It is useful to compare this with the declaration given in Figure 3. The **abstype .... with** construct in ML is essentially an environment manipulation, so that after the construct the declarations appearing between **with** and the corresponding **end** are installed in the subsequent environment, but the type 'comp' is available only in the environment of the declarations after **with.** This is nearly equivalent to the notation in Figure 3, with the following detailed correspondence.

1. In Figure 3 the three **let** clauses introduce the three names into the outer environment whereas in Figure 6 the same three names are left, by being declared after the **with,** in the outer scope.

2. The **begin end** pair delimits a scope level as does a **with end** pair.

3. In Figure 3 the representation of the complex number is introduced by the **structure** declaration which is local to this inner scope only. In Figure 6 the representation of complex is introduced by the **abstype** statement and this binding is available only in the scope by **with** and **end.**

4. In both cases in the inner scope three bindings of names to procedural values are declared.

The similarity is semantically almost complete. As a consequence of the need to define the binding in one scope and introduce the name in another the names have been declared as variables as in Figure 3, whereas they are constants in ML. The other differences are merely syntactic --- the main one being the rather redundant declarations of 'add', 'print' and 'complex'. The designer has the choice of requiring this or adding new constructs such as **abstype** to the language.

Another aspect of using a procedural mechanism is that it provides parametric abstract types. Let us suppose that an abstract type for vectors is required but that different dimensional spaces may be used and that vectors from these require different representations and different operators. Figure 7 shows an appropriate definition.

```
structure vector.pack( proc( pntr,pntr -> pntr )add ; proc( pntr )print ;
                       proc( *real -> pntr )create )

let make.vector.pack = proc( int n -> pntr )
begin
     structure vec( *real rep )

     let check = proc( pntr v -> bool )
                 if v isnt vec then { write "error" ; false }
                 else if upb( v( rep ) ) ≠ n and lwb( v( rep ) ) ≠ 1
                      then { write "dimension error" ; false }
                      else true

     if n < 2 then { write "silly dimension" ; nil }
     else vector.pack(
          proc( pntr a,b -> pntr )
          if check( a ) and check( b ) then
          begin
               let v = vector 1::n of 0.0
               for i = 1 to n do v( i ) := a( rep )( i ) + b( rep )( i )
               vec( v )
          end else nil,

          proc( pntr a )
          if check( a ) do
          begin
               write a( rep,1 )
               for i = 2 to n do write ", ",a( rep )( i )
          end,

          proc( *real r -> pntr )
          if upb( r ) = n and lwb( r ) = 1 then vec(r)
                                           else { write "wrong size" ; nil } )
end ! of make.vector.pack
```

An example of defining a parameterised type

Figure 7

The operators may now be used as shown in Figure 8. To introduce parameterisation of abstract types may mean more complexity than utilising the parametric mechanisms we already have.

```
let Pack.2D = make.vector.pack( 2 )
let Pack.3D = make.vector.pack( 3 )

let add2 = Pack.2D( add ) ; let print2 = Pack.2D( print )
let mk2d = Pack.2D( create )
let add3 = Pack.3D( add ) ; let print3 = Pack.3D( print )
let mk3d = Pack.3D( create )

let v1 = mk2d( @1[ 1.1,2.2 ] )
let v2 = mk2d( @1[ 3.3,4.4 ] )
let v3 = add2( v1,v2 )

print2( v3 )

let w1 = mk3d( @1[ 1.1,2.2,3.3 ] ) .............
```

An example of using the parameterised type

Figure 8

First class procedures can perform as modules

Many languages have also introduced the concept of modules Ada, Clu, ML, Modula2 [27].

These appear to serve three functions:

i) Provide a mechanism for own data, that is data bound with the module over the scope or lifetime of the module, rather than only for individual applications of the module.

ii) To be the unit of program building being used in system construction as a unit of specification, a unit of compilation, testing and assembly.

iii) As a localisation or hiding of certain design decisions, in other words, the provision of abstract types.

We show that, in conjunction with persistence as an orthogonal property, first class procedures perform all these roles. The last has already been demonstrated, the first can depend either on partial application or be obtained in conjunction with the program building facilities. These are simply based on the idea that programs may use procedures which other programs have left in a database. Each of these will now be demonstrated.

It is important to note, once again, though lack of space precludes showing it in every example, that the normal parametric mechanisms of procedures means that we now have modules which may be parameterised, and for which many instances may exist. This is obtained without adding extra constructs or concepts to the language.

Partial application

Another advantage of having procedures as first class data objects is the possibility of having partially applied functions.

Let us provide an abstract structure to maintain lists of things to do, for different people in different contexts. This may be defined as shown in Figure 9.

```
structure list.pack( proc( string )add ; proc()clear ; proc()print )
let make.list.Pack = proc( string person,context -> pntr )
begin
     structure cell( string item ; pntr next )
     let list.start := nil

     list.pack(
     proc( string s ) ; list.start := cell( s,list.start ),
     proc() ; list.start := nil,
     proc()
     begin
          write "'n list of tasks for ",person," doing ",context
          let l := list.start
          while l ≠ nil do
          begin
               write "'n",l( item ) ; l := l( next )
          end
          write "'n"
     end
               )
end
```

Procedure to make various lists and provide routines to maintain them

Figure 9

This can be used the way shown in Figure 10.

```
let RMs = make.list.Pack( "Ron","Finish Paper" )
let MPAs = make.list.Pack( "Malcolm","Finish Paper" )

let RMadd = RMs( add ) ; let RMprint = RMs( print )
let MPAadd = MPAs( add ) ; let MPAprint = MPAs( print )

RMadd( "read Malcolm's notes" ) ; MPAadd( "Write rest of comments" )
RMadd( "type corrections" ) ; MPAadd( "Read next draft" )
RMadd( "Fix references" ) ; MPAadd( "Post last corrections" )
MPAprint() ; RMprint()
```

Using the procedures with local "memory" of lists

Figure 10

Now on the assumption that a given person has tasks in a number of contexts, it may be preferable to partially apply this procedure to yield procedures for each person as in Figure 11.

```
let make.lists.for = proc( string person -> proc( string -> pntr ) )
                        proc( string context -> pntr )
                        make.list.Pack( person,context )
```

Partial application of the make.list.Pack procedure

Figure 11

This can be used as shown in Figure 12.

```
let Rons.list.maker = make.list.for( "Ron" )
let Malcolms.list.maker = make.list.for( "Malcolm" )

let MPA.paper = Malcolms.list.maker( "First Class Fns Paper" )
let MPA.shopping = Malcolms.list.maker( "Shopping" )
```

Using the partially applied list maker

Figure 12

In these examples the procedures yielded by functions have "own" data associated with them (the lists, the tasks and the persons in this example) and so we have demonstrated that the first requirement for modules can be met by first class procedures.

Separate Compilation

Assuming the provision of persistence we now demonstrate how the procedure may be used as the unit of system construction and the unit of definition. Suppose a system is to be built out of the list maintaining program - then to separately compile the list maintainer we could write a program such as that shown in Figure 13.

```
structure list.Pack( proc( string )add ; proc()clear ; proc()print )

let make.list.Pack = proc( string person,context -> pntr )
begin
     let list.start := nil ; structure cell( string item ; pntr next )
     list.Pack(
                proc
                proc                          as in Figure 9
                proc
              )
```

```
end
structure mlp.container( proc( string,string -> pntr )mlp )

let db = open.database( "Library","Gigha","write" )
if db is error.record do { write "Database can''t be opened" ; abort }
s.enter( "make.list.Pack",db,mlp.container( make.list.Pack ) )
commit()
```

A complete PS-algol program to compile a pack of procedures and store them in a database for future use

Figure 13

As the program utilises the persistent mechanisms of PS-algol they are reviewed here, but the reader who requires complete information should read [1,3]. The 'open.database' operation opens the database with the name given by the first parameter, establishing the rights specified by the third parameter by quoting the password given by the second parameter. It also begins a transaction which is completed by a 'commit' or aborted by **abort**. 's.enter' is one of the operations on tables, PS-algol's associative structures. By convention a successful 'open.database' yields one of these tables. 's.lookup' is also available to obtain entries from a table.

We now use the definition in Figure 13 in a program to start a database for a given person, in which are kept lists on various topics. This is shown in Figure 14.

```
structure error.record(string error.context,error.fault,error.explain)
!A program to start a new database for someone's collection of lists
!first get the predefined module for maintaining lists.
let db := nil
repeat
     db := open.database( "library","Gigha","read" )
while db is error.record do
begin
     write "'n sorry the library is being updated"
!     wait( 5 )
end

structure mlp.container( proc( string,string -> pntr )mlp )

let MkListPack = s.lookup( "make.list.Pack",db )
if MkListPack = nil do { write "Make list pack not compiled yet" ; abort }

!find out about the customer
write "Who are you?" ; let p = read.a.line()
!set up his database
write "What password?" ; let pw = read.a.line()
let db2 = open.database( p++".lists",pw,"write" )
if db2 is error.record do { write "Sorry no db space" ; abort }
!insert a table for his lists indexed by topic
s.enter( "topics",db2,table() )
!part apply MkListPack to ensure name always p
let his.make.lists =
                  proc( string topic -> pntr )
                  MkListPack( mlp )( p,topic )
!preserve that for future use
structure his.list( proc( string -> pntr )h.list )

s.enter( "hisMkList",db2,his.list( his.make.lists ) )
commit()
```

An example of using a separately compiled procedure in PS-algol

Figure 14

Examination of Figure 14 shows a number of features. First, a precompiled collection of definitions was obtained from the communal database "Library". The code for this is the loop (normally executed once) to gain access to the program library down to the test that the list package has been defined. This is equivalent to the module being obtained in a typical module based language (ML for example) by

get<Module name>

use<Module name>

It seems that this latter form is more succinct. However if the arrangements for libraries and naming are agreed a standard procedure, such as that shown in Figure 15 can be defined to achieve the same effect equally succinctly.

```
!A standard procedure to obtain a module
let get.from.any = proc( string module,lib,libpw -> pntr )
begin
     repeat
          let db = open.database( lib,libpw,"read" )
     while db is error.record do
     begin
          write "Sorry for the delay, library",lib,"is being updated"
          wait( 5 )
     end
     let wanted.module = s.lookup( module,db )
     if wanted.module = nil do write "Warning: Module",module,"not defined"
     wanted.module
end
let get = proc( string module -> pntr )
          get.from.any( module,"library","Barra" )
```

Standard module fetching procedure defined in PS-algol

Figure 15

In Figure 14, the second part of the program uses the predefined list manipulating module to define a more specific module, which is left for further programs to use. This demonstrates two aspects of module use:

i) the module was used without its implementation being seen by the programmer - giving adequate protection against exploitation of accidents of the present implementation.

ii) modules can be synthesised using other modules, allowing construction of large programs, while the individual program text that has to be read to understand the program at a given level is kept small.

The approach to module collection demonstrated in Figure 15 is just one of many that could be defined. Thus different software construction groups may define their own module naming and module storage conventions, and may have their versions of 'get' and 'get.from.any' carry out authorisation procedures and keep records of what has been used. This gives the basis for constructing a variety of software construction tools within the language.

Comparison of modules with first class functions

We can now compare the anatomy of a module with that of our definition using first class procedures. In a conventional modular language there are three separate components concerned with modules. These are:

i) the module interface definition

ii) the module body definition

iii) the module inclusion statement

The last has already been discussed in connection with Figure 15. The definition of a structure to carry the pack of interfaces is the first class procedure equivalent of the module interface definition. As in module based languages it appears both in the context where the module body is defined and in every context where the module is used. It completely defines the types of all objects that may pass across the interface, and with the type matching rules in PS-algol this ensures that only modules with correctly matching types are assembled together. Although only procedural components of a structure/interface are shown in the examples, other data types may appear allowing direct access between the module and its users to some shared variable.

The module body in a modular language usually contains concepts for defining imported, exported and private variable lists. It usually has a method of defining data storage and data manipulation. All these are defined here by use of the normal algol declarations and block structure without additional concepts.

Where a module has internal storage, there is often a need to make many instances of the module, possibly with different initial data. This can be achieved with these first class procedures by simply calling them repeatedly with different parameters - no special mechanism is required. This is illustrated in Figure 14, where each time that program is used, a new instance of the same module is created, with a different value for person stored within it.

New version installation

With all large systems, constructed out of separate modules, there is a problem of managing the installation of new versions. It is necessary to modify the implementation of modules and then arrange for their subsequent use. Often this can only be done when no part of the system is running, then the new modules are installed by a complete system rebuild. This may take considerable resources. The alternative of replacing a module in situ has to be carefully managed, as it certainly could not be done safely when the module is in use if that execution were affected.

In PS-algol the transaction mechanism makes the concurrent revision and installation of modules safe. The effects of a transaction are not visible to other transactions until the transaction has committed. Programs starting after it will use the new one for the whole program execution if they are written in the style shown in Figure 14.

More sophisticated mechanisms can be implemented with these facilities. For example, a program may arrange to bind a particular version of one module to the package it constructs, by leaving it directly referenced, or leave it to be picked up when the package is run collecting the latest version. Software tools could be written, to build up systems where groups of modules could be installed, retained, replaced etc. using no more language concepts than the features illustrated here.

First class functions as a view mechanism

View mechanisms are used in databases to perform two roles:

i) to provide a stable and appropriate view to the programmer
ii) to implement protection and privacy controls.

The first class functions, together with partial application perform both of these roles. Stability means that the underlying data may be changed without impact upon programs it was not intended to alter apart from possible changes in performance. The person who changes the underlying data is usually responsible for redefining the mapping that provides the view except where the only available mappings are so simple that the new mapping may be inferred. If we interpose a set of functions, then redefinition of these functions will provide the required stability. Similarly, they can be defined so as to provide the appropriate view and the access controls. We have discussed this use of first class persistent functions elsewhere [2].

Figure 14 will again serve as an example. The function saved in the database as 'hisMkList' will now only make up lists, print lists etc. for the one person who created this database. Thus the view of the data has been made appropriate by allowing the person to avoid redundantly giving his own name every time, and has also been restricted to lists concerned with that data. Note that the control and the remapping is quite finely controlled but not over restrictive. For example there is nothing to stop the programmer using this database to hold other data as well, to which he may have any view or access. This seems correct.

In Figure 14 however the view constructed is not as secure as we might wish, as a programmer using it could operate directly on the table which holds the set of topics. To overcome this we refine the definition, as shown in Figure 16. The revised version prevents any misuse of the table of topics by making it available only within the body of the 'make.lists' procedure declaration. The refinement also produces four procedures to work over the data, one to initiate a list on a topic, and the others as before, except that they now take a topic as a parameter and work for any list for the given person. This illustrates the radical revision of views that may be constructed, and the way precise control over the operations on data may be obtained.

```
!Refined Program to start a database for lists
structure error.record( string error.context,error.fault,error.explain )
```

```
write "Who are you?" ; let p = read.a.line()
write "What password?" ; let pw = read.a.line()

let his.make.lists = proc( string p -> pntr )
begin
     let table.for.topics = table()

     let get.topic := proc( string topic -> pntr ) ; nullproc
     get.topic := proc( string topic -> pntr )
     begin
          let pack = s.lookup( topic,table.for.topics )
          if pack = nil then { write "You have not started that topic'n"
                                get.topic("dummy") }
                         else pack
     end

     let db = open.database( "library","Gigha","read" )
     if db is error.record do { write "Cannot open database Library",
                                "'n",db( error.fault ),"'n",
                                     db( error.explain ) }

     structure mlp.container( proc( string,string -> pntr )mlp )
     let mklp = s.lookup( "make.list.Pack",db )( mlp ) !see Figure 14

     structure list.pack( proc( string )add ; proc()clear ; proc()print )

     let start.topic = proc( string topic )
     begin
          let pack = mklp( p,topic )
          s.enter( topic,table.for.topics,pack )
     end

     let add.topic = proc( string topic,task )
                    get.topic( topic )( add )( task )

     let clear.topic = proc( string topic )
                      get.topic( topic )( clear )()

     let print.topic = proc( string topic )
                      get.topic( topic )( print )()

     start.topic( "dummy" )

     structure topic.pack( proc( string )start.t ; proc( string,string )add.t ;
                           proc( string )clear.t,print.t )

     topic.pack( start.topic,add.topic,clear.topic,print.topic )
end

let db = open.database( p++".lists",pw,"write" )
if db is error.record do { write "sorry no db space" ; abort }

s.enter( "hisMkList",db,his.make.lists( p ) )
commit()
```

A refinement of Figure 14 to give a more restrictive and convenient view

Figure 16

Figure 17 then illustrates how this view may be used. Note that the programmer has only the four operations available, and has no knowledge of or access to the way the lists were represented. In this case the view was fairly appropriate for the task. Another view might have provided an extra operation to set the current topic, thus economising on the passing of the 'topic' parameter.

```
!program to provide end user interface to lists

structure error.record( string error.context,error.fault,error.explain )
write "Who are you?" ; let p = read.a.line()
write "Your password?" ; let pw = read.a.line()

let db = open.database( p++".lists",pw,"write" )
if db is error.record do { write "Sorry no db space" ; abort }
!get & unpack saved view
let hML = s.lookup( "hisMkList",db )
```

```
structure topic.pack( proc( string )start.t ; proc( string,string )add.t ;
                      proc( string )clear.t,print.t )
let st = hML( start.t ) ; let ad = hML( add.t ) ; let cl = hML( clear.t )
let pr = hML( print.t )
let current.topic := "dummy" ; let todo := ""
repeat
begin
     write "'n what shall I do?" ; todo := read.a.line()
     case todo of
     "quit"    : {}
     "start"   : { write "topic?" ; current.topic := read.a.line()
                   st(current.topic) }
     "change"  : { write "new topic?" ; current.topic := read.a.line() }
     "add"     : { write "item?" ; ad( current.topic,read.a.line() ) }
     "clear"   : cl( current.topic )
     "print"   : pr( current.topic )
     default   : write "Command not understood"
     write "'n"
end
while todo ~= "quit"
commit()
```

A PS-algol program utilising the view constructed in Figure 16

Figure 17

Conclusions

A number of requirements of modern programming languages, abstract types, modules, control of module assembly, separate compilation and views of data are met by the provision of first class procedures and orthogonal persistence. It has long been understood that it is desirable to be parsimonious in introducing concepts into a language design. The preceding demonstration therefore challenges language designers as to whether it is necessary to introduce a long list of concepts which can be covered by the persistent procedural mechanism.

Considering the semantic properties of languages the case for introducing different concepts rather than depending on these first class procedures appears to be weak. However, the text necessary to 'unpack' and introduce into the local environment, the interface of a module using this method leaves the question of whether extra syntactic constructs are necessary. If they are, they should probably be some general purpose shorthand (such as the patterns of ML) rather than a specific construct for modules.

Using the general properties of persistent procedures seems to have a number of advantages:

i) Software construction tools may be built within the language.
ii) The composition of separately produced software is type checked.
iii) The power of the language is much increased, for example, parameterisation is always available. The structures, interrelationships and naming rules which may be constructed are extremely flexible.

Since readily understood and easily implemented languages are needed as a foundation for software engineering, we argue that serious consideration should be given to languages which support procedures as data objects, which have an orthogonal provision of persistence and which are not overgrown with numerous other concepts.

Acknowledgements

This work was supported in part by SERC grant GRA 86541 at the University of Edinburgh. It is now supported at Edinburgh by SERC grants GRC 21977 and GRC 21960 and at the University of St Andrews by SERC grant GRC 15907. The work is also supported at both Universities by grants from International Computers Ltd. The paper was partly written while Malcolm Atkinson was visiting the University of Pennsylvania, Philadelphia and Ron Morrison the Australian National University, Canberra.

References

1. Atkinson, M.P., Bailey, P.J., Cockshott, W.P., Chisholm, K.J. & Morrison, R. An approach to persistent programming. Computer Journal 26, 4 (1983), 360-365.
2. Atkinson, M.P., Bailey, P.J., Cockshott, W.P., Chisholm, K.J. & Morrison, R. Progress with persistent programming, in **Database - role and structure**, Cambridge University Press, Cambridge, 1984.
3. Atkinson, M.P., Bailey, P.J., Cockshott, W.P. & Morrison, R. PS-algol reference manual. Universities of Edinburgh and St Andrews PPR-8 (1984).
4. Birtwistle, G.M., Dahl, O.J., Myrhaug, B & Nygaard, K. **SIMULA BEGIN.** Auerbach (1973).
5. Cockshott, W.P., Atkinson, M.P., Bailey, P.J., Chisholm, K.J. & Morrison, R. The persistent object management system. Software, Practice & Experience 14 (1984).
6. Evans, A. PAL a language designed for teaching programming linguistics. Proc. ACM 23rd. Nat. Conf. Brandin Systems Press (1968), 395-403.
7. Horning, J.J. Some desirable properties of data abstraction facilities. ACM Sigplan Notices 11 (1976), 60-62.
8. Ichbiah et al,. Rationale of the design of the programming language Ada. ACM Sigplan Notices 14, 6 (1979).
9. Johnston, J.B. A contour model of block structured processes. ACM Sigplan Notices 6, 2 (1971).
10. Lampson, B.W., Horning, J.J., London, R.L., Mitchell, J.G. & Popek, G.J. Report on the programming language Euclid. ACM Sigplan Notices 12, 2 (1977), 1-79.
11. Landin, P.J. The next 700 programming languages. Comm.ACM 9, 3 (1966), 157-164.
12. Liskov, B.H., Synder, A., Atkinson, R. & Schiffert, C. Abstraction mechanisms in CLU. Comm.ACM 20, 8 (1977), 564-576.
13. Liskov, B. & Zilles, S.N. Programming with abstract data types. ACM Sigplan Notices 9, 4 (1974), 50-59.
14. McCarthy, J. et al. Lisp 1.5 Programmers manual. M.I.T. Press Cambridge Mass.

(1962).

15. Milner, R A proposal for standard ML. Technical Report CSR-157-83 University of Edinburgh. (1983).

16. Morris, J.H. Protection in programming languages. Comm.ACM 16, 1 (1973), 15-21.

17. Morrison, R. S-algol language reference manual. University of St Andrews CS/79/1 (1979).

18. Morrison, R. A method of implementing procedure entry and exit. Software Practice and Experience 7, 5 (1977), 535-537.

19. Naur, P. et al. Revised report on the algorithmic language Algol 60. Comm.ACM 6, 1 (1963), 1-17.

20. Nori, K.V. et al. The Pascal P compiler implementation notes. Technical Report, 10 Zurich (1974).

21. Randell, B. & Russell, L.J. **Algol 60 Implementation.** Academic Press (1964).

22. Reynolds, J.C. Gedanken a simple typeless language based on the principle of completeness and the reference concept. Comm.ACM 13, 5 (1970), 308-319.

23. Strachey, C. Fundamental concepts in programming languages. Oxford University (1967).

24. Turner, D.A. SASL language manual. University of St.Andrews CS/79/3 (1979).

25. Wirth, N. & Weber, H. EULER a generalisation of algol. Comm.ACM 9, 1 (1966), 13-23.

26. Wirth, N. The programming language Pascal. Acta Informatica 1, 1 (1971), 35-63.

27. Wirth, N. **Programming in Modula-2** : Second Edition. Springer-Verlag, Berlin, 1983.

28. Wulf, W.A., London, R.L. & Shaw, M. An introduction to the construction and verification of Alphard programs. IEEE Soft. Eng SE-2, 4 (1976), 253-265.

29. Zilles, S.N. Procedural encapsulation : a linguistic protection technique. ACM Sigplan Notices 8, 9 (1973).

30. van Wijngaarden, A. et al. Report on the algorithmic language Algol 68. Numerische Mathematik 14,1 (1969), 79-218.

ABSTRACTION CONCEPTS FOR MODELING SCREEN ORIENTED DIALOGUE INTERFACES

R. Studer
Institut für Informatik
University of Stuttgart
Azenbergstrasse 12
D-7000 Stuttgart 1
Fed. Rep. of Germany

Abstract

We present a formalization of screen oriented dialogue concepts which are widely used in modern dialogue systems. The dialogue concepts which are considered are menus, forms, and windows. With respect to different dialogue styles as e.g. command language oriented dialogues or dialogues based on using a pointing device several different types of abstract models are introduced and discussed.

The presented concepts may be used within a functional specification of a dialogue interface. The specification method which we are using is the Vienna Development Method (VDM).

1. Introduction

With the widespread use of interactive systems by non-DP professionals the design of the user interface of these systems becomes a very important part of the system development.

Currently, a popular approach to user interface design is based on rapid prototyping which was made popular especially in the AI area. Since the only design documentation which is usually provided when using a prototyping approach is the code of the prototype system, design decisions are only recorded on a code level thus resulting in a lack of high-level design documentation which could be used as a communication medium between the users, designers, and implementors. Alternatively, a state transition diagram approach (see /Jako83/) is often used for specifying dialogue interfaces. This approach uses graphic representations and a concrete syntax formalism to represent the states and state transitions of a dialogue interface (see /Wass82/). Unfortunately, this approach has several disadvantages:

(i) By using a concrete syntax formalism a lot of syntactical details have to be considered in an early design phase.

(ii) Only line oriented dialogue types can be specified by using this approach.

(iii) The actions associated with the state transitions are either described informally or on an algorithmic (code) level.

In /Wass84/ the conventional state diagram approach is extended to support the specification of screen oriented dialogue concepts, as e.g. menus, too. However, disadvantages (i) and (iii) are not solved by this extention.

We introduce abstract models of menus, forms, and windows and thus provide a basis for formally specifying the man-machine interface of dialogue systems on an abstract level. By using these models a much more precise specification of the man-machine interface is achieved compared to specifications using the conventional state transition diagram approach. Compared with the models introduced in /Stud84/ more general models for forms and windows are defined. In addition, several types of models are discussed reflecting different types of man-machine interaction styles. All our models are specified by using the Vienna Development Method (VDM) (/BjJo82/) as specification method.

Up to now, only a few approaches have been developed to achieve (a) an abstract specification of dialogue interfaces, thus abstracting from syntactical details, and (b) a formal specification of states and state transitions thus providing a formal basis for specifying the semantics of the dialogue functions. In /Sufr82/ abstract models of text editor concepts are provided. However, dialogue concepts like e.g. forms are not discussed at all. In /GuHo80/ an algebraic approach for specifying dialogue concepts is introduced. Although their specification of "pictures" is to some extent similar to the window model introduced in this paper, they do not consider other dialogue concepts like forms and menus. In /HaHa82/ a very detailed model of forms for describing the screen layout is introduced. However, they do not distinguish between form types and form occurrences and do not consider other dialogue concepts.

The subsequent parts of the paper are organized as follows: after having briefly described the Vienna Development Method (VDM) we will introduce two models of menus, reflecting two different dialogue styles, in section 2. A general model of form types and form occurrences is then defined in section 3. Finally, we introduce two differently abstract models of the window concept in section 4.

1.1 The Vienna Development Method (VDM)

The Vienna Development Method (/BjJo78/, /BjJo82/), which evolved from the programming language area, adopted the denotational semantics approach which uses functions to denote the meaning of programming languages (see e.g. /Stoy77/).

The denotational semantics approach can be characterized as follows: a syntactic domain describing the syntactic objects and a semantic domain containing semantic object classes (domains) and meaning functions can be distinguished. An interpretation function maps each element of the syntactic domain to a meaning function thus defining formally its semantics. I.e. the meaning of a syntactic object is a function having object classes of the semantic domain as its domain and range, respectively.

Beyond this pure functional approach VDM offers various standard data types together with appropriate standard operations. The following standard data types are available in VDM:

(a) set: A VDM-set represents a set of objects in the usual mathematical sense.

(b) tuple: A VDM-tuple represents a finite list of elements which are all taken from the same domain. Operations like hd (head), inds (index-set) or elems (element-set) are defined for tuples.

(c) tree: A VDM-tree combines arbitrary objects to tree structures and provides implicitly defined selctors for accessing the different tree components.

(d) function: A VDM-function is a normal mathematical function.

(e) map: A VDM-map represents a function with finite domains.

In addition, VDM offers a meta language providing an abstract syntax mechanism to define object classes and functions. Since this notation is much more readable than the pure mathematical notation of the denotational approach (see /Stoy77/) VDM has practical importance even in the industrial environment.

2. Models of Menus

When designing abstract models of dialogue concepts a variety of models could be chosen in order to represent the intrinsic characteristics of the dialogue concepts. Actually, the appropriate models and especially the appropriate abstraction levels of the models depend on the interaction style which is used for the user interface.

Subsequently, we will consider two basic types of interaction styles: a "pointing device dialogue", assuming the existence of e.g. a mouse, and a "command language dialogue" assuming that the dialogue is controlled by entering commands via the keyboard.

All the models we will present in this paper are based on the assumption that different types of dictionaries are handled by the dialogue system for recording the different definitions of the dialogue concepts (see /Stud84/).

For modeling our first dialogue concept, i.e. menus, we therefore assume the existence of a menu dictionary containing the definitions of all the menus used in a dialogue system. For defining a menu dictionary we use a VDM map, i.e. a finite function, mapping a menu identifier to the corresponding menu (description). Modeling the dictionary by using a map has two advantages: (a) a single menu may simply be selected by applying the 'MenuDictionary'-map to a given menu identifier. (b) The uniqueness of the menu identifier is guaranteed implicitly.

(2.1) MenuDictionary = MenuId $\overset{m}{\rightarrow}$ Menu.

In order to choose an appropriate abstract representation of menus we have to consider the dialogue type which is used for handling the menus.

a) Pointing Device Dialogue

Assuming the existence of a pointing device a menu is simply represented by its options (see Figure 2-1). In addition, a menu option is selected by pointing to it. According to these characteristics a menu is modeled as a non-empty list of menu options:

(2.2) Menu = MenuOption^{+}
MenuOption = String
(The object class 'Menu' is defined as the set of all non-empty tuples the elements of which are elements of the object class 'MenuOption'.)

```
option1
option2
   .
   .
optionn
```

Figure 2-1: Concrete layout of a menu for a pointing device dialogue

b) Command Language Dialogue

Within the framework of a command language oriented dialogue a menu option may be selected either by entering the name of the menu option or by entering a number identifying the option uniquely (see Figure 2-2)

```
     1 option1
     2 option2
          .
          .
     n optionn
Enter Option:
```

Figure 2-2: Concrete layout of a menu for a command language dialogue

Therefore we model in this case a menu as a VDM map from menu option identifiers (positive natural numbers ('N_+')) to menu options represented by strings.

(2.3) $Menu_2 = N_+ \xrightarrow{m} MenuOption$
      MenuOption = String

When considering the two models introduced for menus it should be clear that it is in general impossible to identify one single model as the best one without considering the context in which the model will be used. Furthermore, by using abstract models we totally abstract from the concrete layout of a menu, which is not important, in order to capture the basic characteristic of a menu.

By using the formal models of menus we could now formally define the semantics of user actions to select one of the options offered by a menu. Due to space limitations we will not formally define such a user action in this paper. An example, based on the command language dialogue model, may be found in /Stud84/.

3. An Abstract Model of Forms

The abstract model of forms we will introduce in this section is based on the following assumptions:

(i) Form handling only makes sense within the framework of a screen oriented dialogue style.

(ii) The structure of a form is defined by its form type ('FormType') and is recorded in the dictionary of form types ('FormType-Dictionary').

(iii) From a given form type several form occurrences may be derived depending on the actual values entered into the form fields. Form occurrences are recorded in a occurrence dictionary ('FormOcc-Dictionary').

The dictionary of form types is modeled in the same way as the menu dictionary by associating a unique form type identifier with the corresponding form type.

(3.1) FormTypeDictionary = FormTypeId m→ FormType

In /Stud84/ the abstract model introduced for forms is rather restrictive: a form could only be decomposed into elementary fields. Subsequently, we will present a general model allowing the definition of arbitrarily complex forms. In principle, a form is hierarchically decomposed into fields which may be either elementary fields or complex fields. Since complex fields again represent forms the form type definition results in a recursive structure.

(3.2) FormType = ElementaryField | ComplexField
ComplexField :: FormType FormType Separation
(An element of 'ComplexField' is represented by a tree having 3 immediate components. Two components are elements of the object class 'FormType', one component is an element of the object class 'Separation'.)

The 'Separation'-component indicates whether a complex field is decomposed in horizontal or vertical direction (see Figure 3-1). In addition, the size of each subfield is determined by specifying the ratio of the sizes as a percentage. Thus a partition value 50 indicates that both subfields should have the same size. By using this approach we only specify the relative size of each subfield of a form. As a consequence, the actual layout of a form can easily be adjusted to its actual size.

(3.3) Separation :: Direction Partition
Direction = {<u>HORIZONTAL</u>, <u>VERTICAL</u>}
Partition = N_+

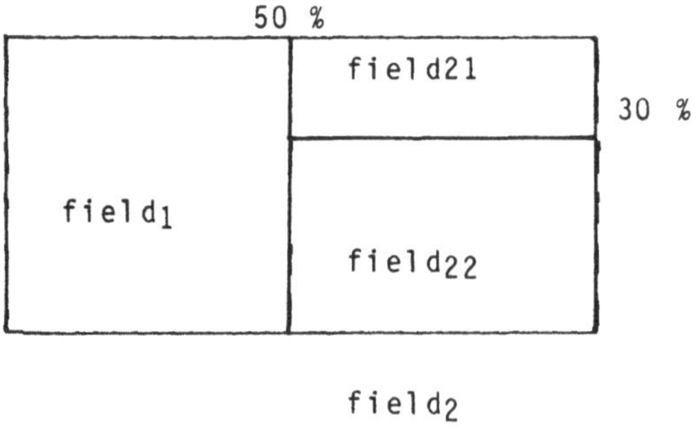

The example form is first horizontally decomposed into 2 fields with partition 50 %. Then field2 is decomposed vertically with partition 30 %.

Figure 3-1: Structure of a form which is decomposed into three fields

An elementary field is described by three elements: (a) a (system internal) field identifier which can be used by the dialogue system to select the corresponding field of the form, (b) an optional prompt value which may be displayed in the field, (c) an indicator whether the field is an input field, an output field, or an input/output field.

```
(3.4) ElementaryField :: FieldId [PromptValue] I/O-Field
                         (The object class '[PromptValue]' is a set con-
                         sisting of the elements of the object class
                         PromptValue' and the special elementary object
                         'NIL').
      PromptValue = String
      I/O-Field = InputField | OutputField | Input/OutputField
```

Each kind of field must be further specified by its field type. Besides the usual basic types we assume the existence of fields of type 'TABLE' (representing column-oriented fields) and fields of type 'GRAPHIC' (representing fields containing a mixture of text and graphical representations) (compare /HaHa82/). In this paper we will not further specify the different types of fields. More details may be found in /Mohr83/.

```
(3.5) InputField :: FieldType
      OutputField :: FieldType
      Input/OutputField :: FieldType
      FieldType = INTEGER | STRING | TABLE | GRAPHIC | ...
```

Considering this form model one realizes that we have totally abstracted from the concept of coordinates. In our opinion, coordinates could be included in a refined, more implementation oriented model of forms. Of course, information about coordinates would be required in order to be able to derive from the position of the cursor on the screen the information in which form field the cursor is currently located.

Our model is oriented towards capturing the basic design decisions for a form oriented user interface: specifying (a) the fields a form is composed of, (b) the relative position of each field, and (c) the type of each field.

Having introduced the abstract model of form types we can now consider the corresponding model of form occurrences. The form occurrences derived from the existing form types are recorded in a corresponding dictionary ('FormOccDictionary') mapping unique form occurrence identifiers to form occurrence descriptions ('FormOccDescr') and type specifications ('FormTypeId'). The type specification determines for each form occurrence the form type it is derived from. Since the structure of a form occurrence is already specified by its form type description the description of a form occurrence simply consists of a specification of the values contained in the different fields. Of course, there may exist form fields which will not contain an actual value.

```
(3.6) FormOccDictionary = FormOccId m→ (FormOccDescr FormTypeId)
      FormOccDescr = FieldId m→ [FieldValue]
      FieldValue = Integer | String | TableFieldValue | ...
```

Having defined the object classes of our form type/occurrence model we have now to specify so-called well-formedness criteria guaranteeing the well-formedness of the object classes, especially the consistency between the form type dictionary and the form occurrence dictionary. In VDM, well-formedness criteria are defined by using boolean functions mapping all elements of an object class, meeting the restrictions of the well-formedness criteria, to 'TRUE'. All other elements are mapped to 'FALSE'.

As an example we will consider the well-formedness criteria 'is- wf-FormDictionary' specifying that (a) the type specification of a form occurrence refers to an existing form type definition, and (b) all the field indentifiers used within a form occurrence are defined in the corresponding form type definition.

```
(3.7) is-wf-FormDictionary (formtypedict,formoccdict) =
         let occspecs = rng(formoccdict)
   .1    (∀ mk(occdescr,typeid) ∈ occspecs:
                             typeid ∈ dom(formtypedict)) ∧
   .2    (∀ occid ∈ dom(formoccdict) :
            let occspec = formoccdict(occid)
            let occdescr = s-FormOccDescr(occspec)
   .3       let typeid = s-FormTypeId(occspec)
   .4       dom (occdescr) = CollectFieldIds(formtypedict(typeid)))
```

Type: (FormTypeDictionary FormOccDictionary) → Bool

Explanations:

1) A form type identifier, representing a form occurrence type specification, must be defined in the form type dictionary.
2) We now consider each form occurrence defined in the form occurrence dictionary.
3) 'occdescr' and 'typeid' represent the form occurrence description and form occurrence type specification of a given form occurrence.
4) 'CollectFieldIds' is an auxiliary function collecting all field identifiers defined within a form type definition. The field identifiers used in a form occurrence have to correspond one-to-one to the field identifiers introduced in the corresponding form type definition.

It should be clear that further well-formedness criteria may be defined in the same way. Based on our abstract model of forms a formal definition of the semantics of user actions manipulating forms may be achieved. However, an example is beyond the scope of this paper and may be found in /Mohr83/.

4. Abstract Modeling of Window Concepts

The third dialogue concept we want to consider is the notion of windows. We will first introduce the basic assumptions our models rely on and will then discuss two types of models: a totally abstract one and a more implementation oriented one.

Our basic assumptions are as follows:

(i) Each window is identified by a unique name.
(ii) The windows which are currently displayed are visible according to an actual visibility order.
(iii) Windows may overlap.
(iv) The names of currently closed windows are displayed in a special area of the screen.

4.1 The More Abstract Model of Windows

The first window model totally abstracts from all location and size aspects, i.e. we only consider the visibility order of the windows currently displayed. Thus the model aims at capturing the first basic design decisions when developing a user interface based on windows: which windows should be displayed in which situation and what should be the visibility order of these windows (see Figure 4-1).

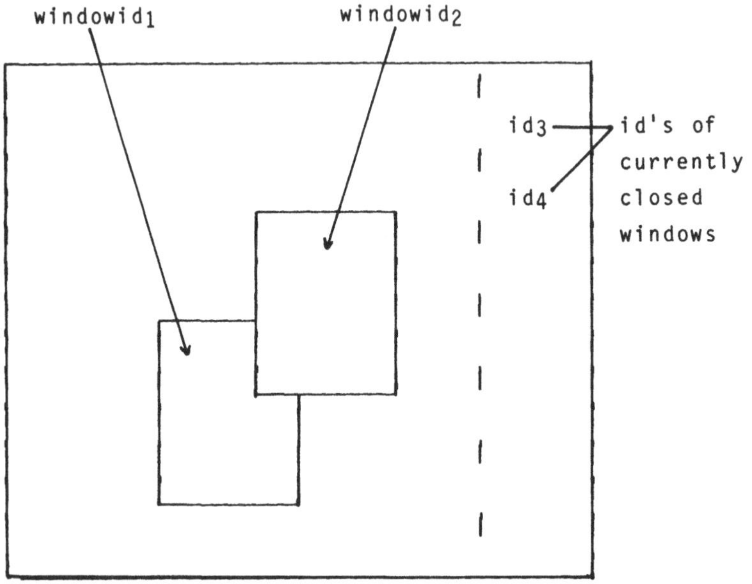

Figure 4-1: Concrete screen layout corresponding to the more abstract window model

For recording all the windows known in the dialogue system we introduce a further dictionary ('WindowDictionary'). A window dictionary is again modeled as a VDM map associating window identifiers with corresponding window specifications ('WindowSpec'). We will not consider the contents of a window ('WindowArea') since it depends on the application which is supported by the dialogue system.

(4.1) WindowDictionary = WindowId m→ WindowSpec
WindowSpec :: WindowArea

For capturing the characteristics of the window concept as described above we introduce an abstract specification of a screen layout ('Screen') defining (a) which windows are currently displayed ('DisplayedWindows'), (b) the visibility order of them ('VisibilityOrder'), and (c) which windows are currently closed ('ClosedWindows'). The visibility order of the windows is simply defined by introducing a VDM-tuple of window identifiers (of the displayed windows) and using the implicitly defined order for tuple elements to represent the visibility order. We assume that the first tuple element refers to the topmost window on the screen. Whereas the displayed windows are modeled by associating their window identifiers with the corresponding window specifications, the closed windows are simply represented by their identifiers.

(4.2) Screen :: VisibilityOrder DisplayedWindows ClosedWindows
VisibilityOrder = WindowId*
(The object class 'VisibilityOrder' is defined as the set of all tuples the elements of which are window indentifiers.)
DisplayedWindows = WindowId m→ WindowSpec
ClosedWindows = WindowId-set
(The object class 'ClosedWindows' is defined as the power set of the object class 'WindowId'.)

Having defined the dictionary of windows and an abstract screen layout using the window concepts we now introduce a specification of a system state consisting of the different dictionaries and the screen specification. System state objects will later on be used as the semantic domain for specifying the meaning of user commands for manipulating windows. Of course, for representing all aspects of a dialogue system more system state components would be required (see /Stud84/).

(4.3) State :: Screen Dictionary
Dictionary :: MenuDictionary FormTypeDictionary FormOccDictionary WindowDictionary

In the same way as we defined well-formedness criteria for our form model we now have to define well-formedness criteria for the window model. However, we will not consider them here (see /Mohr83/ for details) but instead will discuss a user command for manipulating windows.

As an example we will consider a command ('PickWindow') which can be used to select a currently displayed window or a currently closed window as the new topmost window. Subsequently, we assume that the window is selected by using its identifier. However, we do not consider whether the identifier is entered via the keyboard or by e.g. pointing to the window. Thus we totally abstract from any implementation aspects.

```
(4.4) PickWindow :: WindowIdentification
      WindowIdentification = WindowId
```

Assuming the well-formedness of the command with respect to the current system state, we will now introduce the interpretation function 'Elab-PickWindow' mapping the syntactic object class 'PickWindow' to the meaning functions of type (State ⥲ State).

```
(4.5) Elab-PickWindow (mk-PickWindow(ident))(state) =
          let mk-State(screen,dict) = state
          let mk-Screen(visorder,diswindows,closedwindows) = screen
          let mk-Dictionary(,,, windowdict) = dict
   .1     (ident ∈ closedwindows →
             let closedwindows' = closedwindows \ {ident}
   .2        let visorder' = <ident> ^ visorder
             let windowspec' = windowdict(ident)
   .3        let diswindows' = diswindows ∪ [ident → windowspec']
             let screen' = mk-Screen(visorder',diswindows',closedwindows'
   .4        mk-State(screen',dict),
   .5      ident ∈ dom(diswindow) →
             let i ∈ winds (visorder) be s.t. visorder[i] = ident
   .6        let visorder' = <visorder[i]>^
                             <visorder[j] | 1≤j≤ lng(visorder) ∧ j≠i>
             let screen' = mk-Screen(visorder',diswindows,closedwindows)
   .7        mk-State(screen',dict))
```

Type: PickWindow ⥲ (State ⥲ State)

Explanations:

1) We first consider the case that a closed window is selected.
2) The selected window is removed from the set of closed windows and inserted as the new topmost window in the visibility order tuple.
3) The selected window is included into the currently displayed windows (its window specification is first selected from the dictionary).
4) The new system state is composed of the new screen layout and the old dictionary.
5) Now we consider the case that a currently displayed window is selected.
6) The visibility order tuple is rearranged in a way that the selected window is the new first element of the tuple.
7) The new system state is again composed of the new screen layout and

the old dictionary.

When looking at the definition of the meaning of the 'PickWindow'-command it should be clear that we achieve a totally formal semantics definition without considering any implementation aspects.

4.2 The Less Abstract Model of Windows

The second model of windows introduces one additional aspect of modeling window concepts: information about coordinates, i.e. the position of a window on the screen as well as the size of a window are specified. As a consequence, we achieve a model in which we can determine the overlapping and thus the visible parts of the windows.

Within the model the position of a window on the screen is specified by its offset, i.e. the coordinates of its left upper corner (see Figure 4-2) (of course, any other corner of the window could have been used as well to define the offset.) Furthermore, the size of the window is specified by defining its height and length.

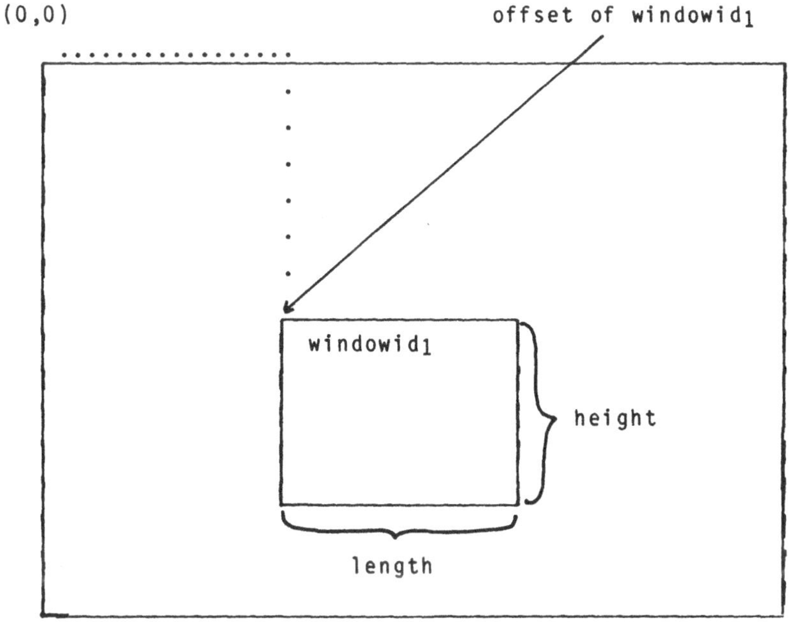

Figure 4-2: Offset and size definition of a window

In the definition of the window dictionary of the second model ('Window-Dictionary$_1$') we introduce a further specification element: a default size for a window which can be used if a currently closed window is displayed again.

(4.6) WindowDictionary$_1$ = WindowId m→ WindowDescr
WindowDescr :: WindowArea [DefaultSize]
DefaultSize = WindowSize
WindowSize :: Length Height
Length = N_+
Height = N_+

When defining the screen model we again have to include appropriate size and coordinate information. Therefore we extend the 'Screen'-definition by a fourth component defining its size. In the same way we have to extend the description of the currently displayed windows by a specification of the current offset and current size. Furthermore, for each identifier, representing a closed window, its position on the screen is defined.

(4.7) Screen$_1$ :: VisibilityOrder DisplayedWindows$_1$ ClosedWindows$_1$ ScreenSize
VisibilityOrder = WindowId*
DisplayedWindows$_1$ = WindowId m→ WindowSpec$_1$
WindowSpec$_1$ :: WindowArea Offset WindowSize
Offset :: Coordinate
Coordinate :: Horizontal Vertical
Horizontal = Z
Vertical = Z
ScreenSize :: Length Height
ClosedWindows$_1$ = ClosedDescr*
ClosedDescr :: WindowId Offset

Based on the detailed model we are able to introduce abstract specifications of window manipulation commands either according to the pointing device or the command language dialogue. As an example we shall use a command for moving a visible window on the screen.

a) Pointing Device Dialogue

For a pointing device dialogue we assume that the window to be moved is selected by pointing to one of its (visible) corners ('VisArgument'). The new position of the window on the screen is then simply determined by the new coordinates of the selected corner. Thus our model integrates the information required for selecting the window (otherwise the window could be selected by pointing to an arbitrary point of it) and for moving it.

```
(4.8) MoveWindowCmd :: VisArgument NewCoordinate
      VisArgument = Coordinate
      NewCoordinate = Coordinate
```

b) Command Language Dialogue

For a command language oriented dialogue a rather different model for our example command is requested. Whereas the window to be moved is selected by specifying its identifier the new position of the window is determined by the new offset of the window.

(4.9) MoveWindowCmd_1 :: WindowId NewOffset
      NewOffset = Coordinate

By comparing the two models of our example command we can again easily recognize that the choice of an appropriate abstract model is strongly influenced by the context it is designed for.

It should be clear that other typical window manipulation commands can be modeled abstractly in the same way. By using the abstract syntax models of the commands as syntactic domain and the screen and dictionary models as semantic domain we could furthermore give a formal definition of the semantics of these commands (see section 4.1). Examples may be found in /Mohr83/.

5. Conclusion

When developing interactive systems the dialogue interface of the system is one of the most important parts to be designed. The abstract models of menus, forms, and windows introduced in this paper provide means for specifying dialogue interfaces, using screen oriented dialogue concepts, in a formal and abstract way. By using such an abstract approach the interface specification can be focused on defining the two most important aspects of a dialogue design:

(i) what should be displayed in which situation, and
(ii) what is the semantics of the user actions.

In our opinion the abstract models may be used in the specification/ design phase of an interactive system for recording design decisions and for providing a communication basis between the system designer and the system user. Our experience shows that these models are very worthwhile for discussing design alternatives since one does not have to consider irrelevant syntactical details when using these abstract models.

Furthermore, these models are well suited to be used in parallel to a rapid prototyping approach for representing basic characteristics of different dialogue concepts or for recording design decisions which are otherwise only recorded informally or in the code of the prototype.

Acknowledgement

The author would like to thank U. Pletat for his critical comments. Thanks also to Ms. Günthör for typing the paper.

References

/BjJo78/ Bjorner, D., Jones, C.B. (eds.): The Vienna Development Method: The Meta-Language, Lecture Notes in Computer Science 61, Springer Verlag, 1978

/BjJo82/ Bjorner, D., Jones, C.B.: Formal Specification and Software Development, Prentice Hall, 1982

/GuHo80/ Guttag, J., Horning, J.J.: Formal Specification as a Design Tool, in: Proc. Principles of Programming Languages, 1980

/HaHa82/ Hansen, M.R., Hansen, B.S.: A Generic Application Programming System, Technical University of Denmark, Lyngby, Master Thesis, 1982

/Jako83/ Jakob, R.J.K.: Using Formal Specifications in the Design of a Human Computer Interface,
in: CACM 26, 4 (April 1983), 259-264

/Mohr83/ Mohrmann, J.: Formal Specification of a Form Oriented Dialogue Interface,
University of Stuttgart, Institut für Informatik, Master Thesis, 1983

/Stoy77/ Stoy, J.E.: Denotational Semantics: The Scott-Strachey Approach to Programming Language Theory,
MIT Press, 1977

/Stud84/ Studer, R.: Abstract Models of Dialogue Concepts.
in: Proc. 7th Int. Conf. on Software Engineering, Orlando, 1984

/Sufr82/ Sufrin, B.: Formal Specification of a Display-Oriented Text Editor,
in: Science of Computer Programming 1 (1982), 175-202

/Wass82/ Wasserman, A.I.: The User Software Engineering Methodology, An Overview,
in: Olle et al. (eds.) Information Systems Design Methodologies: A Comparative Review,
North-Holland Publ. Co., 1982

/Wass84/ Wasserman, A.I.: Extending State Transition Diagrams for the Specification of Human-Computer Interaction,
University of California, San Francisco, Medical Information Science, Technical Report, 1984

VLSI Systems For Design Rule Checks

Rajiv Kane and Sartaj Sahni*
University of Minnesota

lop VLSI designs for the solution of several problems that arise in the design rule check
n automation.

nd Phrases

tems, design rule checks, rectilinear polygons, systolic algorithms.

UCTION

dvances in manufacturing technology have made it possible to fabricate chips of ever nplexity. This has posed a severe challenge to existing design automation tools. Existing ke more computer time than is desirable and in some cases require more time and memory cal.

to meet this challenge is to design new computer architecture and corresponding algo- sign automation tasks. This approach has been the subject of many recent research efforts. ectures for design rule checks are described in [BLAN81], and [SEIL82]; wire routing is [BLAN81],[MUDG82],[NAIR82] and [DAMM82]; [UEDA83], [ISOU83] and [CHYA83] con- placement; and new architectures for simulation are proposed in [ABRA82], [DENN82], d [PFIS82]. It is anticipated that through the use of these specialized architectures, one he circuit size that can be handled by a few order of magnitude.

per is concerned with the development of VLSI systems and in particular, systolic algo- reader unfamiliar with systolic designs is referred to [KUNG79] for an excellent introduc-

NEAR POLYGONS

explicitly with rectilinear polygons only. A rectilinear polygon is composed solely of hor- ertical edges. Further, we assume that all polygons are well formed. This means that open polygons with self overlaps (Figure 1(a) and (b))are not permitted. Polygons are, however, contain holes which are themselves rectilinear polygons (Figure 1(c)).

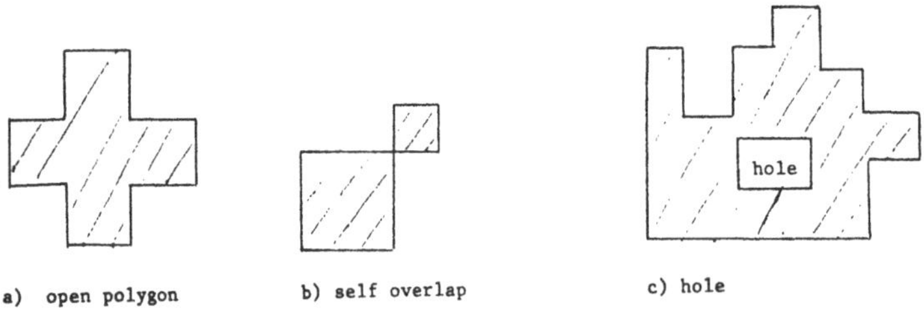

Figure 1

The restriction to rectilinear polygons allows a copmpact representation for each polygon. This representation consists of the following:

Polygon number. Each polygon is assigned a unique number. Holes within a polygon are assigned the same number as the enclosing polygon.

Layer number. The layer number to which the polygon belongs.

A sequence of polygon vertices. This sequence begins at the lowermost left hand vertex of the polygon and is obtained by traversing the polygon so that its interior lies to the left of the edge being traversed. Since all edges are either horizontal or vertical, the polygon vertices (except the first) may be described by providing a single coordinate. Thus , the polygon of Figure 2(a) is represented as:

p, n, l, x_1, y_1, x_2, y_3, x_4, y_5, x_6, y_7, x_8, y_1.

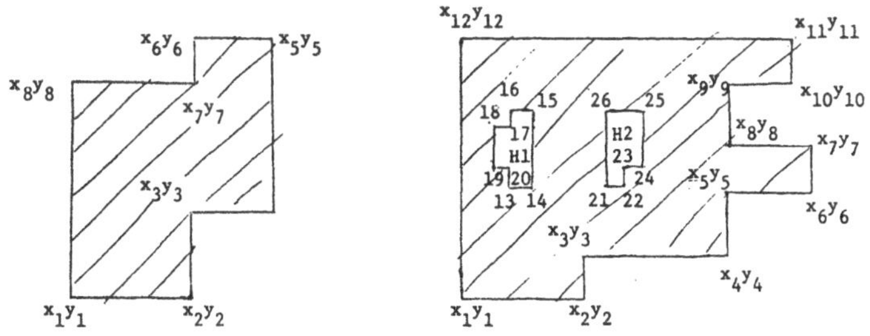

(a) No holes (b) Two holes H1 and H2

Figure 2

The first symbol *p* identifies this as an enclosing polygon. *n* is the polygon number. *l* is the layer number. In case of a hole, an h is used in place of the p. Holes are traversed such that the the interior is to the left of each edge traversed. The representation for the polygon and holes of Figure 2(b) is:

p, n, l, x_1, y_1, x_2, y_3, x_4, y_5, x_6, y_7, x_8, y_9, x_{10}, y_{11}, x_{12}, y_1
h, n, l, x_{13}, y_{13}, x_{14}, y_{15}, x_{16}, y_{17}, x_{18}, y_{19}, x_{20}, y_{13}
h, n, l, x_{21}, y_{21}, x_{22}, y_{23}, x_{24}, y_{25}, x_{26}, y_{21}

3. WIDTH AND SPACING CHECKS

Polygons in a layer are required to satisfy certain spacing and width requirements. Let s be the minimum allowable spacing and d the minimum allowable width. Examples of width and spacing errors are shown in Figure 3. In Figures 3 (g)-(i), the spacing errors are marked with an *.

We develop a systolic system to check for spacing and width errors. This system is called the SWS (systolic width and spacing checker).

3.1. SWS ARCHITECTURE

A block diagram of the SWS appears in Figure 4. The major components of an SWS are two systolic sort arrays (SAX and SAY), controllers for these sort arrays, and a systolic design rule checker (DRC). Note that we use SWS to denote the entire systolic design rule check system of Figure 4 and DRC to refer to a component of SWS that performs the actual design rule checks. This component is also systolic in nature. When design rule checks are to be performed, the CPU sends the compact descriptions of the polygons to the SWS. This description is transformed into explicit edges by the controllers for SAX and SAY. Horizontal edges are created by the controller for SAX and inserted into SAX. Vertical edges are formed by the controller for SAY and inserted into SAY. The sort arrays sort the edges into lexical order. Thus, the SAX sorts edges by y - coordinate and within y - coordinate by x - coordinate. Recall that we have assumed that there are no overlapping edges. So, even though every horizontal edge has two x - coordinates, there is a unique lexical ordering for the horizontal edges. Simi-

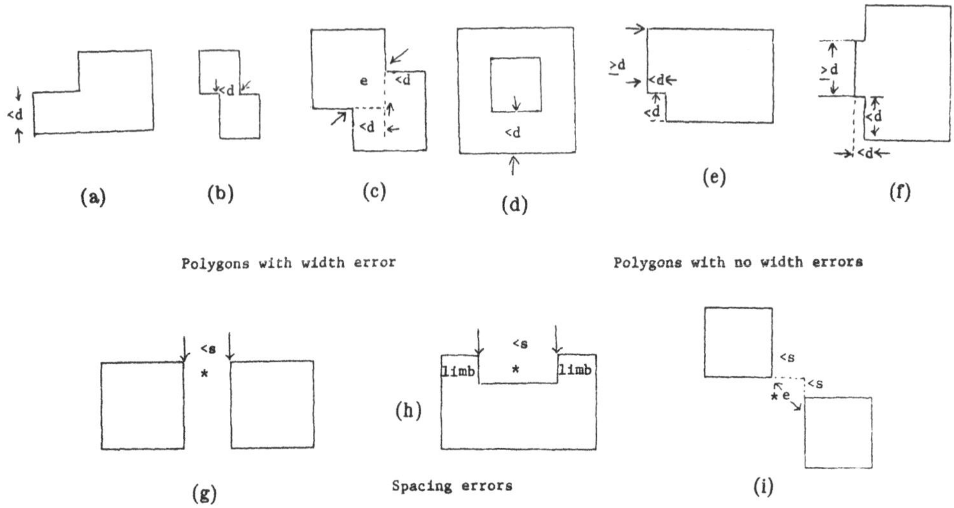

Figure 3

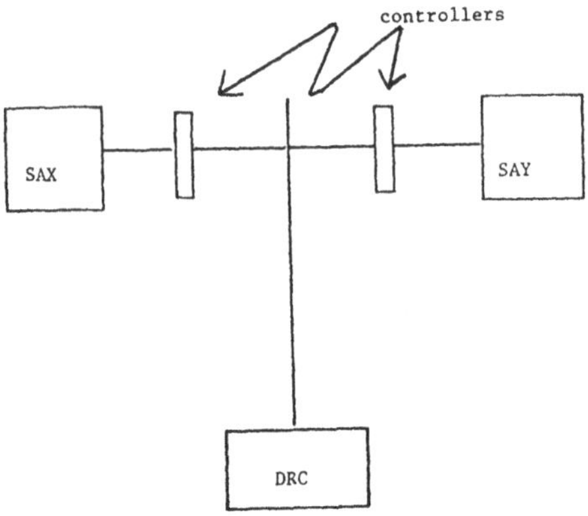

Figure 4 SWS Architecture

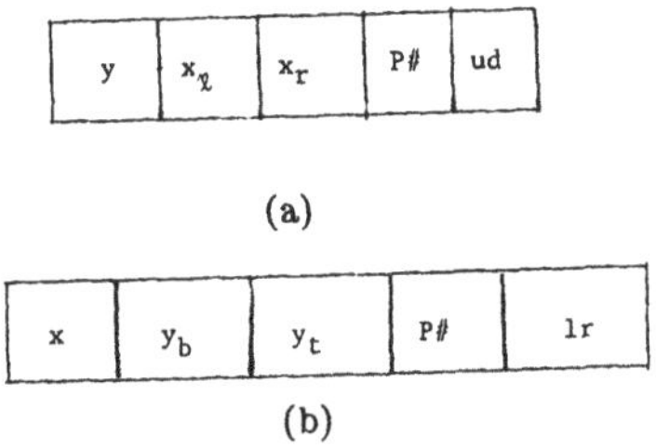

Figure 5

arly there is a unique ordering for the vertical edges.

The SAX and SAY are simply systolic priority queues [LIES79]. Consequently, as soon as the edges have been formed and entered into the SAX and SAY, they may be transmitted in lexical order to the DRC. First SAX sends its edges to the DRC, which examines them for width violations in the y direction and spacing violations in the x direction. All detected errors are transmitted back to SAX. Next SAY transmits its edges to the DRC which examines them for width errors in the x direction and spacing errors in the y direction. These errors are sent back to SAY. The errors collected in SAX and SAY may then be communicated back to the CPU.

Clearly, by using two DRCs, the horizontal and vertical edge processing may be effectively overlapped. Further, by providing a data path for the errors to go directly from the DRC to the CPU, the use of the SWS may be pipelined.

3.2. EDGE FORMING

The descriptor for each edge formed in the sort array controllers consists of 5 fields as shown in Figure 5(a). The terminology used in this figure is with respect to the horizontal edges.

y is the y - coordinate for the edge; x_l the left x coordinate; x_r the right coordinate; p# the polygon number; and ud (up-down) is 0 if the interior of the polygon is above this edge and 1 otherwise. In case the DRC sends errors back to the SAX (rather than directly to CPU) then each edge descriptor will have two additional bits to record the error. For vertical edges we may use the terminology of Figure 5(b) where x is the x-coordinate of the edge; y_b and y_t are, respectively, the bottom and top y-coordinates; p# is the polygon number; and lr (left-right) is 0 if the polygon interior is to the left of the edge and is 1 otherwise. The p# field is used only to identify polygons with errors. This field may be omitted and the detected errors can be associated with polygons by performing a search at the end.

Example 1: The edge descriptors for the horizontal edges of the polygon of Figure 6 are : y_1, x_1, x_2, 1, 0; y_7, x_7, x_8, 1, 1; y_{16}, x_{16}, x_{15}, 1, 0; y_{10}, x_{10}, x_9, 1, 0;; y_{11}, x_{11}, x_{12}, 1, 0;; y_6, x_6, x_5, 1, 1;; y_{14}, x_{14}, x_{13}, 1, 0;; y_4, x_4, x_3, 1, 1;;

The descriptors for the vertical edges are:;

x_1, y_1, y_6, 1, 1; x_7, y_7, y_{16}, 1, 1; x_5, y_5, y_4, 1, 1; x_{15}, y_{15}, y_{14}, 1, 0; x_{10}, y_{10}, y_{11}, 1, 1; x_{12}, y_{12}, y_{13}, 1, 1; x_8, y_8, y_9, 1, 1; x_2, y_2, y_3, 1, 0;

The transformation from the compact polygon representation to the edge descriptors is relatively straightforward.

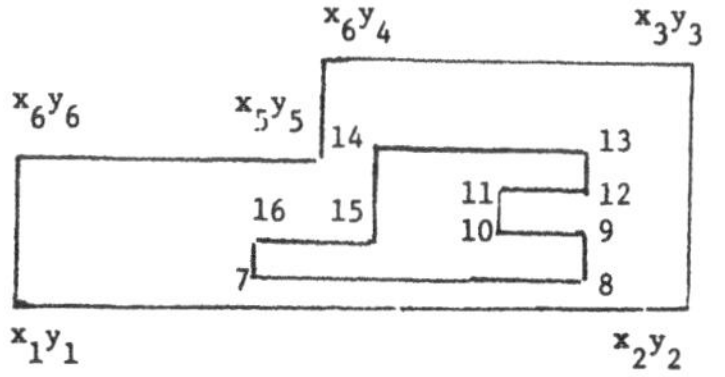

Figure 6

3.3. THE DRC

The DRC is invoked once for horizontal edges and once for vertical edges. Since the processing that occurs with horizontal edges is the same as that for vertical edges, our discussion of the DRC is confined to the case of horizontal edges.

As mentioned earlier, when processing the horizontal edges, the DRC checks for width violations in the y direction and spacing violations in the x direction. In addition, the spacing and width checks of Figure 7 are also performed.

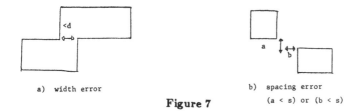

a) width error

b) spacing error (a < s) or (b < s)

Figure 7

The DRC (Figure 8) is a linear systolic array.

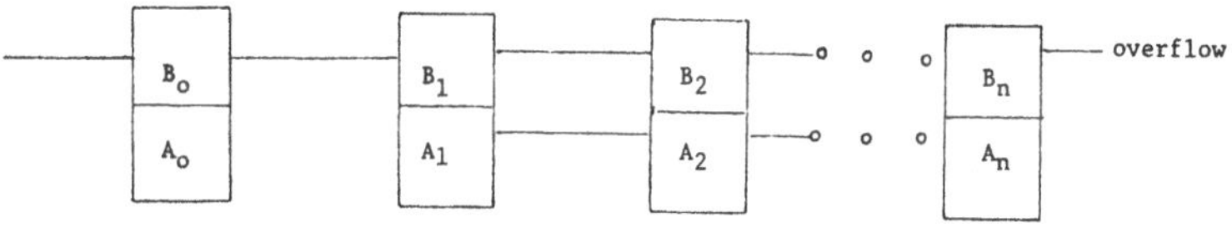

Figure 8

Edges enter the DRC through the B register of PE 0. Output edges, i.e., edges that contain spacing or width errors, exit the DRC through the A register of PE 0. The A registers contain two kinds of edges: (i) edges to be output and (ii) edges not ready for output. This second category of A register edges, called ***settled edges***, have the following properties:

(a) No two edges overlap. If L_i and L_j are the left x coordinates of the edges in PEs i and j respectively, and R_i and R_j, respectively, are their right x coordinates, then either *Rsubj* $\leq L_i$ or $R_i \leq L_j$.

(b) The edges are ordered by their x coordinates. So, if i < j then $R_i \leq L_j$.

The B registers contain edges that are either ready to be output or are looking for a PE to settle into (this can only be done by moving into an A register such that properties (a), and (b) are preserved). Let B be an edge looking for a PE to settle into. B moves to the right (through B registers) until it reaches a PE whose A register edge A lies entirely to its right (Figure 9(a)) or with which it overlaps (Figure 9(b) is *one* such case).

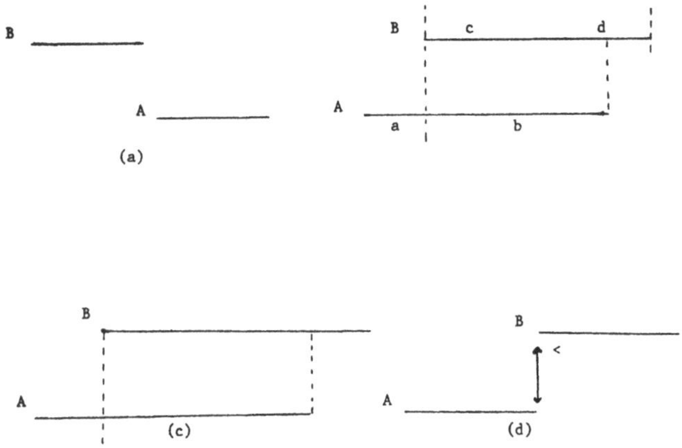

Figure 9

In case B is entirely to the left of A (Figure 9(a)), B settles in this PE and A moves rightwards through the B registers. Edges B and A are checked for possible spacing violations. When B and A overlap as in Figure 9(b), edge A is split into two segments a and b. Edge B is split into the two segments c and d. If the vertical distance between segments b and d is less than w, then a width error is to be reported. This error is recorded in segments a and d. Segments b and c are discarded as they are not needed to detect any further width errors in the y direction or spacing errors in the x direction. Segment d continues to move through the B registers. Observe that segment a isn't ready for output as it is needed to detect further width and spacing errors. Further, observe that by splitting the edges A and B and discarding segments b and c, we ensure that when the segment d eventually settles, it does not overlap with other settled edges.

When the situation depicted in Figure 9(c) arises, we need to check if the vertical distance between the B and A edges is at least s. If it is, then the remaining edges passing over A are too far from A to result in errors. So, edge A may be discarded if no errors have been detected so far with respect to it. If they have, then the status of this edge is changed to "ready for output". In case the vertical seperation between B and A is less than s, then a vertical spacing error between B and A exists. This is recorded and the edge A is declared ready for output. Observe that in this case a y direction spacing error has been detected. While we earlier stated that only x direction spacing errors will be detected in this pass, our implementation at times records y direction errors too. This is essential to catch the spacing error of Figure 9(d).

With this introduction, we present the details of the DRC. We begin with the description of the registers A and B that each PE has. In describing the fields of a register, we shall use the notation A[i].x to mean field x of register A of PE i. Each register in the DRC has all the fields necessary to describe an edge. In addition, the following fields are also present:

PR .. This is a two bit priority field used to control the flow of data in the A and B registers. The four possible values assignable to PR have the following interpretation:

PR = 11: This signifies an empty register. If ud = 0, then this is an empty register to the right of the rightmost edge (i.e. edge 2.1 of Figure 10) in the DRC. If ud = 1, then this is an empty register to the left of the rightmost edge in the DRC.

PR = 10: The register contains an edge that has yet to settle in its place. This value is possible only for B register edges.

PR = 01: This value is possible only for an A register edge. It denotes an edge that has settled.

PR = 00: Denotes an edge for which an error has been detected.

we .. A 1 bit width error field. It is set to 1 if a width error involving this edge has been detected.

se .. A 1 bit space error field that is set to 1 when a spacing error involving this edge is detected.

rightok .. A 1 bit field. This is used only for edges with ud = 0. Let X, Y $\in$ {A, B}. X[i].rightok = 1 iff there is a j such that
(X[i].P# = Y[j].P# and X[i].x_r = Y[j].x_l and Y[j].ud = 0)

y_{right} .. Used in conjunction with rightok. Gives the y-coordinate of the edge that satisfies the condition of rightok

leftok .. A 1 bit field that is used only for edges with ud = 1. Let x $\in$ {A, B}. X[i].leftok = 1 iff there is a limb (i.e., an upward growth of a polygon from one of the ends of a horizontal edge with ud=1) at the left end of the edge.

x_{est} .. When leftok = 1, x_{est} gives the leftmost point of the edge. Since edges may get split during processing, x_{est} may not equal x_l (x_l wil be the current left end of the split edge). Since the rightok and y_{right} fields are used only when ud = 0 while the leftok and x_{est} fields are used only when ud = 1, these fields may use the same physical register space.

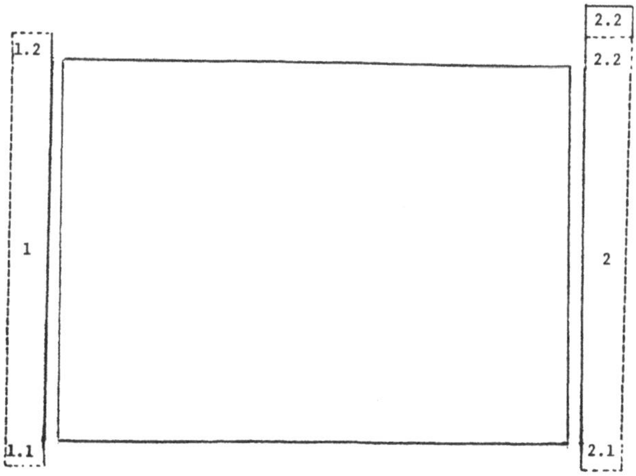

Figure 10

It is assumed that all polygons are to be embedded on a rectangular chip (Figure 10). Thus during processing for horizontal edges, the edges 1.1, 1.2, 2.1, and 2.2 are loaded in the SAX. The edges 1.1 and 1.2 come out of the SAX before any other edges in the layout; whereas the edges 2.1, and 2.2 come out at the end. The DRC is initially loaded with the edge 2.1 for processing edges from SAX and the edge 3.1 for processing edges from the SAY.

At the start of each cycle of the DRC, an edge is inserted in B_0. This edge has PR = 01, and we = se = 0. Since edges come from the SAX (or SAY) only once every two cycles, the cycle time of the DRC must be at least twice that of the sort arrays. Once the edge enters the DRC at B_0, it moves towards the right until it finds its correct position with respect to the edges in the A registers. The A register edges are ordered by their x_l values. As the B register edges move to the right, width and spacing checks are performed against the A register edges in the PEs. Once all the hoizontal edges have been entered into the DRC, we set B[0].PR = 11, B[0].ud = 1 and A[0].PR = 11. This will cause the detected errors to move to the left of the DRC from where they may be removed and sent back to SAX or the CPU.

The basic cycle of the DRC is described in **procedure** cycle.

```
procedure cycle
   {pulsating cycle of the systolic DRC}
   repeat
      { shift B edges right }
      for every PE i, i < n do
         B[i+1] ← B[i]
      B[0] ← new edge
      B[0].leftok ← 0
      A[0].(PR,x_l,x_r, we, se, ud) ← (00, -∞, -∞, 0, 0, 1)
      PROCESS_IN_EACH_PE  { described later }
      { shift A edges as needed }
      for every PE i do
         if
               A[i].PR = A[i+1].PR = 11 and A[i+1].ud = 0
         then { mark i as right of rightmost edge }
               A[i].ud = 0
         end
         for odd i on odd cycles and
               even i on even cycles do
            if A[i].PR > A[i+1].PR
            then
               if ((A[i].PR = 00) or (A[i].PR = B[i].PR = 11))
               then
                  A[i] ←→ A[i+1] { interchange edges }
               end
            endif
      end
   until false  { infinite loop }
end cycle
```

3.4. Procedures Used For Width and Spacing Checks

Before specifying the details of the step 'PROCESS_IN_EACH_PE' ,we describe a few procedures used for this purpose.

Spacecheck 1.1

This is used by a PE that contains an edge in its A register that is to the right of the edge in its B register. Figure 11 depicts two of the situations when the check is performed.

```
procedure spacecheck 1.1
   if A.x_l - B.x_r < s
   then
      [A.se ← 1;B.se ← 1]
   endif
end spacecheck 1.1
```

```
procedure spacecheck 1.2
   if B.x_l - A.x_r < s
   then
      [A.se ← 1;B.se ← 1]
   endif
end spacecheck 1.2
```

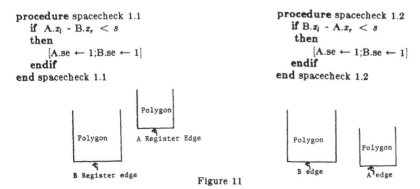

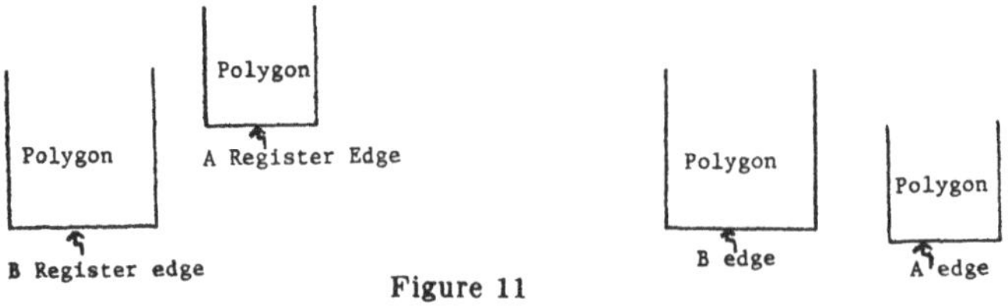

Figure 11

Spacecheck 1.2

This is similar to spacecheck 1.1 except that the B register edge is to the right of the A register edge.

Spacecheck2

This is used to check the interlimb distance in polygons (Figure 12). As edges progress through the DRC, they may get broken. So, the edge in a register may actually be only a segment of a larger edge. The leftmost point on the original whole edge is 'remembered' in the field x_{est} which takes the place of the y_{right} (x_{est} is used when ud = 1 while y_{right} is used when ud = 0).

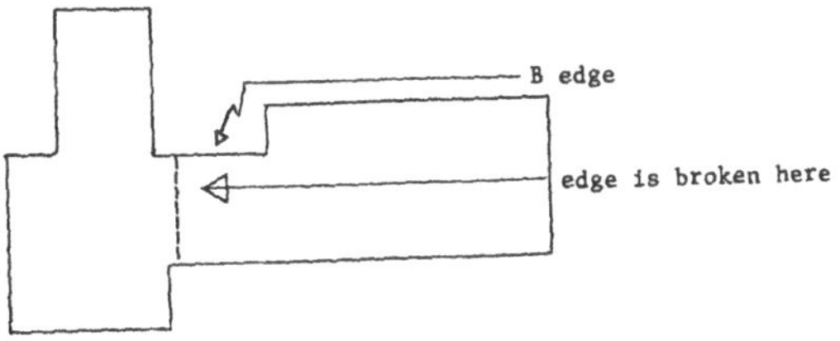

Figure 12 Interlimb distance

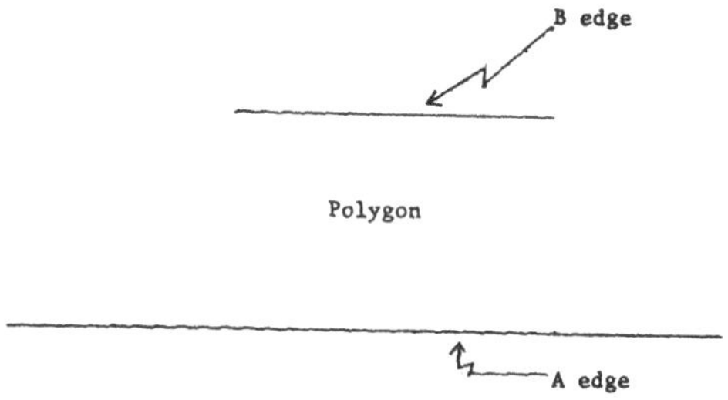

Figure 13

procedure spacecheck2
  if $B.x_r$ - $B.x_{est}$ $< s$
  then
    B.se ← 1
  endif
end spacecheck2

Widthcheck1

This is used when the A and B register edges in a PE belong to the same polygon; have some overlap; and A.ud = 0 and B.ud = 1. Figure 13 depicts a possible situation.

procedure widthcheck1
  if B.y -A.y < d
  then
    [A.we ← 1; B.we ← 1]
  endif
end widthcheck1

procedure widthcheck2
  if B.y - A.y_{right} < d
  then
    B.we ← 1
  endif
end widthcheck2

Widthcheck2

The widthcheck performed by this procedure is shown in Figure 14. The PE that performs this check has edges in its A and B registers that have the same polygon numbers; A.ud = 4 and B.ud = 1; and A.rightok = 1.

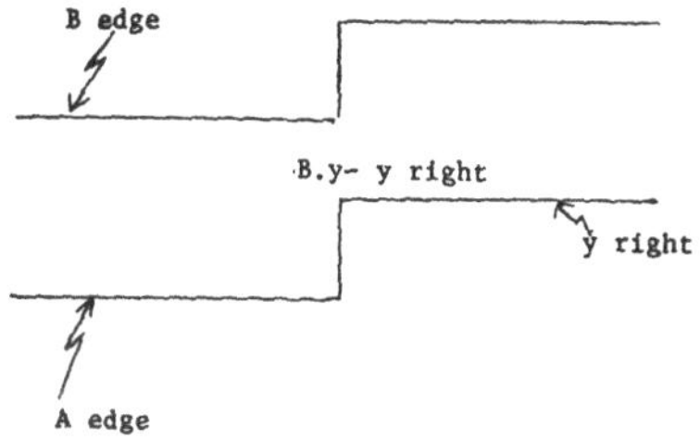

Figure 14

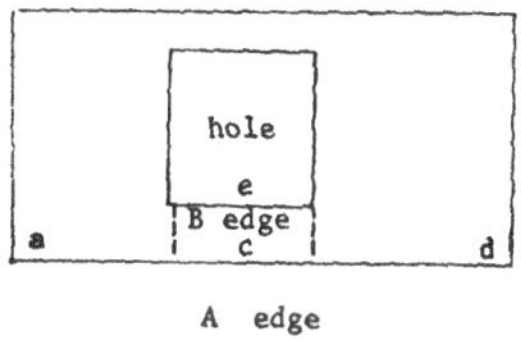

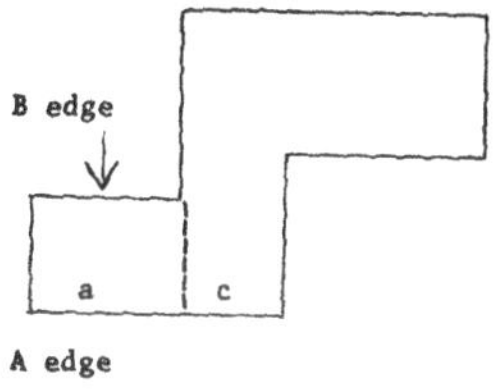

Figure 15

3.5. PROCESS_IN_EACH_PE

In this step of the cycle, each PE examines the edges in the A and B registers and performs the checks based on this. In order to understand the edge processing procedure to be outlined shortly, it is necessory to keep the following in mind.

1. Edges may settle only in A registers. Thus,
   B.PR $\neq$ 01 for any PE.
2. Edges that have not yet settled must do so by moving to the right via B registers. So, the case A.PR = 10 is not possible.
3. Settled edges are ordered by their x values left to right in the A registers. The sequence of settled edges (i.e., PR = 01) may be interspersed with error edges (i.e., PR = 00) and empty edges (i.e., PR = 11).
4. A polygon edge may get split during processing. Figure 15(a) shows a polygon with a hole in it. When edge e is the B edge in the PE that has the edge acd in its A register, the acd edge is split into the three segments a, c, and d. The segments a and c are discarded. In the case of the polygon in Figure 15(b), the edge e causes the edge ac to be split into segments a and c. The segment a is discarded as no new errors with respect to this segment are possible. All errors detected for the edge are retained by the remaining segment.

In general, edge splits and discards are carried out so as to ensure that the set of active edges (i.e., PR= 01 or 10) have no overlap of their x coordinates.

The exact mechanism by which width and spacing errors are detected is best described using algorithmic notation as below.

```
procedure PROCESS_IN_EACH_PE
begin
 case A.PR of
   00 : { A edge has an error; do nothing }

   10 : { A edge hasn't settled. This is not possible.
          Only B edges may have PR = 10 }

   11 : { A register is empty }

        case B.PR of
          00: A ←→ B  { Move error edge to
                        empty A register }

          01: { Not possible as edges can
                settle only in A register }

          10: if A.ud = 0
                then {No edges to the right of PE }
                  [B.PR ← 01; A ←→ B]
                endif
              { B edge must settle here }

          11: { do nothing }
        end case { B.PR of }

   01 : { A edge is in its correct place }

        case B.PR of
          11 : { do nothing }

          00 and 01 :{ not possible }
```

```
10 : case A.ud of

      0:

{ At this point A.PR = 01, B.PR = 10, A.ud = 0.
  The interior of the polygon is above the edge A.}

{ Determine the relationship between the A and B edges }
case

 1: A.x_l ≥ B.x_r :

   { We have the situation of Figure 16 }
   if B.ud = 0
   then {Figure 16(a)}
      [if B.x_r = A.x_l
       then { By assumption on the polygons
                (Figure 2) B.p# = A.p# }
          [B.rightok ← 1; B.y_right ← A.y]
       else { B.P# <> A.P# or B and A are
                from two limbs of the same polygon}
          spacecheck1.1
       endif ]
   endif
  { This is B's place to settle }
  A.PR ← 10; B.PR ← 01; A ←→ B

  { Note that when B.ud = 1, no checks need
    be performed as relevant checks were
    performed when the A edge settled }

 2: A.x_r ≤ B.x_l :

  { This situation is depicted in Figure 17 }
  if B.ud = 0
  then {Figre 17(a)}
     if A.x_r = B.x_l
     then { By assumption on polygons (Figure 2)
               B.p# = A.p# }
        [A.rightok ← 1; A.y_right ← B.y]
     else
        spacecheck1.2
     endif
  else {Figure 17(b)}
     if A.x_r = B.x_l and not B.leftok
     then { Figure 17(c). Set leftok and x_ext
              in case limb test is needed. B edge
              may get split later}
        [B.leftok ← 1; B.x_ext ← B.x_l ]
     endif
     if A.rightok
     then { Figure 17(c). A width check is needed. }
       [if (B.y - A.y < d) and (B.x_l - A.x_r) < d
        then B.we ← 1]
     endif
  endif
```

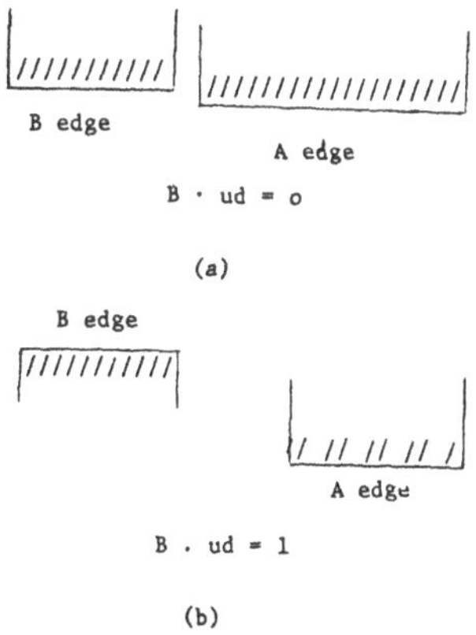

Figure 16

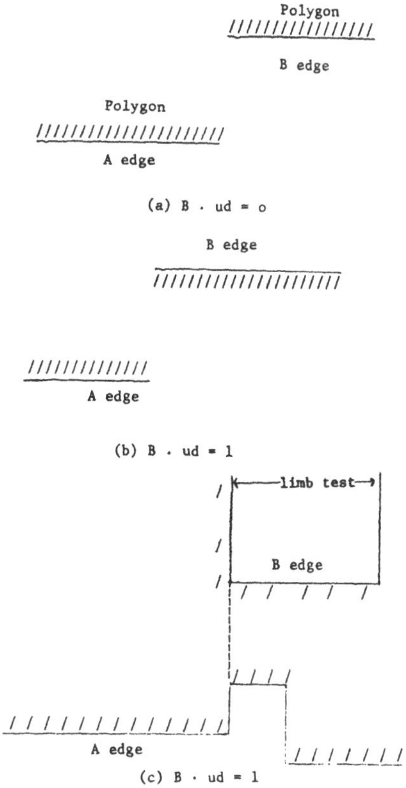

Figure 17

```
3: else : { A and B edges have some overlap and so
            must be part of the same polygon. Hence
            B.ud = 1.
            Note that A.x_l ≤ B.x_l < A.x_r .

            The case B.x_l < A.x_l is not
            possible as this would have caused
            caused the B edge to be split earlier,
            leaving B.x_l = A.x_l  }
       Details appear in [KANE83]
            { Begin last case to consider }

: A.ud = 1:
    { At this time, A.PR = 01, B.PR = 10, and A.ud = 1}

    if B.y - A.y ≥ s

    then { remaining edges are too far
           from A to cause errors}
         [if  A.we or A.se
          then A.PR ← 00
          else  A.PR = 11]
    else
    case

       :A.x_l ≥ B.x_r: {Figure 18}
          if not [(B.ud=1 and B.x_r =A.x_l )
                or A.x_l - B.x_r ≥ s]
          then
              [A.se ← 1; B.se ← 1]
          endif
          { This is B's place to settle }
          A ←→ B; A.PR ← 01; B.PR ← 10

       :A.x_r ≤ B.x_l : {Figure 19 }
           if not [B.ud = 1 and B.x_l = A.x_r
                or B.x_l - B.x_r ≥ s]
           then
               [A.se ← 1; B.se ← 1]
           endif

       :else: { Partial overlap (Figure 20). So, B.ud = 0}
             A.se ← 1; B.se ← 1
             case

               : B.x_r < A.x_r :{Figure 20(a) and (b) }
                     { split A}
                     A.x_l ← B.x_r
                     A ←→ B; A.PR ← 01; B.PR ← 10

               : B.x_r ≥ A.x_r :{Figure 20(c) and (d)}
                     A.PR ← 00

               { The remaining spacing errors involving the left
                 part of the A edge in Figure 20(b) and (d) will
                 be detected when handling vertical edges }
             end case
       end case { else }
     endif { B.y - A.y ≥ s }
  end case { of A.ud }
end. { of PROCESS_INEACH_PE }
```

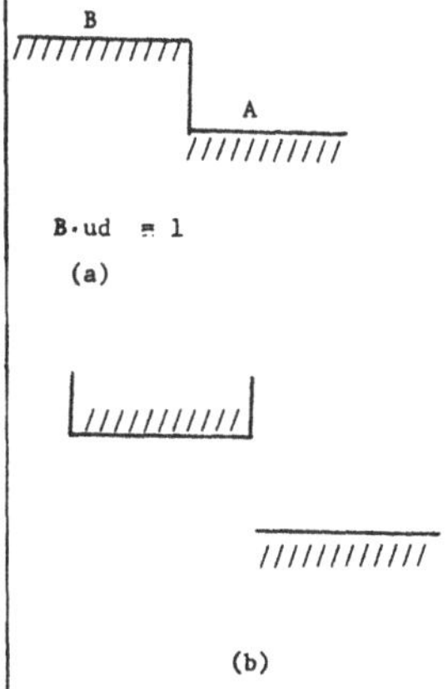

Figure 18

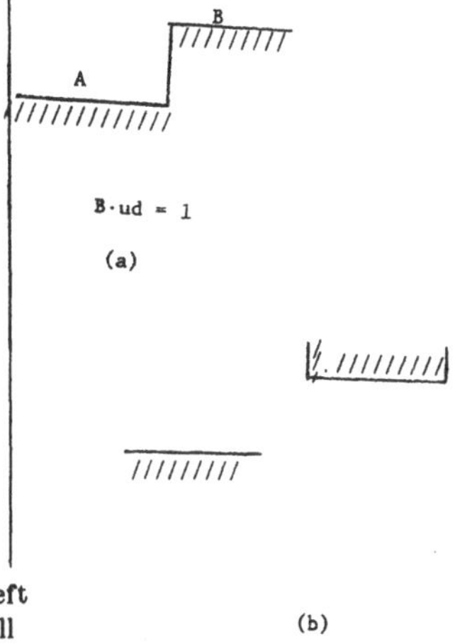

Figure 19

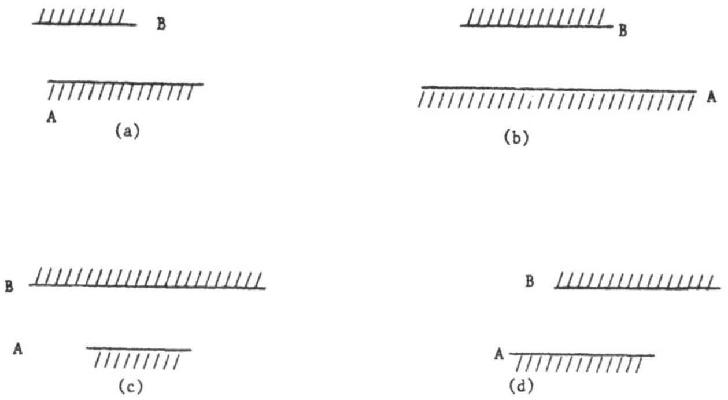

Figure 20

3.6. PERFORMANCE

Under the assumption that the sort arrays and DRC are large enough to accommodate all the edges, the sort time and the DRC time is linear in the number of the edges in all the polygons. Furthermore the time spent extracting the errors from the sort arrays is effectively overlapped with the DRC processing. The edges input to the DRC are sorted on the multikey (y,x_l, ud). Thus the layout effectively is scanned from bottom to top. The edges present at any time in the DRC are:

1. The edges with ud = 0, which have the interior of the polygon above them and the corresponding closing edge (i.e., the edge with ud = 1 and the same x_coordinates) has not yet been encountered.
2. The edges with ud = 1 for which an edge sufficiently above has not been encountered.
3. The errors reported but not yet taken out of the DRC.
4. The segments created due to splitting, with above properties.

No record is kept of the edges with no errors. Thus the number of PEs depends not only on the number of the edges in the layout but also on the number of errors to be reported.

In practice, of course, no matter how large the sort arrays and the DRC, there will be times when the number of edges to be handled exceeds the capacity of the arrays. It would be essential in such cases to partition the layout. A possible partitioning scheme is described in [KANE83].

4. NET GENERATION

4.1. Problem Specification

The input to the net extraction problem is a collection of polygons. We assume that all polygons are well formed and rectilinear. The input representation of each polygon includes the following information:

(a) *Polygon number*
Every polygon is assigned a distinct number. Holes within a polygon are assigned the same number as the bounding polygon.

(b) *Layer number*
Different polygons may lie on different layers. A layer may be a physical or logical layer. Each layer is assigned a distinct number. A polygon (and all its holes) lie on exactly one layer.

(c) *xmin, ymin*
xmin (ymin) is the lowest x coordinate(y coordinate) of any edge in the polygon.

(d) *Polygon vertex sequence* This sequence consists of all vertices in the bounding polygon, followed by those in the first hole, those in the second hole, etc. The order of vertices is obtained by traversing the bounding polygon (or hole) such that the polygon interior lies to the left. The traversal begins at the lowermost left vertex of the polygon.

In addition to the collection of polygons, the input includes a set N of pairs. This set gives the pairs of layers that result in an electrical contact if polygons in those layers ovrlap. For example, suppose that two polygons p1 and p2 overlap in space and that p1 is on layer 1 and p2 is on layer 2. The overlap of p1 and p2 causes an electrical connection iff (1,2) or (2,1) $\in$ N.

Example Let N = { (1, 3), (2, 3), (2, 4)} and let the polygons be as shown in Figure 21. The pair i, j associated with each polygon provides the polygon number (i) and layer number (j). The polygons form two nets {1, 2} and {3, 4, 5}.

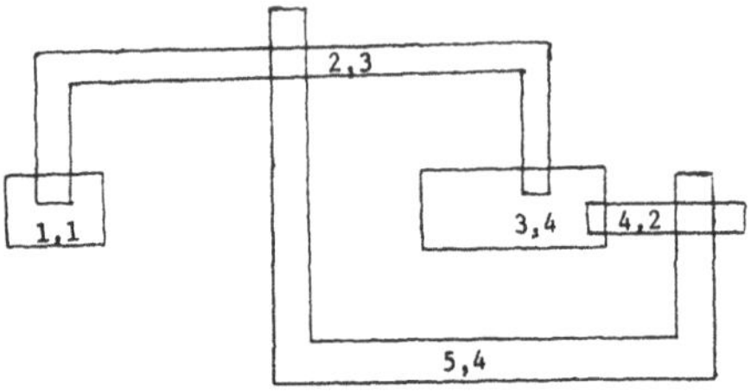

Figure 21

The output for the net extraction problem is a partition of the polygons into equivalence classes such that each equivalence class defines a net.

4.2. Architecture of the Net List Extractor

The net list extractor (NLE) is a hardware device that accepts as input a collection of well formed rectilinear polygons. Its output is a partitioning of polygons into nets. The NLE consists of three architectural blocks: sorter (SORT), pair generator (PAIRGEN), and net generator (NETGEN). A block diagram is provided in Figure 22. The sorter sorts the polygons (*i.e.* their constituent edges) into an order suitable for processing by PAIRGEN. PAIRGEN produces pairs of polygon intersections. Specifically, let i and j be two polygons that overlap. The pair (i, j) is generated by the PAIRGEN iff (i, j) $\in$ N (recall that N is the set of layer pairs that cause electrical equivalence). The NETGEN accepts these pairs as input, and produces the nets or equivalence classes as polygons.

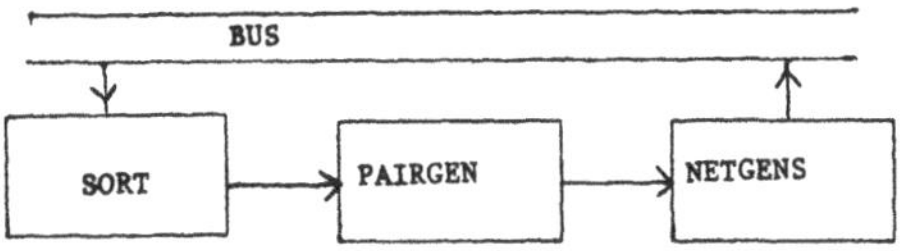

Figure 22 NLE

4.3. SORT

The SORT module of Figure 22 is comprised of a controller and a systolic sort array (Figure 23).

The controller receives the polygon descriptions and generates the horizontal edges of each polygon. For each such edge, a five field descriptor as shown in Figure 24 is created. p# and l# are, respectively, the polygon number and layer in which the polygon resides. y is the y coordinate of the edge and x_l, x_r the left and right x coordinates of the edge.

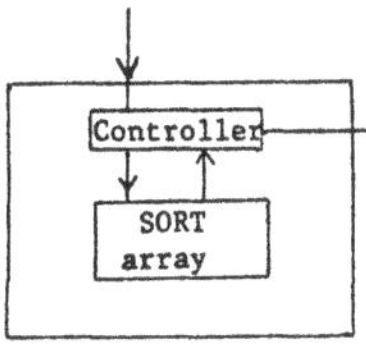

Figure 23

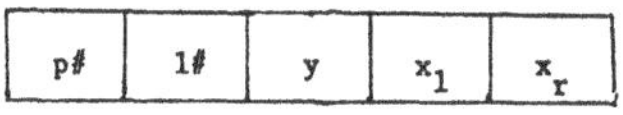

Figure 24 Horizontal edge descriptor

In addition to the horizontal edge descriptors, a bop (beginning of polygon) descriptor is generated for each polygon. The bop descriptor contains the xmin, ymin coordinates (*i.e.*, the lowest x and y coordinates) of the polygon in addition to p# and l#.

The bop descriptor and the edge descriptors for each polygon are input into the sort array. This is a linear array of PEs (processing elements) as described by Leiserson ([LEIS79]). Each PE has two sets of registers A, and B. All input is through the B register of PE 0, and all output is through the A register of this PE. Using a minor modification of the design of [LEIS79], this array can be used to sort the polygons by (ymin, xmin) (*i.e.*, nondecreasing order of (ymin, xmin)). Within a polygon, the edges are sorted in nondecreasing order of (y, x_l). The sorted edge and bop descriptors are then input to the PAIRGEN.

Note that the output of the sort array is sequence of polygons. All edge descriptors of a polygon immediately follow the bop descriptor of that polygon.

4.4. PAIRGEN

PAIRGEN is a one dimensional systolic array of processors (Figure 25). Each processor has four registers. A, B1, B2, and C. Polygons enter PAIRGEN through the B2 register of PE 0. Pairs exit PAIRGEN through the A register of PE 0.

Each register has the following fields: *used*, p#, l#, *function*, *pair*, y_1, x_l, x_r, y_2 and p2. We use the notation X[i].f to refer to field f of register X in PE i. When the PE index is not necessary, we use the notation X.f.

used is a one bit field that enables us to determine whether or not a register is currently in use. X[i].used is true iff register X of PE i is currently in use.

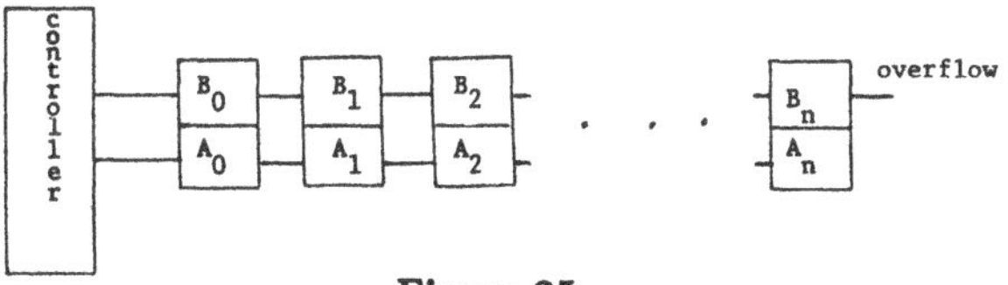

Figure 25

When a register is in use, it contains one of four types of descriptors. The four types are distinguished by their *function* field. The *function* field is two bits long and has the following significance:

function = 00 : register contains an edge descriptor.
= 01 : register contains a rectangle descriptor.
= 10 : register contains a pair descriptor.
= 11 : register contains a bop descriptor.

All descriptors are associated with a polygon. P# and l#, respectively, give the polygon number and layer number of the polygon with which the descriptor is associated.

The usage of the remaining fields depends on the function of the descriptor contained in the register. When function = 00, the register contains an edge. y_1 is the y coordinate of the edge, x_l and x_r are, respectively, the left and right x-coordinates of the edge, and pair is true iff the edge has an unprocessed overlap with a polygon (*i.e.*, an overlap leading to a pair).

When function = 01, the descriptor is a rectangle and y_1, y_2, x_l, x_r, describe the x and y coordinates of the rectangle. The remaining fields are unused.

When function = 10, the descriptor is a pair. (p#, p2) yields the pair to be output. The remaining fields are not utilized.

The last case is function = 11. This time, the descriptor marks the beginning of a polygon (*i.e.*, it is a bop descriptor). The y_2 field is used to record the largest y coordinate of the polygon.

All registers are initialized to have *used* = *false*. In addition, A.x_l is initialized to ∞. The polygons are next input into PAIRGEN in the order they emanate from SORT. *I.e.*, in nondecreasing order of (ymin, xmin). Each polygon is input as a sequence of descriptors. The first descriptor is of type 11 (*i.e.*, a bop, the beginning of a polygon). This has y_2 initialized to miny. This is followed by a sequence of horizontal edge descriptors (*i.e.*, function = 00). The edges enter in nondecreasing order of y coordinate. Edges with same y coordinate enter in increasing order of x_l.

bop and edge descriptors are the only types of descriptors that enter PAIRGEN through B2[0]. The remaining two categories of descriptors are created within PAIRGEN. PAIRGEN decomposes each polygon into its constituent rectangles. These describe the initerior of the polygon. For instance, the polygon of Figure 26 is decomposed into the rectangles a, b, c, d, e, f, g, h. as shown.

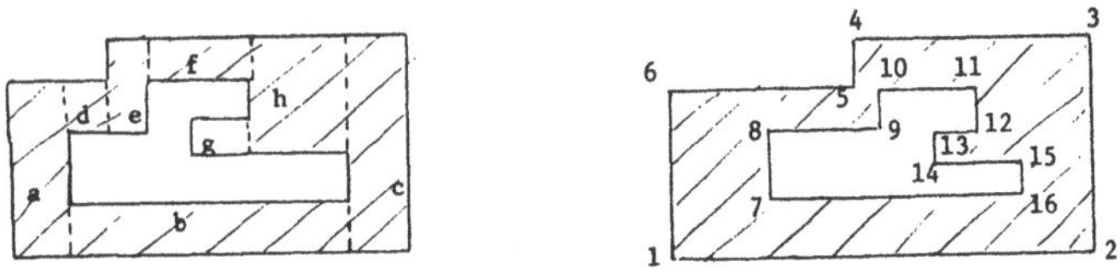

Figure 26

The A registers contain 'settled' descriptors. A settled descriptor can become 'unsettled' at a later time. At this time, it is moved to a B1 or B2 register. The B1 and B2 registers are used to move descriptors to the right and the C register is used to introduce a relative delay in movement between the B2 and B1 registers. A descriptor in a B2 register first moves to the C register in the PE and waits there for one cycle. It moves back to the B2 register on the next cycle for transmission to the neighboring PE on the right.

4.4.1. PAIRGEN Cycle

PAIRGEN is a systolic array which repetitively executes the same code. At the beginning of each cycle, a new descriptor (if any) enters B2[0]. Next, the B1 and B2 registers of each PE send their descriptors to the PE on their right. If the B2 or B1 register of the rightmost PE is used preceding this move, then an overflow occurs. Following the transmission of the B2 and B1 descriptors, each PE performs some processing and then an attempt to move the A register contents leftward, is made. This may cause a pair descriptor to exit the system through PE[0]. The A register data movement is followed by another round of processing in each PE.

Before repeating the above cycle, each PE interchanges the descriptors in its B2 and C registers. This basic cycle is described more formally in Figure 27.

```
procedure PAIRGEN
  Initialize each PE with N;
  Initialize X[i].used = false for all X ∈ {A, B1, B2} and for all i
  Initialize A[i].x_l = ∞ for all i
  repeat {begin systolic cycle}
    if there is a new descriptor
    then B2[0] ← new descriptor
    else B2[0].used ← false;
    endif
    B1[i] ← B1[i-1]; B2[i] ← B2[i-1]; i > 0
    PAIRGEN_PROCESS_IN_EACH_PE;
    if A[0].function = 10 and A[0].used
    then extract pair and set A[0].used = false
    endif
    if not A[i-1].used and [A[i].used or A[i].x_l = ∞]
    then
      [A[i-1] ← A[i]; A[i].used ← false]
    endif
    PAIRGEN_PROCESS_IN_EACH_PE;
    B2 ←→ C; {delay B2}
  until (not A[i].used for all i);
end PAIRGEN
```

Figure 27

4.4.2. PAIRGEN_PROCESS_IN_EACH_PE

This part of the code is concerned with the actual generation of rectangles and pairs. It also determines when an old polygon is too far from the new ones entering the system and no further intersections with it are possible. In reading the description of this code, it is helpful to keep the following in mind:

1. At the beginning of each cycle, all 'settled' descriptors of a polygon are in the A registers of a contiguous group of PEs. The A registers of this contiguous group contain descriptors for this polygon alone (some A registers may be unused).
2. The first PE in the above contiguous group contains a bop descriptor for the polygon.
3. B2 registers never contain rectangle or pair descriptors.
4. B1 registers may contain only those descriptors that result from previously settled descriptors.
5. All polygons are rectilinear and well formed.
6. Polygons and edges enter the PAIRGEN in a specified order.

The processing that actually takes place in each PE is quite minimal. However, it depends on the particular ralationship that exists among the contents of the A, B1, and B2 registers of the PE. A fairly intricate case structure is used to determine the appropriate relationship.

We first provide an informal description of the various cases and the processing for each. This is followed by a more formal description using programming language constructs.

At the top level, the cases are partitioned into two categories depending on whether or not the A register of the PE is in use. In case the A register is not in use and $A.x_l = \infty$ then there are no A registers to the right that are in use. So, the B1 or B2 descriptors can settle here.

The more intricate case occurs when the A register of a PE is in use. At this time we need to determine whether or not the B1 register is in use. If it is, it contains a descriptor derived from a previously settled descriptor. This is coming from the left and we require it to settle here. This of course unsettles the descriptor presently in the A register. In case the B1 register is not in use, the processing is determined by the contents of the register B2.

If B2 is not in use, no processing takes place. If it is in use, we get eight cases depending on the functions of the A and B2 register descriptors. Recall that there are four possibilities for the A register function and only two (bop and edge) for the B2 register.

case 1 A and B register descriptors are both bops.
By this time, all edges belonging to the polygon A.p# have floated over the bop for this polygon and A.y_2 is the maximum y coordinate for the polygon. If A.y_2 < B2.y_1, then polygon A.p# cannot overlap with any of the polygons yet to come (recall that polygons come in nondecreasing order of ymin). Polygon A.p# is no longer needed. Its bop and rectangle descriptors can be discarded and its pair descriptors output. Note that because of the well formedness assumption, all edge descriptors eventually get replaced by rectangle descriptors. The actual elimination of descriptors is accomplished by setting B2.p2 = A.p#. As this B2 descriptor floats over the remaining A.p# descriptors, these take the appropriate action (*i.e.*, set their used value field to false in case of rectangle descriptors).

case 2 A descriptor is a bop and B2 an edge.
At this time we need to determine if the B2 edge detected an overlap for which a pair is to be generated. If so, the pair settles in the A register. The bop previously in this register is moved to the B1 register. In case no pair is to be generated, the only action to take is that of updating A.y_2. If B1.p# = A.p# and A.y_2 < B2.y_1 then B2.y_1 defines a larger y coordinate for A.p# than earlier detected.

There is no need to update A.y_2 in case a pair is generated as the B2 edge will be delayed one cycle relative to the bop (which has been moved to B1). It will catch up with the edge later and the y_2 value will be updated if necessary.

case 3 A descriptor is a pair and B2 a bop.
Nothing needs to be done in this case.

case 4 A descriptor is a pair and B2 an edge.
Something needs to be done only if B2 is set to generate a new pair (B2.pair = true). In this case, we need to verify that the new pair is different from the one in the A register.

case 5 A descriptor is a rectangle and B2 a bop.
In this case we need to verify if B2 has been set to eliminate the A.p# rectangles (*i.e.*, if B2.p2 = A.p#). If so, we set A.used to false.

case 6 A descriptor is a rectangle and B2 an edge.
If the edge and rectangle are from the same polygon nothing is to be done. Similarly if an overlap between B2 and A.p# has already been detected, then also nothing is to de done. If neither of these is the case, then B2 and A need to be examined for possible pair generation. For this, we need to know if an overlap between A.l# and B2.l# is significant (*i.e.* (B2.l#, A.l#) $\in$ N).

case 7 A descriptor is an edge and B2 a bop.
This case cannot arise because of the assumption that polygons are well formed and because of the order in which edges enter the PAIRGEN.

case 8 A and B2 descriptors are both edges.
Because of the assumptions cited under case 7, A.p# = B2.p#. There are eight possibilities for the relationship between the edges in A and B2. These are shown in Figure 28. The three relations shown in Figure 14 cannot arise because of the well formedness assumption of polygons; the order in which polygon edges enter PAIRGEN; and the fact that this order is preserved by the processing of case 8.

Note that because of the well formedness assumption, in cases 2 through 7 of Figure 13 the interior of the polygon lies above the A register edge and below the B2 register edge.

Case 8 of Figure 28 requires no processing. The processing that takes place in each of the remaining seven cases is described in Figure 30.

Labels A, B1, and B2 denote quantities before processing while the labels A',B1', and B2' denote the conditions following the processing. Shaded areas denote the rectangles that get formed. For example, Figure 30(e) denotes case 5 of Figure 28. The edge A gets split into three parts. The left part is an edge from A.x_l to B2.x_l. This resides in register A after processing. The middle part is a rectangle that resides in B1 register after processing. The right part is an edge that extends from B2.x_r to A.x_r. This resides in B2 following the processing. The shaded rectangle is in B1 following the processing.

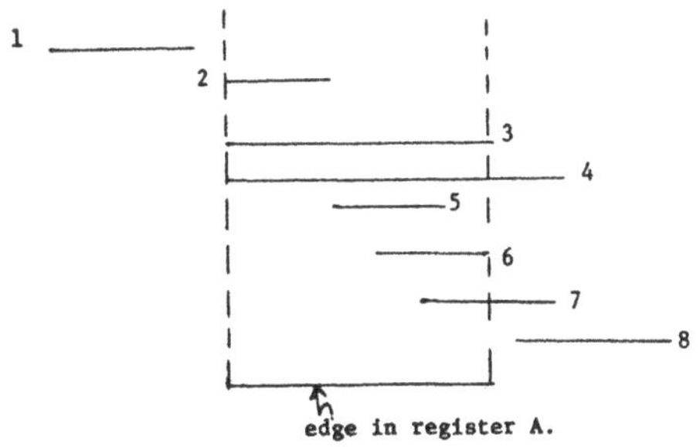

Edge relationships for case 8
Figure 28

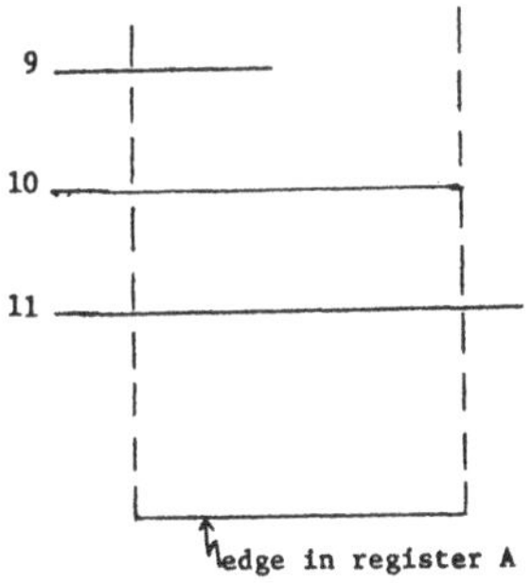

Figure 29

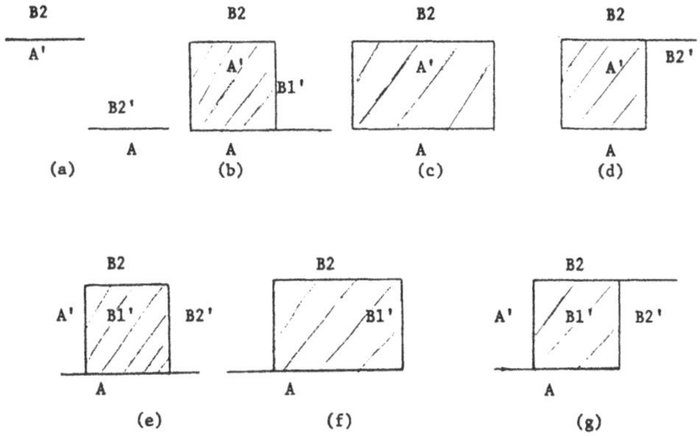

Figure 30

4.5. NETGEN

NETGEN processes the pairs output by PAIRGEN and partitions the polygons into nets. The architecture of NETGEN is shown in Figure 31. We assume there are as many PEs as polygons. PE i represents polygon i. Each PE is able to receive and send messages on the broadcast bus. In addition, each PE is assumed to have one register; net#, which gives the net number to which the polygon belongs. The PEs are also conneted as a chain. The controller, inputs the pairs from PAIRGEN and processes them.

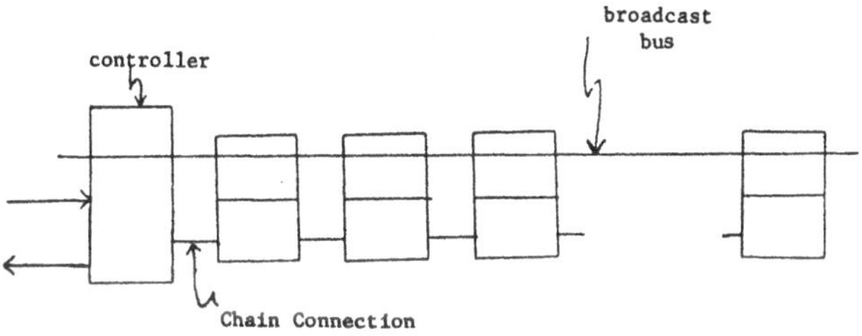

Figure 31

The controller begins by issuing an initialize command along the broadcast bus. This is received by each PE and results in PE i setting its net# register to i. Following this, the controller inputs a pair (i, j) and performs the following instructions:

1. Send a request on the bus to PE i. PE i returns its net# on the bus.
2. Send a request on the bus to PE j. PE j returns its net# on the bus.
3. Send a request to all PEs to examine their net#s. If the net# is net#(i) then change it to net#(j).

The above three steps result in combining together the nets containing i and j. Note that step 3 need be done only when net#(i) $\neq$ net#(j).

When all the pairs have been processed, the PEs transmit (i, net#(i)) leftward along the chain. The algorithm terminates when all these pairs have been output.

As can be seen, the working of NETGEN is described by the three steps:

step1 Initialize net#(i) to i.

step2 Repeatedly input the pairs (i, j) from PAIRGEN. All PEs k with net#(k) = i, change their net#s to net#(j).

step3 Output the net#s.

4.6. PARTITIONING

The discussion thus far has assumed that we have as many PEs as needed. When enough PEs are not available, it is necessary to divide the polygon set into groups containing fewer polygons. This is done by partitioning the x - y space. Each partition should contain a sufficiently small number of poygons (including fractional ones). Following a net extraction on individual partitions, it is necessory to combine together nets from different partitions that have common polygons (common polygons are those that lie in more than one partition). To accomplish this, each net with a common polygon produces a pair (net#, p#). A net produces as many pairs as there are common poygons in it. These pairs are input into a 'modified' NETGEN to relabel nets that get combined. The modified NETGEN uses its PEs to represent both a net and a common polygon. Each PE represents exactly one net or one polygon. The processing is similar to that described in the previous section. At the end each PE representing a net has a new label for that net. Depending on the number of common polygons, this relabeling of nets may have to be done in a hierarchical manner so as to avoid exceeding the hardware capacity.

5. CONCLUSIONS

We have developed algorithm for width and spacing checks as well as for net extraction. These algorithms are suitable for implementation in hardware. The effectiveness of these algorithms will depend on the number of PEs that can be feasibly built for SORT, DRC, PAIRGEN, and NETGEN. With increasing chip densities, it should be possible, in time, to build these hardware components with several thousand PEs. Because of the very regular structure of our design, it should be possible to fully exploit high density fabrication capabilities.

An alternative to hardcoding the algorithms into silicon, is to run them on programmable systolic computer such as the ones being designed and built by H. T. Kung at Carnegie Mellon University. These computers are expected to have about 100 PEs. Each PE will have about 4K words of data space and program space for 100 - 200 instructions.

6. REFERENCES

[ABRA82] M. Abramovici, Y. H. Levendel, and P. R. Menon,"A Logic Simulation Machine" *ACM IEEE Nineteenth Design Automation Conference Proceedings pp 65-73*

[BLAN81] Tom Blank, Mark Stefik, William vanCleemput "A Parallel Bit Map Processor Architecture for DA Algorithms" *ACM IEEE Eighteenth Design Automation Conference Proceedings pp 837-845*

[CHYA83] Dah-Juh Chyan and Melvin A. Breuer, "A Placement Algorithm for Array Processors" *ACM IEEE 20th Design Automation Conference Proceedings pp 182-188*

[DENN82] M. M. Denneau, "The Yorktown Simulation Engine" *CM IEEE Nineteenth Design Automation Conference Proceedings pp 55-59*

[IOSU83] A. Iosupovici, C. King, and M. Breuer, "A Module Interchange Machine' *ACM IEEE 20th Design Automation Conference Proceedings pp 171-174*

[KANE83] R. Kane, S. Sahni, "A Systolic Design Rule Checker" *TR 83-13, Department of Computer Science, University of Minnesota*

[KANE84a] R. Kane, S. Sahni, "Systolic Algorithms for Rectilinear Polygons" *TR 84-2, Department of Computer Science, University of Minnesota*

[KANE84b] R. Mane and S. Sahni, "A hardware algorithm for net extraction", University of Minnesota, Technical Report, 1984.

[KRON82] E. Kronstadt and G. Pfister, "Software Support for the Yorktown Simulation Engine" *ACM IEEE Nineteenth Design Automation Conference Proceedings pp 60-64*

[KUNG79] H. T. Kung, "Let's Design Algorithms for VLSI Systems" *Proceedings of the CALTECH Conference on VLSI, January 1979, pp 65-90*

[KUNG83] H. T. Kung, "A Listing of Systolic Papers", *Department of Computer Science, Carnegie-Mellon University*

[LEIS79] C. E. Leiserson, "Systolic Priority Queues" *Proceedings of Conference on VLSI: Architecture, Design, Fabrication California Institute of Tachnology Jan 79 pp 199-214*

[MUDG82] T. N. Mudge, R. A. Ratenbar, R. M. Lougheed, and D. E. Atkins, "Cellular Image Processing Techniques for VLSI Circuit Layout Validation and Routing" *ACM IEEE Nineteenth Design Automation Conference Proceedings pp 537-543*

[NAIR82] R. Nair, S. Jung, S. Liles, and R. Villani, "Global Wiring on a Wire Routing Machine" *ACM IEEE Nineteenth Design Automation Conference Proceedings pp 224-231*

[PFIS82] G. F. Pfister, "The Yorktown Simulation Engine, Introduction" *ACM IEEE Nineteenth Design Automation Conference Proceedings pp 51-54*

[SEIL82] L. Seiler, "A Hardware Assisted Design Rule Check Architecture" *ACM IEEE Nineteenth Design Automation Conference Proceedings pp 232-238*

[UEDA83] Kazuhiro Ueda, Tsutomu Komatsubara and Tsutomu Hosaka, "A Parallel Processing Approach for Logic Module Placement" *ACM IEEE Transactions on Computer Aided Design Vol. CAD-2 No.1 Jan.83 pp 39-47*

BOUNDS ON THE LENGTH OF CONVEX PARTITIONS OF POLYGONS

Christos Levcopoulos
Andrzej Lingas

The Department of Computer and Information Science
Linköping University
581 83 Linköping, Sweden

Abstract: A heuristic for partitioning rectilinear polygons into rectangles, and polygons into convex parts by drawing lines of minimum total length is proposed. For the input polygon with n vertices, k concave vertices and the perimeter of length p, the heuristic draws partitioning lines of total length $O(plogk)$ and runs in time $O(nlogn)$. To demonstrate that the heuristic comes close to optimal in the worst case, a uniform family of rectilinear polygons Q_k with k concave vertices, $k = 1, 2, \ldots$ and a uniform family of polygons P_k with k concave vertices, $k = 1, 2, \ldots$ are constructed such that any rectangular partition of Q_k has (total line) length $\Omega(plogk)$, and any convex partition of P_k has length $\Omega(plogk/loglogk)$. Finally, a generalization of the heuristic for minimum length of convex partition of simple polygons to include polygons with polygonal holes is given.

1. *Introduction*

Partitioning polygons into simpler parts like convex pieces, rectangles or triangles has a variety of applications in graphics, pattern recognition [12], VLSI and architecture design [10], numerical analysis, database systems [9] and computational geometry itself [3]. There are two main optimality criteria for polygon partition problems:

(1) minimum number of the simpler parts into which the input polygon can be partitioned, and

(2) minimum total length of the lines partitioning the input polygon into its simpler parts.

Chazelle [4] has designed a polynomial time algorithm for minimum number convex partition of polygons. It is an intriguing question whether the problem of minimum length convex partition of simple polygons is solvable in polynomial time or is NP-hard.

A convex partition of a polygon can be viewed as a Steiner planar graph (non-necessarily a tree) for concave vertices of the polygon, lying within the polygon. The NP-hardness of the minimum length planar Steiner tree problem [4] suggests the latter possibility. When polygonal holes are allowed in the input polygon, the problem of minimum length convex partition, as well as its minimum number counterpart become NP-hard (see [7, 10]). The former problem can be viewed as a natural generalization of the problem of minimum length rectangular partition of rectilinear polygons with holes whose decision version has also been shown to be NP-complete [10]. Interestingly, a minimum number rectangular partition of rectilinear polygon with polygonal holes can be found in polynomial time [9] provided that the holes are not degenerate [7]. Minimum length rectangular partition has an application among others in partitioning the area outside already placed modules on a VLSI chip into rectangular channels [10]. In [8], there is presented an $O(n^4)$-time heuristic for minimum length rectangular partition producing solutions whose total length is within a constant factor from the optimum. Also in [8], there is outlined a method of partitioning rectilinear polygon with n corners and the perimeter of length p into rectangles by drawing lines of length $O(plogn)$ in time $O(nlog^2n)$. Here, we implement the idea precisely generalizing it to include the problem of partitioning polygon into convex parts. It turns out that any polygon with n vertices, k concave vertices and the perimeter of length p can be partitioned into convex parts by drawing lines of length $O(plogk)$ in time $O(nlogn)$. When the input polygon is rectilinear, the produced parts are rectangles. The $O(plogk)$ upper bound on the length of rectangular partition is shown to be optimal for a uniform family of polygons Q_k, $k = 1, 2, ...$, with k concave vertices. In the general case, an $\Omega(plogk/loglogk)$ lower bound on the length of convex partition for a uniform family of polygons P_k, $k = 1, 2, ...$, with k concave vertices is established. Finally, the heuristic for minimum length of convex partition of simple polygons is generalized to include polygons with polygonal holes.

2. *Preliminaries*

The following general definitions and lemma are used throughout the paper.

Definition 1: A *vector* is a pair $< v, w >$, where v, w are points in the plane. The point v is a *basis* of the vector. We also say that the vector $< v, w >$ leaves v and incomes w. The Euclidean distance from v to w is the *length* of the vector. The terms $[v, w]$, (v, w), respectively denote the closed and the open straight-line segment with the endpoints v, w. The vector $< v, w >$ intersects another vector, or a straight-line segment, or a line, respectively, if the closed straight-line segment $[v, w]$ intersects the closed straight-line segment corresponding to the other vector, the straight line segment, or the line, respectively.

Definition 2: A (non necessarily simple) *polygon* is a sequence of vectors $< a_1, a_2 >$, $< a_2, a_3 >$, ... $< a_n, a_1 >$ where a_1, a_2, ... a_n are points in the plane. The vectors and the points are respectively called *directed edges* and *vertices* of the polygon. The corresponding closed straight-line segments $[a_1, a_2]$, $[a_2, a_3]$, ... $[a_n, a_1]$ are called *edges* of the polygon. The union of the edges forms the *perimeter* of the polygon. If the non-consecutive edges do not intersect, the polygon is *simple*, its perimeter divides the plane into two connected regions, and the finite open region forms the *inside* of the polygon. A vertex of a polygon is *convex* if the two adjacent edges form an angle of not more than 180 degrees on the right of the vertex if we follow the direction of the edges. Otherwise the vertex is *concave*. If all vertices of a simple polygon are convex, then the polygon is convex. We shall assume that directed edges of simple polygons are always clockwise oriented.

Definition 3: A *convex partition* of a simple polygon P is a set of convex polygons S such that the insides of the convex polygons are pairwise disjoint, and the union of the insides and perimeters of the polygons from S is equal to the inside of P plus the perimeter of P. The *length* of the convex partition is the total length of the edges of the polygons from S that do not overlap with the perimeter of P. A *rectilinear polygon* is a simple polygon whose each edge is either horizontal or vertical. A *rectangle* is a rectilinear polygon with four vertices. A *rectangular partition* of a rectilinear polygon is a convex partition of the polygon consisting only of rectangles.

In the time analysis of the algorithm producing a convex partition of length $O(plogk)$, the following fact whose proof was suggested by D. Wood [15] is useful:

Fact 1 : Let V be a set of k vectors, and let S be a set of n straight-line segments in the plane such that neither two vectors in V nor two segments in S intersect. Next, let U be

the set of all straight-line segments $[v,u]$ for which there exists a vector $< v,w >$ in V, such that the segment $[v,u]$ is an initial fragment of $[v,w]$, u lies on a segment in S, and no segment in S intersects (v,u). Given the sets V and S, the set U can be determined in time $O(nlogn + klogk)$.
Sketch of the Proof: It suffices to modify an algorithm of Bentley and Ottman for reporting intersections of straight-line segments [2]. The endpoints of vectors in V and segments in S are stored in order by x-values as a heap Q. While a vertical line sweeps the plane from left to right, the vectors in V and segments in S that intersect the line are maintained by a balanced tree R, in the above-below order (see [2,13]), and the following procedure is performed. If a left endpoint v of a vector $< v,w >$ in V (i.e. v is the basis of $< v,w >$) is encountered by the sweeping line, $< v,w >$ is inserted in R and checked for intersection with the segments directly below and above it. Whenever such an intersection, say u, is found, the vector is shortened, i.e. w is deleted from Q and u is inserted into Q. When a left endpoint of a segment in S is encountered, the segment is inserted into R and checked for intersection with the vectors in R immediately above and below it. As in the previous case, if such an intersection is found, the intersecting vector is shortened, i.e. Q is appropriately updated. When a left endpoint w of a vector $< v,w >$ in V is encountered, $< v,w >$ is inserted in R. When a right endpoint of a segment or vector in R is encountered, the segment or vector is deleted from R. In the latter case, the vector is inserted into the heap collecting the elements of the set U. In both cases, if the vector and the segment directly above and below, or vice versa, intersect, the vector is shortened. The above procedure takes $O(logn + logk)$ time. Since, for each vector in V, the sweeping line scans at most one intersection of the vector with a segment in S, the $O(nlogn + klogn)$ upper bound follows. The details in large part analogous to these in [2,13], are left to the reader. ∎

3. *The $O(plogk)$ upper bound*

To specify the algorithm producing a convex partition of length $O(plogk)$, we need the following definitions and lemma:

Definition 4: A polygon is *concave — rectilinear* if any edge adjacent to a concave vertex in the polygon is either horizontal or vertical.

The algorithm starts from transforming the input simple polygon into a *concave—rectilinear* simple polygon according to the following lemma:

Lemma 1: A simple polygon P with n vertices, k concave vertices and the perimeter of the length p can be transformed into a concave-rectilinear simple polygon P' in time $O(nlogn)$ such that:

(1) the perimeter of P' lies within P and is of the length $O(p)$,
(2) P' has less than $4n$ vertices, and at most $3k$ concave vertices,
(3) the area between the perimeter of P and P' can be partitioned into convex parts by drawing lines of length $O(p)$ in time $O(n)$.

Proof sketch: Let e be the shortest distance between two vertices of P, and let s be the minimum distance between a concave vertex of P and a non-adjacent edge of P. Next, let $t = min(s/3, e/4)$. We can replace each concave vertex of P by at most three angles of 270 degrees by placing a small square of size at most $t \times t$ of horizontal-vertical orientation slightly overlapping with the angle outside of P formed by the edges adjacent to the vertex

(see Fig. 1). Any pair of such squares is disjoint by the definition of s. The pieces of the perimeters of the rectangles lying within P together with the pieces of the perimeter of P lying outside them form boundaries of the polygon P'.
To determine the size of the small squares (i.e. to find a lower bound on s), we place crosses of horizontal and vertical arms of length e on each concave vertex of P, v, such that v lies in the center of the placed cross (see Fig. 2.). Let V be the set of all vectors $< v, w >$ such that

(a) the segment $[v, w]$ is an arm of the placed cross with the center v,
(b) there is a segment (v, t) that is a fragment of $[v, w]$ and entirely lies inside P.

By applying Fact 1 to the set of vectors V and the set of edges of P, in time $O(nlogn)$, we can find the shortest segment $[v, u]$ for which there is a vector $< v, w >$ in S such that:

the segment $[v, u]$ is a fragment of $[v, w]$,
the point u lies on the perimeter of P or $u = w$,
the perimeter of P is disjoint from (v, u),

It is left to the reader to verify that the length of the shortest segment $[v, u]$ divided by $\sqrt{2}/2$ is a lower bound on s by the definition of e and a simple geometric argument (see Fig. 4). As the closest of N points in the plane can be found in time $O(NlogN)$ [13], the value of e can be determined in time $O(nlogn)$. Thus, the size of the small squares to place can be specified in time $O(nlogn)$ by Fact 1.
The perimeter of P' can be determined in time $O(n)$. If necessary, the area between the perimeter of any of these rectangles and the perimeter of P can be partitioned into convex parts by drawing a straight-line segment of length $\leq t \times \sqrt{2}$. This implies (3) and completes the proof. ∎

The basic observations included in the idea of the algorithm are formalized in the following definitions and lemmas, where P' stands for a concave-rectilinear polygon;

Definition 5: Two vertices of a polygon are *adjacent* if they are endpoints of the same edge of the polygon.

Definition 6. Two vertices of P', v and u in this order, are said to be consecutive concave vertices of P' if they are concave vertices and none of the directed edges leading from v to u has as an endpoint another concave vertex of P'.

Definition 7: Let v and u be two non-adjacent consecutive concave vertices of P', and let $< v', v >$, ($< u, u' >$, respectively) be the directed edge of the polygon incoming v (leaving u, respectively). The vertices v and u are a-*compatible* if the half-line starting from v' and passing through v intersects one of the directed edges of P leading from v to u or the half-line starting from u' and passing through u intersects one of the directed edges of P leading from u to v (see Fig. 3). The vertices v and u are b-*compatible* if the line induced by $[v', v]$ intersects the line induced by $[u, u']$ such that if c stands for the intersection point then v lies between v' and c on the former line, and u lies between u' and c on the latter line, and the segments $[v, c]$, $[c, u]$ are perpendicular (see Fig. 4). If the vertices v and u are a-compatible or b-compatible then they are *compatible*.

Definition 8. Given a straight-line segment, the total length of its vertical projection on X-axis and its horizontal projection on Y-axis is called the $iso - length$ of the segment. The $iso - length$ of a set of segments is the sum of iso-lengths of all segments from this set.

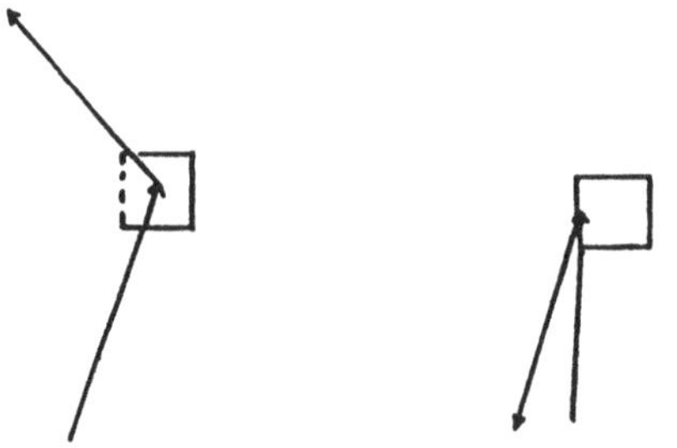

Fig. 1. Replacing a concave vertex by at most three concave vertices of 270°.

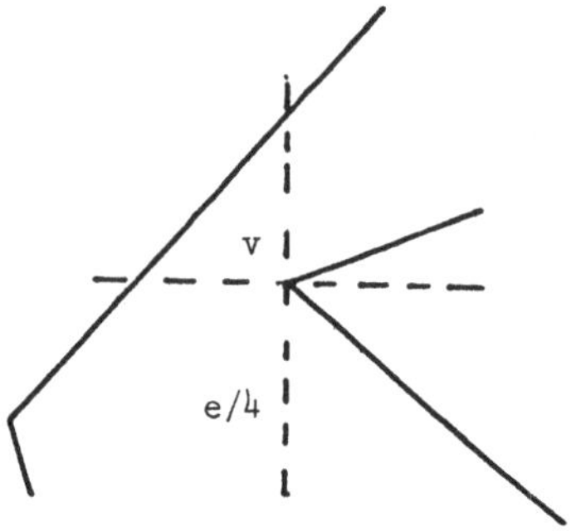

Fig. 2. An example of the cross placed on a concave vertex of P.

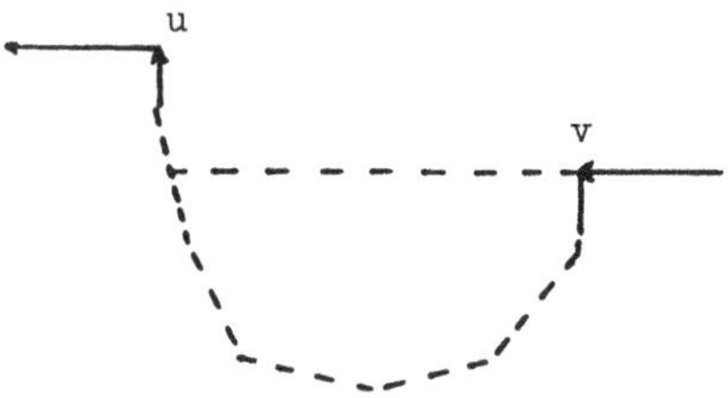

Fig. 3. Two a-compatible vertices of P, v and u.

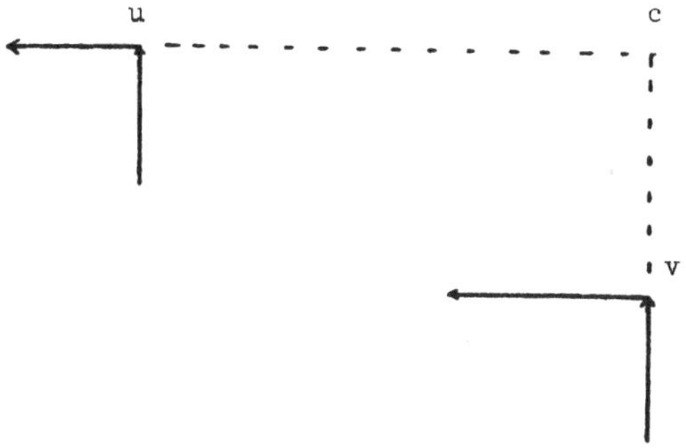

Fig. 4. Two b-compatible vertices of P, v and u.

The basic observations included in the idea of the algorithm are formalized in the following lemmas, where P' stands for a concave-rectilinear polygon.

Lemma 2: If two consecutive concave vertices of P' are neither a-compatible nor b-compatible then they are adjacent.
Proof. The lemma is an easy consequence from Def. 5 and 7.

Lemma 3: Let v and u be two a-compatible consecutive concave vertices of P'. By drawing a straight-line segment of iso-length not exceeding the total iso-length of the directed edges of P' leading from v to u, we can extend either the directed edge of P' incoming v or the directed edge of P' leaving u up to the intersection with the perimeter of P' between v or u.
Proof. The lemma immediately follows from the definition of a-compatibility.

Lemma 4: Let v and u be two b-compatible consecutive concave vertices of P'. By drawing two straight-line segments of total iso-length not exceeding the total iso-length of the directed edges of P' leading from v to u, we can replace the piece of the perimeter of P' between v and u by an L-shape line composed of segments that are extensions of the directed edges of P' incoming v and leaving u respectively.
Proof. Let us assume the notation from Def. 6 and Fig. 4. It is easily seen that the segments $[v, c]$ and $[u, c]$ satisfy the lemma. ∎

Employing the above definitions and lemmas, we specify the algorithm for convex partition of the input polygon P as follows:

Algorithm 1

Transform the input polygon P into the polygon P' according to Lemma 1;
$L \leftarrow$ a list of all concave vertices of P' in clockwise order;
$S1 \leftarrow$ an empty list;
$S2 \leftarrow$ a list of all edges partitioning the area between the perimeter of P and P' into convex parts according to Lemma 1;
<u>*comment*</u> the polygon P' is given as a 2-3 tree (see [1]) storing edges of P' in clockwise order, the sequence L is also given as a 2-3 tree, the global lists $S1, S2$ will eventually contain all edges of the convex partition produced by Algorithm 1 that are not edges of P or P'
<u>*for*</u> $v \in L$ <u>*do*</u>
<u>*begin*</u>
  $h(1, v) \leftarrow$ the half line h co-linear with the directed edge $< v', v >$ of P' such that h starts from v and $v' \notin h$;
  $h(2, v) \leftarrow$ the half line h co-linear with the directed edge $< v, v'' >$ of P' such that h starts from v and $v'' \notin h$;
  <u>*for*</u> $i = 1, 2$ <u>*do*</u>
  $c(i, v) \leftarrow$ the intersection of $h(i, v)$ with the perimeter of P', d, such that $[v, d]$ lies within P' and the distance between v and d is minimum
<u>*end*</u>;
$CONVEX\,PARTITION(P', L)$;
<u>*for*</u> $s \in S2$ <u>*do*</u>
<u>*if*</u> $s = < v, c >$ or s is a half line starting from v and v lies within P' <u>*then*</u> replace s by $[v, c']$ such that $[v, c'] \subset s$ and c' is the closest to v intersection of s with the perimeter of

```
P' or a vector in S1 else delete s from S2;
output the concatenation of a list of all edges in P or P' with S2 and S1;
```

The procedure *CONVEX PARTITION*(*P*', *L*) is defined as follows:

CONVEX PARTITION(*P*', *L*)

```
SP← an empty list;
count←0;
comment count is a counter of the number of consecutively adjacent concave vertices in L;
Lcard← the cardinality of L;
v← the first element in L;
while L contains at least six vertices do
begin
    u ← the member of L immediately succeeding v;
    comment the first member of L immediately succeeds the last member of L;
    if v is a-compatible with u then
    begin
        if v and u lie on the same vertical or horizontal line then
        begin
            add < v, u > to S2;
            delete v and u from L
        end
        else
        begin
            if the path composed of directed edges of P' leading from v to u passes through
            c(1, v) then
            begin
                add h(1, v) to S2;
                delete v from L
            end
            else
            begin
                add h(2, u) to S2;
                delete u from L
            end
        end
        count← − 1
    end
    if v is b-compatible with u then
    begin
        c← the crossing point between h(1, v) and h(2, u);
        add < v, c > and < c, u > to S2;
        replace v and u by c in L
        h(1, c)←h(1, v) − [v, c);
        h(2, c)←h(2, u) − (c, u]
        count← − 1
    end
```

```
    count←count + 1;
    if count = 6 then
    begin
        delete v from L;
        append h(1, v) to SP;
        comment v as the six vertex in a series of six consecutive adjacent concave vertices
        will be canceled;
        count←0
    end
    Lcard←Lcard − 2;
    if Lcard≤1 ∧ SP is not empty then
    begin
        for v ∈ L do
        if v is the beginning point of a half line in SP then replace the half line by
        < v, c(i, v) >;
        Using the vectors in SP partition P' into polygons P_1,..., P_k such that none of the
        polygons contains a concave vertex which is a basis of a vector in SP;
        append the list SP to the list S1;
        Partition the list L into the lists L_1, L_2,..., L_m accordingly;
        for i = 1, m do
        CONVEX PARTITION(P_i, L_i);
        go to E;
    end
    if Lcard ≤ 1 then Lcard← the cardinality of L;
    comment: the new round begins;
    v← the successor of u in L;
E: end;
comment: the while loop ends here ;
for v ∈ L do
append h(1, v) to S2
```

Theorem 1: Let P be a simple polygon with n vertices, k concave vertices and the perimeter of length p. Algorithm 1 applied to P produces a convex partition for P of length $O(plogk)$, and can be implemented in time $O(nlogn)$.

Proof. First, let us prove the $O(plogk)$ upper bound. The segments originally contained in the list $S2$ are of total length $O(p)$ by Lemma 1 (4). The edges of P' non-overlapping with these of P are of total length $O(p)$ by Lemma 1 (2). Let D be the *height* (see [1]) of the recursion tree for $CONVEX\ PARTITION(P', L)$. Given a natural number $d \leq D$, let P_j^d, $j = 1, ..., t_d$, be the polygons, and L_j^d be the lists that are parameters of calls of $CONVEX\ PARTITION$ at the $(D-d)-th$ *level* (see [1]) of the recursion tree of $CONVEX\ PARTITION(P', L)$. To obtain the upper bound, it is sufficient to show that:

(1) the vectors in the list $S1$ partitioning the polygon P' into the polygons P_j^d, $1 \leq d \leq D$, $1 \leq j \leq t_d$, are of total length $O(p)$;

(2) all vectors or half lines inserted in $S2$ during the call of $CONVEX\ PARTITION(P', L)$ are replaced in the last *for* loop of Algorithm 1 by straight-line segments of total length $O(plogk)$.

First, we shall prove (1). Let us project each vector w from $S1$ vertically on the closest boundary of P' below w and horizontally on the closest boundary of P' to the left of w. Suppose that a continuous segment of the perimeter of P', say s_0, is simultaneously a vertical projection (horizontal projection, respectively) of m disjoint pieces of vectors from $S1$ on the perimeter of P'. To prove (1), it is sufficient to show that below (to the left of, respectively) s_0 there are at least $m-1$ pieces of the perimeter of P', u, such that:

(a) u is disjoint from any above vertical (horizontal, respectively) projection of any vector from $S1$ on the perimeter of P';
(b) the vertical (horizontal, respectively) projection of u on the X-axis (Y-axis, respectively) is equal to the analogous projection of each of these m disjoint pieces of vectors from $S1$.

Let v be the basis of a vector in $S1$. Thus, v is the sixth vertex in a series of six consecutively adjacent concave vertices. It follows by computational induction, that each of the edges between consecutive vertices in the series includes an original vertex of the polygon P'. Therefore, the series of concave vertices and the vector have to take one of the two first shapes from Fig. 5 . Consequently, if vertical (horizontal, respectively) projections of m such vectors on the perimeter of P' overlap on some boundary segment of P', the perimeter of P' forms at least m-times folded labirynth, see Fig. 6. For $1 \leq i \leq 2m-1$, let s_i be the piece of the perimeter of P' below (to the left of, respectively) that has the same vertical projection on X-axis (horizontal projection on Y-axis, respectively) as s_0, and is separated from s_0 by $i-1$ boundary lines, see Fig. 6. The segments s_{2i-1}, $i = 1, ..., m$, satisfy (a) and (b).
To prove (2), let us consider the while block in $CONVEX\ PARTITION(P_j^d, L_j^d)$. At the beginning, the 2-3 tree L_j^d represents a sequence of all concave vertices of the polygon P_j^d in a cyclic order. A new vertex is inserted in L_j^d only if it is a corner of an L-shape line adjacent to two b-compatible vertices in L_j^d. It follows by induction on the number of iterations of the while block that the list L_j^d always represents a sequence of all concave vertices of a non necessarily simple polygon (which will be still denoted by P_j^d). Consider a series of consecutive vertices $v_1, v_2, \ldots, v_6$ in L_j^d just after deleting either a pair of compatible vertices from L_j^d or a vertex from L_j^d that were immediate predecessors of the series. Let $S = (v_i, v_i), \ldots (v_i, v_i)$ be the longest sequence of disjoint pairs of consecutive compatible vertices included in the series such that for $q = 1, ..., l$ there is no compatible vertices v_m, v_{m+1}, $1 \leq m \leq 5$, satisfying $m < i_{2q-1}$ and $q > 1 \Rightarrow i_{2q-2} < m$. If the sequence is not empty, then at least one element of each of these pairs is deleted from L_j^d or replaced together with the other element by a corner of an L-shape line. Thus, the series $v_1, \ldots, v_{i_{2l}}$ is replaced by a new one shorter at least by $l \geq 1$. By Lemma 3 and 4, the total iso-length of the straight-line segments produced by the last <u>*loop*</u> of Algorithm 1 from vectors and half lines added to $S2$ during scanning v_1 through $v_{i_{2l}}$ is not greater than the iso-length of the perimeter of P_j^d between v_1 and $v_{i_{2l}}$. If S is empty, the vertices v_m, v_{m+1} are adjacent for $m = 1, 2, ..., 5$, and the series is shortened by the vertex v_6 which is deleted from L_j^d. Neither straight-line nor half-line is inserted in $S2$ in this case.
Let us call a fragment of the performance of the while block in $CONVEX\ PARTITION(P_j^d, L_j^d)$ starting from the moment when $Lcard$ is set to the cardinality of L and lasting until the test $Lcard \leq 1$ is performed and satisfied, a *round*. Next, given $0 \leq d \leq D$, let $l_{k,m}$ and $o_{k,m}$ denote respectively: the total iso-length of the perimeters of P_j^d, $j = 1, ..., t_k$, and the total cardinality of the lists L_j^d, respectively taken at the mo-

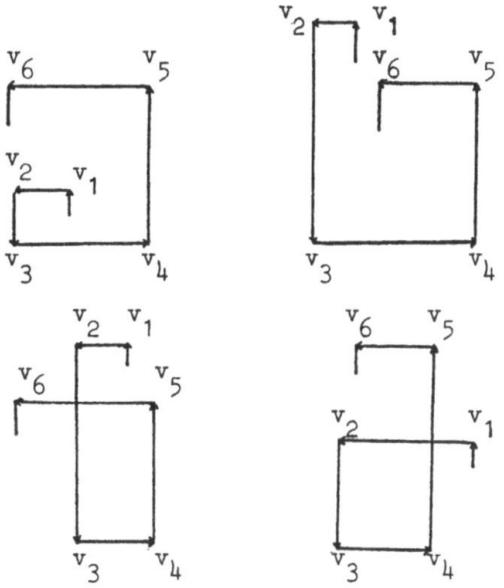

Fig. 5. Four cases of series of six consecutively adjacent concave vertices from L. The two former can only appear.

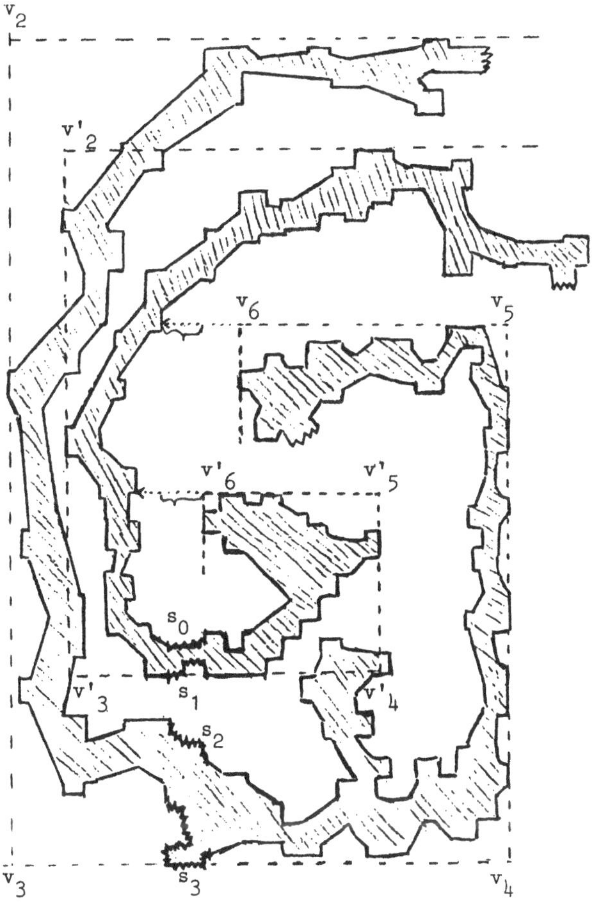

Fig. 6. Twice folded labyrinth. Shadowed areas lie outside the original polygon P'. Edges connecting vertices occuring in series of six consecutively adjacent vertices are marked by dashed lines. Vectors from S1 are marked by dotted lines. The segments s_i are marked by jagged lines.

ment of finishing the $m-th$ round in $CONVEX\ PARTITION(P_j^d, L_j^d)$, or, if there were fewer rounds, in the last round of $CONVEX\ PARTITION(P_j^d, L_j^d)$, $j = 1, ..., t_d$. Finally, let $s_{d,m}$ be the total iso-length of the straight-line segments, inserted in the place of vectors and half-lines (by the last $\underline{for}$ loop of Algorithm 1) that were added to the list $S2$ during the $m-th$ round of $CONVEX\ PARTITION(P_j^d, L_j^d)$, $j = 1, ..., t_d$, or, if there were fewer rounds, the last round,respectively. By the previous observations, we have $l_{d,m+1} \leq l_{d,m}$, $s_{d,m+1} \leq l_{d,m}$ and $o_{d,m+1} \leq max\{(5/6)o_{d,m}, 6\}$. Let $L_1(d)$ be the total iso-length of vectors inserted in the list $S1$ by $CONVEX\ PARTITION(P_j^d, L_j^d)$, $j = 1, ..., t_d$. Moreover, let $m(d)$ be the maximum number of rounds in $CONVEX\ PARTITION(P_j^d, L_j^d)$ over $j = 1, ..., t_d$. It follows that if $d-1 \geq 0$, then : $l_{d-1,1} \leq l_{d,m} + 2L_1(d)$, $s_{d-1,1} \leq l_{d,m} + 2L_1(d)$, and $o_{d-1,1} \leq max\{(5/6)o_{d,m}, 6\}$. By these two above sets of inequalities, we obtain $l_{d,m} \leq iso-length(perimeter(P')) + \sum_{d=0}^{D} L_1(d)$, $s_{d,m} \leq iso-length(perimeter(P')) + \sum_{d=0}^{D} L \supset_1$ (d), for $0 \leq d \leq D$, $1 \leq m \leq m(d)$ and $\sum_{d=1}^{D} m(d) = O(logk)$. Hence, by Lemma 1(1) and the proposition (1), $l_{d,m} = O(p)$ and $s_{d,m} = O(p)$ for $1 \leq d \leq D$, $1 \leq m \leq m(d)$. Clearly, the half-lines added to $S2$ in the $\underline{for}$ loop at the end of the body of $CONVEX\ PARTITION(P_j^d, L_j^d)$, $0 \leq d \leq D$, $1 \leq j \leq t_d$, are replaced by straight-line segments of total length $< 3l_{d,m(d)}$ in the last $\underline{for}$ loop of Algorithm 1. The $O(plogk)$ upper bound on the total iso-length of segments specified in (2) follows.

It remains to estimate the running time of Algorithm 1. The two first steps of Algorithm 1 take $O(nlogn)$ time by Lemma 1. To implement the first $\underline{for}$ loop in Algorithm 1, we apply Fact 1. The half lines $h(j, v)$ are represented by vectors $< v, w >$ such that $[v, w]$ is an initial segment of $h(j, v)$ and w is in the distance of p from v. Let V be the set of the above vectors. By Fact 1 and $\#V = O(k)$, we can find the closest intersections of vectors from V with straight-line segments from P', i.e. $c(i, v)$, $v \in L$, $i = 1, 2$, in time $O(nlogn)$. Analogously, by Fact 1, we can find all $c''s$ in the second $\underline{for}$ loop in Algorithm 1 in time $O(nlogn)$ since $\#S2 = O(k)$ and $\#P' + \#S1 = O(n)$. Given c', we can determine whether the vector basis v is within P' in constant time.

More details on implementing partitions of polygons P_j^d and lists L_j^d is needed in order to derive an upper bound on the total time taken by the splitting process. First of all, when the intersection point $c(i, v)$ in the first $\underline{for}$ loop of Algorithm 1 has been just found, the number of the edge of P' whose intersection with $h(1, v)$ is $c(1, v)$ can be determined in $O(1)$ time. Secondly, let us identify the consecutive edges of P' with numbers 0, 1, 2,...,n-1. Then, with each edge of any polygon P_j^d, e, we can associate a pair of natural numbers (q, r) which represents the directed piece of the perimeter of P' leading from q to r, including q and r. Suppose that we want to perform the partition of a polygon P_j^d and the corresponding list L_j^d induced by a vector $(v, c(1, v))$ from the list SP appended to $S1$. By using the number of the edge of P' on which $c(1, v)$ lies, m, the path in the 2-3 tree for P_j^d from the root to the leaf holding the edge of P_j^d, whose associated pair (q, r) includes m, can be easily found. Next, the 2-3 tree is split into two forests along this path (see [1]). Let e' be the edge of P_j^d incoming v with the associated pair (q', r'). The edge e' is extended up to the intersection with e, the edge e is split into two parts by the intersection point, and a new edge leaving v and incoming the intersection point is introduced (see Fig. 7). One of the forests obtains the extended edge e' with $(q', m-1\ mod\ n)$, and a part of e with (m, r). The other forest obtains the other part of e with (q, m), and the new edge with $(m-1\ mod\ n, r')$ (see Fig. 7). Finally, the two resulting forrests are transformed to two 2-3 trees. The list L_j^d can be split in a similar way. Both splits take $O(logn)$ time (see [1]). The splitting process continues until the set of vectors from SP is exhausted.

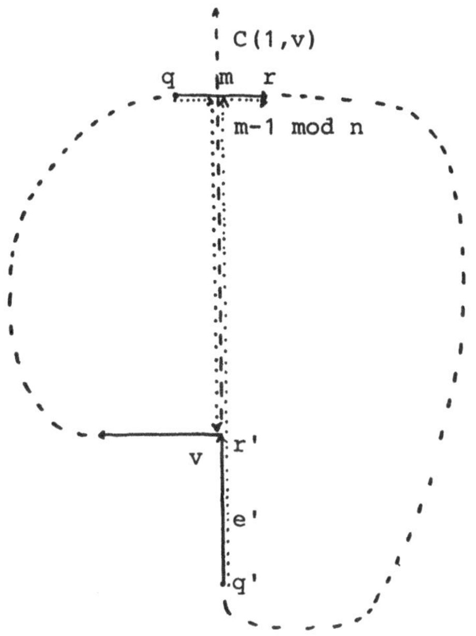

Fig. 7. Partitioning the polygon P_j^d . The vector (v,c(1,v)) and the perimeter of P_j^d are schematically denoted by dashed lines. The new edges are marked by dotted lines.

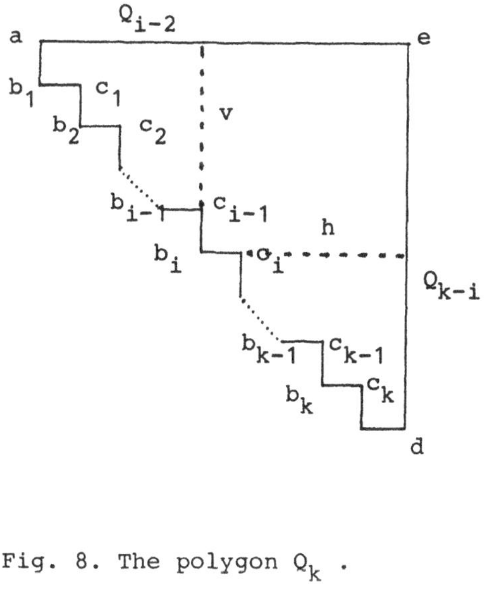

Fig. 8. The polygon Q_k .

Since $S1 = O(k)$, the total time cost of partitioning polygons P_j^d and lists L_j^d is $O(klogn)$. The preprocessing, i.e. the construction of the 2-3 trees to represent P' and L, may be much more costly, as it takes time $O(nlogn)$. The total number of iterations of the while blocks in $PARTITION\ CONVEX(P_j^d, L_j^d)$, $0 \leq d \leq D$, $1 \leq j \leq t_d$, is not greater than the total number of scannings elements from L_j^d which is $\leq h \sum_{i=0}^{t} (5/6)^i k = O(k)$ where h is a constant uniform in k and $t = \lceil logk \rceil$. We can perform any operation, different from partitioning polygons P_j^d and lists L_j^d, in any of these while blocks in time $O(logn)$. Thus, Algorithm 1 can be implemented in time $O(nlogn)$. ∎

When the input polygon P is rectilinear, $P = P'$, and all segments inserted in $S2$ and SP are horizontal or vertical. Hence, we obtain:

Corollary 1: Given a rectilinear polygon with n vertices, k concave vertices and the perimeter of length p, a rectangular partition of the polygon of length $O(plogk)$ can be produced in time $O(nlogn)$.

4. *Lower bounds on the length of convex and rectangular partition of polygons*

By the following theorem, the $O(plogk)$ upper bound on the length of optimal rectangular partition of rectilinear polygons cannot be generally improved:

Theorem 2: There exists an uniform sequence of rectilinear polygons Q_k, $k = 1, 2, ...$, such that:
(a) Q_k has $2(k+2)$ vertices and k concave vertices,
(b) the perimeter of Q_k is of length $4k + 4$, and
(c) any rectangular partition of Q_k is of length $\geq \Omega(klogk)$.
Proof Sketch: For natural k, let Q_k be a rectilinear polygon with vertices $a, b_1, c_1, ..., b_k, c_k, b_{k+1}, d, e$ in counter clockwise order such that the vertices $a, b_1, ..., b_{k+1}, d, e$ are corners of angles of 90 degrees in Q_k, the vertices $c_1, ..., c_k$ are corners of angles of 270 degrees, the edges $[a, b]$, $[b_i, c_i]$, $[c_i, b_{i+1}]$, for $i = 1, ..., k$, and the edge $[b_{k+1}, d]$ are of length 1 (see Fig. 8). To prove the theorem, we show by induction on $k > q$, where q is an appropriate constant, that any rectangular partition of Q_k is of length not less than $k/2log(k/2) = \Omega(plogk)$ (the magnitude of q is determined by the inductive step). Assume inductively that the above statement holds for $k = 1, ..., l$, where $l \geq q$. Let $k = l + 1$, and let P be any minimum length rectangular partition of Q_k. Next, let v be the maximal, horizontal segment in P or on the perimeter of Q_k that touches $[d, e]$ and is closest to e among all such segments. Analogously, let h be the maximal vertical segment in P or on the perimeter of Q_k that touches $[a, e]$ and is closest to e among all such segments. Note that v and h induce a rectangle that is formed by P and has as corners e and b_i for some $1 \leq i \leq k$ (see Fig. 8). Otherwise, by appropriately shifting v or/and h, we could obtain a convex partition of Q_k shorter than P which would contradict the optimality of P. By cutting off the rectangle, Q_k is split into Q_{i-2} and Q_{k-i}. Thus, we have $length(Q) = length(Q_{i-2}) + length(Q_{k-i}) + \mid v \mid + \mid h \mid$. Hence, by the inductive hypothesis, the choice of q and straightforward calculations, P is of length $((i-2)/2)log((i-2)/2) + ((k-i)/2)log((k-i)/2) + k \geq ((k-2)/2)log((k-2)/4) + k \geq (k/2)log(k/2)$ ∎

Naturally, the polygon Q_k can be partitioned into convex parts by drawing lines of length

$O(k)$. Neverthless, the authors are convinced that the $O(plogk)$ upper bound on the minimum length of convex partition given in Theorem 1 cannot be generally improved as it is in the case of rectangular partition by Theorem 2. At this moment, the authors are able to present only an $\Omega(plogk/loglogk)$ lower bound on the length of convex partition for a uniform family of simple polygons P_k , $k = 1, 2, \ldots$, with k concave vertices. To prove the lower bound, we need the following definitions and lemmas:

Definition 9: Given a segment $s = [a, b]$ and an natural even number n, $V^1_{s,n}$ is the chain of n segments of equal length $[a_0, a_1]$, $[a_1, a_2]$, ...,$[a_{n/2}, a_{n/2+1}]$, ..., $[a_{n-1}, a_n]$, where $a = a_0$, $c = a_{n/2}$, $b = a_n$ (see Fig. 9), specified as follows. Let m be the middle point of s, and let l_a and l_b be the lines perpendicular to s and passing through a, b, respectively. Let $[c, m]$ be the segment of length $s/2n$ perpendicular to s. Next, let f_1, f_2, be the points on l_a, respectively l_b, such that $|af_1| = |f_1c| = |cf_2| = |f_2b|$. Finally, let arc_1 and arc_2 be the arcs of the circles with center f_1, respectively f_2, and radius equal to $|af_1|$, such that arc_1 lies between $[f_1, a]$ and $[f_1, c]$, and arc_2 lies between $[f_2, b]$ and $[f_2, c]$. The points $a_0, a_1, \ldots, a_{n/2}$ lie in the above order on arc_1, whereas the points $a_{n/2}, \ldots, a_{n-1}, a_n$ lie in the above order on arc_2 (see Fig. 9).
For the segment s, the even number n, and a positive natural number m, $V^m_{s,n}$ is the chain of n^m segments defined recursively as follows:
(i) $V^0_{s,n} = s$
(ii) if the segments $s_1, s_2, \ldots, s_{n^{m-1}}$ form the chain $V^{m-1}_{s,n}$, then $V^m_{s,n}$ is the chain (of chains) $V^1_{s_1,n}, V^1_{s_2,n}, \ldots, V^1_{s_{n^{m-1}},n}$, such that if the polygon bounded by $V^m_{s,n}$ and s is simple, then it properly includes the polygon bounded by $V^{m-1}_{s,n}$ and s (see Fig. 9).

Definition 10: Given a natural positive number m and a natural even number n, $P'_{m,n}$ is a polygon whose perimeter is composed of a segment s and of the chain of segments $V^m_{s,n}$. The segment s is called the *basis* of $P'_{m,n}$.

Lemma 5: For all natural positive m and all natural even $n \geq m$, $P'_{m,n}$ is a simple polygon.
Proof: If m is arbitrarily large with respect to n, $P'_{m,n}$ can be non-simple (see Fig. 10). For any even natural n, let m_n be the maximal integer m such that $P'_{m,n}$ is simple. Let us assume the notation from Fig. 9. If the angle bac is of x degrees, then it is easily seen that $m_n > 60/x$. Since $abc = arctan(1/n)$, we have $m > \pi/\ (3 \times arctan(1/n)) > \pi n/3 > n$. ∎

Definition 11: Given a natural positive m and a natural even $n \geq m$, P'_n stands for the polygon $P'_{n,n}$, whereas $p_{m,n}$ and p_n denote the length of the perimeters of $P'_{m,n}$ and P'_n respectively.

Lemma 6: For all natural even n, $p_n \leq O(|s|)$.
Proof. Clearly, we have $p_{1,n} \leq |s| \times (1 + \frac{1}{n})$. Moreover, it is easily seen that $p_{i+1,n} \leq p_{i,n} \times (1 + \frac{1}{n})$, for $i \geq 1$. Thus, $p_n = p_{n,n} = |s|(1 + 1/n)^n < |s|e < 2.72 \times |s|$, where e stands for the Euler constant. ∎

Definition 12: For a positive natural m and an even natural n, the minimum length of convex partition of the polygons $P'_{m,n}$ and P'_n is denoted by $c_{n,m}$ and c_n, respectively.

Lemma 7: For all natural even $n \geq 4$, $c_{1,n} \geq \Omega(|s|)$.
Proof: Let the segment s, and the points a_i, $0 \leq i \leq n$ be specified according to Definition 9. Next, let d be the length of the segments in the chain $V^1_{s,n}$. Clearly, we have $d > |s|/n$. Therefore, the shortest segments (of length $< d/2$, perpendicular to s) connecting

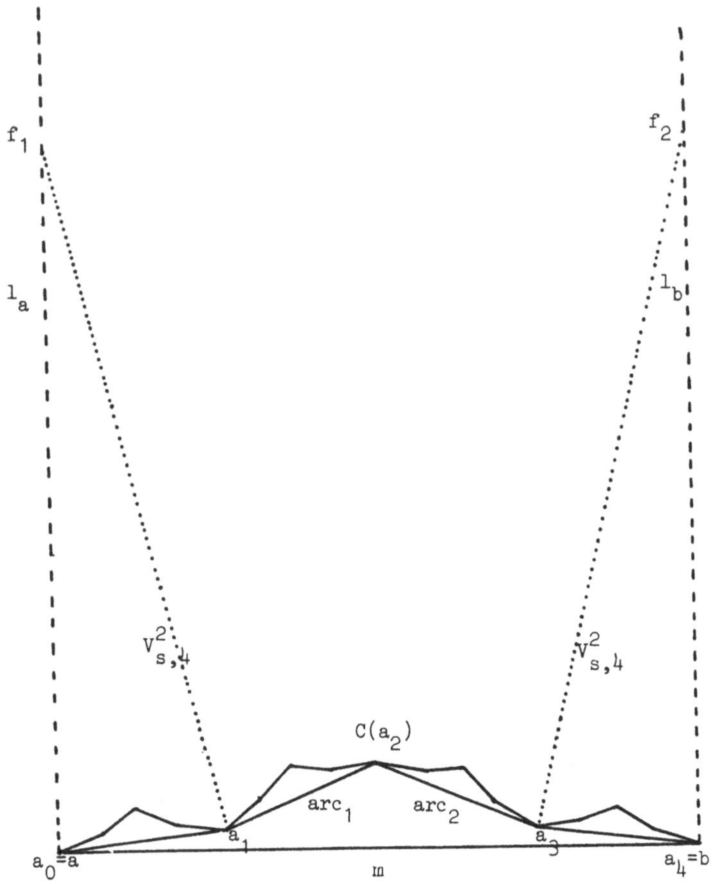

Fig. 9. The chain $V^1_{s,4}$ is composed of the segments $[a_0,a_1]$, $[a_1,a_2]$, $[a_2,a_3]$, $[a_3,a_4]$, whereas the chain $V^2_{s,4}$ is composed of 16 segments above $V^1_{s,4}$.

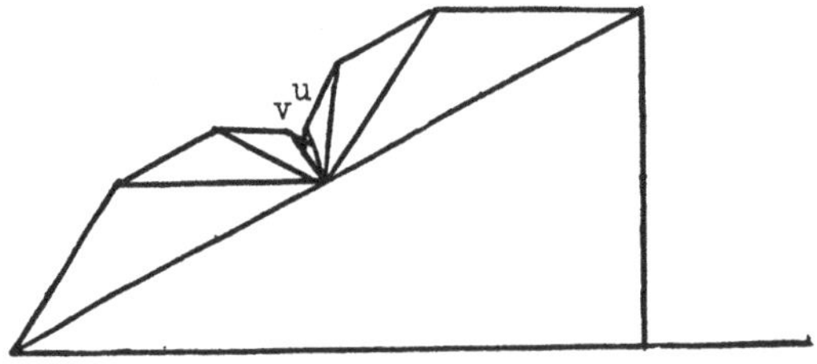

Fig. 10. The piece of the perimeter of the polygon $P_{5,2}$ between v and u crosses itself. Thus, the polygon $P_{5,2}$ is not simple.

the vertices a_i, $i \neq n/2$, $1 \leq i \leq n-1$ with s form a convex partition of $P'_{1,n}$ achieving the minimum length $c_{1,n}$. For any i, where $\lceil n/4 \rceil \leq i \leq \lfloor 3n/4 \rfloor$, the shortest segment connecting a_i with s is of length $\geq \Omega(|s|/n)$. Thus, we have $c_{1,n} \geq (n/2-2) \times \Omega(|s|/n) \geq \Omega(|s|)$. ∎

Lemma 8: For all natural positive m and all natural even $n \geq max(m,4)$, $c_{m,n} \geq \Omega(|s| \times m)$.
Proof: The proof is by induction on m. By Lemma 7, the lemma holds for $m=1$. Let us assume that the lemma holds for $m-1$ and let us consider the figure $P'_{m,n} - P'_{m-1,n}$. Let s, s_1, s_2, ..., $s_{n^{m-1}}$ be the consecutive edges of $P'_{m-1,n}$. The figure $P'_{m,n} - P'_{m-1,n}$ is composed of a sequence of n^{m-1} "copies" of $P'_{1,n}$ in miniature, with basis s_1, s_2, ..., $s_{n^{m-1}}$ respectively. Let $C_{m,n}$ be a minimum length convex partition of $P'_{m,n}$. Next, let C'_1 be the part of $C_{m,n}$ lying within the copy with basis s_1. By Lemma 7, we have $C'_1 \geq \Omega(|s_1|)$. The total length of s_1, s_2, ..., $s_{n^{m-1}}$ is $\geq \Omega(|s|)$. Thus, the part of $C_{m,n}$ lying within $P'_{m,n} - P'_{m-1,n}$ is of length $\geq \Omega(|s|)$. Therefore, we have $c_{m,n} \geq c_{m-1,n} + \Omega(|s|)$. Hence, by the inductive hypothesis, we obtain $c_{m,n} \geq \Omega(|s| \times m)$. ∎

By Lemma 5 and 8, we obtain the $\Omega(plogk/loglogk)$ lower bound as follows:

Theorem 3: There exists a uniform sequence of simple polygons P_k, $k = 1,2,...$, with k concave vertices and the perimeter of length p, such that any convex partition of P_k is of length $\geq \Omega(plogk/loglogk)$.
Proof. It follows from Lemma 8 that $c_n \geq \Omega(|s| \times n)$. The polygon P'_n has n^{n+1} vertices. Thus, if k is the number of vertices in P'_n, then $n > logk/loglogk$. By Lemma 6, the perimeter of P'_n is of length $O(|s|)$. Hence, we have $c_n \geq \Omega(plogk/loglogk)$. So, we can easily construct a sequence of polygons P_k, with k vertices, $k \geq 4$, such that the minimum length convex partition of P_k is of length $\geq \Omega(plogk/loglogk)$. ∎

5. *Partitioning multi — connected polygons into convex parts*

In several applications [10, 12], figures more complicated than simple polygons have to be partitioned or decomposed into convex parts. An example of such figures are polygons with polygonal holes.

Definition 13: A *polygon with polygonal holes* is a figure composed of a simple polygon and a collection of non-overlapping, non-degenerate simple polygons lying inside it. The inside of the figure is equal to the inside of the outer polygon minus the boundaries and insides of the inner polygons. The perimeter of the outer polygon and the perimeters of the inner polygons form *boundaries* of the figure enclosing its inside. The vertices of the inner polygons together with the vertices of the outer polygon are vertices of the figure. A convex partition of the figure is a set of disjoint convex polygons such that the union of the insides and perimeters of the convex polygons is equal to the union of the inside and boundaries of the figure. The length of a convex partition of the figure is the total length of edges of the convex polygons not-overlapping with the boundaries of the figure.

To be able to apply Algorithm 1 to polygon with polygonal holes, we can transform the figure into a simple polygon employing the following lemma:

Lemma 9: Any polygon with polygonal holes, P, with n vertices, k concave vertices, the boundaries of total length b, and the minimum length of its convex partition m, can be transformed into a polygon with $\leq \frac{5}{3}n - 2$ vertices, at most k concave vertices, and the perimeter of length $\leq b + 2m$ in time $O(nlogn)$.

Proof: Imagine a weighted clique where vertices are the inner polygons and the outer polygon in P and the weight of an edge (v, w) is the the minimum Euclidean distance between v and w. To find a minimum weight spanning tree of the clique, we construct a generalized Voronoi diagram of the boundaries of polygons in P (see [5]). The inside of each face of the diagram consists of all points in the plane that are closer to the associated boundary than to any other boundary of P. For each pair of boundaries of P that have adjacent associated Voronoi faces, we can find the minimum Euclidean distance between the boundaries in time linear in the number of Voronoi edges which separate the Voronoi faces associated with the boundaries. Hence, by generalizing the algorithm of Shamos and Hoey for minimum Euclidean spanning tree for a set of points in the plane [14], we can find a minimum weight spanning tree of the clique in time $O(nlogn)$. By drawing the found, planar spanning tree, P is transformed into a simple polygon of at most $\frac{5}{3}n - 2$ vertices and at most k concave vertices. On the other hand, consider a convex partition of P of the minimum length m. By deleting some edges from the partition, we can obtain a planar Steiner tree connecting the polygon boundaries. By the arguments given in [6], the planar spanning tree is of length no greater than the double length of the Steiner tree which is less than $2m$. ▮

Combining Theorem 1 with Lemma 9, we obtain:

Theorem 4: For any polygon with polygonal holes, with n vertices, k concave vertices, the boundaries of length b, and the minimum length of its convex partitions, m, we can produce a convex partition of the polygon of length $O((b+m)logk)$ in time $O(nlogn)$.

References

[1] Aho, A.V., J.E. Hopcroft and J.D. Ullman, *The Design and Analysis of Computer Algorithms*, Addison-Wesley, Reading, Mass., 1974.
[2] Bentley, J.L., T.A. Ottmann, *Algorithms for Reporting and Counting Geometric Intersecti* IEEE Transactions on Computers, Vol. c-28, No. 9, 1979.
[3] Chazelle, B., *Computational Geometry and Convexity*, PhD thesis, Yale Univ. 1980.
[4] Garey, M.R., and D.S. Johnson, *Computers and Intractability*: A Guide to the Theory of NP-completeness, H. Freeman, San Francisco.
[5] D.G. Kirkpatrick, *Efficient Computation of Continuous Skeletons*, Proceedings of 20th Symposium on Foundations of Computer Science (IEEE), 1979.
[6] Kou, L., G. Markowski and L. Berman, *A fast algorithm for Steiner Trees*, Acta Informatica 15, 1981.
[7] A. Lingas, *The Power of Non-rectilinear Holes*, Proc. of 9th ICALP, Aarhus, 1982.
[8] A. Lingas, *Heuristics for Minimum Edge Length Rectangular Partition of Rectilinear Figures*, 6th GI-Conference, Dortmund, January 1983.
[9] Lodi,E., F.Luccio, C.Mugnai, L.Pagli and W.Lipski,Jr., *On Two-dimensional Data Organization 2*, Fundamenta Informatica, Vol. 2, No. 3, 1979.
[10] Lingas, A., R. Pinter, R. Rivest and A. Shamir, *Minimum Edge Length Decompositions of Rectilinear Figures*, Proceedings of 12th Annual Alerton Conference on Communication, Control, and Computing, Illinois 1982.
[11] Masek W., Some NP-complete set covering problems, manuscript, MIT, 1981.
[12] J. O'Rourke, and K. Supowit, *Some NP-hard polygon decomposition problems*, to appear.
[13] M.I. Shamos, *Geometric Complexity*, Proc. of 7th ACM Symp. on the theory of Compt., 1975.
[14] M.I. Shamos and D. Hoey, *Closest Point Problems*, Proceedings of 16th Symposium on Foundations of Computer Science (IEEE), 1975.
[15] D. Wood, *personal communication*, February, 1984.

On Mapping Cube Graphs onto VLSI Arrays +

I.V. Ramakrishnan
Department of Computer Science
University of Maryland
College Park, MD 20742

P.J. Varman
Department of Electrical Enginerring
Rice University
Houston, TX-77001

Abstract

Formal models of *linear, mesh* and *hexagonal arrays* are presented. These arrays are well-suited for VLSI (*very large scale integration*). A model of a *logical linear array,* wherein adjacent processors may be separated by wires of *arbitrary* length, is also presented. Logical linear arrays are important computational structures suitable for implementation on a a wafer where fabrication errors may cause processors to be separated by arbitrarily long distances.

Cube graphs which are data-flow descriptions of some matrix and related computations are introduced. A mathematical technique is developed to construct algorithms for these array models from cube graphs. The technique is illustrated by constructing some published algorithms as well as some new algorithms.

1. Introduction

Specialized array processors have been proposed as a means of handling compute-bound problems in a cost-effective and efficient manner [4,5,6]. These array processors are typically made up of simple, identical processing elements that operate in synchrony. Several array structures have been proposed that include linear arrays, rectangular arrays and hexagonal arrays. Simplicity and regularity of linear, rectangular and hexagonal array processors render them suitable for VLSI implementation. High performance is achieved by extensive use of pipelining and multiprocessing. In a typical application, such arrays would be attached as peripheral devices to a host computer which inserts input values into them and extracts output values from them.

A variety of algorithms have been designed for such arrays [1, 2, 5, 8]. All these algorithms exhibit the following feature. They are composed of streams of data travelling in multiple directions at multiple speeds. Each processing element receives data from each of the streams, performs some simple operation and pumps them out (possibly updated). We will refer to such algorithms as "array algorithms". The array is typically comprised of *identical processors,* that is, they all execute the same set of instructions in every instruction cycle and they do not have any control unit. The array is driven by a single-phase or two-phase global clock [9].

A few methodologies have been presented for VLSI algoritm design [3,8,16]. These methodologies do not shed much insight into the automatic construction of such algorithms. In this paper we describe a mathematical technique for construction of array algorithms from data-flow descriptions of some matrix and other related computations. Such a technique will be useful in compilers that construct array algorithms from high-level specifications. This paper is an extension to our work on automatic transformation of high-level specifications onto linear-array algorithms [12]. We generalize the formal model of a linear array developed in [12] to include *logical linear arrays* and *two-dimensional arrays* (rectangular and hexagonal arrays). Logical linear arrays are important for *wafer-scale integration* [10] wherein an entire system is fabricated on a wafer. A major obstacle to wafer-scale integration, however, is that some of the circuits fabricated on the wafer will be malfunctional due to the presence of imperfections in the wafer or caused by imperfections in the manufacturing process [9].

+ This material is based on work supported by the National Science Foundation under grant number ECS-84-04399.

Fault-free processors in a wafer may be separated by an arbitrary number of faulty processors and algorithms on computational structures in a wafer must be *independent* of such separations. In [14,15] the concept of a logical linear array was proposed as a computational structure to obtain fault-tolerance in a wafer. Such an array is comprised of a sequence of processing elements connected in the form of a one-dimensional pipeline wherein adjacent processors may be separated by wires (unit-delay buffers) of arbitrary length, and algorithms on a logical linear array are insensitive to such separations. A recent paper by Kung and Lam [7] also employs a similar notion of programmable delays to achieve fault-tolerance.

This paper is organized as follows. In Section 2 we formalize the array machine models. We also introduce *cube graphs* which occur as components in data-flow descriptions of many matrix and other related computations (like matrix multiplication, lu-decomposition, dynamic programming, transitive closure and relational database operations). In Section 3 we formulate the concept of transforming cube graphs into array algorithms (henceforth referred ao as *mapping*) precisely. Algorithms for mapping cube graphs onto the array models are also presented in Section 3. In the Appendix we provide a proof that the algorithms in Section 3 correctly transform a cube graph into array algorithms.

2. Computational Models

We now formalize the array models and cube graphs. We begin with a formal definition of an array processor.

2.1. Array Machine Model

Let I_1, I_2, ..,I_z be z sets of sequences of integers where each I_j ranges from 1 to m_j. Let $I \subseteq I_1 \times I_2 \times .. \times I_z$.

Definition 2.1: An *array machine* Ar is a 4-tuple $<N_{Ar}, T_{Ar}, \delta_{Ar}, \psi_{Ar}>$ where:

1. N_{Ar} is a set of identical processors.
2. $T_{Ar}=\{l1, l2, .., lk\}$ is the set of labels.
3. $\delta_{Ar}:N_{Ar}$ is a one-one function that assigns coordinates to every processor in the Euclidean z-space.
4. Every processor in the array has k input ports and k output ports, with each input port and output port assigned a unique label from T_{Ar}.
5. The array is driven either by a single-phase or a two-phase global clock. A phase can be viewed as the instruction cycle of a processor. In a single-phase clocking scheme all processors are activated in every phase and every processor computes a k-ary function ψ_{Ar}. In a two-phase clocking scheme, adjacent processors are activated during opposite phases of the clock and every processor computes ψ_{Ar} in the phase it is active.

The value of z and the communication geometry determine the structure of the array processor. In this paper we will be examining three types of array processors, namely, linear, mesh and hexagonal arrays which are well-suited for VLSI implementation [4,9]. We now formalize these three arrays. Our definition captures the "nearest-neighbor" interconnection of these arrays and also the intuitive notion of a data stream used earlier in the description of array algorithms. $\forall lj \in T_{Ar}$, let n_{lj} be the *neighborhood constant* associated with label lj.

Definition 2.2: Let $n_{lj} \in \{1,-1,0\}$. A *linear array* L_{Ar} is an array processor with z=1, that is, $I \subseteq I_1$. Besides the linear array has the following communication features. Let p be a processor index. Then, $\forall lj \in T_{Ar}$, the output port labelled lj of p is connected to the input port labelled lj of $p+n_{lj}$.

Let L_H, L_V and L_O be three disjoint sets of labels such that $L_H \cup L_V \cup L_O = T_{Ar}$.

Definition 2.3: Let $n_{lj} \in \{1,-1\}$. A *mesh array* M_{Ar} is an array processor with z=2, that is, $I \subseteq I_1 \times I_2$. Besides, the mesh array has the following communication features. Let $<p,q>$ denote the coordinate of any processor in the mesh array. Then,

1. $\forall lj \in L_O$, the output port labelled lj of $<p,q>$ is connected to its own input port labelled lj.

2. $\forall lj \in L_H$, the output port labelled lj is conected to the input port labelled lj of $<p+n_{lj},q>$.

3. $\forall lj \in L_V$, the output port labelled lj is connected to the input port labelled lj of $<p,q+n_{lj}>$.

Let $L_H \bigcup L_V \bigcup L_O \bigcup L_T = T_{Ar}$ be four disjoint sets of labels.

Definition 2.4: Let $c \in \{1,-1\}$ denote the hexagonal array constant. A *hexagonal array* H_{Ar} is similar to a mesh array with the additional communication feature that $\forall lj \in L_T$, the output port labelled lj of $<p,q>$ is connected to the input port labelled lj of $<p+n_{lj}, q+n_{lj}c>$ where $n_{lj} \in \{1,-1\}$.

Fig. 2.1, Fig. 2.2 and Fig. 2.3 illustrate a linear, mesh and hexagonal array processors. In the figures I_1, I_2 and I_3 denote external input ports and O_1, O_2 and O_3 denote external output ports.

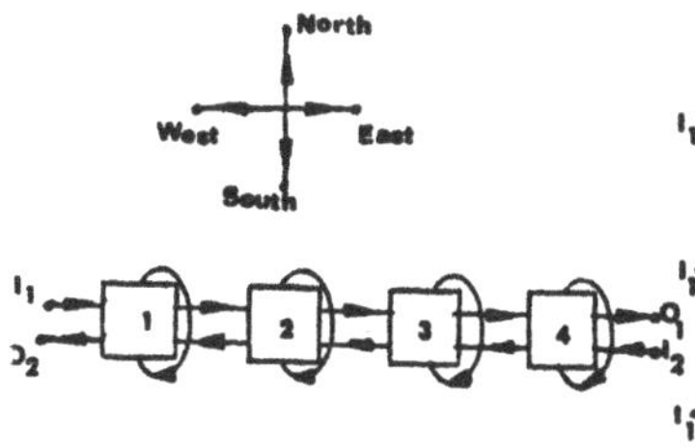

Fig. 2.1

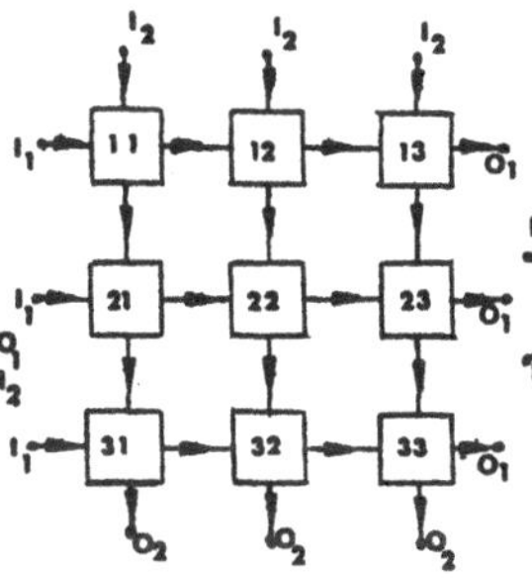

Fig. 2.2

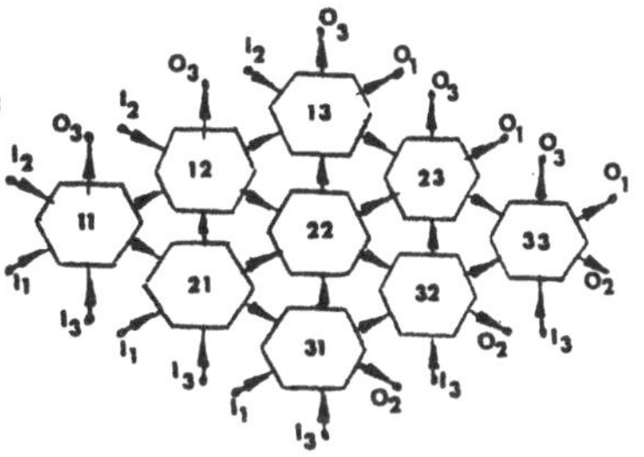

Fig. 2:3

In Fig. 2.1, the links between processors directed from west to east are labelled $l1$ and those directed from east to west are labelled $l2$. The links connecting a processor back to itself are labelled $l3$. The neighborhood constants are $n_{l1} = 0$, $n_{l2} = -1$, and $n_{l3} = 0$.

In Fig. 2.2, the links directed from west to east are labelled $l1$ and the links directed from north to south are labelled $l2$. $L_H=\{l1\}$ and $L_V=\{l2\}$ and $n_{l1} = n_{l2} = 1$.

In Fig. 2.3, the links pointing northeast are labelled $l1$, the links pointing southeast are labelled $l2$ and the links directed from south to north are labelled $l3$. $L_H=\{l1\}$, $L_V=\{l2\}$ and $L_T=\{l3\}$. $n_{l1}=n_{l2}=1$ and $n_{l3}=-1$. The hexagonal array constant $c=-1$.

We will refer to the processor whose input port labelled lj is connected to the output port labelled lj of processor p as its *neighbor with respect to label* lj. If a processor q is the neighbor of p with respect to label lj then q can only receive data from p on the link labelled lj connecting them. Similarly p can only send data to q on the same link. The links connecting any two processors are unidirectional. Impose a direction on the links such that the sender is at the tail end and the receiver at the other end. A stream then, is a directed path through processors and links having the same label.

We model the speed of data in streams by associating a queue of buffers in the communication links. More precisely, let s be a processor in the array. Let $si_t=<si_t^1, si_t^2, .., si_t^k>$ denote the k-tuple input to processor s at time t where si_t^j is the value at the input port labelled lj of processor s at time t. Let $so_t=<so_t^1, so_t^2, .., so_t^k>$ denote the k-tuple output computed by processor s at time t, that is, $\psi_{Ar}(si_t)=so_t$. Elements in a data stream travel at a constant velocity, and hence a non-zero positive *delay constant* d_{lj} is associated with every label lj in T_{Ar} such that so_t^j appears at the output port labelled lj of s at time $t+d_{lj}$. The delay d_{lj} can be implemented as a queue using a shift register of length d_{lj}-1.

2.2. Logical Linear Array

A logical linear array is similar in structure to a linear array (definition 2.2). The main difference is that the communication delay between adjacent processors in a logical array may be arbitrarily long. This notion is precisely captured in the following.

Definition 2.5: A *logical linear array* is similar to a linear array and has the following communication features. Let p be a processor index. Then, $\forall l j \in T_{Ar}$, the logical output port labelled lj of p is connected to the logical input port labelled lj of $p+n_{lj}$ where $n_{lj} \in \{1,-1,0\}$ is the logical neighborhood constant associated with n_{lj}. Besides, for every label $lj \in T_{Ar}$, and for every communication link between the logical output port of a processor indexed p and the logical input port of the processor indexed $p+n_{lj}$, there exists a delay $\delta(lj,p)=d_{lj}+\Delta(lj,p)$ where d_{lj} is the delay constant associated with any communication link labelled lj, and $\Delta(lj,p)$ is the perturbation delay between processor p and $p+n_{lj}$.

A logical linear array is a generalization of the linear array model (see definition 2.2). It is physically realized on a *rooted tree* of processors that are numbered by a depth-first traversal of the tree. On any such tree of processors it is possible to simulate the data flow through a linear array by routing the data streams through a closed path around the periphery of the tree (see Fig. 2.4).

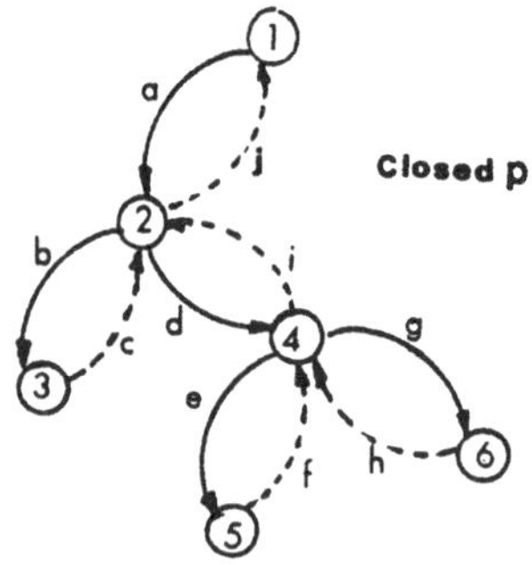

Fig. 2.4

The major difference between this "logical pipeline" in a tree machine and a "physical pipeline" in the linear array model is that in the former, logically adjacent processors (i.e., the pair indexed i and i+1) need not be physically adjacent (that is, processors i and i+1 in the tree need not have a father-son relationship). Since all the data streams flow through the array at a finite velocity, the implication of this physical separation is that the delay encountered by a data element in traversing the array from processors i to i+1 (or vice versa) is a function of both the delay constant associated with the stream to which that element belongs and of the physical separation between the processors.

Our logical linear array model (definition 2.5) is motivated by this idea. The delay for a data stream lj between processors indexed p and $p+n_{lj}$ is represented by $\delta(lj,p) = d_{lj}+\Delta(lj,p)$. The first quantity is the delay constant associated with any link labelled lj and the second quantity is the perturbation in this delay caused by the non-adjacent physical arrangement of the logically adjacent processors p and $p+n_{lj}$.

A method of realizing logical linear arrays is to configure a CHiP-like architecture [13] by "wrapping" a pipeline around the periphery of an arbitrary spanning tree that connects the fault-free processors in the CHiP-like machine. A node in the tree must route the data on its incoming edges onto the appropriate outgoing edges. Such routing can be accomplished by the programmable switches in the CHiP-like machine.

Henceforth, throughout the rest of this paper, neighbors and neighborhood constants in a logical linear array will always refer to logical neighbors and logical neighborhood constants respectively.

2.3. Cube Graphs

We now provide a formal definition of graphs that we will be mapping later on onto linear, mesh, hexagonal and logical linear arrays.

Let $G=<V,E,L_G>$ be a labelled DAG where:

1. $V=V_G \bigcup SO_G \bigcup SI_G$, and V_G, SO_G and SI_G are three disjoint sets of vertices with SO_G the set of source vertices, SI_G the set of sink vertices and V_G the set of remaining vertices, which we shall call computation vertices,
2. $L_G=\{l1,l2,l3\}$ is a set of labels.
3. Every vertex in V_G has three incident edges and three outgoing edges, where each incident and outgoing edge is assigned a unique label from L_G.

In any execution of G on these arrays every computation vertex in G is a single instance of a function evaluation that is performed in a cycle by a processor in the array. As all processors compute the same function, every computation vertex also represents the same function.

We can view the three incoming edges to a computation vertex v_x as representing the three-tuple input value to the processor that evaluates v_x. Similarly, we can view the three outgoing edges from v_x as the three-tuple output value that is computed by the processor on evaluating v_x. Throughout the rest of this paper we will adopt the terminology that a source vertex represents an input value and a sink vertex represents an output value.

Let J_1, J_2 and J_3 be three sequences of integers ranging from 0 to h_1, 0 to h_2 and 0 to h_3 respectively. Let $J \subseteq J_1 \times J_2 \times J_3$.

Definition 2.6: G is a *Cube Graph* iff there exists a one-one function $F:V_G \rightarrow J$ that satisfies the following: Let F_{l1}, F_{l2} and F_{l3} be three projection functions of F, that is, if $F(v_x)=<c_1,c_2,c_3>$ then $F_{l1}(v_x)=c_1$, $F_{l2}(v_x)=c_2$ and $F_{l3}(v_x)=c_3$. Let v_x and v_y be any two computation vertices in V_G. Then, for any label $lj \in L_G$, there exists a path comprised only of edges labelled lj passing through v_x and v_y such that the distance from v_x to v_y is d iff $F_{lj}(v_y)=F_{lj}(v_x)+d$ and $\forall li \in L_G-\{lj\}$, $F_{li}(v_y)=F_{li}(v_x)$.

Data-flow descriptions of relational database operations and many important matrix computations like matrix-matrix multiplication, lu-decomposition and solution of triangular linear systems are either cube graphs or have components that are cube graphs.

Henceforth, throughout the rest of this paper G will denote a cube graph. A cube graph is an object in Euclidean 3-Space and we will refer to the 3 axes as $l1^{st}$, $l2^{nd}$ and $l3^{rd}$ axes. $h_1 \geq 1$, $h_2 \geq 1$ and $h_3 \geq 1$ are the maximum dimensions along $l1^{st}$, $l2^{nd}$ and $l3^{rd}$ axes respectively. If v_x is a computation vertex in a cube graph then we will denote $F_{l1}(v_x)$, $F_{l2}(v_x)$ and $F_{l3}(v_x)$ by x_{l1}, x_{l2} and x_{l3} respectively. Let v_0 denote the vertex whose coordinates are $<0,0,0>$.

3. Mapping Cube Graphs on Arrays

Intuitively mapping of G onto an array assigns each computation vertex of G to a processor in the machine at a particular time step and also fixes the delay and neighborhood constant for every label in L_G. Assuming discrete time steps, let $T=\{0,1,2,..\}$ be the sequence of natural numbers representing the progress of a computation from its start at time 0.

Definition 3.1: A mapping of G onto a linear, rectangular, hexagonal and logical linear array is a 4-tuple <PA,TA,NA,DA> where:

1. $T_{Ar}=L_G$
2. $PA:V_G \rightarrow I$ and $TA:V_G \rightarrow T$ are many-one functions mapping computation vertices onto processors and time steps respectively.
3. Let I^+ be a set of positive non-zero integers. $NA:L_G \rightarrow \{1,-1,0\}$ and $DA:L_G \rightarrow I^+$ are many-one functions assigning neighborhood constants and delay constants respectively.

[Note: $NA(lj)=n_{lj}$ and $DA(lj)=d_{lj}$]

We next formalize a correct mapping.

Definition 3.2: A mapping is *syntactically correct* iff

1. $\forall lj \in L_G$ and for any pair of computation vertices v_x and v_y, if there is an edge labelled lj directed from v_x to v_y, then $PA(v_y)$ is the neighbor of $PA(V_x)$ with respect to label lj,

and

a. $TA(v_y)=TA(v_x)+d_{lj}$ for linear, mesh and hexagonal arrays, and

b. $TA(v_y)=TA(v_x)+\delta(lj,PA(v_x))$ for a logical linear array.

2. No two values appear simultaneously at the same input port of any processor.

3.1. Linear Array Mapping

We now describe the algorithm to map G onto a linear array L_{Ar}. We begin by developing some appropriate terminology for describing the algorithm.

Let $w_L=<w_1,w_2,w_3>$ be a triple where $w_1=1, w_2\in\{1,-1\}$ and $w_3\in\{1,-1\}$.

Definition 3.3: A *linear diagonalization* D_L of a cube graph is a pair $<D,w>$ with the following properties.

1. $D=\{D_1, D_2, .., D_k\}$ is a family of sets of computation vertices and $D_1 \cup D_2 \cup .. \cup D_k = V_G$.
2. $\forall D_p \in D$, if v_x and v_y are in D_p then $w_1x_{l1}+w_2x_{l2}+w_3x_{l3} = w_1y_{l1}+w_2y_{l2}+w_3y_{l3}$.
3. $\forall D_p \in D$ and $\forall D_q \in D$, $p<q$ iff $\forall v_x$ in D_p and $\forall v_y$ in D_q, $\sum_{l=1}^{l=3} w_l x_{l l} < \sum_{l=1}^{l=3} w_l y_{l l}$.

We will refer to w_L as the *linear diagonalization factor* of a cube graph and to any $D_p \in D$ as a *linear diagonal.* If v_x is in D_p then we will refer to $\sum_{l=1}^{l=3} w_l x_{l l}$ as the weight of D_p.

We assign consecutive indices to the diagonals in D in increasing order of their weights with the diagonal having the least weight assigned index 1.

Algorithm

We are now in a position to describe the linear array mapping algorithm.

1. Perform a linear diagonalization $D_L=<D,w_L>$ of the cube graph. For every $D_p \in D$ assign a proceesor indexed p.
2. Choose $n_{l1}=w_1$, $n_{l2}=w_2$ and $n_{l3}=w_3$. This fixes the neighborhood constants of the labels.
3. Choose $d_{l1}=1$. If $n_{l2}=1$ then choose $d_{l2}=2$ else choose $d_{l2}=1$. Choose d_{l3} as follows.

   If $n_{l2}=1$ then if $h_1-h_2+n_{l3}\geq 0$ then choose $d_{l3}=h_1+1+2n_{l3}$ else choose $d_{l3}=h_2+1+n_{l3}$

   If $n_{l2}=-1$ then if $h_2-h_1+n_{l3}\geq 0$ then choose $d_{l3}=2h_2+1+n_{l3}$ else choose $d_{l3}=2h_1+1-n_{l3}$.
4. Map vertices in D_i onto processor i, that is, $\forall v_x$ in D_i , let $PA(v_x)=i$.
5. Let $TA(v_x)=\sum_{l=1}^{l=3} x_{l l} d_{l l} + t_1$ where $TA(v_0)=t_1$

3.2. Mesh Array Mapping

We next describe the algorithm to map G onto a mesh array M_{Ar}.

Let $w_m=<w_1,w_2,w_3>$ be a triple where $w_1=1$, $w_2\in\{1,0,-1\}$, and $w_3=1$. Let $L_G = L_H \cup L_V$. Let $l1\in L_H$ and $l3 \in L_V$.

Definition 3.4: A *mesh diagonalization* D_M of a cube graph is a pair $<D,w_M>$ with the following properties.

1. $D=\{D_{<1,1>}, D_{<1,2>}, .., D_{<m,n>}\}$ is a family of sets of computation vertices and $D_{<1,1>} \cup D_{<1,2>} \cup .. \cup D_{<m,n>} = V_G$.

2. For any $D_{<p,q>} \in D$, if v_x and v_y are in $D_{<p,q>}$ then $\forall l i \in L_H$ and $\forall l j \in L_V$, $\sum_{li} w_{li} x_{li} = \sum_{li} w_{li} y_{li}$ and $\sum_{lj} w_{lj} x_{lj} = \sum_{lj} w_{lj} y_{lj}$

3. $\forall D_{<p,q>} \in D$ and $\forall D_{<r,s>} \in D$, $p<r$ iff $\forall v_x$ in $D_{<p,q>}$ and $\forall v_y$ in $D_{<r,s>}$, and $\forall l i \in L_H$, $\sum_{li} w_{li} x_{li} < \sum_{li} w_{li} y_{li}$. Similarly, $q<s$ iff $\forall l j \in L_V$, $\sum_{lj} w_{lj} x_{lj} < \sum_{lj} w_{lj} y_{lj}$.

We will refer to w_M as the *mesh diagonalization factor* of a cube graph and to any $D_{<p,q>} \in D$ as a *mesh diagonal.* If v_x is in $D_{<p,q>}$ then we will refer to $\sum_{li} w_{li} x_{li}$ where $l i \in L_H$ as the *horizontal weight* and $\sum_{lj} w_{lj} x_{lj}$ where $l j \in L_V$ as the *vertical weight* of $D_{<p,q>}$ respectively. p and q will denote the *horizontal* and *vertical* indices respectively.

We assign consecutive horizontal indices to the diagonals in increasing order of their horizontal weights with the diagonal having the least horizontal weight assigned the horizontal index 1. Similarly, we assign consecutive vertical indices to the diagonals in increasing order of their vertical weights with the diagonals having the least vertical weight assigned the vertical index 1.

Algorithm

We are now in a position to describe the mesh array mapping algorithm.

1. Perform a mesh diagonalization $D_M = <D, w_M>$ of the cube graph. For every $D_{<p,q>} \in D$ assign a processor to the pth row and q^{th} column of a mesh.
2. Choose $n_{l1}=w_1$, $n_{l2}=w_2$ and $n_{l3}=w_3$. This fixes the neighborhood constants of the labels.
3. Choose $d_{l1}=1$, $d_{l3}=1$. If $w_2=1$ then choose $d_{l2}=2$ else choose $d_{l2}=1$.
4. Map vertices on $D_{<p,q>}$ onto the processor in the pth row and q^{th} column, that is, $\forall v_x$ in $D_{<p,q>}$, let $PA(v_x)=<p,q>$.
5. Let $TA(v_x)=\sum_{l=1}^{l=3} x_{li} d_{li} + t_1$ where $TA(v_0)=t_1$.

3.3. Hexagonal Array Mapping

We describe the algorithm to map G onto a hexagonal array H_{Ar}. Let $w_H=<w_1,w_2,w_3>$ be a triple where $w_1=1, w_2=1$ and $w_3 \in \{1,-1\}$. Let the hexagonal array constant $c \in \{1,-1\}$. Let $L_G = L_H \cup L_V \cup L_T$ and let $l1 \in L_H$, $l2 \in L_V$, and $l3 \in L_T$.

Definition 3.4: A *hexagonal diagonalization* D_H of a cube graph is a pair $<D,w_H>$ with the following properties.

1. $D=\{D_{<1,1>}, D_{<1,2>}, .., D_{<m,n>}\}$ is a family of sets of computation vertices and $D_{<1,1>} \cup D_{<1,2>} \cup .. \cup D_{<m,n>} = V_G$.
2. For any $D_{<p,q>} \in D$, if v_x and v_y are in $D_{<p,q>}$ then $w_1 x_{l1} + w_3 x_{l3} = w_1 y_{l1} + w_3 y_{l3}$ and $w_2 x_{l2} + w_3 x_{l3} c = w_2 y_{l2} + w_3 y_{l3} c$.
3. $\forall D_{<p,q>} \in D$ and $\forall D_{<r,s>} \in D$, $p<r$ iff $\forall v_x$ in $D_{<p,q>}$ and $\forall v_y$ in $D_{<r,s>}$ $w_1 x_{l1} + w_3 x_{l3} < w_1 y_{l1} + w_3 y_{l3}$. Similarly, $q<s$ iff $w_2 x_{l2} + w_3 x_{l3} c < w_2 y_{l2} + w_3 y_{l3} c$.

We will refer to w_H as the *hexagonal diagonalization factor* of a cube graph and to any $D_{<p,q>} \in D$ as a *hexagonal diagonal.* If v_x is in $D_{<p,q>}$ then we will refer to $w_1 x_{l1} + w_3 x_{l3}$ as the *horizontal weight* and $w_2 x_{l2} + w_3 x_{l3} c$ as the *vertical weight* of $D_{<p,q>}$ respectively. p and q will denote the *horizontal* and *vertical* indices respectively.

We assign consecutive horizontal indices to the diagonals in increasing order of their horizontal weights with the diagonal having the least horizontal weight assigned the horizontal index 1. Similarly, we assign consecutive vertical indices to the diagonals in increasing order of their vertical weights with the diagonals having the least vertical weight assigned the vertical index 1.

Algorithm

We now describe the hexagonal array mapping algorithm.

1. Perform a hexagonal diagonalization $D_H = <D, w_H>$ of the cube graph. For every $D_{<p,q>} \in D$ assign a processor to the pth row and q^{th} column of a mesh.
2. Choose $n_{l1}=w_1$, $n_{l2}=w_2$ and $n_{l3}=w_3$. This fixes the neighborhood constants of the labels.
3. Choose $d_{l1}=1$, $d_{l2}=1$ and $d_{l3}=1$.
4. Map vertices on $D_{<p,q>}$ onto the processor in the pth row and q^{th} column, that is, $\forall v_x$ in $D_{<p,q>}$, let $PA(v_x)=<p,q>$.
5. Let $TA(v_x)=\sum_{l=1}^{l=3} x_{li}d_{li} + t_1$ where $TA(v_0)=t_1$.

3.4. Logical Linear Array Mapping

Unlike in the linear-array mapping we are required to constrain the choice of w_1, w_2 and w_3. Let $<w_1,w_2,w_3> \in \{<1,1,1>, <1,-1,-1>\}$. A linear diagonalization is performed on the cube graph before being mapped on a logical linear array. The first four steps involved in mapping a cube graph on a logical linear array is the same as the first four steps in mapping cube graphs onto linear arrays. An additional step is involved for fixing the perturbation delays as follows. Let p be a processor index in the tree. (Recall that indexing is done by a depth-first traversal of the tree.)

case 1: If $<w_1,w_2,w_3>=<1,1,1>$ then $\Delta(l1,p)=\Delta(l2,p)=\Delta(l3,p)$.

case 2: If $<w_1,w_2,w_3>=<1,-1,-1>$ then $\Delta(l1,p)=-\Delta(l2,p+1)=-\Delta(l3,p+1)$.

The final step involves fixing the times at which the vertices are mapped. Let $v_x \in D_p$. Then $TA(v_x)=t_1+\sum_{l=1}^{l=3} x_{li}d_{li}+\sum_{j=1}^{p-1}\Delta(l1,j)$ where $TA(v_0)=t_1$.

The constraints on the delay perturbations (cases 1 and 2 above) are motivated by the following discussion. Let T be an arbitrary tree whose vertices are numbered by some depth-first traversal of the tree as shown in Fig. 3.1. The vertex numbered i will be referred to as v_i. Now replace each edge in the tree by a pair of edges between the two vertices and consider a closed path in this graph from v_1 back to itself that visits all the vertices in the order v_1, v_2, ..,.v_n as shown in Fig. 3.2.

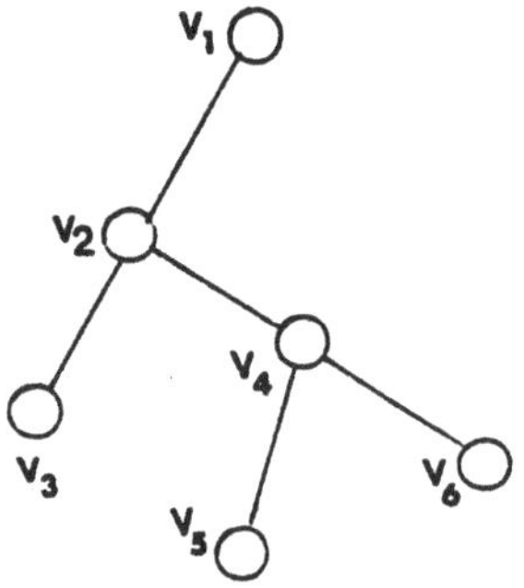

Fig. 3.1

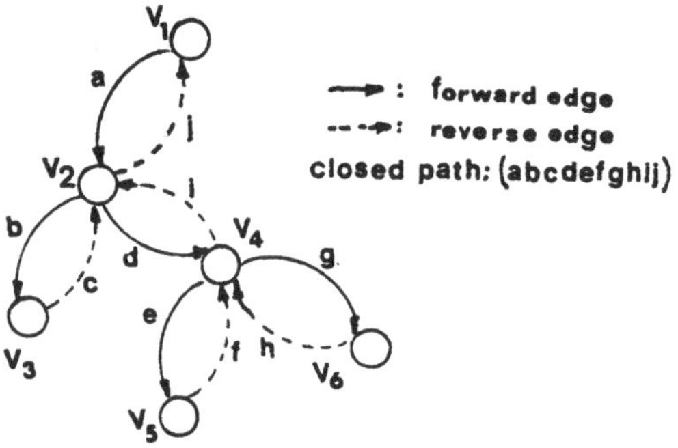

Fig. 3.2

Such a path is composed of *forward* edges (those encountered while traversing from v_i to v_j, $i<j$) and *reverse* edges (those used to backtrack over previously visited vertices). Each reverse edge is assumed to have a constant delay d associated with it; a forward edge has a delay (d_{l1},d_{l2} or d_{l3}) which depends on the label ($l1$,$l2$ or $l3$) of the stream traversing the edge.

In case 1, all the three streams $l1$, $l2$ and $l3$ traverse the closed path mentioned above. If there are x_p reverse edges in this path between v_p and v_{p+1} (note $x_p \geq 0$), then the effective delay for a stream labelled lj in traversing between v_p and v_{p+1} is $\delta(lj,p)=d_{lj}+x_pd$, corresponding to a delay perturbation x_pd. Note that the perturbation delay between v_p and v_{p+1} for any p, is the same for.

all labels.

In case 2, elements of stream $l1$ propagate from v_1 to the leaf vertices in a series of local broadcast steps. An element at v_p is broadcast to all vertices v_q, $q>p$, that are adjacent to v_p in the tree as shown in Fig. 3.3. →, - - → and -8→ denote forward, reverse and broadcast edges respectively.

Fig. 3.3

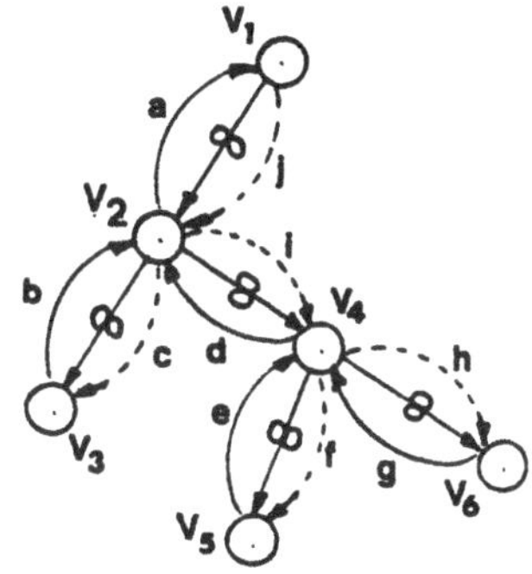

The elements encounter a delay d_{l1} in moving from v_p to v_q. Owing to the depth-first numbering scheme, the difference between the time at which the values of a data element reaches v_{p+1} and the time at which it reaches v_p is $(x_p-1)d_{l1}$, where x_p is the number of reverse edges between v_p and v_{p+1}. Note however, that the element does not traverse these reverse edges, but a copy of its value reaches v_{p+1} by the direct broadcast path. Thus if $x_p=0$ (i.e.,v_p and v_{p+1} are physically adjacent in the tree) then the element will reach v_{p+1}, d_{l1} cycles later than it reaches v_p; else it will reach v_{p+1} at the same or earlier time than it reaches v_p. The effective delay encountered between v_p and v_{p+1} is $\delta(l1,p)=-(x_p-1)d_{l1}$, corresponding to a perturbation $\Delta(l1,p)=-x_pd_{l1}$.

Elements of streams of $l1$ and $l2$ traverse a closed path around the tree as before, but in the direction opposite to that in case 1, that is, in the direction $v_n,v_{n-1},..,v_1$ (*jihgfedcba* in Fig. 3.3). The effective delay for either of these streams (say $l2$) between v_{p+1} and v_p is $d_{l2}+x_pd$, corresponding to a perturbation $\Delta(l2,p+1)=x_pd=\Delta(l3,p+1)$. The conditions in case 2 can be satisfied by choosing $d=d_{l1}$.

In the appendix we have shown that the mapping algorithms correctly map a cube graph. Recall that the host machine inserts input values and extracts the result values from the array. We now describe the evaluation of the times at which insertion and extraction must be done. Also recall that the source vertex represents an initial value and the sink vertex represents a final value. Without loss of generality, let v_x be the computation vertex connected to a source (sink) vertex by an edge labelled l. The delays in the links having identical labels are all the same. Hence, if the distance of the processor (onto which v_x is mapped) from the external input (output) port is k then the input (output) value represented by the source (sink) vertex must be inserted (extracted) into (from) the array by the host at time $t\text{-}k\,n_l$ $(t+k\,n_l)$.

We will now illustrate our mapping technique by constructing three algorithms. In the first example we will construct a linear array matrix multiplication algorithm that we reported in [11]. We will then construct another matrix multiplication algorithm on a logical linear array. Our final example is the construction of an algorithm for multiplication of band matrices on a hexagonal array that appeared in [5].

Example 3.1 Consider multiplication of two dense matrices A and B as shown below.

$$\begin{bmatrix} a_{11} & a_{12} \\ a_{21} & a_{22} \end{bmatrix} \begin{bmatrix} b_{11} & b_{12} & b_{13} \\ b_{21} & b_{22} & b_{23} \end{bmatrix} = \begin{bmatrix} c_{11} & c_{12} & c_{13} \\ c_{21} & c_{22} & c_{23} \end{bmatrix}$$

A program for computing this multiplication is given by the following recurrence.

$$c_{ij}^{(k+1)} = c_{ij}^{(k)} + a_{ik}b_{kj},\ 1 \leq i,k \leq 2 \text{ and } 1 \leq j \leq 3$$

$$c_{ij}^{(1)} = 0$$

The data-flow description of this computation is shown in Fig. 3.4.

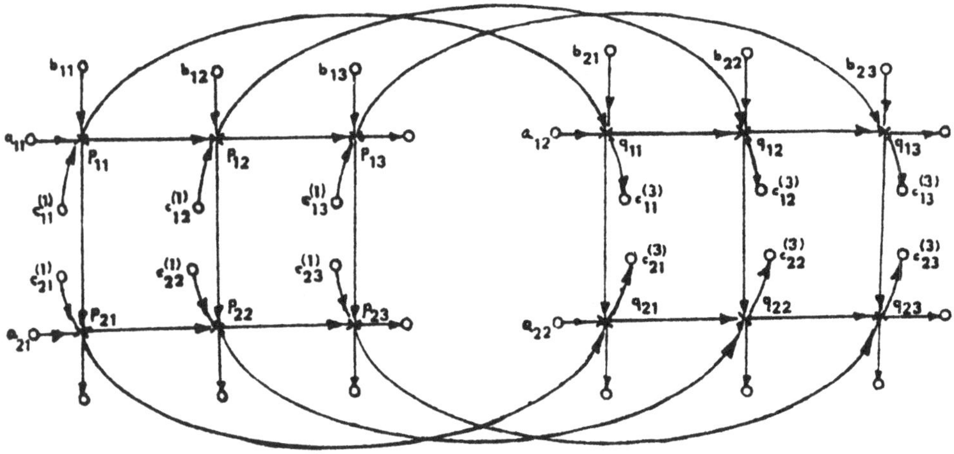

Fig. 3.4

In Fig. 3.4, p_{ij} and q_{ij} denote computation vertices. The horizontal, vertical and oblique incident edges of p_{ij} are labelled $l1$, $l2$ and $l3$ respectively. Similarly the horizontal, vertical and oblique outgoing edges of p_{ij} are labelled $l1$, $l2$ and $l3$ respectively. If the horizontal, vertical and oblique incident edges of p_{ij} or q_{ij} represent the values a, b and c respectively then the horizontal, vertical and oblique outgoing edges of p_{ij} or q_{ij} represent the values a, b and c+ab respectively. In Fig. 3.4, the oblique input edge incident on p_{ij} represents the value $c_{ij}^{(1)}$ which is 0. The oblique outgoing edge from q_{ij} reresents the final (output) value. $c_{ij}^{(3)}$ of c_{ij}, i.e., $a_{11}b_{ij}+a_{12}b_{2j}$.

The graph in Fig. 3.4 is a cube graph as illustrated in Fig. 3.5. The cube graph is shown without the source and sink vertices for purposes of clarity. The maximum dimensions of $l1^{th}$, $l2^{nd}$ and $l3^{rd}$ axes is 2, 1 and 1 respectively, i.e., $h_1=2$, $h_2=1$ and $h_3=1$.

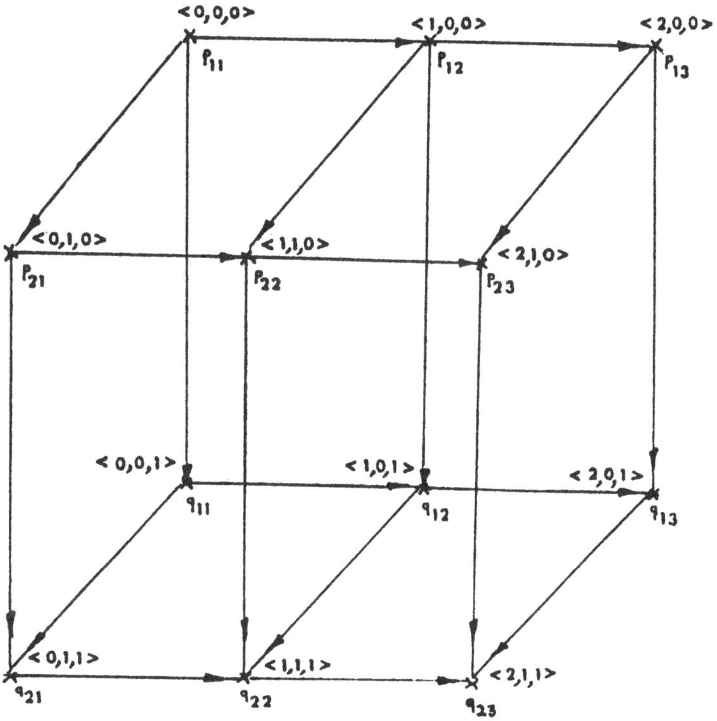

Fig. 3.5

We next map this graph onto a linear array using the linear-array mapping algorithm.

Let $w_L = <w_1, w_2, w_3> = <1,1,-1>$. For this choice of w_L, the set D of diagonals is comprised of $D_1 = \{ q_{11} \}$, $D_2 = \{ p_{11}, q_{12}, q_{21} \}$, $D_3 = \{ p_{12}, p_{21}, q_{13}, q_{22} \}$, $D_4 = \{ p_{13}, p_{22}, q_{23} \}$, $D_5 = \{ p_{23} \}$.

We use $|D| = 5$ processors indexed from 1 to 5. The neighborhood constants for labels $l1$, $l2$ and $l3$ are $n_{l1} = 1$, $n_{l2} = 1$ and $n_{l3} = -1$. The vertices in D_i are mapped onto processor indexed i. The delays for the labels $l1$, $l2$ and $l3$ are $d_{l1} = 1$, $d_{l2} = 2$ and $d_{l3} = 1$. The resulting mapping of the entire cube graph is shown in Fig. 3.6. The times at which a computation vertex is mapped is indicated by the side of the computaion vertex, for instance, p_{21} is mapped onto processor 3 at time $t_1 + 2$. If A and B are $n \times n$ matrices then the constructed algorithm above would require $O(n)$ processors and will take $O(n^2)$ time steps to compute the result matrix.

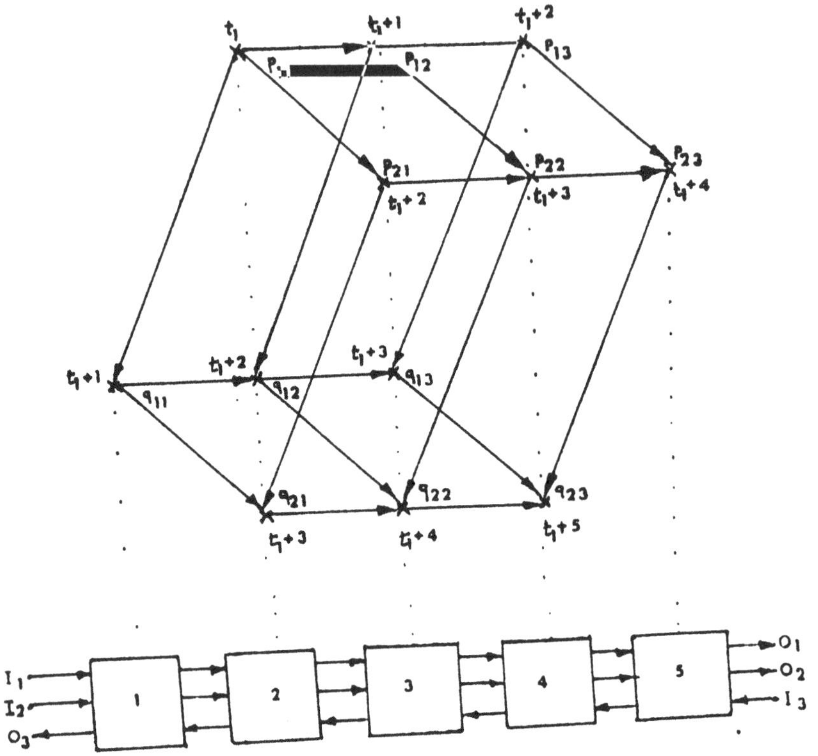

Fig. 3.6

Example 3.2: Consider again multiplication of the two matrices in the previous example. \
construct a logical linear array algorithm for multiplying the two matrices.

Let $w_L=<w_1,w_2,w_3>=<1,-1,-1>$. For this choice of w_L, the set D of diagonals is con
of $D_1=\{ q_{21} \}$, $D_2=\{ q_{22}, q_{11}, p_{21} \}$, $D_3=\{q_{23}, q_{12}, p_{22}, p_{11}\}$, $D_4=\{q_{13}, p_{23}, p_{12} \}$, $D_5=\{p_{13} \}$.

We use $|D|=5$ processors indexed from 1 to 5. The neighborhood constants for labels
and $l3$ are $n_{l1}=1$, $n_{l2}=n_{l3}=-1$. Vertices in D_i are all mapped onto
processor indexed i. The delays for labels $l1$, $l2$ and $l3$ are $d_{l1}=1, d_{l2}=1$ and $d_{l3}=6$.

Let the five vertex tree be as shown in Fig. 3.7 below.

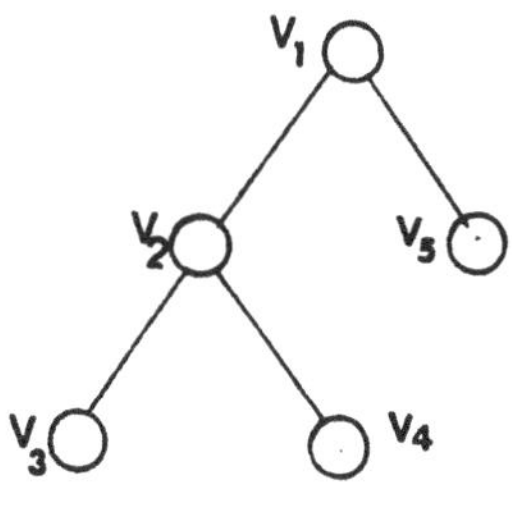

Fig. 3.7

Since the choice of n_{l1}, n_{l2}, and n_{l3} satisfies case 2, we choose the delay d along reverse edges to be equal d_{l1}. The perturbations in the delay for $l1$ satisfy $\Delta(l1,1)=0$, $\Delta(l1,2)=0$, $\Delta(l1,3)=-1$ (there is one reverse edge between v_3 and v_4) and $\Delta(l1,4)=-2$. The perturbations for $l2$ and $l3$ satisfy $\Delta(l2,j)=\Delta(l3,j)=-\Delta(l1,j-1)$, $j=2,..,5$. The effective delay between logically adjacent processors (δ's) is shown in Fig. 3.8 for each stream. The resulting mapping of the cube graph is also shown in the Fig. 3.8. The times at which a computation vertex is mapped is calculated from the final step of the mapping algorithm for logical linear arrays and is indicated by the side of the computation vertex. If A and B were $n \times n$ matrices then this algorithm will require $O(n)$ processors and interestingly, $O(n^2)$ time steps to compute the result matrix !!

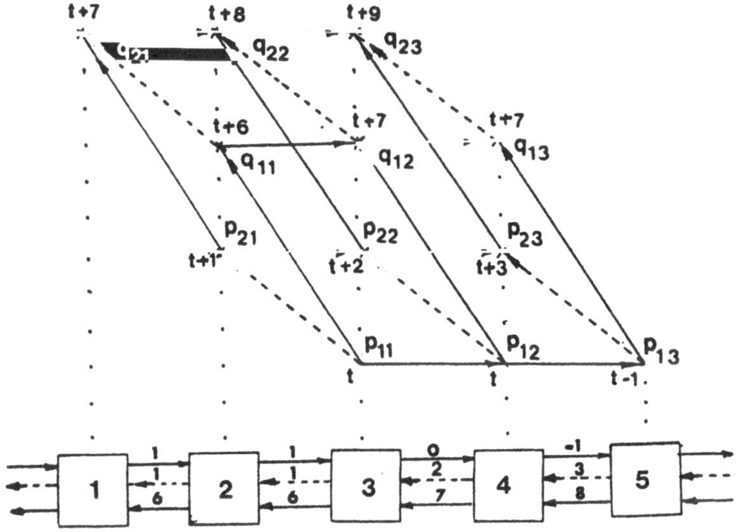

Fig. 3.8

Example 3.3 Consider the multiplication of two band matrices A and B as shown below wherein a_{ij} and b_{ij} denote the $[ij]^{th}$ entries in A and B respectively.

$$
\begin{bmatrix}
a_{11} & a_{12} & & & \\
a_{21} & a_{22} & a_{23} & & \\
a_{31} & a_{32} & a_{33} & a_{34} & \\
 & a_{42} & a_{43} & a_{44} & a_{45} \\
 & & a_{53} & a_{54} & a_{55} \\
 & & & a_{64} & a_{65}
\end{bmatrix}
\quad
\begin{bmatrix}
b_{11} & b_{12} & b_{13} & & & \\
b_{21} & b_{22} & b_{23} & b_{24} & & \\
 & b_{32} & b_{33} & b_{34} & b_{35} & \\
 & & b_{43} & b_{44} & b_{45} & b_{46} \\
 & & & b_{54} & b_{55} & b_{56}
\end{bmatrix}
$$

Let $C=A \times B$ be the result matrix. The data-flow description in Fig. 3.9 represents multiplication of $A \times B$. The horizontal, lateral and vertical edges are labelled $l1$, $l2$ and $l3$ respectively. In Fig. 3.9, v_{ij}^{k+1} is the computation vertex at a vertical distance k from v_{ij}^{1}. Thus, v_{22}^{3} is the computation vertex at a vertical distance 2 from v_{22}^{1}. The program graph in Fig. 3.9 is a cube graph as illustrated in Fig. 3.10. We next map this graph on a hexagonal array using the hexagonal array mapping algorithm.

Let $w_H = \langle w_1, w_2, w_3 \rangle = \langle 1,1,-1 \rangle$ and $c=1$. It can be verified that for this choice of w_H the set of diagonals D is comprised of $\{ D_{ij} \mid 1 \leq i,j \leq 4 \}$.

The hexagonal array is comprised of 4 rows and columns of processors which are identical to the procesors used in example 3.1. $L_H = \{l1\}$, $L_V = \{l2\}$ and $L_T = \{l3\}$. The neighborhood constants for the labels are $n_{l1} = n_{l2} = 1$ and $n_{l3} = -1$. The delays are $d_{l1} = d_{l2} = d_{l3} = 1$. The constant c for the array is 1. Fig. 3.11 illustrates the mapping. All the vertices lying on a "dashed" on a dashed line are all mapped onto the same processor.

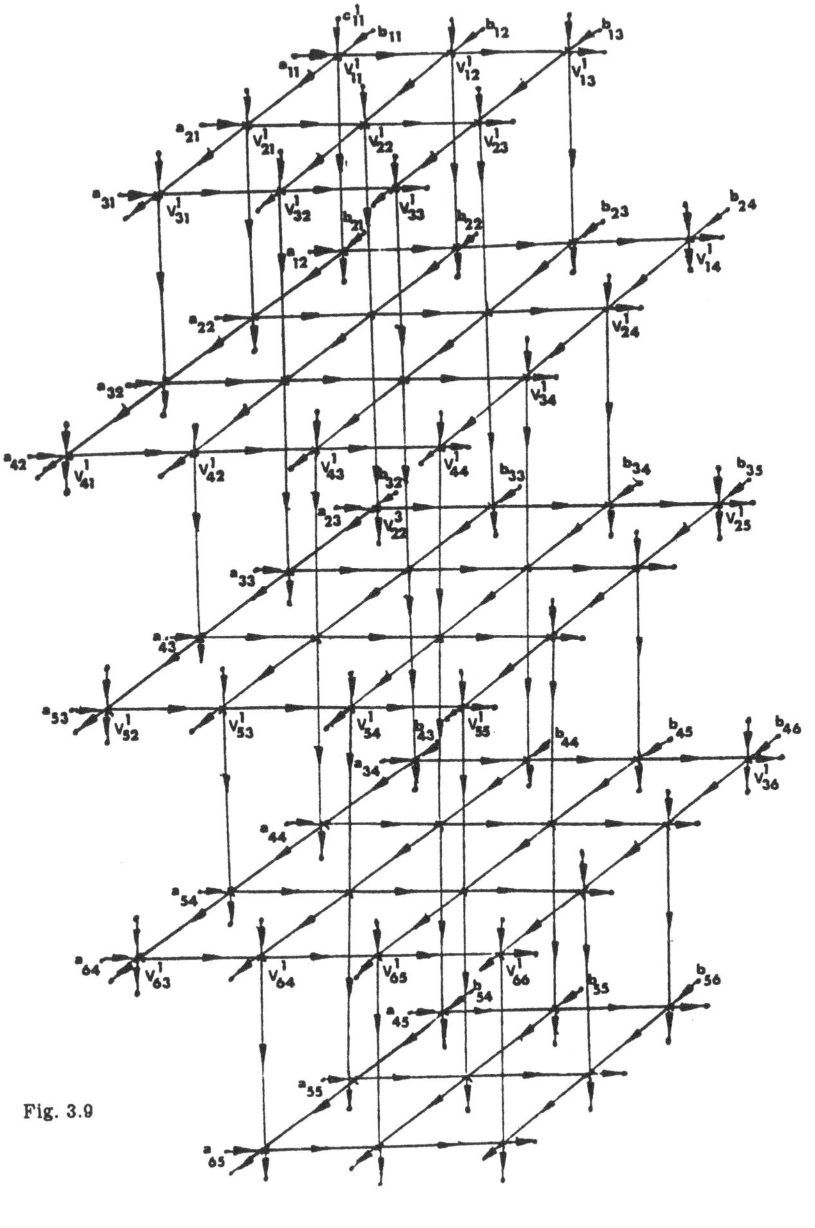

Fig. 3.9

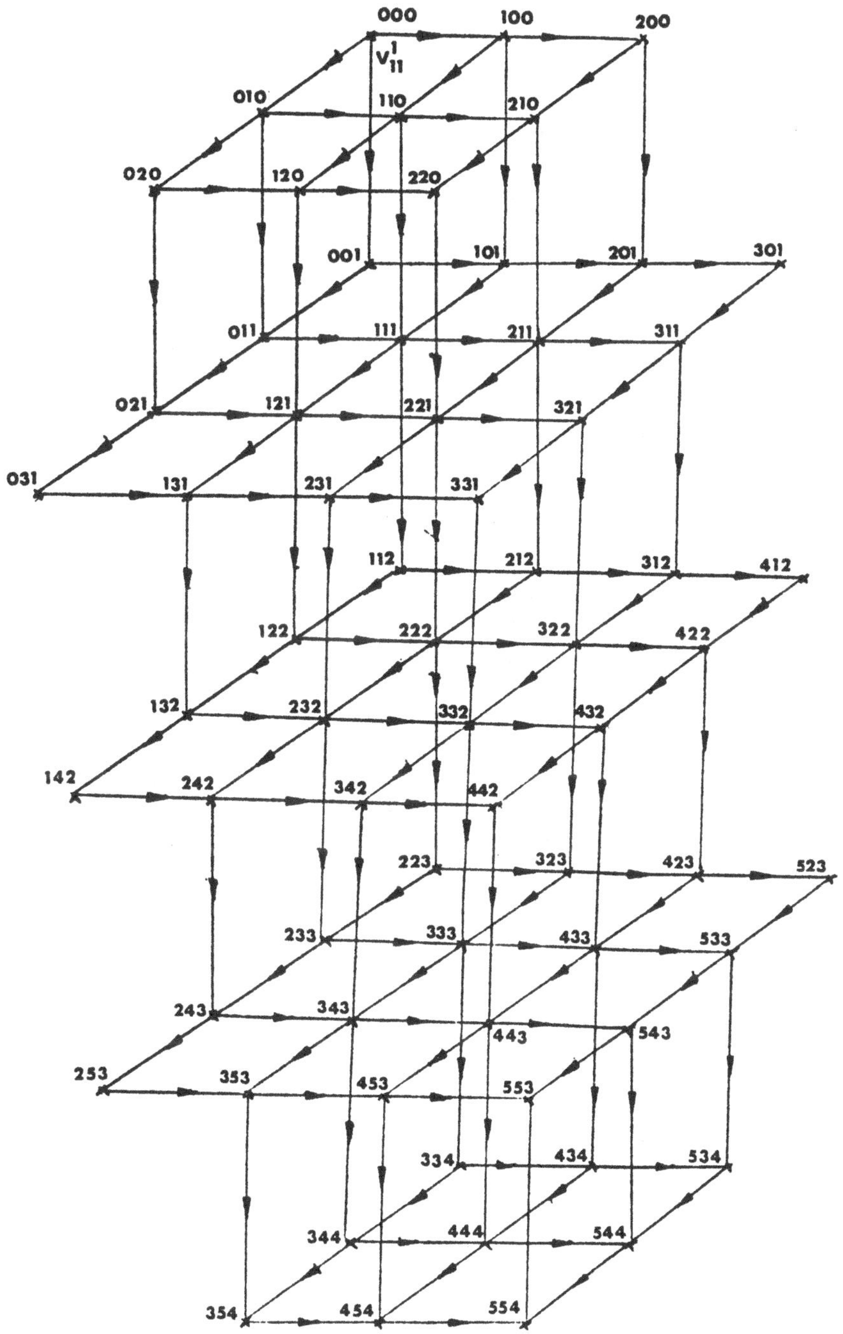
000
100
200
V_{11}^1
010
110
210
020
120
220
001
101
201
301
011
111
211
311
021
121
221
321
031
131
231
331
112
212
312
412
122
222
322
422
132
232
332
432
142
242
342
442
223
323
423
523
233
333
433
533
243
343
443
543
253
353
453
553
334
434
534
344
444
544
354
454
554

Fig. 3.10

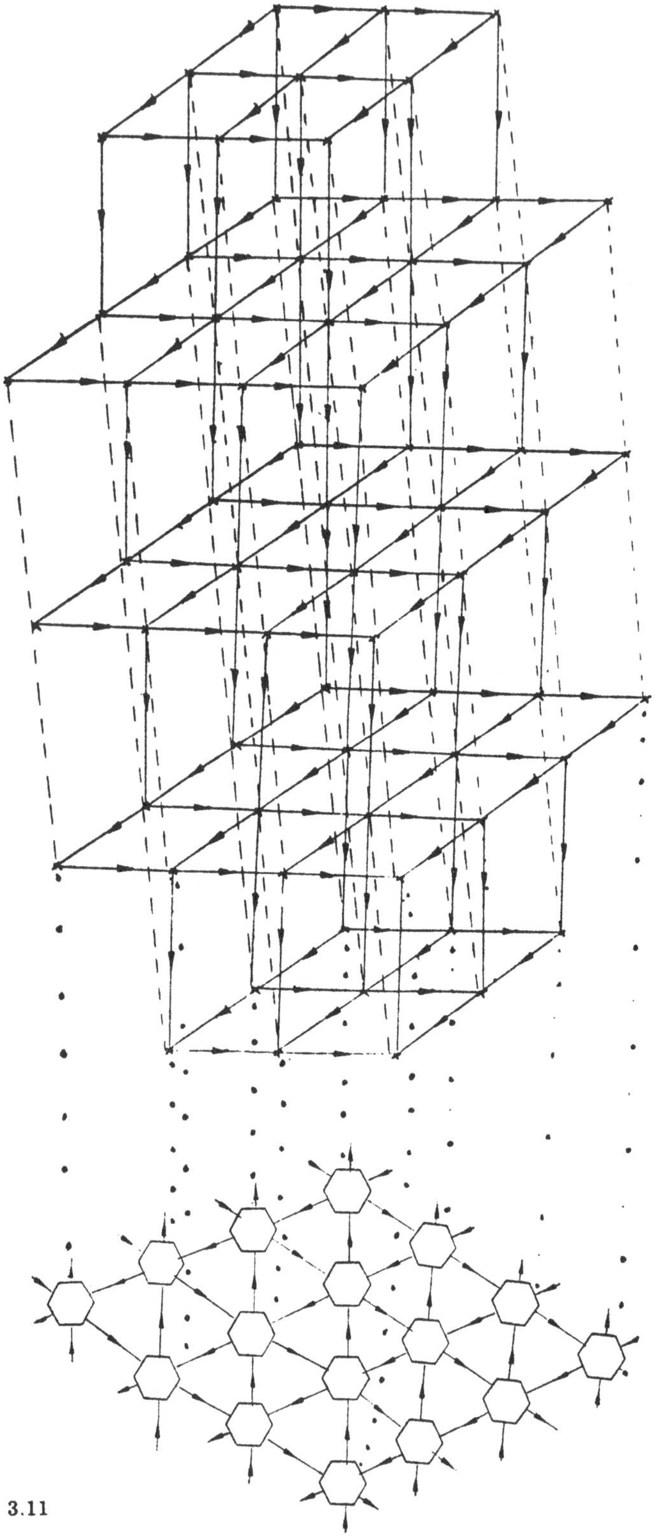

Fig. 3.11

Conclusion

In this paper we formalized linear, mesh and hexagonal array processors suitable for VLSI implementation. We also presented a model of a logical linear array which is an important computational structure for wafer-scale integration. We described a mathematical technique for constructing algorithms for all these array models from cube graphs. We illustrated the technique by constructing the algorithm described in [5] for multiplying two band matrices on a hexagonal array and also constructing new algorithms for multiplying dense matrices on linear and logical linear arrays.

The technique described in this paper will be useful in any compiler that transforms high-level specifications (like data-flow descriptions) onto array algorithms. The next important step in the mechanical construction of algorithms for the array models described in this paper is to investigate the feasibility of "restructuring" arbitrary data-flow descriptions of computations into cube graphs and generalized hypercube graphs.

References

[1] T.C. Chen, V.Y. Lum and C. Tung, "The Rebound Sorter: An efficient Sort Engine for Large Files," *Proceedings of the Fourth International Conference on Very Large Data Bases*, (1978) ,pp. 312-318.

[2] L.J. Guibas and F.M. Liang, "Systolic Stacks, Queues and Counters," *Proceedings of the MIT Conference on Advanced Research in VLSI*, (January, 1982), pp. 155-164.

[3] L. Johnsson and D. Cohen, "A Mathematical Approach to Modelling the Flow of Data and Control in Computational Networks," *VLSI Systems and Computations*, H.T. Kung, R.F. Sproull, and G.L. Steele, Jr., (editors), Computer Science Press, (1981), pp. 213-225.

[4] H.T. Kung, "Let's Design Algorithms for VLSI Systems," *Proceedings of the Caltech Conference on Very Large Scale Integration: Architecture, Design, Fabrication*, (January, 1979), pp. 65-90.

[5] H.T. Kung and C.E. Leiserson, "Systolic Arrays (for VLSI)," *Sparse Matrix Proceedings 1978*, I.S. Duff, and G.W. Stewart, (editors), SIAM, (1979), pp. 256-282.

[6] H.T. Kung, "Why Systolic Architectures," *IEEE Computer 15(1)*, (January, 1980), pp. 37-46.

[7] H.T. Kung and M. Lam, "Wafer-Scale Integration and Two-Level Pipelined Implementation of Systolic Arrays," *Proceedings of the MIT Conference on Advanced Research in VLSI*, (January, 1984).

[8] S.Y. Kung, "VLSI Array Processor for Signal Processing," *Proceedings of the MIT Conference on Advanced Research in Integrated Circuits*, (January, 1980).

[9] C. Mead and L. Conway, *Introduction to VLSI Systems*, Addison-Wesley, (1980).

[10] J.I Raffel, "On the Use of Nonvolatile Programming Links for Restructurable VLSI," *Proceedings of the Caltech Conference on VLSI*, (January, 1979).

[11] I.V. Ramakrishnan, D.S. Fussell and A. Silberschatz, "Systolic Matrix Multiplication on a Linear Array," *Twentieth Annual Allerton Conference on Computing, Control and Communication*, (October, 1982).

[12] I.V. Ramakrishnan, D.S. Fussell, and A. Silberschatz, "On Mapping Homogeneous Graphs on a Linear-Array Processor Model," *Proceedings of the 1983 International Conference on Parallel Processing*, (August, 1983).

[13] L. Snyder, "Introduction to the Configurable, Highly Parallel Computer," *IEEE Computer*, 15(1), (January, 1982).

[14] P.J. Varman, "Wafer-Scale Integration of Linear Processor Arrays," Ph.D Dissertation, The University of Texas at Austin, (August, 1983).

[15] P.J. Varman and D.S. Fussell, "Design of Robust Systolic Algorithms," *Proceedings of the 1983 International Conference on Parallel Processing*, (August, 1983).

[16] U. Weiser, and A. Davis, "A Wavefront Notation Tool for VLSI Array Design," *VLSI Systems and Computations*, H.T. Kung, R.F. Sproull, and G.L. Steele, Jr., (editors), Computer Science Press, (1981), pp. 226-234.

Appendix

We first prove that the mapping algorithm for the tree machine correctly maps the cube graph. We begin by first showing that the mapping preserves the neighborhood constant of the labels.

Theorem A.1: Let $l \in L_G$ and let n_l and d_l be its neighborhood and delay constants respectively. If v_x and v_y are a pair of computation vertices with an edge labelled l directed from v_x to v_y then $PA(v_y) = PA(v_x) + n_l$.

Proof: Let v_x and v_y be the vertices in diagonals D_p and D_q respectively and w_p and w_q be the weights of D_p and D_q respectively. So,

$$w_1 x_{l1} + w_2 x_{l2} + w_3 x_{l3} = w_p, \quad \text{and}$$
$$w_1 y_{l1} + w_2 y_{l2} + w_3 y_{l3} = w_q$$

We will show that the theorem holds for $l = l1$ as the proofs for $l = l2$ and $l = l3$ are similar.

Let e be the edge labelled l directed from v_x to v_y. From the definition of a cube graph we obtain $y_{l1} = x_{l1} + 1$, $y_{l2} = x_{l2}$ and $y_{l3} = x_{l3}$. Consequently, $w_q - w_p = w_1 = 1$. Since the diagonals are indexed in order of their weights, it follows that index of D_q must be one more than the index of D_p, that is, $q = p + 1$.

The mapping algorithm maps vertices in D_p onto processor p and those of D_q onto processor $p + w_1$ and hence $PA(v_y) = PA(v_x) + w_1$. Also from the mapping algorithm $n_{l1} = w_1$. So the theorem holds for $l = l1$. $\square$

Theorem A.2: Let $l \in L_G$ and let n_l and d_l be its neighborhood and delay constants respectively. Let v_x and v_y be a pair of vertices with an edge labelled l directed from v_x to v_y. If v_x is in diagonal D_p then $TA(v_y) = TA(v_x) + \delta(l, p)$.

Proof: We have to consider the two cases when $n_{l1} = n_{l2} = n_{l3} = 1$ and $n_{l1} = 1$, $n_{l2} = n_{l3} = -1$.

case 1: $n_{l1} = n_{l2} = n_{l3} = 1$.

Let $v_y \in D_q$ and $l = l1$ with no loss of generality. From the final step in the mapping algorithm for the tree machine we obtain:

$$TA(v_x) = t_1 + \sum_{i=1}^{3} x_{li} d_{li} + \sum_{j=1}^{p-1} \Delta(l1, j)$$
$$TA(v_y) = t_1 + \sum_{i=1}^{3} y_{li} d_{li} + \sum_{j=1}^{q-1} \Delta(l1, j)$$

By definition of a cube graph we have, $x_{l2} = y_{l2}$, $x_{l3} = y_{l3}$ and $y_{l1} = x_{l1} + 1$. From theorem A.1 we obtain $PA(v_y) = PA(v_x) + 1$, i.e., $q = p + 1$. Therefore,

$$TA(v_y) - TA(v_x) = d_{l1} + \sum_{j=1}^{q-1} \Delta(l1, j) - \sum_{j=1}^{p-1} \Delta(l1, j)$$
$$= d_{l1} + \sum_{j=p}^{q-1} \Delta(l1, j) = d_{l1} + \Delta(l1, p) = \delta(l1, p)$$

case 2: $n_{l1} = 1$, $n_{l2} = n_{l3} = -1$.

If $l = l1$ then the proof is the same as that used in case 1. Else let $l = l2$ with no loss of generality. Again by definition of a cube graph we have, $x_{l1} = y_{l1}$, $x_{l3} = y_{l3}$ and $y_{l2} = x_{l2} + 1$. From theorem A.1 we obtain $PA(v_y) = PA(v_x) - 1$, i.e., $q = p - 1$. So,

$$TA(v_y) - TA(v_x) = d_{l2} + \sum_{j=1}^{q-1} \Delta(l1, j) - \sum_{j=1}^{p-1} \Delta(l1, j)$$
$$= d_{l2} - (\sum_{j=1}^{p-1} \Delta(l1, j) - \sum_{j=1}^{q-1} \Delta(l1, j))$$
$$= d_{l2} - \Delta(l1, q) = d_{l2} + \Delta(l2, q+1) = d_{l2} + \Delta(l2, p)$$
$$= \delta(l2, p)$$

$\square$

We have to next establish that no two values appear simultaneously at the input port of any processor and the following definition and lemma comes in handy for proving it.

Definition A.1 For any label $l \in L_G$, a *major path* labelled l in G is a directed path from a source vertex to a sink vertex such that all the edges in the path are labelled l.

Lemma A.1: Let $l \in L_G$ and $n_l \in \{1,-1\}$. Let P_1 and P_2 be two distinct major paths labelled l in G and let v_x and v_y be the computation vertices adjacent to the source vertices in P_1 and P_2 respectively. Let $PA(v_x) = s_1$, $PA(v_y) = s_2$ where $s_1 \leq s_2$. Let $TA(v_x) = t_1$ and $TA(v_y) = t_2$. If the input/output values represented by the source and sink vertices of P_1 and P_2 appear simultaneously at the input port of a processor then $(t_2 - t_1)n_l = (s_2 - s_1)d_l + n_l(\sum_{j=s_1}^{s_2-1} \Delta(l1,j))$.

Proof: Again we need to consider the two cases when $n_{l1}=n_{l2}=n_{l3}$ and $n_{l1}=1, n_{l2}=n_{l3}=-1$.

case 1: $n_{l1} = n_{l2} = n_{l3} = 1$.

Since $PA(v_x) = s_1$ and $PA(v_y) = s_2$, we have $v_x \in D_{s_1}$ and $v_y \in D_{s_2}$. Assume without loss of generality that the input values represented by the source vertices of P_1 and P_2 appear simultaneously at the input port of processor s. Let $s \leq s_1 \leq s_2$ and the proof will be similar for other values of s. Let t be the time at which both the values appear at the input port labelled l of s. The time taken by the input value represented by the source vertex of P_1 to reach the input port labelled l of s_1 is $t + \sum_{j=s}^{s_1-1} \delta(l,j)$ which is $TA(v_x)$. Similarly, the time taken by the input value represented by the source vertex of P_2 to reach the input port labelled l of s_2 is $t + \sum_{j=s}^{s_2-1} \delta(l,j)$ which is $TA(v_y)$ and hence,

$$t_1 = TA(v_x) = t + (s_1 - s)d_l + \sum_{j=s}^{s_1-1} \Delta(l1, j), \text{ and}$$

$$t_2 = TA(v_y) = t + (s_2 - s)d_l + \sum_{j=s}^{s_2-1} \Delta(l1, j), \text{ and hence,}$$

$$t_2 - t_1 = (s_2 - s_1)d_l + \sum_{j=s_1}^{s_2-1} \Delta(l1,j)$$

Since $n_l = 1$ by hypothesis, we obtain $(t_2 - t_1)n_l = (s_2 - s_1)d_l + n_l(\sum_{j=s_1}^{s_2-1} \Delta(l1,j))$.

case 2: $n_{l1} = 1$, $n_{l2} = n_{l3} = -1$.

If $l = l1$, same proof as case 1 holds else assume $l = l2$ with no loss of generality. $n_{l2} = -1$, and $s_2 \geq s_1 \geq s$. As illustrated in the figure below, if the two values have to meet at s at time t then $t_2 \geq t_1 \geq t$.

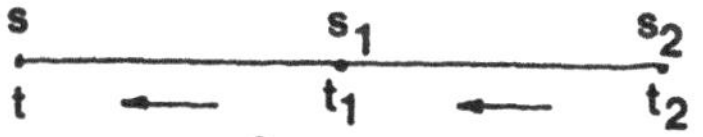

Now $t = t_1 + \sum_{j=s+1}^{s_1} \delta(l2,j) = t_1 + (s_1 - s)d_{l2} + \sum_{j=s+1}^{s_1} \Delta(l2,j)$ is the time taken by the input value represented by the source vertex of P_1 to reach s,

and $t = t_2 + \sum_{j=s+1}^{s_2} \delta(l2,j) = t_2 + (s_2 - s)d_{l2} + \sum_{j=s+1}^{s_2} \Delta(l2,j)$ is the time taken by the input value represented by the source vertex of P_2 to reach s.

Since the values meet at s, the time t is the same in both the equations and hence,

$$(t_2 - t_1) = (s_1 - s_2)d_{l2} + \sum_{j=s+1}^{s_1} \Delta(l2,j) - \sum_{j=s+1}^{s_2} \Delta(l2,j)$$

$$= (s_1 - s_2)d_{l2} - (\sum_{j=s+1}^{s_2} \Delta(l2,j) - \sum_{j=s+1}^{s_1} \Delta(l2,j))$$

$$= (s_1 - s_2)d_{l2} - \sum_{j=s_1+1}^{s_2} \Delta(l2,j)$$

Since $\Delta(l2,j)=-\Delta(l1,j-1)$ we have, $(t_2-t_1)=(s_1-s_2)d_{l2}+\sum_{k=s_1}^{s_2-1}\Delta(l1,k)$

Also as $n_{l2}=-1$, so $(t_2-t_1)n_{l2}=(s_2-s_1)d_{l2}+n_{l2}(\sum_{k=s_1}^{s_2-1}\Delta(l1,k))$. □

We next show that the mapping ensures that no two input/output values appear simultaneously at the input port of any processor.

Theorem A.3 Let $l \in L_G$. Let P_1 and P_2 be two distinct major paths in G labelled l. The mapping ensures that the input/output value represented by the source/sink vertices of P_1 and P_2 never appear simultaneously at the input port labelled l of any processor.

Proof: Let v_x and v_y be the vertices adjacent to the source vertices in P_1 and P_2 respectively. From the mapping algorithm we obtain,

$$PA(v_y)-PA(v_x)=\Delta(P)=\sum_{l=1}^{3}k_l n_{ll} \text{ where } k_l=y_{ll}-x_{ll} \text{ and } -h_l\leq k_l\leq h_l.$$

Let $v_x \in D_p$, $v_y \in D_q$ and $p\leq q$ with no loss of generality. From the mapping algorithm we also obtain,

$$TA(v_y)-TA(v_x)=\Delta T=\sum_{l=1}^{3}(y_{ll}-x_{ll})d_{ll}+\sum_{j=1}^{q-1}\Delta(l1,j)-\sum_{j=1}^{p-1}\Delta(l1,j)$$
$$=\sum_{l=1}^{3}k_l d_{ll}+\sum_{j=p}^{q-1}\Delta(l1,j)$$

Now assume that the input/output value represented by the source/sink vertices of P_1 and P_2 appear simultaneously at the input port labelled $l1$ of a processor. By lemma A.1 we have,

$(\Delta T)n_{l1}=(\Delta P)d_{l1}+n_{l1}(\sum_{j=p}^{q-1}\Delta(l1,j))$ which is the same as

$n_{l1}(\sum_{l=1}^{3}k_l d_{ll})+n_{l1}(\sum_{j=p}^{q-1}\Delta(l1,j))=(\Delta P)d_{l1}+n_{l1}(\sum_{j=p}^{q-1}\Delta(l1,j))$ and hence,

$(\Delta P)d_{l1}=n_{l1}(\sum_{l=1}^{l=3}k_l d_{ll})$ .....(*)

We next show that (*) cannot be satisfied.

1. Let $n_{l2}=1$ and so by the mapping algorithm, $d_{l1}=1$ and $d_{l2}=2$. P_1 and P_2 are distinct major paths labelled $l1$ and so $k_2=k_3\neq 0$.
   a. Let $h_1-h_2+n_{l3}\geq 0$. So $d_{l3}=h_1+1+2n_{l3}$ and (*) reduces to $k_3(h_1+1+n_{l3})+k_2=0$. Now $h_1+1+n_{l3}\geq 1$ and so $k_2\neq 0$ and $k_3\neq 0$. Besides $h_2\leq h_1+n_{l3}$ and $-h_2\leq k_2\leq h_2$ and so (*) cannot be satisfied.
   b. Let $h_1-h_2+n_{l3}<0$ and so $d_{l3}=h_1+n_{l3}$ and (*) reduces to $k_3h_2+k_2=0$. Now $h_2\geq 1$ and so $k_2\neq 0$ and $k_3\neq 0$. Besides $-h_2\leq k_2\leq h_2$ and so (*) cannot be satisfied.
2. Let $n_{l2}=-1$. So $d_{l1}=1$ and $d_{l2}=1$.
   a. Let $h_2-h_1+n_{l3}\geq 0$ and so $d_{l3}=2h_2+1+n_{l3}$. So (*) reduces to $2k_2+k_3(2h_2+1)=0$. As $h_2\geq 1$, so $2h_2+1\geq 3$ and so $k_2\neq 0$ and $k_3\neq 0$. Besides $-h_2\leq k_2\leq h_2$ and so $-(2h_2+1)\leq 2k_2<2h_2+1$ and so (*) cannot be satisfied.
   b. Let $h_2-h_1+n_{l3}<0$ and so $d_{l3}=2h_1+1-n_{l3}$. So (*) reduces to $2k_2+k_3(2h_1+1-2n_{l3})=0$. Now $1\leq h_2<h_1-n_{l3}$. So $2h_1+1-2n_{l3}>1$ and hence $k_2\neq 0$ and $k_3\neq 0$. Besides $-h_2\leq k_2\leq h_2$ and so $-(2h_1+1-2n_{l3})<2k_2<2h_1+1-2n_{l3}$ and hence (*) cannot be satisfied.

Using the inequality relationships between k_1, k_2, k_3 and h_1, h_2, h_3 we can similarly establish that the two equations $\Delta P\ d_{l2}=(\sum_{l=1}^{l=3}k_l d_{ll})\ n_{l2}$ and $\Delta P\ d_{l3}=(\sum_{l=1}^{l=3}k_l d_{ll})\ n_{l3}$ cannot be satisfied and hence no two input/output values will appear simultaneously at the input port of any processor labelled $l2$ or $l3$. □

Proof that the linear-array mapping algorithm correctly maps a cube graph on a linear array follows immediately from the proof of correctness of mapping cube graphs onto tree machines by letting the perturbation delay Δ's be zero in the above proofs.

It can be easily established that if v_x and v_y are two computation vertices connected by an edge labelled l then the mesh-array mapping algorithm maps the vertices on processors which are on the same horizontal row if $l \in L_H$ (like processors 11, 12 and 13 in Fig. 2.2) or on the same vertical column if $l \in L_V$ (like processors 11, 21 and 31 in Fig. 2.2).

It can be similarly established that the hexagonal-array mapping algorithm maps the two vertices on the same row of processors aligned in a north-easterly direction (like processors 11, 12 and 13 in Fig. 2.3) if $l \in L_H$. If $l \in L_V$ they are mapped on a row of processors aligned in a north-westerly direction (like processors 11, 21 and 31 in fig 3.3) and if $l \in L_T$ the vertices are mapped on the same column of processors (like processors 21 and 12 in Fig. 3.3). All these rows and columns constitute a linear array and hence the correctness proof used above can be used to establish that the mesh and hexagonal-array mapping algorithms also map cube graphs correctly.

A linear-time algorithm for determining the intersection type of two star polygons

(Extended Abstract)

S.K. Ghosh

Computer science Group
Tata Institute of Fundamental Research
Homi Bhabha Road, Bombay 400005, India.

Abstract: In this paper, we present a linear time algorithm for determining the intersection type of two star polygons and prove its correctness. The algorithm exploits the sorted angular order of the vertices of a star polygon and, thus, avoiding the general step of sorting the polygonal vertices.

1. Introduction

A frequently occurring geometric problem is to determine whether two figures intersect and if so, to compute their common part. Some applications of intersection algorithms are to the determination of visibility (hidden surface removal) in three-dimensional computer graphics and the checking of design rules in VLSI circuits . The basic intersection problem has several important variants and in two dimensions, the given figure can be a set of line segments or a polygon. The polygon intersection problem consists of deciding: (a) whether two polygons intersect (b) how many pairs of edges intersect or (c) which pair of edges intersect. As all the vertices of a convex (respectively monotone) polygon are sorted with reference to any direction (given direction), the intersection between two convex (monotone) polygons can be computed in linear time(see Shamos[1]). But to detect the intersection between two convex polygons with n and m edges can be obtained in O(log(n+m)) (see Chazelle and Dobkin[5]). As no such structure exists in the case of a set of line segments, to determine the intersection between line segments requires sorting the end points of the given line segments and, therefore, takes O(nlogn) time (Shamos[1]). As any polygon consists of finite set of line segments, determining the intersection between any two polygons with n edges can also be obtained in O(nlogn) time. However, a polygon is a connected set of line segments and thus one can expect a linear time algorithm for detecting the intersection between two polygons by exploiting the polygonal features. In the case of a star polygon, all the vertices are in sorted angular order with respect to its star point and by exploiting this feature , one can obtain a linear time algorithm for this problem. However, finding the intersecting between two star polygons with n and m edges remains O(nm) (Shamos[1]). Montuno and Fournier[2] made an attempt to detect an intersection between two star polygons in linear time but this algorithm uses convex chains for detecting the intersection and therefore, when two convex chains intersect , it does not necessarily mean that the star polygons have intersected and therefore, it requires the checking for intersection between the polygonal edges. So, the complexity in the worst case situtation no longer remains linear. In this paper, we present a linear time algorithm for determining whether the boundary of two star polygons intersect or one contains the other or they are disjoint and prove its correctness.

2.Preliminary definitions and notations

Here,we define various characteristic features of a polygon used in the description of the algorithm and the proof of correctness.

Definition 1.1: A simple polygon is defined as $P=(p_1,p_2,\ldots,p_n)$ i.e. a list of consecutive vertices $p_1,p_2,\ldots,p_n$ with the restriction that no two non-adjacent edges of the polygon intersect.

Notation 2.1: For any two points u and v ,the line segment joining u and v will be denoted as uv.

Definition 2.2: A polygon $P=\{p_1,p_2,\ldots,p_n\}$ is a star polygon if there exists a point z inside P such that, for all p_i, line segment zp_i is contained in the polygon and z is called the star point of P.

Definition 2.3: A vertex u of a polygon is said to be internally (respectively, externally) visible from a point v inside (outside) the polygon if uv lies totally inside (outside) the polygon.

Definition 2.4: Given any triple of vertices in the order p_k,p_{k+1} and p_{k+2} where $p_k=(x_k,y_k)$, one can determine whether or not a reflex angle is defined by them by computing:

$S(p_k,p_{k+1},p_{k+2})= (y_{k+1}-y_k)(x_{k+2}-x_{k+1})+(x_k-x_{k+1})(y_{k+2}-y_{k+1})$

Based upon the value of $S(p_k,p_{k+1},p_{k+2})$ we can assert:

a) $S(p_k,p_{k+1},p_{k+2}) > 0$ implies that the angle subtended at p_{k+1} is not reflex (referred to as right turn).

b) $S(p_k,p_{k+1},p_{k+2}) = 0$ implies that the vertices are collinear.

c) $S(p_k,p_{k+1},p_{k+2}) < 0$ implies that the angle subtended at p_{k+1} is reflex (referred to as left turn).

Definition 2.5 : A Ray[u,v] is defined as a Ray drawn from a point u through a vertex v.

Definition 2.6: A chain (u,v) of a star polygon is defined as a sequence of consecutive vertices from u to v.

Notation 2.2: The distance between two points u and v will be denoted as d(u,v).

3. Intersection algorithm

Consider two given star polygons $A=\{a_1,a_2,...,a_n\}$ and $B=\{b_1,b_2,...,b_m\}$ and their corresponding star points a_0 and b_0. Now, if we join a_0 and b_0 by a line, the line segment a_0b_0 may or may not intersect the boundary of A and B. This leads to the following four possibilities:

Case 1--a_0b_0 intersects both the boundary of A and B: Let us denote the intersection point of a_0b_0 with A as a' and that of B as b' (see Fig.1). It means that either A and B are intersecting polygons or they are disjoint. Without loss of generality, let us choose a_0 as the reference point. Now, find a vertex b_j of B such that all the vertices of B are lying to the right half-plane of the Ray$[a_0,b_j)$. Let us call b_j as b_{min}. Similarly, find a vertex b_k of B such that all the vertices of B are lying to the left half-plane of the Ray$[a_0,b_k)$. Let us call b_k as b_{max}. In other words, if we compute the polar angle for each vertex of B with point a_0 as origin and the Ray$[b_0,a_0)$ as the reference axis where the polar angle around a_0 increases in the clockwise direction, the angle subtended at a_0 will be minimum for b_{min} and maximum for b_{max}. The chain formed by the vertices of B from b_{min} to b_{max} in the counterclockwise order will be referred to as the chain(b_{min},b_{max}) as b' is lying on this chain. Find the intersection point of a_0b_{min} with the boundary of A and denote the point of intersection as a_{min}. Similarly, find the intersection point of a_0b_{max} with the boundary of A and denote it as a_{max}. So, the chain formed by the vertices of A from a_{min} to a_{max} in the clockwise order will be referred to as the chain(a_{min},a_{max}) as a' is lying on this chain. By testing for intersection between the chain (a_{min},a_{max}) and the chain (b_{min},b_{max}), we can decide whether A and B are intersecting or disjoint. The major problem in testing for intersection is that all the vertices of the chain (b_{min},b_{max}) may not be in sorted angular order with respect to a_0. Therefore, we obtain the sorted chain (b_{min},b_{max}) from the chain (b_{min},b_{max}) such that all the vertices are in sorted angular order with respect to a_0. If we obtain the visibility polygon of B from a_0 by the linear time algorithm reported by Lee[4], the visibility polygon of B gives the sorted chain(b_{min},b_{max}) as all the points of the visibility polygon are in sorted angular order with respect to the given point. In other words, if we ignore the polygon A and consider a_0 as merely a point outside the polygon B , the sorted chain (b_{min},b_{max}) will be the portion of B externally visible from a_0. Though under this assumption the sorted chain (b_{min},b_{max}) is totally visible from a_0, it may turn out to be partially visibile or totally visible or totally invisible from a_0 depending upon the position of A relative to B. If the sorted chain (b_{min},b_{max}) is totally invisible from a_0, it means that A and B are disjoint; otherwise, they are intersecting. In other words, for each vertex b_j of the sorted chain (b_{min},b_{max}), if a_0b_j intersects the chain

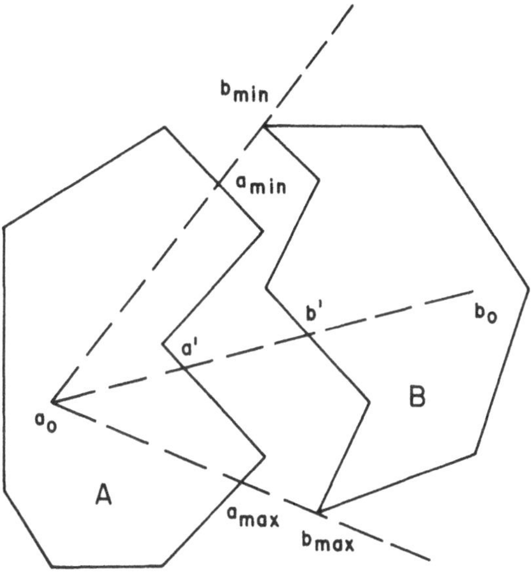

Fig. 1. a_o does not belong to B and b_o does not belong to A

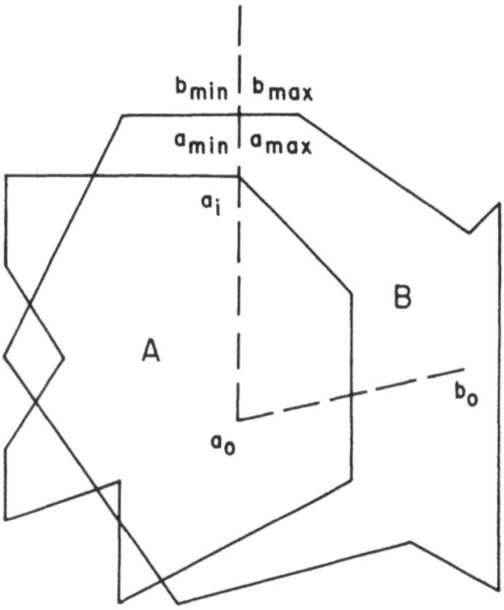

Fig. 2. a_o belongs to B and b_o does not belong to A

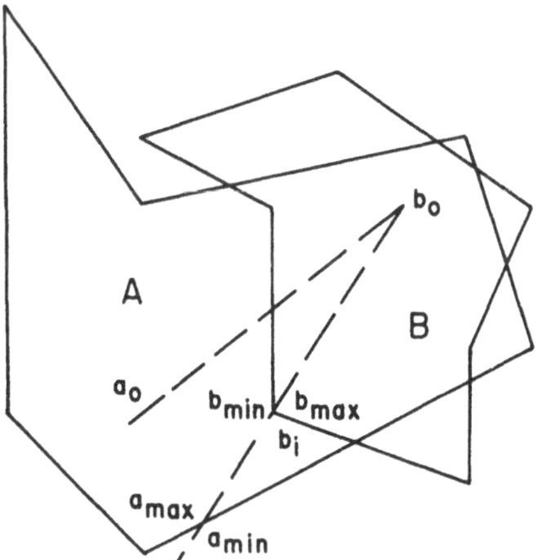

Fig. 3. a_o does not belong to B and b_o belongs to A

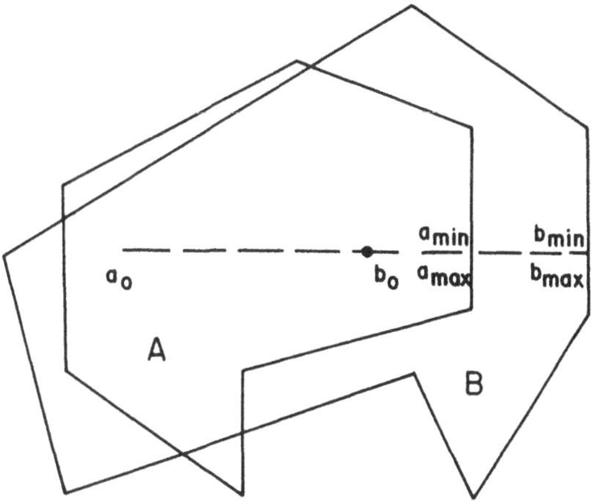

Fig. 4. a_o belongs to B and b_o belongs to A

(a_{min},a_{max}) and for each vertex a_i of the chain (a_{min},a_{max}), if a_0a_i does not intersect the sorted chain (b_{min},b_{max}), the sorted chain (b_{min},b_{max}) is totally invisible from a_0. Computing the visibility in this manner involves checking for intersection between every a_0b_j and all the edges of the chain (a_{min},a_{max}) and every a_0a_i and all the edges of sorted chain (b_{min},b_{max}). This costly procedure can be avoided with the help of the merged list which can be obtained by merging the vertices of the chain (a_{min},a_{max}) and the sorted chain (b_{min},b_{max}) by their relative polar angles with respect to a_0. Now, if we draw rays from a_0 through each vertex of the merged list, these Rays will divide the plane into wedges. In every wedge, there is an edge of the chain (a_{min},a_{max}) and an edge of the sorted chain (b_{min},b_{max}). By checking for intersection between the pair of edges in each wedge, we can decide whether A and B are intersecting or disjoint.

Case 2--$\overline{a_0b_0}$ intersects the boundary of A but does not intersect the boundary of B: In this case, either the boundary of A and the boundary of B intersect or A is contained in B. As a_0 belongs to both A and B, a_0 will be chosen as the reference point(see Fig.2). Let us denote any vertex a_i of A as both a_{min} and a_{max}. Find the closest intersection point of the Ray$[a_0,a_i)$ with the boundary of B and denote it as both b_{min} and b_{max}. The chain (b_{min},b_{max}) and the chain (a_{min},a_{max}) will be the whole polygonal boundary of B and A respectively, both traversed in the clockwise direction. If we ignore the polygon A and consider a_0 as a point inside the polygon B, the sorted chain (b_{min},b_{max}) will be the only portion of B internally visible from a_0. Once the chain (a_{min},a_{max}) and the sorted chain (b_{min},b_{max}) are obtained, merging the vertices of these chains with respect to their relative polar angles and detecting the intersection between these chains follow as in case 1.

Case 3--$\overline{a_0b_0}$ intersects the boundary of B but does not intersect the boundary of A: In this case either the boundary of A and the boundary of B intersect or B is contained in A. As b_0 belongs to both A and B, b_0 will be taken as the reference point and the rest of the computation will be same as stated in case 2 except that the role of A and B will be interchanged (see Fig.3).

Case 4--$\overline{a_0b_0}$ intersects neither the boundary of A nor B: Let us extend the line a_0b_0 in either direction and denote the intersection point with the boundary of A as a' and that of B as b' (see Fig.4). If $d(a',a_0) < d(b',a_0)$ then either the boundary of A and B intersect or A is contained in B. This is same as the case 2. If $d(a',a_0) > d(b',a_0)$ then either the boundary of A and B intersect or B is contained in A. This is same as case 3.

Algorithm: The following notations are used in describing the algorithm and comment is enclosed within curly brackets.

Pred(j) --the predecessor of j (in the counterclockwise order).

Succ(j)--the successor of j (in the clockwise order).

Poly-Intersection, Intersect1 and Intersect2 --boolean variables.

Input: Two star polygons $A=(a_1,a_2,..,a_n)$ and $B=(b_1,b_2,..,b_m)$ where vertices are listed in clockwise order with their x-coordinates and y-coordinates and a_0 and b_0 are star points of A and B respectively given by their x-and y-coordinates.

Output: It can be one of the following:

1. A and B are disjoint polygons.
2. Polygon A is contained inside the polygon B.
3. The boundary of polygon A intersects the boundary of polygon B.

Method:

Step 1: Check for intersection between a_0b_0 and each edge of A and B;

Step 2: If ((a_0b_0 intersects an edge of A) and (a_0b_0 intersects an edge of B)) then

```
    begin {find b_max and b_min}
      find a vertex b_j(respectively,b_k) such that all other vertices of B
       are to the right(left) of the Ray[a_0,bj)(Ray[a_0,b_k)) and call b_j(b_k)
       as bmax(b_min);
      if a_0b_max or a_0b_min does not intersect the boundary of A
        then Poly-intersection:=true
      else
        begin
          denote the intersection point of a_0b_max with A as a_max and a_0b_min
            with A as a_min;
            {chain(b_max,b_min) in the counterclockwise order}
          Interchange succ and pred of the chain(b_min,b_max)}
          Sorted- chain (a_0,b_min,b_max);
          Find - Intersection (a_0,a_min,a_max,b_min,b_max)
        end;
      If Poly-Intersection then
            report 'A and B are intersecting polygons'
      else
            report 'Polygons A and B are disjoint';
    end;
```

Step 3: If (a_0b_0 intersects an edge of A) and (a_0b_0 does not intersect an edge of B) then

```
      begin {denote a_1 as both a_min and a_max}
```

```
a_min:=a_1;
a_max:=a_1;
denote the closest intersection point of the Ray[a_0,a_i) with the
  boundary of B as both b_min and b_max;
if d(a_0,a_min)>d(a_0,b_min)
  then Poly-Intersection:=true
else
   begin  {check for intersection between the chains}
      Sorted-chain(a_0,b_min,b_max);
      Find-Intersection(a_0,a_min,a_max,b_min,b_max);
   end;
if Poly-Intersection then
     report 'A and B are intersecting polygons'
else
     report 'Polygon A is contained in polygon B';
end;
```

<u>Step 4</u>: If (a_0b_0 does not intersect any edge of A) and (a_0b_0 intersects an edge of B) then

```
begin
   interchange A and B ;
   goto step 3
end;
```

<u>Step 5</u>: If (a_0b_0 does not intersect any edge of both A and B) then

```
begin
   denote the intersection point of the Ray[a_0,b_0) with the boundary of
      A as both a_min and a_max and that of B as b_min and b_max;
   if d(a_0,a_min)>d(a_0,b_min) then
    interchange A and B;
   Sorted-chain(a_0,b_min,b_max);
   Find-Intersection(a_0,a_min,a_max,b_min,b_max);
   if Poly-Intersection then
        report 'A and B are intersecting polygons
   else
        report 'Polygon A is contained in polygon B';
end;
```

<u>Step 6</u>: STOP.

```
Procedure Sorted-Chain ( p: star point of A, v,w: vertices of B);
{given a chain(v,w) and a point p, the procedure obtains the sorted chain(v,w)}

Procedure Lookahead;

begin {lookahead}
   {look for a vertex outside the hidden region}
   while S(p,v,u) < 0 do
      u:=Succ(u);
   Find the intersection point z of the Ray[p,v) with the edge (Pred(u),u);
end; {lookahead}

Procedure Backtracking;

begin {backtracking}
   repeat
       {remove the vertices earlier accepted as visible vertices}
      v:=Pred(v);
   until(S(p,v,u)≥0);
   Find the intersection point z between the Ray[p,u) and the edge(v,Succ(v));
end; {backtracking}
begin {sorted-chain}
   u:=Succ(v);
   repeat
     {check the visibility of u from p}
      If S(p,v,u)≥0 then
        begin
           v:=Succ(v);
           u:=Succ(u);
        end
    else {remove the invisible vertices}
      begin
         case S(Pred(v),v,u) of
            left turn: Lookahead;
           right turn: Backtracking;
         end; {case}
      {insert the point of intersection z}
         Succ(v):=z; Pred(z):=v; Succ(z):=u;
         Pred(u):=z; v:=Succ(v);
      end;
   until(u=w); {all vertices of the given chain are considered or not}
end; {sorted-chain}
```

```
Procedure Find-Intersection(p:star point of A;u,q:vertices of A; ,w:vertices of B);
   {All the vertices of the chain (u,q) and the chain (v,w) are in the sorted
      angular order with respect to p}


   begin
     repeat
       case S(p,Succ(u),Succ(v)) of
          right turn: if pSucc(u) intersects the edge(v,Succ(v))
                          then Poly-Intersection:=true
                      else u:=Succ(u);
          collinear : if d(p,Succ(u))≥ d(p,Succ(v))
                         then poly-Intersection:=true
                      else
                         begin
                            u:=Succ(u);
                            v:=Succ(v)
                         end;
          left turn : if pSucc(v) does not intersect edge(u,Succ(u))
                         then Poly-Intersection:=true
                      else v:=Succ(v)
       end; {case}
     until((Poly-Intersection) or (u=q and v=w));
   end;
```

4. Correctness of the algorithm

First, we state the invariant condition of vertices of a star polygon. Star polygon invariant condition: For any two consecutive clockwise vertices a_r and a_{r+1} of a star polygon, $S(a_0,a_r,a_{r+1}) \geq 0$ i.e.vertices a_0,a_r and a_{r+1} either form a right turn or collinear where a_0 is the star point of the star polygon.

Now, we will state all the possible conditions that can arise for detecting the intersection between two star polygons.

Condition 1: Two star polygons A and B are disjoint if $A \cap B = \emptyset$.
Condition 2: Star polygon A is contained in a star polygon B if $A \cap B = A$.
Condition 3: Star polygon B is contained in a star polygon A if $A \cap B = B$.
Condition 4: The boundary of the star polygon A intersects the boundary of star polygon B if none of the above conditions is satisfied.

The algorithm executes step 1 to decide which one of the four subsequent steps will be executed. If step 1 finds $a_0 \notin B$ and $b_0 \notin A$, it means that condition 2 and 3 can not be true. Therefore, step 2 is executed to decide between condition 1 and 4. Taking a_0 as reference point, step 2 obtains b_{min} and b_{max}. If a_0b_{min} does not intersect any edge of A, it means that $b_{min} \in A$ and therefore, condition 4 is true . Similar argument holds if a_0b_{max} does not intersect any edge of A. If a_{min} and a_{max} are found, step 2 checks for intersection between two chains to decide between condition 1 and 4. If step 1 finds $a_0 \in B$ and $b_0 \notin A$, it means that condition 3 and 1 can not be true. Therefore, step 3 is executed to decide between condition 2 and 4. As $a_0 \in B$ and $a_0 \in A$, a_0 is one of the internal points of both A and B . Tacking a_0 as reference point, it obtains a_{min}, a_{max}, b_{min} and b_{max}. If b_{min} is found inside A, it means that condition 4 is true otherwise it checks for intersection between two chains to decide between condition 2 and 4. If step 1 finds $a_0 \notin B$ and $b_0 \in A$, it means that condition 1 and 2 can not be true. Therefore, step 4 is executed to decide between conditions 3 and 4. The step 4 is nothing but the dual of step 3. If step 1 finds $a_0 \in B$ and $b_0 \in A$, it means condition 1 cannot be true and therefore, step 5 is executed to decide among rest of the conditions. After obtaining a_{min},a_{max},b_{min} and b_{max} and depending upon their relative positions, either step 3 or step 4 is executed to arrive at the conclusion.

Once a_{min}, a_{max} , b_{min} and b_{max} are found and appropriate star point is taken as the reference point, the checking for intersection between chains in all the steps 2-5 is identical and we will prove them in the following lemmas.

As we are dealing with only star polygons, overlapping hidden regions and block exterior configuration defined by Freeman and Loutrel[3] do not arise and after removing these cases from the algorithm of Lee[4], the relivant portion of this algorithm is stated here as the procedure Sorted-Chain(p,v,w).

Lemma 1: Procedure 'Sorted-chain (p,v,w)' obtains the sorted chain (v,w) from the given chain (v,w) such that all the points in the sorted chain (v,w) are in sorted angular order with respect to p, i.e. the obtained sorted chain (v,w) is visible from p.

Proof: When the procedure is called, it is assured that v and w are visible from p, i.e. pv and pw will not be intersected by any edge of the chain (v,w). Now, it can be seen from the procedure that the current vertex u is acceptable as a visible vertex iff $S(p,v,u) \geq 0$ i.e. the star polygon invariant condition is satisfied. If $S(p,v,u) < 0$ i.e. the star polygon invariant condition is not satisfied, it means that there exists at least a vertex in the given chain (v,w) that is invisible from p. Therefore, the star polygon invariant condition is restored by removing the invisible vertices of the chain (v,w) either by the procedure Lookahead or by the

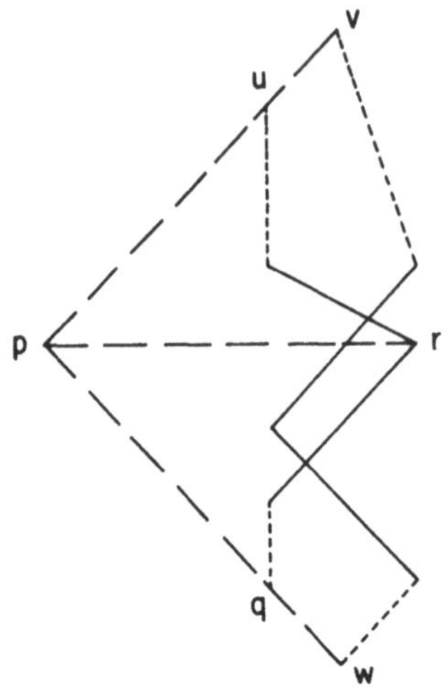

Fig. 5. pr intersects the sorted chain (v, w)

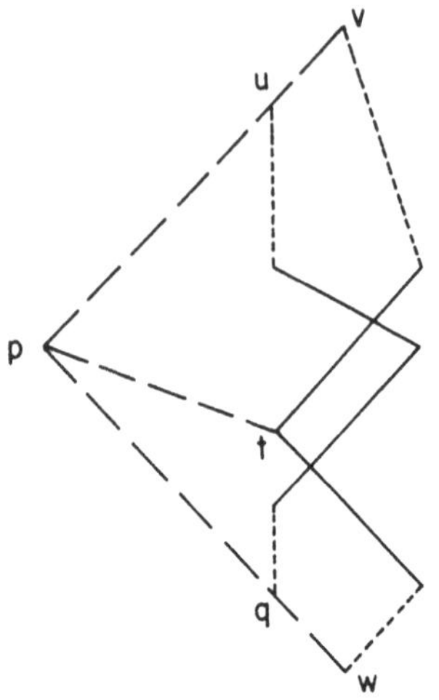

Fig. 6. pt does not intersect the chain (u, q)

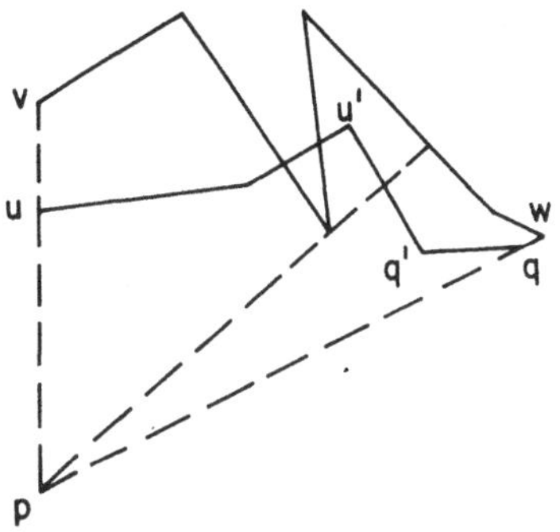

Fig. 7. Preceding edge of u' q' intersects the chain (v, w)

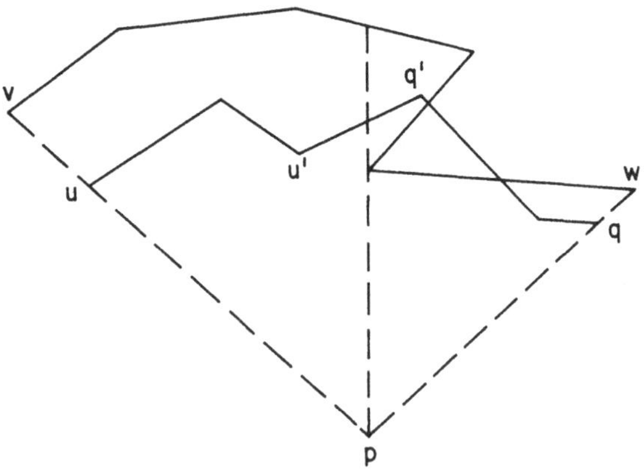

Fig. 8. Succeding edge of u' q' intersects the chain (v, w)

procedure Backtracking. If S(pred(v),v,u)<0, the procedure Lookahead removes invisible vertices from the remaining vertices yet to be scanned in the input list, till the star polygon invariant condition is restored. If S(pred(v),v,u)>0, the procedure Backtracking removes invisible vertices both from the chain of vertices so far accepted as visible vertices and from the remaining vertices yet to be scanned in the input list, till the star polygon invariant condition is restored. It is to be noted that the constructed edges in the sorted chain are collinear with p. So, after removing all the invisible points of the given chain , the sorted chain consists of those vertices that satisfy the star polygon invariant condition. Hence the lemma.

Lemma 2: Procedure 'Find-Intersection (p,u,q,v,w)' finds the intersection between the chain (u,q) and the sorted chain (v,w) correctly.

Proof: When the procedure is called, it is assumed that all the vertices of the chain (u,q) and the sorted chain (v,w) are in the sorted angular order with respect to p. It is also assumed that u lies on pv and q lies on pw. The chain(u,q) intersects the sorted chain(v,w) if there exists at least a vertex (say r) of the chain(u,q) such that pr intersects the corresponding edge of the sorted chain(v,w) (see Fig.5) i.e. r lies inside B or there exists at least a vertex (say t) of the sorted chain(v,w) such that pt does not intersect the corresponding edge of the chain(u,q) (see Fig.6) i.r. t lies inside A. The procedure checks for intersection for each vertex of both the chains and therefore, correctly detects whether there exists any intersection between the two given chains. Hence the lemma.

In the lemma 1, we have shown that all the points of the sorted chain(v,w) are in sorted angular order with respect to p and are constructed edges in the sorted chain(v,w) are collinear with p. In the lemma 2, we have shown that the algorithm correctly detects the intersection between the chain(u,q) and the sorted chain(v,w). If an edge (say u'q') of the chain(u,q) intersects a constructed edge of the sorted chain (v,w), it implies that either any of the preceding edges of u'q'(see fig.7) or any of the succeding edges of u'q'(see fig.8) has intersected the polygonal edge of the chain (v,w) because all the vertices of the chain(u,q) are in sorted angular order with respect to p. So, it is sufficient to check the intersection between the chain(u,q) and the sorted chain(v,w) to determine whether two given star polygons have intersected or not.

5. Analysis of the algorithm

Let n and m be the number of vertices of the given star polygons A and B respectively. Step 1 checks the intersection of a_0b_0 with all the edges of A and B and therefore, it takes O(n+m) time. Finding a_{min}, a_{max}, b_{min} and b_{max} in any of the steps 2-5 can also be performed in O(n+m) time. Procedure 'Sorted-Chain (p,v,w)'scans every vertex of the chain (v,w) once and decides whether to accept it as a visible vertex or not. If the Procedure 'Sorted-Chain (p,v,w)' rejects any vertex, it will not be considered again. Even if a vertex is accepted as a visible vertex, it may turn out to be an invisible vertex subsequently and therefore, will be rejected. Again, once a vertex is rejected, it will not be considered by the procedure later on. Since the procedure considers a vertex of the chain (v,w) at most twice, it obtains the sorted chain (v,w) in linear time. As every vertex of both the chains is considered only once by the procedure 'Find-Intersection(p,u,q,v,w)' for checking the intersection, it can be accomplish in O(n+m) time. Therefore, the algorithm detects the intersection between two given star polygons in linear time.

It is obvious that to detect the intersection as well as to determine the type of intersection between two star polygons in the worst case situation require to consider all the edges of both the star polygons at least once and therefore, our algorithm is optimal within a constant factor.

6. Final remarks

In this paper, we have shown how to determine the type of intersection between two star polygons in linear time and also prove the correctness of the algorithm. Our algorithm determines the type of intersection by exploiting the sorted angular order characteristics of a star polygon and thus it has succeeded in keeping the time complexity linear. Though our algorithm can be used to report some pairs of intersecting polygonal edges , it will not be able to report all the intersecting pairs since one edge of an intersecting pair can be a constructed edge rather than a polygonal edge. So, to obtain all intersecting pairs, additional computation is required in the hidden regions and, therefore, the complexity will be O(n+m+I) where I is the number of intersecting pairs.

Acknowledgements

I gratefully acknowledge the helpful comments and suggestions of R.K. Shyamasundar, Achintya Pal and Pijush Ghosh in production of this paper. Thanks are also due to Ameeta Gupta for developing the program on the DEC system and the referees for pertinent comments.

References

1. M.I.Shamos,Computational Geometry,Ph.D. Thesis,Yale University,1978.
2. D.Montuno and A.Fournier,"Detecting Intersection among Star Polygons",Computer Systems Research Group,University of Toronto, Tech.Rept.CSRG-146(September 1982).
3. H.Freeman and P.P.Loutrel,"An algorithm for the solution of the two dimensional hidden line problem",IEEE Trans. Electron. Comput. EC-16,No.6(December 1967),784-790.
4. D.T.Lee,"Visibility of a Simple Polygon",Computer Vision,Graphics and Image Processing,vol.22,no.2(May 1983),207-221.
5. B.Chazelle and D.P.Dobkin, "Detection is easier than computation", Proc. of 12th ACM Symposium on Theory of Computing, Los Angles (1980), 146-153.

Eliminating Cascading Rollback in Structured Databases*

Gael N. Buckley[1]
A. Silberschatz

Department of Computer Sciences
University of Texas at Austin
Austin, Texas 78712

Abstract

Transaction rollback is a significant performance liability in database systems, and will become increasingly important as the number of concurrent transactions in a database system increases. To minimize or eliminate rollback, several database systems using locking protocols require that the database be structured as a directed acyclic graph. Yannakakis (11) and Fussell (4) have given complete characterizations useful in proving that given protocol is free from transaction rollback. However, it is difficult to use these conditions to construct new protocols that are either rollback free or allow only non-cascading rollback. New protocols to minimize rollback are especially important in databases structured as arbitrary graphs, since the only published protocol for these databases can cause cascading rollback. In this paper we give a constructive characterization for a protocol to ensure either no rollback or only non-cascading rollback in arbitrarily structured graphs. We show that these conditions drastically simplify the proofs of rollback behavior of existing protocols, and use it to construct a new simple rollback protocol that operates in arbitrary databases.

1. Introduction

A database consists of a set D of database items that are required to relate to each other in certain ways, that is, that satisfy *consistency constraints*. The database system is composed of a pair (D,P), where P is the set of all user programs that may access D. A *transaction* in the system is one execution of one program in the set P. In order to insure consistency of the database, it is usual to require that each transaction when executed alone will transform a consistent state into a consistent state. Hency, any serial execution of a set of transactions perserves consistency.

---

*This research was partially supported by NSF Grant Number MCS 81-04017 and by ONR Contract N00014-80-K0987.

[1]Present Location: Dept. of Computer Science, SUNY at Stony Brook, Stony Brook, NY

If a set of transactions can execute concurrently, the database system must ensure that the outcome of a concurrent execution of a set of transactions is the same as an outcome of some serial execution of the same set of transactions. A system that ensures this is said to be *serializable* (3,9).

Almost all systems that ensure serializability divide the database into separate data items, and control access to each item by use of a concurrency control. The most common model for such a system uses a *locking protocol*. Each transaction that executes in the system must lock a data item before any access to that item, and can unlock the item only after all accesses are complete. Thus a locking protocol may be viewed as a restriction on when a transaction may lock and unlock each of the entities in set *D*. A transaction may need to be rolled back if it waits to lock entities presently held by another transaction which waits on it. When this occurs, the transaction must release its locks, undo any writes up until this point, and restart its execution at some future time. Both the bookkeeping and execution overhead becomes quite significant when the degree of concurrency increases the number of restarts necessary.

Eswaran et al. (3) have shown that for systems without restrictions on the order in which data items can be locked, it is necessary and sufficient that a transaction must lock all data items to be accessed before it can unlock any item. This is termed the *two-phase* protocol. However, if the data items in the set *D* are restricted to the locked in some predefined partial order, there are several non-two-phase protocols that allow a transaction to unlock items before all items are locked. The simplest protocol of this type is the tree (X) protocol (8), used in databases organized (logically or physically) as rooted trees. This protocol allows a transaction to lock any data item first, and lock a subsequent item if the transaction currently holds a lock on the father of the item. A transaction can unlock an item at any time.

Other non-two-phase locking protocols were proposed for database systems organized as directed acyclic graphs (see (5,6,7,10)). These protocols can provide more concurrency than the two phase protocol in some sets of transactions which lock exactly the same items in both the two phase and non-two-phase protocols. This follows from the fact that these protocols use the acyclic structure of the graph to ensure either no rollback or only simple rollback. Depending on the derivation for the graph of *D* and the constraints of the locking protocol, the non-two-phase protocol may require more locks in order to gain access to the desired data items.

Non-two-phase graph protocols that operate on arbitrary databases can no longer use a partial order on data items to eliminate transaction rollback. The only published non-two-phase locking protocol operating in arbitrary databases, the *hypergraph* protocol (12), does not guarantee that a transaction which unlocks an item will complete its computation. This implies that cascading rollbacks are possible in systems using this protocol. Cascading rollback occurs when the removal of one incomplete transaction from the system requires removal of other transactions from the system. This is possible whenthe latter transactions are allowed to access data items written by a previous transaction, but the previous transaction cannot complete. Cascading rollback can have serious performance consequences, since transactions which have completed computation using the values of unlocked data items will still need to be restarted. Yannakakis developed the hypergraph policy as a general characterization for serializability of all L policies -- the class of protocols where a transaction uses only its own past history of locks and unlocks and the structure of the database to determine which items the transaction can yet lock.

In this paper we develop general conditions for a protocol to be deadlock free or to allow only non-cascading rollback in an arbitrary database system. These conditions show that the database system operating in arbitrary databases requires more information than is needed for strict serializability. The locking protocols considered are those which only use locks to ensure serializability, and do not use any additional data structures (such as dependency graphs) to determine serializable sequences. We show a simple way to obtain this information, either statically or dynamically. We present a simple protocol (2) that uses two types of structural information about the data items:

- the directed database hypergraph D
- a static set of data items where each element in the set is the first data item locked by some transaction.

This protocol incorporates general two phase behavior, and also extends the set of recognizable histories of locking protocols used in arbitrary databases.

2. Basic Definitions

It is assumed that the set D in the form of an arbitrary directed hypergraph consisting of data items and *hyperedges*. A hypergraph can be thought of as a simple generalization of a directed graph, where each edge can have more than one item in the tail of the edge (13). A hyperedge is used to define the access relations between data items, where a data item in the head of a hyperedge can be accessed if and only if every item in the tail of the hyperedge has previously been accessed. The use of hyperedges rather than simple graph edges allows easier specification of the access restrictions imposed on the database, where a hyperedge can be considered a consistency constraint among items, a physical access path, etc. Each hyperedge has at least one data item in its tail, and exactly one data item as its head. A transaction which will access some data item A for the first time must have previously accessed all data items in the tail of some hyperedge for which A is the head. This restriction does not apply to the first data item accessed by a transaction. If each data item can be accessed independently D is to be considered a complete graph.

Definition 2-1: A *directed path* (or path) from item A to B exists if A is the single item in the tail of a hyperedge with B as its head, or a path exists from A to every item in the tail of one hyperedge with B as its head.

Definition 2-2: A set of items *separates* A from B if some item in the set is in the head of at least one hyperedge in every path from A to B.

A transaction accesses data items according to the restrictions imposed by the hyperedges defined in D, placing a lock on an item before the first access to that item, and releasing the lock after all accesses to the item are complete. In this paper we consider shared and exclusive lock modes (denoted S and X, respectively), where a transaction is restricted to reading the value of item A while A is locked in S mode, and can read or update A which A is locked in X mode. A lock request in S or X mode *conflicts* with a lock issued in X mode, and hence an X lock on item A precludes any other lock on item A. Locks in S mode do not conflict with S mode, which implies several S locks may be held simultaneously on item A. A lock or unlock instruction on item A by T_i is denoted by $LS_i(A)$, $LX_i(A)$, or $UN_i(A)$.

Definition 2-3: A history H is the chronological sequence of the lock and unlock operations of an arbitrary set of transactions $T = \{T_0, \ldots T_{N-1}\}$. Let h be an arbitrary step in H. We define $PAST(T_i,h)$ and $FUTURE(T_i,h)$ at step h as the sets of data items that T_i has locked before step h or will lock at or after step h, respectively. TR(h) is the entire prefix for all transactions in T of H at step h. Hence, TR(h) is the chronological ordering of the lock and unlock instructions issued by all transactions operation in the database up to step h. The set of data items locked is $\bigcup_{i=0}^{N-1} PAST(T_i,h)$.

Definition 2-4: We define the less than relation on a history H of a set T of transactions as follows:

$T_i < T_j \Leftrightarrow$ step h is $LX_j(A)$ or $LS_j(A)$, and TR(h) includes a lock by T_i on A in conflicting mode.

Lemma 2-1: A protocol ensures serializability if and only if all possible executions for a set of transactions produces an acyclic relation.
This is a well known lemma (3) and we do not prove it here.

If transaction T_i holds a lock on a data item A and T_j requests a lock in conflicting mode on A, then T_j must wait for T_i. Deadlock occurs when a set of transactions creates a wait for cycle. For the locking protocols discussed throughout this paper, rollback occurs when some transaction in deadlock must be removed to enable further progress of the other transactions in the same deadlock.

Definition 2-5: Cascading rollback occurs for a history H when it is determined that T_i must be rolled back at step h, and TR(h) includes the subsequence $LX_i(A)$, $UN_i(A)$, $LM_j(A)$ for some item A, where mode M is either S or X. Hence, T_j must be rolled back since it could have read a value which no longer exists.

3. Controlling Transaction Rollback

In this section we present the conditions for deadlock freedom and absence of cascading rollback for a database locking protocol. These conditions are used in this section to prove that many of the existing protocols are deadlock free or only allow non-cascading rollback. More importantly, they indicate how new locking protocols can be constructed that avoid cascading rollback and yet run in arbitrarily structured database systems.

We begin by describing how protocols may allow deadlock. Consider a pair of transactions T_i and T_j such that at step h in H, T_i must precede T_j in the serializable history, either by $T_i < T_j$ or $T_i < T_k < \ldots < T_j$. If there exists a data item $A \in FUTURE(T_i) \cap FUTURE(T_j)$, then T_j can cause rollback by locking A before T_i and creating a deadlock or a nonserializable history. If one version of a locking protocol can be proven serializable, we can additionally restrict the operation of the protocol to ensure that no deadlock occurs after a certain point. If a transaction is not allowed to be rolled back for purposes of serializability, it must be able to complete once it begins execution. Therefore it must be deadlock free at every step, and every lock obtained must be part of a legal serializable sequence. For a transaction that allows only non-cascading rollback, this point must be immediately after the transaction unlocks its first item that it has written. This stems from the fact that the transaction allows any other transaction to use the value it has created, and hence must guarantee that value will not be rolled back.

Definition 3-1: For an arbitrary set of transactions $\mathcal{T}$, we define WATCH(T_i,h) at step h in H to be the sequence of transactions $\langle T_i, T_{i2}, T_{i3}, \ldots, T_{im} \rangle$ as follows (where T_i is identical to T_{i1}):

- o For every $1 \leq j < m$, $\exists$ an item A_j such that $A_j \in$ PAST(T_{ij},h) $\cap$ {PAST(T_{ij+1},h) $\cup$ FUTURE(T_{ij+1},h)}, where A_j is locked in conflicting mode by T_{ij} and T_{ij+1}.
- o $\nexists$ an item A_m such that $A_m \in$ FUTURE(T_i,h) $\cap$ FUTURE(T_{im},h), where T_i and T_{im} lock A_m in conflicting mode.

The first condition constructs the sequence of transactions with a present or future dependency between each pair of transactions in the sequence. This is an acyclic chain. The second condition checks for a future dependency which can create a deadlock or nonserializable sequence if T_{im} obtains a lock on A_m before T_i. We now present a constructive characterization to avoid this occurrence.

Theorem 3-1: A serializable locking protocol P is free from rollback iff for all sequences WATCH(T_{i1},h) constructed for the transaction T_{i1} requesting a lock at step h, the request for T_{im} to lock A_m at step h' > h is delayed until after T_{i1} has locked and unlocked A_m.

Proof: (=>) If a serializable protocol is free from rollback, then it cannot get into deadlock, since at least one transaction in the deadlock must be rolled back. A deadlock free protocol has all transactions in WATCH(T_i,h) execute in a partial order once they conflict lock common items (to conform to the acyclic requirement of the less than relation). Consider the transactions in WATCH(T_i,h), where each item A_j is locked by T_{ij} in conflicting mode before T_{ij+1}, and hence establishes $T_{ij} < T_{ij+1}$ once T_{ij} unlocks A_j and T_{ij+1} locks it. T_{ij+1} has locked or will lock A_j, since $A_j \in$ {PAST(T_{ij+1}, h) $\cup$ FUTURE(T_{ij+1},h)}. Assume by contradiction that T_{im} locks A_m before T_{i1}. If T_{im} does not unlock it before T_{i1} issues a lock request, deadlock ensues, and the hypothesis is contradicted. If T_{im} does unlock A_m before the request, a cyclic < relation is created, and the protocol is nonserializable, which contradicts our assumption.

(<=) Assume by contradiction that protocol P rolls back some transaction. If this results from deadlock, there must be a circuit of transactions where each waits on the next. This implies that for $1 \leq j \leq m$, T_{ij} has a conflict lock on A_j which $T_{i(j+1)\bmod m}$ waits for. This contradicts our assumption that T_{i1} obtains the lock on A_m before T_{im}, and hence the theorem holds. If P rolls back a transaction due to a partial nonserializable sequence, then there must be a cycle in the dependency relation, which implies that there existed a WATCH(T_i,h) sequence where at some future time

T_{im} obtained and released a lock on A_m before T_{i1} obtained a lock, in order to construct a cycle. This contradicts our hypothesis, and hence the theorem holds.

The above result implies that in order to eliminate rollback without unnecessarily restricting concurrency, the system must perform a type of deadlock avoidance algorithm at each step h using both PAST(T_k,h) and FUTURE(T_k,h) for every transaction T_k in $\mathcal{T}$. In order to know both the past and future sequence of lock requests, the database system must know the exact read and write sequences of each transaction in $\mathcal{T}$. Since it is very rare that a database system has this much information, we restrict our attention to a set of protocols whose only information about the set of data items locked by the transactions at step h is the existing prefix TR(h) and the locations where new transactions in $\mathcal{T}$ could enter the graph. Recall that TR(h) is simply the sequence of lock and unlock instructions issued by all transactions up to step h. The database system can use the past sequence of locks to calculate the sequence of transactions that could at some time be in WATCH(T_i,h) by using the structure of the graph. Since these transactions may never actually lock the items the graph allows them access to, these hypothetical sequences may never actually occur. Since we are using only information about the locks already issued, we must assume the worst case. We term these set of transactions STOPWATCH(T_i,h).

<u>Definition</u> <u>3-2</u>: STOPWATCH(T_i,h) is the sequence of transactions $\langle T_{i1}, T_{i2}, \ldots T_{im} \rangle$ in the set $\mathcal{T}$ (where $T_{i1}=T_i$) at step h in H such that:

- o For every $1 \leq j < m$, $\exists$ an item A_j such that there is a path from some set of items in PAST(T_{ij+1},h) to A_j, $A_j \in$ PAST(T_i,h), and T_{ij+1} has locked or could issue a lock in conflicting mode with the lock on A_j issued by T_{ij}.
- o $\exists$ an item A_m such that there is a path from data items in PAST(T_i,h) to A_m and items in PAST(T_{im},h) to A_m, where $A_m \notin \{$PAST(T_i,h) $\cup$ PAST(T_{im},h)$\}$, and A_m can be locked in conflicting mode by T_i and T_{im}.

Recall that T_{ij} and T_{ij+1} lock A_j in conflicting mode if both transactions issue locks on A_j with at least one lock in X mode.

<u>Theorem</u> <u>3-2</u>: A serializable LP protocol P is deadlock free in a structured database iff for every step h in H, P requires that the set of items locked in conflicting mode by T_i with T_{im} in STOPWATCH(T_i,h') (for any step h', where h''$>$h'$>$h) separates the items presently locked or previously locked by T_{im} from A_m until step h'' when T_{i1} issues a lock on A_m.

Proof: (=>) If P is deadlock free in a structured database, let us assume by contradiction that there is some path open between PAST(T_{im},h') and A_m at step h' between h and h''. Construct a history in the following manner. Insert at step h' all locks on all data items along this path, and at the first step after h' for which A_m is unlocked, insert a lock on A_m from T_{im}. Again, if T_{im} unlocks A_m before T_i requests the lock, nonserializability ensues, and if T_{im} does not release the lock, deadlock occurs. Both conditions contradict our assumption, and the theorem holds.

(<=) Assume by contradiction that protocol P gets into deadlock. Hence, there must be some set of transactions $T_{i1}...T_{im}$ which each waits on the previous transaction. In order for T_{i1} to wait on T_{im} to release A_m, T_{im} must have locked A_m earlier. This implies that T_{im} locked a path to A_m following the constraints of the graph protocol P, which contradicts our assumption that the conflict locks on T_{i1} separated all paths between PAST(T_{im},h') and A_m for each step h' between h and h''. Hence the theorem holds.

Theorem 3-3: A serializable LP protocol P allows non-cascading rollback if at every step h after T_i issues its first unlock instruction, P requires that the set of data items locked by T_i in conflicting mode with each T_{im} in every STOPWATCH(T_i,h) separates the items presently locked by T_{im} from A_m.

Proof: Assume by contradiction that there is some transaction which causes cascading rollback, and hence another transaction T_i which unlocked some items is in deadlock or in a nonserializable sequence and must be rolled back. From theorem 3-2, this deadlock must occur before T_i separates PAST(T_{im},h) from A_m, in order for T_{im} to lock A_m first and precipitate the deadlock. Hence, T_i must unlock an item before this separation occurs, which contradicts our assumption, and the theorem holds.

This theorem can be used to prove deadlock freedom of several classes of protocols. We say that a hypergraph is deadlock free for three vertices A, B, and C in a rooted biconnected component that does not contain cycles, if there is a path from A to B and from B to C, then any path from A to C includes B. Most directed acyclic graph protocols operate in such a hypergraph. An L policy (12) is a policy where the set of locks in X mode held by transaction T_i separates in the underlying undirected hypergraph every path between the items it has unlocked and the items T_i has yet to lock.

Corollary 3-1: Every L policy using X locks is deadlock free if it operates in a deadlock free hypergraph.

Proof: From theorem 3-2, T_i must separate T_{im} from A_m until T_i locks A_m. In a deadlock free hypergraph, all transactions in STOPWATCH(T_i,h) must begin above the data items presently locked by T_i, in order to have a path to the common data item to be locked. Hence, since all paths to A_m go through the items locked by T_i, by construction of the deadlock free hypergraph, T_i separates all STOPWATCH(T_i,h) from A_m, and hence the protocol is deadlock free.

Corollary 3-2: Any L policy using X and S locks and operating in a deadlock free hypergraph is deadlock free if it requires that the first lock issued by T_i (which is at step h) is in conflicting mode with any T_{im} in STOPWATCH(T_i,h'), where h' is any step between h and the last instruction of T_i, inclusive.

Proof: From theorem 3-2, T_i must separate T_{im} from A_m. It does so with its first lock, since by construction of the graph, all paths to A_m beginning above this data item contain the data item. If this lock is ever released, any L policy has a set of X locks separating the unlocked item from A_m, which also separated T_{im} from A_m, and the corollary holds.

Corollary 3-2 covers several quite disparate protocols using S and X locks. Two such protocols are the guard protocol (6) using X and S locks with the restriction tha the first lock is in X mode, and the guard protocol which separates transactions into two sets, those which issue only X locks, and those which issue only S locks.

However, the most interesting use of these conditions is in developing new protocols that can be used in arbitrary databases and still allow only non-cascading rollback. In the following section we summarize a protocol which stems directly from the conditions presented above, and has the distinction of being the first simple rollback protocol which takes advantage of the additional concurrency allowed in arbitrary graphs. The detailed protocol and proofs are presented in (2).

4. The Static Entry Point Protocol

In order to efficiently use the general characterization in arbitrary graphs, we need to devise a mechanism which will allow a transaction T_i to statically determine a new set that includes all possible members of any sequence STOPWATCH(T_i,h) at step h before the transaction begins executing. This was not necessary when operating in directed acyclic graphs, since the constraints of the serializable protocols operating in the graphs determined in what sections of the graph $T_{im} \in$ STOPWATCH(T_i,h) could occupy. This is not possible using arbitrary graphs, as is illustrated below.

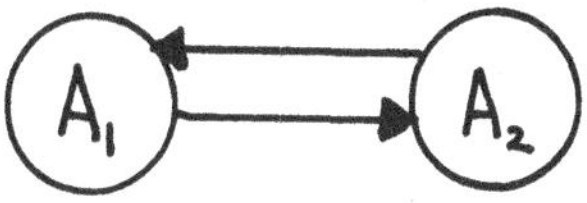

Figure 4-1

Consider the database graph of figure 4-1, where transactions T_1 and T_2 will each lock items A_1 and A_2. If T_1 locks A_1 in X mode and then T_2 locks A_2 in X mode, T_1 cannot release its lock on A, since there is a path from A_2 to A_1.

One efficient way requires that the protocol assumes that the database system has pre-analyzed the set of transactions to determine which data item each transaction locks first when it enters the database system. This concept of pre-analyzing the behavior of transactions has been done before, notably in the distributed database system of SDD-1(1). The first data item locked is denoted E(T_i). The set of all entry points for all transactions is denoted ENTRY(*D*). We assume this set is static for a particular database system and is known in advance.

Wehn transaction T_i enters the database system at data item E(T_i), STOPW(T_i) is statically defined on a set of entry points rather than a set of transactions, and is the set of entry points E(T_{i1})...E(T_{im}) such that:

- for all $1 \leq j < m$ there is a path from E(T_{ij}) and E(T_{ij+1}) to some item A_j, and a path from E(T_{im}) and E(T_{i1}) to some item A_i (where $T_{i1} = T_i$).

Using the definitions given above, we employ the general characterization to derive the general entry point protocol. After a transaction T_i has locked E(T_i) as its first data item, each subsequent lock must conform to the following rules:

1. If a transaction T_i has not unlocked any data items, it can lock item $A_j \neq$ E(T_i) if and only if all vertices in the tail of one hyperedge with A_j as its head are locked by T_i.
2. If T_i has unlocked any data items, it can lock data item $A_j \neq$ E(T_i) if and only if:
   a. T_i holds a lock on all items in the tail of one hyperedge with A_j as its head,
   b. the set of items presently locked in exclusive mode by T_i separates A_j from the unlocked items of T_i and from T_k STOPW(T_i).

Since STOPW(T_i) is defined using only the statically known entry points and the structure of the graph, STOPW(T_i) for every entry point may be calculated at system initialization, and does not add any computational overhead for system execution.

When a transaction has not unlocked any data items, it is said to be operating in 2P mode. Once T_i issues a new lock request after it unlocks a data item, it is said to be operating in N2P mode. Notice that all transactions behave as 2P transactions as long as they do not lock any data items after an item has been unlocked. It should be obvious that any 2P transaction follows Eswaran's two-phase protocol where the precedence relations defined by hyperedges must be followed by every transaction operating in the database. This results from the fact that the chronological access sequenc of the transactions operating in 2P mode is the same access sequence as the original user program operating under the precedence constraints.

We present two simple examples to show how the general entry protocol operates. The first is a simple tree protocol example and the second shows how the use of entry points allows serializable sequences not allowed in the hypergraph protocol.

Example 4-1: Consider the database graph of Figure 4-2 with ENTRY(D)=$\{A_1,A_2,A_3\}$, STOPW(T_1) = $\emptyset$, and STOPW(T_2) = A_1. The partial history of three transactions T_1, T_2, and T_3 is as follows.

T_1	T_2	T_3
		LX(A_3)
LX(A_1)		
LX(A_2)		
U(A_1)		
	LX(A_1)	
	LX(A_2)	
		UN(A_3)
LX(A_3)		

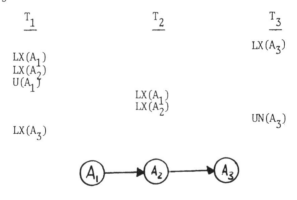

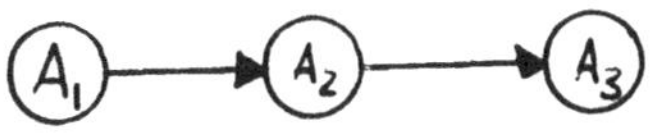

Figure 4-2

This is an example of the simple tree protocol using X locks. Having transactions run in N2P mode provides additional concurrency at no expense of extra locks or the possibility of cascading rollback in the system.

Example 4-2: Consider the database graph of figure 4-3, where entry (D) = (A_1,A_2), STOPW(T_1) = A_1 and STOPW(T_2) = A_2. The partial history of transactions T_1 and T_2 is as follows:

T_1	T_2
$LX(A_2)$	
$LX(A_3)$	
$U(A_2)$	
	$LX(A_1)$
	$LX(A_2)$
$LX(A_4)$	

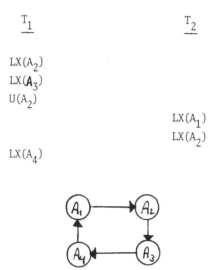

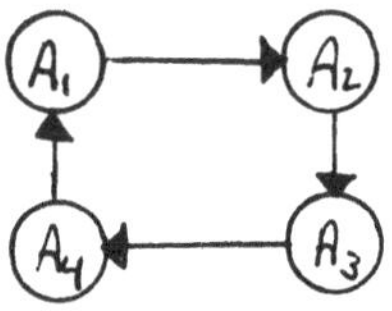

Figure 4-2

Notice that T_1 could not lock A_4 under the only other non-two-phase protocol operating in arbitrary graphs, the hypergraph protocol, since it could not be assured that some transaction starting at A_4 could lock A_1, exit, and produce a nonserializable history. The use of entry points allows the static analysis of the database graph to produce information usable during the execution of transactions.

5. Summary

In this paper we have presented very simple constructive conditions which can be used to prove protocols deadlock free or only allowing simple rollback for databases structured as hypergraphs. These protocols are increasingly important as the number of concurrent transactions operating in a database increases. The conditions given simplify existing proofs of deadlock freedom for published protocols, and shed new light on the amount of information needed by a database to avoid the expense of cascading rollback. The utility of these conditions is illustrated by the presentation of the first graph protocol operating in arbitrary databases which does not admit the possibility of cascading rollback.

REFERENCES

1. Bernstein, P., Shipman, D., and Rothnie Jr, J. "Concurrency Control in a System for Distributed Databases (SDD-1)." *ACM Transactions on Database Systems 5*, 1 (March 1980), 18-51.

2. Buckley, G. and Silberschatz, A. "Beyond Two Phase Locking." *Journal of the ACM* ((to appear)).

3. Eswaran, K.P., Gray, J.N., Lorie, R.A., Traiger, I.L. "The Notions of Consistency and Predicate Locks in a Database System." *Communications of the ACM 10*, 11 (Nov. 1976), 624-723.

4. Fussell, D.S., Kedem, Z., Silberschatz, A. A Theory of Correct Protocols for Database Systems. Proc. Seventh International Conference on Very Large Data Bases, Sept., 1981.

5. Kedem, Z., Silberschatz, A. Controlling Concurrency Using Locking Protocols. Proc. Twentieth IEEE Symposium on Foundations of Computer Science, IEEE, Oct., 1979, pp. 274-285.

6. Kedem, Z., Silberschatz, A. Non-Two-Phase Locking Protocols with Shared and Exclusive Locks. Proc. Sixth International Conference on Principles of Database Systems, March, 1982.

7. Mohan, C., Fussell, D., Silberschatz, A. Compatibility and Commutativity in Non-Two-Phase Locking Protocols. Proc. Conf. on Principles of Database Systems, March, 1982.

8. Silberschatz, A., Kedem, Z. "Consistency in Hierarchical Database Systems." *Journal of the ACM 27*, 1 (Jan. 1980), 72-80.

9. Stearns, R., Lewis, P.M., Rosenkrantz, D.J. Concurrency Control for Database Systems, Proc. Twelfth IEEE Symp. on Foundations of Computer Science, Oct., 1976, pp. 19-32.

10. Yannakakis, M., Papadimitriou, C., Kung, H.T. Locking Protocols: Safety and Freedom from Deadlocks. Proc. Twentieth IEEE Symp. on Foundations of Computer Science, Oct., 1979, pp. 286-297.

11. Yannakakis, M. "Deadlock in Locking Policies," *Siam Journal of Computing 11*, 2 (May 1982), 391-408.

12. Yannakakis, M. "A Theory of Saft Locking Policies in Database Systems." *Journal of the ACM 29*, 4 (July 1982), 718-740.

13. Berge, C. Graphs & Hypergraphs, North Holland, Amsterdam.

RECOGNITION AND TOP-DOWN GENERATION OF β-ACYCLIC DATABASE SCHEMES

V.S. Lakshmanan, N. Chandrasekaran, and C.E. Veni Madhavan
School of Automation
Indian Institute of Science
Bangalore 560 012
INDIA

ABSTRACT

Database schemes can be viewed as hypergraphs with individual relation schemes corresponding to the edges of a hypergraph. Under this setting, a new class of "acyclic" database schemes was recently introduced and was shown to have a claim to a number of desirable properties. However, unlike the case of ordinary undirected graphs, there are several unequivalent notions of acyclicity of hypergraphs. Of special interest among these are α-, β-, and γ-, degrees of acyclicity, each characterizing an equivalence class of desirable properties for database schemes, represented as hypergraphs. In this paper, two complementary approaches to designing β-acyclic database schemes have been presented. For the first part, a new notion called "independent cycle" is introduced. Based on this, a criterion for β-acyclicity is developed and is shown equivalent to the existing definitions of β-acyclicity. From this and the concept of the dual of a hypergraph, an efficient algorithm for testing β-acyclicity is developed. As for the second part, a procedure is evolved for top-down generation of β-acyclic schemes and its correctness is established. Finally, extensions and applications of ideas are described.

1. Introduction

The relational model for organizing data was first introduced by Codd [8]. In this model, a database scheme may be thought of as a collection of relation schemes which are simply tabular formats for storing data. More formally, let U be a finite set of symbols called <u>attributes</u>. U is known as the <u>universal relation scheme</u>. Any subset R of U is a <u>relation scheme</u>. A <u>database scheme D</u> is a set of relation schemes. For complete details on relational databases the reader is referred to [17].

As a natural offshoot of the pioneering work by Beeri and Vardi [5] which introduced and treated the notions of "stems" and "branches" of relation schemes, a simple, yet powerful, class of database schemes called "acyclic" was introduced by Beeri et al [3]. The literature records many advantages of acyclic database schemes [4,12], chiefly in the area of dependency theory [4] and query processing [4,13]. Of prime concern to us in the present context is the desirable property that an acyclic join dependency is equivalent to a set of conflict-free multivalued dependencies [15,16], as established in [4]. There it is also shown that many NP-complete problems for general database schemes have efficient (polynomial) solutions for acyclic schemes. Further, Fagin et al [12] have conjectured that acyclic schemes are general enough to encompass all "real world" situations.

Fagin [11] has argued that there are even "nicer" properties for database schemes not obeyed by the so called acyclic schemes. Corresponding to various classes of such desirable properties he has defined three degrees of acyclicity - α-, β-, and γ-, of the underlying hypergraphs, where α-acyclicity is the same as the type of acyclicity originally studied [4]. He has also shown that there is a linear ordering of the strengths of the three types of acyclicity: γ-acyclicity $\Rightarrow$ β-acyclicity $\Rightarrow$ α-acyclicity. Though each of the three notions of acyclicity is a generalization of the concept of acyclicity (in ordinary undirected graphs) to hypergraphs, we consider β-acyclicity to be the most intuitively appealing. For, β-acyclicity is the least restrictive notion of hypergraph acyclicity that has the hereditary property, analogously to the notion of acyclicity of ordinary graphs. This coupled with the fact that Fagin [11] has identified a number of even nicer properties for β-acyclic schemes, urged us to consider the problem of attempting to design β-acyclic database schemes whenever possible. It should be realized that there are indeed situations warranting the use of β-cyclic, albeit α-acyclic, database schemes, as also situations requiring γ-cyclic, but β-acyclic, database schemes. For an example situation the reader is referred to [11].

In this paper, we have approached this design issue from two complementary angles. For the first part, we introduce the notion of an "independent cycle" and use that to develop a criterion for a database scheme to be β-acyclic. We give a formal proof of its equivalence with existing definitions of β-acyclicity [11]. Using this criterion and the well-known concept of the dual of a hypergraph [6], we develop an efficient algorithm for testing β-acyclicity of hypergraphs. Batini et al [2] have discussed the problem of top-down generation of various subclasses of α-acyclic schemes while D'Atri and Moscarini [10] have studied the problem of top-down generation of γ-acyclic schemes. Our second approach is concerned with building a mechanism for top-down generation of β-acyclic schemes. Specifically, we describe a procedure called <u>B</u>inary <u>D</u>ecomposition <u>W</u>ithout <u>B</u>reaking (BDWB) and prove that it generates β-acyclic database schemes.

The study of β-acyclic schemes in the light of the concept of independent cycles has also lent us insight into the structure of α-acyclic schemes. We have been able to structurally characterize α-acyclic schemes which we have reported in [14]. An important consequence of this is that "securing α-acyclicity" to avoid undesirable answers to certain types of queries on the cyclic schemes which resulted during design, is easy to come by now on a more generalized basis than the methods given in [7]. This matter and its impact on design latitude are also discussed in [14].

Section 2 introduces the preliminaries on databases and hypergraphs. Section 3 deals with the notions of α- and β-acyclicity of hypergraphs. In Section 4, we present our novel idea of an "independent cycle", develop a criterion for β-acyclicity based on it, and formally prove its equivalence with existing definitions of β-acyclicity. Section 5 illustrates with simple examples how an independent cycle differs from other notions of cycles in the literature. Section 6 describes an efficient algorithm for testing β-acyclicity. Section 7 is given over to a discussion of the top-down generation problem of β-acyclic schemes. It also gives a systematic procedure for accomplishing this and formally proves its correctness. Applications and extensions are mentioned in appropriate places. Finally, Section 8 contains conclusions.

2. Preliminaries

In this section we collect together all the relevant notions and terminology.

2.1. Relational Databases

Let U be a finite set of distinct symbols called <u>attributes</u> (or <u>column names</u>). U will be called the <u>universal relation scheme</u> [17]. Any subset X of U is a <u>relation scheme</u>. An X-<u>tuple</u> is a mapping over X, associating a value with each attribute in X [1]. A <u>relation</u> r over X is a finite set of X-tuples. A <u>database scheme</u> $D = \{R_1, R_2, \ldots, R_k\}$ is a finite set of relation schemes R_i, i=1,2,..., k. Finally, a <u>database</u> <u>d</u> <u>with</u> <u>database</u> <u>scheme</u> <u>D</u> is a set $\underline{d} = \{r_1, r_2, \ldots, r_k\}$ of relations each over a corresponding relation scheme in $\underline{D}$.

2.2. Hypergraphs

Hypergraphs are a natural generalization of ordinary undirected graphs [6]. A hypergraph H is a couple $H = (X, \underline{E})$ where $X = \{x_1, x_2, \ldots, x_n\}$ is a finite set of elements called vertices while $\underline{E} = \{E_1, E_2, \ldots, E_m\}$ is a set of subsets of X called edges. The reduction of a hypergraph $(X, \underline{E})$ is the hypergraph $(X, \underline{E}')$ obtained by deleting from $\underline{E}$ each edge that is a subset of some other edge. A hypergraph is reduced if it equals its reduction. Since many properties of hypergraphs are unaffected by reduction [4] we shall henceforth assume that a hypergraph is reduced. Call two sets incomparable if neither is a subset of the other.

Two vertices in X are adjacent if there is an edge in $\underline{E}$ containing them both. Two edges in $\underline{E}$ are adjacent if their intersection is non-empty. A path from vertex x_i to vertex x_j is a sequence $(E_1, E_2, \ldots, E_k)$ of edges in $\underline{E}(k \geqslant 1)$, such that (i) $x_i \in E_1$; (ii) $x_j \in E_k$; (iii) E_i and E_{i+1}, $1 \leqslant i < k$, are adjacent. Such a sequence may also be viewed as an edge path from E_1 to E_k. Two vertices (edges) are connected if there is a path from one to the other. The connected components of a hypergraph are its maximal connected sets of edges. The sub-hypergraph of $H = (X, \underline{E})$ generated by $A \subseteq X$ is defined to be the hypergraph $(A, \underline{E}_A)$ where $\underline{E}_A = \{E_i \cap A : E_i \in \underline{E} \text{ and } E_i \cap A \neq \emptyset\}$. This has also been called node generated set of partial edges, generated by $A \subseteq X$ [4]. The partial hypergraph of H generated by $\underline{F} \subseteq \underline{E}$ is the hypergraph $(X_{\underline{F}}, \underline{E})$ where $X_{\underline{F}} = \bigcup_{(E_i \in \underline{F})} (E_i)$. To avoid confusion, we note that this has been referred to as a subhypergraph in [11]. For other definitions on hypergraphs pertaining to α-acyclicity the reader is referred to [4,11].

To each hypergraph $H = (X; E_1, E_2, \ldots, E_m)$ there corresponds a dual hypergraph $H^* = (E; X_1, X_2, \ldots, X_n)$ where $X = \{x_1, x_2, \ldots, x_n\}$ and $E = \{e_1, e_2, \ldots, e_m\}$, such that $X_j = \{e_i : i \leqslant m, x_j \in E_i\}$, $j = 1, 2, \ldots, n$. One can readily see that the roles of vertices and edges are interchanged between H and H^*. Note that $X_j \neq \emptyset$, $\bigcup_j (X_j) = E$, indeed making H^* a hypergraph, and that H is the dual of H^*. It can be seen that properties true of vertices in a hypergraph carry over to the edges of its dual and conversely.

2.3. Database Schemes as Hypergraphs

Database schemes can be modeled as hypergraphs where attributes are identified with vertices and relation schemes with edges, of the representing hypergraph. In this formalism we notate a hypergraph as $H = (N, \underline{E})$ where N is the set of nodes (vertices) and $\underline{E}$ is the set of edges. We will be using the pairs of terms nodes, edges; and attributes, relation schemes interchangeably. Thus, we will be freely associating hypergraph properties with attributes and relation schemes.

3. On the Notions of Hypergraph Acyclicity

Let us briefly consider α-acyclicity first. Beeri et al [4] have proved that α-acyclicity of hypergraphs is equivalent to each of many desirable properties for the database schemes they represent. We give only one of the several equivalent definitions of α-acyclicity given by them. [4,11] should be consulted for an explanation of the pertinent terminology.

Definition 3.1.

A hypergraph is α-acyclic, if every non-trivial, connected, node generated set of partial edges has an articulation set.

Fagin [11] introduced a stronger notion of acyclicity called β-acyclicity. He has given five equivalent definitions of β-acyclicity three of which will occupy us in the rest of this section. Before that, however, we need a few definitions. A weak β-cycle in a hypergraph is a sequence $(E_1, x_1, E_2, x_2, \ldots, E_k, x_k, E_{k+1})$ where

1) $x_1, x_2, \ldots, x_k$ are distinct nodes;
2) $E_1, E_2, \ldots, E_k$ are distinct edges, with $E_{k+1} = E_1$;
3) $k \geqslant 3$;
4) $x_i \in E_i, E_{i+1}$; $x_i \notin E_j$, $j \neq i$ or $i + 1$; for all $i = 1,2,\ldots, k$.

A Graham cycle in a hypergraph is a sequence $(E_1, E_2, \ldots, E_k, E_{k+1})$ of edges such that

1) $E_1, E_2, \ldots, E_k$ are distinct edges, with $E_{k+1} = E_1$;
2) $k \geqslant 3$;
3) Let $S_i = E_i \cap E_{i+1}$, $i = 1,2, \ldots, m$; then S_i are non-empty and for all $i \neq j$, S_i and S_j are incomparable.

Definition 3.2.

A hypergraph H is β-acyclic if no partial hypergraph of H (including itself) is α-cyclic.

Definition 3.3.

A hypergraph H is β-acyclic if it contains no weak β-cycle.

Definition 3.4.

A hypergraph H is *β-acyclic* if it contains no Graham cycle.

With this introduction, we set about our main task.

4. An Alternative Criterion for β-acyclicity

We present a few additional definitions. Then we introduce the notion of an "independent cycle", prove a few useful lemmas and develop the alternative criterion for β-acyclicity.

In a hypergraph two adjacent edges are said to be *neighbors* of each other. Two neighbors E_2 and E_3 of an edge E_1 are called *independent neighbors* of E_1 if the set intersections $E_1 \cap E_2$ and $E_1 \cap E_3$ are incomparable. Note that "independence" is meaningful only with two (or more) neighbors. In particular, an edge having one or no neighbor (trivially) has no independent neighbors.

Definition 4.1.

A *set* $\underline{F}$ of edges from $\underline{E}$ is said to constitute an *independent cycle* if $\underline{F}$ is connected and each edge in $\underline{F}$ has (at least two) independent neighbors belonging to $\underline{F}$.

It should be emphasized here that our notion of a "cycle" is markedly different from other hypergraph cycles reported in the literature. First of all, an independent cycle is a *set* rather than a *sequence*, (of edges), which the other cycles are. In general, an independent cycle cannot be attributed any ordering, as required of sequences (in the usual sense of a "cycle"), among its edges. The next section makes a comparison of the various types of hypergraph cycles and illustrates the differences with examples. We shall state and prove a few lemmas prior to considering the alternative criterion for β-acyclicity.

Lemma 4.1.

Every weak β-cycle is an independent cycle.

Proof:

Obvious from the definitions. □

Call a property π of hypergraphs *hereditary* if π is true of a hypergraph H implies that π is true of all partial hypergraphs of H.

Lemma 4.2.

β-acyclicity is a hereditary property of hypergraphs.

Proof:

An immediate consequence of Definition 3.2. □

Lemma 4.2 implies that if some partial hypergraph of a given hypergraph H is β-cyclic then H is β-cyclic as well. A Graham cycle is said to be of the shortest length if it involves the least possible number of edges, i.e., no subset of the set of edges would (for any sequence) form a Graham cycle.

Lemma 4.3.

Every Graham cycle of the shortest length is a weak β-cycle.

Proof:

Let $(E_1, E_2, \ldots, E_k, E_{k+1})$, $E_{k+1} = E_1$, be a Graham cycle of the shortest length. From the definition, it is readily possible to choose distinct vertices $x_1, x_2, \ldots, x_k$ such that x_1 belongs to E_1 and E_2 but not E_3, x_2 to E_2 and E_3 but not E_4, and so on. It only remains to show that the choice can ensure that $x_1 \notin E_j$, $3 < j < k$, and so on cyclically. Suppose on the contrary that such a choice is not possible. Thus $x_1 \in E_j$, for some j, $3 < j < k$, no matter what the choice is. Let j be the minimal such index. In this case, however, $(E_2, E_3, \ldots, E_j, E'_{j+1})$ where $E'_{j+1} = E_2$ is a shorter Graham cycle, a contradiction. Hence, $(E_1, x_1, \ldots, E_k, x_k, E_{k+1})$ is indeed a weak β-cycle. □

Our next lemma is concerned with the concept of the dual of a hypergraph and its relevance will become clear when we actually describe our efficient algorithm for testing β-acyclicity.

Lemma 4.4.

A hypergraph is β-acyclic if and only if its dual hypergraph is β-acyclic.

Proof:

Let $H = (X; E_1, E_2, \ldots, E_m)$ be a hypergraph and $H^* = (E; X_1, X_2, \ldots, X_n)$ its dual, where $X = \{x_1, x_2, \ldots, x_n\}$ and $E = \{e_1, e_2, \ldots, e_m\}$. It is more convenient to prove that β-cyclicity of H implies β-cyclicity of H^* and vice versa.

(==>):

Suppose that H is β-cyclic. Then it contains a weak β-cycle, say $(E_1, x_1, \ldots, E_k, x_k, E_{k+1})$, $E_{k+1} = E_1$. (This numbering assumes no loss of generality). Since $x_i \in E_j$ in H translates into $e_j \in X_i$ in H^*, $x_i \in E_i \cap E_{i+1}$ and $x_{i+1} \in E_{i+1} \cap E_{i+2}$ exclusively in H, together imply that $e_{i+1} \in X_i \cap X_{i+1}$ exclusively, in H^*. By using this fact cyclically around $i = 1,2, \ldots, k$, we can readily conclude that $(X_1, e_2, X_2, e_3, \ldots, e_k, X_k, e_1, X_{k+1})$ where $X_{k+1} = X_1$, is a weak β-cycle in H^*, making H^* β-cyclic.

(<==):

Follows identical lines to the first part, except that we start from a weak β-cycle in H^* and identify a corresponding weak β-cycle in H. □

Whereas β-acyclicity is preserved between a pair of dual hypergraphs, it is easy to construct examples where H is α-acyclic and H^* is α-cyclic. The complexity of testing β-acyclicity of a hypergraph H is a function of the number of edges in H. Thus, if the dual hypergraph contains fewer edges, we stand to gain by exploring H^* instead of H for β-acyclicity, since as Lemma 4.4 points out, this property is preserved by the notion of duality. We now introduce some notation used in our proof of the next lemma, the most important one that is of direct use in the proof of our main theorem in this section. Consider an index set $I = \{1,2, \ldots, k\}$, $k \geq 3$. Define the following operations on I:

(1) $i \oplus j = (i+j) \bmod k$, if $(i+j) \bmod k \neq 0$;
$\quad = k$, otherwise,

(2) $i \ominus j = (i-j) \bmod k$, if $(i-j) \bmod k \neq 0$;
$\quad = k$, otherwise,

for $i,j \in I$.

An <u>I-sequence</u> is a sequence $(E_1, E_2, \ldots, E_k)$ of $k \geq 3$ distinct edges satisfying:

(1) Let $S_i = E_i \cap E_{i \oplus 1}$, $i = 1,2, \ldots, k$; then S_i are non-empty;

(2) S_i and $S_{i \oplus 1}$ are incomparable, $i = 1,2, \ldots, k$. Note that every I-sequence is an independent cycle when viewed as a set.

Define $c_{ij} = \min \{j \ominus i,\ i \ominus (j \ominus 1)\}$,
and $I_i = \{j \in I : S_i \subseteq E_j\}$, $i,j \in I$.

Now let $d_i = \min\limits_{(j \in I_i)} \{c_{ij}\}$, if $I_i \neq \emptyset$;
$\quad =$ undefined, otherwise.

By definition, if d_i is defined, then $d_i = c_{ij_i}$ for some $j_i \in I_i$. Let $d_i^+ = j_i \ominus i$ and $d_i^- = i \ominus (j_i \ominus 1)$. Then $d_i = \min \{d_i^+, d_i^-\}$.

Note that $j_i \in \{i \oplus 3, i \oplus 4, \ldots, i \ominus 2\}$ in view of property (2) of an I-sequence. Also, $(j_i \ominus i) + (i \ominus (j_i \ominus 1)) = k+1$. From these it follows that $3 \leqslant d_i \leqslant \lfloor k/2 \rfloor$, a result which will be useful in the proof of the next lemma. Finally, let $d_{i'} = \min_i \{d_i\}$ where i ranges over values in I_i for which d_i is defined.

Lemma 4.5.

For an I-sequence of edges $(E_1, E_2, \ldots, E_k)$, $(k \geqslant 3)$, if $d_{i'}$ is defined then if $d_{i'} = d^+_{i'}$ then $A = \{E_{i' \oplus 1}, E_{i' \oplus 2}, \ldots, E_{j_{i'}}\}$ is an independent cycle; if $d_{i'} = d^-_{i'}$, then $B = \{E_{j_{i'}}, E_{j_{i'} \oplus 1}, \ldots, E_{i'}\}$ is an independent cycle.

Proof:

Assume that $d_{i'}$ is defined. Observe that since $j_{i'} \in \{i' \oplus 3, i' \oplus 4, \ldots, i' \ominus 2\}$, $|A| = (j_{i'} \ominus i') \geqslant 3$; and $|B| = i' \ominus (j_{i'} \ominus i') \geqslant 3$.

Case (a) $d_{i'} = d^+_{i'} = j_{i'} \ominus i'$

At first, observe that $E_{i' \oplus 2}, \ldots, E_{j_{i'} \ominus 1} \in A$ have independent neighbors in A. To prove A to be an independent cycle, therefore we need only show that $E_{i' \oplus 1}$ and $E_{j_{i'}}$ have independent neighbors in A.

1) First let us attend to $E_{i' \oplus 1}$.

Since $S_{i'} \subseteq E_{i' \oplus 1}$ and $S_{i'} \subseteq E_{j_{i'}}$, $S_{i'} \subseteq E_{i' \oplus 1} \cap E_{j_{i'}}$.

We compare $E_{j_{i'}} \cap E_{i' \oplus 1}$ and $E_{i' \oplus 1} \cap E_{i' \oplus 2}$.

If $E_{j_{i'}} \cap E_{i' \oplus 1} \subseteq E_{i' \oplus 1} \cap E_{i' \oplus 2}$ then $S_{i'} \subseteq S_{i' \oplus 1}$ which is impossible with an I-sequence.

If $E_{i' \oplus 1} \cap E_{i' \oplus 2} \subseteq E_{j_{i'}} \cap E_{i' \oplus 1}$, then $S_{i' \oplus 1} \subseteq E_{j_{i'}}$. If $j_{i'} = i' \oplus 3$, this is a direct contradiction for an I-sequence. If $j_{i'} \neq i' \oplus 3$, then $d_{i' \oplus 1} \leqslant j_{i'} \ominus (i' \oplus 1)$. Since, $3 \leqslant d_{i'} \leqslant \lfloor k/2 \rfloor$, this implies that $d_{i' \oplus 1} < d_{i'}$, a contradiction to the minimality assumption on $d_{i'}$; thus, $E_{i' \oplus 1} \cap E_{i' \oplus 2}$ and $E_{i' \oplus 1} \cap E_{j_{i'}}$ are incomparable and hence $E_{i' \oplus 1}$ has two independent neighbors in A.

2) We turn to $E_{j_{i'}}$ now and compare $E_{i' \oplus 1} \cap E_{j_{i'}}$ and $E_{j_{i'}} \cap E_{j_{i'} \ominus 1}$.

If $E_{j_{i'}} \cap E_{i' \oplus 1} \subseteq E_{j_{i'}} \cap E_{j_{i'} \ominus 1}$, then $S_{i'} \subseteq E_{j_{i'} \ominus 1}$ which contradicts with the definition of $d_{i'}$.

If $E_{j_{i'} \ominus 1} \cap E_{j_{i'}} \subseteq E_{j_{i'}} \cap E_{i' \oplus 1}$, then $S_{j_{i'} \ominus 1} \subseteq E_{i' \oplus 1}$.

Thus, $d_{j_{i'}\ominus 1} \leqslant (j_{i'} \ominus 1) \ominus (i' \oplus 1 \ominus 1)$
$= (j_{i'} \ominus 1) \ominus i'$.

Since, $3 \leqslant d_{i'} \leqslant \lfloor k/2 \rfloor$, $d_{j_{i'}\ominus 1} < d_{i'}$, contradicting the assumption on the minimality of $d_{i'}$. Thus, $E_{j_{i'}}$ also has two independent neighbors in A. Hence A is an independent cycle.

<u>Case (b)</u> $d_{i'} = d^-_{i'} = i' \ominus (j_{i'} \ominus 1)$.

That B is an independent cycle follows from arguments similar to those for case (a).

Since case (a) and case (b) were handled independently of each other, when $d_{i'} = d^+_{i'} = d^-_{i'}$, both A and B are independent cycles. □

We say that a set $\{E_1, E_2, \ldots, E_k\}$ of $k \geqslant 3$ edges <u>constitutes a weak β-cycle</u> if for some sequence $(E_{i_1}, E_{i_2}, \ldots, E_{i_k})$, where $1 \leqslant i_1, \ldots, i_k \leqslant k$, there is a choice of distinct vertices $x_{i_1}, x_{i_2}, \ldots, x_{i_k}$ such that $(E_{i_1}, x_{i_1}, \ldots, E_{i_k}, x_{i_k}, E_{i_{k+1}})$ where $E_{i_{k+1}} = E_{i_1}$, is a weak β-cycle.

<u>Theorem 4.6.</u>

A hypergraph H is β-cyclic if and only if it contains an independent cycle.

<u>Proof</u>:

(==>):

Assume that H is β-cyclic. Then by Definition 4.4 it contains a weak β-cycle, which by Lemma 4.1 is an independent cycle.

(<==):

We prove this part by induction. Let H contain an independent cycle.

<u>Basis</u>

Let H have only three edges, say E_1, E_2, E_3. Since $\{E_1, E_2, E_3\}$ is an independent cycle, E_2 and E_3 are independent neighbors of E_1 and so on cyclically. Thus, $E_1 \cap E_2$, $E_2 \cap E_3$, and $E_1 \cap E_3$ are pairwise incomparable enabling a choice of distinct nodes x_1, x_2, x_3, such that

$(E_1, x_1, E_2, x_2, E_3, x_3, E_1)$ is a weak β-cycle. Thus H is β-cyclic.

Induction

Assume that for any hypergraph with fewer than k edges, if it contains an independent cycle then it is β-cyclic. Let H be a hypergraph with k edges $E_1, E_2, \ldots, E_k$. Two cases arise.

Case (i)

The independent cycle involves fewer than k edges. Clearly, the partial hypergraph generated by the edges in the independent cycle is β-cyclic by inductive hypothesis. By Lemma 4.2 H is also β-cyclic.

Case (ii)

The independent cycle involves all the k edges in H. Two subcases arise.

Subcase (ii) (a)

The independent cycle has a proper subset which is also an independent cycle. An argument similar to that for case (i) would show that H is β-cyclic.

Subcase (ii) (b)

The independent cycle has no proper subset of edges which is also an independent cycle. In this case we shall show that there is a sequence involving all the edges such that it is a weak β-cycle. For this purpose execute a "traversal" of edges as follows. Start at an arbitrary edge say E_{i_1} and "visit" it. Visit one of its independent neighbors and follow it recursively upto (k+1) stages such that the sequence of edges traced by the traversal say, $(E_{i_1}, E_{i_2}, \ldots, E_{i_k}, E_{i_{(k+1)}})$ satisfies the following properties. $E_{i_{j-1}}$ and $E_{i_{j+1}}$ are distinct independent neighbors of E_{i_j}, $j = 2, \ldots, k$. We now claim that (1) $E_{i_1}, \ldots, E_{i_k}$ are distinct edges and (2) $E_{i_{k+1}} = E_{i_1}$. For (1) let $j < k+1$ be the first occurrence of a repetition such that $E_{i_{j'}} = E_{i_j}$ (say), where $E_{i_{j'}}$ precedes E_{i_j} in the traversal sequence. By the method of traversal, $j' < j - 2$. However, the method also implies that $\{E_{i_{j'}}, E_{i_{j'+1}}, \ldots, E_{i_j}\}$ is an independent cycle, which contradicts the assumption for case (ii) (b). For (2) let $E_{i_{k+1}} = E_{i_j}$, for some $j \neq 1$. Note that $j < k - 1$. However, $\{E_{i_j}, E_{i_{j+1}}, \ldots, E_{i_k}\}$ would then be an independent cycle.

In view of (1) and (2), $(E_{i_1}, E_{i_2}, \ldots, E_{i_k})$ is an I-sequence. We shall show that it is a Graham cycle of the shortest length. Without loss of generality let $i_j = j$, $j = 1,2,\ldots, k$. Now, define $S_i = E_i \cap E_{i \oplus 1}$ $i = 1,2, \ldots, k$. We know that S_i and $S_{i \oplus 1}$, $i = 1,2,\ldots, k$, are incomparable. We have to show that for any $i \neq j$, S_i and S_j are incomparable. If for at least one i, $S_i \subsetneq S_j$ for some j, then trivially $S_i \subsetneq E_j$. Thus d_i and hence $d_{i'}$ are defined. By Lemma 4.5, corresponding to $d_{i'}$ two sets A and B (see Lemma 4.5) which are proper subsets of $\{E_1, E_2, \ldots, E_k\}$, can be identified, at least one of which is an independent cycle. This is a contradiction. Thus, $(E_1, E_2, \ldots, E_k, E_{k+1})$ where $E_{k+1} = E_1$ is a Graham cycle. From the preceding arguments it should be obvious that it is in fact a Graham cycle of the shortest length. Lemma 4.3 shows that $\{E_1, E_2, \ldots, E_k\}$ then constitutes a weak β-cycle. H is thus β-cyclic. □

5. A Comparison of the Different Definitions of β-acyclicity

The three notions of β-acyclicity using the notions of weak β-cycle, Graham cycle, and independent cycle are all equivalent (see Section 4). Indeed, superficially the three types of cycles appear to be very close to each other. It will be the aim of this section to illustrate the differences. In particular, we feel that it is essential to understand the difference between a Graham cycle and an independent cycle. We take recourse to a couple of examples for our illustration.

Example 5.1

Consider the database scheme $\underline{D} = \{R_1, R_2, R_3, R_4, R_5\}$ where $R_1 = ABC$, $R_2 = CDE$, $R_3 = EFG$, $R_4 = CGI$, $R_5 = AHJ$, (See Fig.5.1). $S_i = R_i \cap R_{i \oplus 1}$ are given in the diagram. Clearly, $(R_1, R_2, \ldots, R_5, R_6)$ where $R_6 = R_1$, is a Graham cycle. However, it can be seen from Fig.5.1 that no sequencing among R_i would produce a weak β-cycle involving all the relation schemes $R_1, \ldots, R_5$. However, $\underline{D}$ does contain two weak β-cycles. (See Fig. 5.1). □

Example 5.2

Consult Fig.5.2(a). It depicts a database scheme $\underline{D} = \{R_1, R_2, R_3$ $R_4, R_5\}$ with $R_1 = ABC$, $R_2 = ADE$, $R_3 = CEFGH$, $R_4 = GIK$, $R_5 = HJK$. All neighbors of each R_i are independent. Hence $\underline{D}$ constitutes an independent cycle. However, no ordering among R_i would produce a Graham cycle involving all the relation schemes. $\underline{D}$ contains two Graham cycles, however.

Now consider the structure of the database scheme depicted in Fig.5.2(b). It can be shown to be an independent cycle! Curiously, a portion of it possesses "Chain-like" structure, which is no part of any "conventional" (weak β-, or Graham) cycles. □

Example 5.2 suggests just how much more structurally powerful, independent cycles are compared to other cycles. In fact, independent cycles can be "synthesized" from blocks of simpler independent cycles by providing appropriate links of edges as in Fig.5.2.

Interestingly, similar to the linear ordering of the strengths of acyclicity proved by Fagin [11], we have the following ordering on the three types of primitives composing a β-cyclic hypergraph.

Theorem 5.1

Every weak β-cycle is a Graham cycle and every Graham cycle is an independent cycle. But none of the reverse implications holds.

Proof:

Obvious from the discussion in Section 4 and Examples 5.1 and 5.2. □

The notion of an independent cycle is usefully employed in the next section in coming up with an efficient algorithm for testing β-acyclicity of hypergraphs. It is also used in proving the main result of Section 7. Finally, its use in structurally characterizing α-acyclic schemes is the central theme of [14].

6. An Algorithm for Recognition of β-acyclicity

In this section we actually give two algorithms for testing β-acyclicity. The first is a natural development from the notion of independent cycles while the second is more efficient. We will need the following definitions. An <u>isolated node</u> in a hypergraph is one which belongs to exactly one edge. The <u>representative graph</u> L(H) of a hypergraph H is an edge-labeled ordinary undirected graph whose nodes correspond to the edges of H. There is an edge between two nodes in L(H) if the associated edges in H are adjacent. The edge in L(H) is labeled by the set intersection of the corresponding edges in H. The <u>weight</u> of an edge is its label. We identify the nodes of L(H) with the edges of H. Thus, we speak of independent neighbors of nodes of L(H), which can be understood in the obvious way.

Before we present the algorithms, we explain why our algorithms are to be expected to perform better than the one reported in [11]. First, weak β-cycles are a finer structure than independent cycles. Thus, an algorithm based on weak β-cycles has to explore a hypergraph much deeper for detecting β-cyclicity than one based on independent cycles. We assume that the input hypergraph contains no isolated nodes. (If isolated nodes are present they can always be removed). This is because such nodes translate into edges containing a single node, which are proper subsets of some other edges, in the dual hypergraph.

The Algorithms

Input:

Of the two hypergraphs - H and its dual H^*, the one with fewer edges is selected for input. Let it be H without loss of generality. Its representative graph L(H) in the form of adjacency lists is input as an array NL [1:m], indexed by the nodes of L(H). The weights of the edges of L(H) are stored in W[1:m, 1:m]. For Algorithm 6.2, in addition the incidence matrix of L(H) is also input.

Output:

'Yes' or 'No' depending on whether H is β-acyclic or not.

Comment:

H is assumed to be connected. If it is not, apply any one of the algorithms to each connected component of H. H is β-acyclic if and only if all connected components, as pronounced by the algorithm, are β-acyclic. Let $v_1, v_2, \ldots, v_m$ be the vertices of L(H).

Algorithm 6.1

```
begin flag := false;
  current-set := {v1, v2, ..., vm};
  repeat flag := true;
    for each vi in current-set do
      if ∄ two incomparable weights W(vi, vj), W(vi, vk)
```

```
          where v_j, v_k ∈ NL(v_i) then
          begin
               current-set:= current-set -{v_i};
               flag := false;
            for each v_j in NL(v_i) do
              NL(v_j) := NL(v_j) -{v_i}
          end
     until (flag);
          If current-set = ∅ then return ('Yes')
           else return ('No')
   end.
```

Algorithm 6.2

```
   begin Node-set := {v_1, v_2, ..., v_m};
       for each v_i ∈ Node-set do
          begin for each v_j in NL(v_i) do
                 if ∄ v_k in NL(v_i) such that
                    W(v_i, v_j) and W(v_i, v_k) are incomparable
                    then
                      begin delete v_j from NL(v_i);
                            delete v_i from NL(v_j);
                            update incidence matrix of L(H)
                      end
          end;
       If ∃ v_i in Node-set such that NL(v_i) ≠ ∅
          then return ('No')
          else return ('Yes')
   end.
```

Algorithm 6.1 works by successively pruning the current-set which initially contains all the nodes in L(H). It deletes nodes without independent neighbors in the current set. Thus, this is a natural development on the notion of an independent cycle. Its correctness is obvious. If the maximum degree in L(H) is a constant, then it has an $O(m^2)$ performance. If the maximum degree is O(m) then it appears that in the worst case, the performance could degrade to $O(m^4)$.

Algorithm 6.2 is a modification of Algorithm 6.1. For a fixed maximum degree of L(H) the complexity of Algorithm 6.2 is O(m)! The worst-case complexity is $O(m^3)$; for each vertex v_i, for each of its neighbors in the worst case $O(m)$ time is spent; the outer <u>for</u> loop executes exactly m times. Correctness can be established as follows. If H is β-acyclic then since it contains no independent cycle, each subset of nodes has at least one node with no independent neighbors (see Section 7). Thus NL of all nodes would become empty when the algorithm terminates. If H is β-cyclic, since it contains an independent cycle, a stage will be reached when the algorithm does not delete nodes from the NL of a set of nodes, signifying an independent cycle. Again the algorithm correctly terminates. Its termination is trivially guaranteed. In [11] Fagin gives an algorithm for testing β-acyclicity, which consists in cycling through all triples of three edges of H, constructing another set of edges for each case, and testing for some property. Its complexity is $O(m^4)$. Clearly Algorithm 6.2 exhibits better performance. It should be interesting to explore if β-acyclicity can be tested in linear time, thereby reinforcing the natural correspondence between β-acyclicity of hypergraphs and acyclicity of ordinary undirected graphs.

7. Top-down Generation of β-acyclic Database Schemes

Decomposition of database relation schemes was advocated by Codd [9] as a remedy to certain insertion and deletion anomalies and problems such as redundancy in storage. Decomposition is carried out with the aid of given data dependencies which may be functional, multivalued, or join dependencies [17]. In this section a special procedure for top-down generation of β-acyclic schemes is presented. The motivation is threefold. First, in general, top-down generation of database schemes with prescribed structures possessing nice properties is a well-motivated problem. E.g., Batini et al [2] have studied the problem of top-down generation of various subclasses of α-acyclic schemes. D'Atri and Moscarini [10] have considered top-down generation of γ-acyclic schemes. Second, Beeri et al [4] have shown that join dependencies whose underlying scheme is α-acyclic are equivalent to a set of conflict-free multi-valued dependencies [15, 16]. The result of this section sheds some light on the nature of multi-valued dependencies equivalent to a join dependency whose scheme is β-acyclic Third, there is as yet no complete axiom system for acyclic join dependencies. The result of this section can be used in developing an inference rule for such dependencies.

In what follows, we shall employ the hypergraph formalism for database schemes. Let $H = (N, \underline{E})$ be a database scheme where N is the set of attributes and $\underline{E}$ is the set of relation schemes. Define <u>the neighborhood of a relation scheme</u> $R_i \in \underline{E}$ as $A(R_i) = \{R_j \in \underline{E} : R_j \neq R_i, R_j \cap R_i \neq \emptyset\}$. We define <u>binary decomposition</u> as the process of decomposing a relation scheme R_i into two other relation schemes R_{i_1} and R_{i_2}, denoted by $R_i \rightarrow R_{i_1}, R_{i_2}$. A sequence of such binary decompositions applied to the existing relation schemes, starting from the universal relation scheme is a <u>binary decomposition process</u>. We start with the universal relation scheme at stage 2. For convenience, stage 1 is assumed to make no decomposition. At stage i, a relation scheme is decomposed into two other relation schemes, taking us to stage (i+1). It should be obvious that at the end of stage m there will be exactly m relation schemes, say $R_1, R_2, \ldots, R_m$. Define $C(R_i) = \{R_i \cap R_j : R_j \in A(R_i)\}$, $i = 1,2,\ldots, m$. Let $C_R(R_i)$ be the reduction of $C(R_i)$ viewed as a hypergraph. Now, a decomposition $R_i \rightarrow R_{i_1}, R_{i_2}$ is said to <u>break the neighborhood of</u> R_i, if

$$\exists \quad S \in C_R(R_i) \text{ such that } S \not\subseteq R_{i_j},\ S \cap R_{i_j} \neq \emptyset; \text{ for } j = 1 \text{ or } 2.$$

Intuitively "breaking the neighborhood" can be understood as follows. If for some $S \in C_R(R_i)$, in the decomposition $R_i \rightarrow R_{i_1}, R_{i_2}$ a portion of S is taken away by each of R_{i_1} and R_{i_2}, then we say that the decomposition above breaks the neighborhood of R_i.

A binary decomposition process in which at no stage does a decomposition break the associated neighborhood is said to satisfy the <u>no-breaking property</u> and is termed <u>Binary Decomposition Without Breaking</u> (BDWB).

Before we can get on with proving properties about the BDWB process, it would be convenient to prove a useful lemma. Let $\underline{D}$ be a database scheme. Let $\Pi(\underline{D})$ be the property that $\underline{D}$ has at least one relation scheme with no independent neighbors. Define $\Pi'(\underline{D})$ as the property that all subsets of $\underline{D}$ satisfy Π.

<u>Lemma 7.1</u>

A database scheme $\underline{D} = \{R_1, R_2, \ldots, R_k\}$ is β-acyclic if and only if $\Pi'(\underline{D})$ is true.

<u>Proof</u>:

(<==):

Let $\underline{D}$ be β-acyclic. Then it contains no independent cycle. Thus $\Pi(\underline{D})$ is true. Since, β-acyclicity is a hereditary property, Π is true of all subsets of $\underline{D}$, making $\Pi'(\underline{D})$ true.

(==>):

Let $\underline{D}$ be β-cyclic. Then it contains at least one independent cycle. Thus, there is a subset of $\underline{D}$ which does not satisfy Π. Therefore $\Pi'(\underline{D})$ is false. □

Theorem 7.2

A BDWB process always generates β-acyclic schemes.

Proof:

We shall give an inductive proof.

Basis

At stage 1 or 2, we have less than three relation schemes. Trivially the associated hypergraph contains no independent cycle, and hence is β-acyclic.

Induction

Assume that the scheme generated upto stage m, say $\underline{D}_m = \{R_1, R_2, \ldots, R_m\}$, is β-acyclic. We shall show that $\underline{D}_{m+1}$ generated from $\underline{D}_m$ by the decomposition $R_i \rightarrow R_{i_1}, R_{i_2}$, such that there is no breaking, is also β-acyclic. In other words, we shall show that $\Pi'(\underline{D}_m) \Rightarrow \Pi'(\underline{D}_{m+1})$. This is easily done by considering all subsets S of $\underline{D}_{m+1}$ and proving that $\Pi(S)$ is true. Any subset S of $\underline{D}_{m+1}$ falls into one of the following four cases.

Case (i)

$R_{i_1}, R_{i_2} \notin S$. In this case $S \subseteq \underline{D}_m$ also and $\Pi(S)$ is automatically true.

Case (ii)

$R_{i_1} \in S$; $R_{i_2} \notin S$.

Let S' be obtained from S by replacing R_{i_1} with R_i. Now since $S' \subseteq \underline{D}_m$, $\exists\, R_k$ in S', having no independent neighbors, in order that $\pi(S')$ be true.

<u>Subcase (ii) (a)</u>

$$R_k \neq R_i$$

If $R_k \cap R_i = \emptyset$ then $R_k \cap R_{i_1} = \emptyset$; R_k continues to have no independent neighbors in S also.

If $R_k \cap R_i \neq \emptyset$, then let R_k have other neighbors. Since R_k has no independent neighbors in S', $\exists R_{k'}$ in S' such that $R_{k'}$ is a neighbor of R_k and $R_k \cap R_i \subseteq R_k \cap R_{k'}$ <u>or</u> $R_k \cap R_{k'} \subseteq R_k \cap R_i$. In the first case, $R_k \cap R_{i_1} \subseteq R_k \cap R_{k'}$; R_k has no independent neighbors in S. In the second case, by virtue of the no-breaking property, $R_k \cap R_i \subseteq R_{i_1}$ <u>or</u> $(R_k \cap R_i) \cap R_{i_1} = \emptyset$.

This implies that

$$R_k \cap R_{k'} \subseteq R_k \cap R_{i_1} \quad \underline{\text{or}} \quad R_k \cap R_{i_1} = \emptyset$$

Again, R_k has no independent neighbors in S.

Thus $\pi(S)$ is true.

<u>Subcase (ii) (b)</u>

$$R_k = R_i$$

Let R_i have, in general, two or more (dependent) neighbors in S'. Then there should be two neighbors R_{k_1} and R_{k_2} of R_i such that

$$R_i \cap R_{k_1} \subseteq R_i \cap R_{k_2} \quad \underline{\text{and}} \quad R_i \cap R_{k_2} \in C_R(R_i)$$

$R_i \cap R_{k_2}$ is not broken up by the decomposition $R_i \rightarrow R_{i_1}$, R_{i_2}. Thus, $R_i \cap R_{k_2} \subseteq R_{i_1}$ <u>or</u> $(R_i \cap R_{k_2}) \cap R_{i_1} = \emptyset$. Hence, $R_{i_1} \cap R_{k_1} \subseteq R_{i_1} \cap R_{k_2}$, and R_{i_1} does not have independent neighbors in S also.

<u>Case (iii)</u>

$R_{i_1} \notin S$; $R_{i_2} \in S$. By symmetry, this part has a proof similar to that for case (ii).

<u>Case (iv)</u>

$R_{i_1}, R_{i_2} \in S$.

Obtain S' from S by removing R_{i_1} and R_{i_2} and including R_i.

$\Pi(S)$ directly follows from the observations below.

(1) $(R_k \cap R_i) \subseteq (R_k \cap R_{k'})$ where $R_{k'}$ and R_i are dependent neighbors of R_k, implies that $(R_k \cap R_{i_j}) \subseteq (R_k \cap R_{k'})$, $j = 1,2$.

(2) Similarly, $(R_k \cap R_{k'}) \subseteq (R_k \cap R_i)$ implies that $(R_k \cap R_{k'}) \subseteq (R_k \cap R_{i_j})$ <u>or</u> $(R_k \cap R_{i_j} = \emptyset)$, $j = 1,2$.

(1) and (2) prove that $R_k (\neq R_i)$ defined in case (ii) continues not to have any independent neighbors in S also.

(3) For $R_k = R_i$, as before,

$(R_i \cap R_{k_1}) \subseteq (R_i \cap R_{k_2})$ implies that

$(R_{i_j} \cap R_{k_1}) \subseteq (R_{i_j} \cap R_{k_2})$ <u>or</u> $R_{i_j} \cap R_{k_2} = \emptyset$,

$j = 1,2$. Thus, R_{i_1} and R_{i_2} have no independent neighbors in S for this case. Hence $\Pi(S)$ is true.

Since all possible cases for a general subset S of $\underline{D}_{m+1}$ have been exhausted, $\forall S \subseteq \underline{D}_{m+1}$, $\Pi(S)$ is true. In other words, $\Pi'(\underline{D}_{m+1})$ is true and hence $\underline{D}_{m+1}$ is β-acyclic by Lemma 7.1. □

At this stage it appears that the set of multi-valued dependencies, satisfying the property that a binary decomposition process using them one by one suffers no breaking, is a subset of conflict-free multi-valued dependencies [15,16,4]. This is very much in keeping with the fact that β-acyclic schemes form a subset of α-acyclic schemes. The complete characterization of such multi-valued dependencies is being investigated. Besides, the condition of "no-breaking" is only a sufficient condition for a binary decomposition process to generate β-acyclic schemes. The necessity problem is as yet open. The no-breaking condition can be used for one of the inference rules for deducing acyclic join dependencies, whose axiomatization (an open problem) we are trying to build. Specifically, if a necessary and sufficient condition for a binary decomposition process to generate β-acyclic schemes is found, then a complete axiomatization, at least, of β-acyclic join dependencies should be possible.

8. Conclusions

In this paper, the problem of designing β-acyclic database schemes has been approached from two complementary angles. For the first part, an efficient recognition algorithm for β-acyclic schemes was developed using a new notion of an independent cycle. For the other, a decomposition process for top-down generation of β-acyclic schemes was described. Applications and extensions of the ideas provided in this paper were discussed.

REFERENCES

1. ARMSTRONG, W.W. Dependency structures of database relationships. In Proc. IFIP 74, North Holland, Amsterdam, 1974, pp. 580-583.

2. BATINI, C., D'ATRI, A., AND MOSCARINI, M. Formal tools for top-down and bottom-up generation of acyclic relational schemata. In Proc. Int. Conf. on Graph-Theoretic Concepts in Computer Science, Linz, Austria, 1981.

3. BEERI, C., FAGIN, R., MAIER, D., MENDELZON, A.O., ULLMAN, J.D., AND YANNAKAKIS, M. Properties of acyclic database schemes. In Proc. 13th Ann. ACM Symp. on Theory of Computing, ACM, New York, 1981, pp. 355-362.

4. BEERI, C., FAGIN, R., MAIER, D., AND YANNAKAKIS, M. On the desirability of acyclic database schemes. J. ACM 30, 3 (July 1983), pp. 479-513.

5. BEERI, C., AND VARDI, M.Y. On the properties of join dependencies, In Advances in Database Theory, H. Gallaire, J. Minker, and J-M Nicolas, Eds., Plenum, New York, 1981, pp. 25-72.

6. BERGE, C., Graphs and Hypergraphs. North Holland, Amsterdam, 1976.

7. CHASE, K. Join graphs and acyclic database schemes. In Proc. 7th Int. Conf. on Very Large Databases, ACM, New York, 1981, pp. 95-100.

8. CODD, E.F., A relational model of data for large shared data banks. Commun. ACM 13, 6 (June 1970), pp. 377-387.

9. CODD, E.F., Further normalization of the relational database model. In Data Base Systems, Courant Computer Science Symposia 6, R. Rustin, Ed., Prentice Hall, 1971, pp.65-98.

10. D'ATRI, A., AND MOSCARINI, M. Acyclic hypergraphs: Their recognition and top-down versus bottom-up generation. Tech.Rep. R.29, Consiglio Nazionale Delle Richerche, Institute di Analisi dei Sistemi ed Informatica, 1982.

11. FAGIN, R. Degrees of acyclicity for hypergraphs and relational database schemes. J. ACM 30, 3(July 1983), pp. 514-550.

12. FAGIN, R., MENDELZON, A.O., AND ULLMAN, J.D., A simplified universal relation assumption and its properties. ACM Trans. Database Syst. 7,3 (Sept. 1982), pp. 343-360.

13. GOODMAN, N., AND SCHMUELI, O. Tree queries: A simple class of queries. ACM Trans. Database Syst. 7,4 (Dec. 1982), pp. 653-677.

14. LAKSHMANAN, V.S., VENI MADHAVAN, C.E., AND CHANDRASEKARAN, N. A structural characterization of α-acyclic database schemes, under preparation.

15. LIEN, Y.E. On the equivalence of database models. J. ACM 29,2 (Apr. 1982), pp. 333-362.

16. SCIORE, E. Real-world MVDs. In Proc. Int. Conf. on Management of Data, ACM, New York, 1981, pp.121-132.

17. ULLMAN, J.D., Principles of Database Systems. Computer Science Press, Potmac, Md., 1984.

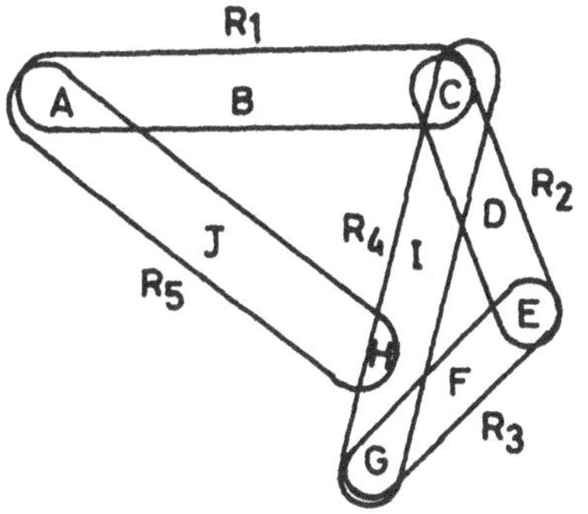

Fig.5.1

$\underline{D} = \{R_1, R_2, R_3, R_4, R_5\}$ is a database scheme. $S_1 = C$; $S_2 = E$; $S_3 = G$; $S_4 = H$; $S_5 = A$. $(R_1, R_2, R_3, R_4, R_5)$ is a Graham cycle. The only weak β-cycles in $\underline{D}$ are $(R_1, C, R_4, H, R_5, A, R_1)$ and $(R_2, E, R_3, G, R_4, C, R_2)$.

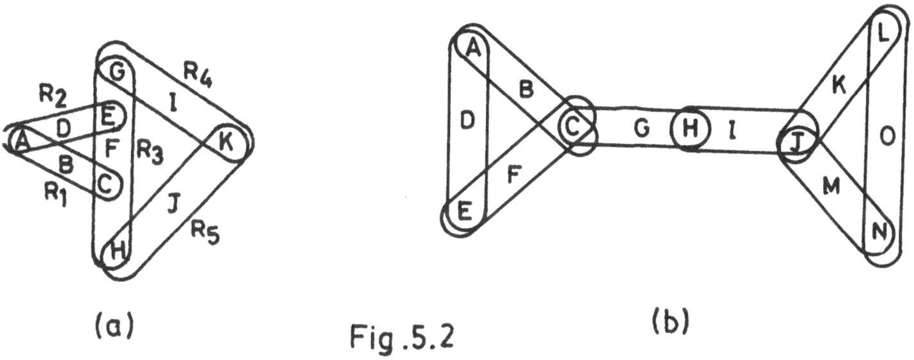

Fig.5.2

(a) $\underline{D} = \{R_1, R_2, R_3, R_4, R_5\}$ is a database scheme. $\underline{D}$ is an independent cycle. The only Graham cycles in $\underline{D}$ are (R_1, R_2, R_3, R_1) and (R_3, R_4, R_5, R_3).

(b) An example structure of an independent cycle.

UNIVERSAL AND REPRESENTATIVE INSTANCES USING UNMARKED NULLS

Sushil Jajodia*
Department of Computer Science
University of Missouri-Columbia
Columbia, Missouri 65211

ABSTRACT

Representative instances are important since in addition to the universal relation view they permit updates in the individual relations; if these updates are locally valid, then they do not violate global consistency. In this paper, we first give conditions under which we can construct a universal instance I which uses only one type of nulls (unmarked nulls) and whose total projections onto the relation schemes yield exactly the database relations. Then, we give a necessary and sufficient condition under which this I is actually a representative instance. Our conditions are simple and easily maintained.

I. Introduction

The most important motivation which led to the origin of the relational model was the "objective of providing a sharp and clear boundary between the logical and physical aspects of database management" [Codd]. By separating the logical and physical structures, the relational model frees the users from navigation in the physical database. However, it does not free the users from navigation within the conceptual database; they must understand the relational scheme and navigate between various relations. The universal relation (UR) systems go one step further than the relational model by removing from the users concern about not only the physical organization of data, but some of the logical organization as well.

The UR systems permit the users to have a universal relation view [Ullm1, Ullm2] which means that the users can regard the data stored in various relations as a single universal relation over all the attributes of the relation schemes. With an UR view, the users can phrase their queries simply and succinctly in terms of attribute names; they do not need to remember how the various attributes are grouped together to form the different relation schemes.

One way to support an UR view is via the classical "universal in-

---

*This work was supported in part by the University of Missouri Summer Research Fellowship.

stance assumption" which requires that the relations in a database must be projections of a single, null-free universal relation. There are many objections to this assumption [AP, BG, HLY, Kent, Maiel, Ullm1] which make it unacceptable. Thus, it is generally agreed that nulls--marked or unmarked--must be permitted in the universal relation. The introduction of nulls, however, pose some difficult technical problems. In particular, the work of Bernstein and Goodman [BG] pointed out the need for a consistent theory of updates for an UR system. To this end, Sagiv introduced the notion of representative instance [Sagi2] which in addition to the UR view, permits updates (insertions and deletions) in the individual relations; if these updates are locally valid, then they are globally valid as well (Precise definitions are given in the next section.).

Sagiv and others [Sagi1, Sagi2, KU, Maie1, Hone, Vass] use marked (or unique) nulls in their work. Works such as [KU] and [Maie1] use marked nulls to enforce a universal instance. As Sagiv [Sagi2] points out, their approach is costly to maintain since the chase [MMS] is required whenever updates are performed on the database and there is a need to store many null values which do not provide any information. In [Sagi1, Sagi2], Sagiv has weakened the notion of a "universal instance" to a "containing instance" where a universal relation is said to be a containing instance for the database $\underline{r}$ if its projections onto the relation schemes contain the relations in $\underline{r}$. But this means that we cannot recover the original relations in $\underline{r}$ from its universal relation [Riss].

We, on the other hand, take a different approach. We use unmarked nulls in the universal relation and insist that the universal relation be actually a universal instance whose projections onto the relation schemes yield exactly the database relations. More precisely, we show that if a relational scheme $\underline{R}$ is γ-acyclic, then we can construct from any database $\underline{r}$ over $\underline{R}$, satisfying the subset condition, a universal instance I, possibly containing unmarked nulls, whose total projections onto $\underline{R}$ yields exactly the set $\underline{r}$. Moreover, this I is a representative instance if $\underline{R}$ satisfies additionally the following natural condition: For any functional dependency (FD) $X \to A$ where A is a single attribute, whenever XA is contained in two relation schemes R and R' of $\underline{R}$, we have that $R \cap R'$ is a relation scheme of $\underline{R}$, having X as one of its keys.

We begin the next two sections with a review of basic definitions and the concepts of null-valued relations and of their satisfaction of FDs. In the two sections that follow, we give our results. The conclusion is given in the last section.

II. γ-acyclic Relational Schemes

We first review the definitions and basic facts essential to understand our results. The reader is presumed familiar with relational database theory as explicated in [Ullm2] or [Maie2]. We denote single attributes by A, B, C,... and sets of attributes by ...,X, Y, Z. The notation r(X) means that the relation r is defined over attributes X and r[X'] denotes the restriction $\{t[X'] : t \in r\}$ of tuples of r to attributes $X' \subset X$. Let R be a set of attributes, and let $K = \{K_1,\ldots,K_m\}$ be a set of Keys of R (i.e., each K_i in K functionally determines R and no K_j, $j \neq i$, is properly contained in K_i). The set R is said to embody the FDs $\{K_1 \to R,\ldots,K_m \to R\}$.

We assume that there is a universal set U of distinct attribute names and F is the set consisting of all FDs imposed on U. A relational scheme $\underline{R}$ over attributes U is a set of ordered pairs $<R_1,K_1>,\ldots,<R_n,K_n>$ such that each relation scheme $R_i \subseteq U$, $\bigcup_{i=1}^{n} R_i = U$, K_i is a set of keys for R_i, and $\bigcup_{i=1}^{n} F_i$ is a cover of F where F_i denotes the set of FDs embodied in R_i. For the sake of simplicity, we omit K_i's and simply write $\underline{R} = \{R_1,\ldots,R_n\}$. A database $\underline{r}$ over $\underline{R}$ is a set of relations $\{r_1,\ldots,r_n\}$ such that each r_i is a relation over R_i and satisfies the FDs in F_i. We wish to allow relation schemes R_i and R_j in $\underline{R}$ such that $R_i \subset R_j$, and speak of a database $\underline{r}$ over $\underline{R}$ as satisfying subset condition* if $r_j[R_j] \subseteq r_i$ whenever $R_i \subset R_j$. We denote by SUBCON($\underline{R}$) the collection of all databases $\underline{r}$ which satisfy the subset condition.

A hypergraph $\underline{H}$ is a pair $<N,\underline{E}>$ where N is a set of nodes and $\underline{E}$ is a set of edges which are arbitrary nonempty subsets of N. To each relational scheme $\underline{R}$, we can associate a hypergraph $\underline{H} = <U,\underline{R}>$, i.e., the attributes in U are the nodes of the hypergraph and relation schemes R_i of $\underline{R}$ becomes its edges. Without loss of generality, in this paper we assume that $\underline{R}$ or more precisely, the associated hypergraph $\underline{H}$ is connecte

Definition [Fagi]. A hypergraph $H = <N,\underline{E}>$ is said to be γ-acyclic if it does not contain any γ-cycle which is a sequence of the form

$$(E_1,n_1,E_2,n_2,\ldots,E_m,n_m,E_{m+1})$$

where

1) $n_1,n_2,\ldots,n_m$ are distinct nodes in N,

---

*Subset condition has been referred by us and others as existence constraints [JNS1, JNS2, Lien, Yann] and should not be confused with existence constraints of Maier [Maie1, Maie2] which are quite different

2) $E_1, E_2, \ldots, E_m$ are distinct edges in $\underline{E}$ and $E_{m+1} = E_1$,
3) $m \geq 3$
4) n_i is in E_i and E_{i+1}, $1 \leq i \leq m$
5) if $1 \leq i \leq m$, then n_i is no E_j except E_i and E_{i+1}.

We call a relational scheme $\underline{R}$ γ-acyclic if its associated hypergraph $\underline{H} = \langle U, \underline{R} \rangle$ is γ-acyclic.

There is a beautiful polynomial-time algorithm for testing γ-acyclicity, due to D'atri and Moscarini [DM, Fagi]. It is similar in spirit to Graham's algorithm for determining α-acyclicity of relational schemes [Grah].

Theorem 1 [DM, Fagi]. A relational scheme $\underline{R}$ is γ-acyclic if and only if $\underline{R}$ can be reduced to the empty set by an exhaustive application of the following operations:

a) delete a node if it belongs to precisely one relation scheme,
b) delete a relation scheme if it contains exactly one attribute,
c) if two relation schemes contain precisely the same attributes, delete one of these relation schemes, and
d) if two attributes are in precisely the same relation schemes, then delete one of them from every relation scheme that contains it.

There are two weaker degrees of acyclicity for relational schemes, called γ-acyclicity (or simply acyclicity [FMU, BFMY]) and β-acyclicity [Fagi2]. Each type of acyclic schemes enjoys several desirable properties. In particular, a relational scheme is γ-acyclic iff its Bachman diagram is loop-free [Lien, Yann, Fagi2].

We call a database $\underline{r}$ over $\underline{R}$ pairwise consistent if for any pair of relations $r_i(R_i)$ and $r_j(R_j)$ in $\underline{r}$, $r_i[R_i \cap R_j] = r_j[R_i \cap R_j]$. We call $\underline{r}$ pairwise inconsistent if it is not pairwise consistent. The database $\underline{r}$ is said to be globally consistent if there is a universal instance $I(U)$ such that $I[R_i] = r_i$, $i = 1, 2, \ldots, n$. Such a universal instance I is called a representative instance if I satisfies the FDs in F which, by definition, is the closure of $\bigcup_{i=1}^{n} F_i$.

In the absence of nulls, it is obvious that global consistency implies pairwise consistency, but the converse does not hold in general. In fact, every pairwise consistent database over $\underline{R}$ is globally consistent iff $\underline{R}$ is α-acyclic [BFMY]. We consider pairwise consistency condition unacceptable on practical grounds. No real-world database will satisfy this condition since the information is often partial or missing. Thus, we investigate under what condition will a pairwise inconsistent database *r* over *R* have a *universal/representative* instance I(U). Since *r* is not pairwise consistent, such an I will contain nulls--marked or unmarked. We prefer to work with a single unmarked null since there is no benefit gained by marking them here.

III. Relations with Null Values

Since we wish to introduce the null δ into relations, we need to define some notions and notations used with relations which may contain nulls. There are various different semantics of δ; for example, 1) as an unknown value, which exists but is not recorded (for whatever reason), 2) as a non-existent value, such as an unassigned phone number, or 3) inapplicable value, such as maiden name of a male employee. Basically, we take the approach of [Zani] and assume no information semantic for δ, which does not prejudge whether δ can ever be replaced by a "real" value or not. (If it ever is, nothing is lost!) Hence a tuple <Smith, 301 Main Street, 345-3113> carries the same information as <Smith, 301 Main St., 345-3113, δ, δ> but more information than <Smith, 301 Main Street, δ>.

Let X be a collection of attributes, and let S(X) be a relation defined on X, possibly containing null values, denoted by δ. For a tuple t in S and $Y \subseteq X$, we continue to use the notation t[Y] to denote the Y-value of t, which may now contain δ. The tuple t is said to be *Y-total* if $t[A] \neq \delta$ for all attributes A in Y. For $Y \subseteq X$, the *Y-total projection* of S is the set {t[Y] : t is a Y-total tuple of S} and is denoted by S[Y]. Note that S[Y] does not contain δ. Let t and s be two tuples in relation S(X). We say t *subsumes* s if for every attribute A in X, either t[A] = s[A] or s[A] = δ. S is said to be *subsumption-free* if it does not contain two tuples such that one subsumes the other. In the sequel, all relations are assumed to be subsumption-free. We say that the *functional dependency with nulls* (NFD) $Y \rightarrow A$ holds in the relation S if, for all Y-total tuples s and t of S, s[Y] = t[Y] implies s[Z] t[Z], where the latter may both contain δ. By a *universal instance* I for a database $\underline{r} = \{r_1, \ldots, r_n\}$, where each r_i is a total relation over the relation scheme R_i, we mean a subsumption-free relation I over $U = \bigcup_{i=1}^{n} R_i$ such that the total projections $I[R_i] = r_i$ for $i = 1, \ldots, n$. Let F denote the set of FDs defined on U. Then a universal instance I is said to be a *representative instance* if for each FD $X \rightarrow A$ in F, its null counterpart, the NFD $X \rightarrow A$, holds in I. A complete set of inference rules for NFD appears in [Lien, Theorem 1, p. 342]. It should be noted that transitivity rule which holds for traditional non-null FDs, does not hold for NFDs.

Throughout this paper, null values are not allowed in database relations; they are permitted only in universal relations. We should note here that the universal relation is imaginary and not stored physically. Hence, we do not actually store null values.

IV. From γ-acyclic Relational Databases to Universal Databases

We first show that given a γ-acyclic relational scheme R and a database r ε SUBCON(R), it is possible to construct a universal instance I, possibly containing null values δ, whose total projections satisfy $I[R_i] = r_i$ for all relations $r_i(R_i)$ in r.

Let $\{t_1(R_1),\ldots,t_m(R_m)\}$ be a set of tuples from distinct relations in r such that the hypergraph consisting of edges $R_1,\ldots,R_m$ is connected and for any two relation schemes R_i and R_j, whenever $R_i \cap R_j \neq \emptyset$, we have that $t_i[R_i \cap R_j] = t_j[R_i \cap R_j]$. We call the natural join of tuples $t_1,\ldots,t_m$ the traversal of these tuples and denote it by $trav(t_1,\ldots,t_m)$. If no traversals can be defined from a superset of $trav(t_1,\ldots,t_m)$, we call a traversal maximal. Then, using all maximal traversals, we define

$$I = \{t(U) : t[R_1\ldots R_m]\ trav(t_1,\ldots,t_m) \text{ and } \tag{1}$$
$$t[U - R_1\ldots R_m] = \delta \text{ where } trav(t_1(R_1),\ldots,t_m(R_m))$$
$$\text{is a maximal traversal}\}.$$

Thus, tuples of I correspond to maximal traversals where we extend each traversal to a tuple over U by adding δ wherever necessary.

We should add here that I can be constructed algorithmically and efficiently using a "minimal information" extension of the usual natural join operation. We refer the reader to [JNS1, JNS2] for details.

Working with pairwise inconsistent databases, Lien has shown how to construct a universal instance, denoted by maxtrav(b), from a network database b for a loop-free Bachman diagram B [Lien]. Now a γ-acyclic connected relational scheme R with database r ε SUBCON(R) can be regarded as a loop-free Bachman diagram B with a network database b for B, and conversely. It turns out that I in (1) coincides with Lien's maxtrav(b). Hence, we can restate his result as follows:

Theorem 2. Let <R,r> be a relational database such that R is γ-acyclic and r ε SUBCON(R). Then I in (1) is a universal instance such that its total projections satisfy $I[R_i] = r_i$ for $i = 1,\ldots,n$.

The following examples show that Theorem 2 fails if either the condition of γ-acyclicity of R or the subset condition on r are weakened.

Example 1. Consider $\underline{R}$ = {AB,BC,ABC}. This $\underline{R}$ is β-acyclic (the next weaker acyclic condition; see [Fagi2]), but γ-cyclic. Consider the database $\underline{r}$ ε SUBCON($\underline{R}$) consisting of relations

r_1:

A	B
0	1

r_2:

B	C
1	0
1	1

r_3:

A	B	C
0	1	0

The I in (1) is given by

I:

A	B	C
0	1	0
0	1	1

which is not a universal instance since I[ABC] ≠ r_3.

Example 2. Consider $\underline{R}$ = {AB,ABC}, a γ-acyclic relational scheme and the database $\underline{r}$ consisting of relations:

r_1:

A	B
0	1

r_2:

A	B	C
0	1	0
1	0	1

$\underline{r}$ does not satisfy the subset condition. The I in (1) is identical to r_2, and I is not a universal instance since I[AB] ≠ r_1.

Example 1 can easily be generalized to show that any γ-cyclic $\underline{R}$ has some database $\underline{r}$ ε SUBCON($\underline{R}$) for which the instance I in (1) is not universal (i.e., I does not project onto r_i via R_i-total projections).

Theorem 3. A relation scheme $\underline{R}$ is γ-acyclic iff the instance I in (1) constructed from any database $\underline{r}$ ε SUBCON(R) is a universal instance.

Proof. If $\underline{R}$ is γ-acyclic and $\underline{r}$ ε SUBCON(R), then I in (1) is a universa instance by Theorem 2. Conversely, suppose $\underline{R}$ is not γ-acyclic. Then by [Fagi2, p. 525], it follows that $\underline{R}$ contains at least one of these two cycles: 1) there is a sequence of relation schemes $R_1,\ldots,R_m,R_{m+1}$ such that i) $R_1,\ldots,R_m$ are distinct and $R_{m+1} = R_1$, ii) $m \geq 3$, and iii) for $1 \leq i \leq m$, $R_i \cap R_j$ is nonempty iff $j = i+1$ (see Fig. A) or 2) there exist relation schemes R_1, R_2, and R_3 such that $R_1 \cap R_2 \cap R_3$, $(R_1 \cap R_3)-R_2$, and $(R_2 \cap R_3)-R_1$ each contains at least one attribute (see Fig. B).

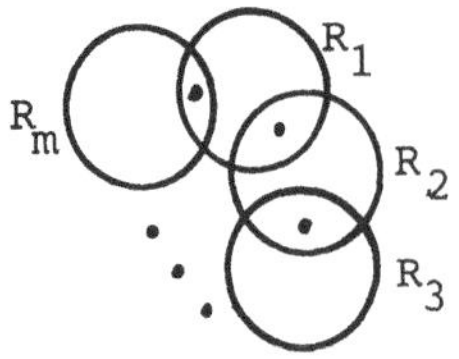

Fig. A

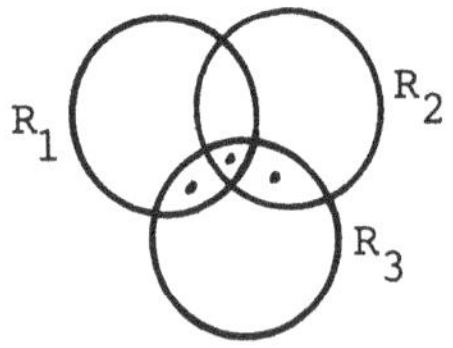

Fig. B

In either case it is easy to construct a database $\underline{r} \in \text{SUBCON}(\underline{R})$ for which I in (1) is not a universal instance.

V. From Universal Instances to Representative Instances

In this section, we investigate when the universal instance I constructed in the previous section is actually a representative instance, i.e., satisfies the NFD counterpart of each FD in F. We show that some natural conditions are enough to guarantee that I would be a representative instance for $\underline{r}$.

Theorem 4. Let $\underline{R} = \{R_1,\dots,R_n\}$ be a γ-acyclic relational scheme over attributes U, F_i denote the set of FDs embodied in R_i, and $\bigcup_{i=1}^{n} F_i$ form a cover for F, the set of all FDs imposed on U. Let I denote the universal instance (given by (1)) for the database $\underline{r} \in \text{SUBCON}(\underline{R})$. Then I is a representative instance iff $\underline{R}$ satisfies the following condition:

whenever $X \to A$ is an FD in $\bigcup_{i=1}^{n} F_i$ such that XA is contained in

(*) two relation schemes R and R' of $\underline{R}$, it follows that $R \cap R'$ is

a relation scheme of $\underline{R}$, having X as one of its keys.

We will not prove this theorem here, but give two examples which show why the condition (*) is natural and necessary.

Example 3. Consider $\underline{R} = \{\underline{X}AB, \underline{X}AC\}$ where we have underlined the key in each case. Clearly $\underline{R}$ does not obey the condition (*). Now consider the database $\underline{r} \in \text{SUBCON}(\underline{R})$ consisting of relations

X	A	B
x	a_1	b

X	A	C
x	a_2	c

The universal instance I is given by

X	A	B	C
x	a_1	b	δ
x	a_2	δ	c

which does not satisfy the NFD $X \to A$.

Note that this $\underline{R}$ can be made to satisfy condition (*) by adding the relation scheme $\underline{X}A$ to $\underline{R}$. In general, such additions do not affect the γ-acyclicity of $\underline{R}$ since $\underline{R}$ is γ-acyclic iff $\underline{R} \cup \{R \cap R'\}$ is.

Example 4. Let $\underline{R} = \{XA, \underline{X}AB\}$. Again $\underline{R}$ does not satisfy (*) since X is not a key of XA. Now consider $\underline{r} \in \text{SUBCON}(\underline{r})$ consisting of relations

X	A
x	a_1
x	a_2

X	A	B
x	a_1	b

The universal instance I is given by

X	A	B
x	a_1	b
x	a_2	δ

which does not satisfy the NFD $X \to A$.

Again, this example shows that (*) is a quite natural condition. If we do not enforce $X \to A$ in r(XA), there is no way that the NFD $X \to A$ can hold in I since r(XA) is "contained in" I.

We conclude this section with a final remark. In this paper, we consider relational schemes of the form $\langle R_1,K_1\rangle,\dots,\langle R_n,K_n\rangle$ where each K_i is a set of keys of R_i. Starting with the universe U of attributes and a set F of FDs, such an $\underline{R}$ can be obtained using either a decomposition or a synthetic approach (see [Fagi1] or [Ullm2], for example). Relational schemes obtained by using either approach have the property that each FD $X \to A$ is embodied in a unique relational scheme R_i of $\underline{R}$. Thus, they trivially satisfy the condition (*). As a simple example, consider the industrial database scheme of [Fagi1]. The attributes of U are PROJECT, PART, SUPPLIER, LOCATION, COST, EMPLOYEE, SALARY, HIREDATE, AND MANAGER. The set of constraints consist of these dependencies:

{SUPPLIER,PART} $\to$ COST (2)

PROJECT $\to$ MANAGER (3)

EMPLOYEE $\to$ {SALARY,HIREDATE} (4)

SUPPLIER $\to\to$ LOCATION

PROJECT $\to\to$ {EMPLOYEE,SALARY,HIREDATE}.

The semantics of these dependencies are explained in [Fagi1]. Using the decomposition approach, Fagin derives the relational scheme $\underline{R}$ consisting of these six relation schemes:

R_1(SUPPLIER,PART,PROJECT),

R_2(SUPPLIER,PART,COST),

R_3(EMPLOYEE,SALARY,HIREDATE),

R_4(EMPLOYEE,PROJECT),

R_5(PROJECT,MANAGER), and

R_6(SUPPLIER,LOCATION).

Using the Theorem 1, it is easy to verify that $\underline{R}$ is γ-acyclic. Since each FD is contained in a single relation scheme, the condition (*) is automatically satisfied. Since no relation scheme of $\underline{R}$ is contained in any other relation scheme of $\underline{R}$, it follows that any database $\underline{r}$ will have a representative instance provided the FDs (2), (3), (4) are enforced in relations $r(R_2)$, $r(R_5)$, and $r(R_3)$ respectively.

VI. Conclusion

In this paper we have shown that if a relational scheme $\underline{R}$ is γ-acyclic, then any database $\underline{r}$ for $\underline{R}$, satisfying the subset condition, has a universal instance I, possibly containing unmarked nulls, whose total projection onto $\underline{R}$ yields exactly the set $\underline{r}$. Moreover, we have characterized those $\underline{R}$ for which this I is actually a representative instance.

γ-acyclic relational schemes are desirable since the absence of γ-cycles makes choices of navigational routes in the database unambiguous. In general, however, there are many well-designed relational schemes which are γ-acyclic. In these cases, the cycles can always be eliminated by renaming the "overloaded" attributes to fit their role in each relation scheme (see [CK] or [Fagi2]). It has been argued that this approach may not be acceptable in a practical environment since renaming quickly leads to large attribute names which are complex and not easy to use and many additional edges in the hypergraph [AP, Kent]. We feel that the UR system can be effective iff the total number of attributes in the relational scheme is small and the connections among attributes are starkly evident. Hence, this renaming is not a problem.

References

[AP] Atzeni, P. and Parker, D. S., Assumptions in relation database theory, Proc. ACM Symp. on Principles of Database Systems, (1982), 1-9.

[BFMY] Beeri, C., Fagin, R., Maier, D., and Yannakakis, M., On the desirability of acyclic database schemes, Journal of ACM, (30)3 (1983), 479-513.

[BG] Bernstein, P. A., and Goodman, N., What does Boyce-Codd normal form do? Proc. 6th Int'l. Conf. on Very Large Data Bases, (1980), 245-259.

[CK] Carlson, C. R., and Kaplan, R. S., A generalized access path model and its application to a relational database system, Proc. ACM SIGMOD Conf. on Management of Data, (1976), 143-154.

[Codd] Codd, E. F., Relational database: a practical foundation for productivity, Comm. of ACM, (25)2(1982), 109-116.

[DM] D'atri, A. and Moscarini, M., Acyclic hypergraphs : their recognition and top-down versus bottom-up generation. Tech. Rep. Consiglio Nazionale Delle Richerche, Instituto di Analisi dei Sistemi ed Informatica, (1982).

[Fagi1] Fagin, R., The decomposition versus the synthetic approach to relational database design, Proc. 3rd Int'l. Conf. on Very Large Data Bases, (1977), 441-446.

[Fagi2] Fagin, R., Degrees of acyclicity for hypergraphs and relational database schemes, Journal of ACM, (30)3(1983), 514-550.

[FMU] Fagin, R., Mendelzon, A. O., and Ullman, J. D., A simplified universal relation assumption and its properties, ACM Trans. Database Systems, (7)3(1982), 343-360.

[Grah] Graham, M. H., On the universal relation, Technical Report, University of Toronto (1979).

[HLY] Honeyman, P., Ladner, R. E., and Yannakakis, M., Testing the universal instance assumption, Info. Proc. Letters, (10)1(1980), 14-19.

[Hone] Honeyman, P., Testing satisfaction of functional dependencies, Journal of ACM, (29)3(1982), 668-677.

[JNS1] Jajodia, S., Ng, P. A., and Springsteel, F. N., On universal and representative instances for inconsistent databases, in Entity-Relationship Approach to Software Engineering (C. Davis et al., eds.) North-Holland, Amsterdam (1983), 279-295.

[JNS2] Jajodia, S., Ng, P. A., and Springsteel, F. N., Constructive universal instances over incomplete information, in preparation.

[Kent] Kent, W., Consequences of assuming a universal relation, ACM Trans. on Database Systems, (6)4(1981), 539-556.

[KU] Korth, H. F., and Ullman, J. D., SYSTEM/U : a database system based on the universal relation assumption Proc. XP/1 Conference, (1980).

[Lien] Lien, Y. E., On the equivalence of database models, Journal of ACM, (29)2(1982), 333-362.

[MMS] Maier, D., Mendelzon, A. O., and Sagiv, Y., Testing implications of data dependencies, ACM Trans. on Database Systems, (4)4(1979), 455-469.

[Maie1] Maier, D., Discarding the universal instance assumption : preliminary results, Proc. XP/1 Conf., (1980).

[Maie2] Maier, D., The Theory of Relational Databases, Computer Science Press, Rockville, Maryland (1983).

[Riss] Rissanen, J., On equivalence of database schemes, Proc. ACM Symp. on Principles of Database Systems, (1982), 23-26.

[Sagi1] Sagiv, Y., Can we use the universal instance assumption without using nulls?, Proc. ACM SIGMOD Int'l. Conf. on Management of Data, (1981), 108-130.

[Sagi2] Savig, Y., A characterization of globally consistent databases and their correct paths, ACM Trans. on Database Systems, (8)2 (1983), 266-286.

[Ullm1] Ullman, J. D., The U. R. strikes back, Proc. ACM Symp. on Principles of Database Systems, (1982), 10-22.

[Ullm2] Ullman, J. D., Principles of Database Systems, 2nd Ed., Computer Press, Rockville, MD. (1982).

[Vass] Vassiliou, T., Functional dependencies and incomplete information, Proc. 6th Int'l. Conf. on Very Large Data Bases, (1980), 260-269.

[Yann] Yannakakis, M., Algorithms for acyclic database schemes, Proc. 7th Int'l. Conf. on Very Large Data Bases, (1981), 82-94.

[Zani] Zaniolo, C., Database relations with null values, Proc. ACM Symp. Principles of Database Systems, (1982), 27-33.

On Some Computational Problems Related to Data Base Coding*

F.de Santis, M.I. Sessa

Dipartimento di Informatica e Applicazioni
Facolta di Scienze
Universita di Salerno
I84100 Salerno, Italy

Abstract

A very frequent problem arising in the retrieval of information from data bases is to search for elements matching a given one subject to well defined constraints. Efficiency considerations about the searching algorithms obviously suggest to arrange elements in such a way that the processing time is minimum. Nevertheless, investigations about ordering relations to be established on the key coding set for file access appear much more interesting and results prone. In this paper we show that some interesting properties hold for ordering relations on the key codings; moreover, such properties constitute the starting point to design efficient algorithms for the above mentioned search problems.

* Final manuscript not received in time for inclusion in the proceedings.

Generic Oracles*

Bruno Poizat

Mathematique
Universite Pierre & Marie Curie (Paris 6)
4 Place Jussieu
75230 Paris Cedex 05
France

Summary

If for some oracle the polynomial hierarchy does not collapse before level n, then this is true for any generic oracle.

* Final manuscript not received in time for inclusion in the Proceedings.

APPROXIMATION ALGORITHM FOR MAXIMUM INDEPENDENT SET IN PLANAR TRAINGLE-FREE GRAPHS

C.E. Veni Madhavan
School of Automation
Indian Institute of Science
Bangalore 560-012
INDIA

ABSTRACT

The maximum independent set problem is NP-complete even when restricted to planar graphs, cubic planar graphs or triangle free graphs. The problem of finding an absolute approximation still remains NP-complete. Various polynomial time approximation algorithms, that guarantee a fixed worst case ratio between the independent set size obtained to the maximum independent set size, in planar graphs have been proposed. We present in this paper a simple and efficient, $O(|V|)$ algorithm that guarantees a ratio $\frac{1}{2}$, for planar triangle free graphs. The algorithm differs completely from other approaches, in that, it collects groups of independent vertices at a time. Certain bounds we obtain in this paper relate to some interesting questions in the theory of extremal graphs.

1. Introduction

The problem of determining independence number, chromatic number, clique number and clique cover number for arbitrary graphs have led to many interesting theoretical and algorithmic results in graph theory. These numbers or indices, for a graph $G = (V,E)$, denote respectively, the cardinality of the largest set of non-adjacent vertices (independent set), the minimum number of independent sets required to cover V, the cardinality of the vertex subset inducing a complete subgraph (clique), and the minimum number of cliques required to cover V. While all four problems are NP-complete for general graphs, researchers have naturally focussed their attention on polynomial time algorithms for restricted graphs and on polynomial time approximation algorithms. These problems are also of great interest in the theory of extremal graphs and the theory of random graphs.

The maximum independent set problem is NP-complete even when restricted to planar graphs, cubic planar graphs or triangle free graphs [6]. While the maximum independent set in bipartite graphs (planar or not), a sub-class of triangle free graphs, can be determined in polynomial time by a simple algorithm, the problem in triangle free graphs (planar or not) is NP-complete. These considerations motivate the development of an approximation algorithm for finding an independent set $I(G)$, of size $|I(G)|$ as close as possible to the maximum independent set size $\alpha(G)$, on a given graph $G = (V,E)$, $|V| = n$, $|E| = e$. It is known that the problem of finding an absolute approximation $I(G)$ such that $\alpha(G) - |I(G)| \leq k$ for any fixed constant k is also NP-complete [5]. While the problem of devising an ϵ-approximation algorithm that ensures a ratio $|I(G)|/\alpha(G) \geq \epsilon$, $0 < \epsilon < 1$, still remains NP-complete for arbitrary graphs, the class of planar graphs lend themselves to polynomial time ϵ-approximation algorithms.

Various polynomial time algorithms ensuring different worst-case ratios have been proposed for the problem on planar graphs. Albertson [1], developed an algorithm with $\epsilon = 2/9$, which was recently refined to an $O(n^2)$ algorithm by Chiba et al [3]. It is possible to develop an $O(n^2)$ algorithm with $\epsilon = \frac{1}{4}$ based on the four-colour theorem. In their two recent works Chiba et al [2], [4], have devised respectively, an $O(n)$ algorithm with $\epsilon = 1/5$ and an $O(n \log n)$ algorithm with $\epsilon = 1/2$. Lipton and Tarjan [9] have applied their planar separator theorem to obtain $O(n \log n)$ algorithm with an asymptotic worst case ratio of $1 - O(1/\sqrt{\log \log n})$ as $n \rightarrow \infty$.

In this paper, we develop a simple ϵ-approximation algorithm that guarantees in $O(n)$ time an independent set of size at least half the maximum independent set size (i.e., $\epsilon = \frac{1}{2}$) for planar triangle free graphs. The worst-case ratio ϵ of our algorithm is even better in various special cases. In particular, it obtains the maximum independent set in bipartite graphs (planar or not) in $O(n)$ time.

Certain problems in extremal graph theory related to bounds on the Ramsey number $R(3,k)$, have led to many recent interesting results on the bounds for the independence number in triangle free graphs. Griggs [7] and Shearer [10] have reported such bounds in terms of the average degree in a graph. A conjecture due to Albertson, cited in [7], states that $\alpha \geq n/3$ for arbitrary planar triangle free graphs. We demonstrate in this paper that our approximation algorithm, indeed, guarantees this lower bound. We also deduce certain upper bounds in the course of our proofs of the fact that the worst-case ratio $\epsilon \geq 1/2$.

In section 2, we prove the NP-completeness result and certain bounds. We describe our algorithm and its complexity in section 3.

In section 4, we present the various results and proofs required to establish that our algorithm achieves the desired ratio.

2. NP-completeness and other results

Theorem 2.1 : Finding a maximum independent set in planar triangle free graphs is NP-complete.

Proof: The problem of finding maximum independent set in arbitrary graphs and, in particular, in planar triangle free graphs, is clearly in NP. Indeed, the set of all subsets of vertices can be input to a non-deterministic Turing machine program, that verifies in polynomial time, the independent sets and picks the maximum cardinality independent set.

We next show that the problem of finding a vertex cover in planar graphs which is NP-complete [6] can be polynomially transformed to the problem of finding a vertex cover in planar triangle free graphs. The latter problem is trivially equivalent to the problem of finding a maximum independent set.

Construction : Given a planar graph G with n vertices and e edges, we can construct in O(n+e) a graph H, in which every edge of G is represented by a path of length three through two additional vertices. The graph H has n + 2e vertices and 3e edges and H is planar triangle free. We then show that G has a vertex cover of size VC(G) if and only if H has a vertex cover of size VC(H) = VC(G) + e.

Proof of claim that the problem of finding vertex cover in G is equivalent to that in H: Since a vertex cover of G must have at least one of any two adjacent vertices, the path representing this edge in H can be covered by exactly one of the two vertices on this path. Thus VC(H) = VC(G) + e.

To prove the converse, we assume without loss of generality that the graphs under consideration have a least degree, $\delta \geq 2$ and a maximum degree, $\Delta \geq 3$ (Note: the other cases can be dealt with individually in a trivial manner). A vertex cover for H must obviously have atleast one of the two vertices on the paths representing the edges of G. Since the original vertices of G all have degree greater than or equal to the degree of these two vertices (= 2), a vertex cover on H, being a minima cover, must consequently have at most one of these two vertices in its cover set, in addition to the number of vertices in the vertex cover of G. Hence VC(G) = VC(H) - e.

We next deduce some bounds on the independence number as a consequence of the Euler polyhedron formula. We use these bounds, in section 4, to determine the worst-case ratio of our approximation algorithm. Lemma 2.1 (Harary [8], pp.104) : If G is a planar graph with $|V| = n$, $|E| = e$, in which every face is a k-cycle, then $e=k(n-2)/(k-2)$.

Since every face is a 3-cycle in a maximal planar graph on $n \geq 3$ vertices and every face is a 4-cycle in a planar bipartite graph or a maximal planar triangle free graph on $n \geq 4$ vertices, we have:

Corollary 2.1 : If G is planar, then $e \leq 3n - 6$.
Corollary 2.2 : If G is planar and bipartite, then $e \leq 2n - 4$.
Corollary 2.3 : If G is planar and triangle free, then $e \leq 2n-4$.
Corollary 2.4 : If G is planar triangle free, then $\delta \leq 3$.

Since $\sum_{v \in V} \deg(v) = 2e \leq 4n - 8$, the average degree $\bar{d} \leq 4 - 8/n$ and $\delta \leq \bar{d} \Rightarrow \delta \leq 3$.

Lemma 2.2 : If G is planar triangle free and $\delta = 3$, then $\alpha \leq 2n/3$.

Proof: Consider the bipartite graph G_B, with the two partite sets of maximum independent set $I^*(G)$ and the vertex cover set $V - I^*(G)$, obtained by deleting the edges between the vertices in $V - I^*(G)$. The graph G_B is planar and bipartite. Therefore we have by corollary 2.2 and the assumption of $\delta = 3$,

$$2n - 4 \geq |E(G_B)| = \sum_{v \in V-I^*(G)} \deg(v) = \sum_{v \in I^*(G)} \deg(v)$$
$$\geq 3\,|I^*(G)| = 3\alpha$$
$$\text{or, } \alpha \leq 2n/3. \qquad \square$$

For planar triangle free cubic graphs, we have an even tighter upper bound.

Lemma 2.3 : If G is planar, triangle free and $\delta = \Delta = 3$, then $\alpha \leq n/2$.

Proof : Consider the bipartite graph G_B as in the proof of lemma 2.2. Assume $\alpha > n/2$. Then $3n/2$ edges are incident on the vertex cover set $V - I^*(G)$ having less than $n/2$ vertices which implies that there is at least one vertex in this set of degree > 3, a contradiction. $\square$

Corollary 2.5: If G is planar, triangle free and $\delta = \Delta = 2$, then $\alpha \leq n/2$.

Lemma 2.4 : In a planar triangle free graph (with arbitrary Δ) $\alpha \leq (2n + k)/3$, where k is the number of degree-2 vertices.

Proof: Let the number of degree 2 vertices be k and let m of these vertices be in the maximum independent set $I^*(G)$. In the planar bipartite graph G_B considered in the proof of lemma 2.2, we now have

$$2n - 4 \geq |E(G_B)| = \sum_{v \in I^*(G)} \deg(v) \geq 2m + 3(\alpha - m),$$

or,

$$\alpha \leq (2n + m)/3 \leq (2n + k)/3.$$

This slightly loose bound on α suffices for our estimates as we show in section 4.

3. Approximation algorithm

3.1. Algorithm and data structures:

The algorithm MAIN is essentially based on the simple scheme of classifying recursively a set of vertices and their neighbours into an independent set (ind-list) and a dependent set (dep-list). The idea is to exploit the property of triangle free nature, namely, neighbours of any single vertex are independent. The neighbours of a set of vertices, however, do not in general form an independent set unless the graph is bipartite or a tree. We therefore employ another sub-algorithm SIFT to scan the neighbour set and identify a large set of independent vertices. The existence of such a set is proved in section 4. We initiate the algorithm with the set of degree 2 vertices.

We use both, the adjacency matrix and adjacency list representation of G with two links (a row link and a column link) from the adjacency matrix to the adjacency lists. We also link all the vertices of same degree (particularly the degree 2 vertices). We use a doubly linked list representation for the independent sets (<u>ind-list</u>) and a singly linked list for the dependent sets (<u>dep-list</u>). We associate with every vertex two Boolean flags - <u>ind-flag</u> and <u>dep-flag</u>.

A sketch of the algorithm follows:

<u>Algorithm : MAIN</u>

<u>begin</u>

<u>step 1</u>. Traverse the list of degree 2 vertices, copy it into the doubly linked <u>ind-list</u> and set appropriate <u>ind-flag</u> True. Call this list A_1.
$j := 1$

<u>repeat</u> step 2 and step 3

<u>step 2</u>. (a) examine adjacency lists of $x \in A_j$ and 'shift' dependent vertices in A_j to a new <u>dep-list</u> B_j using algorithm SIFT
(b) reset <u>ind-flag</u> and <u>dep-flag</u> accordingly.

(c) traverse ind-list A_j, pick the neighbours of $x \in A_j$ and chain them to list B_j if they are not in the list B_j

(d) delete the elements of A_j and B_j from all adjacency lists in which they are present (note: the adjacency matrix links are used in performing this deletion efficiently)

(e) count (ind-set) := count(ind-set) + length (A_j)

count (dep-set) := count(dep-set) + length (B_j)

step 3. create a new doubly linked ind-list A_{j+1} with the neighbours of $y \in B_j$ as members and set appropriate ind-flag True.

j := j+1

until (count (ind-set) $\geq$ n/3) OR (count (ind-set) + count(dep-set) $\geq$ n)

end

Given a set of vertices S in the form of a doubly linked list A_j in step 2a of MAIN, the algorithm SIFT identifies in O($|S|$) time a subset of S of size at least $|S|/2$ such that the vertices in this subset are all independent. The algorithm SIFT given below deletes recursively vertices of S which have the largest number of dependent vertices belonging to S. Vertices of S are initially organized into lists in a decreasing order of count of dependencies within S. This can be achieved in O($|S|$) time using Δ number of inverted lists. The vertex deletion and appropriate list update operations are highlighted in the algorithm SIFT. These Δ inverted lists are also doubly linked to the ind-list A_j.

Algorithm : SIFT

```
{Pass 1 - Dependency ordering of the ind-list Aj in step 2a of MAIN}
 max-deg := 0; tot-dep-count := 0
 for  x ∈ Aj  do
 begin
   C := count of neighbours of x that belong to Aj
   if C > 0  then include x in sift-list of count C, doubly
                  link ind-list Aj with this and
                  tot-dep-count := tot-dep-count + C
   if C ≥ max-deg then max-deg := C
 end
```

```
if max-deg = 0 then  all vertices in A_j are independent and continue
                     with step 2c of MAIN
else
{pass 2: Dependent vertices elimination}
  while  max-deg > 0  do
  begin
    while sift-list corresponding to max-deg is not-empty do
    begin
      consider a vertex  x  in this list
      delete x from ind-list  A_j and insert in dep-list B_j
      delete x from sift-list
      tot-dep-count := tot-dep-count-max-deg.
      {reposition the neighbours of x, belonging to A_j in sift-list}
      for y ∈ neighbours(x) ∩ A_j do
      begin
        let y ∈ sift-list C_1, then delete y from sift-list C_1,
        insert y in sift-list C_1 - 1 if C_1 > 1,
        tot-dep-count := tot-dep-count-1
      end
    end
   max-deg := max-deg - 1
   end
```

We illustrate the working of the algorithms MAIN and SIFT by means of the following example consider a graph $G = (V,E)$, $V = 1,2,\ldots, 12$, with the adjacency lists: $a_1 = (2,9,12,3)$, $a_2 = (1,4)$, $a_3 = (1,4,5)$, $a_4 = (2,6,3)$, $a_5 = (3,8)$, $a_6 = (4,8,10,7)$, $a_7 = (6,11)$, $a_8 = (5,9,6)$, $a_9 = (1,8,10)$, $a_{10} = (6,9,11,12)$, $a_{11} = (10,7)$, $a_{12} = (10,1)$. There are five degree-two vertices, which are collected first by MAIN.

step 1. of MAIN results in

ind-list $A_1 = (2,5,7,11,12)$

ind-flag $= (F,T,F,F,T,F,T,F,F,F,T,T)$.

Then algorithm SIFT is invoked in step 2a, resulting in

sift-list $C{:}1 = (7,11)$ with appropriate links to

ind-list A_1, max-deg = 1, tot-dep-count = 2,

after the execution of the for loop.

Since max-leg > 0, the sifting action is carried out to remove the fewest number of dependent vertices from ind-list A_1, in pass 2 of the algorithm SIFT. Thus the vertex 7 is removed from list A_1 and inserted in a new dep-list B_1. It is also deleted from the sift-list. Then the neighbours of vertex 7, which are present in the ind-list A_1(i.e., vertex 11) is transferred to a lower sift-list (in this case null). Since max-deg now reduces to zero, sifting is complete.

step 2b now renders

ind-flag : F,T,F,F,T,F,F,F,F,F,T,T

dep-flag : T,T,F,F,F,F,T,F,F,F,F,F

step 2c augments the B_1 list, B_1 = (7,1,4,3,8,10)

At the end of steps 2d and 2e, we have count(ind-set) = 4,count(dep-set)=6.

step 3 creates a new ind-list A_2 = (6,9).

The algorithm now terminates without any further sifting, since count(ind-set) = $4 \geq |V| /3$.

3.2 Complexity of the algorithms MAIN and SIFT

The adjacency matrix, adjacency lists, the mutual links and the degree links can all be initialized in O(n) space and O(n) time (since $e \leq 2n-4$ for planar triangle free graphs). The ind-list, dep-list, the two flags of algorithm MAIN together with the sift-list of algorithm SIFT and the mutual links, all require O(n) space.

The complexity of the algorithm can be estimated from two different points of view. In MAIN, the steps 2 and 3 are repeated at most $\lceil \log_d n \rceil$ times, where d stands for the average degree. In each repetition, however, the number of vertices dealt with grow geometrically in d. It is easy to visualize the situation, if we consider the case of a bipartite graph or a tree with average degree d(if regular, then $d = \delta = \Delta$). In such a case the algorithm SIFT returns with max-deg=0, in every pass through step 2a of MAIN and thus the graph structure is easily recognized. The maximum independent set will, however, be given by the larger of the two lists ind-list and dep-list.

A second approach to the analysis of MAIN, is to observe that the two lists ind-list and dep-list are constructed sequentially without backtracking. These lists partition the vertex set and the total operations involved are essentially, examination of adjacency lists of all vertices and building of links in lists of total size n. Thus MAIN works in O(n) time. The 'seemingly' redundant operations involved in step 3 and step 2a, which first include a set of neighbouring vertices in ind-list and then removes some of the dependent vertices by invoking SIFT, are also accomplished in O(n) time. The algorithm SIFT traverses the ind-list twice-once to perform the ordering of dependency and a second time to carry out the dependent vertices elimination. Since the maximum list sizes can be n, these operations are also performed in O(n) time. By using a maximum of Δ (maximum degree) lists, the ordering is achieved in O(1) without recourse to sorting. Thus the overall complexity in the worst case is O(n).

4. Proof of correctness of the algorithm

We now state and prove the main result.

Theorem 4.1 : The algorithm described in section 3, finds a maximum independent set of size greater than $\alpha/2$ in a planar triangle free graph.

The proof of the theorem requires certain auxiliary results which we prove first.

Lemma 4.1 : From a set S of k vertices in a graph G, removal of atmost k/2 vertices leaves the remaining vertices independent.

Proof : Order the set of k vertices according to their degree as $d_1 \geq d_2 \geq \dots \geq d_k$. Deletion of a vertex of maximum degree (= max-deg as in algorithm SIFT of section 3.1) at each stage reduces the total degree by 2. max-deg. Thus by removing at most k/2 vertices, of maximum degree at each stage, the total degree reduces to zero leaving the remaining vertices independent. □

Lemma 4.2: In a planar bipartite graph with $\delta = 2$, in which the edges are forbidden from crossing the face F (as shown) the number of vertices in the partite set P_2 is atleast $\left\lceil \frac{k+2}{2} \right\rceil$ if $|P_1| = k$.

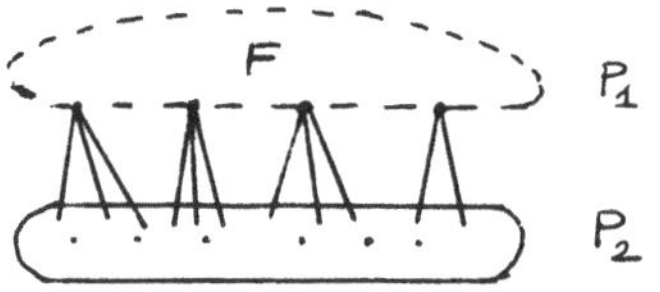

Proof : $|P_1| = k$. Since all edges of G lie on the complement of face F and since every face is bounded by a four-cycle, no more than four edges can be incident on any vertex of P_2. Thus $4\,|P_2| \geq e \geq 2k$ or $|P_2| \geq k/2$. In fact, all but the two extreme vertices of P_2 (which can have degree 2) can have degree four. Hence $4\,|P_2| - 4 \geq 2k$ or $|P_2| \geq k+2/2$. □

Proof of theorem 4.1: In a planar triangle free graph with k degree 2 vertices, we have, by lemma 2.4 an upper bound on the maximum independent set $\alpha \leq (2n + k)/3$. We shall now show that our approximation algorithm obtains an independent set $I(G)$ of size at least $k/2+(n-k)/3=(2n+k)/6$. These two together imply that $|I(G)|/\alpha \geq 1/2$.

To show that $|I(G)| \geq (2n+k)/6$, we observe that our algorithm SIFT finds atleast $k/2$ independent degree 2 vertices (see lemma 4.1). It remains to show that of the remaining $(n-k)$ vertices of degree greater than two, the algorithm finds $(n-k)/3$ independent vertices. It suffices to prove this for the general case with $\delta = 3$.

<u>Claim</u> : The algorithm finds an independent set $I(G)$ of size atleast $n/3$ in a planar triangle free graph with $|V| = n$ and $\delta = 3$.

We prove this by induction.

It is easy to verify that the algorithm produces an independent set of atleast $n/3$ vertices for all graphs with $n \leq 8$. We assume as the inductive hypothesis that the claim holds for all graphs with less than n vertices. Let $G = (V,E)$ with $|V| = n$ be a planar triangle free graph with $\delta = 3$.

At each stage in the algorithm we have a set D of dependent vertices and a set N of neighbours of vertices in D, of sizes, say, k and x respectively. Our algorithm finds atleast y independent neighbours from N. We then restrict our attention to the graph $G' = (V', E')$ obtained by removing the $k+x$ vertices from G after adding y vertices to the independent set $I(G)$. Thus, we have, by the induction hypothesis,

$|I(G')| \geq |V'|/3$, and by construction

$|I(G)| \geq |I(G')| + y$

$|V| \leq |V'| + k + x$.

These three inequalities together imply that

$$|I(G)| \geq |V|/3 + (y - (k+x)/3).$$

We next show that the ratio $y/(k+x)$ 1/3, which would prove our claim that $|I(G)|/|V| = |I(G)|/n \geq 1/3$.

To show this we observe that the graph G' constructed during the stages of the algorithm MAIN partitions the vertices successively into independent and dependent sets. Thus at any stage we have a set of dependent vertices D and its neighbour set N. The sets D and N satisfy the hypothesis of lemma 4.2, with $|D| = k$ and $|N| = x$. Lemma 4.2 implies that $y \geq k/2$ if $x \leq k$ and lemma 4.1 implies that $y \geq x/2$ if $x \geq k$, and our algorithms MAIN and SIFT obtain these y independent vertices. Thus, in either case, we can bunch the remaining $x-y$ dependent vertices of the set N as belonging to the dependent set D considered in the next stage along with the neighbours of the resulting independent vertices of N. This implies that we need only to consider the ratio y/(k+y). Now

$$\frac{y}{k+y} \geq \frac{k/2}{k+k/2} > 1/3 \qquad \text{if } x \leq k,$$

$$\frac{y}{k+y} \geq \frac{x/2}{k+x/2} > 1/3 \qquad \text{if } x \geq k,$$

thereby proving our claim and hence the theorem. □

Conclusion : In this paper we have developed an O(n) time approximation algorithm for finding an independent set of size atleast half of the maximum independent set, in planar traingle free graphs. Our technique is therefore an algorithmic verification of a conjecture that $\alpha \geq n/3$. While the algorithm may produce an independent set with a much better ratio than 1/2, the difficulty lies in evolving a proof technique to improve this worst case lower bound.

Our algorithm produces larger independent sets if a large proportion of the set of neighbours of a set of vertices are mutually independent in a planar triangle free graph. This would depend upon the probability that the triangle free property related to a single vertex is carried over to a set of vertices. The theory of random graphs is likel to aid in such studies, and to devise probabilistic algorithms that produce a 'large' independent set 'almost surely' or with very high probability.

References

1 M.O. ALBERTSON, Finding an independent set in planar graphs. In Graphs and Combinatorics, R.A. Bari and F. Harary, Eds.Springer, Berlin (1974) pp.173-179.

2 N. CHIBA, T.NISHIZEKI AND N. SAITO, A linear 5-coloring algorithm of planar graphs, J. Algorithms, 2(1981), pp.317-327.

3 N. CHIBA, T. NISHIZEKI AND N. SAITO, An algorithm for finding a large independent set in planar graphs, Networks 13(1983), pp. 247-252.

4 N.CHIBA, T. NISHIZEKI AND N. SAITO, An approximation algorithm for the maximum independent set problem on planar graphs, SIAM J.Comput. 11(1982), pp.663-675.

5 M.R.GAREY AND D.S.JOHNSON, Computers and Intractability: A guide to the theory of NP-completeness, W.H.Freeman, San Francisco, 1979.

6 M.R.GAREY, D.S.JOHNSON AND L.STOCKMEYER, Some simplified NP-complete graph problems, Theoret.Comput.Sci., 1(1976), pp.237-267.

7 J.R.GRIGGS, Lower bounds on the independence number in terms of degree, J.Comb.Th.Ser.B. 34 (1983), pp.22-39.

8 F.HARARY, Graph Theory, Addison-Wesley, Reading, MA, 1972.

9 R.J. LIPTON AND R.E. TARJAN, Applications of the planar separator theorem, SIAM J. Comput., 9(1980), pp.615-627.

10 J.B.SHEARER, A note on the independence number of triangle free graphs, Disc.Math., 46, (1983), No.1, pp.83-87.

GRID FILE ALGORITHMS: AN ANALYSIS IN THE BIASED CASE

Mireille REGNIER

INRIA

Rocquencourt

78153-Le Chesnay (France)

ABSTRACT

Multi-key access to records in a dynamically growing file may be performed using grid file algorithms[7] . *We specify two of them , that generalize mono-dimensional dynamic hashing. Then, we derive the average sizes of the associated directories and provide an asymptotic analysis for uniform and biased distributions. The growth of the indexes is non linear; for uniform distributions, sizes are:* $O(n^{1+\frac{1}{b}})$ *or* $O(n^{1+\frac{s-1}{sb+1}})$, *where* s *is the number of attributes being used,* n *the file size, and* b *the page capacity of the system. At last, we compare exact values and asymptotics and study the robustness of grid file algorithms with respect to the bias of the distribution.*

INTRODUCTION

We are dealing with *dynamic multidimensional structures* for datas stored on secondary memory and accessed by an *index*. Several such physical access methods have been proposed for data bases systems [12, 3, 8, 14] . and, in particular, the so-called ***grid file algorithms***[7] Generalizing some usual single key retrieval search techniques, they apply to the search of records characterized by several keys or attributes. The index is a multidimensional array - **a grid-** which contains addresses of records on secondary memory. When the size of the data set varies, it may grow (or shrink) dynamically, still ensuring a constant access cost to the file: say two disk accesses on the average. The two of them we study generalize Extendible Hashing [5] and Dynamic Hashing [9] to the multidimensional case. Thus we name them : Multidimensional Extendible (resp. Dynamic) Hashing and note MEH (resp. MDH). We specify them in Section 1. Then we provide an analysis on the average for uniform and biased distributions. These problems were left unsolved in [7] . To do so we derive in Section 2 the exact values of the average sizes of indexes . And in Section 3, we compute their asymptotic expansions. Using some elaborate asymptotic techniques (Mellin transform,Laplace method...), we prove that the growth is *non linear*. We also discuss the robustness of the algorithms. Finally, in Section 4, we compare MEH and MDH with respect to their asymptotic behaviours and transient phases. And we suggest choices in relation to the capacity of pages in secondary memory.

1. Grid File Algorithms

We define here the *grid file* algorithms (see [7]) and make precise two of them that we analyse below. Our general assumption about the system used is the existence of virtual memory. More precisely, secondary memory is divided in pages with a fixed capacity b that the system may allocate or remove.

1.1. Geometric partitions and grid file algorithms

The basic idea of grid file algorithms is to use *geometric partitions of the data set* that may be naturally defined, provided some hypotheses are satisfied. We assume in the following that records are identified by a key formed on s attributes that range in $[0,1]$. Thus, these attributes may be seen as reals in $[0,1]$ or, equivalently, infinite sequences of bits 0–1. Using their values as coordinates, we may represent them geometrically in the domain $[0,1]^s$.

We describe the algorithms for two attributes, the generalization to $s>2$ is easy. A geometric partition of any set of n records in subsets that contain at most b records is created by using the recursive procedure *PARTITION* (see below). At the first step, one calls *PARTITION*$([0,1],[0,1],b,0,0)$.

```
procedure PARTITION(INT1,INT2,b,var k1,k2:integer);
begin
if      INT1 × INT2 contains more than b records
then    if      k1=k2
        then    begin
                split INT1 into two adjacent subintervals, INT1_l and INT1_r;
                PARTITION(INT1_l,INT2,b,k1+1,k2);
                PARTITION(INT1_r,INT2,b,k1+1,k2);
                end
        else    begin (* k1=k2+1*)
                split INT2 into two adjacent subintervals,
                INT2_l and INT2_r;
                PARTITION(INT1,INT2_l,b,k1,k2+1);
                PARTITION(INT1,INT2_r,b,k1,k2+1);
                end
end;
```

Three examples are given in Figure A., where the records are represented by × and the elements of the partition by the closed regions. Notice that when the partition is done (see Figure A.), the shape of the final regions are quite pecular: they are either square or they may be split into two squares by a horizontal line. As a matter of fact, a rectangular region R, defined as $INT1 \times INT2$ with $k_1 = k_2$, which contains more than b records is split by PARTITION into two rectangular regions by a vertical line. Simultaneously, the records in R are divided into two subsets, according to the value of their first attribute. At the next step, a rectangular region -with $k_1 = k_2 + 1$ - is divided, if necessary i.e. if it containsmore than b records, into two squares by a horizontal line. The corresponding subset is divided according to the value of the second attribute. Then, one may speak of *vertical* and *horizontal* splits.

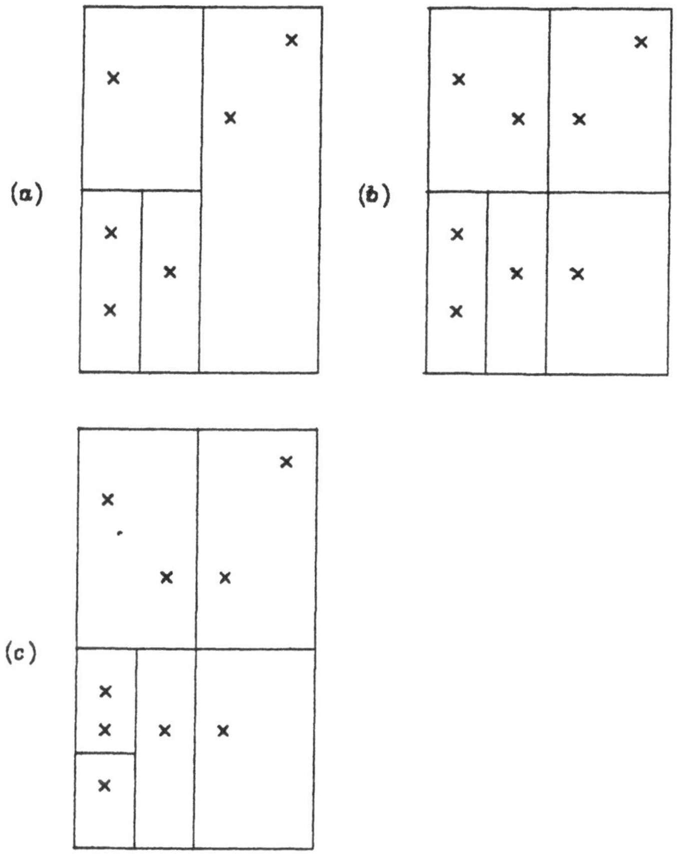

Fig.A.: *Three possible partitions of* $[0,1] \times [0,1]$ *,when* $b=2$.

These partitions organize secondary memory: a page is allocated for each element of the partition. To adress these pages, one uses an index or a directory. When the data set grows (or shrinks), the partition may be refined and the index must be maintained dynamically, according to grid file algorithms. One may distinguish two types of indexes and algorithms. The division of intervals by PARTITION may depend on the values of the data already inserted in the file or it may be fixed in advance by some law. We are dealing now with this second type, and we even assume that intervals are always split into two subintervals of equal lengths (see the *buddy system* in [5]). Thus, grid file algorithms generalize dynamic hashing algorithms to the multidimensional case. Moreover, we will study directories that are independent of the history of insertions (which makes the implementation easier).

1.2. MEH and MDH algorithms

We present here Multidimensional Extendible Hashing and Multidimensional Dynamic Hashing algorithms that will be analysed in Sections 2 and 3. In both of them, the partition of the plane domain previously defined is refined by some embedding in a 2-dimensional array -represented as a ***grid*** -, containing pointers to secondary memory.

The construction of the MEH directory is described in [14] as *EXCELL* method. Considering in the partition the element of smallest surface, one may "embed" the whole partition in a refined one where all the regions are of equal surface σ. For example, the Figure A.a. may be embedded in the 2-dimensional array of Figure B.a., where the numbers represent the different pages in secondary memory. Remark that pages may be addressed several times. We shall see below that this will make easier the allocations of memory. In order to save space, one also defines Multikey Dynamic Hashing (or MDH) directories. Intuitively, every ***line*** that appears in the partition is extended to the whole space. For example, the Figure A.a. may be embedded in the directory of Figure B.b.

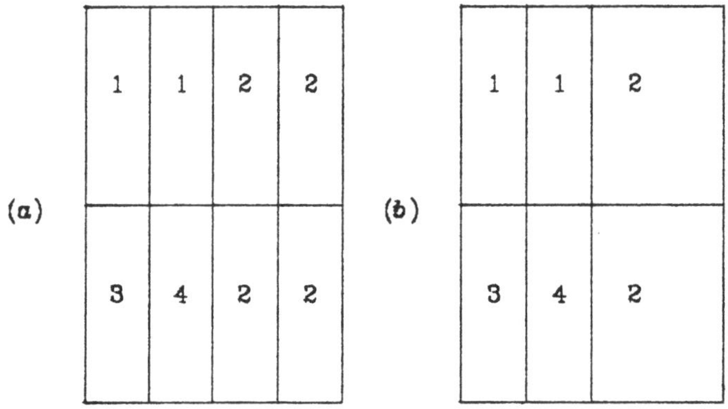

Fig.B.: *MEH* and *MDH indexes associated to geometric partitions of A.*

The first advantage of such directories is to allow retrieving records with only one disk access, provided that the index may be kept resident in core. As a matter of fact, to access some record, one uses the values of its attributes to chose an entry of the index. Then, following the pointer found in that entry, one retrieves the page containing the record sought. The second advantage is that such structures are suitable for dynamically varying sets of data. When the data set grows, the partition may be modified by a local refinement according to procedure PARTITION. Such an evolution is represented in Figure A: (a),(b) and (c). Whenever a new record is addressed to a region that already contains b records, this region has to be split into two parts: the corresponding page m is full and *overflows*. Such events are called *collisions*. Some new page m_2 is allocated and the $b+1$ records are shared among m_1 and m_2 according to the new partition.

This modification of the organization of secondary memory is taken into account in the index in two possible ways.

In the first -and easy- case, the refinement has no effect on the embedding (see for example the change from Figure A.a. to A.b). The new subdivision already exist in the MEH and MDH directories. associated to A.a. (see B.a and B.b.). Thus, we get the directories in Figure C.a. and C.b., corresponding to the data set in Figure A.b. Notice that we may have to modify several pointers (see C.a.).

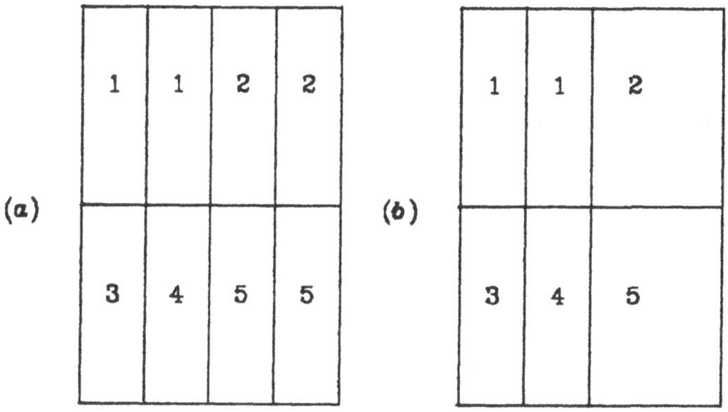

Fig.C.: *MEH* and *MDH indexes associated to Figure A.b.*

In the second case, collisions produce a modification of the structure of the index. This is lustrated in the change from A.b. to A.c. and the associated indexes are drawn in Figure D. In EH algorithms, whenever a collision occurs on an element of the partition of smallest size, ne must double in size the directory, copy m pointers and finally update one of them: see .a. In MDH algorithms, a "new line is drawn". Some pointers are copied, a new one, pointing o the newly allocated page, is written: see D.b.

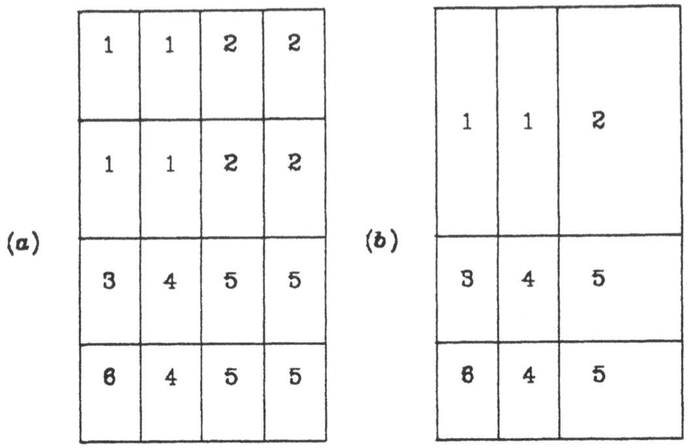

Fig.D.: *MEH* and *MDH indexes associated to Figure A.c.*

One must remark that such definitions imply that MEH and MDH directories uniquely depend on the data distribution and are ***independent of the history of insertions***. It is worth illustrating this assertion for MDH. Assume a collision happens on the rightmost lower case in A.c. One should not use the horizontal line creating two entries to page 5 in C.b. (such an impossible directory is drawn in E.a.). But one forces a vertical line to be drawn and gets the directory in Figure E.b. One may verify that this index is the one that would have been obtained if the collision on page 5 had occurred before the collision on page 3 that changed A.b. to A.c.

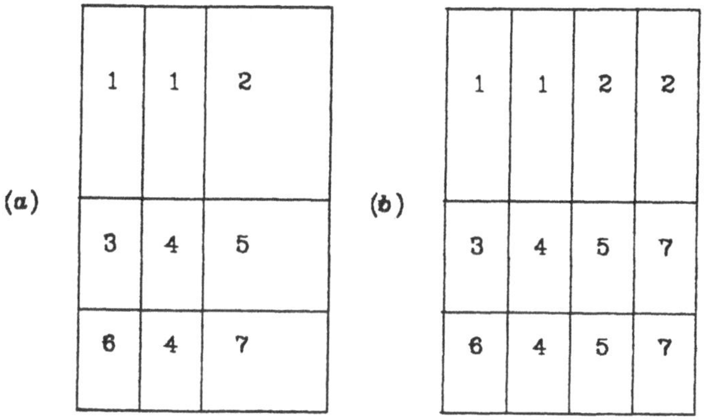

Fig.E.: *Independency of the history of insertions.*

Remark 1: Notice also that for $s=1$, i.e. when records are characterized by a single key ranging in [0,1], MEH and MDH reduce to Extendible and Dynamic Hashing (EH or DH). [5, 9]

Remark 2: As the intervals are split into two subintervals of equal length, we consider the attributes of a record as infinite sequences of bits 0-1. This helps choosing the region in the partition it belongs to. As a matter of fact, whenever an interval is split, one must use one more bit of the key to address it. For example, page 5 contains all the keys (1..,1..) in D.b. and (10..,1..) in E.b. Generalizing a notion of monodimensional dynamic hashing, we call **depth of an interval** the number of bits of the keys necessary to address records in this interval.

To sum up, we may say that both MDH and MEH directories are associated to the same geometric partitions of the space and are independent of the history of insertions. Moreover, they can manage dynamically growing sets and records are retrieved with a constant number of disk access. In the next sections, we are dealing with performances. It is pointed out in [14] that the algorithm MEH is the algorithm Extendible Hashing on one key obtained by shuffling the s keys. Thus, the occupation of the file, obviously the same for MEH and MDH, is the one studied for EH and DH in [9, 10, 13, 15], see Theorem A.

Theorem A: *When the data are uniformly distributed according to a Bernoulli or Poisson law, for both EH and DH, the average load factor of the data part α fluctuates around* $\log 2$, *or* $p\log\frac{1}{p}+q\log\frac{1}{q}$ *when the distribution is biased.*

Moreover, the average size of the directory of EH or MEH satisfies asymptotically:

$$S_{MEH}(n) = P(\{(1+\frac{1}{b})\log_2(n)\})n^{1+\frac{1}{b}} + O(n).$$

where P is a continuous periodic function with period 1 and mean:

$$\frac{1}{\log 2}[(b+1)!]^{\frac{-1}{b}}\Gamma(1-\frac{1}{b}).$$

We study below the size of MEH and MDH directories, for uniform and biased distributions. The size of EH indexes have been derived for uniform distributions [2, 1] and are reminded in Theorem A. Moreover, when MDH is used, some information about splits on the attributes should be kept in core. One creates *axial directories* (see a possible implementation in [11]). Their sizes are also studied below.

2. Analysis:

2.1. The Statistical Model:

In order to derive an analysis on the average, we make precise here some hypotheses on the data distribution. We assumed in the first part that records were identified by a key formed with s attributes ranging in [0,1]. Eventually, hashing would reduce to that case. We make two hypotheses on the distribution *on the attributes* of the keys, considered as infinite sequences of bits.

(i) the values of the keys on the s attributes are independent.

(ii) for any attribute i, for any j, the bit b_j^i satisfies either:

(a) $Pr(b_j^i=0)=Pr(b_j^i=1)=\frac{1}{2}$

(b) $Pr(b_j^i=0)=p$, $Pr(b_j^i=1)=q$, $p+q=1$

In (a) the distribution is *uniform*, in (b), it is *biased*.

It appears that the analysis can be done when we know the distribution of the keys hashed to r disjoint *volumes*, where the volumes are finite products of intervals. The distribution induced by (i) and (ii) is given in Proposition 2. To simplify the calculations, we make a Poisson approximation in multidimensional case. This is justified by the fact that Poisson and Bernoulli results are asymptotically equivalent [6] .

Proposition 2: *Let us assume that the number of records in the file follows a Poisson law with mean ν. Then, the random variables $J_1,\ldots,J_r$ of the number of records hashed to r disjoint* *blocks $I_1,\ldots,I_r$ of volumes $v_1,\ldots,v_r$ are r independent random variables, following Poisson laws with parameters: $\nu v_1,\ldots,\nu v_r$.*

Remark: Biased distributions define a new measure on $[0,1]^s$. Proposition 2 still holds if we generalize the notion of *volume*. Consider only surfaces $2^{kv}\times 2^{kh}$ obtained by splits of intervals into 2 parts. All records adressed to such a surface S have keys of the form: $(b_1\ldots b_{kv}\ldots,c_1\ldots c_{kh}\ldots)$ with identical sequences (b_i) and (c_i). In the uniform case, the distribution on S only depends on the sum $kv+kh$ (see above), in the biased case one uses two more parameters k_1 and k_2, the number of 0-bits in sequences (b_i) and (c_i). These parameters also count the number of left vertical (resp. horizontal) splits performed to "draw this rectangular surface". According to hypotheses (ii.b), the number of records addressed to S is $\nu p^{k_1} q^{kv-k_1} p^{k_2} q^{kh-k_2}$ and one may call "volume" the quantity: $p^{k_1} q^{kv-k_1} p^{k_2} q^{kh-k_2}$.

We derive below the exact expressions of the average sizes of axial and main directories, for uniform and biased distributions.

Notation: Let $f_b(x)$ be the real function : $e_b(x)e^{-x}$ where:

$$e_b(x) = 1+\frac{x}{1!}+\ldots+\frac{x^b}{b!}.$$

2.2. Average sizes of axial directories:

Theorem 1

The expectation of the number of vertical (resp. horizontal) subdivisions is in the uniform case:

$$E_V(\nu) = \sum_{k\geq 0} 2^k\left(1-f_b(\nu 2^{-2k})^{2^k}\right). \qquad (a)$$

$$E_H(\nu) = \sum_{k\geq 0} 2^k\left(1-f_b(\nu 2^{-2k-1})^{2^{k+1}}\right).$$

or, in the biased case:

$$E_V(\nu) = \sum_{k\geq 0}\sum_{k_1=0}^{k}\binom{k}{k_1}\left(1-\prod_{k_2} f_b\left(\nu p^{k_1+k_2} q^{k-k_1+k-k_2}\right)^{\binom{k}{k_2}}\right) \qquad (b)$$

$$E_H(\nu) = \sum_{k\geq 0}\sum_{k_1=0}^{k}\binom{k}{k_1}\left(1-\prod_{k_2} f_b\left(\nu p^{k_1+k_2} q^{k-k_1+k+1-k_2}\right)^{\binom{k+1}{k_2}}\right)$$

The expectation of entries in the vertical (resp. horizontal) index is:

$$N_V(\nu) = 1+E_V(\nu)\ , \ (resp.\ N_H(\nu) = 1+E_H(\nu)\ ).$$

To prove this, we estimate, for all the possible subdivisions, their probabilities to exist. We must introduce a new notion. We have already defined the ***depth of a subdivision or a line***. Notice that a line at depth k splits some associated column or row of width 2^{-k}. This column (or row) contains records from the data set with keys of the form: $b_1 \ldots b_k$. Let the **left split number** be the number of 0-bits in this sequence. For example, the dotted vertical or horizontal line in Figure 2.2. are associated to 1 and 0 while their depths are 1 and 2. We get now:

Lemma 1:

Let Δ_V (resp. Δ_H) be a vertical (resp. horizontal) line at depth k, with left split number k_1. We have, in the uniform case:

$$P(\Delta_V) = 1-f_b(\nu 2^{-2k})^{2^k}\ ,$$

$$P(\Delta_H) = 1-f_b(\nu 2^{-2k-1})^{2^{k+1}}\ .$$

and, in the biased case:

$$P(\Delta_V) = (1-\prod_{k_2} f_b(\nu p^{k_1+k_2} q^{k-k_1+k-k_2})^{\binom{k}{k_2}})$$

$$P(\Delta_H) = (1-\prod_{k_2} f_b(\nu p^{k_1+k_2} q^{k-k_1+k+1-k_2})^{\binom{k+1}{k_2}})$$

Proof: We establish Lemma 1 for the vertical subdivisions. We first consider the uniform case.

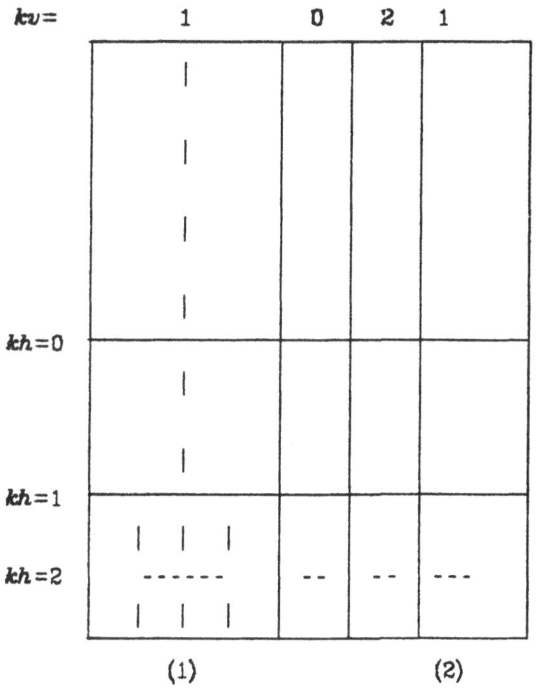

Figure 2.2.b: *Intersection of* Δ_H *at depth* $kh=2$ and Δ_V *at depth* $kv=1$

The column of width 2^{-k} associated to a vertical line Δ_V at depth k may be logically divided in 2^k squares of dimensions $2^{-k}\times 2^{-k}$. This line will not exist iff no vertical split has been performed on any of these squares. This means that none of them contains more than b elements. We know that the probability that such a square of surface 2^{-2k} contains at most b elements is, according to Proposition 2:

$$\sum_{i=0}^{b} e^{-\nu 2^{-2k}} \frac{(\nu 2^{-2k})^i}{i!} = f_b(\nu 2^{-2k}) .$$

As the 2^k squares are disjoint and the distributions are independent, the probability of such an event is thus: $f_b(\nu 2^{-2k})^{2^k}$, and we get:

$$P(\Delta_V) = 1-f_b(\nu 2^{-2k})^{2^k} .$$

We derive in the same manner the results on horizontal lines, considering 2^{k+1} rectangles of dimensions $2^{-(k+1)}\times 2^{-k}$ (see for example the dotted line for $kh=2$).

We are dealing now with biased distributions. Consider again the 2^k squares associated to a vertical line Δ_V at depth k. For all records in a given square, the second attribute keys start with the same sequence: $b_1 \ldots b_k$, with k_2 0-bits. Then the volume is: $p^{k_1}q^{k-k_1}p^{k_2}q^{k-k_2}$, $k_2=0..k$, and the probability that it contains less than b records is: $f_b(\nu p^{k_1+k_2}q^{k-k_1+k-k_2})$. As distributions are independent, we get:

$$P(\Delta_V) = \prod_{k_2=0}^{k} f_b(\nu p^{k_1+k_2} q^{k-k_1+k-k_2})^{\binom{k+1}{k_2}}$$

Theorem 1 follows. The expectation of the number of subdivisions is obtained by summation. There are 2^k possible lines at depth k, and $\binom{k}{k_1}$ among them with a parameter k_1.

2.3..Average sizes of main directories:

Theorem 2:

The total number of grid blocks is , on the average:

$$S_{MDH}(\nu) = N_H(\nu)\ .\ N_V(\nu) - T(\nu) - 1$$

where N_H and N_V are the average sizes of axial directories, and $T(\nu)$ is, in the uniform case:

$$\sum_{kv,kh\geq 0} 2^{kv+kh} f_b(\nu 2^{-2kv})^{2^{kv}} f_b(\nu 2^{-2kh-1})^{2^{kh+1}}$$

$$\times(1-f_b(\nu 2^{-2kv})^{-2^{kv-kh}}\delta_{kv>kh}-f_b(\nu 2^{-2kh-1})^{-2^{kh+1-kv}}\delta_{kv\leq kh}),$$

and, in the biased case:

$$\sum_{kv,kh}\sum_{k_1=0}^{kv}\sum_{k_2=0}^{kh}\binom{kv}{k_1}\binom{kh}{k_2}\prod_{k_4} f_b(\nu p^{k_4}q^{kh+1-k_4}p^{k_2}q^{kh-k_2})^{\binom{kh+1}{k_4}}\prod_{k_3} f_b(\nu p^{k_1}q^{kv-k_1}p^{k_3}q^{kv-k_3})^{\binom{kv}{k_3}}$$

$$(1-\frac{\delta_{kv>kh}}{\prod_{m=0}^{kv-kh} f_b(\nu p^{k_1}q^{kv-k_1}p^{k_2+m}q^{kv-k_2-m})^{\binom{kv-kh}{m}}}$$

$$-\frac{\delta_{kv\leq kh}}{\prod_{m=0}^{kh+1-kv} f_b(\nu p^{k_1+m}q^{kh+1-m}p^{k_2}q^{kh-k_2})^{\binom{kh+1-kv}{m}}})$$

To prove this, we first remark that the number of grid blocks is the number of intersections of lines. Thus we study in Lemma 2 the probability that the intersection of a vertical line Δ_V at depth kv with parameter k_1 and of a horizontal line Δ_H at depth kh with parameter k_2 exist.

Lemma 2:

Let Δ_V and Δ_H be two vertical and horizontal lines (or subdivisions). Let kv and kh be their depths, k_1 and k_2 their left split numbers. We note $P((\text{no}\,\Delta_V)\cap(\text{no}\,\Delta_H))$ the probability that none of them exist. This quantity is, for uniform or biased distributions :

(i) if $kv>kh$:

$$f_b(\nu 2^{-2kh-1})^{2^{kh+1}}\times f_b(\nu 2^{-2kv})^{2^{kv}(1-2^{-kh})} \quad \text{(a)}$$

$$\frac{\prod_{k_4} f_b(\nu p^{k_4}q^{kh+1-k_4}p^{k_2}q^{kh-k_2})^{\binom{kh+1}{k_4}}\prod_{k_3} f_b(\nu p^{k_1}q^{kv-k_1}p^{k_3}q^{kv-k_3})^{\binom{kv}{k_3}}}{\prod_{m=0}^{kv-kh} f_b(\nu p^{k_1}q^{kv-k_1}p^{k_2+m}q^{kv-k_2-m})^{\binom{kv-kh}{m}}} \quad \text{(b)}$$

(ii) if $kv\leq kh$:

$$f_b(\nu 2^{-2kv})^{2^{kv}}\times f_b(\nu 2^{-2kh-1})^{2^{kh+1}(1-2^{-kv})} \quad \text{(a)}$$

$$\frac{\prod_{k_4} f_b(\nu p^{k_4}q^{kh+1-k_4}p^{k_2}q^{kh-k_2})^{\binom{kh+1}{k_4}}\prod_{k_3} f_b(\nu p^{k_1}q^{kv-k_1}p^{k_3}q^{kv-k_3})^{\binom{kv}{k_3}}}{\prod_{m=0}^{kh+1-kv} f_b(\nu p^{k_1+m}q^{kh+1-m}p^{k_2}q^{kh-k_2})^{\binom{kh+1-kv}{m}}} \quad \text{(b)}$$

Proof of Lemma 2: We derive the result when $kv \le kh$: see the intersection of dotted lines in Figure 2.2. We write:

$$P((no\,\Delta_V) \cap (no\,\Delta_H)) = P(no\,\Delta_V).P((no\,\Delta_H)/\,(no\,\Delta_V)).$$

where $P((no\,\Delta_V) \cap (no\,\Delta_H))$ is the probability that neither Δ_V nor Δ_H exist. The line Δ_V (resp. Δ_H)does not exist iff none of the rectangles in the surfaces (1) and(2) contains more than b elements. As surface (1) is included in a square defined by Δ_V -and thus unsplit- we get:

$$P((no\,\Delta_H)/\,(no\,\Delta_V)) = P(no\ rectangle\ in\ (2)\ contains\ more\ than\ b\ elements)$$

$$= \frac{P(\Delta_H)}{P(no\ rectangle\ in\ (1)\ has\ more\ than\ b\ elements)}$$

When the distribution is uniform, all the rectangles have the same volume: 2^{-2kh-1} and there are $2^{kh+1-kv}$ of them in (1). The result is then established. When it is biased, the volumes are different. For all records in rectangles defined by Δ_H, the second attribute keys have the kh first bits identical, with k_2 0-bits. For rectangles in (1), the first attribute keys have the kv first bits identical. As they are included in the surface defined by Δ_V they have k_1 0-bits. Moreover, the next $kh+1-kv$ that also characterize them contain m 0-bits. Thus the volumes are: $p^{k_1+m} q^{kh+1-k_1-m} p^{k_2} q^{kv-k_2}$, and Lemma 2 follows.

■

Proof of Theorem 2: We note $P(\Delta_V \cap \Delta_H)$ the probability that Δ_V and Δ_H both exist. As:

$$E(\Delta_V \cap \Delta_H) = E(\Delta_V) + E(\Delta_H) + E((no\,\Delta_V) \cap (no\,\Delta_H)) - 1,$$

summing over all the possible intersections, we get Theorem 2. For example, for a uniform distribution and $kv \le kh$, we write:

$$E(\Delta_V \cap \Delta_H) = (1 - f_b(\nu 2^{-2kv})^{2^{kv}}) \times (1 - f_b(\nu 2^{-2kh-1})^{2^{kh+1}})$$

$$- f_b(\nu 2^{-2kh-1})^{2^{kh+1}} f_b(\nu 2^{-2kv})^{2^{kv}} (1 - f_b(\nu 2^{-2kh-1})^{-2^{kh+1-kv}}) .$$

There are 2^{kv+kh} possible pairs of lines at depths kv and kh.Thus,we count 2^{kv+kh} intersections of lines (Δ_V, kv) and (Δ_H, kh). We count too half of the intersections with the edges. Finally, considering also the case $kv > kh$, we get:

$$S_{MDH}(\nu) = \sum_{kv,\,kh \ge 0} 2^{kv+kh} (1 - f_b(\nu 2^{-2kv})^{2^{kv}})(1 - f_b(\nu 2^{-2kh-1})^{2^{kh}}) + E_H(\nu) + E_V(\nu) - T(\nu)$$

$$= (E_H(\nu)+1) \times (E_V(\nu)+1) - T(\nu) - 1 = N_H(\nu) \times N_V(\nu) - T(\nu) - 1 .$$

3. Asymptotic behaviour of MDH directories:

The expressions we derived in Section 2 are quite intricated. In order to know the variations of these quantities with the number n of records, we study their asymptotic expansions. The techniques involve both Mellin transform methods and the Laplace method for integrals. We recall some general principles in Section 3.1. More details are given in[6] . Then we study in 3.2. axial directories sizes, $N_V(\nu)$ and $N_H(\nu)$. Finally, in 3.3. we prove that the main directory size $S_{MDH}(\nu)$ is asymptotically equivalent to $N_V(\nu).N_H(\nu)$.

3.1. Mellin Transform:

The Mellin transform of a continuous function $f:[0,+\infty[\longrightarrow\mathbf{R}$ is:

$$f^*(s)=\int_0^\infty f(x)x^{s-1}dx=\mathbf{M}(f,s).$$

We have:

$$\begin{cases}(f+g)^*(s)=f^*(s)+g^*(s) & (i)\\ \mathbf{M}(f(ax),s)=a^{-s}\,\mathbf{M}(f,s) & (ii)\end{cases}.$$

The asymptotic expansion of such a function f is related to the singularities of its Mellin transform f^*. A pole α of f^* of order k, with the expansion, as $s\longrightarrow-\alpha$.:

$$f^*(s)=\frac{a_0}{s+\alpha}+\cdots+\frac{a_{k-1}}{(s+\alpha)^k},$$

is associated [4] in the asymptotic development of f to the term:

$$(a_0+\ldots+a_{k-1}(\log x)^{k-1})x^{-\alpha}.$$

In the following, we are dealing with *harmonic power sums*, i.e. functions F of the form:

$$F(x)=\sum_k \alpha_k f_b(\beta_k x)^{\gamma_k}\times g(\beta_k x),$$

where: $\gamma_k\to\infty$, $\beta_k\to 0$. A general treatment of such functions is done in [6, 13]. Under some conditions of regularity on f and g, we may replace $Log f$ and g by the first term of their development around 0. If G is the new simpler function obtained from F, we have:

$$F(x) \sim G(x)$$

and the order of approximation only depends on the next terms of the developments of *Logf* and g. Then, to expand G, we use again its Mellin transform. As G may be written as an ***harmonic sum:***

$$G(x) = \sum \alpha_k{}^* f\,(\beta_k{}^* x),$$

using properties of Mellin transform (see above), one gets:

$$G^*(s) = (\sum \alpha_k{}^* \beta_k^{*-s}).f^*(s)$$

whose singularities are usually easy to study.

3.2. Asymptotic Behaviour of Axial Directories sizes:

In grid file algorithms with $s=2$, we always perform vertical splits before horizontal ones. For any s, we may define an order of splitting on the attributes and number them $1,\ldots,j,\ldots,s$ accordingly. Thus, we prove:

Theorem 3: *The expected size of an axial directory associated to the attribute j satisfies, asymptotically, for uniform distributions:*

$$N_j(\nu) \sim 2^{-\frac{(j-1)b}{sb+1}} \nu^{\frac{1}{s}(1+\frac{s-1}{sb+1})} A_b P(\{\frac{1}{s}(1+\frac{s-1}{sb+1})\log_2\nu\}) + O(\nu^{\frac{1}{s}(1-\frac{(s-1)^2}{sb+1})}),$$

where:

$$A_b = \frac{1}{\log 2}[(b+1)!]^{-\frac{1}{sb+1}}\Gamma(1-\frac{1}{sb+1}).$$

$P(u)$ is a fluctuating function with small amplitude and period 1:

$$P(u) = \sum_{l=\infty}^{\infty} c_l e^{-2il\pi u},$$

with:

$$c_l = [(b+1)!]^{\chi_l} \frac{\Gamma(-\frac{1}{sb+1}+\chi_l)}{[(sb+1)\log 2\,\Gamma(1-\frac{1}{sb+1})]};\ \chi_l = \frac{2il\pi}{sb+1\log 2}$$

Proof:

We prove the theorem for $N_V(\nu)$, when $s=2$. Thus, $j=1$. To get the asymptotic expansion of: $N_V(\nu)$, we integrate the asymptotic expansion of:

$$\frac{d}{d\nu}N_V(\nu) = \frac{\nu^b}{b!}\sum_k 2^{-2kb} f_b(\nu 2^{-2k})^{2^k} \quad \times \frac{1}{e_b(\nu 2^{-2k})}.$$

If we define $F(\nu)$ by : $\frac{d}{d\nu}N_V(\nu) = \frac{\nu^b}{b!}F(\nu)$, we may apply the results of 3.1. As:

$$\begin{cases} \log f_b(x) = \log[e_b(x)e^{-x}] \sim -\frac{1}{(b+1)!}x^{b+1} \\ g(x) = \frac{1}{e_b(x)} \sim 1. \end{cases}$$

we get:

$$G(x) = \sum_k 2^{-2kb} e^{-\frac{2^{-k(2b+1)}\nu^{b+1}}{(b+1)!}}.$$

As: $\mathbf{M}(e^{-ax^{b+1}},s) = a^{-\frac{s}{b+1}}\Gamma(\frac{s}{b+1})$, we have:

$$G^*(s) = \frac{1}{b+1}\Gamma(\frac{s}{b+1})[(b+1)!]^{\frac{s}{b+1}} \quad \sum_k 2^{k\frac{s(2b+1)-2b(b+1)}{b+1}}$$

The series is analytic in the stripe: $0< Re(s) <s_1 = \frac{2b(b+1)}{2b+1}$ and meromorphic in $0<Re(s)$. Its poles in the stripe $<0,+\infty>$ are:

$$p_l = b(1+\frac{1}{2b+1}) + \frac{2il(b+1)\pi}{(2b+1)\log 2}, \quad l\in\mathbf{Z}$$

The residues at these poles are:

$$r_l = \frac{1}{(2b+1)\log 2}\Gamma(1-\frac{1}{2b+1}+\chi_l)[(b+1)!]^{\frac{2b}{2b+1}},$$

with:

$$\chi_l = \frac{2il\pi}{2b+1\log 2}.$$

From the correspondence (see 3.1.): $(p_l,r_l)\to r_l x^{-p_l}$, we get asymptotics for $G(\nu)$ and $F(\nu)$, and, by integration, of $N_V(\nu)$. Note that the periodicity of the function Q is a consequence of the fact that the poles p_l are regularly distributed on the vertical axis. We do not prove here the order of approximation: see the method in [6, 13].

3.3. Main Indexes:

In section 2, we derived $S_{MDH}(\nu) = N_V(\nu).N_H(\nu) + T(\nu)$. We show here that T is negligeable when compared to $N_V.N_H$. The meaning of this result is that the average size of the index is the product of the average sizes of the axial directories. This result still holds for $s>2$. We establish it first for uniform distributions.

Theorem 4:

The average size of the index of MDH satisfies, for a uniform distribution :

$$S_{MDH}(\nu) = \nu^{1+\frac{s-1}{sb+1}} c_b Q(\{\frac{1}{s}(1+\frac{1}{sb+1})\log_2(\nu)\}) + O(\nu^{\frac{1}{s}(1+\frac{1}{sb+1})}\log\nu)$$

where

$$c_b = \frac{2^{-\frac{(s-1)sb}{2(sb+1)}}}{(log\,2)^s}[(b+1)!]^{\frac{-s}{sb+1}}\Gamma(1-\frac{1}{sb+1})^s .$$

and $Q(u)$ *a periodic function with period* 1.

Proof of Theorem 4: We give the proof for $s=2$, and we use one lemma.

Lemma 3:

Let V be the double series:

$$V(\nu) = \frac{1}{(b+1)!}\sum_{a=1}^{\infty}\sum_{k=0}^{\infty} 2^{2(a+k)}(g_{a,k}(2^{-2(a+k)}x)+2^{-1}g_{a,k}(2^{-2(a+k)+1}x)),$$

with

$$g_{a,k}(x) = x^{b+1}f_b(x)^{2^{a+k-1}}.$$

Then:

$$V(\nu) = O(\nu^{\frac{1}{2}(1+\frac{1}{2b+1})}\log_2\nu)$$

and for any ν*:*

$$|T(\nu)| \le V(\nu) + N_H(\nu) + N_V(\nu) - 2 .$$

Theorem 4 follows immediately. We have $T(\nu) =_{as} O(\nu^{\frac{1}{2}(1+\frac{1}{2b+1})}\log_2\nu)$ and the order of the leading term of $N_H(\nu).N_V(\nu)$ is $\nu^{1+\frac{1}{2b+1}}$.

Proof of lemma 3 :

We first prove the inequality. We consider the terms in series T corresponding to $kv > kh$ and note $a = kv - kh$, $k = kd$. As:

$$\begin{cases} f_b(x2^{-2hd}-1)^{2^{kh}} \leq 1 \\ f_b(x2^{-2vd})^{2^{kv}(1-2^{-kd})} \leq f_b(x2^{-2vd})^{2^{kv}-1}, \; kh > 0. \\ |1-f_b(x)^m| \leq m\frac{x^{b+1}}{(b+1)!} \end{cases}$$

we get the result. When $kh \geq kv$, we let a be $kh+1-vd$ and k be kv.

We derive now the order of magnitude of V, which appears to be an harmonic power sum. As in 3.1., we replace $Log f_b(x)$ by its development in 0. Then:

$$V(x) \sim W(x).$$

where:

$$W(x) = \frac{x^{b+1}}{(b+1)!}\sum_{a=1}^{\infty}\sum_{k=0}^{\infty} 2^{-2(a+k)b}\left(e^{-\frac{x^{b+1}2^{-2(a+k)(2b+1)-1}}{(b+1)!}} + 2^b e^{-\frac{x^{b+1}2^{-2(a+k)(2b+1)}2^b}{(b+1)!}}\right).$$

Then, from properties (i) and (ii) in 3.1.:

$$W^*(s) = \frac{1}{b+1}\Gamma\left(\frac{s+b+1}{b+1}\right)2^{\frac{s+b+1}{b+1}} \times \sum_a 2^{a\frac{s(2b+1)+b+1}{b+1}} \sum_k 2^{k\frac{s(2b+1)+b+1}{b+1}}$$

This function $W^*(s)$ is analytic in the stripe $<-(b+1), -\frac{1}{2}(1+\frac{1}{2b+1})>$ and meromorphic in $<-(b+1), +\infty>$. Its poles in this stripe are:

$$r_l = -\frac{1}{2}\left(1+\frac{1}{2b}\right) + \frac{2il\pi}{2b+1}\frac{(b+1)}{\log 2},$$

with the order of multiplicity 2 . Note p_l the residues. Then:

$$V(\nu) \sim \nu^{\frac{1}{2}(1+\frac{1}{2b+1})}\log\nu \sum_{l\in\mathbb{Z}} p_l e^{\frac{2il\pi}{2b+1}(b+1)\log_2\nu} = O(\nu^{\frac{1}{2}(1+\frac{1}{2b+1})}\log_2\nu).$$

We may derive the same analysis for biased distributions, for $s=2$.

Theorem 5: *The average size of the index of MEH with 2 attributes and biased distribution (p,q) is*

$$S_{MEH}(\nu) = \sum_{k\geq 0} 2^k \Big(1 - \prod_{k_1=0}^{k} f_b(\nu p^{k_1} q^{k-k_1})^{\binom{k}{k_1}}\Big)$$

and satisfies asymptotically:

$$S_{MEH}(\nu) \sim \frac{\nu^{(b+1)a_p}[(b+1)!]^{-a_p}\Gamma(-a_p)a_p}{\log 2} P(\{(b+1)a_p \log_2 \nu\})$$

where $P(u)$ is a periodic function with mean 1 and $a_p = -\dfrac{1}{\log_2(p^{b+1}+q^{b+1})}$

Under the same hypotheses, the average size of MDH index has for asymptotic order:

$$A_\sigma \nu^{2(b+1)\sigma}$$

where σ is the smallest real (positive) root of:

$$(p^{b+1}+q^{b+1})^\sigma (p^{(b+1)\sigma}+q^{(b+1)\sigma}) = 1.$$

and

$$\begin{cases} A_\sigma = [(b+1)!]^{-2\sigma}\Gamma(-\sigma)^2(p^{b+1}+q^{b+1})^\sigma(ae^{\sigma a}+be^{\sigma b})^{-2} \\ a = \log(p^{b+1}+q^{b+1})+(b+1)\log p \\ b = \log(p^{b+1}+q^{b+1})+(b+1)\log q \end{cases}$$

First, we give some hints for the proof for MDH algorithms. We use the expressions in Theorem 2. Once more, we replace $Log f_b(x)$ by $-\dfrac{x^{b+1}}{(b+1)!}$. We get:

$$E_V(\nu) \sim F_V(\nu) \text{ and } E_H(\nu) \sim F_H(\nu).$$

with:

$$\begin{cases} F_V(\nu) = \displaystyle\sum_{k\geq 0}\sum_{k_1}\binom{k}{k_1}\Big(1-e^{-\frac{\nu^{b+1}}{(b+1)!}(p^{k_1}q^{k-k_1})^{b+1}(p^{b+1}+q^{b+1})^k}\Big) \\ F_V(\nu) = \displaystyle\sum_{k\geq 0}\sum_{k_1}\binom{k}{k_1}\Big(1-e^{-\frac{\nu^{b+1}}{(b+1)!}(p^{k_1}q^{k-k_1})^{b+1}(p^{b+1}+q^{b+1})^{k+1}}\Big) \end{cases}.$$

We have: $\mathbf{M}(1-e^{-ax^{b+1}},s) = \Gamma(\frac{s}{b+1}).a^{-\frac{s}{b+1}}$. Then:

$$F^*_v(s) = -[(b+1)!]^{\frac{s}{b+1}}.\sum_k (p^{b+1}+q^{b+1})^{-\frac{ks}{b+1}}(p^{-s}+q^{-s})^k.$$

We set $\sigma=-\frac{s}{b+1}$. $F^*{}_{\nu}(s)$ is analytic when $\Gamma(\frac{s}{b+1})$ and the series are both analytic, i.e. when $0<\sigma<\sigma_0$ where σ_0 satisfies the equation above in Theorem 6.

To compute the expression of the average size of MEH indexes, we consider the probability that no cell of surface 2^k exist -and there are $\begin{bmatrix}k\\k_1\end{bmatrix}$ among them of volume $p^{k_1}q^{k-k_1}$. we get them the desired expression as in the uniform case[5] . The derivation of the asymptotics is quite analogous to the computation in 3.1.

We are now concerned with robustness. We see first that $a_p\to\frac{1}{b}$ and $\sigma\to\frac{1}{2b+1}$ when $(p,q)\to(\frac{1}{2},\frac{1}{2})$. Thus, $(b+1)a_p\to\frac{b+1}{b}$ and $2(b+1)\sigma\to1+\frac{1}{2b+1}$. The constants involved in Theorem 6: $\frac{[(b+1)!]^{-a_p}\Gamma(-a_p)a_p}{\log 2}$ and A_σ converge to the corresponding constants in Theorem A and 3. But in Theorem 3, the leading term is multiplied by a periodic function Q. The periodic terms are associated to a first set of poles of the Mellin transform regularly distributed on the vertical axis (D). Such a phenomenon seems to disappear for MDH, as Equation 1) has a unique solution with real part σ.

Nevertheless, a more careful study shows it admits a set of poles "almost regularly distributed on some convex curve (C). (C) is symmetric with respect to the real axis, the intersection with this axis is σ and the closest p is to $\frac{1}{2}$, the closest (C) is to (D). Analytically, we have:

$$S_{MDH}(\nu)\sim\nu^{2(b+1)\sigma}(1+\sum_{l\in\mathbb{Z}}p_l n^{-\varepsilon}e^{-2il\pi[(b+1)\sigma-\varepsilon]\log_2\nu})$$

which is almost periodical, when n is not too big. Then, MEH and MDH algorithms appear to be robust when the distribution is slightly biased.

. Discussion:

We have seen in Section 1 that the organization of secondary memory is the same for both MEH and MDH. We are concerned here with the size of directories. We have seen previously that MDH was asymptotically better than MEH. However, to compare them, one must consider the constants involved and the convergence of real sizes to the asymptotics. To do so, we will consider the uniform case. Then, we will use the asymptotics to discuss the robustness.

We plot the directory sizes when n ranges. They are obtained either by simulations-30-, or by computation of the exact values (Theorem 1) or by computation of the asymptotics. On may see some general properties. First, the periodicity phenomenon clearly appears. Second, the sizes grow step by step and, the biggest b is and the more uniform is the distribution, the quicker are the transitions.

In Figure 4.a. and 4.b., we are concerned with the uniform case for $b=10$, (resp. 50). We have computed S_{MEH} and S_{MDH} using the MACSYMA system; the corresponding graphs are (1) and (2). The two graphs coincide when b is 50. This result is general when b is big. $\frac{\nu^{1+\frac{1}{b}}}{\nu^{1+\frac{1}{2b+1}}}$ remains close to 1 , even for large ν, and the constants involved are almost equal as: $\frac{A_b}{C_b} \approx 2^{\frac{1}{2}} \log 2 \approx 1$.

When b is smaller: $b=10$, the curves are quite distinct and MDH seems asymptotically better. To study transient phases we plot the curves (3) and (4) obtained by simulation that correspond to MDH and MEH. In both cases, MDH appears to be better. The difference is about 30% when $b=10$, 10% when $b=50$ and would be even less for bigger b.

We assume now that the distribution is slightly biased (see 2.1.) and that $s=2$. To compare the robustness of algorithms in the transient phases, we have computed the expressions of the average sizes of directories for $p \neq q$, given in Theorem A for MEH and Theorem 1 for MDH. In Figures 4.c. (resp. 4.d.), we plot the sizes of directories for MEH when $b=100$ (resp. for MDH, when $b=50$). Curves (1), (2), (3) and (4) are associated to $(p,q)=(0.5,0.5)$, $(0.48,0.52)$, $(0.45,0.55)$, $(0.4,0.6)$. It appears that MEH is very sensitive to the bias of the distribution. For $p=0.45$, the size of the directory is already twice the one we get when p is 0.5 or 0.48. For MDH, the performances deteriorate more slowly and remain good enough even for $p=0.45$.

We can now suggest some choices. When b is small (say $b<20$), MDH should be used. When b is bigger, MEH, which is easily implemented, is to be chosen when the distribution is uniform. If the distribution is slightly biased ($0.45 \leq p \leq 0.55$) the performances of MDH are much better. Else, one should use a hashing function in order to get a (nearly) uniform distribution.

References

1. M. Regnier., "On the Average Height of Trees in Digital Search and Dynamic Hashing," *IPL* **13** pp. 64-66 (1981).

2. Ph. Flajolet , "On the Performance Evaluation of Extendible Hashing and Trie Searching," *Acta Informatica* **20** pp. 345-369 (1983).

3. W.A. Burkhard, "Interpolation-Based Index Maintenance," *BIT* **23** pp. 274-294 (1983).

4. Doetsch, *Handbuch der Laplace Transformation*, Birkhauser (1950).

5. R. Fagin, J. Nievergelt, N. Pippenger, and H.R. Strong, "Extendible Hashing:A Fast Access Method for Dynamic Files," *ACM TODS* **4,3** pp. 315-344 (1979).

6. Ph. Flajolet, M. Regnier, and R. Sedgewick, "Mellin Transform Techniques for the Analysis of Algorithms ," *in preparation*, (1984).

7. J.Nievergelt, H. Hinterberger, and K.C. Sevcik, "The Grid-file: an Adaptable Symmetric Multi-Key File Structure," *ACM TODS* **9,1**(1984).

8. J.W.Lloyd and K. Ramamohanarao, "Partial-Match Retrieval for Dynamic Files," *BIT* **22** pp. 150-168 (1982).

9. P.A. Larson, "Dynamic Hashing," *BIT* **18** pp. 184-201 (1978).

10. H. Mendelson, "Analysis of Extendible Hashing," *IEEE Trans. on Software Engineering*, pp. 611-624 (1982).

11. T.H. Merrett and E.J. Otoo, "A Storage Scheme for Extendible Arrays," *Computing*, (1983). To appear

12. C. Puech and Ph. Flajolet , "Tree Structure for Partial Match Retrieval," *INRIA Research Report* **233**(1983). submitted to JACM

13. M. Regnier, "Evaluation des performances du hachage dynamique," *These de 3-eme cycle, Universite d'Orsay*, (1983).

14. M. Tamminen, "The Extendible Cell Method for Closest Point Problems," *BIT* **22** pp. 27-41 (1982).

15. A.C. Yao, "A Note on the Analysis of Extendible Hashing," *IPL* **11** pp. 84-86 (1980).

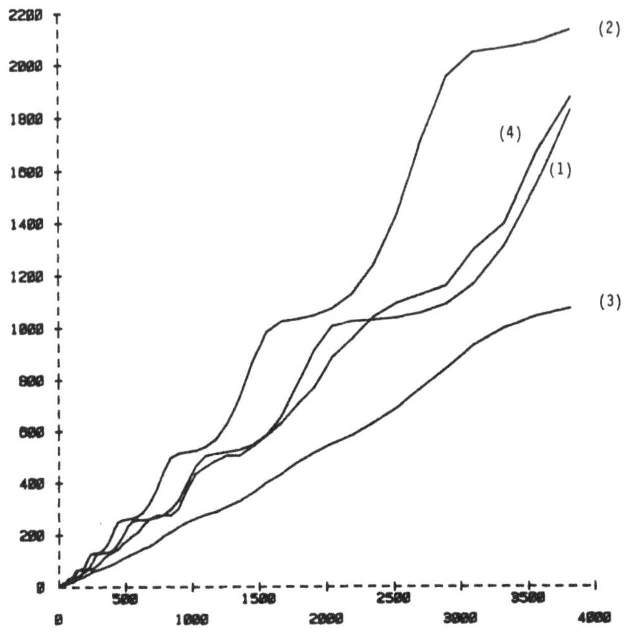

Figure 4.a. : MEH and MDH directory sizes when b=10
(1) and (2) : Asymptotic values for MDH and MEH
(3) and (4) : Simulations for MDH and MEH

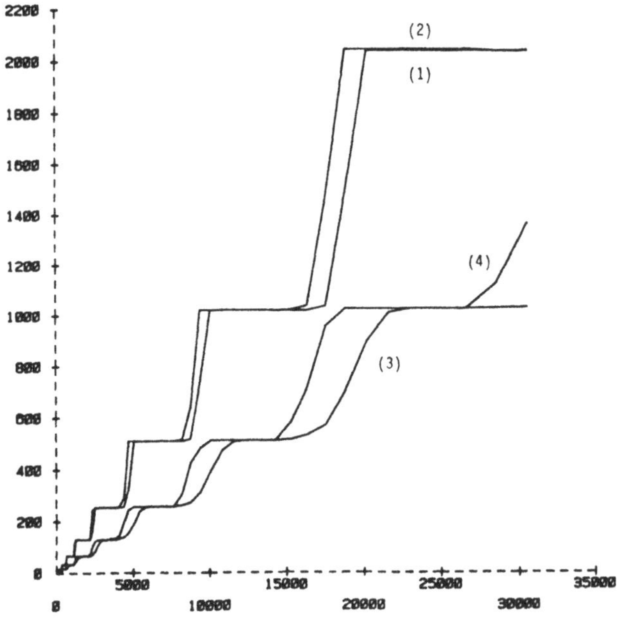

Figure 4.b. : MDH and MEH directory sizes when b=50

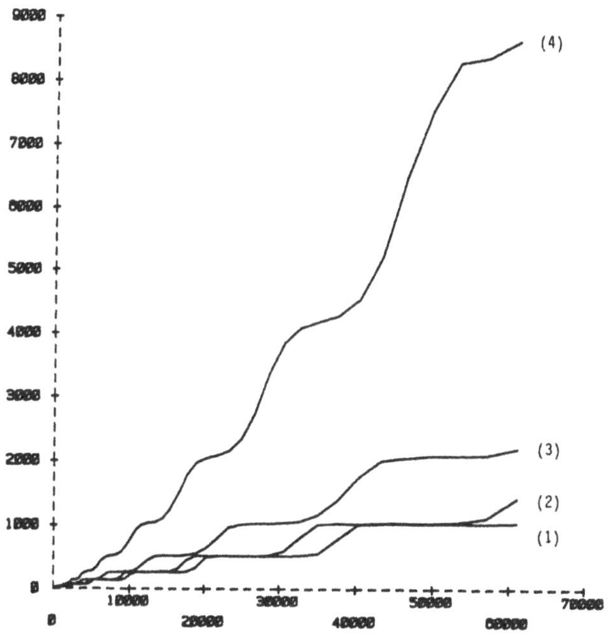

Figure 4.c. : Directory size of MEH when p varies and b=100
In curves (1), (2), (3) and (4), p=0.5, 0.48, 0.45 and 0.4

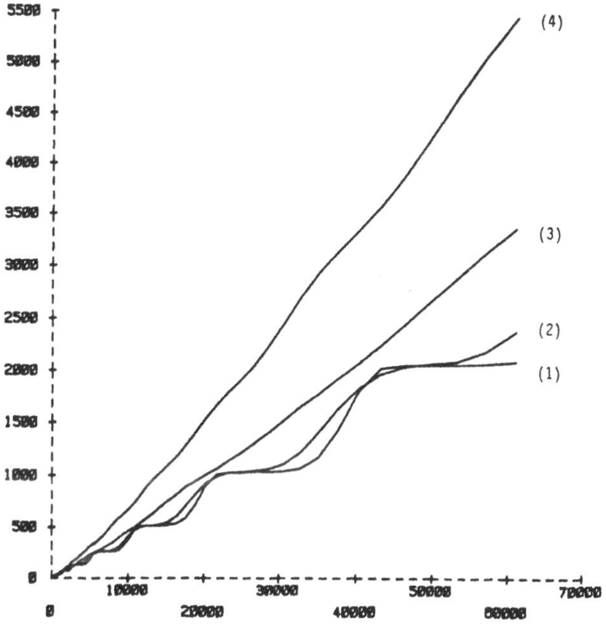

Figure 4.d. : Directory size of MDH when p varies and b=50
In curves (1), (2), (3) and (4), p=0.5, 0.48, 0.45 and 0.4

On The Mean Weight Balance Factor Of Binary Trees

by

A. K. Pal and A. Bagchi

Indian Institute of Management Calcutta
P. O. Box 16757
Calcutta - 700 027
I N D I A

Abstract :

A new performance measure for binary trees, called the mean weight balance factor (MWBF), is introduced. For any binary tree T, $0 < \mathrm{MWBF}(T) \leq 1$. Very unbalanced trees have MWBF close to 0, while complete binary trees have MWBF close to 1. The expected MWBF of a binary tree under random insertions is derived. It is shown that an AVL tree has an MWBF of atleast 0.73. Bounds are also obtained on the expected MWBF of an AVL tree under random insertions.

Section 1 : Introduction

The binary tree is a very widely used data structure in computer sorting and searching. Since the number of binary trees that have n internal nodes grows exponentially with n, we need to be able to distinguish between trees that can play a useful role in sorting and searching and those that cannot. A commonly used performance measure is the average number of comparisons for a successful search, and for an n - node tree we want this to be logarithmic in n. When good worst-case performance is to be guaranteed, we also want the worst-case number of comparisons for a successful search to be logarithmic in n, i.e. we want the tree to be well "balanced". AVL trees are examples of such balanced trees. (For details, see Knuth [5].)

In this paper we propose a new performance measure, which we call the mean weight balance factor (MWBF) of a binary tree. Our measure has the following properties :

i) For any binary tree T, $0 < MWBF(T) \leq 1$.

ii) If a binary tree is very unbalanced, for example if it is a linear binary tree, then its MWBF approaches 0 as the number of nodes n becomes large.

iii) If a binary tree is very well balanced, for example if it is a complete binary tree, then its MWBF is close to 1.

iv) An AVL tree has an MWBF of atleast 0.73; it is very likely (although we have not been able to prove it) that no AVL tree has an MWBF less than 0.82 .

v) It is possible to compute the expected MWBF of a binary tree under random insertions (see Knuth [5], p.427).

vi) It is also possible, using the results of Brown [3], to get bounds on the expected MWBF of an AVL tree under random insertions. No good bounds on the average number of comparisons for a successful search in AVL trees under random insertions are known as yet.

The MWBF measure, although less intuitively appealing than the average (or worst-case) number of comparisons, has the convenient property of permitting both bottom-up and top-down analyses. It is derived from the notion of the weight balance factor of a node, as defined for example in Reingold, Nievergelt and Deo [7], p.244 (see also Bagchi and Reingold [2]). We introduce the MWBF concept in Section 2 and look at some of its basic properties. In Section 3 we derive the expected MWBF of a binary tree under random insertions. In the next section we describe various ways of getting a lower bound on the MWBF of an AVL tree. This problem is difficult and much remains to be done. Using the results of this section and the results of Brown [3] we are able in Section 5 to get upper and lower bounds on the expected MWBF of an AVL tree under random insertions. We summarize our conclusions and state some open problems in Section 6.

Section 2 : MWBF - Definition and Basic Properties

Let T be a binary tree, and u be a node in T. Let there be n nodes in T, n_1 nodes in the subtree of T rooted at u, n_2 nodes in the left subtree of u, and n_3 nodes in the right subtree of u. Clearly, $n \geq n_1 = n_2 + n_3 + 1$.

Definition 2.1 :

i) The weight balance factor (WBF) of the node u is given by

$$\mathrm{WBF}\ (u) = 2 \cdot \frac{1 + \min\ (n_2, n_3)}{1 + n_1} \cdot$$

ii) The mean weight balance factor (MWBF) of the binary tree T is the average of the weight balance factors of the nodes in T, i.e.

$$\mathrm{MWBF}\ (T) = \frac{1}{n} \sum_{u \in T} \mathrm{WBF}\ (u).$$

For each node $u \in T$, we have $0 < \mathrm{WBF}(u) \leq 1$.
Hence $0 < \mathrm{MWBF}(T) \leq 1$.

Example 2.1 : Consider the binary trees T_1 and T_2 of Fig.1. The WBF's of the nodes are shown beside the nodes. Here, $\mathrm{MWBF}(T_1) = \frac{13}{15}$, while $\mathrm{MWBF}(T_2) = \frac{17}{20}$. ⊠

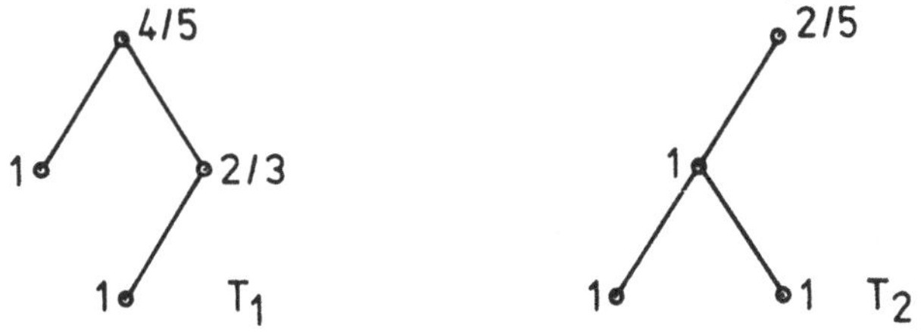

Figure 1

If no node in the binary tree T has a non-null right successor, i.e. if the tree is linear, then the MWBF is

$$\frac{2}{n}\ (H_{n+1} - 1), \text{ where } H_n = \sum_{i=1}^{n} \frac{1}{i} \cdot$$

This approaches 0 as $n \to \infty$, since the value of H_n is close to ln n (see Knuth [4], pp.73-78). On the other hand, the MWBF of a complete binary tree (see Knuth [4], pp.400-401) is always close to 1; in fact, it is exactly equal to 1 if $n = 2^k - 1$ for some positive integer k.

There exist examples of trees for which the MWBF is close to 1, and yet the average number of comparisons for a successful search is worse than logarithmic in n.
Let $0 < \epsilon < 1$. The MWBF of the tree shown in Fig. 2 approaches 1 as $n \to \infty$. But the average number of comparisons for a successful search assuming each key is equally likely to be searched is $O(n^{\epsilon}) > O(\ln n)$. This points out a limitation of the MWBF concept.

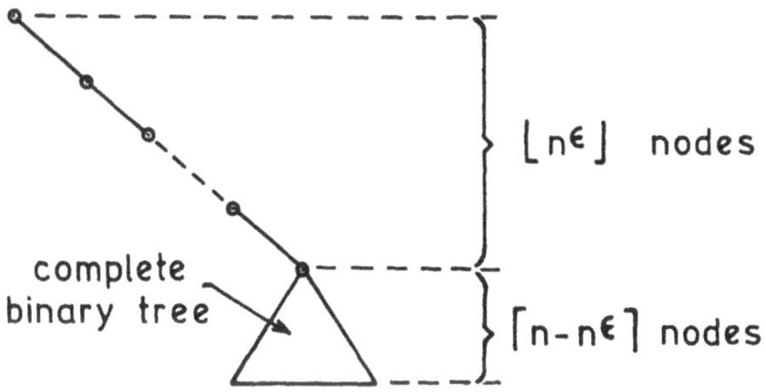

Figure 2

For purposes of illustration we derive an expression for the MWBF of a Fibonacci tree which is the least balanced of AVL trees (see Knuth [5], p.453). Let T'_h be the Fibonacci tree of height h. Then T'_h has $F_{h+2} - 1$ nodes, where $\{F_i, i \geq 0\}$ is the Fibonacci sequence satisfying $F_0 = 0$, $F_1 = 1$, and $F_i = F_{i-1} + F_{i-2}$, $i \geq 2$. Let $m_h = \text{MWBF}(T'_h)$. Then

$$m_h = \frac{1}{F_{h+2} - 1} \left[m_{h-1} (F_{h+1} - 1) + m_{h-2} (F_h - 1) + \frac{2F_h}{F_{h+2}} \right]$$

for $h \geq 2$, with $m_0 = m_1 = 1$. Algebraic manipulation yields

$$m_h = \frac{2}{F_{h+2} - 1} \sum_{i=1}^{h} \frac{F_i \, F_{h+1-i}}{F_{i+2}}$$

for $h \geq 1$. It can be checked that $m_h \to 0.8288$ as $h \to \infty$.

It would be natural to surmise that Fibonacci trees have the lowest MWBF among AVL trees. This however is not true. The AVL tree of Fig. 3 has 8 nodes u_1 through u_8 and is of height 4. Its MWBF is 0.8333, which is less than $m_4 = 0.8405$. Again, there is an AVL tree of 88 nodes having an MWBF of 0.8330, while the Fibonacci tree of 88 nodes has an MWBF of 0.8362.

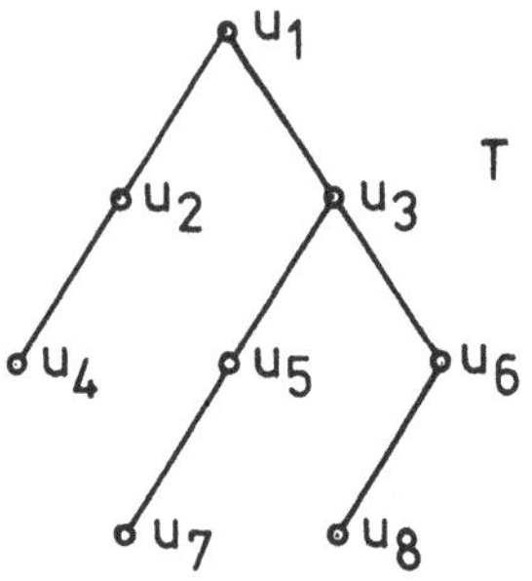

Figure 3

Section 3 : MWBF of Binary Trees Under Random Insertions

Let x_n be the expected MWBF of a binary tree with n keys under random insertions. Then $x_0 = 1$, and for $n \geq 1$,

$$n^2 x_n = \sum_{i=0}^{n-1} \left[ix_i + (n-i-1)\, x_{n-i-1} + \frac{2 \min (i+1,\ n-i)}{n+1} \right] ,$$

since each i+1, $0 \leq i \leq n-1$, is equally likely to be the root with probability 1/n. Putting
$y_i = ix_i$, $0 \leq i \leq n$, we get

$$ny_n = 2 \sum_{i=0}^{n-1} \left[y_i + \frac{\min (i+1,\ n-i)}{n+1} \right]$$

for $n \geq 1$, with $y_0 = 0$. Since

$$\sum_{i=0}^{n-1} \min (i+1,\ n-i) = \left\lfloor \frac{n+1}{2} \right\rfloor \left\lceil \frac{n+1}{2} \right\rceil$$

we have, for $n \geq 2$,

$$ny_n - (n+1)y_{n-1} = \frac{2}{n+1}\left\lfloor\frac{n+1}{2}\right\rfloor\left\lceil\frac{n+1}{2}\right\rceil - \frac{2}{n}\left\lfloor\frac{n}{2}\right\rfloor\left\lceil\frac{n}{2}\right\rceil .$$

Thus, for $n \geq 2$,

$$\frac{y_n}{n+1} - \frac{y_{n-1}}{n} = \begin{cases} \dfrac{1}{2(n+1)^2}, & n \text{ even} \\[2ex] \dfrac{1}{2n^2}, & n \text{ odd.} \end{cases}$$

Finally, for $n \geq 1$,

$$x_n = \begin{cases} \frac{1}{2}\left(1+\frac{1}{n}\right)\left[2\,H_{n+1}^{(2)} - \frac{1}{2}\,H_{n/2}^{(2)} - 1 - \dfrac{1}{(n+1)^2}\right], & n \text{ even,} \\[2ex] \frac{1}{2}\left(1+\frac{1}{n}\right)\left[2\,H_{n}^{(2)} - \frac{1}{2}\,H_{\frac{n-1}{2}}^{(2)} - 1\right], & n \text{ odd,} \end{cases}$$

where $H_n^{(2)} = \sum_{i=1}^{n} \frac{1}{i^2}$ (see Knuth [4], pp.73-78).

Since $\lim_{n\to\infty} H_n^{(2)} = \frac{\pi^2}{6}$, we have

$$\lim_{n\to\infty} x_n = \frac{\pi^2}{8} - \frac{1}{2} = 0.7337 .$$

Section 4 : Lower Bound on MWBF of AVL Trees

How can we obtain a good lower bound on the MWBF of AVL trees ? Let T be an AVL tree having n nodes. Let us suppose that T has the least MWBF among all AVL trees with n nodes. Let M_n = MWBF(T) and h_n = height(T).

We have the recurrence

$$nM_n = \min\left[kM_k + (n-1-k)M_{n-1-k} + \frac{2(k+1)}{n+1} \;\middle|\; 1 \leq k \leq \frac{n-1}{2} \text{ and } -1 \leq h_{n-1-k} - h_k \leq 1\right] .$$

Unfortunately, it appears difficult to solve this recurrence directly, the constraint on the heights of the subtrees being the complicating factor. However, the recurrence can be used for tabulating M_n values with the help of a computer. Our results show that for $n \leq 1024$, $M_n \geq 0.8275$, and it does not seem likely that for larger n the value of M_n dips much lower.

We now propose some alternative methods for getting a lower bound on the MWBF of AVL trees. While the methods do not yield very good lower bounds, they clearly indicate that no AVL tree can have an MWBF below about 0.73 .

Let T be a binary tree of height h, and let S be the set of nodes of T. We define a sequence $S_0, S_1, \ldots, S_h$ of disjoint sub-sets of S as follows :

$$S_0 = \emptyset$$

$$S_i = \left\{ u \;\middle|\; u \in S - \bigcup_{j<i} S_j \text{ and all non-null successors of } u \text{ are in } \bigcup_{j<i} S_j \right\}, \quad 1 \leq i \leq h .$$

Example 4.1 : For the binary tree T of Figure 3,

$$S = \{u_1, u_2, u_3, u_4, u_5, u_6, u_7, u_8\}$$
$$S_0 = \emptyset$$
$$S_1 = \{u_4, u_7, u_8\}$$
$$S_2 = \{u_2, u_5, u_6\}$$
$$S_3 = \{u_3\}$$
$$S_4 = \{u_1\} . \qquad \boxtimes$$

Definition 4.1 :

i) Let a_i be the number of nodes in S_i .

ii) Let $A_i = \sum_{j=1}^{i} a_j$, $i \geq 1$.

We note the following simple facts :

Lemma 4.1 : Let T be an AVL tree of height h having n nodes.

i) $a_i \geq 1$ for $1 \leq i < h$,

$a_h = 1$.

ii) $\sum_{i=1}^{h} a_i = n$.

iii) For $1 \leq i < h$, if the A_i nodes belonging to $\bigcup_{j \leq i} S_j$ are removed from T (along with the associated arcs), then the resulting tree is AVL and has height $h-i$.

Proof : Clear. ⊠

Lemma 4.2 : Let T be an AVL tree of height h having n nodes. Then for $1 \leq i < h$,

$$a_i \leq n+1-A_i \leq a_i + a_{i+1} .$$

Furthermore, the bounds are achievable.

Proof : Let T' be the AVL tree obtained from T when the A_i nodes in $\bigcup_{j \leq i} S_j$ are removed. The lemma follows from the observation that every node in S_i must be an external node of T' ; moreover, both sons of a node in S_{i+1} must be external, and atleast one son must be in S_i. Since T' is AVL, all successors of nodes in S_{i+2} belong only to S_i and S_{i+1}. Hence T' has no more external nodes than $a_i + a_{i+1}$.

To see that the bounds are achievable, again consider Figure 3. Here n = 8, and

$$a_1 = 3, \quad A_1 = 3,$$
$$a_2 = 3, \quad A_2 = 6,$$

so that

$$a_2 = n+1-A_2$$

and $n+1-A_1 = a_1+a_2$.

Similar examples for other n can be readily constructed. ⊠

The following results follow directly from the above lemmas.

Corollary 4.1 : Let T be an AVL tree of height h having n nodes. Then

i) $a_{i+1} \leq a_i, \quad 1 \leq i < h$

ii) $\left\lceil \frac{n+1}{3} \right\rceil \leq a_1 \leq \left\lfloor \frac{n+1}{2} \right\rfloor$

iii) $a_i \leq \left\lfloor \frac{n+1-A_{i-1}}{2} \right\rfloor, \quad 2 \leq i \leq h$

iv) $a_i \geq \max \left\{ n+1-A_{i-1} - a_{i-1}, \left\lceil \frac{n+1-A_{i-1}}{3} \right\rceil \right\}, \quad 2 \leq i \leq h$

v) $a_i \leq 2a_{i+1} + a_{i+2} \leq 3a_{i+1}, \quad 1 \leq i < h-1$

vi) $a_i + A_i \leq n+1, \quad 1 \leq i \leq h$

vii) The bounds in (i) through (vi) are achievable.

<u>Proof</u> : i) By Lemma 4.2,

$$a_{i+1} \leq n+1-A_{i+1} = (n+1-A_i) - a_{i+1}$$

$$\leq a_i + a_{i+1} - a_{i+1}$$

$$= a_i .$$

ii) Since $A_1 = a_1$, by Lemma 4.2,

$$a_1 \leq n+1-a_1$$

so $a_1 \leq \frac{n+1}{2}$.

Again,

$$n+1-a_1 \leq a_1 + a_2$$

$$\leq 2a_1 \text{ by (i),}$$

so that $a_1 \geq \frac{n+1}{3}$.

iii) By Lemma 4.2 .

iv) Again by Lemma 4.2,

$$a_i \geq n+1-A_{i-1} - a_{i-1} .$$

But $n+1-A_i \leq a_i + a_{i+1}$

$$\leq 2a_i \quad \text{by (i)}$$

so that $a_i \geq \frac{n+1-A_{i-1}}{3}$

as well.

v) By Lemma 4.2,

$$a_i \leq n+1-A_i$$

$$= n+1-A_{i+1} + a_{i+1}$$

$$\leq 2a_{i+1} + a_{i+2}$$

$$\leq 3a_{i+1} \qquad \text{by (i).}$$

vi) Clear.

vii) Examples are easily constructed, as in the proof of Lemma 4.2. ⊠

Note that it is possible for a non-AVL tree to satisfy Lemmas 4.1 and 4.2. Moreover, two AVL trees having different MWBF may have an identical set of a_i values.

Example 4.2 : In Figure 1, T_1 is an AVL tree while T_2 is not. But for both trees, $a_1 = 2$, $a_2 = 1$, $a_3 = 1$.

The two AVL trees T_1 and T_2 of Figure 4 both have $n = 8$, $a_1 = 4$, $a_2 = 2$, $a_3 = a_4 = 1$.
But $MWBF(T_1) = 0.8750$ while $MWBF(T_2) = 0.9194$. ⊠

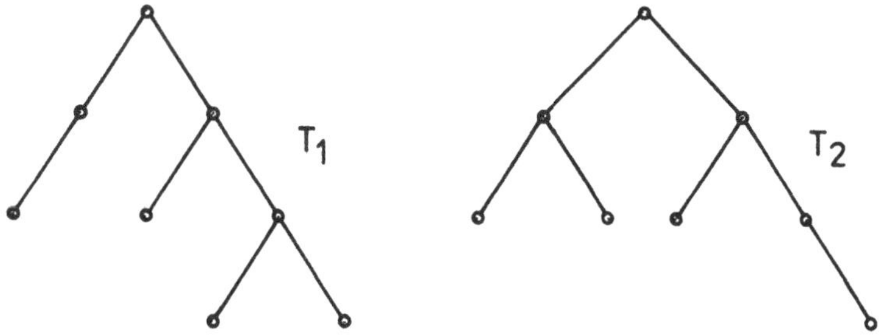

Figure 4

We can nevertheless use the a_i's to obtain a lower bound on the MWBF of an AVL tree. Let T be an AVL tree of n nodes and height h, with a_i nodes in S_i for $1 \leq i \leq h$. Let

$$c_i = \frac{2F_i}{F_i + 2^{i-1}}, \quad i \geq 1$$

$$C(T) = \frac{1}{n} \sum_{i=1}^{h} c_i a_i .$$

A node in S_i has a weight balance factor of atleast c_i, since at the very worst one of its subtrees is a Fibonacci tree of height i-2, while the other subtree is a complete binary tree of height i-1.
Thus $MWBF(T) \geq C(T)$,
so that

$$M_n \geq \min C(T)$$

where the minimum is taken over all AVL trees having a n nodes. One way of getting a lower bound on M_n therefore is by minimizing the sum

$$C_n = \frac{1}{n} \sum_{i \geq 1} c_i a_i$$

subject to just the two conditions

$$\sum_{i \geq 1} a_i = n,$$

$$\left\lceil \frac{n - A_{i-1} + 1}{3} \right\rceil \leq a_i \leq \left\lfloor \frac{n - A_{i-1} + 1}{2} \right\rfloor , \quad i \geq 1$$

where $A_0 = 0$.

Theorem 4.1 : When the a_i's are subject to the above two conditions, C_n is minimal for

$$a_1 = \left\lceil \frac{n+1}{3} \right\rceil$$

$$a_i = \left\lceil \frac{n - A_{i-1} + 1}{3} \right\rceil , \quad i \geq 2.$$

Proof : Let the a_i's be as given. Then there exists i_0 such that for $i > i_0$, $a_i = 0$, while $a_{i_0} = 1$.

Clearly, $\sum_{i=1}^{i_0-1} a_i = n$.

To see that these a_i minimize C_n, we note that

$$c_i \geq c_{i+1}, \quad i \geq 1.$$

Thus C_n will be smallest if a_1 is made as small as possible subject to the given conditions, which forces $a_1 = \left\lceil \frac{n+1}{3} \right\rceil$. Now a_2 should be made as small as possible subject to the given conditions, which forces $a_2 = \left\lceil \frac{n - A_1 + 1}{3} \right\rceil$ and so on. A more formal proof would proceed by induction on n. ⊠

For large n, using the above expressions for a_i we find that C_n works out to 0.7052. To get a better bound we must impose more conditions on the a_i's. Let n be large, and let us ignore the fact that the a_i's must be integers. Let

$$b_i = \frac{a_i}{n}$$

$$B_i = \frac{A_i}{n}$$

for $i \geq 1$. We can fix n, then minimize C_n using a linear programming package. The constraints derived in Lemmas 4.1 and 4.2 on the a_i's are all linear and can be supplied to the package. For n = 28655 =

$F_{23} - 2$, we get a lower bound on C_n of 0.7315, and

$$\begin{aligned} b_1 &= b_2 = 1/3 \\ b_3 &= 0.1273 \\ b_4 &= 0.0787 \\ b_5 &= 0.0486 \\ b_6 &= 0.0301, \text{ etc.} \end{aligned}$$

The values of c_i were supplied to the package only to 20 terms, since no binary tree of 28655 nodes has height greater than 20. The results are of course approximate, since we get a_i's with non-integer values, but n being large the error is not likely to be significant. Nor does the computed bound depend significantly on n as Table 1 shows.

Table 1

MINIMUM VALUES OF C_n

(obtained using LP package)

n	Minimum value of C_n
25	0.7510
50	0.7430
100	0.7380
200	0.7347
500	0.7328
1000	0.7405
2000	0.7318
5000	0.7316
10945	0.7315
28655	0.7315

We now present an alternative formulation. Let T again be an AVL tree of height h having n nodes. Let

$$D(T) = \frac{1}{n}\sum_{i=1}^{h} d_i a_i$$

where

$$d_i = \frac{2\,F_i}{1 + \frac{A_i}{a_i}}, \quad i \geq 1.$$

Lemma 4.3 : The mean of the weight balance factors of the a_i nodes in S_i is $\geq d_i$, $1 \leq i \leq h$. Consequently, $MWBF(T) \geq D(T)$.

Proof : Let w_i be the mean of the weight balance factors of the nodes in S_i. Then

$$w_i \geq \frac{1}{a_i} \sum_{j=1}^{a_i} \frac{2F_i}{1+R_j}$$

where R_j is the total number of nodes in the subtree rooted at the j-th node in S_i. Now

$$\sum_{j=1}^{a_i} R_j = A_i \ .$$

Moreover, the harmonic mean of the numbers

$$1 + R_j \ , \ j \in S_i$$

cannot exceed their arithmetic mean. Thus

$$w_i \geq \frac{2\ F_i}{a_i} \sum_{j=1}^{a_i} \frac{1}{1 + R_j}$$

$$\geq \frac{2\ F_i}{1 + \frac{A_i}{a_i}} = d_i \ .$$

The lemma follows. ⊠

We can thus try to get a lower bound on M_n by minimizing the sum

$$D_n = \frac{1}{n} \sum_{i \geq 1} d_i a_i$$

where the a_i's are subject to the conditions given in Lemmas 4.1 and 4.2. Unfortunately, and somewhat unexpectedly, this method gives a poor lower bound on M_n, as we can see by putting

$$b_1 = 1/2$$

$$b_i = \frac{1 - B_{i-1}}{2} \ , \ i \geq 2$$

which gives, for large n,

$$D_n = \frac{8}{11} = 0.7273,$$

so the minimum must be even smaller.

A possible way of getting better bounds could be as follows. Let us minimize C_n and D_n for a specified value of a_1. Let

$$E_n\,(a_1) = \max\left\{\min C_n(a_1),\ \min D_n(a_1)\right\}.$$

It is easy to see that

$$M_n \geq \min\left\{E_n(a_1)\ \middle|\ \left\lceil\frac{n+1}{3}\right\rceil \leq a_1 \leq \left\lfloor\frac{n+1}{2}\right\rfloor\right\}.$$

While a detailed study appears difficult and has not yet been attempted, some preliminary calculations indicate that $\min C_n(a_1)$ increases as a_1 increases from $\left\lceil\frac{n+1}{3}\right\rceil$ to $\left\lfloor\frac{n+1}{2}\right\rfloor$. Table 2 shows the nature of variation of $\min C_n(a_1)$ with a_1. The minimization has been achieved using an LP package. On the other hand, $\min D_n(a_1)$ first decreases as a_1 increases, then reaches a minimum when $b_1 = a_1/n = 0.44$, and increases subsequently. The values shown for $\min D_n(a_1)$ are somewhat approximate, since an exhaustive search must be made. The actual minima will be smaller than the table entries, so we find that under the restrictions of Corollary 4.1, $\min D_n(a_1)$ always appears to be smaller than $\min C_n(a_1)$ for each a_1. But the conditions given in Corollary 4.1 are only necessary, not sufficient. If better conditions can be imposed on the a_i, then the study of $E_n(a_1)$ could give superior lower bounds on M_n. Further study of this interesting problem appears desirable. We summarize the results of this section in the following theorem.

Theorem 4.2 : For large n, $M_n \geq 0.73$.

Proof : See discussion above. ⊠

Table 2

VARIATION OF $\min C_n(a_1)$ AND $\min D_n(a_1)$ WITH a_1

a_1	$\min C_n(a_1)$	$\min D_n(a_1)$
1/3	0.7315	0.7277
0.34	0.7328	0.7265
0.36	0.7366	0.7232
0.38	0.7405	0.7207
0.40	0.7485	0.7189
0.42	0.7569	0.7179
0.44	0.7652	0.7175
0.46	0.7736	0.7179
0.48	0.7820	0.7191
0.50	0.7904	0.7209

Section 5 : MWBF of AVL Trees Under Random Insertions

Let x_n be the expected MWBF of an AVL tree under random insertions. We can use the results of Brown [3] to get bounds on x_n. Brown shows that under random insertions when n is large, the expected value of $b_1 = \frac{3}{7}$, while the expected value of $b_2 \geq \frac{1}{7}$; moreover, the expected fraction of nodes with a weight balance factor of 2/3 is atleast $\frac{1}{7}$. In computing the lower bound on x_n we face a difficulty. Although C_n is linear in a_1 (and hence in b_1), min $C_n(a_1)$ may not be linear in a_1, so it may not be quite correct to work with expected values of a_1. We get around the problem in the following way. It has been shown by Bagchi and Pal [1] that the process of random insertion in a 2-3 tree or an AVL tree can be modelled using a generalized Polya-Eggenberger urn scheme. Their results imply that for large n the standardized random variable corresponding to a_1 is asymptotically normal; moreover, a_1 has a standard deviation of $O(n^{\frac{1}{2}})$. Since the standard deviation is of lower order than n, we can conclude that for large n the possible nonlinear variation of min $C_n(a_1)$ as a function of a_1 is of no significance, so that $x_n \geq \min C_n(b_1 = 3/7)$. Using the linear programming formulation we thus get $x_n \geq 0.760$. Again,

$$x_n \leq 1 - \frac{1}{3} \cdot \frac{1}{7} = \frac{20}{21} = 0.952 .$$

Thus for large n, $0.760 \leq x_n \leq 0.952$.

The bounds are not very good because Brown's analysis does not extend to subtrees of height greater than 2. It may be possible to get a somewhat better lower bound on x_n by using $E_n(b_1 = \frac{3}{7})$ in place of min $C_n(b_1 = \frac{3}{7})$. Again, $E_n(a_1)$ may be nonlinear in a_1, but the problem is resolved as argued above when n is large.

Section 6 : Conclusion

MWBF, as a performance measure for binary trees, has many desirable properties, and is convenient for different kinds of analyses. If some kind of relationship can be derived between the MWBF of a binary tree and the average (or worst-case) number of comparisons, then MWBF would become a more appealing concept. It may be worth investigating whether there would be any gain in taking a weighted mean of the weight balance factors of the nodes of a tree, instead of just a simple mean as has been done here.

In this paper we have not been able to derive analytically a really satisfactory lower bound on the MWBF of an AVL tree. This is an interesting problem and further work is needed. There is another area that has not been touched upon at all. This concerns 2-3 trees and 3-trees (see Pal and Bagchi [6]). Is it possible to extend the MWBF idea to 3-trees and thence to 2-3 trees ? Would we be able to get any further insight into the propertiesof 2-3 trees by use of the MWBF measure ?

REFERENCES

1. A. Bagchi and A. K. Pal
Asymptotic Normality in the Generalized Polya-Eggenberger Urn Model, With an Application to Computer Data Structures
SIAM Jr. Alg. Disc. Meth., (to appear) .

2. A. Bagchi and E. M. Reingold
A Naturally Occurring Function Continuous Only at Irrationals
American Math. Monthly, Vol.89, No.6, June-July 1982, pp.411-417.

3. M. R. Brown
A Partial Analysis of Random Height-Balanced Trees
SIAM Jr. Comp., Vol.8, No.1, Feb. 1979, pp.33-41.

4. D. E. Knuth
The Art of Computer Programming, Vol.I, Fundamental Algorithms (2nd Ed.,
Addison Wesley, 1975.

5. D. E. Knuth
The Art of Computer Programming, Vol.III, Sorting and Searching
Addison Wesley, 1975.

6. A. K. Pal and A. Bagchi
Analysis of a Simple Insertion Algorithm for 3-trees
Proc. 3rd Ann. Conf. on Foundations of Software Tech. and Theo. Comp. Sc., Bangalore (India), Dec. 12-14, 1983, pp.390-417.

7. E. M. Reingold, J. Nievergelt and N. Deo
Combinatorial Algorithms
Prentice Hall, 1977.

AN EFFICIENT ALGORITHM FOR RANDOM SAMPLING WITHOUT REPLACEMENT

P. Gupta
IPAD/RSA
Space Applications Centre (ISRO)
Ahmedabad 380 053
INDIA

and

G.P. Bhattacharjee
Department of Mathematics
Indian Institute of Technology
Kharagpur 721 302
INDIA

Abstract

An algorithm for drawing a random sample of size M from the population of size N ($M \leq N$) has been proposed. The algorithm has the time complexity of MIN $\{O(M\log_2 M), O[(N-M)\log_2(N-M)]\}$ and the space complexity of $O(M)$.

INTRODUCTION

One of the basic problems in sampling is to design efficient algorithms for drawing a sample from a finite population. The population from which the sample is to be drawn can be assumed to be represented by the integers (1,2,....,N), N being the size of the population. Let M be the size of the sample. If any subset of size M has an equal probability of being in the sample, then the technique of drawing the sample is known as 'simple random sampling'. There are other useful sampling techniques where items of the population are selected in some systematic fashion or in clusters or items are selected with probabilities proportional to some known characteristic of the items. Most of the general sampling techniques are based on either sampling with replacement in which items may be repeated in the sample or sampling without replacement.

The problem of drawing a random sample without replacement occurs in many statistical experiments, data processing and game problems, computer simulation studies. Several algorithms for random sampling without replacement are available; some of these are discussed in [2], [3]. Since the correctness and the efficiency with respect to time and storage requirements are the criteria of a good algorithm, a sampling algorithm which is fast and requires minimum time is of interest.

In [3] Goodman and Hedetniemi have presented an algorithm SELECT for drawing a random sample without replacement. The algorithm has the time- and space-complexity of O(N) where N is the size of the population from which the sample has been drawn. The algorithm has been modified by Ernvall and Nevalainen [1]. The modified algorithm, HSELECT, has the time complexity of $O(M^2)$ in the worst case, O(M) in the average case and the storage requirements of O(M) where M is the size of the sample. The algorithm, HSELECT, has been improved by Teuhola and Nevalainen [5]. The improved algorithm, HSEL, requires $O(M^2)$ units of time in the worst case, O(M) units of time in the average case and only 2M storage locations.

In this paper an algorithm for drawing a random sample without replacement has been proposed. The algorithm has the time-complexity of $\text{MIN}\{O(M\log_2 M), O[(N-M)\log_2(N-M)]\}$ in worst case and space complexity of O(M).

2. RELATED ALGORITHMS

This section describes three published algorithms which are relevant to our work.

Algorithm SELECT, proposed by Goodman and Hedetniemi in [3] selects M items of the population in M stages. Without any loss of generality let the items of the population be represented by the integers 1,2,3,...,N. Let A(1:N) be an array with A(i)=i, i=1,2,3,...,M. It selects, at random, an integer k from among the integers 1,2,3,...,N-i+1 and then selects the item A(k) as the ith item in the sample; the item selected is deleted from the array A and is replaced by the item A(N-i+1). Thus at every stage Algorithm SELECT maintains an array A of unselected items of the population. The algorithm has the time and the space complexity of O(N).

Algorithm HSEL, presented by Teuhola and Nevalainen in [5], maintains and manupulates an array B(1:M). The ith element B(i) of the array B initially contains a random integer lying between 1 and N-i+1 where both 1 and N-i+1 are inclusive; it finally gives after a chain of substitution, the index of the ith selected item. The substitution is based on the recursive relation.

$$B(i)=N+1-\text{MAX}\{s \mid B(i)=B(s), s=1,2,..,M; i=1,2,..,M\}$$

In order to avoid repeated traversal of the same substitution chain, the substitutions are done in reverse order i.e. from the last index to the first index. It has been shown in [5] that Algorithm HSEL is based on the principle of Algorithm SELECT [3] and is an improvement over Algorithm SELECT since it selects the same sample in time of $O(M^2)$ in worst case or O(M) in the average case and requires storage of O(M) only. The substitution process of Algorithm HSEL is illustrated in Figure 1 for N=10 and M=5.

Algorithm BAL-SRH-INT, proposed by Gupta and Bhattacharjee in [4] considers a table search and insertion problem. Given a table of records which form a balanced binary tree and argument k, Algorithm BAL-SRH-INT determines a non-negative integer u, updates k by k+u and inserts into the tree a node containing k such that the rank of the inserted node when records are arranged in increasing order of their keys is u+1 and rebalance the tree, if necessary, to make the tree balanced. In this algorithm each node of the balanced tree is assumed to have six fields : the key (KEY) of the node, the pointer (RL) to the right subtree of the node, the pointer (LL) to the left subtree of the node, the balance factor (B) which is equal to the height of the left subtree minus the height of the right subtree of the node, the right information (RI) field and the left information (LI) field give the number of nodes in the right subtree and in the left subtree of the node respectively. Thus a node p of the tree is of the form

LI(p)	KEY(p)	RI(p)
LL(p)	B(p)	RL(p)

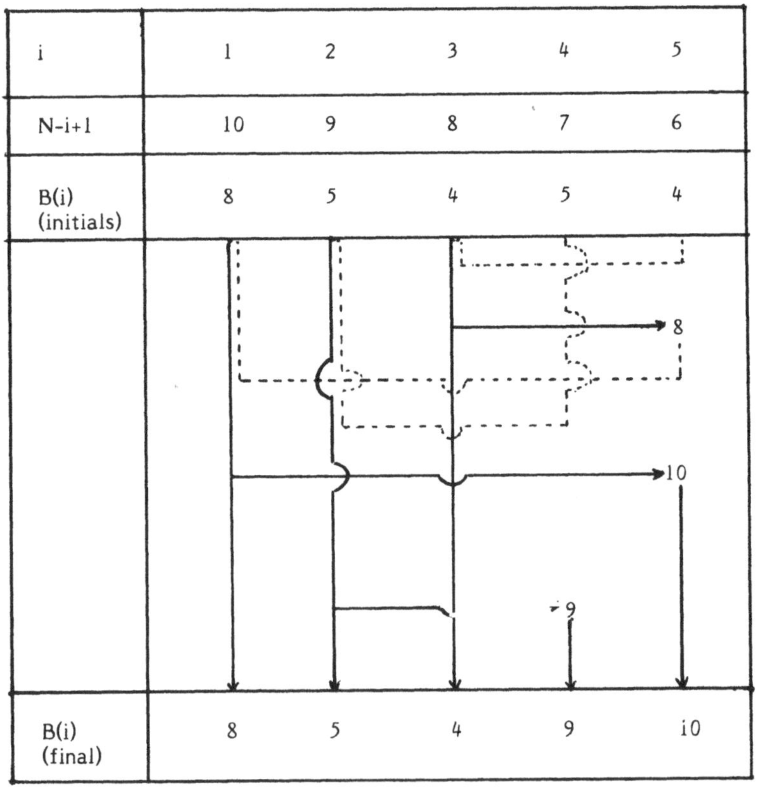

Figure 1 : An illustration of Algorithm HSEL for N=10, M=5

The total number of nodes in the subtree TREE(p) with root p is LI(p)+RI(p)+1. A special header node appears at the top of the tree in location h; the pointer RL(h) points to the root of the tree and LL(h) is used to keep track of the overall height of the tree. The tree is assumed to be non-empty. The inputs to the algorithm are k, N_1, h and AVAIL where

(i) k is the given argument,

(ii) N_1 is the total number of records in the table,

(iii) $T(1{:}N_1)$ is the table of records where records are represented in the storage by a balanced binary tree with header h, i.e. for any node p other than the header h of the tree we have

(1) $KEY[LL(p)] < KEY(p) < KEY[RL(p)]$

(2) $B(p) = -1, 0, +1$

(iv) AVAIL refers to the top of a list of available spaces.

Algorithm BAL-SRH-INT uses a top-down search of the tree to find an appropriate value of u and insert k+u into the tree. It has been shown in [4] that

THEOREM 1 : The key k+u of the inserted node is unique and its rank is u+1.

THEOREM 2 : Algorithm BAL-SRH-INT requires $O(\log_2 N_1)$ units of time .

3. AN IMPROVED ALGORITHM

As in Algorithm SELECT consider an array A(1:N) of N elements where A(i)=1, $1 \leq i \leq N$. The improved sampling procedure, GSEL, given in Figure 2, consists of M stages. At the $(N_1+1)^{-th}$ stage ($N_1 < M$) there exist N_1 selected elements for the sample and a random integer k lying between 1 and $N-N_1+1$ (both 1 and $N-N_1+1$ are inclusive). The procedure finds the kth element of unselected elements of A to consider as a $(N_1+1)^{th}$ selected element for the sample. Let $C(1{:}N_1)$ be an array of N_1 elements which are selected in N_1 stages and arranged in such a way that $C(i) < C(j)$, $1 \leq i < j \leq N_1 < M$. Obviously the set of elements of C is a subset of the elements of A. At the $(N_1+1)^{th}$ stage the kth smallest element of the unselected elements of A is to be selected for the sample. To find the kth smallest element one can use Algorithm BAL-SRH-INT [4]. For a given integer k Algorithm BAL-SRH-INT finds a non-negative integer u such that exactly u elements of C are less than k+u and the remaining (N_1-u) elements of C are greater than k+u. Since A contains first N natural numbers and exactly u elements of C are less than k+u, so there must exist exactly (k-1) elements of A which are less than k+u and are not the elements of C. Similarly, it can be shown that there exist exactly $(N-N_1-k)$

elements of A but not of C which are greater than k+u. It follows that:

LEMMA 1 : Let A (1:N) and $C(1:N_1)$ be two arrays such that

$A(i) = i \quad 1 \leq i \leq N$

$C(i) < C(i) \quad 1 \leq i < j \leq N_1$

and the set of elements of C is a subset of the elements of A. The kth smallest element of the set of elements of A which are not the elements of C is k+u where u is non-negative interger satisfying

$C(u) < k+u < C(u+1)$ where $1 \leq K \leq N-N_1$ and $0 \leq u \leq N_1$

The inputs of GSEL are N, the population size and M, the sample size and the output is an array C(1:M).

Step 1 : Initialize $i = 1$;

Step 2 : Generate a random variate r_i, $0 < r_i < 1$;

Step 3 : Set $k = \lceil r_i(N-i+1) \rceil$;

Step 4 : If i = 1 then execute step 5, else execute step 6;

Step 5 : Set $q \Leftarrow$ AVAIL; RL(h) = q; KEY(q) = k; B(q) = 0;
LL(h) = 1; LL(q) = RL(q) = $\wedge$; LI(q) = RI(q) = 0;
Go to step 7

Step 6 : Call Algorithm BAL-SRH-INT(k,i-1,h,AVAIL);

Step : Set C(i) = k; i = i+1;
If i = M+1 then terminate; else go to step 2;

Figure 2 : Steps of GSEL

The notation $\lceil x \rceil$ used in Figure 2 denotes the smallest integer greater than the variable x and AVAIL denotes the top node of a list of available spaces.

LEMMA 2 : GSEL selects exactly M items

Proof : From Step 7 it is clear that no more than M items are selected since GSEL terminates as soon as the Mth item has been selected. At step 3 it is observed that if i items have been selected and only M-i items remain to be selected, then all the remaining

N-i items will be considered. Since $N \geq M$, atleast M items are selected. Thus exactly M items are selected.

LEMMA 3 : GSEL produces an unbiased sample .

Proof : If any subset of size M of the original population has an equal chance of being the sample drawn, then the sample is unbiased. Let p_j be the probability that the integer j has been selected for the sample. Since j can occur in the first draw, or in the second draw, ..., or in the Mth draw and let $p_j(i)$ be the probability that j occurs in the ith draw, then

$$p_j = \sum_{i=1}^{M} p_j(i)$$

The probability of drawing j in the ith draw is given by

$$p_j(i) = p_j^c(1)\, p_j^c(2)\ldots\ldots p_j^c(i-1)\; p_j(i)$$

where $p_j^c(k)$ is the probability that j does not occur in the kth draw. Thus

$$p_j(i) = \frac{N-1}{N}\,\frac{N-2}{N-1}\,\cdots\cdots\,\frac{N-(i-1)}{N-(i-2)}\cdot\frac{1}{N-(i-1)}$$

$$= 1/N$$

Therefore,

$$p_j = M/N$$

Hence the proof .

It follows from LEMMA 1 that

LEMMA 4 : Items selected for the sample by GSEL are distinct and lying between 1 and N (both 1 and N are inclusive) .

LEMMA 5 : GSEL requires $O(M \log_2 M)$ units of time at worst and O(M) storage locations .

Proof : Assume that any arithmetic operation requires 0(1) unit of time. It is clear from Figure 2 that steps of GSEL except step 6 are of 0(1) unit of time. Step 6 is repeated for M-1 times. At the ith repetition Algorithm BAL-SRH-INT finds the ith index

Stage i	Random integer 1 j N-i+1	u	tree T(1:i-1)	Balance tree T(1:i-1)	Selected item
1	8	0	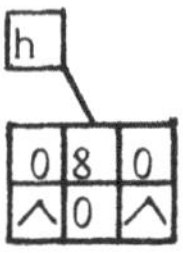	-	8
2	5	0	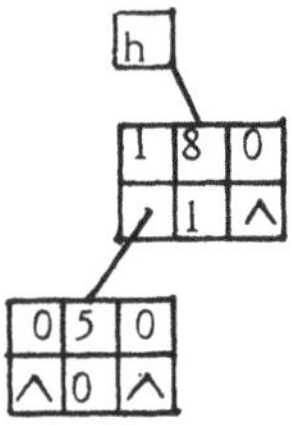	-	5
3	4	0	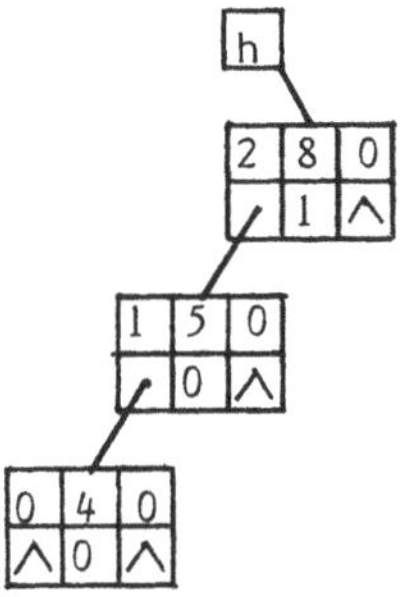	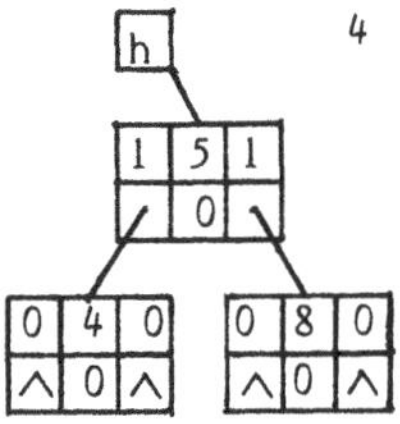	4
4	5	2	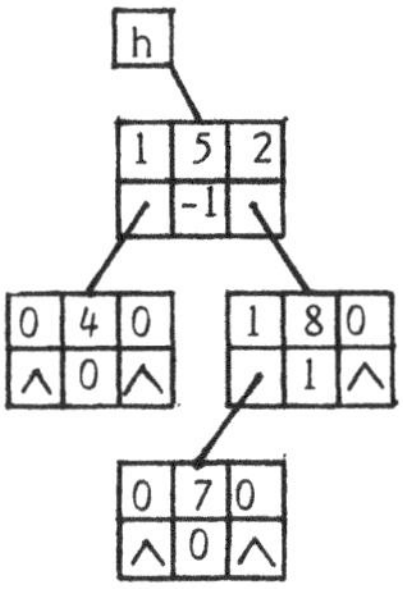		7
5	6	4	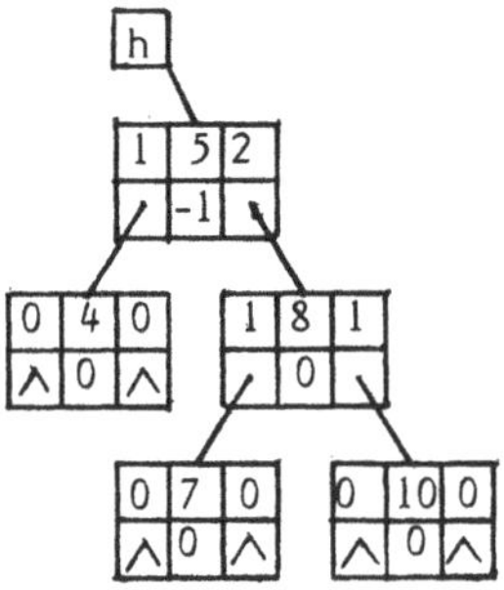		10

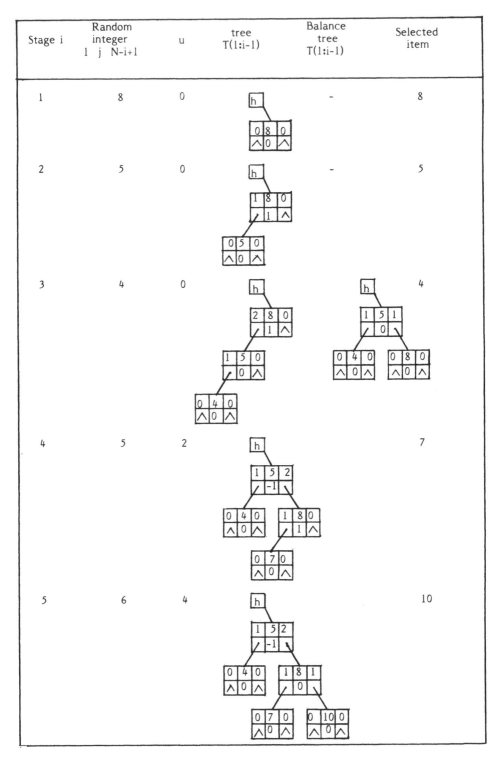

Figure 3 : An Example of GSEL

of the sample which satisfies LEMMA 1 and requires $0[\log_2(i-1)]$ units of time (by THEOREM 1). Thus step 6 requires $0[\log_2(M-1)!]$ units of time. Hence GSEL has the time complexity of $0(M\log_2 M)$.

Again each node considered in Algorithm BAL-SRH-INT consists of six fields. There are M nodes in the tree at the end of the Mth repetition of Algorithm BAL-SRH-INT. So GSEL requires 0(M) storage locations.

Hence the proof.

This sampling algorithm also produces an ordered sample if one traverses the balanced tree of M nodes inorder. The algorithm can further be improved when $M > N/2$. Instead of selecting M indices ($M > N/2$) for the sample by the algorithm GSEL, it is suggested to use GSEL to select N-M indices and then to consider the integers which are not selected by GSEL but are lying between 1 and N (both 1 and N are inclusive) as the indices of the sample. It follows that:

LEMMA 6 : The algorithm to draw a sample of size M from a population of size N ($M \leq N$) has the time-complexity of $\mathrm{Min}\{0(M\log_2 M), 0[(N-M)\log_2(N-M)]\}$ and the sapce complexity of 0(M).

Consider the example of drawing a random sample of size 5 from the population of size 10. Figure 3 shows how GSEL selects the indices of items for the random sample.

REFERENCES

[1] Ernvall J. and O. Nevalainen, An Efficient Algorithm For Unbiased Random Sampling, Computer J., Vol. 25, No. 1, pp. 45-47, 1982.

[2] Fan C.T., M.E. Muller and Ivan Rezucha, Development of Sampling Plans By Using Sequential (Item by Item) Selection Techniques And Digital Computers, JASA, Vol. 57, No. 298, pp. 387-402, 1962.

[3] Goodman S.E. and S.T. Hedetniemi, Introduction To The Design And Analysis Of Algorithm, McGraw Hill, 1977.

[4] Gupta P. and G. P. Bhattacharjee, Parallel Generation Of Permutations, Computer J., Vol. 26, No. 2, pp. 97-105, 1983.

[5] Knuth D.E., The Art of Computer Programming, Vol. 2 (Seminumerical algorithms), Addison-Wesley Pub., (Reading Mass), 1981.

[6] Teuhola J. and O. Nevalainen, Two Efficient Algorithms For Random Sampling Without Replacement, IJCM, Vol. 11, No. 2, pp. 127-140, 1982.

Proof Rules for Communication Abstractions

by
Gadi Taubenfeld and Nissim Francez
Computer Science dept.
Technion - Israel Institute of Technology
Haifa 32000, Israel

Abstract

A modular proof system is presented for proving partial correctness and freedom from deadlock of concurrent programs using scripts (including recursive scripts). Its applications to augmentations of CSP and a subset of ADA are discussed. The proof rules are a generalization of both the procedure rules and the concurrency rules. Correctness proofs for examples are presented.

C.R. Categories: D.3.3, F.3.1, F.3.3

Key Words: proof rule, verification, concurrent programming, deadlock, script, invariants.

1. INTRODUCTION

In [FH83] a programming language construct named script was introduced, to serve as a communication abstraction mechanism, to be added to any programming language in which concurrency and communication are expressible. The exposition there was informal and concentrated on the concurrency and communication related issues.

The purpose of this paper is to present a more formal definition of the concept by means of *proof rules* for proving partial correctness - and freedom from deadlock - assertions about concurrent programs which employ scripts. There are two main aspects of the script that dictate an approach towards the formulation of the required rules.

(i) The script, viewed as an abstraction, is a multi-party communication and synchronization construct, generalizing the primitives found in most languages for concurrent computation, which involve *binary* communication and synchronization.

(ii) The (joint) script-enrollment of processes to roles in a script can be viewed as a generalization of the procedure-call mechanism, whereby a "distributed call" consists of each process calling "its piece" of a procedure, namely a *role* in the script. The overall effect of a script is reached by means of parameter passing.

Thus, the task is to find a proper amalgamation of proof rules dealing with concurrency and communication with those related to procedures, in order to produce a uniform proof system defining the script construct.

As far as concurrency and communication are concerned, our system is a natural extension of what has become known as "cooperation proofs". We had to generalize both the sequential proof rules for a process/role to deal with enrollment, and the notion of cooperation, dealing with the concurrent composition. A major design goal is to introduce into the proof system the same degree of modularity induced by the script construct on the program.

Thus, we adopted the idea, derived from the proof-theory of procedures, to prove a "parametric assertion" about a script, which is then adapted to the enrolling environment by means of a generalization of the procedure rule and the recursive rule for procedure calls.

To preserve this kind of modularity in proofs of deadlock freedom, we had also to modify the concept of a "blocked situation" [AFR80,OG76]. Thus, an enrollment to a script that has a danger of potential deadlock is itself considered a blocked situation.

The presentation consists of two parts. The first part presents the verification ideas in a host-language independent way. In the second part we assume CSP [HO78] as a host language, and consider an augmentation of the proof system presented in [AFR80] to suit our needs. CSP has been chosen because of its natural suitability in our context, the availability of an established proof systems for it and the familiarity of the authors with both. We also devote a small section to the discussion of adopting the ideas to the framework of an ADA subset dealing with concurrency, for which a version of cooperating proofs also exists. Nowhere is the dependency on the host language essential.

The results of the paper can be best understood on the basis of previous knowledge of proof systems for concurrency and procedures. For partial self-containment a brief review of the functional structure of a script is presented in the next section. The rest of the paper is organized as follows. In section 3 and 4 we introduce the partial correctness proof system. Section 5 contains a case study in full details. Section 6 generalizes the proof system to freedom from deadlock. Finally, in section 7 we extend the proof system for partial correctness and freedom from deadlock to apply also to recursive scripts.

2. THE STRUCTURE OF A SCRIPT

The main purpose of a *script* is to serve as an *abstraction* mechanism, hiding the implementation details of various *communication patterns* among communicating processes. It is viewed also as a programming language construct that can be added to any *host* programming language for expressing concurrent programs. It is best conceived in analogy with the *procedure* construct in languages for sequential programming.

More details about the script (including examples) can be found in [FH83]. We briefly repeat here the functional structure of a script, for the (partial) self containment of the paper.

Basically, a script is a parametrized concurrent program section, to which processes *enroll* in order to participate. It consists of the following components :

body – this is a concurrent composition of disjoint formal processes (i.e no shared variables), each of which is called a *role*. Communication among the various roles of a script is achieved using the inter-process communication primitives of the host language.

roles – these are formal processes, to which (actual) processes enroll. Parameter passing is used for interface with a script.

data parameters – these are formal data parameters (as in the case of ordinary procedures) associated with the roles.

In this paper we assume, for simplicity, that the actual parameters, transferred by an actual process to a role, are expressions referring to distinct identifiers. This assumption is motivated similarly to the analogous assumption regarding procedures, avoiding aliasing.

There are two methods of *partners –policy enrollment* :

* *partners –unnamed enrollment* : upon enrollment a process specifies only its own role (and, of course, the script name).
* *partners –named enrollment* : a process not only specifies the role to which it enrolls, but also names the identities of (some or all of) the other processes it wants to communicate with in the script and their intended roles. In such cases, the processes will jointly enroll in the script only when their enrollment specifications match.

There are also two methods of *script initiation* and *termination*

* *delayed initiation* : processes must first enroll in the roles of a given script; only then may the execution of that script start.
* *immediate initiation* : the script is activated upon the enrollment of its first participating process. Other processes may enroll while the script is in progress.
* *delayed termination* – will free (together) the processes enrolled in a script after of the roles have terminated.
* *immediate termination* – will free each process as soon as it completes its own role.

The case where both initiation and termination are immediate is not treated by this paper. Note that, in this case, a given process may enroll in several roles of the same script, provided these roles do not communicate with each other within the script's body.

For simplicity, we assume that there is only one instance of a script; however, the proof system can also allow the case of multiple instances of a script.

The collective activation of all the roles of a script is called a *performance*. The minimum requirement assumed, for the semantic of successive activation of a script, is that all of the roles of a given performance must terminate before a subsequent performance of the same script can begin. Note that a delayed-initiation or delayed-termination policy would automatically guarantee that the successive activations requirement is met.

In the examples presented, a mixture of CSP [HO78] and Pascal notations is used as the host language.

CSP's convention for distributed termination of loops is not assumed in this paper.

Example 1: Broadcast:

The first example is of a star-like broadcast script in which a transmitter(R_1) communicates non-deterministically with each of two recipients(R_2, R_3).

```
SCRIPT broadcast ::
  INITIATION  : ****;
  TERMINATION: ****;
  [ ROLE R1 (VALUE x1: item) ::
       VAR send: ARRAY [2..3] OF boolean;
       send[2..3] := 2*false;
       *[ [](k=2,3) ¬send[k]; Rk!x1→ send[k]:=true]
   ||
   ROLE (i=2,3) Ri (RESULT zi: item) ::
         R1?zi
  ].
```

The stars '****' stand for DELAYED or ~~IMMEDIATE which~~ determine the method of initiation and termination (which is of no concern in this example).

A process may enroll as the transmitter by:

ENROLL IN broadcast AS R_1 $(u*v-1)$;

and as the first recipient by:

ENROLL IN broadcast AS R_2 (w);

In this paper we further restrict the Script in two ways:

(1) A role can directly communicate only with other roles of the *same* script.

(2) The processes enrolling to the same performance of some script are all roles in some other script. The external (main) program is also considered to be a script regarding this restriction.

These restrictions ensure that apart from the actual processes that enroll to some script, no other process can influence the result of a performance of the script. This is so because a process (different from the script roles) cannot communicate with the script's roles, either (1) directly or (2) indirectly, via another script in which it and the role(s) would enroll. These restrictions simplify the design of an inference rule for the script. Without them we would not be able, because of the interaction between scripts, to handle each script separately, as we do later. It also avoids some scoping problems.

A nested enrollment, where a role in one script can enroll in some other script, is allowed. Recursive scripts, where a role can enroll in its own script, and mutual recursion among scripts are allowed only in section 7, where the issue of recursive scripts is treated separately.

Finally, in order to avoid cumbersome presentation, we consider only scripts that use exclusively either inter-role communication or *enroll* commands (not both in the same script). External processes can communicate only via enroll commands. The extension to any mixture of primitive inter-process communication and script enrollment is possible but rather technical. The possibility of having nested enroll commands within the body of an accept in the extension to arbitrary mixtures when using ADA is briefly discussed at the end of section four.

3. PROVING PROPERTIES OF SCRIPT BODIES

The way we intend to prove partial correctness of programs that use scripts is closely related to the way procedures are treated [AP81,GL80,HO71]. First, for each script body some assertion, relating pre- and post-conditions, is proved; then, using these proofs, an assertion about the main program is proved.

In the case of nested enrollments a script regards another script that enrolls in it as a main program, while it is regarded itself as a main program by a script it enrolls in. Thus, to avoid the artificial distinction, we will from now on only use the term script. Everything we say about a script relates also to the main program.

With each script we associate an invariant SI called the ***script invariant***, (i.e. each script has its own invariant). Each SI expresses global information about a script. It may refer to the formal parameters and local variables of all of the roles in the script.

When a script uses only primitive inter-role communication, the pre- and post-assertions associated with its body are proved using any proof system for the host language. In the case in which it uses *enroll* commands (i.e. there are nested enrollments) the system described in the sequel is used.

As in the case of the procedure inference rule [HO71], which is used as interface between the procedure call and its body, we present a new proof rule which is a generalization of the procedure rule.

3.1 Script enrollment

The definition, $ROLE\ \ R_j\ (VALUE\ \vec{x_j};\ VALUE-RESULT\ \vec{y_j};\ RESULT\ \vec{z_j}){::}\ B_j$ defines a role R_j with *value* parameters $\vec{x_j}$, *value*-*result* parameters $\vec{y_j}$, *result* parameters $\vec{z_j}$ and body B_j.

For a script S with roles as defined above, the notation $SCRIPT\_S\ (\vec{x},\vec{y},\vec{z}){::}\ B_s$ is used. Here $\vec{x},\vec{y},\vec{z}$ denote the formal parameters of the roles $\vec{x}_1,\ldots,\vec{x}_{ns};\ \vec{y}_1,\ldots,\vec{y}_{ns};\ \vec{z}_1,\ldots,\vec{z}_{ns}$ respectively, where $ns=|S|$ denotes the number of roles in the script S. Also, B_s denotes the script body $(\mathop{||}\limits_{j=1}^{ns} B_j)$.

As mentioned above, with a given script S with body B_s an assertion $\{pre(S)\}\ B_s\ \{post(S)\}$ can be associated. Both $pre(S)$ and $post(S)$ are constructed by conjoining, respectively, the preconditions and postconditions of all of the various roles with the script invariant.

The formal data parameters referred to by the predicates $pre(S)$,$post(S)$ may only be $\vec{x},\vec{y}$ and $\vec{y},\vec{z}$, respectively. They may also refer to constants and *free variables* to describe initial and final values (called 'logical variables' in [GL80]). Note that $\vec{z}$ must be initialized inside B_s, which explains why $pre(S)$ may not refer to the result parameters. Also since the value parameters $(\vec{x})$ are inrelevant to the enrolling processes upon termination of a performance of a script, $post(S)$ may not refer to the value parameters. Again, these restrictions are motivated similarly to the analogous restrictions regarding procedures and do not restrict generality.

When applying the proof system presented in [AFR80] to a script S which uses CSP's primitive communication commands, the script roles and the predicate $pre(S)$ correspond, respectively, to processes and the precondition over the initial state in CSP programs.

Example 1.1: Consider again the *broadcast* example. Using the proof system for CSP described in [AFR80], we may prove: $\{x_1=C\}\ B_{broadcast}\ \{z_2=z_3=C\}$

The *proof outline* for the script:

```
[ R1:  {x1 = C} send[2..3]:=false;
       LI: {x1 = C}
       *[ [](k=2,3) ¬send[k]; Rk!x1→ send[k]:=true {LI}]
       {LI}
  ||
  Ri(i=2,3):  {true } R1?zi {zi=C}
]
```

In this case, $SI_{1.1}\equiv$true.

For establishing cooperation we have to prove:

$$\{x_1=C\}\ R_k!x_1 \| R_1?z_i\ \{x_1=C \wedge z_i=C\} \qquad (for\ k=i),$$

which is done by applying the communication and preservation axioms and conjunction rule. By the parallel composition and consequence rules the proof is finished. ▯

C is a free variable "freezing" the initial value of the transmitter and final value of all of the roles. Because $\{x_1=C\}B_{broadcast}\{z_2=z_3=C\}$ is universally true, C may be replaced by any term to yield another universally true statment.

A process P_i can enroll as role R_j in script S using the command $E_j^s(\vec{a_i},\vec{b_i},\vec{c_i})$, where the variables $\vec{a_i}$ $\vec{b_i}$ and $\vec{c_i}$ are the arguments corresponding to the parameters $\vec{x_j}$, $\vec{y_j}$ and $\vec{z_j}$, respectively. The value arguments $\vec{a_i}$ can be expressions. E_j^s is a shorthand notation for ENROLL IN S AS R_j.

Definition: $E_1^s, \ldots, E_{ns}^s$ are *matching enrollments* if they may enroll to different roles in the same preformance of S. ▯

By the assumption that initiation and termination are not both immediate, no two $E$is, E_j^s $i \neq j$ belong to the same process.

This notion is a natural generalization of that of matching communication commands that is used in verifying CSP programs [AFR80].

Note that from restriction (2) in the script definition above, matching enrollments consist only of enroll commands which are all made by roles from the same script.

We now introduce a new inference rule used as an interface between the enrolling processes and the script. Again, this rule naturally generalizes the 'rule of adaptation' used for procedures.

enrollment rule: for a script S and matching enrollments $E_1^s, \ldots, E_{ns}^s$,

$$\frac{\{pre(S)\}\ B_s\ \{post(S)\}}{\{pre(S)[\vec{a};\vec{b}/\vec{x};\vec{y}]\}\ \ [\overset{ns}{\underset{j=1}{\|}} E_j^s(\vec{a_{k_j}},\vec{b_{k_j}},\vec{c_{k_j}})]\ \ \{post(S)[\vec{b};\vec{c}/\vec{y};\vec{z}]\}}$$

where $\vec{a},\vec{b},\vec{c}$ denote $\vec{a_{k_1}}, \ldots, \vec{a_{k_{ns}}}$; $\vec{b_{k_1}}, \ldots, \vec{b_{k_{ns}}}$; $\vec{c_{k_1}}, \ldots, \vec{c_{k_{ns}}}$; respectively. By definition all of the processes P_{k_j} $(k_j=1..n)$ and the roles R_j $(j=1..ns)$ are disjoint.

Here $p[\vec{u}/\vec{v}]$ denotes the assertion obtained from p by substituting (simultaneously) $\vec{u}$ for all free occurrences of $\vec{v}$.

Explanation: The script S operates on the actual parameters $\vec{a};\vec{b};\vec{c}$ in exactly the same way as the body B_s would do with the formal parameters $\vec{x};\vec{y};\vec{z}$. Thus it is expected that $post(S)[\vec{b};\vec{c}/\vec{y};\vec{z}]$ is true after execution of the script provided that $pre(S)[\vec{a};\vec{b}/\vec{x};\vec{y}]$ is true beforehand.

Furthermore, let SI be the script invariant for B_s which refers to the formal parameters. Then, after passing the actual parameters, SI remains invariant (i.e. parameter passing does not affect the invariance of SI).

Example 1.2: consider a program $P :: [P_1 \| P_2 \| P_3]$ using the broadcast script specified above, where:

$P_1 :: E_1(5)$
$P_2 :: E_2(c_2)$
$P_3 :: E_3(c_3)$

(E abbreviates here $E^{broadcast}$)

We prove : $\{\text{true}\}\ [P_1 \| P_2 \| P_3]\ \{c_2=c_3=5\}$.

Using the proof that $\{x_1=C\}\ B_{broadcast}\ \{z_2=z_3=C\}$ which was given before, we take C to be 5 and get : $\{x_1=5\}\ B_{broadcast}\ \{z_2=z_3=5\}$

By the enrollment rule we get :

$$\frac{\{x_1=5\}\ B_{broadcast}\ \{z_2=z_3=5\}}{\{x_1=5[5/x_1]\}\ [E_1(5) \| E_2(c_2) \| E_3(c_3)]\ \{z_2=z_3=5[c_2,c_3/z_2,z_3]\}}$$

After substitution we obtain :

$$\{5=5\}\ [E_1(5) \| E_2(c_2) \| E_3(c_3)]\ \{c_2=c_3=5\} \quad ▯$$

Note that, as in case of the procedure-call rule (see [GL80]), the enrollment rule is independent of the script body; it depends only on the specification of the body, namely the pre- and post-conditions of the script body. This is a strong argument in support of the use of scripts as an abstraction mechanism.

Before continuing, we would like to contemplate on the meaning of the enrollment rule as a semantic definition of enrollments. As the rule uses substitutions into global states, one may falsly conclude that both delayed initiation and delayed termination are implied.

Enrolling processes need to be synchronized in order for such a global state to be an actual state in the computation satisfying, in particular, the script invariant (after substitution), so that the usual inductive argument can be applied to deduce the invariant upon total termination.

This, however, is not so. It suffices that at least one event, either initiation or termination be delayed, the other one possibly being immediate. The argument for showing this is a variant on the one used in [EF82], as each preformance of a script under such conditions satisfies similar properties to these of communication-closed layers ; the only difference is that these layers do not form a cross-section of the whole program, only of the participating processes. We refer the reader to [EF82] for further discussions.

We would like to note also, that the kind of execution induced by these rules is such that processes do local activities until all face enrollments. Then, a whole group, forming a matching enrollment, is advanced one "big step". This generalizes the execution of CSP programs induced by the [AFR80] system, where processes are advanced one pair at the time. For a proof that an arbitrary execution is equivalent to such a serialized one, see [AP83].

Finally, we introduce two new proof rules which are also a natural generalization of those for procedures. The names chosen for the rules are the same as those used for procedures [AP81]. Both of them refer to script S and matching enrollments $E_1^s, \ldots, E_{ns}^s$.

parameter substitution rule

$$\frac{\{p\}\ [\,\|_{j=1}^{ns} E_j^s(\vec{a_{k_j}},\vec{b_{k_j}},\vec{c_{k_j}})]\ \{q\}}{\{p\ [\vec{d};\vec{e}\,/\,\vec{a};\vec{b}]\}\ \ [\,\|_{j=1}^{ns} E_j^s(\vec{d_{k_j}},\vec{e_{k_j}},\vec{f_{k_j}})]\ \ \{q\ [\vec{e};\vec{f}\,/\,\vec{b};\vec{c}]\}}$$

where $\quad var(\vec{d};\vec{e};\vec{f}) \cap free(p,q) \subseteq var(\vec{a};\vec{b};\vec{c})$.

$\vec{a}$, $\vec{d}$: denote a sequence of expressions,

$\vec{b},\vec{c},\vec{e},\vec{f}$: denote a sequence of variables,

$p[\vec{d};\vec{e}\,/\,\vec{a};\vec{b}]$: stands for simultaneous substitution of the expressions and variables from $\vec{d}$ and $\vec{e}$ for those from $\vec{a}$ and $\vec{b}$,

$var(\vec{a};\vec{b};\vec{c})$ denotes the set of all variables appearing in $\vec{a};\vec{b}$ and $\vec{c}$.

$free(p,q)$: denotes the set of all free variables of p and q.

A similar restriction appear and is explained in [AP81, p. 464].

variable substitution rule

$$\frac{\{p\}\ [\,\|_{j=1}^{ns} E_j^s(\vec{a_{k_j}},\vec{b_{k_j}},\vec{c_{k_j}})]\ \{q\}}{\{p\ [\vec{s}\,/\,\vec{r}]\}\ [\,\|_{j=1}^{ns} E_j^s(\vec{a_{k_j}},\vec{b_{k_j}},\vec{c_{k_j}})]\ \{q\ [\vec{s}\,/\,\vec{r}]\}}$$

where $\quad var(\vec{s};\vec{r}) \cap var(\vec{a};\vec{b};\vec{c}) = \phi$

The variable substitution rule is used to rename free variables which are not used as actual parameters. Those free variables are typically used to "freeze" the value of the parameters before enroll command.

Both rules are useful but not necessary when recursion is not allowed. They are vital when the proof system is later extended to deal with recursion. Example for using the rules appear in section 7.

4. PROVING PROPERTIES OF ENROLLMENTS

We now introduce the method for proving pre- and post- assertion about a script that uses enroll commands. This proof system is structured similarly to the one for CSP introduced in [AFR80].

We use the term *process* generically for both a role and an external process. That is so because when a role enrolls in some other script S, it can be regarded by S, as an external process in case of nested enrollments.

A proof of pre- and post- assertions about a script is done in two stages:

(1) separate proofs are constructed in isolation for each component process.

(2) the separate proofs are combined by showing that they *cooperate*.

To generate separate proofs for each process we need the following axiom:

Enrollment Axiom: Let E denote any *enroll* command.

$$\{p\}E\{q\}.$$

where p and q refer only to variables local to the process from which E is taken.

This axiom indicates that any post-assertion q can be deduced after an enroll command. Note, however, that q cannot be arbitrary since at stage (2) it must pass the cooperation test. This axiom is a natural generalization of the input/output axioms introduced in [AFR80] for CSP's communication commands. There the "arbitrariness" of q is explained in more detail.

Using the enrollment axiom and the first eight rules of inference (I1-I8) which are listed in the appendix, we can establish separate proofs for each process. This is presented, as in [OG76], by a *proof outline* in which each substatment of a process is preceded and followed by a corresponding assertion.

Remark: the rules for the Alternative and Repetitive statements listed in the appendix are in a format suitable for CSP. The use of another host language might require suitable modifications to be made.

In this proof outline a process '*guesses*' the value its parameters will receive after enrollment. When the proofs are combined, these guesses have to be checked for consistency in some way. This is done by the cooperation test.

Note the role of the 'guess' in this proof rule. We may distinguish three levels of "guessing"

(i) "small guess" - as present in proof system for CSP in the form of a "communication axiom" [AFR80]. The "guess" is over the effect of a single communication.

(ii) "moderate guess" - as presented in the proof system for an ADA subset (for concurrency) using the call-accept primitives [GR]. Here the "guess" is over a chain of entry calls, when an *accept* or *call* appears within the body of another *accept*.

(iii) "big guess" - as present in the current system, "guessing" the effect of an enrollment, that may involve an unbounded number of primitive communications.

We now explain how, at stage (2), the separate proofs are combined.

First we need the concept of *bracketing*.

Definition: A process P_i is *bracketed* if the brackets "<" and ">" are interspersed in its text so that

(i) for each program section <B>, B is of the form $B_1;E;B_1'$ where B_1 and B_1' do not contain any *enroll* commands, and

(ii) all *enroll* commands appear only within brackets as above. []

The purpose of the brackets, as in [AFR80], is to delimit the script sections within which the script invariant need not necessarily hold. Again, a generalization of the situation in the script-free programs is easily recognizable.

With each proof of $\{p\}[P_1 \| \cdots \| P_n]\{q\}$ we now associate a script invariant SI and an appropriate bracketing. The proof rule concerning parallel composition has the following form:

Parallel Composition rule

$$\frac{\textit{proofs of } \{p_i\}P_i\{q_i\},\ i=1,\ldots,n,\ \textit{cooperate}}{\{p_1\wedge\cdots\wedge p_n\wedge SI\}[P_1\|\cdots\|P_n]\{q_1\wedge\cdots\wedge q_n\wedge SI\}}$$

provided no variable free in SI is subject to change outside a bracketed section.

Intuitively proofs cooperate if each performance of a script validates all the post-assertions ('guesses') of the *enroll*-commands enrolling in this performance.

We now define precisely what it means for proofs to cooperate. Assume a given bracketing of a script $[P_1 \| \cdots \| P_n]$ and a script invariant SI associated with it.

Definition: $\langle B_1 \rangle, \ldots, \langle B_{ns} \rangle$ are matching bracketed sections if they contain matching enrollment $(E_1^s, \ldots, E_{ns}^s)$ to some script S. []

Definition: The proofs $\{p_i\} P_i \{q_i\}, i=1,\ldots,n$, *cooperate* if

(*i*) the assertions used in the proof of $\{p_i\} P_i \{q_i\}$ have no free variables subject to change in P_j for $i \neq j$;

(*ii*) $\{ \bigwedge_{j=1}^{ns} pre(B_j) \wedge SI \} [\,\|_{j=1}^{ns} B_j] \{ \bigwedge_{j=1}^{ns} post(B_j) \wedge SI \}$

holds for all matching bracketed sections $\langle B_1 \rangle, \ldots, \langle B_{ns} \rangle$. []

The following axiom and proof rule are needed to establish cooperation:

Enrollment rule, *Parameter substitution rule* and *Variable substitution rule* : as described in the previous section.

Rearrangement rule:

$$\frac{\{p\}\ B_1;\ldots;B_{ns}\ \{p_1\},\ \{p_1\}\ [\,\|_{j=1}^{ns} E_j^s]\ \{p_2\},\ \{p_2\}\ B_1';\ldots;B_{ns}'\ \{q\}}{\{p\}\ [\,\|_{j=1}^{ns} (B_j;\, E_j^s;\, B_j')\ ]\ \{q\}}$$

provided $B_1, B_1', \ldots, B_{ns}, B_{ns}'$ do not contain any enroll commands and $E_1^s, \ldots, E_{ns}^s$ above are matching enrollments.

The rearrangement rule reduces the proof of cooperation to sequential reasoning, except for an appeal to the enrollment rule. Note that the rearrangement of $B_1, \ldots, B_{ns}$, and $B_1', \ldots, B_{ns}'$ is arbitrary, since they are disjoint in variables. This is a generalization of the binary rearrangement used for CSP, called the 'formation rule' in [AFR80]

For proving cooperation we also need the preservation rule (I9. in the appendix). Finally, to complete the proof system, the substitution rule (I10) and the auxiliary variable rule (I11) are needed.

Example 1.3 Consider the program $P::[P_1 \| P_2 \| P_3]$, where:

$P_1 :: E_2(a_1)$
$P_2 :: a_2:=5;\ E_1(a_2+1)$
$P_3 :: E_3(a_3)$

for the rest of the section $E \equiv E^{broadcast}$.

Note that P_2 enrolls as the transmitter and P_1, P_3 enroll as recipients.

Using the system above we can prove: $\{\text{true}\}\ [P_1 \| P_2 \| P_3]\ \{a_1=a_3=6 \wedge a_2=5\}$

The proof outline is:

P_1 : $\{\text{true}\}\ E_2(a_1)\ \{a_1=6\}$
P_2 : $\{\text{true}\}\ a_2:=5\ \{a_2=5\}\ E_1(a_2+1)\ \{a_2=5\}$
P_3 : $\{\text{true}\}\ E_3(a_3)\ \{a_3=6\}$

and we may choose $SI_{1.3} \equiv \text{true}$.

There is only one matching enrollment, so for *cooperation* we must prove:

$$\{a_2=5\}\ [E_1(a_2+1) \| E_2(a_1) \| E_3(a_3)]\ \{a_1=a_3=6 \wedge a_2=5\}$$

Using the proof that $\{x_1=C\} B_{broadcast} \{z_2=z_3=C\}$ which was given before, we take C to be 6 and get : $\{x_1=6\}\ B_{broadcast}\ \{z_2=z_3=6\}$

By the enrollment rule we get :

$$\frac{\{x_1=6\} B_{broadcast} \{z_2=z_3=6\}}{\{x_1=6[a_2+1/x_1]\}\ [E_1(a_2+1) \| E_2(a_1) \| E_3(a_3)]\ \{z_2=z_3=6[a_1,a_3/z_2,z_3]\}}$$

and after substitution: $\{a_2+1=6\}\ [E_1(a_2+1) \| E_2(a_1) \| E_3(a_3)]\ \{a_1=a_3=6\}$.

By the preservation axiom : $\{a_2=5\}\ [E_1(a_2+1) \| E_2(a_1) \| E_3(a_3)]\ \{a_2=5\}$.

Using the conjunction rule the required cooperation is obtained.

Finally, by applying the parallel composition rule, the proof is completed. □

The cooperation test between proofs requires comparisons of all syntactically matching enrollments, even though some of them will never take place during any performance of the script considered.

In this context, the main role of the script invariant SI is to carry global information helping to determine which of the syntactic matches also match semantically. This information is expressed using *Auxiliary Variables* (different from the program variables), [OG76].

Consider *example* 1.4

P_1 ::	P_2 ::	P_3 ::
$E_1(5)$;	$E_2(a_2)$;	$E_3(a_3)$;
$E_2(a_1)$	$E_1(a_2+1)$	$E_3(a_3)$

In this example there are four syntactically matching enrollments (denoted: 1,2,3,4). Two of them, namely (3,4), are not semantically matching enrollment (i.e. will ***never*** take place). The other two, namely (1,2), are semantically matching.

We use this example to demonstrate the concept of bracketing and script invariant.

To verify the program, three auxiliary variables i,j,k are used.

proof outline (for the bracketed program)

P_1' ::	P_2' ::	P_3' ::
$\{i=0\}$	$\{j=0\}$	$\{k=0\}$
$<E_1(5);\{\text{true}\}i:=1>$	$<E_2(a_2);\{a_2=5\}j:=1>$	$<E_3(a_3);\{\text{true}\}k:=1>$
$\{i=1\}$	$\{a_2=5 \wedge j=1\}$	$\{k=1\}$
$<E_2(a_1)>$	$<E_1(a_2+1)>$	$<E_3(a_3)>$
$\{a_1=6\}$	$\{a_2=5\}$	$\{a_3=6\}$

We choose $SI_{1.4} \equiv i=j=k$,

We now show that the two semantically matching enrollments (1,2) pass the cooperation test. In the other syntactic matching enrollments (3,4), the conjunction of the preconditions contradicts the invariant, so they trivially passes the cooperation test.

(1) We must prove

$$\{SI_{1.4} \wedge i=j=k=0\}\ [<E_1(5);i:=1> \| <E_2(a_2);j:=1> \| <E_3(a_3);k:=1>]\ \{SI_{1.4} \wedge a_2=5 \wedge i=j=k=1\}$$

Taking C to be 5, we get by the *enrollment rule*

$$\{\text{true}\}\ [E_1(5) \| E_2(a_2) \| E_3(a_3)]\ \{a_2=a_3=5\}.$$

By the assignment and preservation axioms:

$$\{a_2=5\}\ i:=1;j:=1;k:=1\ \{i=j=k=1 \wedge a_2=5\}$$

By applying the consequence and rearrangement rules the proof of (1) is finished.

(2) We must prove

$$\{SI_{1.4} \wedge a_2=5 \wedge i=j=k=1\}\ [<E_1(a_2+1)> \| <E_2(a_1)> \| <E_3(a_3)>]\ \{SI_{1.4} \wedge a_1=a_3=6 \wedge a_2=5\}$$

from example 1.3 we know that

$$\{a_2=5\}\ [E_1(a_2+1) \| E_2(a_1) \| E_3(a_3)]\ \{a_1=a_3=6 \wedge a_2=5\}$$

applying the preservation axiom and the conjunction rule the proof of (2) is finished.

Hence, by the parallel composition, consequence, and auxiliary variables rules:

$$\{i=0 \wedge j=0 \wedge k=0\}\ [P_1 \| P_2 \| P_3]\ \{a_1=a_3=6 \wedge a_2=5\}.$$

Finally by applying the substitution rule we obtain

$$\{\text{true}\}\ [P_1 \| P_2 \| P_3]\ \{a_1=a_3=6 \wedge a_2=5\}. \quad \square$$

Before ending this section we want to clarify a point concerning the extension of the proof system for ADA (presented in [GR]), to any mixture of primitive call-accept communications and script enrollments.

Such an extension enables the possibility of having occurrences of enroll commands within the body of an accept; such a phenomenon is not possible in extending the rule to mixtures in CSP.

A similar problem, of having occurrences of calls or accepts, within the body of another accept was resolved in [GR, sec. 3] by restricted the notation of bracketing in such way that the invariant also holds when such inner calls or accepts are reached.

Applying that method in exactly the same way to enroll commands nested within accept gives an easy and smooth solution. We present below a modified definition for bracketed task; the rest of the details in the extension, as we said before, are rather technical.

Definition: A task is called bracketed if the brackets '<' and '>' are interspersed in its text, so that:

(1) for each bracketed section, $<B>$, B is of the form

(a) B_1; *CALL T.a(arguments)*; B_2,

(b) B_1; *ENROLL IN s AS* R_j*(arguments)*; B_2,

(c) *ACCEPT b(parameters) DO* B_1,

(d) B_2 *ENDACCEPT*;

where B_1 and B_2 do not contain any entry call or accept or enroll, and may be the null statement.

(2) each call, accept and enroll is bracketed as above. $\square$

5. EXAMPLES

In this section we present a somewhat larger case study in full detail. We present a script and two different patterns of enrollment to this script, yielding two different effects in the enrolling program.

First the script ROTATE is introduced. It consists of *m roles* arranged as a ring configuration. Each role R_i has a formal parameter x_i with an initial value denoted by the free variable C_i. Each role R_i non-deterministically sends its own initial value to its right neighbor R_{i+1} and receives the initial value of its left neighbor R_{i-1}. (In this section, + and - are interpreted cyclically in {1,...,m}). The action in which each role transfers its initial value to its right neighbor is called rotate right. The indices are used in order to clarify the presentation.

The script declaration,

```
SCRIPT rotate ::
  [ ROLE (i=1,m) R_i (VALUE_RESULT x_i: integer) ::
      VAR send_i,receive_i: boolean; temp_i: integer;
      send_i:=false; receive_i:=false;
      *[ ¬send_i;  R_{i+1}!x_i  →  send_i:=true
        □
         ¬receive_i; R_{i-1}?temp_i → receive_i:=true
      ]; x_i:=temp_i
  ].
```

Using the proof system for CSP described in [AFR80] we prove:

$$\{\bigwedge_{i=1}^{m}(x_i=C_i)\}\ B_{rotate}\ \{\bigwedge_{i=1}^{m}(x_i=C_{i-1})\}$$

To verify the script two auxiliary variables s_i and r_i are introduced for each role R_i. Following is the *proof outline* for the script:

R_i : $\{x_i = C_i \wedge s_i = r_i = \text{false}\}$
  $send_i$:=false; $receive_i$:=false;
  LI_i: $\{x_i = C_i \wedge send_i = s_i \wedge receive_i = r_i\}$
  $*[\ \neg send_i$; <$R_{i+1}!x_i \rightarrow s_i$:=true ; $send_i$:=true> $\{LI_i\}$
   $\square$
   $\neg receive_i$; <$R_{i-1}?temp_i \rightarrow r_i$:=true; $receive_i$:=true> $\{LI_i\}$
   $]\{LI_i \wedge receive_i \wedge send_i\}$ $x_i := temp_i$ $\{s_i \wedge r_i \wedge x_i = temp_i\}$

We choose the script invariant $SI \equiv \bigwedge_{i=1}^{m}[(s_i \wedge r_{i+1}) \rightarrow temp_{i+1} = C_i]$. SI means that "when R_i has send and R_{i+1} has received then $temp_{i+1}$ holds the value C_i. (note that SI refers also to local variables).

Matching bracketed sections consist of the first alternative of some R_i and the second alternative of R_{i+1}. So, for establishing cooperation, we have to prove

$\{\neg send_i \wedge \neg receive_{i+1} \wedge LI_i \wedge LI_{i+1} \wedge SI\}$
[<$R_{i+1}!x_i \rightarrow s_i$:=true ;$send_i$:=true>$\|$<$R_i?temp_{i+1} \rightarrow r_{i+1}$:=true; $receive_{i+1}$:=true>]
$\{LI_i \wedge LI_{i+1} \wedge SI\}$

By the arrow rule (see [AFR80]) it remains to prove that

$$\{\neg send_i \wedge \neg receive_{i+1} \wedge LI_i \wedge LI_{i+1} \wedge \bigwedge_{\substack{j=1\\ j\neq i}}^{m}[(s_j \wedge r_{j+1}) \rightarrow temp_{j+1} = C_j] \wedge temp_{i+1} = x_i\}$$

s_i:=true; $send_i$:=true; r_{i+1}:=true; $receive_{i+1}$:=true $\{LI_i \wedge LI_{i+1} \wedge SI\}$

holds, where the precondition above is postcondition of: $R_{i+1}!x_i \| R_i?temp_{i+1}$ inferred by the axioms of communication ([AFR80]) and preservation.

Using the assignment axiom and consequence rule the required cooperation is obtained. By the parallel composition rule:

$$\{SI \wedge \bigwedge_{i=1}^{m}[x_i = C_i \wedge s_i = r_i = \text{false}]\}\ B_{rotate}\ \{SI \wedge \bigwedge_{i=1}^{m}[r_i \wedge s_i \wedge x_i = temp_i]\}$$

The post-assertion $(SI \wedge \bigwedge_{i=1}^{m}[r_i \wedge s_i \wedge x_i = temp_i])$ implies $\bigwedge_{i=1}^{m}[x_i = C_{i-1}]$

So, finally, by the consequence, auxiliary variables and substitution rules the required result is obtained. $\square$

In the next two examples we have again *m processes* arranged as a ring configuration. In the first program, using the rotate-script, the effect of "rotate right" is achieved. In the second example, using a different pattern of enrollment to the rotate-script, the effect of "rotate left" is achieved. For the rest of the section $E \equiv E^{rotate}$.

Example 2.1 (rotate right) let

$P :: [\ \|_{i=1}^{m} P_i\ ]$

$P_i :: a_i := i;\ E_i(a_i)$

We prove: $\{true\}\ P\ \{\bigwedge_{i=1}^{m}(a_i = i-1)\}$

proof outline: $P_i : \{true\}\ a_i := i\ \{a_i = i\}\ E_i(a_i)\ \{a_i = i-1\}$

and we may choose $SI_{2.1} \equiv$ true.

for *cooperation* we must prove: $\{\bigwedge_{i=1}^{m}(a_i = i)\}\ [\|_{i=1}^{m} E_i(a_i)]\ \{\bigwedge_{i=1}^{m}(a_i = i-1)\}$.

We take C_i to be i and get : $\{\bigwedge_{i=1}^{m}(x_i = i)\}\ B_{rotate}\ \{\bigwedge_{i=1}^{m}(x_i = i-1)\}$.

By the enrollment rule:

$$\frac{\{\bigwedge_{i=1}^{m}(x_i=i)\}\ B_{rotate}\ \{\bigwedge_{i=1}^{m}(x_i=i-1)\}}{\{\bigwedge_{i=1}^{m}(x_i=i)[a_i/x_i]\}\ [\mathop{\|}_{i=1}^{m}E_i(a_i)]\ \{\bigwedge_{i=1}^{m}(x_i=i-1)[a_i/x_i]\}}$$

which after substitution yields the required result.
By the parallel composition rule the proof is finished. □

Example 2.2 (rotate left) let

$P :: [\mathop{\|}_{i=1}^{m} P_i\ ]$

$P_i :: a_i:=i;\ E_{m-i+1}(a_i)$

For simplicity, we denote $m-i+1$ by k_i. $\{k_1, \ldots, k_m\}$ is permutation of $\{1,\ldots,m\}$, so P has exactly one matching enrollment.

We prove: $\{true\}\ P\ \{\bigwedge_{i=1}^{m}(a_i=i+1)\}$.

Proof outline: $P_i : \{true\}\ a_i:=i\ \{a_i=i\}\ E_{k_i}(a_i)\ \{a_i=i+1\}$

and we may choose $SI_{2.2} \equiv$ true.

for *cooperation* we must prove: $\{\bigwedge_{i=1}^{m}(a_i=i)\}\ [\mathop{\|}_{i=1}^{m}E_i(a_{k_i})]\ \{\bigwedge_{i=1}^{m}(a_i=i+1)\}$

(because $[\mathop{\|}_{i=1}^{m}E_{k_i}(a_i)]$ is the same as $[\mathop{\|}_{i=1}^{m}E_i(a_{k_i})]$ we can interchange them)

We take C_i to be k_i and get : $\{\bigwedge_{i=1}^{m}(x_i=k_i)\}\ B_{rotate}\ \{\bigwedge_{i=1}^{m}(x_i=k_{i-1})\}$

Because $k_{i-1} = m-(i-1)+1 = k_i+1$, $\{\bigwedge_{i=1}^{m}(x_i=k_i)\}\ B_{rotate}\ \{\bigwedge_{i=1}^{m}(x_i=k_i+1)\}$

By the enrollment rule we get :

$$\frac{\{\bigwedge_{i=1}^{m}(x_i=k_i)\}\ B_{rotate}\ \{\bigwedge_{i=1}^{m}(x_i=k_i+1)\}}{\{\bigwedge_{i=1}^{m}(x_i=k_i)[a_{k_i}/x_i]\}\ [\mathop{\|}_{i=1}^{m}E_i(a_{k_i})]\ \{\bigwedge_{i=1}^{m}(x_i=k_i+1)[a_{k_i}/x_i]\}}$$

and after substitution: $\{\bigwedge_{i=1}^{m}(a_{k_i}=k_i)\}\ [\mathop{\|}_{i=1}^{m}E_i(a_{k_i})]\ \{\bigwedge_{i=1}^{m}(a_{k_i}=k_i+1)\}$ which is clearly the same as the required proof.
By parallel composition the proof is finished. □

Remark: other definitions of k_i can cause interesting results, such as rotate k times ...

6. DEADLOCK FREEDOM

In this section we assume every script has an unlimited number of identical instances. When there exist matching enrollments to a script, one of its instances (transparent to the enrolling processes) starts a performance, despite the possibility that other performances of that script are taking place at this moment. From the enrolling processes point of view the script is always available, and there is no need to wait till one performance terminates in order to start a new one. The assumption is essential for the proof system presented in the sequel.

We show how the proof system can be used for proving deadlock freedom of a given program. We assume that there exists a deadlock freedom proof system for the host language (for example the proof systems presented in [AFR80,GR] for CSP and ADA, respectively).

As in [GR] we use a notion called *frontiers of computation* (f.o.c) which characterizes the set of all commands executing at a given moment. Note that these commands may belong to different scripts, their number is bounded by the number of the (main) program processes, and no two commands may belong to the same process.

A script that started a performance and has not terminated yet is called an active script. A process of an active script, which has not terminated yet, is called an active process.

Deadlock means a state in which the execution cannot proceed, although the program is still active. In the context of scripts this means that at least one process is active, each active process waits in front of a communication command (either an enroll command or a communication primitive of the host language), and no process can proceed. Thus, at the f.o.c , neither primitive communication nor matching enrollment are present in a deadlock.

Definition: A program P is deadlock free relative to a precondition p if no execution of P, starting in an initial state satisfying p, ends in a deadlock. $\Box$

The approach we use in proving freedom of deadlock is similar to that of the previous sections. Each script S is proved to be deadlock free relative to some assertion denoted by $\boldsymbol{df}(S)$.

Note that $\boldsymbol{df}(S)$ and $\boldsymbol{pre}(S)$ (from the partial correctness proof) need not necessarily be the same. For example for each script S, $\{\text{true}\}S\{\text{true}\}$ holds but if there exists an initial state in which S ends in a deadlock then, for proving deadlock freedom, $\boldsymbol{df}(S)$ has to be stronger then true. Similar to $\boldsymbol{pre}(S)$, $\boldsymbol{df}(S)$ may only refer to value parameters, value result parameters and constants. It may not refer to free variables.

The approach we present is slightly different to the one introduced in [AFR80,OG76,GR] where, in order to prove deadlock freedom, all possible deadlock situations (also called blocked situation in [AFR80,OG76] and blocked f.o.c in [GR]) are first show to be unreachable. Using this method would have forced us to give up modularity handling all of the scripts together instead of separately, as we wish to do.

The main idea is that, before a script can end in a deadlock it has to pass through a situation which we call a ***potentially blocked situation*** ($p.b.s$). A necessary (but not sufficient) condition for a situation to be a $p.b.s$ is that each of the scripts own active processes is waiting in front of an enroll command. Note that in contrast with the f.o.c which may include commands from different scripts, the p.b.s is characterized by a single script's own processes only. Proving deadlock freedom of a script is now done by identifying all of its p.b.s and proving that they are unreachable.

When a script uses only primitive inter-role communication its deadlock-freedom proof is done using a proof system for the host language. In case it uses enroll command, the system described below is used.

Example: The example demonstrates a $\boldsymbol{df}(S)$ predicate associated with a script S which uses CSP's primitive communication only. It is also used later to illustrate the new concept of p.b.s .

SCRIPT S::
[[ROLE R_1(*VALUE−RESULT* x_1:integer):: $[x_1>5 \rightarrow R_2!x_1 \; [] \; x_1\leq 5 \rightarrow R_2?x_1]$
[ROLE R_2(*VALUE−RESULT* x_2:integer):: $[x_2>5 \rightarrow R_1?x_2 \; [] \; x_2\leq 5 \rightarrow R_1!x_2]$
].

Using the CSP proof system it is easy to prove that S is deadlock free relative to $\boldsymbol{df}(S) \equiv (x_1>5 \wedge x_2>5) \vee (x_1\leq 5 \wedge x_2\leq 5)$.

The rest of this section is devoted to the formulation of a theorem which provides a sufficient condition for a script, using enroll commands, to be deadlock free. We assume that a specific proof outline is given for each process P_i $i=1,\ldots,n$ and that SI is the script invariant associated with that proof.

Definition: A matching enrollment, $E_1^t, \ldots, E_{nt}^t$, is ***df −matching enrollments*** if $\bigwedge_{i=1}^{nt} [\boldsymbol{pre}(E_i^t(\vec{a_{k_i}}, \vec{b_{k_i}}, \vec{c_{k_i}}))] \wedge SI$, (the conjunction of all of the preassertions of the enroll commands and the script invariant of the enrolling processes) implies $\boldsymbol{df}(t)[\vec{a},\vec{b}/\vec{x},\vec{y}]$. $\Box$

It is easy to see that a performance initiated by a ***df −matching enrollment*** will not end in a deadlock.

Definition: $\langle B_1 \rangle, \ldots, \langle B_{ns} \rangle$ are ***df −matching bracketed sections*** if they contain a df-matching enrollment $(E_1^s, \ldots, E_{ns}^s)$ to some script S. $\Box$

Next we introduce the new concept of ***potential blocking***. Consider the situation of an active script in which each of its own active processes waits in front of an enrollment command. Although the processes cannot continue immediately, the state is not necessarily a deadlock because there may be matching enrollments among the enroll commands.

Such a situation is characterized by an n-tuple of enrollment capabilities (e.c) associated with the corresponding processes and is defined as follows.

Assume that each process is waiting in front of an enroll command or has terminated; then:

(i) in case it has terminated its e.c consists of signalling its termination.

(ii) in case it is waiting in front of an enroll command its e.c consists of the bracketed section surrounding this enroll command.

The bracketed sections forming an n-tuple may be partitioned in different ways to form matching bracketed sections. Such a composition of bracketed sections is called a combination. A number of different combinations may be obtained from an n-tuple, each one indicating a possible path of execution. Note that a combination which does not include any df-matching bracketed sections indicates an execution path which may end in a deadlock, where the script is still in the same situation (i.e. the situation characterized by the n-tuple that the above combination is obtained from).

Definition: A situation, as described above, is a **p.b.s** if the following two conditions hold:

(a) Among the combinations obtained from the n-tuple of an e.c there exists a combination which does not include any df-matching bracketed sections.

(b) Not all processes signalling their termination (i.e the script is active).

Formally, condition (a) is:

$$\exists\ C \in combination(n\_tuple)\ \underset{match}{\forall} <B_1>, \ldots, <B_{nt}> \in C\ [\neg(\bigwedge_{i=1}^{nt}(pre(<B_i>)) \wedge SI \Longrightarrow df(t))]$$

where $combination(n\_tuple)$ is the set of all combination obtained from the n_tuple of e.c.'s which characterize the above situation, C describe one of those combinations and $<B_1>, \ldots, <B_{nt}>$ are some matching bracketed sections belonging to C.

To illustrate the concept of potential blocking, consider the following examples and their proof outlines. All of the enroll commands refer to the script S introduced in the previous example. The invariant is identically true in all the examples. In all of the examples we consider the situation in which *each* process waits to enroll, so condition (b) holds trivially.

(1) let P:: $[\{a_1=6\}E_1\{\text{true}\} \parallel \{a_2=6\}E_2\{\text{true}\}]$. There exists one combination only, including a matching enrollment which is a df-matching enrollment. Hence, condition (a) does not apply, and it is not a p.b.s .

(2) let P:: $[\{a_1=6\}E_1\{\text{true}\} \parallel \{a_2=6\}E_1\{\text{true}\}]$. There exists one combination only, which does not include any matching enrollments. Hence, condition (a) holds, and the situation is a p.b.s .

(3) let P:: $[\{a_1=6\}E_1\{\text{true}\} \parallel \{a_2=4\}E_2\{\text{true}\}]$. There exists one combination only, including a matching enrollment which, clearly, is not a df-matching enrollment. Hence, condition (a) holds, and again we have a p.b.s .

(4) let P:: $[\{a_1=4\}E_1\{\text{true}\} \parallel \{a_2=6\}E_1\{\text{true}\} \parallel \{a_3=6\}E_2\{\text{true}\}]$. Two combinations can be obtained. In the first combination, the third and second processes form a df-matching enrollment, while in the second combination the third process can also form a matching enrollment which is not a df-matching enrollment, with the first process. Hence condition (a) holds, and it is a p.b.s .

(5) let P:: $[\{a_1=4\}E_1\{\text{true}\} \parallel \{a_2=4\}E_1\{\text{true}\} \parallel \{a_3=6\}E_2\{\text{true}\} \parallel \{a_4=6\}E_2\{\text{true}\}]$. Two combinations can be obtained, both include exactly two matching enrollments which are clearly not df-matching enrollments. Hence condition (a) holds, and it is a p.b.s .

(6) let P:: $[\{a_1=6\}E_1\{\text{true}\} \parallel \{a_2=4\}E_1\{\text{true}\} \parallel \{a_3=6\}E_2\{\text{true}\} \parallel \{a_4=6\}E_2\{\text{true}\}]$. Two combinations can be obtained, both include exactly two matching enrollments where one of them is a df-matching enrollment. Hence condition (a) does not hold, and it is not a p.b.s .

(7) let P:: $[\{a_1=4\}E_1\{\text{true}\} \parallel \{a_2=6\}E_1\{\text{true}\} \parallel \{a_3=4\}E_2\{\text{true}\} \parallel \{a_4=6\}E_2\{\text{true}\}]$. Two combinations can be obtained. In the first combination, the first and third processes and the second and fourth processes form two df-matching enrollments, but the second combination includes two matching enrollments which are both not df-matching enrollments. Hence condition (a) holds, and it is a p.b.s .

Note that if the n-tuple may form only one combination, which does not include any matching bracketed sections, then it is a state of deadlock (as in example (2)).

With each p.b.s we associate an n-tuple of assertions, consisting of the assertions associated with the corresponding processes.

The assertion p_i associated with a blocked process P_i is either post(P_i) in case it has signalled it termination, or, otherwise, it is the preassertion of the bracketed section in front of which it waits.

We call an n-tuple $<p_1, \ldots, p_n>$ of assertions associated with a p.b.s a ***potentially blocked*** n-tuple.

It is now clear that a script has to pass through a p.b.s before it can end in deadlock. Thus, if it can be proved that all p.b.s's are not reachable then deadlock cannot occur and the script is proved to be deadlock free.

This argument is formally expressed in a theorem (similar to theorem 1 in [AFR80, sec. 4]).

Theorem: Given a proof of $\{df(S)\}S\{q\}$ with a script invariant SI, S is deadlock free (relative to $df(S)$) if for every potentially blocked n-tuple $<p_1, \ldots, p_n>$, $\neg(\bigwedge_{i=1}^{n} p_i \wedge SI)$ holds.

This theorem provides a method for proving deadlock freedom. The expressed condition is not a necessary one since it depends on a *given* proof .

In order to prove that S is deadlock free, we have to identify all potentially blocked n-tuples, and the SI should be such that a contradiction can be derived from the conjunction of the SI and the given potentially blocked n-tuple. The arguments supporting this theorem are similar to those appearing in previous discussion of proof of absence of deadlocks, e.g [AFR80, p. 378].

7. RECURSIVE SCRIPTS AND THEIR VERIFICATION

7.1 The notation of recursive scripts

In [FH83] recursive scripts, where a role can enroll in its own script, were mentioned as natural generalization of scripts. The purpose of this section is to further investigate this option by extending the proof system for partial correctness and deadlock freedom of non-recursive scripts, presented in the previous sections, to apply also to recursive scripts. The presentation here is in terms of ***direct recursion***, but the extension handles mutual recursion as well.

In case of recursion it is obvious that multiple instances of recursive scripts are assumed. The first two restrictions imposed on the script are now applied to each individual instance of a script.

(1) A role can directly communicate only with other roles of the same script instance, and

(2) The processes enrolling to the same performance of some script are all roles in some other script instance.

All other restrictions and assumptions, mentioned in section 2, remain intact.

When initiation is immediate a single recursive enrollment, where a role enrolls in its own script, is sufficient to open a new nested performance. In case of delayed initiation a nested performance is opened *only* when every role in a script recursively enrolls to its own script to compose a recursive matching enrollments.

Note that a role can recursively enroll to *any* one of its own script roles, thus the roles which have been enrolled to a nested preformance are a permutation of the roles they enrolled to.

To further demonstrate the idea of recursive scripts we now introduce an extensive case study in full detail. Later on, this example will also be verified using the extended proof system presented in the sequel.

7.2 An example: The 'Towers of Hanoi'

The 'Towers of Hanoi' is a game played with three poles, named ***source***, ***destination*** and ***spare***, and a set of discs. Initially all the discs are on the source pole where no disc is placed on top of a smaller one. The purpose of the game is to move all of the discs onto the destination pole. Each time a disc is moved from one pole to another, two constrains must be observed:

(1) Only the top disc on a pole can be moved.

(2) No disc may be placed on top of a smaller one.

The spare pole can be used as temporary storage.

First, we introduce the well known sequential solution to the game. It make use of a recursive procedure which has four parameters. Three of them represent the poles and the fourth is an integer to decide the number of discs to be moved. It consists of three steps. In step one, N-1 discs are moved, using a recursive call, from the source to the spare using the destination as spare. In step two, a single disc is moved from the source to the destination. In step three, N-1 discs are moved, using again a recursive call, from the spare to the destination, using the source as spare.

Next, a solution by a recursive script is introduced. It is similarly structured to the sequential one, and makes use of the same three steps. Although it is distributed, no parallel computation is involved. In a generalization of the game where more then three poles are allowed, parallel computation may take place.

The recursive script, named Hanoi, implementing a winning strategy for the game, is defined as follows. Each one of the three poles is "in possession" of a different role, represented as a stack of discs. Due to this representation the first constraint is observed trivially. Each of the three roles has two parameters. The first parameter is the number of discs to be moved and the second parameter is the stack itself. We also use an auxiliary simple script named move, which has two roles, named give and take. Each role has one parameter of type stack of disks. The purpose of this script is to move a single element (disc) from the give-role stack onto the take-role stack.

The strategy of the hanoi script which will correctly play the Towers of Hanoi game with three roles (named also source, destination and spare) and N discs is described using the same three steps introduced in the sequential solution.

step 1: If $N>1$ then $N-1$ discs are moved from the source to the spare using the destination as spare. This is done by the source, destination and spare roles *recursively* enrolling to the source, spare and destination respectively, with first parameter equal to $N-1$, while the second parameter is the stack which the role possess.

step 2: A single disc is moved from the source to the destination. This is done by the source and destination roles respectively enrolling to the give and take roles in the move script.

step 3: If $N>1$ then $N-1$ discs are moved from the spare to the destination, using the source as spare. This is done by the source, destination and spare roles *recursively* enrolling to the spare, destination and source role respectively, with first parameter equal $N-1$, the second parameter, as before, is the stack.

7.3 proving partial correctness

Next we extend the proof system presented before to recursive scripts. The new proof rule we introduce to deal with recursion is a natural generalization of that for recursive procedures (see [HO71, AP81]). Consider a (recursive) script declaration $SCRIPT\ \ S(\vec{x},\vec{y},\vec{z});B_s$, as in section 3.1, where B_s may include also recursive enrollments. The rule is referring to recursive script S and matching enrollments $E_1^s, \ldots, E_{ns}^s$.

recursion rule

$$\frac{\{pre(S)\}\ [\mathop{\|}_{j=1}^{ns} E_j^s(\vec{x_j},\vec{y_j},\vec{z_j})]\ \{post(S)\} \vdash \{pre(S)\}\ B_s\ \{post(S)\}}{\{pre(S)\}\ [\mathop{\|}_{j=1}^{ns} E_j^s(\vec{x_j},\vec{y_j},\vec{z_j})]\ \{post(S)\}}$$

The reasoning presented by the recursion rule is the the following: infer $\{pre(S)\}\ [\mathop{\|}_{j=1}^{ns} E_j^s(\vec{x_j},\vec{y_j},\vec{z_j})]\ \{post(S)\}$ from the fact that $\{pre(S)\}\ B_s\ \{post(S)\}$ can be proved (using the other rules and axioms) from the assumption $\{pre(S)\}\ [\mathop{\|}_{j=1}^{ns} E_j^s(\vec{x_j},\vec{y_j},\vec{z_j})]\ \{post(S)\}$.

This is the usual circularity encountered when treated recursion.

We now supplement the proof system presented in sections 3 and 4, with the recursion rule. the extension is enough for dealing with recursion script. It may seem peculiar, but no further extension is needed for the cooperation test. The explanation is that once a recursive script is proved (such a proof also involves cooperation tests), that proof applied

```
SCRIPT hanoi ::
 INITIATION : DELAYED
 TERMINATION: DELAYED
 [ ROLE source (VALUE n1: integer, VALUE_RESULT A: stack of discs) ::
     [ n1≠1 → ENROLL IN hanoi AS source(n1−1, A) [] n1=1 → skip ];
     ENROLL IN move AS give(A);
     [ n1≠1 → ENROLL IN hanoi AS spare(n1−1, A)  [] n1=1 → skip ]
 ||
  ROLE destination (VALUE n2: integer, VALUE_RESULT B: stack of discs) ::
     [ n2≠1 → ENROLL IN hanoi AS spare(n2−1, B) [] n2=1 → skip ];
     ENROLL IN move AS take(B);
     [ n2≠1 → ENROLL IN hanoi AS destination(n2−1, B) [] n2=1 → skip ]
 ||
  ROLE spare (VALUE n3: integer, VALUE_RESULT C: stack of discs) ::
     [ n3≠1 → ENROLL IN hanoi AS destination(n3−1, C) [] n3=1 → skip ];
     [ n3≠1 → ENROLL IN hanoi AS source(n3−1, C) [] n3=1 → skip ]
  ].
```

Figure 1. Towers of Hanoi

```
SCRIPT move ::
 INITIATION : DELAYED
 TERMINATION: DELAYED
 [ ROLE give  (VALUE_RESULT X: stack of discs) ::
    VAR temp1: integer
    temp1:=pop(X);
    take ! temp1
 ||
  ROLE take (VALUE_RESULT Y: stack of discs) ::
    VAR temp2: integer
    give ?  temp2;
    push(Y,temp2)
  ].
```

Figure 2. move

automatically to each instance of that script. It is so, because of using free variables to denote the initial values of the parameter. Therefore, no matter which parameters are transferred to some nested performance, the proof ensures that the instance executing that performance will do it as expected.

7.4 Verifying the 'Towers of Hanoi'

Using the new rules presented, we can now verify the example presented before. First, consider the script *move*. Using the proof system for CSP ([AFR80]) we may prove:

$$\{X=s \bullet X_0 \wedge Y=Y_0\}\ Body_{move}\ \{X=X_0 \wedge Y=s \bullet Y_0\}$$

X_0 and Y_0 represent ordered stacks of discs and s denotes a single disc. They are used to "freeze" the initial state of the stacks X and Y. By $s \bullet X_0$ we mean that s is placed on top of the disc denoted by X_0.

It is required that the s disc will be smaller then any disc in the stacks X_0 or Y_0 and that initially no disc is placed on top of a smaller one. Note that those requirements are satisfied (by the actual parameters) when the move script is used (in step 2) by the hanoi script.

The proof outline for move script:

```
[ give : {X=s • X0}
         temp1=pop(X)
         {temp1=s ∧ X=X0}
         take ! temp1
         {X=X0}
||
  take :{Y=Y0}
         give ? temp2
         {temp2=s ∧ Y=Y0}
         push(Y,temp2)
         {Y=s • Y0}
].
```

The script invariant *SI* is identically true.

Cooperation is proved easily using the communication axiom, preservation axiom and consequence rule. By applying the parallel composition rule the proof is finished. □

It is simple to see that the constrain that *no disc may be placed on top of a smaller one* is observed by this script if the initial requirements are satisfied.

Finally, we verify the hanoi script. What we first prove is:

(*) $\{A=A[1..W] \wedge B=B_0 \wedge C=C_0 \wedge n_1=n_2=n_3=N\}$

$[E^{hanoi}_{source}(n_1,A) \,||\, E^{hanoi}_{dest}(n_2,B) \,||\, E^{hanoi}_{spare}(n_3,C)]$

$\{A=A[N+1..W] \wedge B=A[1..N]\bullet B_0 \wedge C=C_0 \wedge n_1=n_2=n_3=N\}$

$A[1..W]$, B_0, C_0 are used for freezing the initial state of the stacks A,B,C respectively. $A[1..W]$ denote an order stack of W discs, where for each i,j such that $1 \le i < j \le W$, disk $A[i]$ is smaller then disc $A[j]$. N is an integer $1 \le N \le W$.

For the sake of the proof we assume that any one of the A[1..W] discs is smaller then any disc of B_0 or C_0. Later we explain why that assumption can be removed. Based on the game definition we assume that initially, no disc is placed on top of a smaller one

By the recursion rule it suffices to prove:

(*) $\vdash \{A=A[1..W] \wedge B=B_0 \wedge C=C_0 \wedge n_1=n_2=n_3=N\}\ Body_{hanoi}$

$\{A=A[N+1..W] \wedge B=A[1..N]\bullet B_0 \wedge C=C_0 \wedge n_1=n_2=n_3=N\}$

Assume (*).

The *proof outline* for the hanoi script:

```
[ source:   {A=A[1..W] ∧ n1=N}
            [ n1≠1 → E^hanoi_source(n1−1, A) {A=A[N..W] ∧ n1=N}
             □
             n1=1 → skip                    {A=A[N..W] ∧ n1=N}
            ] {A=A[N..W] ∧ n1=N}
            E^move_give(A);
```

$\{A=A[N+1..W] \wedge n_1=N\}$
$[\ n_1 \neq 1 \rightarrow E^{hanoi}_{spare}(n_1-1,\ A)\ \ \{A=A[N+1..W] \wedge n_1=N\}$
$\square$
$n_1=1 \rightarrow \text{skip} \qquad \{A=A[N+1..W] \wedge n_1=N\}$
$]\ \{A=A[N+1..W] \wedge n_1=N\}$

||

destination: $\{B=B_o \wedge n_2=N\}$
$[\ n_2 \neq 1 \rightarrow E^{hanoi}_{spare}(n_2-1,\ B)\ \ \{B=B_o \wedge n_2=N\}$
$\square$
$n_2=1 \rightarrow \text{skip} \qquad \{B=B_o \wedge n_2=N\}$
$]\ \{B=B_o \wedge n_2=N\}$
$E^{move}_{take}(B);$
$\{B=A[N]\bullet B_o \wedge n_2=N\}$
$[\ n_2 \neq 1 \rightarrow E^{hanoi}_{dest}(n_2-1,\ B)\ \ \{B=A[1..N]\bullet B_o \wedge n_2=N\}$
$\square$
$n_2=1 \rightarrow \text{skip} \qquad \{B=A[1..N]\bullet B_o \wedge n_2=N\}$
$]\ \{B=A[1..N]\bullet B_o \wedge n_2=N\}$

||

spare: $\{C=C_o \wedge n_1=N\}$
$[\ n_3 \neq 1 \rightarrow E^{hanoi}_{dest}(n_3-1,\ C)\ \{C=A[1..N-1]\bullet C_o \wedge n_3=N\}$
$\square$
$n_3=1 \rightarrow \text{skip} \qquad \{C=A[1..N-1]\bullet C_o \wedge n_3=N\}$
$]\ \{C=A[1..N-1]\bullet C_o \wedge n_3=N\}$
$[\ n_3 \neq 1 \rightarrow E^{hanoi}_{source}(n_3-1,\ C)\ \{C=C_o \wedge n_3=N\}$
$\square$
$n_3=1 \rightarrow \text{skip} \qquad \{C=C_o \wedge n_3=N\}$
$]\ \{C=C_o \wedge n_3=N\}$

].

The script invariant is again identically true.

There are exactly three matching enrollments corresponding to steps 1-3, which must be shown to pass the cooperation test.

step (1): we must prove:

(1) $\{A=A[1..W] \wedge B=B_o \wedge C=C_o \wedge n_1=n_2=n_3=N\}$

$[E^{hanoi}_{source}(n_1-1,A) \,||\, E^{hanoi}_{dest}(n_3-1,C) \,||\, E^{hanoi}_{spare}(n_2-1,B)]$

$\{A=A[N..W] \wedge B=B_o \wedge C=A[1..N-1]\bullet C_o \wedge n_1=n_2=n_3=N\}$

The proof starts with (*).

By variable substitution rule, preservation, conjunction and consequence rules, (exchanging N with N-1)

$\{A=A[1..W] \wedge B=B_o \wedge C=C_o \wedge n_1=n_2=n_3=N-1\}$

$[E^{hanoi}_{source}(n_1,A) \,||\, E^{hanoi}_{dest}(n_2,B) \,||\, E^{hanoi}_{spare}(n_3,C)]$

$\{A=A[N..W] \wedge B=A[1..N-1]\bullet B_o \wedge C=C_o \wedge n_1=n_2=n_3=N-1\}$

Now, by the parameter substitution rule (substituting B, C, n_2, n_3, for C, B, n_3, n_2 respectively) and variable substitution rule (substituting B_o, C_o for C_o, B_o respectively),

$\{A=A[1..W] \wedge B=B_o \wedge C=C_o \wedge n_1=n_2=n_3=N-1\}$

$[E^{hanoi}_{source}(n_1,A) \,||\, E^{hanoi}_{dest}(n_3,C) \,||\, E^{hanoi}_{spare}(n_2,B)]$

$\{A=A[N..W] \wedge B=B_0 \wedge C=A[1..N-1]\bullet C_0 \wedge n_1=n_2=n_3=N-1\}$

Finally, by the parameter substitution rule (substitute n_1-1, n_2-1, n_3-1 for n_1, n_2, n_3 respectively), the required result is obtained. **end step (1).**

step (2): we must prove:

(2) $\{A=A[N..W] \wedge B=B_0 \wedge n_1=n_2=N\}$ $[E^{move}_{give}(A) \,||\, E^{move}_{take}(B)]$

$\{A=A[N+1..W] \wedge B=A[N]\bullet B_0 \wedge n_1=n_2=N\}$

Using the the proof that $\{X=s\bullet X_0 \wedge Y=Y_0\}$ $Body_{move}$ $\{X=X_0 \wedge Y=s\bullet Y_0\}$ which was given before, we take s, X_0, Y_0 to be $A[N], A[N+1..W], B_0$ respectively and get: $\{X=A[N..W] \wedge Y=B_0\}$ $Body_{move}$ $\{X=A[N+1..W] \wedge Y=A[N]\bullet B_0\}$

Note that $A[N]$, $A[N+1..W]$, B_0 satisfy the initial requirements of the move script.

By the enrollment rule we get:

$$\frac{\{X=A[N..W] \wedge Y=B_0\}\ Body_{move}\ \{X=A[N+1..W] \wedge Y=A[N]\bullet B_0\}}{\{X=A[N..W] \wedge Y=B_0[A,B/X,Y]\}[E^{move}_{give}(A) \,||\, E^{move}_{take}(B)]\{X=A[N+1..W] \wedge Y=A[N]\bullet B_0[A,B/X,Y]\}}$$

and after substitution:

$$\{A=A[N..W] \wedge B=B_0\}\ [E^{move}_{give}(A) \,||\, E^{move}_{take}(B)]\ \{A=A[N+1..W] \wedge B=A[N]\bullet B_0\}$$

By the preservation axiom: $\{n_1=n_2=N\}$ $[E^{move}_{give}(A) \,||\, E^{move}_{take}(B)]$ $\{n_1=n_2=N\}$

Using the conjunction rule the required cooperation is obtained. **end step (2).**

step (3): we must prove:

(3) $\{A=A[N+1..W] \wedge B=A[N]\bullet B_0 \wedge C=A[1..N-1]\bullet C_0 \wedge n_1=n_2=n_3=N\}$

$[E^{hanoi}_{source}(n_3-1, C) \,||\, E^{hanoi}_{dest}(n_2-1, B) \,||\, E^{hanoi}_{spare}(n_1-1, A)]$

$\{A=A[N+1..W] \wedge B=A[1..N]\bullet B_0 \wedge C=C_0 \wedge n_1=n_2=n_3=N\}$

The proof starts with (1).

By the parameter substitution rule (substituting respectively, A,B,C for B,C,A and n_1-1, n_2-1, n_3-1 for n_2-1, n_3-1, n_1-1), and the variable substitution rule (substituting $A[N+1..W]$, $A[N]\bullet B_0$, C_0 for B_0, C_0, $A[N..W]$ respectively)

the required result is obtained. **end step 3**

By applying parallel composition rule, the required result about the body ($Body_{hanoi}$) is obtained.

Finally, by the recursion rule the proof of (*) is obtained. □

Consider, again, the constrain that *no disc may placed on top of a smaller one*. The only place where that constrain has to be checked is within the move script. It was pointed out that if the initial requirements of the move script are satisfied this constrain is observed, and that always (step 2) the requirements are satisfied. Thus we informally proved that the constrain is observed within the hanoi script, which means that it is an invariant, as required by the game definition.

Consider again the definition of the game. The claim we have just proved is stronger then needed. So, if we now take (*) and use the consequence rule and variable substitution rule to substitute, *empty*, *empty*, *empty* for $A[N+1..W]$, B_0, C_0, where *empty* denote an empty stack, we get:

$\{A=A[1..N] \wedge B=C=empty \wedge n_1=n_2=n_3=N\}$

$[E^{hanoi}_{source}(n_1, A) \,||\, E^{hanoi}_{dest}(n_2, B) \,||\, E^{hanoi}_{spare}(n_3, C)]$

$\{A=empty \wedge B=A[1..N] \wedge C=empty\}$

which is exactly what was defined as the object of the game.

Note that the last formula can not be proved directly using the recursion rule because of step 3. Note also that once the proof is finished the assumption assuming that any one of the A[1..W] discs is smaller then any disc of B_0 or C_0, is not needed any more. That is so because of the substitution of empty stacks for B_0 and C_0 .

7.5 Deadlock freedom

In this section we extend the proof system introduced for proving deadlock freedom of non recursive scripts, presented in section 6, to apply also to recursive scripts. All assumption made there are also adopted here.

In such an extension it has to be shown how to prove that a recursive script S is deadlock free relative to some assertion denoted by $df(S)$. When using the 'old' proof system the problem which arises is how to decide whether a *recursive* matching enrollments is a df_matching enrollments or not. Such a decision is based on knowing the assertion relative to which the script, which the matching enrollments enroll to, is deadlock free. In the case of recursive matching enrollments that assertion ($df(S)$) is actually the one to be proved. The solution is the one usually encountered when treating recursion, to permit the use of the desired conclusion about an enrollment as an assumption in the proof of the body.

Thus, to decide whether a recursive matching enrollments to script S is a df_matching enrollment or not, we assume that S is deadlock free relative to $df(S)$. After all the recursive matching enrollments have been decided, we 'forget' the above assumption and continue as usual. If from that point, using the already known proof system, it is provable that S is deadlock free relative to $df(S)$, then indeed it is.

8. CONCLUSION

We have presented a proof system for proving partial correctness and deadlock-freedom of concurrent programs using scripts.

By separating the proof of the whole program and handling each script separately we achieved the goal of modularizing the proof system with the same degree of modularity as has been achieved by use of the script construct. To achieve this modularity in the system the enrollment rule and the recursive rule, which are used as interface between the enrolling processes and the script, are introduced. Those proof rules are generalization of the procedure rule and recursive rule for procedure call. Also, the idea of cooperating proofs was extended to meet our needs. Although we have mentioned only CSP and ADA, we believe that the basic ideas of the proof system can be applied to most concurrent programming languages if they are augmented with scripts.

In future research, the question of the completeness of the proof system should be studied, as well as its extension for proving termination. Another issue is extending the enrollment mechanism to serve as a guard. Finally, efficient implementations, especially distributed ones, are of primary concern.

Acknowledgment: The 2nd author was partially supported by the fund for the promotion of research, the Technion.

APPENDIX

Notations

S : script named S.

$|S|$, ns : number of roles in the script S.

$E_j^s(\vec{a})$: enroll in S as R_j $(\vec{a})$.

$R_j^s(\vec{x_j})$: role R_j in script S with formal data parameters $\vec{x_j}$, and body B_j.

B_s : Body of S $\left(\mathop{\|}_{j=1}^{|S|} B_j \right)$.

$pre(R_j^s)$: pre-condition of R_j^s.

$post(R_j^s)$: post-condition of R_j^s.

SI : script invariant.

$pre(S)$: pre-condition of B_s.

$post(S)$: post-condition of B_s. $\left(\bigwedge_{j=1}^{ns} post(R_j^s) \wedge SI \rightarrow post(S) \right)$.

$df(S)$: predicate relative to which S is proved to be deadlock free.

Axioms and proof rules.

I1. *Assignment axiom*

$$\{p[t/x]\}\ x:=t\ \{p\}.$$

I2. *Skip axiom*

$$\{p\}\ skip\ \{p\}.$$

I3. *Alternative Command rule*

$$\frac{\{p \wedge b_i\}\ S_i\ \{q\},\ i=1,\dots,m}{\{p\}\ [[](i=1,\dots,m)\ b_i \rightarrow S_i]\ \{q\}}.$$

I4. *Repetitive Command rule*

$$\frac{\{p \wedge b_i\}\ S_i\ \{p\},\ i=1,\dots,m}{\{p\}\ *[[](i=1,\dots,m)\ b_i \rightarrow S_i]\ \{p \wedge \neg(b_1 \vee \cdots \vee b_m)\}}.$$

I5. *Composition rule*

$$\frac{\{p\}S_1\{q\},\ \{q\}S_2\{r\}}{\{p\}\ S_1;\ S_2\ \{r\}}.$$

I6. *Consequence rule*

$$\frac{\{p\} \rightarrow \{p_1\},\ \{p_1\}S\{q_1\},\ \{q_1\} \rightarrow \{q\}}{\{p\}S\{q\}}.$$

I7. *Conjunction rule*

$$\frac{\{p\}S\{q\},\ \{p\}S\{r\}}{\{p\}S\{q \wedge r\}}.$$

I8. *Disjunction rule*

$$\frac{\{p_1\}S\{q\},\ \{p_2\}S\{q\}}{\{p_1 \vee p_2\}S\{q\}}.$$

I9. *Preservation axiom*

$$\{p\}\ S\ \{p\}.$$

provided no free variable of p is subject to change in S.
Note that the *skip axiom* is subsumed by the *preservation axiom*.

I10. *Substitution rule*

$$\frac{\{p\}\ S\ \{q\}}{\{p[t/z]\}\ S\ \{q\}}$$

provided z does not appear free in S and q.

The *substitution rule* is needed to eliminate auxiliary variables from the preassertion.

I11. *Auxiliary Variables rule*

Let AV be a set of variables such that $x \in$ AV implies x appears in S' only in assignments $y:=t$, where $y \in$ AV. Then if q does not contain free any variables from AV, and S is obtained from S' by deleting all assignments to variables in AV,

$$\frac{\{p\}\ S'\ \{q\}}{\{p\}\ S\ \{q\}}.$$

list of the new rules

enrollment rule

$$\frac{\{pre(S)\}\ B_s\ \{post(S)\}}{\{pre(S)[\vec{a};\vec{b}/\vec{x};\vec{y}]\}\quad [\mathop{\|}_{j=1}^{ns} E_j^s(\vec{a_{k_j}},\vec{b_{k_j}},\vec{c_{k_j}})]\quad \{post(S)[\vec{b};\vec{c}/\vec{y};\vec{z}]\}}$$

parameter substitution rule

$$\frac{\{p\}\ [\mathop{\|}_{j=1}^{ns} E_j^s(\vec{a_{k_j}},\vec{b_{k_j}},\vec{c_{k_j}})]\ \{q\}}{\{p\ [\vec{d};\vec{e}\,/\,\vec{a};\vec{b}]\}\ \ [\mathop{\|}_{j=1}^{ns} E_j^s(\vec{d_{k_j}},\vec{e_{k_j}},\vec{f_{k_j}})]\ \ \{q\ [\vec{e};\vec{f}\,/\,\vec{b};\vec{c}]\}}$$

where $\quad var(\vec{d};\vec{e};\vec{f}) \cap free(p,q) \subseteq var(\vec{a};\vec{b};\vec{c})$.

variable substitution rule

$$\frac{\{p\}\ [\mathop{\|}_{j=1}^{ns} E_j^s(\vec{a_{k_j}},\vec{b_{k_j}},\vec{c_{k_j}})]\ \{q\}}{\{p\ [\vec{s}\,/\,\vec{r}\}\ [\mathop{\|}_{j=1}^{ns} E_j^s(\vec{a_{k_j}},\vec{b_{k_j}},\vec{c_{k_j}})]\ \{q\ [\vec{s}\,/\,\vec{r}]\}}$$

where $\quad var(\vec{s};\vec{r}) \cap var(\vec{a};\vec{b};\vec{c}) = \phi$

enrollment axiom

$$\{p\}E\{q\}.$$

rearrangement rule

$$\frac{\{p\}\ B_1;\ldots;B_{ns}\ \{p_1\}\ ,\ \{p_1\}\ [\mathop{\|}_{j=1}^{ns} E_j^s]\ \{p_2\}\ ,\ \{p_2\}\ B_1';\ldots;B_{ns}'\ \{q\}}{\{p\}\ [\mathop{\|}_{j=1}^{ns}\ (B_j;\ E_j^s;\ B_j')\ ]\ \{q\}}$$

recursion rule

$$\frac{\{pre(S)\}\ [\mathop{\|}_{j=1}^{ns} E_j^s(\vec{x_j},\vec{y_j},\vec{z_j})]\ \{post(S)\} \vdash \{pre(S)\}\ B_s\ \{post(S)\}}{\{pre(S)\}\ [\mathop{\|}_{j=1}^{ns} E_j^s(\vec{x_j},\vec{y_j},\vec{z_j})]\ \{post(S)\}}$$

REFERENCES

[AFR80] Apt,K.R., Francez, N., and de Roever, W.P. A proof system for communicating sequential processes. *ACM Trans. Prog. Lang. Syst.* 2,3 (July 1980), 359-385.

[AP81] Apt,K.R., Ten years of Hoare logic: A survey-part 1. *ACM Trans. Prog. Lang. Syst.* 3,4 (October 1981), 431-483.

[AP83] Apt,K.R., Formal justification of proof system for communicating sequential processes. *ACM Trans. Prog. Lang. Syst.* 30,1 (January 1983), 197-216.

[EF82] Elrad, T., Francez, N. Decomposition of distributed programs into communication-close layers. Science of Computer Programming 2 (1982) 155-173, North-Holland.

[FH83] Francez, N., and Hailpern, B. Script: A communication abstraction mechanism. *ACM−SIGACT 2nd annual PODC conf., Montreal*, (August 1983).

[GL80] Gries, D., and Levin, G. Assignment and procedure call proof rules. *ACM Trans. Prog. Lang. Syst.* 2,4 (October 1980), 564-579.

[GR] Gerth, R., and de Roever, W.P. A proof system for concurrent ada programs. to appear in SCP. Tech. Rep. RUU-CS-83-2, U. of Utrecht, October 1983.

[HO71] Hoare, C.A.R. Procedures and parameters: An axiomatic approach. In Symp. Semantics of Algorithmic Languages, E. Engeler, Ed., Notes in Mathematics 188, Springer-Verlag, New York, 1971, 102-116.

[HO78] Hoare, C.A.R. Communicating sequential processes. *Commun. ACM* 21,8 (August 1978), 666-677.

[OG76] Owicki, S.S., and Gries, D. An axiomatic proof technique for parallel programs. *I. Acta Inf.* 6, 1976, 319-340.

LIST OF AUTHORS

M P Atkinson
Department of Computing Science
University of Glasgow
Glasgow G12 8QQ
Scotland
U.K.

A Bagchi
Indian Institute of Management
P.O. Box 16757
Calcutta 700 027

M Beynon
Department of Computer Science
University of Warwick
Coventry CV4 7AL
England

G P Bhattacharjee
Department of Mathematics
Indian Institute of Technology
Kharagpur 721 302

B B Bhattacharya
Electronics Unit
Indian Statistical Institute
Calcutta 700 035

G N Buckley
Department of Computer Science
University of Texas
Austin, Texas 78712-1188
U.S.A.

N Chandrasekharan
School of Automation
Indian Institute of Science
Bangalore 560 012

A T Cohen
Department of Computer and
Information Sciences
University of Delaware
Newark, Delaware 19716
U.S.A.

A Das
Department of Computer Science
and Engineering
Indian Institute of Technology
Madras 600 036

S K Debray
Department of Computer Science
SUNY at Stony Brook
Stony Brook, New York 11794
U.S.A.

N Francez
Computer Science Department
Technion
Haifa 32000
Israel

A J Frank
Department of Computer Science
SUNY at Stony Brook
Stony Brook, New York 11794
U.S.A.

S Ghosh
Electronics Unit
Indian Statistical Institute
Calcutta 700 035

S K Ghosh
Computer Science Group
Tata Institute of Fundamental Research
Colaba
Bombay 400 005

A K Goswami
School of Automation
Indian Institute of Science
Bangalore 560 012

P Gupta
IPAD/RSA
Space Applications Centre (ISRO)
Ahmedabad 380 053

H Heller
Mathematik
ETH Zentrum
CH 8092 Zurich
Switzerland

S Jajodia
Department of Computer Science
University of Missouri-Columbia
Columbia, Missouri 65211
U.S.A.

K Krithivasan
Department of Computer Science
and Engineering
Indian Institute of Technology
Madras 600 036

V S Lakshmanan
School of Automation
Indian Institute of Science
Bangalore 560 012

C Levcopoulos
Department of Computer and
Information Science
Linkoping University
581 83 Linkoping
Sweden

A Lingas
Department of Computer and
Information Science
Linkoping University
581 83 Linkoping
Sweden

T S E Maibaum
Department of Computing
Imperial College of Science
and Technology
University of London
180 Queen's Gate
London SW7 2BZ
U.K.

R Morrison
University of St. Andrews
St. Andrews, Fife
Scotland
U.K.

T J Myers
Department of Computer and
Information Science
University of Delaware
Newark, Delaware 19716
U.S.A.

N Natarajan
NCSDCT
Tata Institute of Fundamental
Research
Colaba
Bombay 400 005

A K Pal
Indian Institute of Management
P.O. Box 16757
Calcutta 700 027

L M Patnaik
School of Automation
Indian Institute of Science
Bangalore 560 012

B Poizat
Mathematiques
University P & M Curie
4 Place Jussieu
75230 Paris Cedex 05
France

I V Ramakrishnan
Department of Computer Science
University of Maryland
College Park, Maryland 20742
U.S.A.

R Ramanujam
Computer Science Group
Tata Institute of Fundamenta
Research
Colaba
Bombay 400 005

M Regnier
INRIA
Rocquencourt
B.P. 105
78153 Le Chesnay Cedex
France

M R Sadler
Department of Computing
Imperial College of Science
and Technology
University of London
180 Queen's Gate
London SW7 2BZ
U.K.

F de Santis
Departmento di Informatica e
Applicazioni
Facolta di Scienze
Universita di Salerno
184100 Salerno
Italy

M I Sessa
Departmento di Informatica e
Applicazioni
Facolta di Scienze
Universita di Salerno
184100 Salerno
Italy

R K Shyamasundar
Computer Science Group
Tata Institute of Fundamental Research
Colaba
Bombay 400 005

A Silberschatz
Department of Computer Sciences
University of Texas
Austin, Texas 78712-1188
U.S.A.

B P Sinha
Electronics Unit
Indian Statistical Institute
Calcutta 700 035

S A Smolka
Department of Computer Science
SUNY at Stony Brook
Stony Brook, New York 11794
U.S.A.

P K Srimani
Indian Institute of Management
P.O. Box 16757
Calcutta 700 027

R Studer
Institut fur Informatik
University of Stuttgart
Azenbergstrasse 12
D-7000 Stuttgart 1
Federal Republic of Germany

G Taubenfeld
Computer Science Department
Technion
Haifa 32000
Israel

P J Varman
Department of Electrical Engineering
Rice University
Houston, Texas 77001
U.S.A.

P A S Veloso
Departmento de Informatica
Pontificia Universidade Catolica
Rua Marques de Sao Vicente, 225
22453 Rio de Janeiro, RJ
Brazil

C E Veni Madhavan
School of Automation
Indian Institute of Science
Bangalore 560 012

S Zachos
Mathematik
ETH Zentrum
CH 8092 Zurich
Switzerland

Vol. 142: Problems and Methodologies in Mathematical Software Production. Proceedings, 1980. Edited by P.C. Messina and A. Murli. VII, 271 pages. 1982.

Vol. 143: Operating Systems Engineering. Proceedings, 1980. Edited by M. Maekawa and L.A. Belady. VII, 465 pages. 1982.

Vol. 144: Computer Algebra. Proceedings, 1982. Edited by J. Calmet. XIV, 301 pages. 1982.

Vol. 145: Theoretical Computer Science. Proceedings, 1983. Edited by A.B. Cremers and H.P. Kriegel. X, 367 pages. 1982.

Vol. 146: Research and Development in Information Retrieval. Proceedings, 1982. Edited by G. Salton and H.-J. Schneider. IX, 311 pages. 1983.

Vol. 147: RIMS Symposia on Software Science and Engineering. Proceedings, 1982. Edited by E. Goto, I. Nakata, K. Furukawa, R. Nakajima, and A. Yonezawa. V. 232 pages. 1983.

Vol. 148: Logics of Programs and Their Applications. Proceedings, 1980. Edited by A. Salwicki. VI, 324 pages. 1983.

Vol. 149: Cryptography. Proceedings, 1982. Edited by T. Beth. VIII, 402 pages. 1983.

Vol. 150: Enduser Systems and Their Human Factors. Proceedings, 1983. Edited by A. Blaser and M. Zoeppritz. III, 138 pages. 1983.

Vol. 151: R. Piloty, M. Barbacci, D. Borrione, D. Dietmeyer, F. Hill, and P. Skelly, CONLAN Report. XII, 174 pages. 1983.

Vol. 152: Specification and Design of Software Systems. Proceedings, 1982. Edited by E. Knuth and E. J. Neuhold. V, 152 pages. 1983.

Vol. 153: Graph-Grammars and Their Application to Computer Science. Proceedings, 1982. Edited by H. Ehrig, M. Nagl, and G. Rozenberg. VII, 452 pages. 1983.

Vol. 154: Automata, Languages and Programming. Proceedings, 1983. Edited by J. Díaz. VIII, 734 pages. 1983.

Vol. 155: The Programming Language Ada. Reference Manual. Approved 17 February 1983. American National Standards Institute, Inc. ANSI/MIL-STD-1815A-1983. IX, 331 pages. 1983.

Vol. 156: M.H. Overmars, The Design of Dynamic Data Structures. VII, 181 pages. 1983.

Vol. 157: O. Østerby, Z. Zlatev, Direct Methods for Sparse Matrices. VIII, 127 pages. 1983.

Vol. 158: Foundations of Computation Theory. Proceedings, 1983. Edited by M. Karpinski, XI, 517 pages. 1983.

Vol. 159: CAAP'83. Proceedings, 1983. Edited by G. Ausiello and M. Protasi. VI, 416 pages. 1983.

Vol. 160: The IOTA Programming System. Edited by R. Nakajima and T. Yuasa. VII, 217 pages. 1983.

Vol. 161: DIANA, An Intermediate Language for Ada. Edited by G. Goos, W.A. Wulf, A. Evans, Jr. and K.J. Butler. VII, 201 pages. 1983.

Vol. 162: Computer Algebra. Proceedings, 1983. Edited by J.A. van Hulzen. XIII, 305 pages. 1983.

Vol. 163: VLSI Engineering. Proceedings. Edited by T.L. Kunii. VIII, 308 pages. 1984.

Vol. 164: Logics of Programs. Proceedings, 1983. Edited by E. Clarke and D. Kozen. VI, 528 pages. 1984.

Vol. 165: T.F. Coleman, Large Sparse Numerical Optimization. V, 105 pages. 1984.

Vol. 166: STACS 84. Symposium of Theoretical Aspects of Computer Science. Proceedings, 1984. Edited by M. Fontet and K. Mehlhorn. VI, 338 pages. 1984.

Vol. 167: International Symposium on Programming. Proceedings, 1984. Edited by C. Girault and M. Paul. VI, 262 pages. 1984.

Vol. 168: Methods and Tools for Computer Integrated Manufacturing. Edited by R. Dillmann and U. Rembold. XVI, 528 pages. 1984.

Vol. 169: Ch. Ronse, Feedback Shift Registers. II, 1–2, 145 pages. 1984.

Vol. 171: Logic and Machines: Decision Problems and Complexity. Proceedings, 1983. Edited by E. Börger, G. Hasenjaeger and D. Rödding. VI, 456 pages. 1984.

Vol. 172: Automata, Languages and Programming. Proceedings, 1984. Edited by J. Paredaens. VIII, 527 pages. 1984.

Vol. 173: Semantics of Data Types. Proceedings, 1984. Edited by G. Kahn, D.B. MacQueen and G. Plotkin. VI, 391 pages. 1984.

Vol. 174: EUROSAM 84. Proceedings, 1984. Edited by J. Fitch. XI, 396 pages. 1984.

Vol. 175: A. Thayse, P-Functions and Boolean Matrix Factorization, VII, 248 pages. 1984.

Vol. 176: Mathematical Foundations of Computer Science 1984. Proceedings, 1984. Edited by M.P. Chytil and V. Koubek. XI, 581 pages. 1984.

Vol. 177: Programming Languages and Their Definition. Edited by C.B. Jones. XXXII, 254 pages. 1984.

Vol. 178: Readings on Cognitive Ergonomics – Mind and Computers. Proceedings, 1984. Edited by G.C. van der Veer, M.J. Tauber, T.R.G. Green and P. Gorny. VI, 269 pages. 1984.

Vol. 179: V. Pan, How to Multiply Matrices Faster. XI, 212 pages. 1984.

Vol. 180: Ada Software Tools Interfaces. Proceedings, 1983. Edited by P.J.L. Wallis. III, 164 pages. 1984.

Vol. 181: Foundations of Software Technology and Theoretical Computer Science. Proceedings, 1984. Edited by M. Joseph and R. Shyamasundar. VIII, 468 pages. 1984.